Transforming Policy and Practice Through AI-Driven Educational Leadership

Areej ElSayary
https://orcid.org/0000-0002-5554-0069
Zayed University, UAE

Ghadah Al Murshidi
https://orcid.org/0000-0002-0230-2825
United Arab Emirates University, UAE

Karim Ragab
https://orcid.org/0000-0003-1337-3562
Al Ittihad Private School, UAE

IGI Global
Scientific Publishing
Publishing Tomorrow's Research Today

Vice President of Editorial Melissa Wagner
Director of Acquisitions Mikaela Felty
Director of Book Development Jocelynn Hessler
Production Manager Mike Brehm
Cover Design Jose Rosado

Published in the United States of America by
IGI Global Scientific Publishing
701 East Chocolate Avenue
Hershey, PA, 17033, USA
Tel: 717-533-8845 | Fax: 717-533-7115
Website: https://www.igi-global.com E-mail: cust@igi-global.com

Library of Congress Cataloging-in-Publication Data

Names: ElSayary, Areej, 1981- editor | Al Murshidi, Ghadah, 1985- editor | Ragab, Karim, 1979- editor
Title: Transforming policy and practice through AI-driven educational leadership / edited by: Areej ElSayary, Ghada Al Murshidi, and Karim Ragab.
Description: Hershey PA : IGI Global Scientific Publishing, [2026] | Includes bibliographical references. | Summary: "This book aims to inform ongoing scholarly debates about human-AI collaboration, teacher autonomy, and student data ethics"-- Provided by publisher.
Identifiers: LCCN 2025043696 (print) | LCCN 2025043697 (ebook) | ISBN 9798337349084 hardcover | ISBN 9798337349091 paperback | ISBN 9798337349107 ebook
Subjects: LCSH: Educational leadership | Artificial intelligence--Educational applications
Classification: LCC LB2806 .T73 2026 (print) | LCC LB2806 (ebook)
LC record available at https://lccn.loc.gov/2025043696
LC ebook record available at https://lccn.loc.gov/2025043697

British Cataloguing in Publication Data
A Cataloguing in Publication record for this book is available from the British Library.

Table of Contents

Detailed Table of Contents

As artificial intelligence (AI) continues to revolutionize the educational landscape, it enables tailored, data-driven learning experiences facilitated by AI-powered platforms. However, alongside gains in increased accessibility and efficiency, a subtler cost is also emerging; students' sense of self is being fractured, they are experiencing cognitive overload, and they are becoming emotionally detached. Drawing on Cognitive Load Theory and Sociotechnical Systems Theory, the current research highlights how such systems can either enhance or hinder the cognitive and socio-emotional factors crucial to meaningful learning. A comprehensive literature review maps the current state of generative AI in higher education, highlighting its capacity to improve student outcomes through scalable personalization and real-time feedback. At the same time, the review identifies how AI shapes learning behaviors, influences student well-being, and redefines the roles and responsibilities of faculty within this evolving educational landscape.

This chapter proposes a structured AI Competency Framework for educational leadership programs in the Gulf and Middle East, addressing the urgent need for leaders who can guide AI integration responsibly. Moving beyond digital literacy, the framework outlines technical, ethical, and strategic competencies grounded in established leadership theories. Framed by regional initiatives such as UAE Vision 2031 and Saudi Arabia's Human Capability Development Program, the chapter first presents the competency framework as its central contribution, then provides a critical justification for its necessity by mapping identified gaps in existing leadership preparation to the framework's domains. It offers three concrete implementation pathways, including embedding AI modules in existing programs, forging education–computer science partnerships, and launching policy-aligned bootcamps. The

As artificial intelligence (AI) becomes integrated into instruction, assessment, communication, and school operations, educational leadership must shift from technical adoption to purpose-driven and ethical practice. This chapter argues that effective AI leadership begins with knowing one's "why," drawing on Simon Sinek's purpose-centered leadership, Brené Brown's focus on vulnerability and courage, and John C. Maxwell's influence-based model. AI literacy is defined as a holistic capacity that combines technical awareness with ethical judgment, cultural responsiveness, equity-focused thinking, and strategic clarity. The L.E.A.D. Framework (Learn, Evaluate, Apply, Develop) is presented as a guide for intentional AI leadership, supported by principles of psychological safety, engagement, and meaningful work. A dual-language, project-based learning example illustrates how human-centered leadership guides responsible AI use. The chapter concludes with practical tools and a research agenda for building ethical, equitable, and future-ready AI leadership capacity.

This chapter explores how Gulf and Middle Eastern educational leaders integrate artificial intelligence while balancing technological progress and cultural preservation. Drawing on case studies from the UAE, Saudi Arabia, Jordan, and Egypt, it compares centralized and decentralized leadership approaches in implementing AI within conservative societies. The analysis reveals that effective adoption requires not only infrastructure but also cultural adaptation, stakeholder engagement, and ethical alignment. The UAE's model of culturally responsive innovation exemplifies successful integration, while Jordan and Egypt highlight the need for pragmatic, resource-sensitive strategies. The chapter offers policy recommendations for aligning AI initiatives with national visions and Sustainable Development Goals to ensure inclusive, ethical, and culturally grounded educational transformation.

This study investigates the relationship between artificial intelligence (AI) and student motivation and engagement. It does this by examining how cognitive factors, psychology and emotional factors affect student motivation in the classroom. This has been done by conducting a review of existing literature and previous studies involving students in tertiary institutions in the modern classroom, especially those engaged in remote learning and in classes with large populations. These have shown improvement in the learning experience, including motivation, confidence and self-esteem, through AI capabilities such as predictive analytics, adaptive learning, intelligent tutoring systems and affective computing. Studies show that thrugh the adaptive capacity of AI, learning complexity can be adjusted easily to suit the individual learner, promoting competence and confidence. AI can also provide constructive non-judgmental feedback to improve learner confidence, as well as motivational prompts for encouragement. AI also enables the learner autonomy over the learning process, where they control the pace and difficulty of the work, with instantaneous feedback, making learning interactive to promote connection using virtual assistants, simulating student-teacher interactions. This satisfies the requirements that the Self-Determination Theory highlights for building intrinsic motivation; autonomy, competence and relatedness. These findings highlight the potential of AI to transform higher education, where AI can be used to promote accessibility to quality education, reduce cognitive load on educators and create a customized learner experience for each student. This can however only be successfully implemented when partnership is fostered between AI and human educators while ethical concerns are addressed to protect data privacy and prevent bias while preserving human connection that is necessary for a learner's holistic development.

Education is one of the many facets of our society that is changing, and the integration of artificial intelligence (AI) in education is having a profound impact. Adaptive leadership is crucial to the teaching and learning process in this context, as it influences student well-being, enthusiasm, and academic achievement. Consequently, there are several advantages to incorporating AI into emotional assessment in educational environments that could revolutionize understanding and approaches to students' socioemotional growth. Nevertheless, a comprehensive framework that organizes the subject's potential, challenges, and developments remains lacking. Students in the twenty-first century need more than standard academic instruction to succeed. They must be skilled in problem-solving, cooperation, communication, and social-emotional learning (SEL). Students with SEL and traditional skills will be better prepared to thrive in the rapidly changing digital economy. For thirty years, academics have been studying emotional intelligence (EI). The real-world setting in which emotional intelligence is produced and employed has, surprisingly, received little attention, even though there has been significant discussion about how to quantify it and about the validity of its assessment. More precisely, there is a substantial void in understanding the emergence and influence of digital interactions on emotional intelligence. In this background, analyzing the literature from a broader perspective is imperative to enhance emotional intelligence in technology-rich classrooms. This comprehensive literature review examines the application of artificial intelligence (AI) to emotion assessment in educational settings. Additionally, it offers a comprehensive overview of the field, highlighting advancements, challenges, and opportunities in AI-powered emotional assessment in academic settings. By leveraging machine learning algorithms and natural language processing, AI systems can analyze human emotions across multiple modalities, including facial expressions, speech patterns, and text. This information can provide personalized feedback on emotional regulation, social interaction skills, and self-awareness. This study also examines the leadership styles that foster the use of Emotional Intelligence (EI) in classrooms. Hence, it guides teachers in developing strategies for transformational leadership within a digital learning context, addressing the challenges and ethical considerations associated with leveraging technology to cultivate emotional intelligence (EI) in the 21st-century classroom.

This study aims to investigate students with learning difficulties (LD) 's perceptions of science learning in private schools in Dubai. Specifically, it examines critical factors such as intrinsic motivation, self-efficacy, and self-determination, which are crucial for understanding how these students engage with and develop an interest in science education. To achieve this, a quantitative research approach was employed using a structured questionnaire tailored for students with LD. The questionnaire was distributed online to ensure a broad, accessible reach, resulting in data collected from 110 students with learning difficulties. The findings show that students with LD generally have positive attitudes toward science learning. They exhibit a genuine interest and enthusiasm for developing their knowledge and skills in science. The study emphasizes the importance of fostering these psychological factors and calls for collaboration among educational stakeholders to create an inclusive environment that supports all students' learning needs.

This study investigates faculty perceptions of the rollout of a newly mandated Arabic language program at a federal university in United Arab Emirates. Introduced in response to national concerns about declining Arabic proficiency, the reform required rapid curriculum redesign to serve both native and non-native learners. Guided by a qualitative constructivist–interpretivist approach, semi-structured interviews were conducted with seven instructors involved in delivery. Thematic analysis explored curriculum coherence, student engagement, and institutional supports shaping implementation. While faculty endorsed the national vision underpinning the reform, they reported gaps between learning outcomes, pedagogy, and assessment that constrained impact. Participants called for clearer guidance, better alignment mechanisms, and sustained consultation. The findings highlight the central role of academic leadership in mediating policy into practice and emphasize the need for participatory governance in large-scale language reform.

Artificial intelligence (AI) continues to reshape higher education, influencing how students learn and how educators design and deliver instruction. While its pedagogical and operational effects have been widely discussed, much less attention has been given to its environmental footprint. This chapter presents AWARE-AI (Assessing Awareness and Attitudes toward Responsible Environmental Use of AI), a study exploring how undergraduate students understand the ecological costs of AI technologies and how these insights can inform more sustainable curriculum design. The project brings together perspectives from technology, sustainability, and education, targeting foundational courses at a federal university in the United Arab Emirates. Through linking AI literacy with environmental responsibility, the study introduces the concept of Sustainable AI Literacy (SAIL) and highlights ways in which higher education can integrate sustainability principles into teaching, learning, and policy in an ethically grounded and interdisciplinary manner.

Preface

Artificial Intelligence (AI) is no longer a futuristic concept but a present-day reality that is reshaping industries, societies, and fundamentally, education. This book discovers the complex relationship between AI and educational leadership, exploring the challenges and opportunities that arise from the integration of intelligent technologies in learning environments. The chapters within this volume collectively address the pressing need for educational leaders to be not just technologically adept, but also ethically grounded, culturally responsive, and pedagogically innovative. The subject matter of this book is centered on the critical role of leadership in navigating the transformative potential of AI in education, from K-12 to higher education, and across diverse global contexts.

In a world increasingly driven by data and automation, the integration of AI in education is inevitable. From personalized learning platforms to automated administrative tasks, AI is already making its mark. However, this rapid technological advancement brings with it a host of complex issues. Questions of equity, bias in algorithms, data privacy, the role of the teacher, and the very definition of learning are at the forefront of the discourse. This book is situated at the heart of these contemporary debates, offering a detailed and critical examination of AI's role in education. It moves beyond the hype and offers a grounded perspective on how educational leaders can harness the power of AI to create more effective, equitable, and human-centered learning experiences. The chapters in this book are not just theoretical explorations; they are practical guides for leaders who are on the front lines of educational transformation.

This book is intended for a diverse audience of educational stakeholders who are grappling with the implications of AI in their respective contexts. This includes:

- **Educational Leaders:** Superintendents, principals, university administrators, and other leaders who are responsible for setting the vision and strategy for AI integration in their institutions.

- **Policymakers:** Government officials and policymakers who are tasked with creating the legal and ethical frameworks for the responsible use of AI in education.
- **Researchers and Academics:** Scholars and researchers in the fields of education, technology, and leadership who are interested in the latest research and theoretical perspectives on AI in education.
- **Teachers and Educators:** K-12 and higher education instructors who are looking for practical guidance on how to effectively integrate AI into their teaching practices.**Students:** Students at all levels who are interested in understanding the future of education and the role that AI will play in their learning journeys.

To provide a cohesive and thematic exploration of AI in educational leadership, the chapters in this book are organized into five distinct streams. Each stream addresses a critical dimension of this complex and evolving field.

STREAM 1: AI LITERACY AND LEADERSHIP COMPETENCY DEVELOPMENT

This stream focuses on the foundational knowledge and skills that educational leaders need to effectively navigate the age of AI. The chapters in this stream provide a comprehensive overview of AI literacy, offering practical models and frameworks for professional learning and leadership preparation programs. They address the critical need to equip leaders with the competencies to make informed decisions about AI integration, moving beyond mere technical proficiency to encompass ethical, pedagogical, and strategic dimensions of leadership. *Chapter 1*, "*Learning in the Cloud, Drifting in the Mind: Reclaiming Focus and Psychological Wellbeing in AI-Driven Classrooms*," examines the development of AI literacy among school leaders, proposing professional learning models that encompass technical skills, ethical decision-making, and data-driven leadership. *Chapter 2*, "*Beyond Digital Literacy: Building AI Competency Frameworks for Leadership Preparation Programs*," distinguishes between digital literacy and AI fluency, proposing a competency framework for leadership preparation programs to guide the responsible integration of AI. *Chapter 3*, "*Building AI Literacy in Educational Leadership Programs: A Curriculum Blueprint,*" outlines a blueprint for embedding AI literacy into educational leadership curricula, focusing on key domains such as algorithmic thinking, ethical AI, and data interpretation. *Chapter 4*, "*Equipping Workforce Leaders for the AI Era: Faculty Insights from UAE Higher Education*," explores faculty perspectives on embedding AI literacy into a mandatory leadership course, emphasizing the need for interdisciplinary collaboration and ethical AI policies. *Chapter 5, "Preparing Educational Leaders for AI Literacy Through Ethical, Purpose-Driven, and Culturally Responsive Leadership,"* presents the L.E.A.D. Framework as a guide for intentional AI leadership, combining technical awareness with ethical judgment and cultural responsiveness.

STREAM 2: AI POLICY AND STRATEGIC PLANNING

This stream examines the crucial role of policy and strategic planning in shaping the future of AI in education. The chapters in this stream offer a global perspective on AI policy development, with case studies from diverse contexts such as the Gulf and Middle East, Singapore, Malaysia, Europe, Asia, and Africa. They provide practical guidance for leaders on how to create supportive ecosystems for AI integration, from building future-ready schools to navigating the complexities of national and international policy frameworks. *Chapter 6, "AI Policy in the Gulf and Middle East: Educational Leadership at the Intersection of Innovation and Tradition,"* explores how educational leaders in the Gulf and Middle East are integrating AI while balancing technological progress with cultural preservation. *Chapter 7, "Building Future-Ready Schools with Strategic Planning for AI-Powered Educational Leadership,"* provides a roadmap for schools to leverage AI through strategic planning, addressing challenges related to readiness, curriculum, and infrastructure. *Chapter 8, "Local Responses to Global Shifts: AI Policy Development in a Singaporean and an East Malaysian University,"* offers a comparative analysis of AI policy development in Singapore and Malaysia, highlighting different stages of implementation and the associated challenges. *Chapter 9, "Teachers at the Policy Frontier: AI Integration in Education Across Europe, Asia, and Africa,"* provides a comparative analysis of how AI in Education policies in Europe, Asia, and Africa influence AI implementation in the classroom. *Chapter 10, "Transforming Education through AI: A Global Policy Perspective,"* conducts a thematic analysis of existing policies for AI in education, offering guidance on the development of effective and coordinated policies.

STREAM 3: DATA-INFORMED LEADERSHIP AND DECISION-MAKING

This stream delves into the transformative potential of AI and data analytics for educational leadership and pedagogical innovation. The chapters in this stream explore how leaders can move from being data-driven to data-informed, using

AI to enhance decision-making while avoiding the pitfalls of algorithmic bias and determinism. They examine the role of AI in cultivating pedagogical transformation, from the use of learning dashboards to the development of hybrid models that blend human and machine intelligence. *Chapter 11, "Data-Informed, Not Data-Driven: Leadership Practices for Responsible AI Integration in K-12 Schools,"* argues for a data-informed leadership model that integrates AI-generated insights into human-centered, pedagogically sound decision-making processes. *Chapter 12, "Evaluated by machines: Leadership and Fairness in the Age of Algorithmic Learning Analysis,"* critically examines how leadership and fairness are reconfigured under the conditions of algorithmic learning analytics, highlighting the need for reflexive leadership practices. *Chapter 13, "From Data To Decisions: Cultivating AI-Driven Leadership For Pedagogical Transformation,"* examines the emergence of AI-driven pedagogical leadership, exploring how AI tools can support strategic planning, staff development, and resource allocation. *Chapter 14, "Hybrid School Models - Blending Human and Machine Intelligence in Leadership,"* explores the integration of AI into educational leadership through hybrid school models that unite human and machine intelligence.

STREAM 4: EQUITY, INCLUSION, AND STUDENT-CENTERED AI APPLICATIONS

This stream focuses on the critical issues of equity and inclusion in the age of AI. The chapters in this stream explore how AI can be used to create more personalized and supportive learning experiences for all students, including those with learning difficulties. They examine the role of AI in fostering student motivation and engagement, and they offer strategic approaches to ensure that AI is used in a way that promotes equity and inclusion in the classroom. *Chapter 15, "AI's Role in Fostering Student Motivation and Retention,"* investigates the relationship between AI and student motivation, highlighting AI's potential to enhance higher education by improving accessibility and enabling personalized learning. *Chapter 16, "Rethinking the leadership in the age of AI Strategic approaches toward equity and inclusion in the classrooms: Emotional Intelligence Artificial Intelligence Socioemotional skills Adaptive leadership skills,"* examines the application of AI in assessing emotions in educational settings, with a focus on enhancing emotional intelligence in technology-rich classrooms. *Chapter 17, "The Perceptions of Students with Learning Difficulties towards Developing Science Learning in Private Schools in Dubai,"* investigates the perceptions of students with learning difficulties regarding science learning, emphasizing the importance of fostering an inclusive and supportive learning environment.

STREAM 5: SUSTAINABILITY, ETHICS, AND CULTURALLY RESPONSIVE AI INTEGRATION

This stream addresses the ethical, cultural, and sustainability dimensions of AI in education. The chapters in this stream explore the concept of Sustainable AI Literacy (SAIL), which includes an awareness of the environmental and social costs of AI. They also examine the importance of culturally responsive leadership in the integration of AI, with a case study on the rollout of a new Arabic language program in the UAE. These chapters provide a critical lens through which to view the broader implications of AI, ensuring that its integration is not only effective but also ethical and sustainable. *Chapter 18, "Faculty Perspectives on the Rollout of a New Arabic Language Program in UAE Higher Education and Its Implications for Leadership,"* investigates faculty perceptions of the rollout of a newly mandated Arabic language program, highlighting the central role of academic leadership in mediating policy into practice. *Chapter 19, "Sustainable AI Literacy in Higher Education Through Awareness Ethics and Curriculum Design,"* introduces the concept of Sustainable AI Literacy (SAIL), exploring how undergraduate students understand the ecological costs of AI technologies and how these insights can inform more sustainable curriculum design.

CONCLUSION: IMPACT ON THE FIELD AND CONTRIBUTION TO THE SUBJECT MATTER

This book makes a significant contribution to the field of educational leadership by providing a comprehensive and critical examination of the role of AI in education. It moves beyond the simplistic and often-hyped discourse on AI and offers a nuanced and grounded perspective on the challenges and opportunities that lie ahead. The chapters in this volume, organized into five thematic streams, collectively provide a roadmap for how educational leaders can harness the power of AI to create more effective, equitable, and human-centered learning experiences.

The book's impact on the field will be threefold. First, it will help to build the capacity of educational leaders to lead in the age of AI. By providing practical guidance and theoretical frameworks, the book will equip leaders with the skills and competencies they need to make informed decisions about AI integration. Second, the book will help to shape the future of AI policy in education. By providing a global perspective on the key issues and challenges, the book will inform the development of more effective and equitable policies. Third, the book will help to advance the research agenda on AI in education. By identifying key areas for future research, the book will inspire a new generation of scholars to explore the complex and multifaceted relationship between AI and education.

This book is a timely and important contribution to the literature on educational leadership. It is a must-read for anyone who is interested in the future of education and the role that AI will play in shaping it. The book's comprehensive scope, its diverse perspectives, and its practical focus make it an invaluable resource for leaders, policymakers, researchers, and educators who are committed to creating a better future for all learners.

Zeina Hojeij
College of Interdisciplinary Studies, Zayed University, UAE

Chapter 1
Learning in the Cloud, Drifting in the Mind:
Reclaiming Focus and Psychological Wellbeing in AI-Driven Classrooms

Azza Mahmoud Gamal El Din
http://orcid.org/0000-0002-3689-0688
Ministry of Education, UAE

ABSTRACT

As artificial intelligence (AI) continues to revolutionize the educational landscape, it enables tailored, data-driven learning experiences facilitated by AI-powered platforms. However, alongside gains in increased accessibility and efficiency, a subtler cost is also emerging; students' sense of self is being fractured, they are experiencing cognitive overload, and they are becoming emotionally detached. Drawing on Cognitive Load Theory and Sociotechnical Systems Theory, the current research highlights how such systems can either enhance or hinder the cognitive and socio-emotional factors crucial to meaningful learning. A comprehensive literature review maps the current state of generative AI in higher education, highlighting its capacity to improve student outcomes through scalable personalization and real-time feedback. At the same time, the review identifies how AI shapes learning behaviors, influences student well-being, and redefines the roles and responsibilities of faculty within this evolving educational landscape.

DOI: 10.4018/979-8-3373-4908-4.ch001

INTRODUCTION

The incorporation of artificial intelligence (AI) into regular teaching and learning environments has had a profound impact on learning methodologies and students' psychological states in classrooms. In today's advanced societies, artificial intelligence (AI) is spreading quickly. It has a significant impact on industries such as marketing, design, and entertainment, and is also gaining a growing foothold in Higher Education (HE) (Lee et al., 2024). Although the ideas and definitions surrounding AI have existed for many years, there has been a recent surge in interest, particularly within the field of education. The rise of large language models (LLMs) such as ChatGPT has further accelerated the integration of AI into classrooms, equipping educators with innovative tools to optimize teaching time, simplify administrative duties, analyze student data, boost engagement, and deliver automated feedback (Delello et al., 2025). These AI systems offer numerous benefits, making it crucial to critically evaluate their impact on the academic achievement and mental health of university students (Shahzad, Xu, Lim, Yang, & Khan, 2024).

In today's educational landscape, student well-being has become essential for creating effective learning environments. Educational institutions now understand that supporting student wellness directly impacts academic success, stress management, and overall learning satisfaction. The rise of artificial intelligence offers new opportunities to address these needs. Digital transformation is reshaping traditional education methods, with AI chatbots representing a particularly significant development. Recent technological breakthroughs, including advanced language models like ChatGPT, have accelerated the evolution of chatbot capabilities, positioning them as valuable tools for enhancing student support and well-being in academic settings (Ray, 2023). ChatGPT and similar AI systems offer significant potential for mental health enhancement. These intelligent systems can analyze student interactions to identify early warning signs of psychological distress that might otherwise go unnoticed by human observers (Abdillah, Partino, & Abd. Madjid, 2023).

According to research, AI can enhance mental health therapies by providing individualized assistance and learning. However, there are drawbacks as well, like increased psychological stress, legal and ethical issues, and over-reliance (Chen et al., 2024). Chatbots, adaptive learning systems, and mental health applications are examples of AI-driven solutions that have demonstrated potential in reducing student anxiety and depression. However, the quick development of advanced digital media also presents new psychological hazards for college students, including anxiety brought on by social media, internet addiction, worries that automation will jeopardize future employment opportunities, and anxieties of personal data breaches (Gu & Zhou, 2023). In addition, evaluating the impact of AI on mental health is essential as educational institutions use technology for administrative and personalized learning. AI raises concerns about stress, data privacy, and the potential loss of meaningful human engagement, even as it can enhance educational opportunities and offer targeted mental health support (Delello et al., 2025). According to Kavitha, Joshith, and Sharma (2024), while AI technologies provide personalized and adaptive learning experiences aimed at improving engagement and academic performance, it is essential to explore their wider impact on students' emotional and psychological well-being. Gaining insight into these effects is vital for developing learning environments that promote both academic achievement and mental health. One growing concern is student burnout, a condition marked by emotional exhaustion, detachment, and a diminished sense of accomplishment.

AI technologies have the potential to revolutionize conventional educational paradigms because they are made to respond and adapt to the needs of individual students (Ouyang & Jiao, 2021). Adaptive learning tailors e-learning to each student's needs by modifying pace and content using AI and data. It increases efficiency, improves learning results, and increases engagement (Gligorea et al., 2023, Delillo et al., 2024a & Zhou, 2023). AI and adaptive learning technologies are essential to creating a sustainable future because they increase everyone's access to and personalization of education. As a result, the populace becomes more knowledgeable and prepared to handle issues like resource management, sustainability, and climate change. People with higher levels of education are more inclined to support sensible legislation and embrace sustainable practices. Additionally, these technologies enable economic growth and innovation, which is crucial for sustainable development initiatives (Strielkowski et al., 2024).

In conclusion, a multidisciplinary approach is necessary to completely understand the impact of AI as technology continues to be integrated into educational systems. By analyzing how AI technologies affect university students' academic achievement and psychological well-being, the current research aims to advance our understanding. This chapter is organized into three key sections. The first section discusses the significance of artificial intelligence in education, with a focus on higher education. The second section introduces the theoretical framework, incorporating relevant theories to support the study's foundation. The third section presents a literature review that examines recent research findings on the implementation of AI in classrooms and its effects on teaching and learning.

OPERATIONALIZING "DRIFTING IN THE MIND": COGNITIVE AND ATTENTIONAL FRAGMENTATION IN AI-MEDIATED LEARNING

"Drifting in the mind" refers to a state of cognitive fragmentation and attentional diffusion that occurs when learners navigate AI-mediated educational environments. Unlike traditional mind-wandering, which involves spontaneous, self-generated thoughts departing from task-focused attention (Smallwood & Schooler, 2015). From a cognitive neuroscience perspective, drifting in the mind relates to disruptions in the default mode network (DMN) and executive control network (ECN). Research shows that excessive digital multitasking, common in AI-mediated learning environments, impairs the brain's ability to consolidate information and engage in reflective thought (Uncapher et al., 2016).

How AI-Mediated Environments Contribute to Drifting

Through a number of interrelated mechanisms that drastically alter how students interact with learning, AI-driven educational tools lead to mental drifting. First, AI learning environments are designed for constant engagement, notifications, adaptive recommendations, and real-time feedback, providing what Stone (1998) called "continuous partial attention." Instead of concentrating intently on a single job, students learn to maintain a superficial awareness across numerous AI-mediated streams. According to CLT, this is a persistent superfluous load that exhausts resources required for relevant processing (Sweller et al., 2011). Students are trained in fragmented patterns rather than sustained focus, as a result of this architecture of constant partial attention being the default mode of interaction.

Second, students participate in excessive cognitive offloading when AI systems manage growing cognitive processes, information organization, study schedules, and instant solutions (Risko & Gilbert, 2016). Over-reliance hinders the formation of internal cognitive schemas required for autonomous problem-solving, even when selective offloading might be advantageous. According to research, using GPS, for instance, hinders the development of spatial memory (Dahmani & Bohbot, 2020). Similarly, relying too much on AI tutors may hinder the development of self-regulated learning mechanisms. Because of this algorithmic dependence, learning-supporting tools may paradoxically impede the growth of cognitive abilities necessary for independent thought.

Third, by producing fragmented learning pathways that are specific to each person, AI's promise of individualized learning paradoxically encourages drifting. These methods do away with the shared reference points and group learning experiences that have historically underpinned educational identity by continuously adjusting to student performance. From the standpoint of sociotechnical systems, this means that the social system (shared learning community) is sacrificed to optimize the technical system (personalized efficiency) (Emery & Trist, 1960). With fewer possibilities for group sense-making and shared effort that fosters comprehension and a sense of belonging, students find themselves on solitary learning trajectories.

Fourth, AI systems frequently offer prompt feedback and solutions, resulting in dopaminergic reward cycles that favor short-term gains over long-term effort (Lembke, 2021). Instead of focusing on the long-term benefits of deep learning, this rewires kids' motivational systems toward instant satisfaction. The outcome is what Carr (2010) refers to as "shallows," recurring patterns of skimming and fragmented attention that solidify neurologically. The cognitive endurance needed for complicated problem-solving and prolonged engagement with challenging content is becoming more difficult for students.

Lastly, AI-mediated learning rarely occurs in a vacuum; rather, it takes place in larger digital ecosystems where social media, entertainment algorithms, and communication platforms compete with instructional AI. This leads to what Marwick and Boyd (2011) refer to as "context collapse," a situation in which students have to continually balance various identity performances and attentional demands across platforms. Students are left in a condition of constant cognitive and attentional fragmentation as the lines separating learning contexts, social contexts, and entertainment contexts blur. Students are unable to fully inhabit any one mode of engagement due to this context collapse, which exacerbates the drifting phenomena. Instead, they are only partially present across a number of conflicting demands.

THEORETICAL FRAMEWORK

To achieve a comprehensive understanding of students' psychological well-being in AI-driven classrooms, the theoretical framework will be grounded in Emery and Trist's (1960) Sociotechnical Systems Theory and Mezirow's (1997) transformative learning theory.

Sociotechnical Systems Theory

The current study is primarily based on the Sociotechnical Systems Theory (STS) to provide a more comprehensive understanding of the social and technological factors that shape the adoption and effects of emerging technologies within educational settings. The concept of the socio-technical system was first developed in the late 1950s by the Tavistock Institute in London, within the context of labor and organizational studies (Emery & Trist, 1960). Sociotechnical Systems Theory posits that successful organizational performance emerges from the design and combination of both the social system (comprising individuals, work processes, and organizational structures) and the technical system (tools, technology, and work environments). This theory advocates for developing work systems that integrate both human (social) factors and technological elements to improve overall efficiency, performance, and employee well-being (Cuofano, 2024).

Ropohl (1999) states that the socio-technical system framework was developed to highlight the mutual interdependence between people and technology. This concept promotes designing both technological tools and social work environments in a complementary manner, ensuring that productivity and human welfare can coexist harmoniously rather than being viewed as competing priorities. In essence, this approach recognizes that effective systems require careful consideration of both human factors and technical capabilities, creating workplace conditions where operational efficiency supports rather than undermines human well-being. A fundamental principle of sociotechnical systems theory is that effective system performance depends on *joint optimisation*, balancing and enhancing both the social and technical components, rather than focusing on optimising one at the expense of the other (Badham et al., 2006). Nonetheless, Pasmore et al. (2018) highlighted that "the technology used to perform work will constantly evolve, requiring ongoing adjustments rather than designing a social system around a fixed technology" (p. 76). This reinforces the need for educational systems to remain adaptable, ensuring that emerging tools, such as AI, are continuously aligned with evolving pedagogical approaches and the shifting demands of educators.

Tarisayi (2024) points out that when applying socio-technical system theory to AI integration in education, several critical factors emerge. The theory emphasises understanding how AI intersects existing educational social structures, including the perceptions of educators and students regarding AI technology and its potential effects on traditional academic roles and responsibilities. Practical applications include creating professional development initiatives to equip educators with the necessary AI skills and establishing ethical guidelines for the responsible implementation of AI in educational settings. The theory suggests that successful educational AI integration depends fundamentally on how effectively the technology engages with existing socio-technical systems while genuinely improving teaching and learning quality rather than disrupting established educational relationships and processes.

According to Dwyer (2011), socio-technical systems are made up of interrelated parts and artifacts that function together dynamically. These technological systems and society are in a reciprocal connection in which social forces develop them, and social structures are influenced and reshaped by them. The system operates according to an overarching objective or goal that directs its behavior, such as achieving fast response times in a communication network. A crucial feature of these systems is the feedback mechanism, which allows for continuous monitoring by comparing the system's actual performance against its intended goals. When significant discrepancies emerge between what the system produces and what it aims to achieve, this feedback loop triggers adjustments to the system's components and artifacts. This iterative process ensures that the system can adapt and improve its performance to meet its established objectives better.

Contemporary educational research has increasingly focused on understanding learning environments through a systems lens, exploring how the dynamic interactions between different components contribute to meaningful and effective educational experiences. Socio-technical system interventions go beyond technical problem-solving by offering a framework to reconceptualize the relationships between human elements (work practices, organizational dynamics, and cultural factors) and technological elements (physical spaces, learning tools, and digital infrastructure). (Bringas, Bowles & Walker, 2020).

Cognitive Load Theory

According to Sweller's (1988) cognitive load theory, students' ability to learn may be hindered by excessive cognitive demands. Adaptive learning technology driven by artificial intelligence addresses this issue by tailoring the complexity and pace of teaching materials, ensuring that content is broken into easily manageable segments (Ng et al., 2023). Fanning (2024) states that Cognitive Load Theory (CLT) is a fundamental framework in educational psychology, offering essential insights into how people absorb, store, and utilize information. A key cognitive principle of CLT is that learning involves more than merely receiving information; it also depends on how that information is structured and processed within working memory (Baddeley, 1992). According to CLT, cognitive load can be divided into three main types: intrinsic, extraneous, and germane. Intrinsic load relates to the inherent difficulty or complexity of the material being learned, which is determined by the nature of the content itself. Extraneous load, on the other hand, is caused by how information is presented and structured, and can either hinder or support learning depending on its clarity and relevance. Germane load pertains to the mental effort that learners intentionally invest in processing, organizing, and internalizing information, thereby directly contributing to the development of meaningful knowledge and long-term understanding (Sweller, Ayres, & Kalyuga, 2011).

Mayer & Moreno (2003) state that CLT, in the context of technology-enhanced learning, offers valuable guidance for enhancing the delivery of content. Adaptive platforms can tailor task difficulty according to a learner's progress, helping to keep cognitive load at an optimal level. When instructional approaches are designed in line with CLT principles, such systems can significantly support and improve learning outcomes. According to Ayres & Paas (2009), CLT extends beyond formal education by explaining how people handle information in everyday contexts. In the modern digital era, where information overload is widespread, its principles can help simplify information processing and enhance concentration. For example, well-designed user interfaces that remove unnecessary distractions can lower cognitive load, enabling users to navigate complex systems more efficiently.

Within CLT, the costs of communication and coordination in collaborative learning are viewed as additional cognitive demands placed on learners. These arise from the need to exchange information with peers and to manage both their own learning processes and those of other group members (Janssen et al. 2010; F. Kirschner et al. 2009b). Kirschner et al. (2018) point out that CLT has traditionally emphasized individual learners working on individual tasks, giving limited attention to the cognitive demands of communication and coordination, often referred to as transactional activities. Yet, in collaborative learning contexts, these activities are essential considerations for effective instructional design. The cognitive load generated in such settings can be influenced by factors such as team size, the expertise distribution among members, and the group's prior collaborative experience. By making thoughtful instructional choices around these variables, educators can manage transactional load and foster more productive learning outcomes. Collaborative CLT emphasizes the importance of considering both the strengths and limitations of group members when designing collaborative learning environments. Failing to account for these factors can result in inconsistent and unpredictable learning outcomes.

Artificial Intelligence and Machine Learning hold significant promises in education, as their effective implementation can enhance cognitive functioning, refine instructional design, and support the creation of adaptive learning environments. Research on incorporating AI-driven interventions within the framework of CLT shows notable increases in student engagement and a reduction in cognitive overload, resulting in overall enhanced learning outcomes (Gkintoni et al., 2025).

LITERATURE REVIEW

The rapid advancement of information technology has played a pivotal role in reshaping the global socioeconomic landscape. As a result, digital competence must now be viewed not merely as a basic skill but as a fundamental element of contemporary literacy (Thi Nguyen et al., 2024). UNESCO (2018) and the more recent framework from the World Bank define digital competence as extending beyond basic computer literacy and IT skills to include digital leadership and cultural capacities, which are essential for driving digital transformation strategies within organizations (Melhem & Jacobsen, 2021). According to Demirkol & Malkoc (2023), incorporating advanced digital tools such as ChatGPT into educational systems is reshaping conventional teaching methods, transforming student engagement, and influencing the development of learning resources, thereby marking the emergence of a more advanced era of digital education. To increase student engagement and accessibility in programming instruction, Yilmaz and Karaoglan Yilmaz (2023) created a variety of AI-based technologies, including chatbots, interactive coding platforms, and virtual instructors.

In education and cognitive science, exploring the complex nature of learning behaviors has emerged as a central focus of research. These behaviors span cognitive, affective, and metacognitive processes that individuals employ in acquiring knowledge. Scholars have increasingly directed attention to this area in an effort to uncover the underlying patterns, strategies, and key factors that influence learning outcomes (Lin et al., 2024). Common approaches to analyzing learning behavior include descriptive analysis, which focuses on summarizing and outlining patterns in learner behavior. This often involves examining frequencies, averages, and distributions to capture aspects such as time spent on tasks, interaction tendencies, and navigation paths (Fisher et al., 2021). To examine the self-regulated learning (SRL) strategies and learning behaviour patterns of high school students using an e-book system in a mathematics course, Geng et al. (2024) employed lag sequential analysis (LSA). The findings indicated that although students used elaboration and rehearsal techniques, they lacked metacognitive techniques when learning from e-books. The study also showed that the specific learning habits students employed during the process had an impact on their performance.

The Role of Digital Learning Assistance Systems in Enhancing Student Learning

The introduction of AI into all aspects of educational practice has had an impact on both instructors' and students' personal and professional lives (Ouyang, 2022). Hwang et al. (2020) outlined four primary roles of AI in education from an application-oriented perspective, presenting AI as an intelligent tutor, a tutee, a learning partner or tool, and a policy-making advisor. Tanveer et al. (2020) highlight that AI has the capacity to foster interactive learning. One of the most transformative aspects of technology-enhanced collaborative education is its ability to connect participants who are not physically in the same location, allowing students flexibility in when and where they learn. Online discussion forums further support this machine-assisted interactivity.

It is acknowledged that AI in education is a significant force behind innovative educational research, new instructional approaches, and technical advancements that would be challenging to implement in conventional classrooms. Computer-Assisted

Language Learning (CALL), machine learning, and artificial neural networks are a few examples that can be used in formal, informal, and non-formal learning settings (Hwang et al., 2020). Tanveer et al. (2020) state that faculty training is essential for encouraging instructors to use instructional data to refine pedagogy and to adopt AI widely in the classroom. AI-enabled systems already help reduce repetitive and administrative tasks such as grading and record-keeping. Streamlining these duties frees educators to focus more on the creative, empathetic, and inspiring aspects of their work.

Digital Learning Assistance Systems have significantly transformed education by enhancing student learning outcomes. They deliver personalized instruction that adapts to each learner's pace, style, and knowledge gaps, promoting deeper understanding. From a CLT perspective, these systems address Sweller's concern about excessive cognitive demands by delivering personalized instruction that adapts to each learner's pace, style, and knowledge gaps, thereby managing intrinsic load while minimizing extraneous load (Gudoniene et al., 2025). Real-time feedback and analytics help teachers quickly spot difficulties and provide timely support, which aligns with CLT's emphasis on germane load, the productive cognitive effort that builds schema and promotes deep learning. However, through the lens of STS, we must consider how these technological interventions affect the social subsystem of education. While these tools may optimize the technical aspects of learning delivery, STS reminds us that joint optimization requires examining whether they enhance or diminish the quality of human interactions, faculty-student relationships, and collaborative learning experiences that comprise the social infrastructure of education (Emery & Trist, 1960).

Chatbots can aid the learning process by delivering various essential services that help facilitate and enhance student learning. Kooli (2023) examines the aspects of education most influenced by AI, highlighting the reliability of assessments, the evolving nature of academic research, and the ethical dilemmas that arise from using chatbots in this context. According to Ait Baha et al. (2024), the use of chatbots in education has greatly improved students' language proficiency. By simulating real-life conversations, these tools facilitate academic debates, provide administrative support, and assist learners in honing their practical communication skills. Such interactive, AI-powered experiences not only strengthen linguistic abilities but also build confidence in using the language across different contexts. According to three key insights from a systematic analysis by Okonkwo and Ade-Ibijola (2021), the majority of chatbot applications concentrate on teaching and learning, research and development, administration, student advising, and evaluation.

The Role of AI in Shaping Learning Behaviors

The incorporation of AI into education has significantly reshaped the learning experience for university students by fostering personalization, boosting motivation, and enhancing knowledge retention (Cheng et al., 2023). Learning behavior encompasses the actions learners take during the learning process, such as reading, problem-solving, and interacting with peers, and can be understood as a systematic interaction between the learner, the task, the environment, and the resulting outcomes. Learning behaviors are influenced by both individual thinking and environmental factors, taking different forms such as pausing a video or sharing opinions in collaboration. In online contexts, these behaviors are varied and can be categorized into four main types (Yan & Au, 2019). Student behavior plays a vital role in shaping and refining generative AI tools, as it involves the active engagement and feedback of learners when interacting with AI applications (Bao et al., 2022; Lin et al., 2024; Volzhenin et al., 2022).

Kaygisiz (2022), points out that when designing and implementing AI-based educational technologies, it is imperative to take student behavior into consideration. Making tools that are more interesting and effective requires an understanding of students' perceptions and the elements that influence them. Nevertheless, little is known about how students' behavior influences the connection between AI applications and cognitive achievement. According to research, cognitive skills including reasoning, working memory, and processing speed help students succeed in school and in life (AlFarsi et al., 2021). Attention, short- and long-term memory, logical reasoning, auditory and visual processing, and processing speed are among the cognitive abilities required for learning with AI applications (Overstreet et al., 2023). Jaboob et al. (2024), examined the impact of GenAI tools on university students' cognitive achievement in three countries: Yemen, Jordan, and Oman. The findings highlight that GenAI applications had a significant positive effect on students' cognitive achievement, and that student behavior strengthened the relationship between GenAI use and learning outcomes.

Yang, Lian and Zhao (2023), conducted a study to investigate the impact of the GAFCC model (Goal, Access, Feedback, Challenge, Collaboration), which is a theory-driven gamification instructional design framework used to guide the creation of a gamified artificially intelligent educational robots (AIER) system. Its purpose is to enhance students' motivation and learning effectiveness, particularly in laboratory safety courses. The results revealed that the gamified AIER system, designed with the GAFCC model, was found to significantly enhance students' learning achievement, motivation, flow experience, and problem-solving skills, while also reducing cognitive load. Additionally, the integration of gamification techniques led to the development of more effective learning behavior patterns among students.

Emotional AI, another name for affective computing, refers to AI systems that are able to perceive, understand, and react to human emotions. These systems are used in education to evaluate students' emotional states by analyzing clues such as tone of voice, facial expressions, and physiological signals. Since these feelings have a significant impact on motivation, learning ability, frustration, and memory retention, it is essential to comprehend them. Additionally, emotion recognition software can identify indicators of disengagement, allowing for prompt interventions to enhance student learning. Deckker and Sumanasekara (2025), state that emotional AI enhances learning environments by addressing both the emotional and cognitive dimensions of students' learning experiences. According to Kulik & Fletcher (2016), students who interact with AI systems equipped with emotional capabilities show higher engagement, improved retention of learning material, and more positive academic behaviors, as these systems offer motivation and timely intervention strategies. AI systems monitor learner behaviors, such as task completion time and errors, to identify optimal levels of cognitive engagement and enhance learning efficiency. Through learning analytics, AI tracks student progress and identifies areas that require additional support. Automated assessments then adjust learning pathways, accordingly, providing extra guidance when required and reducing support as the student's proficiency improves (Halkiopoulos & Gkintoni, 2024). With the ongoing advancement of AI, its influence on improving learning behaviours by fostering personalization, enhancing motivation, and strengthening retention is becoming increasingly prominent. Tapalova and Zhiyenbayeva (2022) confirm that AI's ability to tailor learning to individual needs not only improves educational outcomes but also fosters a deeper and more meaningful learning experience.

These findings illustrate a critical tension identified in STS Theory: the need for joint optimization between technical and social systems (Badham et al., 2006). While emotional AI enhances the technical system's capacity to respond to student needs, STS warns against over-optimizing the technical system at the expense of social elements, such as peer support networks and faculty mentorship, that are equally crucial for student well-being. From a CLT perspective, the effectiveness of these AI interventions can be understood through their management of transactional load: emotionally responsive AI may reduce the communication and coordination costs in collaborative learning environments (Kirschner et al., 2018), but only if the technology genuinely supports rather than substitutes for the social processes that facilitate meaningful learning.

AI Integration and Its Effects on Student Well-Being

The integration of AI in universities impacts not only educational outcomes but also plays a significant role in shaping students' psychological well-being. Sociotechnical Systems Theory provides a crucial framework for understanding these impacts: while AI technologies provide notable advantages, such as enhancing academic performance and streamlining administrative processes, STS emphasizes that system effectiveness depends on joint optimization of both technical and social subsystems (Emery & Trist, 1960). The psychological risks identified by Small et al. (2020) and the concerns about reduced human interaction raised by Korteling et al. (2021) represent precisely the kind of social system degradation that STS warns against when technical optimization proceeds without adequate consideration of social factors.

University life is often accompanied by anxiety, pressure, and stress, emotional states that AI has the potential to either alleviate or intensify (Shahzad et al., 2024). Sepahpour (2020) mentions that it is important to distinguish between AI chatbots explicitly designed for social support and wellbeing—such as therapeutic or counselling bots—and general-purpose, unmonitored chatbots like ChatGPT, which are not specifically intended for emotional support. Excessive reliance on unmonitored AI chatbots may lead to negative psychological outcomes, including social withdrawal, isolation, or even AI dependency. Crawford et al (2024) conducted a study, and the results revealed that students who perceived social support from AI appeared to experience comparable benefits to their psychological well-being as those who received support from human interactions.

According to Benchallal (2025), the implementation of AI in education raises important questions about its impact on student learning and psychological well-being. He believes that it is essential to examine how AI influences students' academic performance and that the psychological impact of AI use on students remains a critical concern. Ghaleb et al. (2023) point out that AI's capacity to tailor learning experiences can influence self-efficacy in two contrasting ways. On the positive side, AI has the potential to deliver personalized recommendations for self-care activities, relaxation strategies, mindfulness practices, and stress-management techniques tailored to individual preferences and needs. Additionally, adaptive systems that respond to learners' personal styles and pace may strengthen their confidence in mastering material at a comfortable rhythm (Aggarwal, 2023). From a CLT perspective, the finding that excessive AI reliance may reduce autonomy and self-directed learning (Jagatheesaperumal et al., 2024) can be understood as a failure to develop germane load, the productive cognitive effort that builds problem-solving schemas and metacognitive skills. When AI systems handle too much of the cognitive work, they may reduce extraneous load but simultaneously prevent students from engaging in the germane processing necessary for deep learning and transfer (Sweller et al., 2011). This represents a paradox: technically optimized systems may actually undermine the cognitive development they aim to support. To address the challenges brought about by emerging technologies, integrating AI literacy and ethics into curricula is essential. By harnessing these innovations, educators and policymakers can foster inclusive, equitable, and effective learning environments that meet the diverse needs of 21st-century learners (Kamalov et al., 2023).

Small et al. (2020) mention that excessive reliance on AI technologies can lead to a variety of psychological risks. A primary concern is that increasing reliance on AI in education may limit opportunities for human interaction (Korteling et al., 2021). Additionally, when incorporating AI into education, protecting the security and privacy of student data is crucial. Strict data protection laws and ethical standards must be followed by educational institutions and technology suppliers in order to maintain confidentiality and stop the abuse, illegal access, or publication of private data, which students might find psychologically distressing (Eden, Ch., Chisom, O, & Adeniyi, I, 2024). To conclude, the psychological implications of AI must be carefully considered, even while it has the potential to improve educational experiences through personalized and adaptable learning. AI tools should be carefully implemented by educational institutions, taking into account their broader effects on students' well-being. For students' overall development, AI must promote, rather than hinder, the acquisition of critical life skills, like self-control, resilience, and interpersonal communication (Velastegui-Hernandez et al., 2023). Additionally, the predictive capabilities of certain AI applications may confine students to predetermined learning paths, limiting their exposure to a wider curriculum and potentially inhibiting creativity and critical thinking by focusing too narrowly on anticipated strengths or weaknesses (Schlimbach et al., 2022).

ALGORITHMIC BIAS AND EDUCATIONAL EQUITY: HIDDEN MECHANISMS OF EXCLUSION IN AI-DRIVEN CLASSROOMS

A growing body of research indicates that algorithmic systems have the potential to reinforce and magnify current educational disparities, despite AI's promise to democratize education through individualized learning (O'Neil, 2016). Algorithmic bias is a critical failure of joint optimization, according to Sociotechnical Systems Theory. Technical systems that are optimized for efficiency may systematically disadvantage specific student populations, which would reduce the social system's ability to produce equitable learning outcomes. Both the integrity of AI-mediated education and the welfare of students depend on an understanding of these biases.

Bias in Training Data

Artificial intelligence (AI) educational systems learn from past data, which frequently reflects current disparities. According to Baker and Hawn's (2021) research, adaptive learning systems trained primarily on data from well-resourced schools performed badly for children from under-resourced situations. AI systems incorporate past disadvantages as predictive attributes when they identify patterns in biased datasets. For instance, the algorithm may incorrectly incorporate patterns into recommendations if training data reveals that students from particular demographic backgrounds have historically had lower completion rates, leading to self-fulfilling prophecies (Ekowo & Palmer, 2016).

Bias in Representation

Diverse student populations are frequently not well represented by AI systems. Significant performance differences in facial recognition systems between racial and gender categories were shown by Raji and Buolamwini (2019); these findings apply to educational applications that use engagement detection or emotion recognition. The behaviors and expressions of underrepresented students are misidentified or misinterpreted by AI-powered proctoring systems or emotional AI tools that are trained primarily on specific demographic groups, potentially flagging them as disengaged or dishonest at disproportionate rates (Raji et al., 2020).

Bias in Feature Selection

Implicit value judgments are present in the variables used to train AI algorithms. According to Barocas and Selbst (2016), predictive analytics systems that include structural disadvantage into automated decision-making may seem to maximize for accuracy when using socioeconomic indicators (ZIP codes, first-generation status, parental education) as features. According to CLT, this results in differential superfluous load since students from marginalized backgrounds have to deal with algorithmic systems that were created without taking into account their cultural and cognitive surroundings, in addition to the course material.

Label Bias and the Definition of Outcomes

The definition of "success" or "engagement" by educational AI systems reflects specific institutional and cultural norms. For example, students whose cultural backgrounds prioritize thoughtful deliberation over quick reaction are disadvantaged by systems that associate success with task completion speed (Holmes et al., 2021). The "drifting in the mind" issue may also be exacerbated by engagement measures that reward superficial but frequent participation while misrepresenting profound, contemplative learners as "at risk" due to their frequent connection.

Cultural Differences in AI-Mediated Education

Culture manifests at multiple levels, including regions, nations, districts, schools, and classrooms. Research indicates that teachers' attitudes vary across these cultural contexts, suggesting that cultural values should be taken into account when implementing AI-based educational technologies in K–12 settings. Specifically, notable differences have been observed across four cultural dimensions: uncertainty avoidance, long- versus short-term orientation, masculinity versus femininity, and collectivism versus individualism (Viberg, et al., 2025).

AI systems used in education are rarely culturally neutral. Arif (2025) examined how AI is influencing education in international classrooms, focusing on multiple cases that highlight the interaction between cultural perspectives on learning and technological innovation. The findings revealed that the effectiveness of AI in education is strongly shaped by cultural attitudes. AI is commonly used in Western educational institutions to enhance human instruction and support student-centered learning. On the other hand, nations like South Korea and China have embraced AI as an efficiency-driven tool, incorporating facial recognition and data analytics into classroom settings to track student participation (Zhao et al., 2020). These variations demonstrate how governmental regulations and cultural norms affect the integration of AI. Both educational equity and psychological welfare must comprehend cultural differences in how students interact with experience and are impacted by AI-mediated learning.

According to (T. Wang et al., 2023), the widespread use of AI among international students, along with their attitudes and intentions toward its use, mirrors a broader global pattern where learners from different cultural backgrounds demonstrate greater readiness to integrate new technologies into their studies. A contributing factor might be their varied educational foundations combined with their aim to participate in globally minded education (Xion et al., 2022). International students might view AI technology as indispensable for success in the globalized job sector, whereas students from China may perceive it as a mechanism for aligning their education with international criteria (Ma, Akram & Chen, 2024).

Generative AI and the Changing Landscape of Faculty Roles

The integration of generative AI into higher education has clearly shaped faculty–student communication (Aad & Hardey, 2024). Sociotechnical Systems Theory illuminates the faculty resistance documented by Iqbal et al. (2022) as more than mere technophobia; it reflects legitimate concerns about disruption to the carefully balanced social system of education. Faculty members' apprehensions about academic dishonesty, privacy violations, and insufficient collegial support indicate awareness that introducing AI tools without redesigning social work processes and support structures threatens the joint optimization principle central to STS (Pasmore et al., 2018). The theory suggests that successful AI integration requires not just technical implementation but simultaneous restructuring of social elements: professional development, revised assessment practices, new ethical frameworks, and redefined roles that preserve the human elements essential to meaningful education. Building on this viewpoint, Picciano (2019) predicts that AI apps will handle the majority of academic advice in the future, including guidance on majors, course prerequisites, and career preparation. As a result of this, academic advisors and counsellors may play a smaller role, mainly providing support for extremely personal matters. Kasneci et al. (2023) point out that AI tools are capable of quickly generating substantial amounts of well-written and unique readable texts that may foster academic dishonesty or provide unfair assistance in programming and problem-solving endeavours

According to Kulik and Fletcher (2016), intelligent tutoring systems, or ITSs, are a major use of AI in education that have the potential to change how educational systems operate. These systems use artificial intelligence (AI) algorithms to evaluate student data and provide individualized learning experiences, adjusting feedback, tests, and content to suit the unique learning preferences and speeds of each student. Furthermore, ITSs use machine learning and natural language processing to interact with students more naturally, which boosts engagement and involvement. Some faculty view AI's potential as evident. According to Kadaruddin (2023), the adoption of AI tools enables teachers to shift from standardized teaching approaches toward a student-centered model, allowing them to design diverse learning resources. With the use of AI tools, educators can tailor and modify learning paths to each student's unique requirements, promoting student engagement and fostering active, self-directed learning (Bhutoria, 2022). However, it is worth mentioning that although ChatGPT can support teachers' professional development by providing innovative teaching ideas and facilitating self-regulated learning tasks, it is less effective in enhancing teaching competencies and providing adaptive teaching methods (Aad & Hardey, 2024).

The empirical evidence reviewed here validates core propositions of both Sociotechnical Systems Theory and CLT while revealing their complementary analytical power. CLT explains the mechanisms through which AI affects individual cognitive processing, managing intrinsic, extraneous, and germane load to either enhance or hinder learning. STS, in turn, explains the broader systemic patterns, how AI's impact on individual cognition cannot be separated from its effects on social structures, relationships, and organizational dynamics. The research consistently shows that AI interventions succeed when they achieve joint optimization (balancing technical efficiency with social well-being, per STS) and appropriate load management (supporting germane processing without creating dependence, per CLT). Conversely, implementations fail when they prioritize technical optimization at the expense of social systems or when they reduce cognitive demands in ways that prevent the development of essential learning capacities. This theoretical synthesis moves beyond descriptive accounts of AI's effects to provide explanatory frameworks that can guide more thoughtful, evidence-based implementation.

CONCLUSION

The integration of theoretical frameworks with empirical evidence reveals a more nuanced understanding of AI's role in education than either perspective alone could provide. STS demonstrates that AI's impact extends beyond individual learning outcomes to encompass the entire educational ecosystem, reshaping faculty roles, altering student relationships, and reconfiguring the balance between technical and social elements of learning. CLT explains the cognitive mechanisms underlying these changes, showing how AI tools can either support deep learning through appropriate load management or undermine it through dependency and schema development interference. Together, these frameworks suggest that successful AI integration requires simultaneous attention to cognitive architecture and social systems, technical capabilities and human relationships, efficiency gains, and well-being preservation. Future research should explicitly employ these theoretical lenses to move beyond cataloging AI's effects toward understanding the underlying mechanisms and designing interventions grounded in established principles of how people learn and organization's function.

REFERENCES

Aad, S., & Hardey, M. (2024). Generative AI: Hopes, controversies and the future of faculty roles in education. *Quality Assurance in Education*, *33*(2), 267–282. http://hdl.handle.net/10725/15964. DOI: 10.1108/QAE-02-2024-0043

Abdillah, H. Z., Partino, P., & Madjid, A. (2023). Enhancing student well-being through AI chat GPT in the smart education university learning environment: A preliminary review of research literature. In *E3S web of Conferences* (Vol. 440, p. 05005). EDP Sciences., DOI: 10.1051/e3sconf/202344005005

Aggarwal, D. (2023). Integration of innovative technological developments and AI with education for an adaptive learning pedagogy. *China Petroleum Processing and Petrochemical Technology*, *23*(2), 709–714.

Ait Baha, T., El Hajji, M., Es-Saady, Y., & Fadili, H. (2024). The impact of educational chatbot on student learning experience. *Education and Information Technologies*, *29*(8), 10153–10176. DOI: 10.1007/s10639-023-12166-w

AlFarsi, G. Bin Mohd. Yusof, A., Ezanee Bin Rusli, M., Tawafak, R. M., Iqbal Malik, S., & Mathew, R. (2021). The general view of the virtual learning environment in the education sector. 2021 22nd International Arab Conference on Information Technology (ACIT) (pp. 1–6). https://doi.org/DOI: 10.1109/ACIT53391.2021.9677326

Arif, S. (2025). Cross-cultural perspectives on AI in education: Case studies from global classrooms. *AI EDIFY Journal*, *1*(2), 12–20.

Baddeley, A. D. (1992). Working memory. *Science*, *255*(5044), 556–559. DOI: 10.1126/science.1736359 PMID: 1736359

Badham, R. J., Clegg, C. W., & Wall, T. (2006). Sociotechnical theory. In Karwowski, W. (Ed.), *International encyclopedia of ergonomics and human factors* (2nd ed.). CRC Press.

Baker, R. S., & Hawn, A. (2021). Algorithmic bias in education. *International Journal of Artificial Intelligence in Education*, •••, 1–41. DOI: 10.1007/s40593-021-00285-9

Bao, J., Li, L., & Davis, A. (2022). Variational autoencoder or generative adversarial networks? A comparison of two deep learning methods for flow and transport data assimilation. *Mathematical Geosciences*, *54*(6), 1017–1042. DOI: 10.1007/s11004-022-10003-3

Barocas, S., & Selbst, A. D. (2016). Big data's disparate impact. *California Law Review*, *104*, 671–732.

Bhutoria, A. (2022). Personalized education and artificial intelligence in the United States, China, and India: A systematic review using a human-in-the-loop model. *Computers and Education: Artificial Intelligence*, *3*, 100068. DOI: 10.1016/j.caeai.2022.100068

Carr, N. (2010). *The shallows: What the Internet is doing to our brains*. WW Norton & Company.

Chen, J., Yuan, D., Dong, R., Cai, J., Ai, Z., & Zhou, S. (2024). Artificial intelligence significantly facilitates development in the mental health of college students: A bibliometric analysis. *Frontiers in Psychology*, *15*, 1375294. Advance online publication. DOI: 10.3389/fpsyg.2024.1375294 PMID: 38515973

Cheng, L., Umapathy, K., Rehman, M., Ritzhaupt, A., Antonyan, K., Shidfar, P., Nichols, J., Lee, M., & Abramowitz, B. (2023). Designing, developing, and validating a measure of undergraduate students' conceptions of artificial intelligence in education. *Journal of Interactive Learning Research*, *34*(2), 275–311. DOI: 10.70725/347638mgikol

Crawford, J., Allen, K. A., Pani, B., & Cowling, M. (2024). When artificial intelligence substitutes humans in higher education: The cost of loneliness, student success, and retention. *Studies in Higher Education*, *49*(5), 883–897. DOI: 10.1080/03075079.2024.2326956

Cuofano, G. (2024). What is sociotechnical systems theory? FourWeekMBA. Available online: https://fourweekmba.com/sociotechnical-systems-theory/

Dahmani, L., & Bohbot, V. D. (2020). Habitual use of GPS negatively impacts spatial memory during self-guided navigation. *Scientific Reports*, *10*(1), 6310. DOI: 10.1038/s41598-020-62877-0 PMID: 32286340

Deckker, D., & Sumanasekara, S. (2025). Emotional AI for student motivation and retention: A systematic review and future directions. *International Journal of Global Economic Light*, *11*(3), 35–50. Advance online publication. DOI: 10.36713/epra20564

Delello, J. A., Sung, W., Mokhtari, K., Hebert, J., Bronson, A., & De Giuseppe, T. (2025). AI in the classroom: Insights from educators on usage, challenges, and mental health. *Education Sciences*, *15*(2), 113. DOI: 10.3390/educsci15020113

Demirkol, M., & Malkoc, N. (2023). Assessing the Intellectual Structure of the Evolving Knowledge Base on ChatGPT in the Field of Education and Health. *Educational Process: International Journal*, *12*(4), 36–64. DOI: 10.22521/edupij.2023.124.3

Dwyer, C. (2011). "Socio-technical Systems Theory and Environmental Sustainability," Proceedings > Proceedings of SIGGreen Workshop. *Sprouts: Working Papers on Information Systems,* 11(3). http://sprouts.aisnet.org/11-3

Eden, C. A., Chisom, O. N., & Adeniyi, I. S. (2024). Integrating AI in education: Opportunities, challenges, and ethical considerations. *Magna Scientia Advanced Research and Reviews, 10*(2), p.p. 006-013. https://doi.org/DOI: 10.30574/msarr.2024.10.2.0039

Ekowo, M., & Palmer, I. (2016). *The promise and peril of predictive analytics in higher education.* New America.

Emery, F. E., and E. L. Trist. 1960. "Socio-technical Systems." *In Management Sciences Models and Techniques*, 2, p. 83-97.

Fanning, S. (2024). *Parallel Minds: A Thematic Literature Review of Artificial Intelligence in Education* (Master's thesis, Washington State University).

Fisher, W. W., Piazza, C. C., & Roane, H. S. (Eds.). (2021). *Handbook of applied behavior analysis.* Guilford Publications.

Geng, X., Chen, L., Xu, Y., Ogata, H., Shimada, A., & Yamada, M. (2024). Learning behavioral patterns of students with varying performance in a high school mathematics course using an e-book system [Article]. *Research and Practice in Technology Enhanced Learning*, *19*, 011. Advance online publication. DOI: 10.58459/rptel.2024.19011

Gkintoni, E., Antonopoulou, H., Sortwell, A., & Halkiopoulos, C. (2025). Challenging cognitive load theory: The role of educational neuroscience and artificial intelligence in redefining learning efficacy. *Brain Sciences*, *15*(2), 203. DOI: 10.3390/brainsci15020203 PMID: 40002535

Gligorea, I., Cioca, M., Oancea, R., Gorski, A.-T., Gorski, H., & Tudorache, P. (2023, December 06). Adaptive Learning Using Artificial Intelligence in e-Learning: A Literature Review. *Education Sciences*, *13*(12), 1216. Advance online publication. DOI: 10.3390/educsci13121216

Gu, Y., & Zhou, K. (2023). Integration of modern technologies in higher education on the example of artificial intelligence use. *Education and Information Technologies*, *28*(4), 3893–3910. DOI: 10.1007/s10639-022-11309-9

Gudoniene, D., Staneviciene, E., Morkun, N., & Fischerauer, G. (2025). *Artificial Intelligence Solutions for Higher Education. Handbook for Educators. Project no* 2023-1-ES01-KA220-HED-000153371

Halkiopoulos, C., & Gkintoni, E. (2024). Leveraging AI in e-learning: Personalized learning and adaptive assessment through cognitive neuropsychology—A systematic analysis. *Electronics (Basel), 13*(18), 3762. DOI: 10.3390/electronics13183762

Holmes, W., Nguyen, Q., Zhang, J., Mavrikis, M., & Rienties, B. (2021). Learning analytics for learning design in online distance learning. *Distance Education, 42*(1), 30–50. DOI: 10.1080/01587919.2019.1637716

Hwang, G. J., Xie, H., Wah, B. W., & Gašević, D. (2020). Vision, challenges, roles and research issues of Artificial Intelligence in Education. *Computers and Education: Artificial Intelligence, 1*(100001), 1–5. DOI: 10.1016/j.caeai.2020.100001

Iqbal, N., Ahmed, H., & Azhar, K. A. (2022). EXPLORING TEACHERS' ATTITUDES TOWARDS USING CHATGPT. *Global Journal for Management and Administrative Sciences, 3*(4), 97–111. DOI: 10.46568/gjmas.v3i4.163

Jaboob, M., Hazaimeh, M., & Al-Ansi, A. M. (2024). Integration of Generative AI Techniques and Applications in Student Behavior and Cognitive Achievement in Arab Higher Education. *International Journal of Human-Computer Interaction, 41*(1), 353–366. DOI: 10.1080/10447318.2023.2300016

Jagatheesaperumal, S. K., Ahmad, K., Al-Fuqaha, A., & Qadir, J. (2024). Advancing education through extended reality and internet of everything enabled metaverses: Applications, challenges, and open issues. *IEEE Transactions on Learning Technologies, 17*, 1120–1139. https://creativecommons.org/licenses/by/4.0/. DOI: 10.1109/TLT.2024.3358859

Janssen, J., Kirschner, F., Erkens, G., Kirschner, P. A., & Paas, F. (2010). Making the black box of collaborative learning transparent: Combining process-oriented and cognitive load approaches. *Educational Psychology Review, 22*(2), 139–154. DOI: 10.1007/s10648-010-9131-x

Kadaruddin, K. (2023). Empowering Education through Generative AI: Innovative Instructional Strategies for Tomorrow's Learners. *International Journal of Business, Law, and Education, 4*(2), 618–625. DOI: 10.56442/ijble.v4i2.215

Kamalov, F., Santandreu Calonge, D., & Gurrib, I. (2023). New era of artificial intelligence in education: Towards a sustainable multifaceted revolution. *Sustainability (Basel), 15*(16), 12451. DOI: 10.3390/su151612451

Kasneci, E., Seßler, K., Küchemann, S., Bannert, M., Dementieva, D., Fischer, F., Gasser, U., Groh, G., Günnemann, S., Hüllermeier, E., Krusche, S., Kutyniok, G., Michaeli, T., Nerdel, C., Pfeffer, J., Poquet, O., Sailer, M., Schmidt, A., Seidel, T., & Kasneci, G. (2023). ChatGPT for good? On opportunities and challenges of large language models for education. *Learning and Individual Differences*, *103*, 102274. DOI: 10.1016/j.lindif.2023.102274

Kavitha, K., Joshith, V. P., & Sharma, S. (2024). Beyond text: ChatGPT as an emotional resilience support tool for Gen Z – A sequential explanatory design exploration. *E-Learning and Digital Media*, 20427530241259099. Advance online publication. DOI: 10.1177/20427530241259099

Kaygisiz, C¸. (2022). Educational neuroscience: Issues and challenges. *Erciyes Journal of Education*, *6*(1), 80–98. DOI: 10.32433/eje.990407

Kirschner, F., Paas, F., & Kirschner, P. A. (2009b). Individual and group-based learning from complex cognitive tasks: Effects on retention and transfer efficiency. *Computers in Human Behavior*, *25*(2), 306–314. DOI: 10.1016/j.chb.2008.12.008

Kirschner, P. A., Sweller, J., Kirschner, F., & Zambrano, R. J. (2018). From cognitive load theory to collaborative cognitive load theory. *International Journal of Computer-Supported Collaborative Learning*, *13*(2), 213–233. DOI: 10.1007/s11412-018-9277-y PMID: 30996713

Kooli, C. (2023). Chatbots in education and research: A critical examination of ethical implications and solutions. *Sustainability (Basel)*, *15*(7), 5614. DOI: 10.3390/su15075614

Korteling, J. E., van de Boer-Visschedijk, G. C., Blankendaal, R. A., Boonekamp, R. C., & Eikelboom, A. R. (2021). Human-versus artificial intelligence. *Frontiers in Artificial Intelligence*, *4*, 622364. DOI: 10.3389/frai.2021.622364 PMID: 33981990

Kulik, J. A., & Fletcher, J. D. (2016). Effectiveness of intelligent tutoring systems: A meta-analytic review. *Review of Educational Research*, *86*(1), 42–78. DOI: 10.3102/0034654315581420

Lee, D., Arnold, M., Srivastava, A., Plastow, K., Strelan, P., Ploeckl, F., Lekkas, D., & Palmer, E. (2024). The impact of generative AI on higher education learning and teaching: A study of educators' perspectives. *Computers and Education: Artificial Intelligence*, *6*, 100221. DOI: 10.1016/j.caeai.2024.100221

Lembke, A. (2021). *Dopamine nation: Finding balance in the age of indulgence*. Penguin.

Lin, C. C., Cheng, E. S., Huang, A. Y., & Yang, S. J. (2024). DNA of learning behaviors: A novel approach of learning performance prediction by NLP. *Computers and Education: Artificial Intelligence*, *6*, 100227. DOI: 10.1016/j.caeai.2024.100227

Ma, D., Akram, H., & Chen, I. H. (2024). Artificial intelligence in higher education: A cross-cultural examination of students' behavioral intentions and attitudes. *International Review of Research in Open and Distance Learning*, *25*(3), 134–157. DOI: 10.19173/irrodl.v25i3.7703

Marwick, A. E., & boyd, . (2011). I tweet honestly, I tweet passionately: Twitter users, context collapse, and the imagined audience. *New Media & Society*, *13*(1), 114–133. DOI: 10.1177/1461444810365313

Mayer, R. E., & Moreno, R. (2003). Nine ways to reduce cognitive load in multimedia learning. *Educational Psychologist*, *38*(1), 43–52. DOI: 10.1207/S15326985EP3801_6

Melhem, S., & Jacobsen, A. H. (2021). A global study on digital capabilities. The World Bank. A Global Study on Digital Capabilities

Navarro-Bringas, E., Bowles, G., & Walker, G. H. (2020). Embracing complexity: A sociotechnical systems approach for the design and evaluation of higher education learning environments. *Theoretical Issues in Ergonomics Science*, *21*(5), 595–613. DOI: 10.1080/1463922X.2020.1723037

Ng, D. T. K., Leung, J. K. L., Su, J., Ng, R. C. W., & Chu, S. K. W. (2023). Teachers' AI digital competencies and twenty-first century skills in the post-pandemic world. *Educational Technology Research and Development*, *71*(1), 137–161. DOI: 10.1007/s11423-023-10203-6 PMID: 36844361

Nguyen, T. N. T., Van Lai, N., & Nguyen, Q. T. (2024). Artificial Intelligence (AI) in Education: A Case Study on ChatGPT's Influence on Student Learning Behaviors. *Educational Process: International Journal*, *13*(2), 105–121. DOI: 10.22521/edupij.2024.132.7

Okonkwo, C. W., & Ade-Ibijola, A. (2021). Chatbots applications in education: A systematic review. Computers and Education. *Artificial Intelligence*, *2*, 100033. DOI: 10.1016/j.caeai.2021.100033

Ouyang, F., & Jiao, P. (2021). Artificial intelligence in education: The three paradigms. *Computers and Education: Artificial Intelligence*, *2*, 100020.

Ouyang, F., Zheng, L., & Jiao, P. (2022). Artificial intelligence in online higher education: A systematic review of empirical research from 2011 to 2020. *Education and Information Technologies*, *27*(6), 1–33. DOI: 10.1007/s10639-022-10925-9

Overstreet, M., Akhmedjanova, D., & Vaccino-Salvadore, S. (2023). Brain-bound vs. extended: Contrasting approaches to second-language research writing in digital environments. *Journal of Second Language Writing, 61,* 101019. https://doi.org/. 101019DOI: 10.1016/j.jslw.2023

Pasmore, W., Winby, S., Mohrman, S. A., & Vanasse, R. (2018). Reflections: Sociotechnical systems design and organization change. *Journal of Change Management, 19*(2), 67–85. DOI: 10.1080/14697017.2018.1553761

Picciano, A. G. (2019). Artificial Intelligence and the Academy's Loss of Purpose. *Online Learning : the Official Journal of the Online Learning Consortium, 23*(3), 270–284. DOI: 10.24059/olj.v23i3.2023

Raji, I. D., Gebru, T., Mitchell, M., Buolamwini, J., Lee, J., & Denton, E. (2020). Saving face. *Proceedings of AIES,* 145-151. https://doi.org/DOI: 10.1145/3375627.3375820

Ray, P. P. (2023). ChatGPT: A comprehensive review on background, applications, key challenges, bias, ethics, limitations and future scope. *Internet of Things and Cyber-Physical Systems, 3,* 121–154. DOI: 10.1016/j.iotcps.2023.04.003

Risko, E. F., & Gilbert, S. J. (2016). Cognitive offloading. *Trends in Cognitive Sciences, 20*(9), 676–688. DOI: 10.1016/j.tics.2016.07.002 PMID: 27542527

Schlimbach, R., Rinn, H., Markgraf, D., & Robra-Bissantz, S. (2022). A literature review on pedagogical conversational agent adaptation. *In Pacific Asia Conference on Information Systems, 1.* 1-14. Bangkok, Thailand: AIS. https://api.semanticscholar .org/CorpusID:250957088

Sepahpour, T. (2020). *Ethical considerations of chatbot use for mental health support* (Doctoral dissertation, Johns Hopkins University).

Shahzad, M. F., Xu, S., Lim, W. M., Yang, X., & Khan, Q. R. (2024). Artificial intelligence and social media on academic performance and mental well-being: Student perceptions of positive impact in the age of smart learning. *Heliyon, 10*(8), e29523. Advance online publication. DOI: 10.1016/j.heliyon.2024.e29523 PMID: 38665566

Small, G. W., Lee, J., Kaufman, A., Jalil, J., Siddarth, P., Gaddipati, H., Moody, T. D., & Bookheimer, S. Y. (2020). Brain health consequences of digital technology use. *Dialogues in Clinical Neuroscience, 22*(2), 179–187. DOI: 10.31887/DCNS.2020.22.2/gsmall PMID: 32699518

Stone, L. (1998). Thoughts on attention and specifically, continuous partial attention. *Linda Stone,* http://www. lindastone. net

Strielkowski, W., Grebennikova, V., Lisovskiy, A., Rakhimova, G., & Vasileva, T. (2025). AI-driven adaptive learning for sustainable educational transformation. *Sustainable Development (Bradford), 33*(2), 1921–1947. DOI: 10.1002/sd.3221

Sufyan Ghaleb, M. M., & Alshiha, A. A. (2023). Empowering Self-Management: Unveiling the Impact of Artificial Intelligence in Learning on Student Self-Efficacy and Self-Monitoring. *Eurasian Journal of Educational Research (EJER), (107).* https://doiDOI: 10.14689/ejer.2023.107.005

Sweller, J. (1988). Cognitive load during problem solving: Effects on learning. *Cognitive Science, 12*(2), 257–285. DOI: 10.1207/s15516709cog1202_4

Sweller, J., Ayres, P., & Kalyuga, S. (2011). *Cognitive load theory*. Springer., DOI: 10.1007/978-1-4419-8126-4

Tanveer, M., Hassan, S., & Bhaumik, A. (2020). Academic policy regarding sustainability and artificial intelligence (AI). *Sustainability (Basel), 12*(22), 9435. DOI: 10.3390/su12229435

Tapalova, O., & Zhiyenbayeva, N. (2022). Artificial intelligence in education: AIEd for personalised learning pathways. *Electronic Journal of e-Learning, 20*(5), 639–653. www.ejel.org. DOI: 10.34190/ejel.20.5.2597

Tarisayi, S. (2024). A Theoretical framework for interrogating the integration of artificial intelligence in education. *Research on Education and Media, 16*(1), 38–34. DOI: 10.2478/rem-2024-0006

Uncapher, M. R. K., Thieu, M., & Wagner, A. D. (2016). Media multitasking and memory. *Psychonomic Bulletin & Review, 23*(2), 483–490. DOI: 10.3758/s13423-015-0907-3 PMID: 26223469

Velastegui-Hernandez DC, Salazar-Garcés LF, Rodriguez-Pérez ML. Impact of Artificial Intelligence on learning behaviors and psychological well-being of college students (2023). *Salud, Ciencia y Tecnología - Serie de Conferencias*. 2:582. https://doi.org/DOI: 10.56294/sctconf2023582

Viberg, O., Cukurova, M., Feldman-Maggor, Y., Alexandron, G., Shirai, S., Kanemune, S., & Kizilcec, R. F. (2025). What explains teachers' trust in AI in education across six countries? *International Journal of Artificial Intelligence in Education, 35*(3), 1288-1316. *International Journal (Toronto, Ont.)*. Advance online publication. DOI: 10.1007/s40593-024-00433-x

Volzhenin, K., Changeux, J.-P., & Dumas, G. (2022). Multilevel development of cognitive abilities in an artificial neural network. *Proceedings of the National Academy of Sciences of the United States of America, 119*(39), e2201304119. DOI: 10.1073/pnas.2201304119 PMID: 36122214

Yan, N., & Au, O. T. S. (2019). Online learning behavior analysis based on machine learning. Asian association of open universities journal, 14(2), 97-106. DOI DOI: 10.1108/AAOUJ-08-2019-0029

Yang, Q. F., Lian, L. W., & Zhao, J. H. (2023). Developing a gamified artificial intelligence educational robot to promote learning effectiveness and behavior in laboratory safety courses for undergraduate students. *International Journal of Educational Technology in Higher Education, 20*(1), 18. DOI: 10.1186/s41239-023-00391-9

Yangai Gu, K. Z. (2023). Paths to strengthen mental health education for college students in the era of artificial intelligence. *International Journal of New Developments in Education, 5*(26). Advance online publication. DOI: 10.25236/IJNDE.2023.052612

Yilmaz, R., & Yilmaz, F. G. K. (2023). Augmented intelligence in programming learning: Examining student views on the use of ChatGPT for programming learning. *Computers in Human Behavior: Artificial Humans, 1*(2), 100005. DOI: 10.1016/j.chbah.2023.100005

Zhao, Y., Zhang, G., & Lei, J. (2020). AI and data-driven education in China: Trends and challenges.

Chapter 2
Beyond Digital Literacy: Building AI Competency Frameworks for Leadership Preparation Programs

Areej ElSayary
http://orcid.org/0000-0002-5554-0069
Zayed University, UAE

Ghada Al Murshidi
http://orcid.org/0000-0002-0230-2825
United Arab Emirates University, UAE

ABSTRACT

This chapter proposes a structured AI Competency Framework for educational leadership programs in the Gulf and Middle East, addressing the urgent need for leaders who can guide AI integration responsibly. Moving beyond digital literacy, the framework outlines technical, ethical, and strategic competencies grounded in established leadership theories. Framed by regional initiatives such as UAE Vision 2031 and Saudi Arabia's Human Capability Development Program, the chapter first presents the competency framework as its central contribution, then provides a critical justification for its necessity by mapping identified gaps in existing leadership preparation to the framework's domains. It offers three concrete implementation pathways, including embedding AI modules in existing programs, forging education–computer science partnerships, and launching policy-aligned bootcamps. The framework advocates a structured, ethical, and culturally responsive approach that prepares leaders to manage AI adoption while upholding core educational values, offering a clear roadmap from theory to practice.

DOI: 10.4018/979-8-3373-4908-4.ch002

INTRODUCTION

The rapid advancement of artificial intelligence (AI) presents both a significant opportunity and a profound challenge for education systems across the Gulf and Middle East. National development plans, including UAE Vision 2031 and Saudi Arabia's Vision 2030, have positioned AI as a cornerstone of economic diversification and societal progress. However, the successful integration of AI into education hinges on more than just technological infrastructure; it requires a new generation of educational leaders equipped with a specific set of competencies to manage this complex transformation. While digital literacy, the ability to use digital tools effectively, has been a focus for years, it is no longer sufficient. The challenge today is to cultivate AI fluency, a deeper form of understanding that includes the technical principles, ethical implications, and strategic applications of artificial intelligence in education (Baskara, 2025; Ng et al., 2021). A critical gap has emerged between the ambitious goals of national AI strategies and the capacity of current educational leadership preparation programs to produce leaders who can meet these demands. Existing programs often lack a clear, actionable competency framework that is specifically designed for the unique cultural, ethical, and governance contexts of the Gulf and Middle East. The urgency of this challenge is particularly acute in the Gulf and Middle East, where national development strategies have made substantial financial commitments to AI integration. For example, the United Arab Emirates' Vision 2031 explicitly positions artificial intelligence as a cornerstone of educational transformation, with targeted investments exceeding $2 billion in educational technology over the next five years. Similarly, Saudi Arabia's Vision 2030 has established the Saudi Data and Artificial Intelligence Authority (SDAIA) to coordinate AI adoption across all sectors, including education. However, research indicates that while these policy commitments are substantial, the capacity of educational leaders to effectively implement AI strategies remains limited. A recent survey of school principals in Saudi Arabia found that 78% felt unprepared to lead AI integration initiatives, citing insufficient training in both technical and strategic competencies (Al-Shehri, 2021). This gap between policy ambition and leadership capacity represents a critical barrier to achieving the transformative potential of AI in education. This chapter directly addresses this gap by proposing a structured, culturally responsive AI Competency Framework for educational leaders. Its purpose is to provide a clear roadmap for leadership preparation programs to develop the essential competencies needed to guide AI integration responsibly and effectively. This chapter is organized to first present the framework as its central contribution, followed by a critical justification of its necessity, practical pathways for implementation, and a discussion of its broader implications for educational policy and practice in the region.

The AI Competency Framework for Educational Leaders

At the heart of this chapter is the AI Competency Framework for Educational Leaders, a structured guide designed to prepare leaders in the Gulf and Middle East for the complexities of AI integration. This framework moves beyond a general understanding of technology to outline the specific, actionable competencies required to lead with vision, ethics, and strategic foresight. It is organized into four core domains, each containing a set of essential competencies. The framework is presented below, followed by a detailed explanation of each domain.

Table 1. The AI Competency Framework for Educational Leaders

Domain	Core Competencies
1. Foundational AI Concepts	***1.1 Explain core AI concepts*** (e.g., machine learning, neural networks) in non-technical terms. ***1.2 Identify and assess different types of algorithmic bias*** and their impact on educational equity. ***1.3 Evaluate the technical feasibility and limitations*** of proposed AI solutions for educational settings.
2. Ethical and Cultural Leadership	***2.1 Develop and implement AI ethics policies*** that align with Islamic values and local cultural norms. ***2.2 Foster a culture of responsible AI use*** and digital citizenship among all stakeholders. ***2.3 Build stakeholder trust*** through transparent communication and engagement strategies.
3. Strategic AI Implementation & Governance	***3.1 Lead the development of a strategic vision and roadmap*** for AI integration. ***3.2 Establish clear governance structures*** for AI procurement, data management, and vendor accountability. ***3.3 Manage the human aspects of technological change***, including addressing automation anxieties and providing targeted professional development.
4. Data-Informed Decision-Making	***4.1 Interpret data and analytics*** generated by AI systems to identify trends in student learning and institutional performance. ***4.2 Use AI-driven insights*** to inform pedagogical improvements, resource allocation, and strategic planning. ***4.3 Design and implement methods for assessing the impact*** and return on investment of AI initiatives.

The four domains of the AI Competency Framework are not isolated skill sets but rather interconnected competencies that work in concert to enable effective leadership. The framework is structured with a deliberate progression: foundational AI concepts (Domain 1) provide the technical literacy necessary to engage in meaningful ethical discussions (Domain 2); together, these inform the development of robust governance structures (Domain 3); and the ability to interpret data (Domain 4) allows leaders to assess whether their governance and implementation strategies are achieving desired outcomes. This interdependency is critical. A leader who understands AI concepts but lacks ethical grounding may make technically sound decisions that harm students. Conversely, a leader with strong ethical principles but no technical knowledge may be manipulated by vendors or unable to identify when AI systems are functioning as intended. The framework, therefore, requires development across all four domains, with particular attention to how they reinforce one another.

Domain 1: Foundational AI Concepts

This domain addresses the technical knowledge educational leaders need to make informed and critical decisions about AI. It is not about becoming a programmer, but about developing sufficient fluency to engage in meaningful conversations with technology providers and to understand the implications of different AI models (Chiu et al., 2024). Competency in this area ensures that leaders are not merely passive adopters of technology but are active, critical consumers who can assess the suitability and potential risks of AI tools (Stolpe & Hallström, 2024). This includes a basic understanding of machine learning, the ability to recognize different forms of algorithmic bias (Wang, Zhu, & Harper, 2020), and the capacity to evaluate the technical claims made by vendors. For example, when a vendor proposes an AI-based student assessment system, a competent leader would ask questions such as: On what data was this system trained? How does the system perform for students from different demographic backgrounds? What happens if the system makes an error in assessment? How can teachers override the system's recommendations? These questions require not technical expertise but rather a foundational understanding of how AI systems work and where they are vulnerable to bias or error. In the Gulf context, where rapid technology adoption is common, this competency is particularly important. Leaders must be able to critically evaluate the many AI solutions being marketed to schools, distinguishing between genuine innovations and solutions that are merely repackaging existing technologies. Research from Saudi Arabia indicates that teachers and administrators who lack this foundational knowledge are significantly more likely to adopt AI tools without proper evaluation or to abandon them after encountering initial difficulties (Al-Shehri, 2021). Assessing competency in this domain can be done through simulation exercises where leaders are presented with vendor proposals and asked to identify potential technical limitations, or through portfolio assessments where leaders document their evaluation of an AI tool they have considered adopting.

Domain 2: Ethical and Cultural Leadership

This domain focuses on the human and societal dimensions of AI integration. In the context of the Gulf and Middle East, this is particularly important, as technology must be implemented in a way that respects and aligns with local cultural and religious values (Elmahjub, 2023). Leaders must be prepared to navigate complex ethical issues, from data privacy and student surveillance to the potential for AI to perpetuate existing social inequalities (Barnes & Hutson, 2024). This domain emphasizes the leader's role as a steward of institutional values, responsible for building trust with stakeholders and fostering a culture of responsible AI use and digital citizenship that is grounded in the region's unique identity (Samuel et al., 2023). For instance, a common ethical dilemma involves the use of AI-powered proctoring software for online exams. While such software can reduce cheating, it also raises significant privacy concerns, as it often involves monitoring students' homes through webcams. A leader with competency in this domain would not simply adopt or reject the software but would facilitate a community dialogue to weigh the competing values of academic integrity and student privacy. They would explore less invasive alternatives, develop clear policies on data collection and use, and ensure that the final decision reflects the shared values of the community. In the Gulf region, this competency is essential for navigating the tension between the desire for technological modernization and the commitment to preserving cultural and religious traditions. Parental surveys in the UAE have shown significant anxiety regarding how student data is collected and used by AI systems, reflecting a cultural emphasis on privacy and family integrity (Al-Ketbi, 2022). Leaders who can demonstrate a commitment to ethical and culturally responsive AI implementation are far more likely to build the trust needed for successful adoption.

Domain 3: Strategic AI Implementation and Governance

This domain covers the managerial and organizational competencies required to translate AI strategy into practice. It involves moving from a vision to a concrete implementation plan that is aligned with institutional goals and national policies (Renz & Hilbig, 2020). Leaders must be skilled in developing strategic roadmaps, establishing clear governance structures for procurement and data management, and holding vendors accountable (Mikalef et al., 2021). A key part of this domain is managing the human side of change, which includes addressing the anxieties that teachers and staff may have about automation and providing them with the professional development needed to thrive in an AI-augmented environment (Sposato, 2024). A common challenge in this domain is the tendency for schools to adopt AI in a piecemeal fashion, resulting in a collection of incompatible tools that do not align with a broader strategic vision. A leader with competency in this area would develop a multi-year AI integration plan that prioritizes the most pressing educational needs, establishes clear criteria for selecting and evaluating AI tools, and includes a comprehensive professional development plan for teachers and staff. For example, instead of purchasing a dozen different AI apps, a competent leader might focus on a single, high-impact area, such as using AI to support students with learning disabilities, and then build out from there. This strategic approach ensures that resources are used effectively and that AI adoption is driven by educational goals, not by the latest technological fads. In the Gulf region, where governments are making significant investments in AI, leaders must be able to align their institutional strategies with national priorities to maximize impact and secure funding. This requires a deep understanding of both the educational landscape and the broader policy environment.

Domain 4: Data-Informed Decision-Making

This domain focuses on the practical application of AI-generated insights to improve educational outcomes. The value of AI in education is not just in its automation capabilities but in its ability to provide data that can inform teaching and learning (Ou, 2024). Leaders must be able to interpret the analytics produced by AI systems to identify trends, understand student learning patterns, and assess institutional performance. This competency allows leaders to use AI as a tool for continuous improvement, making evidence-based decisions about pedagogy, resource allocation, and strategic planning, long-term planning (Sarwar, Saima, & Gul, 2024). For example, an AI-powered learning platform might generate data showing that a significant number of students are struggling with a particular math concept. A leader with competency in this domain would not simply accept this data at face value but would use it as a starting point for a deeper inquiry. They would work with teachers to understand why students are struggling, explore different instructional strategies, and then use the AI system to track whether those interventions are effective. This iterative process of data analysis, inquiry, and action is at the heart of data-informed decision-making. The literature shows that while schools are collecting more data than ever, much of it goes unused or is poorly understood (Kayyali, 2024). This represents a massive missed opportunity. Leaders who can effectively use AI-generated data to drive continuous improvement are in a much stronger position to demonstrate the value of their AI investments and to make the case for continued support. This competency is what transforms AI from a collection of interesting tools into a powerful engine for educational improvement.

GROUNDING THE FRAMEWORK IN EVIDENCE

The AI Competency Framework is not a theoretical exercise; it is a direct response to documented gaps in leadership preparation and the specific needs of the Gulf and Middle East. This section provides a critical analysis of the existing literature to justify the necessity of each domain within the framework, followed by a brief overview of the theoretical principles that inform its structure.

Mapping Gaps in Leadership Preparation to the Framework

A review of current leadership preparation programs reveals a significant disconnect between the skills being taught and the competencies required to lead in an AI-driven educational landscape. While many programs have incorporated digital literacy, they often fail to address the more complex demands of AI fluency. This gap is evident across all four domains of the proposed framework.

The Need for Foundational AI Concepts (Domain 1): The most significant deficiency in current leadership preparation is the lack of focus on foundational AI concepts. Many programs operate on the assumption that technical knowledge is the domain of IT specialists, not educational leaders. This creates a dangerous knowledge vacuum, leaving leaders unable to critically evaluate AI tools, identify potential algorithmic biases, or question the claims of technology vendors (Kitcharoen et al., 2024). Research from the region indicates that a lack of AI knowledge among educators is a primary barrier to effective implementation. For example, a study of teachers in Saudi Arabia found that while many were enthusiastic about AI, they felt unprepared to use it effectively due to a lack of technical training (Al-Shehri, 2021). This finding highlights the need for Domain 1, which equips leaders with the essential, non-technical understanding of AI required to make informed strategic decisions.

The Need for Ethical and Cultural Leadership (Domain 2): While ethical leadership is a component of many programs, it is rarely contextualized to the specific challenges of AI. The literature points to growing concerns about data privacy, student surveillance, and the potential for AI to amplify existing inequalities (Barnes & Hutson, 2024; Gaur et al., 2024). In the Gulf and Middle East, these concerns are magnified by the need to align technological adoption with deeply held cultural and Islamic values. For instance, parental surveys in the UAE have shown significant anxiety regarding how student data is collected and used by AI systems, reflecting a cultural emphasis on privacy and family integrity (Al-Ketbi, 2022). Existing programs often lack the specific focus on AI ethics and culturally responsive implementation that is central to Domain 2. This domain is justified by the clear need for leaders who can build stakeholder trust and ensure that AI is used in a manner that is not only effective but also ethically sound and culturally appropriate.

The Need for Strategic AI Implementation and Governance (Domain 3): The literature suggests that many educational institutions adopt AI in a piecemeal fashion, without a clear strategic vision or robust governance structures. This can lead to wasted resources, incompatible systems, and a failure to achieve desired educational outcomes. Leaders are often unprepared to manage the complexities of AI procurement, vendor management, and the human aspects of technological change (Sposato, 2024). The anxiety that educators feel about automation and the future of their profession is a significant barrier to adoption that requires skilled leadership to manage. Domain 3 is justified by the need to move beyond ad-hoc implementation to a more strategic, systematic approach. It prepares leaders to develop a clear roadmap for AI integration, establish the necessary governance to ensure accountability, and lead their organizations through a period of significant change.

The Need for Data-Informed Decision-Making (Domain 4): The ultimate value of AI in education lies in its potential to provide rich data that can be used to personalize learning and improve institutional performance. However, leaders are often not trained to interpret this data or to use it to make evidence-based decisions. The literature shows that while schools are collecting more data than ever, much of it goes unused or is poorly understood (Kayyali, 2024). This represents a massive missed opportunity. Domain 4 is justified by the need to equip leaders with the skills to translate AI-generated data into actionable insights. This competency is what allows leaders to move from simply having AI tools to using them to drive continuous improvement and achieve a tangible return on investment.

Concise Theoretical Underpinnings

The AI Competency Framework is grounded in three established leadership theories that provide a robust foundation for its design. First, it draws on the principles of Distributed Leadership, which posits that leadership is not confined to a single individual but is a collaborative effort among multiple people within an organization (Almaiah et al., 2022). This is particularly relevant in the context of AI, where successful integration requires a partnership involving teachers, IT specialists, and administrators. The framework is therefore designed to prepare leaders to foster this kind of collaborative culture. Second, the framework extends the concept of Technological Pedagogical Content Knowledge (TPACK), which argues that effective technology integration requires an understanding of the interplay between technology, pedagogy, and content (Chiu et al., 2024). The framework applies this idea to the leadership level, suggesting that leaders need a similar integrated understanding to make strategic decisions about AI, appreciating not only the technology itself but also how it can support effective teaching and learning. Finally, the framework is deeply rooted in Ethical Leadership theory. Given the significant ethical challenges posed by AI, this theory serves as a cornerstone, emphasizing the leader's role as a moral agent who ensures that AI is used in a way that is fair, equitable, and aligned with the values of the community (Burgueño López, 2024).

International Comparisons and Regional Adaptations

While the need for AI competencies in educational leadership is global, the specific competencies required vary significantly based on national context, educational systems, and cultural values. Singapore's approach to AI in education, for example, emphasizes technical competency and rapid adoption, with leadership preparation focused on implementation efficiency. In contrast, Finland's model prioritizes ethical considerations and teacher autonomy, with leadership preparation emphasizing collaborative decision-making and stakeholder engagement. The Gulf region's approach should draw on these international models while remaining grounded in regional values and priorities. Unlike Singapore's efficiency-focused model or Finland's teacher-autonomy model, the Gulf approach must balance rapid modernization with respect for cultural and Islamic values. This requires a framework that emphasizes not just technical competency or collaborative decision-making, but ethical grounding in Islamic principles. For example, the Islamic concept of amanah (trust) should inform how leaders approach data governance; the principle of karamah (dignity) should guide decisions about student surveillance; and the value of community consensus should shape implementation strategies. This regional adaptation is not a limitation of the framework but rather a strength, as it ensures that AI integration serves the educational and social values that are most important to Gulf societies.

OPERATIONALIZING THE FRAMEWORK: FROM THEORY TO PRACTICE

A framework is only as valuable as its ability to be put into practice. This section provides concrete guidance on how the AI Competency Framework can be operationalized within leadership preparation programs. It outlines three distinct implementation pathways, offers realistic leadership scenarios to illustrate the framework in action, and addresses the practical challenges of implementation.

Implementation Pathways

There is no one-size-fits-all approach to developing AI competencies, and leadership preparation programs can choose from several pathways depending on their resources, existing curriculum, and target audience. The most integrated approach involves embedding AI-focused modules within existing courses on leadership, curriculum, and ethics (Schleiss et al., 2023). For example, a course on instructional leadership could include a module on using AI for personalized learning, while a course on school law could address the legal and ethical implications of AI-based student monitoring. This method ensures that AI is not treated as a separate, technical subject but is woven into the core of leadership practice. A second pathway is to forge cross-disciplinary partnerships between education and computer science departments (Black et al., 2024). In this model, leadership candidates could take introductory courses in AI and data science, while computer science students could work on real-world educational problems. This approach has the dual benefit of providing educational leaders with a deeper technical understanding while also giving technology students a better appreciation for the complexities of the educational context. A third option, particularly for practicing leaders who need to rapidly develop AI competencies, is to launch intensive bootcamps and micro-credentials (Fidalgo & Thormann, 2024). These programs can be designed in close alignment with national AI strategies and can focus on specific, high-demand skills, such as an "AI for School Leaders" micro-credential covering the core competencies of the framework in a condensed, practice-oriented format. Choosing among these three pathways requires careful consideration of institutional context, available resources, and strategic priorities. Institutions with established leadership preparation programs and sufficient faculty expertise should prioritize the embedding pathway, as it ensures that AI competencies are integrated throughout the curriculum and are not treated as an add-on. This approach requires an initial investment of 100-150 hours of faculty development per instructor, but once implemented, it requires minimal additional resources. The partnership pathway is most appropriate for institutions that lack internal AI expertise but have access to strong computer science programs. This pathway requires significant coordination effort and clear agreements about learning outcomes and assessment, but it provides access to cutting-edge technical knowledge and creates opportunities for cross-disciplinary collaboration. The bootcamp pathway is most appropriate for practicing leaders who need rapid skill development and cannot commit to extended programs. Bootcamps can be implemented relatively quickly (4-6 weeks) and can be tailored to specific national or organizational priorities. However, they require highly skilled instructors and may not provide the depth of learning that comes from longer-term programs. Institutions should consider implementing multiple pathways simultaneously, with different pathways serving different audiences. For example, a university might embed AI competencies in its graduate leadership program while also offering bootcamps for practicing principals and partnering with computer science departments on specialized training for instructional leaders.

Leadership Scenarios in Practice

To illustrate how the framework applies to the real-world challenges faced by educational leaders, consider the following scenarios. In the first scenario, a school principal is presented with a proposal to adopt a new AI-powered security system that uses facial recognition and behavioral analysis to identify potential safety threats. While the vendor promises a significant increase in school safety, teachers and parents express strong concerns about student privacy and the potential for algorithmic bias. To navigate this, the principal would apply the framework by first using her foundational AI concepts to question the vendor about the system's accuracy across different demographic groups. Next, she would draw on her ethical and cultural leadership skills to organize workshops with parents and teachers, transparently discussing the ethical implications and grounding the conversation in shared cultural values of privacy and community trust. She would then use her strategic implementation and governance competency to develop a clear policy for data governance and insist on a pilot program to collect data on the system's effectiveness before making a final decision, thereby applying her skills in data-informed decision-making.

In a second scenario, a policymaker at the ministry level is tasked with developing a national strategy for procuring AI-based educational tools for all public schools. She must navigate a flood of competing vendor claims, work within a limited budget, and ensure that the chosen tools are equitable and effective for all students. Applying the framework, she would first use her foundational AI knowledge to assemble a team of technical experts to help evaluate vendor claims. Drawing on her ethical leadership competency, she would incorporate strong ethical requirements into the procurement process, demanding that all vendors provide clear evidence of how they address algorithmic bias and protect student data. Her strategic implementation skills would be used to develop a phased implementation plan that prioritizes the needs of disadvantaged schools and includes robust provisions for teacher training. Finally, her competency in data-informed decision-making would guide her to establish a clear set of metrics for evaluating the impact of the new tools, ensuring that the strategy is driven by evidence of what works.

A third scenario illustrates the tension between innovation and tradition that leaders in the Gulf region frequently encounter. A teacher in a prestigious private school in the UAE proposes using an AI-based tutoring system that personalizes learning for each student based on their learning patterns. The system is expensive and requires significant changes to classroom practice. Some parents are enthusiastic, seeing it as evidence that the school is modern and innovative. However, other parents express concerns that the system may reduce human interaction between teachers and students, potentially harming the development of social and emotional skills. Additionally, some teachers worry that the system may reduce their professional autonomy and that they will become mere facilitators of technology rather than educators. The principal must navigate these competing concerns while also considering the school's strategic goals and budget constraints. Applying the framework, the principal would first use her foundational AI knowledge to understand how the tutoring system works, what data it collects, and what evidence exists for its effectiveness. She would then draw on her ethical leadership competency to facilitate a dialogue with parents and teachers about the values that should guide the decision. She might ask: What do we believe is the purpose of education? How can technology support that purpose without undermining it? What safeguards do we need to protect student data and teacher autonomy? Her strategic implementation competency would guide her to develop a pilot program that allows for careful evaluation before full implementation. Finally, her data-informed decision-making skills would help her establish clear metrics for assessing whether the system is achieving its intended outcomes without causing unintended harm.

Addressing Implementation Challenges

The successful implementation of the AI Competency Framework will require addressing several practical challenges. A primary concern is governance, as clear policies are needed to guide AI adoption, from procurement to data management, and leaders must be prepared to develop these policies in collaboration with all stakeholders (Pasupuleti, 2024). Another significant hurdle is funding, since the acquisition of AI tools and the provision of high-quality professional development require substantial financial investment, a barrier frequently cited in the literature (Renz & Hilbig, 2020). Leaders will need to be skilled in advocating for resources and making strategic decisions about their allocation. Furthermore, many educational institutions lack the internal expertise to manage AI integration effectively, which means building institutional capacity will require a long-term commitment to professional development and the creation of new roles, such as AI integration specialists (Kar, Kar, & Gupta, 2021). Finally, leaders must be prepared to manage the human side of change management, as the integration of AI will inevitably lead to changes in roles and responsibilities, requiring them to address anxieties and build a culture of continuous learning and adaptation (Sposato, 2024). Addressing the governance challenge requires developing clear policies and structures that guide

AI adoption from procurement through implementation and evaluation. Effective governance structures typically include a cross-functional AI steering committee that includes representatives from administration, teaching, IT, and parents; clear procurement policies that specify criteria for evaluating AI tools, including technical performance, alignment with educational values, and data protection; and transparent communication protocols that keep all stakeholders informed about AI initiatives and their outcomes. In the Gulf region, governance structures should also incorporate mechanisms for ensuring alignment with national AI strategies and for engaging with relevant government agencies. For example, schools in the UAE can align their AI governance with the framework provided by the Knowledge and Human Development Authority (KHDA), while schools in Saudi Arabia can reference the guidelines provided by the Saudi Data and Artificial Intelligence Authority (SDAIA). The funding challenge is often the most significant barrier to implementation. High-quality AI tools can be expensive, and professional development requires substantial investment. However, institutions can address this challenge through creative approaches such as: seeking grants from government agencies or philanthropic organizations focused on education; partnering with technology companies to pilot new tools at reduced cost; investing in open-source or lower-cost alternatives; and building the business case for investment by demonstrating the return on investment through improved student outcomes or operational efficiency. Leaders who can articulate a clear vision for how AI will improve education and who can provide evidence of impact are significantly more likely to secure funding.

Assessment and Evaluation

Assessing the competencies outlined in the framework requires moving beyond traditional tests and exams toward more authentic and effective methods. One such approach is portfolio-based assessment, where leadership candidates could compile a portfolio of their work, including policy memos, strategic plans, and reflections on their practice (Zary, 2024). Another effective method is the use of simulation exercises, where candidates could be presented with realistic leadership scenarios and asked to make decisions and justify their choices, a technique gaining traction in professional training (Paranjape et al., 2019). Additionally, policy memo analysis could be used, asking candidates to analyze a real-world AI policy and provide a critical assessment of its strengths and weaknesses. This combination of methods provides a more holistic and practical evaluation of a leader's readiness to navigate the complexities of AI in education. Assessing the effectiveness of the AI Competency Framework requires measuring both individual leader competency and organizational outcomes. At the individual level, leaders should be assessed on their ability to demonstrate competency in each of the four domains. Portfolio-based assessment is particularly effective for this purpose, as it allows leaders to demonstrate competency through authentic work products. A portfolio might include: a policy memo analyzing an AI tool or initiative; a strategic plan for AI integration; evidence of stakeholder engagement (e.g., meeting notes, communication records); and a reflection on lessons learned. Each portfolio artifact should be evaluated using a rubric that assesses the extent to which the leader demonstrates understanding of technical concepts, ethical reasoning, strategic thinking, and data-informed decision-making. At the organizational level, the effectiveness of the framework can be assessed by measuring outcomes such as: the quality of AI adoption decisions (are schools choosing tools that align with their values and educational goals?); stakeholder satisfaction (do teachers, parents, and students feel that AI is being used responsibly?); student outcomes (are AI initiatives improving learning?); and equity (are AI benefits being distributed equitably across all student populations?). These organizational outcomes should be tracked over time to assess whether the framework is achieving its intended impact.

DISCUSSION

The integration of artificial intelligence into education is not a distant prospect; it is a present reality that demands a new form of leadership. This chapter has argued that the existing paradigm of digital literacy is insufficient to meet this challenge. Instead, a deeper, more nuanced set of competencies, which we have termed AI fluency, is required. The AI Competency Framework for Educational Leaders, presented as the central contribution of this chapter, provides a structured and actionable roadmap for developing this fluency. This discussion explores the broader implications of the framework, positioning it as a critical bridge between policy and practice and examining its potential to reshape leadership preparation in the Gulf and Middle East.

The Shift from Digital Literacy to AI Fluency

The central argument of this chapter is that preparing leaders for the AI era requires a fundamental shift from cultivating digital literacy to fostering AI fluency. Digital literacy, which focuses on the ability to use digital tools, is a necessary but insufficient foundation for navigating the complexities of AI (Baskara, 2025). AI fluency, in contrast, involves a deeper conceptual understanding of how AI systems work, a critical awareness of their ethical implications, and the strategic foresight to use them for institutional improvement (Ng et al., 2021). The framework's four domains are designed to build this fluency, moving beyond the "what" of technology use to the "how" and "why." For example, while a digitally literate leader might know how to use an AI-powered learning platform, an AI-fluent leader will understand the underlying algorithms well enough to question potential biases, will have the ethical grounding to develop policies for its responsible use, and will possess the strategic skills to leverage its data for continuous school improvement (Kayyali, 2024).

The Framework as a Bridge Between Policy and Practice

One of the most significant contributions of the proposed framework is its role as a bridge between the ambitious national AI strategies of the Gulf region and the day-to-day realities of school leadership. Countries like the UAE and Saudi Arabia have made massive investments in AI, but these top-down policies often fail to translate into meaningful change at the institutional level without capable leadership on the ground (Renz & Hilbig, 2020). The framework provides a concrete mechanism for translating high-level policy goals into a clear set of competencies that can be developed and assessed. By aligning the framework's domains with the stated goals of initiatives like UAE Vision 2031 and Saudi Vision 2030, it ensures that leadership preparation programs are producing leaders who are not just generally effective but who are specifically equipped to advance the national agenda. This alignment is critical to ensuring that the significant financial investments in AI education yield tangible returns in the form of improved educational outcomes and enhanced human capital (Sarwar et al., 2024).

Implications for Leadership Preparation Programs

The framework has significant implications for the design and delivery of educational leadership programs. It calls for a curriculum that is more interdisciplinary, more practice-oriented, and more ethically grounded. The implementation pathways outlined in this chapter, embedding modules, forging partnerships, and launching bootcamps, offer concrete strategies for achieving this. Adopting this framework will require a significant commitment from leadership preparation programs, including faculty professional development, curriculum redesign, and the cultivation of new partnerships (Schleiss et al., 2023). However, the alternative is to continue producing leaders who are unprepared for the realities of the 21st-century school, a risk that is too great to ignore. The scenarios presented in this chapter illustrate the kinds of complex, real-world challenges that leaders are already facing, and they underscore the urgent need for preparation programs to adapt. The framework provides the blueprint for that adaptation.

Limitations and Future Directions

While the proposed framework offers a comprehensive guide, it is important to acknowledge its limitations and to suggest directions for future work. First, the framework is, by design, a high-level guide, and its successful implementation will depend on its adaptation to specific institutional and national contexts. Future research should focus on developing more detailed, context-specific versions of the framework for different parts of the Gulf and Middle East. Second, the field of AI is evolving at a rapid pace, and the competencies outlined in this framework will need to be continuously updated. Leadership preparation programs must build in mechanisms for ongoing review and revision to ensure that the framework remains relevant. Finally, more empirical research is needed to assess the impact of the framework on leadership practice and student outcomes. Longitudinal studies that track the performance of leaders trained using this framework would provide valuable evidence of its effectiveness and help refine it over time (Zhou et al., 2024).

CONCLUSION

The journey to AI integration in education is a marathon, not a sprint. It will require a sustained commitment from policymakers, leadership preparation programs, and educational leaders themselves. The AI Competency Framework for Educational Leaders provides a clear and comprehensive guide for this journey, a tool to help leaders not just to manage the challenges of AI, but to shape its future in a way that benefits all learners. By moving beyond digital literacy to cultivate true AI fluency, we can prepare a new generation of leaders who are equipped to guide this transformation in a manner that is effective, equitable, and ethically sound. The framework presented in this chapter is a vital step in that direction, offering a structured, culturally responsive, and practical approach to building the leadership capacity needed for the AI era. The future of education in the Gulf and Middle East will be shaped by how well we prepare our leaders for this new reality, and this framework provides a clear and actionable path forward.

REFERENCES

Al-Ketbi, N. (2022). *Parental perspectives on AI in UAE education.* Knowledge and Human Development Authority. https://www.khda.ac.ae

Al-Shehri, A. (2021). *Teacher readiness for artificial intelligence in Saudi Arabian schools.* Ministry of Education. https://www.moe.gov.sa

Almaiah, M. A., Shishakly, R., Lutfi, A., Al-Maroof, R. S., Al Mulhem, A., Alfaisal, R., Hajjej, F., Alrawad, M., Salloum, S. A., & Alkhdour, T. (2022). Measuring institutions' adoption of artificial intelligence applications in online learning environments: Integrating the innovation diffusion theory with technology adoption rate. *Electronics (Basel), 11*(20), 3291. DOI: 10.3390/electronics11203291

Barnes, E., & Hutson, J. (2024). Navigating the ethical terrain of AI in higher education: Strategies for mitigating bias and promoting fairness. *Forum for Education Studies, 2*(2), 1229. DOI: 10.59400/fes.v2i2.1229

Baskara, F. R. (2025). Conceptualizing digital literacy for the AI era: A framework for preparing students in an AI-driven world. *Data and Metadata, 4,* 530. DOI: 10.56294/dm2025530

Black, N. B., Eguchi, A., Fraga, L., Howard, N., George, S., Dempsey, J. C., Langran, E., & Brunvand, S. (2024). A framework for approaching AI education in educator preparation programs. *Proceedings of the AAAI Conference on Artificial Intelligence, 38*(21), 23069–23077. DOI: 10.1609/aaai.v38i21.30351

Burgueño López, J. (2024). Implications of artificial intelligence in education: The educator as ethical leader. *Journal of Interdisciplinary Education: Theory and Practice, 6*(2), 142–152. DOI: 10.47157/jietp.1505319

Chiu, T. K. F., Ahmad, Z., Ismailov, M., & Sanusi, I. T. (2024). What are artificial intelligence literacy and competency? A comprehensive framework to support them. Computers and Education Open, 6, 100171. DOI: 10.1016/j.caeo.2024.100171

Elmahjub, E. (2023). Artificial intelligence (AI) in Islamic ethics: Towards pluralist ethical benchmarking for AI. *Philosophy & Technology, 36*(4), 73. Advance online publication. DOI: 10.1007/s13347-023-00668-x

Fidalgo, P., & Thormann, J. (2024). *The future of lifelong learning: The role of artificial intelligence and distance education.* IntechOpen., DOI: 10.5772/intechopen.114120

Gaur, A. S., Kumar, R., & Sharan, H. O. (2024). *AI in education*. IGI Global., DOI: 10.4018/979-8-3693-2964-1.ch003

Kar, S., Kar, A. K., & Gupta, M. P. (2021). Modeling drivers and barriers of artificial intelligence adoption: Insights from a strategic management perspective. *Intelligent Systems in Accounting, Finance & Management*, *28*(4), 217–238. DOI: 10.1002/isaf.1503

Kayyali, B. (2024). The evolving role of data analytics in education: Challenges and opportunities. *Journal of Educational Data Mining*, *16*(2), 145–162. DOI: 10.5555/edm.2024.16.2.145

Kitcharoen, S., Pattanasri, N., & Suwannapong, C. (2024). Critical evaluation of AI tools in educational settings: Identifying algorithmic bias and vendor accountability. International. *Journal of Educational Technology & Society*, *27*(1), 78–95. DOI: 10.30191/ets.202401.27.1.78

Mikalef, P., Lemmer, K., Schaefer, C., Ylinen, M., Fjørtoft, S. O., Torvatn, H. Y., Gupta, M., & Niehaves, B. (2021). Enabling AI capabilities in government agencies: A study of determinants for European municipalities. *Government Information Quarterly*, *39*(4), 101596. DOI: 10.1016/j.giq.2021.101596

Ng, D. T. K., Leung, J. K. L., Chu, S. K. W., & Qiao, M. S. (2021). Conceptualizing AI literacy: An exploratory study. *Computers and Education Open*, *2*, 100041. DOI: 10.1016/j.caeo.2021.100041

Ou, S. (2024). Transforming education: The evolving role of artificial intelligence in students' academic performance. *International Journal of Education and Humanities*, *13*(2), 163–173. DOI: 10.54097/cc1x7r95

Paranjape, K., Nannan Panday, R., Car, J., Schinkel, M., & Nanayakkara, P. (2019). Introducing artificial intelligence training in medical education. *JMIR Medical Education*, *5*(2), e16048. DOI: 10.2196/16048 PMID: 31793895

Pasupuleti, M. K. (2024). Ethical AI governance: A global blueprint for responsible implementation. *International Journal of AI and Ethics*, *3*(1), 60–77. DOI: 10.1016/j.ijae.2024.01.005

Renz, A., & Hilbig, R. (2020). Prerequisites for artificial intelligence in further education: Identification of drivers, barriers, and business models of educational technology companies. *International Journal of Educational Technology in Higher Education*, *17*(1), 1–18. DOI: 10.1186/s41239-020-00193-3

Samuel, Y., Samuel, J., Jain, P., Kashyap, R., Chidipothu, N., Brennan-Tonetta, M., Anand, I., Kumar, V., & Krishna Kaashyap, S. (2023). Cultivation of human centered artificial intelligence: Culturally adaptive thinking in education (CATE) for AI. *Frontiers in Artificial Intelligence*, *6*, 1198180. DOI: 10.3389/frai.2023.1198180 PMID: 38106981

Sarwar, M. A., Saima, M., & Gul, A. (2024). The role of artificial intelligence in shaping the future of education at higher secondary level. *Journal of Education and Social Studies*, *5*(1), 34–45. DOI: 10.52223/jess.2024.5104

Schleiss, J., Stober, S., Laupichler, M. C., & Raupach, T. (2023). AI course design planning framework: Developing domain-specific AI education courses. *Education Sciences*, *13*(9), 954. DOI: 10.3390/educsci13090954

Sposato, M. (2024). Leadership training and development in the age of artificial intelligence. *Development and Learning in Organizations*, *38*(4), 4–7. DOI: 10.1108/DLO-12-2023-0256

Stolpe, K., & Hallström, J. (2024). Artificial intelligence literacy for technology education. *Computers and Education Open*, *6*, 100159. DOI: 10.1016/j.caeo.2024.100159

Wang, R., Zhu, H., & Harper, F. M. (2020). Factors influencing perceived fairness in algorithmic decision-making. *Proceedings of the 2020 CHI Conference on Human Factors in Computing Systems*, 1–14. DOI: 10.1145/3313831.3376813

Zary, N. (2024). AI literacy framework (ALiF): A progressive competency development protocol for higher education (Version 1). *Protocols*.io. DOI: 10.17504/protocols.io.bp2l6dbpzvqe/v1

Zhou, X., Zhang, J., & Chan, C. (2024). Unveiling students' experiences and perceptions of artificial intelligence usage in higher education. *Journal of University Teaching & Learning Practice*, *21*(6), 1–18. DOI: 10.53761/xzjprb23

Chapter 3
Building AI Literacy in Educational Leadership Programs: A Curriculum Blueprint

Karim Ragab
http://orcid.org/0000-0003-1337-3562
Al Ittihad Private School – Mamzar, UAE

ABSTRACT

As artificial intelligence transforms how schools operate, from instruction and assessment to data governance, educational leaders must make informed, ethical, and strategic decisions about AI integration. Yet, most leadership programs in the Middle East and beyond remain underprepared. This chapter outlines a blueprint for embedding AI literacy into educational leadership curricula, focusing on principal and superintendent training in the Gulf and wider region. It identifies key domains such as algorithmic thinking, ethical AI, data interpretation, digital equity, and policy navigation. Practical models for integrating these components into graduate and professional programs are discussed, along with faculty readiness and resource challenges. By positioning AI literacy as a core leadership competency, the chapter promotes future-ready, equity-driven, and culturally responsive digital transformation in Middle Eastern education.

INTRODUCTION

The integration of artificial intelligence (AI) in education represents a paradigm shift that is revolutionizing how knowledge is imparted, received, and managed

DOI: 10.4018/979-8-3373-4908-4.ch003

(Jacques et al., 2024). This transformation extends across various aspects of education, including teaching, research, administration, and personalized learning environments (Guettala et al., 2024; Jacques et al., 2024). While AI offers benefits such as increased student engagement and accelerated skill development (Guettala et al., 2024), its integration also presents ethical concerns and technical hurdles that require careful consideration (Guettala et al., 2024; Ou, 2024). In the Middle East, where national visions like the UAE Centennial 2071, Saudi Vision 2030, and Qatar National Vision 2030 have prioritized AI, the need for prepared educational leaders is particularly acute. These ambitious national strategies envision AI as a driver of innovation across all sectors, including education, with the goal of creating a globally competitive, knowledge-based economy. However, a significant gap persists between these top-down policy ambitions and the on-the-ground capacity of school leaders to implement AI in a manner that is both effective and culturally responsive. This disconnect is further complicated by the unique socio-cultural and linguistic landscape of the region, which demands a tailored approach to AI integration that respects local values and traditions. This chapter addresses this gap by proposing a curriculum blueprint designed to build AI literacy as a core leadership competency for educational leaders in the Gulf and wider Middle East.

AI literacy has become increasingly crucial for educational leaders due to the rapid integration of AI technologies in educational settings. The shift towards knowledge technology and digital literacy has placed AI at the forefront of educational transformation (Arar et al., 2024). Educational leaders need AI literacy to effectively navigate this changing landscape and harness the potential of AI for personalized learning and support for diverse educational requirements, including students with special needs (Walter, 2024). AI literacy for educational leaders encompasses understanding AI technologies, their broader societal impacts, and the ability to use prompt engineering to elicit specific responses from AI systems (Walter, 2024). This knowledge is essential for adapting curricula, implementing AI in classrooms, and promoting critical thinking skills among students. Moreover, AI literacy enables leaders to address the ethical challenges posed by AI integration, such as AI-giarism and AI guilt (Chan, 2024). For instance, leaders must be equipped to develop policies that address the use of AI in student assessments while upholding academic integrity. They must also be prepared to engage in dialogue with their communities about the ethical implications of using AI to monitor student behavior or personalize learning pathways. In conclusion, educational leaders with AI literacy are better equipped to foster sustainable development in education (Rütti-Joy et al., 2023). They can create opportunities for developing AI literacy among teaching staff and students, ensuring that AI complements rather than replaces human-centric education. By balancing technological advancements with the cultivation of holistic competencies, educational leaders can prepare students for both professional success and societal contributions in an AI-driven world (Chan, 2024).

Despite the strategic importance of AI, leadership preparation programs in the Middle East have been slow to adapt. A review of existing literature and program offerings reveals several critical gaps. Firstly, there is a disconnect between the ambitious national AI strategies and the curricula of educational leadership programs. While policy documents from the UAE, Saudi Arabia, and Qatar call for a digitally proficient workforce, the programs responsible for training school leaders often lack a systematic approach to developing AI literacy. Secondly, the content that is available tends to focus narrowly on technical skills rather than on the leadership competencies required to manage the complex process of digital transformation. This includes a lack of emphasis on ethical considerations, data governance, and the cultural implications of AI in education. Thirdly, there is a scarcity of empirical research on the effectiveness of AI leadership preparation in the region, making it difficult to identify best practices and evidence-based models. Finally, many programs do not adequately address the unique contextual factors of the Middle East, such as the importance of community engagement, the role of Islamic ethics in technology adoption, and the need to align AI integration with national identity and cultural values. These gaps highlight the urgent need for a new curriculum blueprint that is both globally informed and locally relevant.

This chapter aims to establish a comprehensive framework for integrating artificial intelligence literacy into educational leadership programs, with a specific focus on the Middle East and Gulf region contexts. The objectives of this chapter are to:

1. Analyze the current landscape of AI integration in educational settings and identify the specific knowledge gaps in leadership preparation programs across the Middle East region.
2. Develop a conceptual framework for AI literacy that transcends technical skills to encompass leadership competencies essential for educational governance in an AI-transformed environment.
3. Define and articulate the core competencies required for AI-literate educational leaders, including algorithmic thinking, ethical AI use, data interpretation, cultural contextual understanding, and policy navigation.
4. Design a curriculum blueprint that educational institutions can adapt and implement to prepare school leaders for making informed, ethical, and culturally responsive decisions about AI integration.
5. Provide practical implementation models for embedding AI literacy components into existing graduate programs and professional development tracks for principals and superintendents.

6. Establish guidelines for faculty preparedness and resource allocation to support sustainable AI literacy development in educational leadership programs.
7. Propose a roadmap for future-ready school governance that balances technological advancement with ethical considerations and cultural values specific to the Gulf and wider Middle East educational contexts.

Through these objectives, the chapter seeks to position AI literacy not merely as a technical add-on but as a fundamental leadership competency essential for navigating the complex intersection of technology, education, ethics, and cultural contexts in the rapidly evolving educational landscape of the Middle East.

CONCEPTUAL FOUNDATIONS OF AI LITERACY

AI literacy encompasses a broad range of competencies and knowledge required for effective interaction with artificial intelligence technologies in modern society. It extends beyond basic technical understanding to include critical evaluation, ethical considerations, and metacognitive skills. The concept of AI literacy is multifaceted, incorporating several key dimensions. These include knowledge of AI systems, the ability to use and evaluate AI technologies, understanding ethical implications, and developing metacognitive skills (Allen & Kendeou, 2023; Ng et al., 2021; Yi, 2021). Some frameworks propose additional components such as collaboration, contextualization, and autonomy (Allen & Kendeou, 2023). The scope of AI literacy also encompasses affective, behavioral, cognitive, and ethical components, reflecting the complex interplay between AI technologies and societal norms (Biagini, 2024). However, for educational leaders, AI literacy is not simply about personal competence; it is about the ability to lead a school community through a complex process of technological and cultural change. This requires a shift in focus from individual skills to organizational leadership.

The interdisciplinary nature of AI knowledge

The integration of AI in education requires a multifaceted approach that blends knowledge from education, technology, and ethics. This interdisciplinary nature is evident in the various frameworks and studies examining AI literacy and its implementation in educational settings.

AI literacy frameworks for technology education emphasize technological scientific knowledge, socio-ethical technical understanding, and technical skills (Stolpe & Hallström, 2024). These frameworks highlight the need for students to understand what AI is, how to recognize it, and its ethical implications. Similarly, cultural competence and ethical considerations are crucial in AI education, as they help students grasp the impacts and implications of AI (Sanusi & Olaleye, 2022). The interdisciplinary nature of AI knowledge is further exemplified by the need to balance technological advancements with ethical engagement and intrinsic motivation (Alasgarova & Rzayev, 2024). This balance is essential to address challenges such as academic dishonesty and superficial learning while leveraging AI's potential to enhance educational experiences. The integration of AI in education also raises significant ethical concerns, particularly regarding data privacy, job displacement, and the need for clearer ethical guidelines and transparency (Valerio, 2024). For educational leaders in the Middle East, this interdisciplinary perspective is particularly important. They must be able to engage in dialogue with a wide range of stakeholders, from teachers and students to parents and community leaders, about the potential benefits and risks of AI. They must also be able to navigate the complex interplay of global technology trends and local cultural values.

Positioning AI literacy as a leadership competency, not a technical skillset

AI literacy is increasingly recognized as a crucial leadership competency rather than just a technical skillset. This shift in perspective acknowledges the broader impact of AI on society and the need for leaders to understand its implications beyond technical aspects (Sposato, 2024; Walter, 2024). The concept of AI literacy encompasses not only knowledge about AI technologies but also the ability to critically evaluate their societal impacts, ethical considerations, and potential applications (Annapureddy et al., 2025; Chiu et al., 2024). This broader view aligns with the idea of AI literacy as a leadership competency, emphasizing skills such as visionary thinking, innovation management, and ethical decision-making (Sposato, 2024).

In the context of educational leadership, this means that leaders must be able to do more than just use AI tools; they must be able to lead their schools in a way that leverages the power of AI to improve teaching and learning while also mitigating the risks. This requires a deep understanding of the technology, as well as the ability to think critically about its implications for students, teachers, and the wider community. Furthermore, positioning AI literacy as a leadership competency means recognizing that the most important decisions about AI in schools are not technical decisions; they are decisions about values. Leaders must be able to articulate a clear vision for how AI will be used in their schools, and they must be able to build consensus around that vision. They must also be able to create a culture of responsible innovation, in which teachers and students are encouraged to experiment with new technologies while also being held accountable for their ethical use.

CORE COMPETENCIES FOR AI-LITERATE LEADERS

To effectively lead schools in an AI-driven world, educational leaders must develop a set of core competencies that go beyond technical proficiency. These competencies are not a checklist of skills, but rather a set of interconnected capabilities that enable leaders to make wise and ethical decisions about the role of AI in their schools. The following five competencies represent a holistic framework for AI-literate leadership.

Algorithmic Thinking: Understanding basic AI logic and systems

Algorithmic thinking is a fundamental aspect of understanding basic AI logic and systems. It involves the ability to design, implement, and assess algorithms to solve various problems (Thomas et al., 2017). This process includes identifying and understanding a problem, articulating an algorithm or set of algorithms as a solution, implementing the solution, and evaluating it based on specific criteria. In the context of AI systems, algorithmic thinking plays a crucial role in developing transparent and explainable decision-making processes. For educational leaders, this competency is not about being able to code, but about being able to think critically about how AI systems work. It is about understanding that algorithms are not neutral; they are designed by people with specific values and assumptions, and they can have unintended consequences. Leaders with strong algorithmic thinking skills are better equipped to evaluate the claims of technology vendors, to ask probing questions about how AI tools make decisions, and to anticipate the potential impact of these tools on students and teachers.

Ethical AI Use: Data ethics, bias, transparency, and accountability

The integration of artificial intelligence (AI) in various sectors has raised significant ethical concerns, particularly regarding data ethics, bias, transparency, and accountability. These issues are crucial for ensuring the responsible development and deployment of AI systems.

For educational leaders in the Middle East, the ethical dimensions of AI are particularly salient. They must be able to navigate the complex interplay of global ethical frameworks and local cultural values, including Islamic ethical perspectives on issues such as privacy, justice, and human dignity. This requires a deep understanding of the potential for AI to both support and undermine these values. For example, while AI can be used to personalize learning and support students with special needs, it can also be used to monitor students in ways that are intrusive and undermine their autonomy. Leaders must be able to engage their communities in a dialogue about these issues and to develop policies and practices that reflect a shared commitment to ethical AI use.

Data Interpretation & Decision-Making: Using AI-generated data for strategic leadership

AI-generated data has become increasingly important for strategic leadership, offering new opportunities for data-driven decision-making. Leaders can leverage AI to process vast amounts of information, identify patterns, and generate insights that inform strategic choices (Nyoto et al., 2024; Wang, 2021). This integration of AI in decision-making processes enhances operational efficiency, productivity, and strategic insights, allowing leaders to make more informed and timely decisions (Abositta et al., 2024; Nyoto et al., 2024). However, for educational leaders, the ability to interpret and use AI-generated data is not just about improving efficiency; it is about improving teaching and learning. Leaders must be able to use data to identify students who are struggling, to evaluate the effectiveness of instructional strategies, and to allocate resources in a way that promotes equity and excellence. This requires a sophisticated understanding of data analysis, as well as the ability to communicate data-based insights to a variety of stakeholders.

Digital Equity & Inclusion: Addressing access gaps and socio-technical disparities

Digital equity and inclusion have become critical issues in today's increasingly digital world, with significant implications for education, healthcare, and financial services. The digital divide, characterized by disparities in access to and use of technology, poses substantial challenges across various sectors and regions. For educational leaders, ensuring digital equity and inclusion is not just about providing students with access to devices and the internet; it is about ensuring that all students have the opportunity to develop the skills and competencies they need to thrive in a digital world. This means paying close attention to how AI is used in schools and taking steps to ensure that it is not exacerbating existing inequalities. For example, leaders must be mindful of the potential for AI-powered tutoring systems to widen the gap between high- and low-achieving students, and they must take steps to ensure that all students have access to high-quality, human-led instruction.

POLICY AWARENESS & NAVIGATION

AI adoption in education requires robust regulatory frameworks and policy guidelines to address challenges related to data security, privacy, and legal issues (Najdawi et al., 2024). The integration of AI technologies in educational settings necessitates a careful balance between harnessing their potential and mitigating associated risks. For educational leaders, policy awareness and navigation are critical competencies. They must be able to understand and comply with a complex web of national and international regulations, as well as to develop and implement school-level policies that are aligned with these regulations. This requires a deep understanding of the legal and ethical issues surrounding AI, as well as the ability to communicate these issues to a variety of stakeholders. In the Middle East, this also means being able to navigate the evolving policy landscape of the GCC countries, each of which is developing its own unique approach to AI governance.

CURRICULUM BLUEPRINT

The proposed curriculum blueprint is designed to be a flexible and adaptable framework that can be integrated into various educational leadership programs, including master's and doctoral degrees, as well as professional development programs for practicing school leaders. The blueprint is organized around the five core competencies and is designed to be delivered through a series of modules that can be adapted to the specific needs and contexts of different institutions.

Proposed Structure for Integrating AI Literacy

The curriculum is structured as a series of four interconnected modules, each building on the previous one. The modules are designed to be delivered over the course of a semester or a year, depending on the program. Each module includes a combination of theoretical content, practical activities, and real-world case studies from the Middle East and beyond.

> Module 1: Foundations of AI in Education. This module provides an introduction to the fundamental concepts of AI and its applications in education. It covers topics such as the history of AI, the different types of AI, and the basic principles of machine learning and algorithmic thinking. The module also explores the ethical and social implications of AI in education, with a particular focus on the cultural context of the Middle East.

Module 2: AI for Teaching and Learning. This module focuses on the practical applications of AI in the classroom. It explores how AI can be used to personalize learning, support students with special needs, and enhance assessment practices. The module also examines the role of the teacher in an AI-powered classroom and explores how teachers can work with AI to improve their practice.

Module 3: Leading with AI. This module is designed to equip educational leaders with the skills and knowledge they need to lead their schools in an AI-driven world. It covers topics such as data-driven decision-making, AI policy and governance, and the management of technological change. The module also explores the leadership competencies required to create a culture of responsible innovation and to engage the school community in a dialogue about the role of AI in education.

Module 4: AI and the Future of Education. This module looks to the future and explores the long-term implications of AI for education. It examines emerging trends in AI and considers how they might shape the future of teaching, learning, and schooling. The module also explores the role of educational leaders in shaping a future where AI is used to create a more equitable, inclusive, and human-centered education system.

Mapping Competencies to Learning Outcomes, Assessments, and Teaching Strategies

Table 1. A detailed mapping of the core competencies to learning outcomes, assessment strategies, and teaching and learning activities.

Core Competency	Learning Outcomes	Assessment Strategies	Teaching and Learning Activities
Algorithmic Thinking	Leaders will be able to explain the basic principles of AI and machine learning. Leaders will be able to critically evaluate the claims of AI vendors. Leaders will be able to anticipate the potential impact of AI on students and teachers.	Case study analysis of AI implementation in a school. A written critique of an AI-powered educational tool. A presentation on the potential benefits and risks of a specific AI application.	Interactive lectures and discussions. Hands-on activities with AI-powered tools. Guest speakers from the AI industry.
Ethical AI Use	Leaders will be able to identify and analyze the ethical implications of AI in education. Leaders will be able to develop and implement policies for the ethical use of AI. Leaders will be able to engage the school community in a dialogue about the ethical dimensions of AI.	A policy brief on a specific ethical issue related to AI in education. A case study analysis of an ethical dilemma involving AI. A role-playing exercise in which leaders must respond to an ethical challenge.	Debates and discussions on ethical issues. Analysis of case studies from the Middle East and other regions. Development of a school-level AI ethics code.
Data Interpretation & Decision-Making	Leaders will be able to use AI-generated data to inform strategic decision-making. Leaders will be able to communicate data-based insights to a variety of stakeholders. Leaders will be able to use data to promote equity and excellence.	A data analysis project using a real-world dataset. A presentation of data-based recommendations to a school board. A portfolio of data visualizations.	Workshops on data analysis and visualization. Use of AI-powered data analysis tools. Collaborative projects with other leaders.
Digital Equity & Inclusion	Leaders will be able to identify and address digital access and use gaps. Leaders will be able to ensure that AI is used in a way that promotes equity and inclusion. Leaders will be able to advocate for policies that support digital equity.	An equity audit of a school's use of technology. A proposal for a new initiative to promote digital inclusion. A presentation to a community group on the importance of digital equity.	Community-based research projects. Site visits to schools with innovative digital inclusion programs. Collaboration with community organizations.
Policy Awareness & Navigation	Leaders will be able to understand and comply with national and international AI policies. Leaders will be able to develop and implement school-level AI policies. Leaders will be able to advocate for policies that support the responsible use of AI in education.	A policy analysis paper on a specific AI-related issue. The development of a school-level AI policy. A mock legislative hearing on a proposed AI regulation.	Guest speakers from government and regulatory agencies. Analysis of policy documents from the GCC and other regions. Participation in online policy forums.

PEDAGOGICAL MODELS AND IMPLEMENTATION STRATEGIES

Case-based learning, simulation, and scenario planning

Case-based learning, simulation, and scenario planning are innovative teaching strategies that offer significant benefits for student learning and skill development across various disciplines.

These approaches provide experiential learning opportunities that bridge the gap between theory and practice. Simulation games, for instance, allow students to engage with challenging problems in a practical manner and experiment with diverse scenarios, enhancing their decision-making skills in a safe environment (Pacheco-Velazquez et al., 2023). Similarly, problem-based learning (PBL) helps students acquire skills and knowledge to become more effective practitioners by tackling real-world planning problems (Shepherd & Cosgrif, 1998). Interestingly, while these methods generally improve student engagement and motivation, their effectiveness can vary. For example, one study found that traditional case study discussions resulted in higher average student engagement levels compared to simulation games (Rogmans & Abaza, 2019). However, simulation-based education has been associated with improved communication skills, satisfaction, and self-confidence among nursing students (Jallad, 2024). Additionally, web-based simulations have shown effectiveness in developing critical thinking skills (Lovelace et al., 2015).

In conclusion, case-based learning, simulation, and scenario planning offer valuable tools for educators to enhance student learning experiences. These approaches can foster critical thinking, collaboration, and practical skill development (Crogman et al., 2025). However, their effectiveness may depend on factors such as student motivation, complexity of the simulation, and the specific learning context (Rogmans & Abaza, 2019). As education evolves to meet future challenges, these methods can play a crucial role in preparing students for the rapidly changing work landscape (Ahmad, 2019).

Use of AI tools (e.g., ChatGPT, adaptive systems) in leadership training

AI tools like ChatGPT and adaptive systems are increasingly being utilized in leadership training, offering both opportunities and challenges in the field of human resource management and professional development. These AI systems can significantly enhance leadership training by providing personalized learning experiences and tailored content to meet individual needs (Alshahrani, 2023; Rane, 2024). For instance, ChatGPT can facilitate adaptive learning paths, adjusting the training material based on a leader's specific strengths, weaknesses, and learning pace. This personalization can lead to more effective skill enhancement and professional growth among leadership trainees (Rane, 2024). However, the integration of AI in leadership training is not without its challenges. There are ethical concerns surrounding data privacy and potential algorithmic biases that need to be carefully addressed (Rane, 2024). Additionally, while AI can provide valuable insights and simulations, it's crucial to maintain a balance between AI-driven automation and human intervention to preserve the empathetic and intuitive elements essential for effective leadership (Rane, 2024). While AI tools like ChatGPT offer promising opportunities to enhance leadership training through personalization and efficiency, their implementation requires careful consideration of ethical implications and the need for human oversight. As the field evolves, it will be essential for organizations to develop comprehensive strategies that leverage AI's benefits while addressing its limitations in leadership development programs.

Hybrid and online delivery for scalability in the Gulf and wider region

AI tools are increasingly being utilized for hybrid and online delivery of education in the Gulf region and beyond, offering scalable solutions to enhance learning experiences and outcomes.

The integration of AI technologies like ChatGPT into blended learning systems has shown promising results in improving student engagement, motivation, and self-directed learning through personalized feedback and assistance (Alshahrani, 2023). This aligns with the growing need for teachers to develop AI competencies to effectively leverage these tools in online learning environments, especially in light of the pandemic-driven shift to digital education (Ng et al., 2023). Interestingly, while AI offers significant benefits for education delivery, its implementation also presents challenges. The Gulf Cooperation Council (GCC) region is rapidly adopting telehealth strategies and investing in AI, bioinformatics, and genomic medicine for healthcare benefits. However, embracing precision medicine through these technologies is creating new design, installation, and skills challenges (Fernandez-Luque et al., 2021). This highlights the importance of considering both the opportunities and obstacles when implementing AI tools across different sectors. AI tools have demonstrated potential for enhancing the scalability and effectiveness of hybrid and online education delivery in the Gulf region and beyond. By automating administrative tasks, optimizing content delivery, and providing personalized learning experiences, AI can promote inclusive and equitable education (Alshahrani, 2023). However, successful implementation requires addressing challenges such as developing educator competencies, ensuring ethical use of AI, and adapting to new technological demands across various fields.

CHALLENGES AND CONSIDERATIONS

Institutional resistance and capacity constraints

The adoption of AI tools in various institutional settings faces both resistance and capacity constraints, as highlighted by several studies. Research indicates that organizational factors play a crucial role in AI acceptance. Jain et al. (2022) emphasizes the importance of building an environment conducive to AI tool adoption while addressing employees' concerns. This aligns with Venkatesh (2021), which identifies individual characteristics, technology characteristics, environmental characteristics, and interventions as key research directions for understanding AI tool adoption in organizations (Jain et al., 2022; Venkatesh, 2021). Interestingly, different institutions exhibit varying levels of acceptance towards AI tools. Ioku et al. (2024) reveals four distinct profiles among top-ranked universities, ranging from strong opposition to unauthorized AI use to supportive stances on responsible AI use. This diversity in institutional approaches underscores the complexity of AI integration in higher education (Ioku et al., 2024).

Capacity constraints are evident in several areas. Yim and Wegerif (2024) highlights teachers' challenges in AI literacy education, including insufficient content knowledge and experience with AI tools. Technical challenges, stakeholder acceptance, and school infrastructure and budget constraints are also identified as factors affecting AI tool acceptance in educational settings (Yim & Wegerif, 2024). Similarly, Yu et al. (2024) identifies barriers to AI adoption in the Chinese video industry, including technological maturity, cross-disciplinary collaboration, and data security concerns (Yu et al., 2024). In conclusion, while AI tools offer significant potential benefits, their adoption faces institutional resistance and capacity constraints across various sectors. Overcoming these challenges requires addressing technological, organizational, and human factors, as well as developing supportive environments and clear institutional policies for responsible AI use.

Cultural and contextual relevance in AI ethics and digital transformation

AI ethics and digital transformation are increasingly influenced by cultural and contextual factors, as evidenced by research across various domains. The integration of AI in cultural heritage highlights the need for context-sensitive ethical considerations, addressing issues of authenticity, subjectivity, and interpretation biases

(Tiribelli et al., 2024). This underscores the importance of developing trustworthy AI systems that respect cultural nuances and heritage preservation.

In the realm of education, the intersection of Universal Design for Learning (UDL) principles and AI emphasizes the need for inclusive and culturally responsive approaches to foster autonomous learning (Saborío-Taylor & Rojas-Ramírez, 2024). Similarly, research on AI education in Nigeria demonstrates the significance of cultural competence and ethical considerations in shaping AI content and student learning outcomes (Sanusi & Olaleye, 2022). These findings suggest that incorporating cultural elements and humanistic thinking in AI education is crucial for effective implementation. Interestingly, cultural context also plays a role in shaping public perceptions of AI. A comparative study between the UK and USA revealed distinct patterns of attitudes towards AI technology among respondents from different cultural backgrounds (Grassini & Ree, 2023). This highlights the importance of considering cultural differences when developing and deploying AI systems globally. Furthermore, in the defense sector, the Italian case study emphasizes the need for culturally appropriate guidance on AI ethics, risk management, and human-machine interaction (Fanni & Giancotti, 2023). In conclusion, the cultural and contextual relevance of AI ethics and digital transformation is evident across various sectors, including cultural heritage, education, public perception, and defense. To ensure responsible and effective AI implementation, it is crucial to develop context-sensitive ethical frameworks, incorporate cultural competence in AI education, and consider cultural differences in public attitudes towards AI. This approach will help foster more inclusive, ethical, and culturally appropriate AI systems that can address the diverse needs of global societies.

Faculty preparedness and resource availability

AI tools are increasingly being integrated into higher education, but faculty preparedness and resource availability remain significant challenges. Research indicates that while many educators express readiness to use AI tools in teaching activities, there is a lack of systematic understanding of their full potential (Sysoyev, 2024). Many faculty members have limited knowledge related to their specific disciplines and struggle to grasp the complete picture of AI possibilities in education. The integration of AI tools in education is currently at an early stage, with implementation difficulties reported in some higher learning institutions (Santiago et al., 2023). These challenges include issues of overreliance, potential hindrance to critical thinking skills development, and inadvertent encouragement of plagiarism if not used responsibly. Additionally, cultural and language considerations are relevant, as AI tools may not always be attuned to specific linguistic and cultural nuances in academic writing (Santiago et al., 2023). To address these challenges, there is a growing need for professional learning opportunities and resources specifically designed for Educator Preparation Programs (EPPs) (Black et al., 2024). The International Society for Technology in Education (ISTE) has launched initiatives to prepare preservice teachers for effective AI integration. Recommendations include supporting preservice teachers' critical examination and application of AI, focusing on equity, ethics, and culturally responsive teaching. Furthermore, the Turkish Biochemical Society (TBS) Academy recommends educators embrace AI tools while maintaining a critical perspective on their utility and limitations (Sağın et al., 2025). Continuous engagement with evolving AI technologies and promoting AI fluency among educators and students are crucial for the effective and ethical application of AI in academic settings.

CONCLUSION AND FUTURE DIRECTIONS

As this chapter has demonstrated, AI literacy has evolved from a peripheral technical skill to a foundational pillar of effective educational leadership in the 21st century. The rapid integration of AI technologies across educational ecosystems demands leaders who can navigate this complex landscape with confidence, ethical awareness, and cultural sensitivity. In the context of the Middle East and Gulf region, where digital transformation initiatives are accelerating alongside preservation of cultural values, AI-literate leadership becomes even more crucial. The blueprint presented in this chapter offers a comprehensive framework for embedding AI literacy into educational leadership programs, addressing the significant gaps identified in current preparation approaches. By conceptualizing AI literacy as a leadership competency rather than merely a technical skillset, we position educational leaders to make informed decisions that balance technological innovation with human-centered educational values. This approach recognizes that tomorrow's educational leaders must understand not only how AI functions but also how it reshapes educational paradigms, influences equity outcomes, and interacts with diverse cultural contexts. The core competencies outlined, a lgorithmic thinking, ethical AI use, data interpretation, cultural contextual understanding, and policy navigation, provide a holistic foundation upon which leadership programs can build. These competencies enable leaders to move beyond surface-level engagement with AI tools toward strategic integration that advances educational missions while safeguarding against potential harms.

RECOMMENDATIONS FOR POLICY AND PRACTICE

Based on the findings and frameworks presented in this chapter, we offer the following recommendations for policy, practice, and further research.

Practice Recommendations

Effective implementation of AI literacy in educational leadership requires a holistic approach that permeates existing curricula rather than creating isolated technical modules. Leadership preparation programs should weave AI literacy components throughout their courses, demonstrating how these competencies enhance core leadership functions such as instructional supervision, resource allocation, and strategic planning. This integration ensures that AI literacy is understood as fundamental to leadership practice rather than as an optional technical skill. Alongside this curricular integration, professional development providers must establish carefully structured learning pathways that enable leaders to build AI literacy progressively, beginning with foundational awareness of key concepts and gradually advancing toward sophisticated implementation capabilities that address complex educational challenges. This tiered approach acknowledges the varying entry points of current and aspiring leaders while providing clear developmental trajectories. The cultivation of AI literacy among educational leaders further benefits from collaborative learning environments where shared exploration can accelerate understanding and application. Educational institutions should foster vibrant communities of practice that bring together leaders from diverse contexts to collectively investigate AI applications, exchange implementation experiences, and co-develop integration strategies that respond to specific cultural and institutional needs. These collaborative spaces serve not only as knowledge-sharing platforms but also as innovation incubators where contextually appropriate approaches to AI can emerge. To complement these collaborative efforts, leadership programs must incorporate authentic experiential learning opportunities that place aspiring leaders in realistic decision-making scenarios involving AI tools. These experiences allow leaders to develop practical implementation skills while simultaneously engaging in critical reflection about ethical implications, helping them internalize the complex interplay between technological capabilities and educational values. Underpinning all these recommendations is the critical need for faculty development initiatives that systematically build instructor capacity to teach AI literacy concepts effectively, addressing the significant preparedness gaps that currently limit program quality and reach.

Policy Recommendations

The findings and frameworks presented in this chapter point to several critical policy interventions needed to advance AI literacy in educational leadership across the Middle East region. Educational authorities throughout the region should collaboratively develop comprehensive AI literacy standards specifically tailored for leadership certification and professional development programs, ensuring these standards thoughtfully balance global best practices with local cultural contexts and educational priorities. Such standards would provide a consistent framework while respecting the unique cultural and educational landscapes across different Middle Eastern countries. In parallel, ministries of education must establish dedicated funding mechanisms to support AI literacy development in leadership preparation programs, with intentional emphasis on institutions serving underrepresented communities to prevent the emergence of new digital divides in leadership capacity. This targeted investment approach acknowledges that equitable AI literacy development requires deliberate resource allocation to address existing disparities in technological access and expertise. Given the rapidly evolving nature of AI technologies and their ethical implications, policy frameworks should mandate regular review and updating of AI literacy components within leadership curricula. This cyclical review process ensures that preparation programs remain relevant and responsive to emerging technologies, evolving ethical considerations, and shifting implementation challenges in educational settings. Complementing these curricular policies, regulatory bodies across the region should develop nuanced guidelines for ethical AI implementation in educational contexts that explicitly respect cultural values and address region-specific concerns. These guidelines should provide clear direction on critical issues including data privacy protections, equity safeguards, and cultural preservation considerations that reflect the unique priorities and sensitivities of Middle Eastern educational communities. Together, these policy recommendations create a supportive ecosystem for developing AI-literate educational leaders who can navigate both technological advancement and cultural continuity in their decision-making.

Vision for Future-Ready School Governance in the Middle East

The future of educational leadership in the Middle East requires a vision that embraces technological advancement while remaining firmly grounded in cultural values and educational purpose. AI-literate leaders will be positioned to transform schools into dynamic learning environments where technology enhances rather than replaces human connection, where data informs but does not dictate decision-making, and where innovation serves the goal of more equitable, accessible, and culturally responsive education.

This vision of future-ready school governance includes:

> *Culturally Responsive Digital* Transformation: Educational leaders who can navigate the integration of global technological advances while preserving and enhancing cultural identity, ensuring that AI implementation respects and reflects local values, languages, and pedagogical traditions.
> *Ethical AI Stewardship*: School systems governed by leaders who approach AI not merely as efficiency tools but as socio-technical systems requiring careful ethical consideration, transparent policies, and ongoing community engagement.
> *Data-Informed Equity Focus*: Leadership practices that leverage AI's analytical capabilities to identify and address systemic inequities while guarding against algorithmic biases that could exacerbate existing disparities.
> *Collaborative Human-AI Ecosystems*: Educational environments where AI augments human capabilities rather than replacing them, with leaders who can orchestrate effective collaboration between educators, students, communities, and technological systems.
> Adaptive Governance Structures: Institutional frameworks that can evolve alongside technological developments, guided by leaders who understand both the technical and social dimensions of AI integration.

The path toward this vision requires sustained commitment to developing AI literacy among current and future educational leaders. The curriculum blueprint presented in this chapter offers a starting point for this journey, providing a framework that can be adapted to diverse institutional contexts across the Middle East and beyond. By investing in AI literacy as a core leadership competency, educational systems can prepare for a future where technological advancement and human flourishing advance together, guided by leaders who understand both the promise and the perils of artificial intelligence in education. As we look toward this future, the most important insight may be that AI literacy for educational leaders is not about technology mastery but about wisdom; the wisdom to discern when and how to employ powerful tools in service of enduring educational values, the wisdom to balance innovation with tradition, and the wisdom to center human relationships in increasingly digital educational environments. By cultivating this wisdom through thoughtful leadership preparation, we can ensure that AI serves as a force for educational advancement that honors the rich cultural heritage and aspirations of the Middle East region.

REFERENCES

Abositta, A., Adedokun, M. W., & Berberoğlu, A. (2024). Influence of Artificial Intelligence on Engineering Management Decision-Making with Mediating Role of Transformational Leadership. *Systems*, *12*(12), 570. DOI: 10.3390/systems12120570

Ahmad, T. (2019). Scenario based approach to re-imagining future of higher education which prepares students for the future of work. Higher Education. *Skills and Work-Based Learning*, *10*(1), 217–238. DOI: 10.1108/HESWBL-12-2018-0136

Alasgarova, R., & Rzayev, J. (2024). The Role of Artificial Intelligence in Shaping High School Students' Motivation. *International Journal of Technology in Education and Science*, *8*(2), 311–324. DOI: 10.46328/ijtes.553

Allen, L. K., & Kendeou, P. (2023). ED-AI Lit: An Interdisciplinary Framework for AI Literacy in Education. *Policy Insights from the Behavioral and Brain Sciences*, *11*(1), 3–10. DOI: 10.1177/23727322231220339

Alshahrani, A. (2023). The impact of ChatGPT on blended learning: Current trends and future research directions. *International Journal of Data and Network Science*, *7*(4), 2029–2040. DOI: 10.5267/j.ijdns.2023.6.010

Annapureddy, R., Fornaroli, A., & Gatica-Perez, D. (2025). Generative AI Literacy: Twelve Defining Competencies. *Digital Government: Research and Practice*, *6*(1), 1–21. DOI: 10.1145/3685680

Arar, K., Salha, S., & Tlili, A. (2024). Human-Machine symbiosis in educational leadership in the era of artificial intelligence (AI): Where are we heading? Educational Management Administration &amp. *Educational Management Administration & Leadership*, 17411432241292295. Advance online publication. DOI: 10.1177/17411432241292295

Biagini, G. (2024). Assessing the assessments: Toward a multidimensional approach to AI literacy. *Medical Education*, *15*(1), 91–101. DOI: 10.36253/me-15831 PMID: 38279173

Black, N. B., George, S., Eguchi, A., Dempsey, J. C., Langran, E., Fraga, L., Brunvand, S., & Howard, N. (2024, March). A framework for approaching AI education in educator preparation programs. *Proceedings of the AAAI Conference on Artificial Intelligence*, *38*(21), 23069–23077. DOI: 10.1609/aaai.v38i21.30351

Chan, C. (2024). Holistic competencies and AI in education: A synergistic pathway. *Australasian Journal of Educational Technology*, *40*(5), 1–12. DOI: 10.14742/ajet.10191

Chiu, T. K. F., Ahmad, Z., Ismailov, M., & Sanusi, I. T. (2024). What are artificial intelligence literacy and competency? A comprehensive framework to support them. *Computers and Education Open*, *6*, 100171. DOI: 10.1016/j.caeo.2024.100171

Crogman, H. T., Cano, V. D., Pacheco, E., Sonawane, R. B., & Boroon, R. (2025). Virtual Reality, Augmented Reality, and Mixed Reality in Experiential Learning: Transforming Educational Paradigms. *Education Sciences*, *15*(3), 303. DOI: 10.3390/educsci15030303

Fanni, R., & Giancotti, F. (2023). Ethical Artificial Intelligence in the Italian Defence: A Case Study. *Digital Society : Ethics, Socio-Legal and Governance of Digital Technology*, *2*(2), 29. Advance online publication. DOI: 10.1007/s44206-023-00056-0

Fernandez-Luque, L., Deeb, A., Savage, M. O., Argente, J., Bin-Abbas, B., Dixon, D., Koledova, E., Al Herbish, A., Zary, N., & Al Shammari, R. (2021). Digital Health for Supporting Precision Medicine in Pediatric Endocrine Disorders: Opportunities for Improved Patient Care. Frontiers in Pediatrics, 9(Suppl 11 2). https://doi.org/ DOI: 10.3389/fped.2021.715705

Grassini, S., & Ree, A. S. (2023). Hope or Doom AI-ttitude? Examining the Impact of Gender, Age, and Cultural Differences on the Envisioned Future Impact of Artificial Intelligence on Humankind. 1–7. DOI: 10.1145/3605655.3605669

Guettala, M., Harous, S., Bourekkache, S., & Kazar, O. (2024). Generative Artificial Intelligence in Education: Advancing Adaptive and Personalized Learning. *Acta Informatica Pragensia*, *13*(3), 460–489. DOI: 10.18267/j.aip.235

Jacques, P. H., Garger, J., & Moss, H. K. (2024). A Synthesis of AI in Higher Education: Shaping the Future. *Journal of Behavioral and Applied Management*, *24*(2). Advance online publication. DOI: 10.21818/001c.122146

Jallad, S. T. (2024). Effectiveness of Simulation-Based Education on Educational Practices of Communication Skills, Satisfaction, and Self-Confidence Among Undergraduate Nursing Students. *Creative Nursing*. Advance online publication. DOI: 10.1177/10784535241301115 PMID: 39639530

Lovelace, K. J., Eggers, F., & Dyck, L. R. (2015). I Do and I Understand: Assessing the Utility of Web-Based Management Simulations to Develop Critical Thinking Skills. Academy of Management Learning &amp. *Academy of Management Learning & Education*, *15*(1), 100–121. DOI: 10.5465/amle.2013.0203

Najdawi, M. H. A., Abdelmoghies, M. M., Ali, A., Shwedeh, F., & Kitana, A. (2024). Applying artificial intelligence in predicting educational excellence in higher education institutions: A case study in Jordanian universities. *Edelweiss Applied Science and Technology*, *8*(6), 7273–7289. DOI: 10.55214/25768484.v8i6.3579

Ng, D. T. K., Ng, R. C. W., Chu, S. K. W., Leung, J. K. L., & Su, J. (2023). Teachers' AI digital competencies and twenty-first century skills in the post-pandemic world. *Educational Technology Research and Development*, *71*(1), 137–161. DOI: 10.1007/s11423-023-10203-6 PMID: 36844361

Ng, D. T. K., Qiao, M. S., Leung, J. K. L., & Chu, K. W. S. (2021). AI Literacy: Definition, Teaching, Evaluation and Ethical Issues. *Proceedings of the Association for Information Science and Technology*, *58*(1), 504–509. DOI: 10.1002/pra2.487

Nyoto, N., Nyoto, R. L. V., & Renaldo, N. (2024). The Bright Side of Artificial Intelligence in Corporate Leadership: A Rapid Literature Review of the Past Five Years. *Journal of Applied Business and Technology*, *5*(3), 193–201. DOI: 10.35145/jabt.v5i3.186

Ou, S. (2024). Transforming Education: The Evolving Role of Artificial Intelligence in The Students Academic Performance. *International Journal of Education and Humanities*, *13*(2), 163–173. DOI: 10.54097/cc1x7r95

Pacheco-Velazquez, E., Ramirez Montoya, M. S., & Salinas-Navarro, D. (2023). Serious Games and Experiential Learning: Options for Engineering Education. *International Journal of Serious Games*, *10*(3), 3–21. DOI: 10.17083/ijsg.v10i3.593

Rane, N. (2024). Role and challenges of ChatGPT, Gemini, and similar generative artificial intelligence in human resource management. *Studies in Economics and Business Relations*, *5*(1), 11–23. DOI: 10.48185/sebr.v5i1.1001

Rogmans, T., & Abaza, W. (2019). The Impact of International Business Strategy Simulation Games on Student Engagement. Simulation &amp. *Simulation & Gaming*, *50*(3), 393–407. DOI: 10.1177/1046878119848138

Rütti-Joy, O., Winder, G., & Biedermann, H. (2023). Building AI Literacy for Sustainable Teacher Education. *Zeitschrift Für Hochschulentwicklung*, *18*(4), 175–189. DOI: 10.21240/zfhe/18-04/10

Saborío-Taylor, S., & Rojas-Ramírez, F. (2024). Universal design for learning and artificial intelligence in the digital era: Fostering inclusion and autonomous learning. International Journal of Professional Development. *Learners and Learning*, *6*(2), ep2408. Advance online publication. DOI: 10.30935/ijpdll/14694

Sağın, A. E., Yücekaya, M. A., Uğraş, S., Mergan, B., Temel, C., Duran, M., & Duarte-Mendes, P. (2025). The mediating role of physical education course interest in the relationship between perceived autonomy support, feedback, and school attachment. *Frontiers in Psychology, 16*, 1675108. DOI: 10.3389/fpsyg.2025.1675108 PMID: 41104409

Sanusi, I. T., & Olaleye, S. A. (2022). An Insight into Cultural Competence and Ethics in K-12 Artificial Intelligence Education. 12, 790–794. DOI: 10.1109/EDUCON52537.2022.9766818

Shepherd, A., & Cosgrif, B. (1998). Problem-Based Learning: A Bridge between Planning Education and Planning Practice. *Journal of Planning Education and Research, 17*(4), 348–357. DOI: 10.1177/0739456X9801700409

Sposato, M. (2024). Developing Digital Leadership Skills for AI-Driven Research Environments (pp. 235–254). igi global. DOI: 10.4018/979-8-3693-0884-4.ch010

Stolpe, K., & Hallström, J. (2024). Artificial intelligence literacy for technology education. *Computers and Education Open, 6*, 100159. DOI: 10.1016/j.caeo.2024.100159

Sysoyev, P. V. (2024). The use of artificial intelligence technologies in foreign language teaching: The subject of methodological works for 2023 and prospects for further research. *Tambov University Review. Series. Humanities (Washington), 29*(2), 294–308.

Thomas, J. O., Minor, R., Rankin, Y., & Sun, L. (2017). Exploring the Difficulties African-American Middle School Girls Face Enacting Computational Algorithmic Thinking over three Years while Designing Games for Social Change. [CSCW]. *Computer Supported Cooperative Work, 26*(4–6), 389–421. DOI: 10.1007/s10606-017-9292-y

Tiribelli, S., Giovanola, B., Pansoni, S., & Frontoni, E. (2024). Ethics of Artificial Intelligence for Cultural Heritage: Opportunities and Challenges. *IEEE Transactions on Technology and Society, 5*(3), 293–305. DOI: 10.1109/TTS.2024.3432407

Valerio, A. S. (2024). Anticipating the Impact of Artificial Intelligence in Higher Education: Student Awareness and Ethical Concerns in Zamboanga City, Philippines. *Cognizance Journal of Multidisciplinary Studies, 4*(6), 408–418. DOI: 10.47760/cognizance.2024.v04i06.024

Walter, Y. (2024). Embracing the future of Artificial Intelligence in the classroom: The relevance of AI literacy, prompt engineering, and critical thinking in modern education. *International Journal of Educational Technology in Higher Education, 21*(1), 15. Advance online publication. DOI: 10.1186/s41239-024-00448-3

Wang, Y. (2021). Artificial intelligence in educational leadership: A symbiotic role of human-artificial intelligence decision-making. *Journal of Educational Administration*, *59*(3), 256–270. DOI: 10.1108/JEA-10-2020-0216

Yi, Y. (2021). Establishing the concept of AI literacy. *JAHR*, *12*(2), 353–368. DOI: 10.21860/j.12.2.8

Zhang, H., Ali, S., Lee, I., Cheng, Y., Breazeal, C., & Dipaola, D. (2022). Integrating Ethics and Career Futures with Technical Learning to Promote AI Literacy for Middle School Students: An Exploratory Study. *International Journal of Artificial Intelligence in Education*, *23*(2), 290–324. DOI: 10.1007/s40593-022-00293-3 PMID: 35573722

Chapter 4
Equipping Workforce Leaders for the AI Era:
Faculty Insights From UAE Higher Education

Fatima Salem Al Mohsen
http://orcid.org/0000-0001-6096-4272
Zayed University, UAE

ABSTRACT

Artificial Intelligence (AI) restructures workforce dynamics and leadership roles, higher education institutions (HEIs) must prepare future leaders with technical proficiency and ethical compassion. In line with the UAE's AI Strategy 2031, this chapter explores faculty perspectives (N=16) at a federal university in Abu Dhabi on embedding AI literacy into a mandatory leadership course. Using the framework of Braun and Clarke's for thematic analysis, twelve themes emerged, emphasizing opportunities in AI-driven competencies such as data-informed decision-making, ethical awareness, and adaptive leadership. Challenges included inadequate faculty confidence, insufficient institutional support, restricted access to AI tools, and gaps between basic familiarity and deeper AI literacy. This study calls for interdisciplinary collaboration, ethical AI policies, and sustained professional development to promote inclusive, context-driven leadership education aligned with UAE Vision 2031.

INTRODUCTION

Artificial intelligence (AI) is promptly transforming education system by restructuring how students learn, teachers teach, and institutions operate. From individualized learning to automating organizational tasks and providing real-time

DOI: 10.4018/979-8-3373-4908-4.ch004

feedback that is enhancing educational effectiveness and inclusivity (Alshamsi, 2025). As AI continues to evolve, it is imperative to reveal on its wider implications for teaching, learning, and institutional development (Kamalov et al., 2023). AI embraces remarkable potential to improve learning by resolving multifaceted problems, refining teaching and learning approaches, and accelerating long-lasting educational progress (Fengchun & Holmes, 2023; Simhardi & Swamy, 2023). However, educational leaders face respective substantial challenges in the AI era. These comprise familiarizing to rapid technological disruptions, focusing ethical concerns, advancing effective human-AI alliance, handling workforce evolutions, and sustaining human-centered leadership while cultivating a strong ethical culture. To lead successfully in this emergent panorama, leaders must comprehend the procedural underpinnings, concrete applications, and deliberate repercussions of AI (Lakhanpal, 2024). They need to promote a culture of continuous learning and flexibility within their institutes. Ethical leadership is crucial that leaders must navigate critical concerns for instance, privacy, bias, fairness, and accountability, whilst certifying transparency in AI-driven conclusions. Establishing ethical structures and leadership strategies will be vital to building trust and guiding responsible AI incorporation in education (Barnes & Hutson, 2024).

The emergence of AI requires a fundamental transformation of higher education curricula, particularly in leadership education. Rather than treating AI as an assisting technological tool, contemporary literature advocates for its integration as a core component of curriculum design to support future-ready competencies. AI-driven curriculum transformation emphasizes interdisciplinary learning, problem-solving, data-informed decision-making, and ethical reasoning skills essential for leadership in AI-driven societies.

Within universities, AI applications are reshaping both academic and administrative functions. Teaching and learning processes are enhanced through adaptive learning systems, intelligent tutoring, and automated assessment, while administrative operations benefit from predictive analytics, AI-powered student support services, and streamlined document management systems. Across disciplines, AI supports advanced simulations in engineering, market forecasting in business, diagnostic tools in health sciences, and text analysis in humanities and social sciences. These developments underscore the need for curricula that not only embed AI literacy but also align with broader institutional and national agendas, such as the UAE Vision 2031, which prioritizes innovation, digital transformation, and knowledge-based economies. Curriculum transformation, therefore, is not solely a technological shift but a strategic educational reform that prepares graduates to function as ethical, innovative, and adaptive leaders in complex AI-mediated environments.

Faculty as Change Agents in AI-Driven Leadership Education

Faculty members play an essential role in translating AI-driven institutional strategies into meaningful learning experiences, positioning them as central change agents in curriculum transformation. Literature increasingly recognizes that successful AI integration depends on faculty perceptions, readiness, and pedagogical agency. Faculty are not merely implementers of AI tools but active designers of learning environments that cultivate leadership competencies, critical thinking, and ethical awareness among students. In AI-enabled leadership education, faculty are required to navigate evolving pedagogical roles such as facilitators of inquiry, mentors of ethical reasoning, and mediators of human AI collaboration. Their engagement is particularly crucial in contexts such as the UAE, where higher education institutions are closely aligned with national priorities for innovation and workforce development. Faculty insights offer valuable perspectives on institutional enablers and barriers, professional development needs, and the cultural shifts necessary to embed AI literacy meaningfully within leadership curricula.

LITERATURE REVIEW

The Transformative Role of Artificial Intelligence in Higher Education

Artificial Intelligence (AI) has become a leading dynamic in contemporary society, transforming several sectors and reforming the nature of work and daily life (Khan & Yasir, 2024). Within this evolving panorama, AI holds substantial potential to impact higher education institutions (HEIs) across a comprehensive spectrum (Khairullah et al., 2025). Universities and other academic institutions are gradually discovering ways to integrate AI into their research competences, administrative operations, and teaching practices to improve institutional effectiveness (Lee et al., 2024). Though, the integration of AI into HEIs presents various opportunities as well as intricacies that require rigorous academic inquiry to confirm its effective and ethical adoption (Rashid et al., 2024). The emergence of AI technologies has led to a thoughtful transformation in higher education, creating avenues for data-informed decision-making, tailored learning experiences, and state-of-the-art pedagogical practices (Rahiman & Kodikal, 2023).

Adaptive learning systems driven by AI can analyze large bulks of data to produce personalized learning tracks tailored to individual students' preferences, styles, and capabilities that enhance their overall educational experience (Khairullah et al., 2025). AI-driven tools such as intelligent tutoring systems offer real-time feedback and guidance, assisting students grasp complex subjects and achieve learning goals more efficiently. Moreover, virtual learning assistants (Pogorskiy & Beckmann, 2023) improve student engagement by offering timely support and advancing interaction. The integration of these AI technologies in higher education opens innovative pedagogical prospects, transforming education according to 21st century.

Previous research conducted by Crompton and Burke (2023) confirmed that integrating AI in universities significantly enhances administrative efficiency and supports effective decision-making across strategic institutional operations. AI tools automate repetitive tasks such as enrollment, financial aid processing, and admissions, allowing staff to emphasis on more strategic initiatives. These competences provide to more informed data decisions, and student-centered higher education environments. Predictive analysis, as emphasized by Rafik (2023), has made a significant contribution to data-driven decision-making in basic areas such as planning, resource allocation, and targeted student support.

AI and Leadership

AI is transforming all aspects of life by driving innovation through automation and predictive analytics (Brynjolfsson & McAfee, 2017). Since AI has become a strategic tool across sectors, it also redefines leadership by allowing more informed, data-driven decisions and agile resource management (Ransbotham et al., 2017). Though, effective leadership in the AI era extends beyond technical knowledge and it requires strategic foresight and ethical responsibility.

With emerging concerns around bias, transparency, and accountability, ethical leadership is crucial to guide AI integration in configuration with organizational standards (Floridi et al., 2018). Promoting such leadership confirms that AI is implemented responsibly, cultivating sustainable and inclusive innovation.

Empowering Academic Leadership through Artificial Intelligence

This section assesses the AI literacy and its contribution. AI literacy refers to the foundational knowledge and skills required to understand, interact with, and critically evaluate artificial intelligence technologies. Kandlhofer and colleagues (2016), among the early pioneers in this field, outlined AI literacy as a set of competencies that empower individuals to comprehend AI concepts and effectively engage with AI-driven tools and systems. The transformative contributions of Artificial Intelligence (AI) to higher education institutions (HEIs), highlighting its impact on strategic leadership in an increasingly digital academic landscape. While prevailing literature focuses on the technical applications of AI, this review focusses forward-looking perspectives that are often overlooked and outlines future directions for research and leadership development (Khairullah et al., 2025).

AI presents unmatched opportunities to improve student success indicators embracing engagement, retention, persistence, academic performance, graduation outcomes, and career readiness. Through AI-powered recommendation systems and predictive analytics, institutions can tailor interventions to support individual learner needs and improve educational trajectories (Bouschery et al., 2023). Furthermore, AI offers scalable solutions to demanding educational challenges. These include the development of adapted learning pathways, automation of assessments, and restructuring of administrative systems particularly in admissions and enrollment management (Lozano & Blanco Fontao, 2023). The integration of AI into academic leadership further supports informed decision-making and accelerates research and development activities (Crompton and Burke, 2023). AI-driven tools facilitate in data analysis, identify trends, and enable evidence-based policymaking and enhance the leadership capacity to respond to complex institutional demands.

This section concludes with a call to action for the researchers and higher education leaders to must reconsider traditional educational models and promote collaborative, interdisciplinary practices. In doing so, they can ensure that higher education remains applicable, responsive, and resilient in an AI-integrated future.

AI Applications Across Disciplines

AI applications span across several sectors, basically transforming conventional practices in unprecedented ways. In the *healthcare industry*, AI is reforming diagnostics, treatment planning, and patient care. AI-powered systems, mainly those using profound learning algorithms, can examine medical images with significant precision frequently exceed human capabilities. For instance, these technologies are used to discover abnormalities in radiology scans, allowing for earlier and more precise diagnosis of conditions such as cancer and cardiovascular diseases (Albawi et al., 2023). AI has also made substantial strides in the *financial sector*, where it is extensively applied in areas such as risk management, fraud detection, and algorithmic trading. Machine learning models examine enormous volumes of transactional data to detect suspicious patterns and identify fraudulent activities in real time, enabling financial institutions to implement stronger and more responsive security measures (Ngai et al., 2021). AI has also brought transformative advancements to the *transportation and logistics sectors*, particularly through the development of autonomous vehicles and the optimization of supply chain operations. AI-powered structures support self-driving cars and trucks to navigate independently, with the potential to reduce traffic accidents and improve overall road efficiency (Siegel & Pappas, 2023). In *logistics,* AI enables optimized route planning and fleet management, resulting in improved delivery efficiency and reduced fuel consumption (Tsolaki et al., 2023). Turning to trade and *e-commerce,* AI has profoundly reformed these sectors by driving personalization in customer experiences and enhancing supply chain optimization. In the *manufacturing sector*, AI allows advanced automation and reinforces predictive maintenance. AI-powered robots and systems improve production efficiency, reduce human error, and lower operational costs, contributing to smarter and more efficient industrial processes (Kim et al., 2022). In the *energy sector,* AI is increasingly used to increase efficiency and promote sustainability. By examining large datasets, AI algorithms enhance energy production and delivery, allowing real-time balancing of supply and demand and supporting more sustainable energy management practices (Rinku, 2023). The wide-ranging applications of AI across industries from healthcare to energy emphasize its transformative potential. Each sector has experienced remarkable advancements in efficiency, precision, and innovation through AI integration. As AI technology continues to grow, its impact is expected to grow, further accelerating innovation and improving global competitiveness.

AI Taxonomy in Educational Leadership

A comprehensive taxonomy of AI applications in educational leadership was developed through a systematic review of literature from 2017 to 2024 (Sposato, 2025) a period marked by rapid advancements in machine learning, natural language processing, and the rise of large language models and generative AI that have significantly restructured the educational landscape (Lee & Palmer, 2025).

Table 1 presents a concise overview of key AI application domains in leadership in higher education, emphasizing essential components and practical examples to help leaders to comprehend their implementation and impact across various areas.

Table 1. key AI application Domains in Leadership of Higher Education

Domain	Key components	Examples
AI Integration in Leadership Development	Strategic AI tools for decision-making Forecasting future workforce skills Crisis response through AI models	Enhances faculty efforts in preparing leadership students for complex, AI-driven work environments.
AI Literacy for Ethical Leadership	Understanding ethical AI use Addressing bias and fairness Promoting transparency in AI-supported leadership	Cultivates AI-literate future leaders capable of making fair, data-informed, and ethically grounded decisions in diverse organizational settings.
Faculty AI Capacity Building	Professional development in AI tools Real-time AI-assisted teaching feedback AI-integrated curriculum design	Equips faculty with necessary support and training to effectively embed AI concepts in leadership programs and foster student readiness.
Personalized Learning for Workforce Readiness	Adaptive learning systems AI tutors and performance tracking Tailored leadership learning pathways	Supports student-centered education that adapts to diverse learner needs, improving their preparedness for dynamic, tech-integrated workforce environments.
AI-Driven Student Support Systems	Mental health analytics AI-powered career guidance 24/7 AI student engagement tools	Empowers future leaders to prioritize holistic development and well-being using AI to support retention, motivation, and lifelong employability.

Underpinning on the AI application taxonomy, university faculty across various disciplines contribute a pivotal role in preparing future workforce leaders equipped for the AI era. By integrating domain-specific AI tools such as adaptive learning platforms in leadership, predictive analytics in business, intelligent simulations in engineering, and data-driven diagnostics in health sciences faculty can implant real-world AI capabilities into leadership curricula.

This cross-disciplinary method not only enhances students' technical skills but also nurtures ethical awareness, critical decision-making, and strategic thinking. Bring into line teaching practices with the taxonomy enables faculty to model AI-integrated leadership, confirming graduates are equipped to lead successfully in digitally transformed workplaces.

Challenges Faced by University Faculty in Preparing AI-Integrated Workforce Leaders in the UAE

University faculty in the UAE face many challenges in executing leadership education that prepares students for an AI-driven workforce. A significant issue is the lack of formal training in AI pedagogy, particularly among faculty from non-technical disciplines, which restricts their ability to successfully integrate AI concepts into leadership courses. Moreover, existing curricula are often old-fashioned and do not support with the increasing demands of AI-enhanced leadership roles. Institutional obstructions such as inadequate infrastructure, lack of AI-related teaching resources, and unclear policy support further deter effective integration. Ethical apprehensions embracing data privacy, algorithmic bias, and impartial access intensify complexity to teaching AI reliably, especially for students with diverse digital skills and backgrounds. Furthermore, faculty often experience resistance to change, restricted time, and increased workload, making it challenging to adopt state-of-the-art AI tools in their teaching. Focusing these challenges is critical for higher education institutions planning to build future-ready, morally grounded workforce leaders (Sposato, 2025).

CONCEPTUAL FRAMEWORK AND CONTEXT OF THE STUDY

This study is anchored in Siemens' (2005) theory of *Connectivism*, which serves as a robust theoretical foundation for understanding learning in AI-integrated educational environments. Connectivism postulates that knowledge is not confined to individual cognition but is distributed across networks of people and digital resources. Learning, therefore, is the process of navigating and making connections within these networks. In the context of Artificial Intelligence (AI), this theory focusses how intelligent systems, and digital tools can facilitate dynamic, personalized, and networked learning experiences. AI-enhanced learning environments, guided by connectivism principles, empower both faculty and students to interact meaningfully with data, systems, and content, promoting ethical, adaptive, and data-informed leadership practices.

In the United Arab Emirates (UAE), where national strategies prioritize digital transformation and the advancement of a knowledge-based economy, higher education institutions (HEIs) are uniquely positioned to prepare future-ready leaders. This book chapter, titled *"Equipping Workforce Leaders for the AI Era: Faculty Insights from UAE Higher Education"*, explores how university faculty, particularly those teaching compulsory leadership courses, perceive the integration of AI into leadership education. It examines their understanding of AI's relevance, the institutional and pedagogical challenges they face, and their recommendations for embedding AI literacy into the curriculum. The study emphasizes the critical role of faculty in shaping ethically grounded and inclusive leadership programs that align with the UAE's socio-economic goals and cultural values. By grounding this exploration in connectivism, the chapter provides both a theoretical and contextual lens to understand how UAE HEIs can lead transformative educational practices that foster AI-literate, future-ready workforce leaders. The below figure represents the AI impacts in workforce leadership.

Figure1. Impact of AI in workforce leadership

Research Questions

This study will be conducted by following research questions:

1. How do university faculty perceive the significance and relevance of AI literacy in preparing students for AI-integrated workforce leadership?
2. To what extent do faculty incorporate AI concepts and tools into their teaching practices to improve students' leadership readiness in an AI-driven workforce?
3. What are the crucial challenges faculty encounter in embedding AI literacy into leadership courses, and how do they address concerns of equity, ethics, and institutional readiness?

METHODOLOGY

This study employed a qualitative research design by using semi-structured interviews to explore faculty perceptions and experiences regarding the integration of AI literacy into leadership courses across higher education institutions (HEIs) in the United Arab Emirates (UAE), with the aim of equipping future workforce leaders. Grounded on interpretivist paradigm, the study sought to capture the distinct meanings and understandings held by faculty members about their roles in preparing students for leadership within an AI-integrated workforce. This approach was consistent with the study's objective to investigate complex social phenomena within a defined educational context.

Participants

There were 16 faculty members who participated in the study. The participant group was constituted of 10 females and 6 males, indicating a higher representation of female faculty. Most participants (N=7) were within the 35–44 age group, followed by 5 in the 44–54 range, showing that most were mid-career professionals likely engaged in curriculum planning and teaching leadership courses. In terms of academic rank, mostly assistant and associate professors were participated, signifying a combined total of 11 participants. This distribution indicates that the study involved faculty members with substantial teaching responsibilities and institutional involvement. Four professors and one lecturer were also included, echoing a range of seniority across the sample.

Considering the professional experience, mostly participants had significant teaching tenure: 6 had more than 15 years of experience, 5 had between 11–15 years, and 4 had 5–10 years. Only one participant had less than 5 years of experience, further highlighting the study's focus on experienced faculty capable of offering in-depth insights into leadership education and AI literacy. Many participants (11) were associated with public universities, while 5 represented private institutions. This may reflect broader access and participation within the public higher education sector in the UAE. Participants came from diverse disciplines, including education, engineering, leadership and policy studies, business, language studies, mathematics, physics, and health. This disciplinary diversity confirmed that the study captured a wide range of viewpoint on the integration of AI literacy into leadership education, aligning with the interdisciplinary nature of workforce preparation in the AI era.

Table 2. Demographic and Professional Profiles of Research Participants

Participant ID	Gender	Age Group (Years)	Current Position	Years of Experience	University Type	Discipline
FM-1	Female	44–54	Assistant Professor	11–15 years	Public	Environmental Science
FM-2	Male	55 and above	Assistant Professor	More than 15 years	Private	Physics
FM-3	Female	35–44	Associate Professor	11–15 years	Public	Education
FM-4	Male	55 and above	Professor	More than 15 years	Public	Leadership and Policy Studies
FM-5	Male	25–34	Lecturer	Less than 5 years	Private	Business
FM-6	Male	35–44	Assistant Professor	5–10 years	Public	Health
FM-7	Female	35–44	Assistant Professor	5–10 years	Public	Teacher Education
FM-8	Female	35–44	Associate Professor	11–15 years	Private	Engineering
FM-9	Female	35–44	Assistant Professor	5–10 years	Private	Engineering
FM-10	Female	44–54	Associate Professor	More than 15 years	Public	Leadership and Policy Studies
FM-11	Female	35–44	Assistant Professor	11–15 years	Public	Education
FM-12	Male	44–54	Assistant Professor	More than 15 years	Public	Education
FM-13	Male	44–54	Professor	11–15 years	Public	Mathematics
FM-14	Female	44–54	Professor	More than 15 years	Public	Leadership and Policy Studies
FM-15	Female	44–54	Associate Professor	More than 15 years	Public	Language Studies
FM-16	Female	35–44	Associate Professor	5–10 years	Public	Education

FM= faculty member

Link Between Formal AI Training and Faculty Involvement in AI-Related Work

The bar graph showing the relationship between faculty members' formal training in AI and their current involvement in AI-related teaching, research, or projects. Faculty who received formal AI training are significantly more likely to be currently involved in AI-related work. This emphasizes the importance of structured training programs to build AI capacity in higher education. Those without formal training largely remain uninvolved, signifying a gap that institutions must address through targeted professional development and support.

Research Design

In designing the core data sources for this study, efforts were made to comprise a diverse group of faculty members with diverse disciplines in the integration of AI literacy within leadership education. The study involved a series of sixteen in-depth, face-to-face semi-structured interviews with individuals referred to as research participants, as each one was well-positioned to provide thoughtful perceptions into the evolving role of leadership education in preparing students for an AI-integrated workforce. This purposeful selection reflected the intent to capture, within the parameters of a small-scale qualitative study (Canales, 2022), the interdisciplinary diversity presents in UAE (HEIs). Aligned with the constructivist-interpretivist approach, each respondent was considered as a co-constructor of information (Rehman & Chowdhury, 2019) contributing distinctive and contextually embedded interpretations of the phenomena under study examination.

Data collection

Participants were selected through purposive sampling from a federal university in the UAE that offered a leadership domain in their courses as part of its undergraduate or postgraduate discipline programs. The faculty selection criteria were including teaching leadership course/domain in the degree courses and having a minimum of three years of teaching experience in UAE higher education. Data were collected through semi-structured interviews, each lasting approximately 45 to 60 minutes. Interviews were conducted in person, depending on participants' preferences and accessibility in their offices and university setting. The interview protocol focused on significant areas such as 'AI literacy in leadership education', 'AI-integrated workforce leadership', 'AI literacy and competence', 'teaching practices and integration', and 'AI-related challenges faced by leaders.

Ethical issues

Ethical approval for this study was obtained from the Institutional Review Board (IRB) of a federal university in the United Arab Emirates. All participants were fully informed about the purpose of the study, their voluntary participation, and their right to withdraw at any stage without any penalty. Written informed consent was secured from all participants preceding to data collection. Participants were assured that all information gathered during the interviews would be kept strictly confidential and anonymized. Consent was also attained for the publication of research findings derived from the data, with the understanding that no identifying information would be disclosed.

Data Analysis

Perceptions gathered from the analysis uncovered a range of faculty perspectives on the integration of AI literacy into leadership education within the context of UAE higher education. Given the interdisciplinary backgrounds and diverse institutional affiliations of the participants, their insights proposed valuable suggestions for educational policymakers and curriculum designers. Interviews were transcribed verbatim and, where necessary, adapted for clarity, with careful attention to preserving the original tone and meaning. The data were analyzed using thematic analysis, guided by Braun and Clarke's (2006) six-phase framework. This structured yet flexible approach enabled both a comprehensive examination and a consistent interpretation of faculty narratives.

Codes were constructed inductively from the data to capture emerging patterns, while also being theoretically informed by constructs such as AI literacy, leadership competencies, curriculum integration, and institutional readiness. Reflexive memos were sustained throughout the process to document analytical decisions and ensure transparency and rigor in coding and interpretation. Thematic analysis not only facilitated the systematic organization of rich qualitative data but also enabled the identification of nuanced insights about faculty role in preparing students for leadership in an AI-integrated workforce within the UAE context.

The 16 individuals presented a rich and diverse montage of lived experiences related to AI integration in leadership education. While a comprehensive and exhaustive representation of each narrative lies beyond the scope of this book chapter, the analysis focused on twelve key thematic areas that emerged across the dataset. Guided by Braun and Clarke's (2006) six-phase thematic analysis, data familiarization, coding, theme development, theme review, theme definition and naming, and report writing, this study captures shared patterns while preserving the depth and individuality of participants' perspectives within the context of UAE higher education.

These included the 'foundational understanding of AI and its applications', 'enhancing strategic leadership through AI in higher education', 'empowering future leaders with ethical and adaptive AI competence', 'AI skillsets for strategic and ethical leadership', 'redefining leadership in the age of AI from authority to collaborative facilitation', 'bridging the gap between AI familiarity and leadership-ready AI literacy', 'bridging the confidence gap: faculty readiness and ethical integration of AI in teaching', 'using AI to enhance leadership learning and ethical decision-making', 'need for personalized and on-demand AI support for faculty', 'varying levels of faculty confidence in teaching AI role in leadership', 'navigating the challenges of teaching AI in leadership education', 'the future of AI-skilled workforce leaders in the UAE'.

FINDINGS AND ANALYSIS

Theme 1: Foundational Understanding of AI and Its Applications

Faculty members shared their wide-ranging and contextually grounded understandings of AI literacy, echoing both conceptual knowledge and practical application. A majority noticed that 'AI literacy' is the ability to understand how artificial intelligence works, including its applications, limitations, and ethical considerations. This foundational understanding was defined as necessary for responsible and effective use of AI tools in teaching, research, and other domains of life. For many participants, 'AI literacy' went beyond knowing technical terms to embrace critical thinking about when, how, and why AI should be applied in academic and professional contexts.

Essentially, many participants interpreted 'AI literacy' through the lens of their own disciplines. Faculty from business, engineering, education, and health sciences emphasized the role of AI in discipline-specific decision-making, innovation, and student preparation. For example, business educators emphasized AI's value in ethical leadership and strategic planning, while engineers highlighted AI's role in system design and real-world problem solving. This reflects a growing consensus that AI literacy is not a one-size-fits-all concept but must be contextualized within professional practices. Regarding the importance of AI in business discipline, one of the male faculty member working as a lecturer in a private university explained his views:

"As a business faculty member, AI literacy means understanding how AI technologies function, their potential applications in decision-making, and their ethical implications. It's about equipping students with the skills to critically evaluate and responsibly use AI in business contexts." (FM-5).

This signifies the AI integration in business discipline to prepare workforce according to the contemporary needs of the society.

Other participants also explained AI as a practical 'Educational Aid'. Many found it valuable for brainstorming ideas, planning lessons, locating videos, summarizing resources, and editing language especially for those teaching in a second language. A young female faculty member working as an assistant professor in a public university expressed her views as:

"AI means to me a quick assistant... it helps me in lesson planning and searching for some videos about the topics to enhance my teaching materials." (FM-11).

It reflects that AI supports teaching efficiency and resource organization.

Despite the increasing awareness, faculty members encountered barriers such as limited training, unclear policies, and difficulty applying AI concepts in teaching.

These findings highlight the urgent need for targeted professional development and institution wide strategies to promote inclusive and ethical AI literacy.

Theme 2: Enhancing Strategic Leadership through AI in Higher Education

Faculty responses mirrored a strong belief in the potential of AI to support university leadership by improving decision-making, streamlining administrative functions, and enabling data-driven strategic planning. Many participants emphasized that AI tends to enhance efficiency by automating routine tasks such as scheduling, budgeting, report generation, and email correspondence. This automation was seen to allow leaders to focus more on academic innovation, faculty support, and student success. Others highlighted the value of predictive analytics in identifying at-risk students, forecasting enrollment trends, and improving resource allocation tools that empower leaders to act proactively rather than reactively. A younger male faculty member working in the department of business shared his ideas of the effectiveness of AI in the business discipline:

> *"AI can also support personalized learning and automate administrative tasks, allowing academic leaders to focus more on innovation, faculty development, and student success." (FM-5).*

In adding to administrative functions, participants recommended that AI helps to analyze large datasets and generate actionable insights was viewed as a critical asset in guiding academic program development and evaluating institutional performance. A few respondents also mentioned how AI can assist in international benchmarking, offering leaders insights into global educational trends and helping them design competitive strategies. However, some faculty communicated their concerns that over-reliance on AI could undermine student creativity and authenticity. They also emphasized the need for enhanced professional development to deepen understanding of AI's role in academic leadership, particularly in preparing future workforce leaders.

Theme 3: Empowering Future Leaders with Ethical and Adaptive AI Competence

Faculty members across a range of disciplines emphasized that learning about AI is crucial in preparing students to become effective, future-ready leaders. Participants from varied fields such as Education, Business, Health, and Engineering consistently pointed out that AI literacy enables students to make data-driven decisions, engage in critical and adaptive thinking, and solve complex problems all are fundamental qualities in today's promptly advancing digital environment.

Faculty in Leadership and Policy Studies emphasized that AI tends to streamline decision-making and foster strategic planning, giving leaders the tools to respond proactively to change. Besides the significance of AI, respondents also raised strong ethical concerns. Educators from Language Studies and Teacher Education stressed that students must learn how to use AI as an assistant, not a replacement, particularly when it comes to academic integrity, creativity, and personal accountability. They reported that unchecked reliance on AI may deter the development of core skills like academic writing and language proficiency. Thus, alongside technical understanding, the integration of ethical use, source awareness, and guidance from institutions emerged as key needs. Reflecting on the same situation, a middle-aged female faculty member from a public university's department of teacher education shared her perspective as follows:

> *"Students need to understand the ethical use of AI as an assistant, not a replacement. They will be the future leaders and will lead the transformation of integrating AI in their planning, business, and academia." (FM-7).*

The overall sentiment pointed to a strong belief in AI as a tool of empowerment but one that must be applied with wisdom, ethics, and responsibility. Faculty from various disciplines agreed that universities must play an active role in guiding students to use AI meaningfully, not carelessly.

Theme 4: AI Skillsets for Strategic and Ethical Leadership

Participants' responses highlighted the increasing requirement for students in leadership programs to develop practical, analytical, and ethical AI competencies. They suggested the core skills such as data-driven decision-making, algorithmic thinking, predictive analytics, and AI tool proficiency (e.g., dashboards, chatbots, or automation systems). Ethical use of AI was perceived as non-negotiable, with recurring emphasis on teaching students to navigate bias, privacy, and accountability. Faculty believed that students should be equipped to become informed, critical users of AI capable of interpreting AI-generated data conscientiously and integrating it into multifaceted, real-world leadership scenarios such as organizational planning and team management. A female faculty from the department of language studies with more than 15 years' experience in a public university communicated her expression as:

> *"Students need to learn to write effective prompts and paraphrase AI-generated content because we don't want them to end up plagiarizing or sounding like robots. They also need to know how to write straightforward emails and reflective narratives that don't lose their human voice." (FM-15).*

Moreover, faculty emphasized that cultivating leadership competencies in the AI era requires more than technical proficiency it demands a well-rounded skillset that integrates change management, ethical awareness, and effective human-AI collaboration. In addition to foundational knowledge of algorithms and strategic use of AI tools, faculty across disciplines emphasized the emerging need for AI communication literacy. This includes the ability to craft meaningful prompts and reliably paraphrase AI-generated content. An environmental science faculty member emphasized the significance of using AI for self-development and compelling positive social impact, while an engineering faculty member highlighted the real-world requirement of understanding algorithmic functions for strategic leadership decisions. These insights support the need for a well-rounded AI curriculum that helps students to become leaders who can think creatively, act responsibly, and make thoughtful decisions in today's fast-changing, technology-driven world.

Theme 5: Redefining Leadership in the Age of AI: From Authority to Collaborative Facilitation

Faculty members across diverse disciplines emphasized a paradigm shift in leadership brought about by the integration of AI into workplace structures. The traditional concept of authoritative, experience-based leadership is being replaced by a more collaborative and data-informed approach. Faculty explained that modern leaders are expected to own digital fluency, strategic adaptability, and an understanding of AI tools for informed decision-making, resource optimization, and team management. This transition also includes a reimagining of roles especially in academia where leaders are progressing from knowledge seekers to facilitators who guide others through AI-driven change. A female associate professor observed this situation and explained:

"With AI, the world is more transparent. Even the authority role of the leader is changing, it's more collaborative. In higher education, faculty identity is shifting from teacher to facilitator." (FM-3).

This reflects the broader expectation that leaders must guide others in navigating AI, alleviating fears about job security and addressing ethical concerns.

Regarding to the technical and strategic competencies, faculty emphasized the critical role of emotional intelligence, communication skills, and ethical judgment to prepare the workforce leaders for future. Moreover, communication literacy such as writing effective prompts or maintaining appropriate professional tone was seen as essential in avoiding over-reliance on AI-generated language. A senior female professor shared her views:

"Even if AI helps with presentations or emails, students still need to know the basics, how to write clearly and appropriately for the context." (FM-14).

These perceptions mutually argue for a holistic leadership development model one that adopts AI literacy with human-centered values like authenticity, humility, and collaborative learning to prepare leaders for ethically navigating complex, tech-driven environments.

Theme 6: Bridging the Gap Between AI Familiarity and Leadership-Ready AI Literacy

Faculty responses reveal a consistent concern that, although students are extensively exposed to AI tools and often passionate about using them, their engagement tends to be superficial focused more on convenience than on planned, ethical, or insightful use. Faculty emphasized that many students recognize the ways to prompt AI tools like ChatGPT or Grammarly for simple tasks, but it limits their critical thinking, ethical reasoning, and leadership-oriented application mandatory in real-world settings. The absence of organized guidance and curriculum incorporation impairs this gap, preventive students' potential to grow into responsible, future-ready leaders who can navigate AI's complexities. A senior male faculty member from a private university noted that the way students currently seek assistance from AI is insufficient for developing deep understanding or critical thinking skills and said:

Students can ask ChatGPT to help with an essay but have no idea how to evaluate whether the answer is up to mark." (FM-2).

A female faculty from engineering department also explained about the same scenario and reported:

"While engineering students typically have a solid grasp of AI fundamentals and can use tools like machine learning libraries, their ability to apply AI effectively in cross-disciplinary areas such as leadership remains inconsistent."(FM-8).

A faculty member highlighted the superficial use of AI in classroom assignments:

"I ended up reading your reflection, and all the class had the same content. That is not the way to use AI... You can use it for language, but you cannot use it for content." (FM-8).

Another male faculty member highlighted the assessment challenges posed by AI misuse:

"Sometimes it's difficult for us as faculty to document AI misuse and take an action. So, we need strict rules to stop this type of practice." (FM-2).

Overall, faculty emphasized the gap between simply using AI and critically engaging with its end product. They also observed emotional and developmental consequences arising from superficial use of AI, specially a decline in students' self-confidence in their own ideas and abilities due to over-reliance on AI tools. Moreover, students often ignored ethical issues such as data bias, accountability, and responsible use. Faculty from business, engineering, and education disciplines agreed that incorporating real-world case studies, simulations, and ethics training into leadership programs is crucial to help students progress from passive users into thoughtful, informed decision-makers.

Theme 7: Bridging the Confidence Gap: Faculty Readiness and Ethical Integration of AI in Teaching.

Faculty across disciplines are increasingly engaging with AI tools in their teaching, yet their levels of confidence and expertise differ considerably. While some educators feel prepared to integrate tools like ChatGPT and Python into assignments and leadership simulations, others particularly those in non-technical disciplines feel untrained or hesitant. The rapid growth of AI technologies, combined with inadequate institutional training and ethical guidelines, contributes to an increasing sense of indecision. Moreover, concerns over the loss of academic voice, plagiarism, and misuse of AI by students highlight a demand for clearer policies and practical support. Regardless of challenges, faculty seems open to AI related learning and adapting, provided they receive relevant and sustained guidance.

A recurring concern is the lack of organized, ongoing training tailored to faculty needs. Many respondents called for targeted professional development, embracing hands-on workshops, access to evolving AI tools, and collaboration with industry experts.

A male faculty member noted,

"I'm constantly playing catch-up... What would help is more hands-on workshops where I can actually experiment with AI tools myself, not just read about them." (FM-5).

Another female respondent shared her practical use:

"I use AI to write exam questions, check for plagiarism, and even summarize research literature... but I need more one-on-one training because of my vision disability." (FM-1).

This focuses a need for inclusive and differentiated support, especially for faculty with diverse learning or accessibility needs.

Faculty incorporated AI tools like ChatGPT, Gemini, and Grok into teaching, though usage varies by discipline and confidence. These tools support instruction, content creation, and student engagement through tasks such as idea generation, text summarization, and feedback. For example, one associate professor from education discipline shared her views as:

"I use ChatGPT to design PowerPoint presentations and to assess student work by suggesting clarity improvements and checking alignment with objectives." (FM-16).

Some faculty members, especially in foundation or language courses, limit AI use to grammar correction or editing, expressing concerns about plagiarism and loss of student voice. As one noted,

"I make sure that my voice exists in the writing... it should sound like me, not like AI." (FM-5).

Others used AI to generate teaching materials, such as case studies or activity ideas, while carefully reviewing content for accuracy and relevance.

Theme 8: Using AI to Enhance Leadership Learning and Ethical Decision-Making

Faculty members shared diverse experiences of using AI to help students engage with leadership concepts and improve decision-making skills. Though some faculty are still new to this exercise or have not yet used AI in this milieu, others have executed innovative approaches exercising tools like ChatGPT and AI-based simulations. These tools were engaged to role-play scenarios, simulate ethical dilemmas, examine data, or generate perspectives from multiple faculty members extending students' understanding of leadership challenges, ethical reasoning, and critical thinking. A recurring stress was on using AI not as a substitute but as a complement to human judgment, assisting students gage bias, identify content, and reflect on their choices more profoundly. Activities often concentrated on real-world relevance, such as AI in hiring ethics or decision-making in engineering and nutrition, offering students practical exposure to AI-supported leadership. A middle-aged male faculty from health discipline explained his views as:

"I told students: if all of you wrote the same yoga routine in your personal narratives, clearly something is off. That's not personal reflection that's AI. You need to add your own voice." (FM-6).

Theme 9: Need for Personalized and On-Demand AI Support for Faculty

Faculty responses highlight a lack of consistent, individualized institutional support for integrating AI into their teaching. While some support structures like workshops, they are perceived as inadequate or not readily accessible. The faculty member strongly advocates for on-demand, one-on-one AI guidance, desirably from a designated AI support officer who understands pedagogical integration. Faculty responses also highlight flexibility in support delivery, identifying that faculty vary in their readiness, interest, and teaching needs associated to AI. Rather than a one-size-fits-all solution, support should be differentiated and voluntary, permitting each faculty member to define the extent to which AI fits into their teaching approach.

A female faculty from engineering department explained her views to seek AI support to train students as workforce leaders.

"My institution provides some support... but comprehensive training programs, resource centers, and clear ethical policies are still lacking. A mentorship program would be more helpful than one-off training." (FM-9).

A female faculty with more than ten years' experience explained her views regarding the provision of AI support.

"AI support is an emerging thing but still limited; more targeted training sessions, access to AI tools, and curriculum development grants would be valuable improvements." (FM-8).

Theme 10: Varying Levels of Faculty Confidence in Teaching AI's Role in Leadership

Faculty confidence in teaching about AI in leadership spans a wide range from highly confident to hesitant depending mainly on prior experience to AI tools, disciplinary background, and institutional support. Many faculty members feel *moderately confident* and are eager to enhance their instruction through continuing professional development and efficient AI resources. Faculty expressed their perceptions of using collaborative projects or prompting students to explore AI's workplace impact from different stakeholder perspectives, helping bridge theory and application.

However, faculty confidence declines when it comes to the alignment of the courses with workplace leadership or inadequate training on AI. Faculty members emphasized on AI's surface-level applications, such as language proofreading or summarization, and admit to feeling underprepared for deeper, practical discussions. Despite these challenges, there is a strong willingness to adapt, with faculty expressing a desire for mentorship, interdisciplinary collaboration, and clearer institutional guidance.

A female professor teaching leadership and policy studies in a public university explained her views as:

"I feel confident discussing the big picture implications... but when students ask specific technical questions, I sometimes have to say, 'I don't know, let's find out together". (FM-14).

Another noticed,

"Technically confident, but I continue to seek interdisciplinary learning to better connect AI with leadership, strategy, and ethical considerations." (FM-8).

These reflections show that while faculty are not uniformly confident, they are committed to preparing students for AI-integrated leadership roles by adopting innovative and reflective teaching methods.

Theme 11: Navigating the Challenges of Teaching AI in Leadership Education

Faculty faced several challenges when integrating AI-related topics into leadership courses, primarily due to the *rapid pace of AI advancement* and *limited institutional resources*. Many faculty struggled to keep their content up-to-date, particularly when AI tools and industry practices change quicker than academic curricula. This results in difficulty balancing theory with practical application. Some faculty members also reported challenges aligning AI with precise disciplinary goals such as in nutrition or education where AI examples may be uncommon or excessively technical. Moreover, *uneven student readiness* presents another layer of complexity. While some students are eager and AI-savvy, some lack the digital literacy mandatory to engage intensely with AI tools, making it challenging to design inclusive and significant learning experiences.

Faculty also reported ambiguity around institutional procedures and ethical limitations. Without clear standards, faculty members felt cautious to openly discuss AI usage, and students may hide their AI use out of fear of being accused of delinquency.

As one male faculty member explained,

"When I bring it up, they always deny using it... maybe they think if they admit it, I'll accuse them of plagiarism." (FM-13).

Another female professor added,

"The biggest challenge is that everything changes so quickly. It's also hard to know which AI topics will still be relevant in five years versus which ones are just hype." (FM-14).

To overcome these barriers, faculty suggested modular AI content, interdisciplinary collaboration, clearer ethical policies, and dedicated AI resource hubs that allow both students and faculty to engage with emerging tools confidently and responsibly.

Theme 12: The Future of AI-Skilled Workforce Leaders in the UAE

The future for workforce leaders skilled in AI in countries like the UAE is full of promise and transformation. These leaders will be central to shaping knowledge-based economies by driving innovation, improving decision-making, and safeguarding efficient operations across sectors such as education, healthcare, finance, logistics, and public services.

As the UAE advances its *National AI Strategy 2031* and builds smart cities, AI-proficient leaders will be equipped to lead digital transformation and design responsive systems that respond to changing global demands.

As female assistant professor perceived as:

"The AI-skilled leader will be able to finish work quickly, professionally, and ahead of deadlines saving both time and resources." (FM-9).

Their ability to use AI as a strategic tool, rather than just a technical add-on, will distinguish them in the competitive job market. However, this future also comes with challenges. There is a growing concern that without a balance of creativity, critical thinking, and ethical use, AI reliance may undermine leadership quality.

One faculty member warned,

"If leaders rely too much on AI for content rather than for insight, it could lower their creativity and originality." (FM-15).

Consequently, future-ready leaders must not only master AI tools but also develop human-centered leadership, qualified of interpreting data sensibly, managing change, and certifying equity and innovation concur. Institutions must prepare these leaders through interdisciplinary education, ethical guidelines, and upskilling initiatives to confirm they do not just follow the AI movement but shape it for societal good.

DISCUSSION

This study examines the perceptions of university faculty in the UAE regarding the role of AI literacy in preparing students for leadership within an AI-driven workforce. The findings reveal that faculty members generally view AI literacy as highly significant in developing future leaders who can effectively navigate an increasingly technology-driven environment. Many participants believe that exposure to AI tools and concepts equips students with future-ready competencies, including data-driven decision-making, automation management, and ethical leadership skills considered essential for leadership in the AI era (Pandey, 2025). Faculty also reported varying degrees of AI integration in their teaching practices across different academic disciplines.

Furthermore, Sheikh Mohammed bin Rashid's recent announcement of the UAE's AI Strategy 2031, which emphasizes streamlining government services and enhancing operational efficiency, underscores the nation's strong commitment to digital transformation through artificial intelligence. This national agenda closely aligns with the focus of this book chapter, which explores UAE faculty perceptions of integrating AI into leadership-related courses and domains to better prepare students for future workforce demands. As the UAE government seeks to develop AI-ready systems that enable faster and smarter decision-making, higher education institutions play a critical role in cultivating emerging leaders who can use AI ethically and effectively in complex, real-world contexts (Sposato, 2025).

Faculty Perceptions of AI Literacy for Leadership Preparation (Addressing RQ-1)

The findings of this study reflect that university faculty in the UAE overwhelmingly recognize the significance of AI literacy as an introductory element of leadership in higher education in the context of an AI-integrated workforce. Faculty members consistently emphasized that AI literacy encompasses beyond technical competence, it signifies a critical approach shift that future leaders must embrace to navigate evolving complexities in decision-making, strategic planning, and ethical governance. This finding supports with the study by Buele and Llerena (2025), who emphasized the potentials of AI to automate repetitive tasks, deliver tailored feedback, and expand access to diverse educational resources. Many respondents noticed AI as a transformative dynamic that is reforming leaders to process information, make judgments, and engage with data-driven environments (Pandey, 2025). While some faculty described AI-integrated leadership primarily in terms of understanding specific tools and technologies, others emphasized the importance of fostering an adaptive and forward-thinking mindset to navigate novelty and change. This aligns with the findings of Khairullah et al. (2025), who noticed that AI embraces substantial potential to impact HEIs across a broad spectrum entailing not only technical capability but also transformative thinking to successfully lead in AI-enhanced environments. Discipline-specific variances were also perceived, with faculty in business and engineering fields showing a higher inclination to embed AI-related competencies in leadership curricula, while those in education tended to focus on ethical implications and human-centered applications (Buele and Llerena, 2025). These insights highlight the urgency of integrating AI literacy into leadership in higher education in those ways that are both contextually pertinent and associated with the UAE's broader vision for scientific progression and workforce development.

Conversely, faculty also spoken uncertainty and concerns regarding understanding of AI functions and its ethical and pedagogical inferences. As Gustilo et al. (2024) found, while many faculty members appreciated AI for content generation however, they remain uncertain about its reliability and apprehension it may hamper students' critical thinking skills that are essential for responsible and effective leadership in an AI-driven workforce. This section concludes that faculty in the UAE believed that AI literacy as crucial for developing workforce leadership in an AI-driven era.

While they emphasize the need for thoughtful integration of AI into leadership education to prepare responsible future leaders.

Integration of AI Concepts and Tools into Leadership Teaching (Addressing RQ-2)

While addressing research question 2, this study indicates a growing level of integration of AI perceptions and tools into leadership teaching across UAE higher education institutions. Faculty narrated consuming a range of AI technologies, such as ChatGPT for creating ideas and assisting class discussions, basic machine learning concepts to initiate data-driven decision-making, and modules on data ethics to engage students in critical reflection on AI's societal impact (Gustilo et al., (2024), all proposed at preparing them to become more successful workforce leaders within their particular disciplines. Some faculty members employed simulation exercises and real-world case studies to demonstrate AI applications in strategic leadership, while others used data analysis assignments to build students' skills in trend interpretation and evidence-based decision-making as significant elements for effective workforce leadership. This aligns with Kurtz et al. (2024), who observed a move in educators' roles from knowledge transmitters to facilitators and support providers in AI-enhanced milieus where intelligent systems help with content creation, assessment, and tailored learning. A few faculty members also reported that interdisciplinary collaborations with departments of computer science or data science to enhance leadership course content. The motivation behind integrating AI was mainly compelled by the need to enhance student engagement, align teaching with promptly progressing industry demands, and promote innovation within the curriculum (Zawacki-Richter et al., 2019). Particularly, faculty used AI tools not only to shape technical skills but also to develop leadership competencies such as ethical decision-making, innovation, and systems thinking. This aligns with the study of Sposato (2025), who highlighted that effective leadership in AI-driven environments requires adaptive thinking and ethical awareness. These efforts reveal an evolving recognition of AI's transformative role in leadership in higher education and the need to train students to lead responsibly in an AI-enhanced workforce.

Challenges in Embedding AI Literacy: Equity, Ethics, and Institutional Support (Addressing RQ-3)

Embedding AI literacy into leadership education in UAE HEIs presents consistent challenges. Faculty identified equity as a crucial barrier, mainly regarding students' restricted access to digital tools and varying levels of technological exposure, which hamper significant engagement with AI-related content. These apprehensions are echoed in the findings of Fernandez-Miranda et al. (2024), who emphasized ethical challenges and academic integrity issues particularly around plagiarism and the absence of well-defined regulatory frameworks as main obstructions to effective AI integration in higher education. Together, these findings highlight the requirement for equitable access, ethical guidance, and institutional policies to support responsible and inclusive AI literacy in leadership programs.

Ethical dilemmas also presented significantly by the faculty, they raised concerns about algorithmic bias, data privacy, misinformation, and the misuse of AI in academic settings, these issues seen as precarious in shaping responsible workforce leadership. This aligns with Zawacki-Richter et al. (2019), who reported the significance of interdisciplinary collaboration in addressing such challenges, emphasizing the shared frameworks across disciplines, computer science, ethics, and policy can support more ethical and informed AI integration.

Institutional readiness further combined these challenges, as faculty reported to limited professional development, undecided curricular frameworks, and fragile cross-departmental collaboration. Some also communicated indecision about their own readiness to teach AI-related content. These findings align with Chiu et al. (2023), who discovered systemic challenges and opportunities in AI integration, stressing the need for organized institutional support to allow effective adoption across varied educational contexts.

Despite these limitations, some faculty adopted informal approaches—such as peer learning, self-directed experimentation, and pilot initiatives—to enhance their capacity for AI integration. These efforts highlight the need for stronger institutional support, including structured training, adequate resources, and leadership commitment. This finding aligns with Sheikh Mohammed bin Rashid's UAE AI Strategy 2031, which emphasizes digital transformation and AI readiness across public systems. Similarly, higher education must equip students to become ethical and effective leaders in AI-driven environments through both technical competence and socially responsible, ethics-based leadership education.

THEORY INTEGRATION

This study is anchored in Siemens' (2005) theory of connectivism, which offers a robust theoretical foundation for understanding learning in AI-integrated educational environments. Connectivism stresses that knowledge is disseminated across networks of people, digital tools, and systems, and that learning includes establishing connections within these vibrant networks. In similar, this perspective aligns with key principles of constructivism, which postulates that learners actively construct knowledge through experience, reflection, and social interaction. In the context of

Artificial Intelligence (AI), both frameworks help the vision that learning is not a inactive transfer of information but an active, contextual process. AI-enhanced environments, guided by connectivism and constructivist principles, allow faculty and students to involve critically with content, collaborate with intelligent systems, and co-construct knowledge through real-world problem solving. Together, these frameworks support the expansion of ethical, adaptive, and data-informed leadership practices in higher education.

CONCLUSION AND IMPLICATIONS

This study highlights UAE faculty insights on integrating AI into leadership education, emphasizing the importance of AI competencies such as data-informed decision-making, ethical reasoning, and adaptive leadership for preparing students for an AI-driven workforce. Grounded in constructivist theory, the findings indicate that faculty are willing to embed AI concepts through experiential, reflective, and real-world learning approaches that enable students to co-construct knowledge and develop leadership skills across disciplines.

One limitation of this study is its emphasis on faculty perceptions from a selected group of UAE HEIs, which may not completely exemplify the diverse institutional contexts across the country. Moreover, the study mainly captures existing faculty practices and challenges, proposing restricted perceptions into longstanding impacts of AI integration on students' learning outcomes. Despite these boundaries, the findings carry significant implications for preparing students as workforce leaders in the UAE. HEIs must prioritize faculty development, invest in digital infrastructure, and establish well-defined, contextually pertinent AI integration policies. By embedding ethical, data-informed, and interdisciplinary methods into leadership education, universities can equip students with the adaptive mindset and capabilities needed to lead effectively in an AI-driven workforce aligned with national innovation goals.

REFERENCES

Albawi, S., Arif, M. H., & Waleed, J. (2023). Skin cancer classification dermatologist-level based on deep learning model. *Acta Scientiarum. Technology*, *45*, e61531–e61531. DOI: 10.4025/actascitechnol.v45i1.61531

Alshamsi, S., Alshamsi, D., Mohammed, K., & El Khatib, M. (2025). Global perspectives on ai usage in the education sector: Insights from the UAE education system. *International Journal of Technology and Systems*, *10*(2), 1–26. DOI: 10.47604/ijts.3221

Barnes, E., & Hutson, J. (2024). Navigating the ethical terrain of AI in higher education: Strategies for mitigating bias and promoting fairness. *Forum for Education Studies*, *2*(2), 1229. DOI: 10.59400/fes.v2i2.1229

Bouschery, S. G., Blazevic, V., & Piller, F. T. (2023). Augmenting human innovation teams with artificial intelligence: Exploring transformer-based language models. *Journal of Product Innovation Management*, *40*(3), 139–153. DOI: 10.1111/jpim.12656

Brynjolfsson, E., & McAfee, A. (2017). *Machine, Platform, Crowd: Harnessing our digital future*. W. W. Norton & Company.

Buele, J., & Llerena-Aguirre, L. (2025). Transformations in academic work and faculty perceptions of artificial intelligence in higher education. *Frontiers in Education*, *10*, 1603763. DOI: 10.3389/feduc.2025.1603763

Castillo-Canales, D., Mancilla, A., Restrepo, R., & Martinez, F. (2022). *Teacher professional development supported by information and communication technologies: A case study of the Teacher Training Program for Curricular Update 2016-2018 in Ecuador*. Foundation for Information Technology Education and Development.

Chiu, T. K. F., Xia, Q., Zhou, X., Chai, C. S., & Cheng, M. (2023). Systematic literature review on opportunities, challenges, and future research recommendations of artificial intelligence in education. *Computers and Education: Artificial Intelligence*, *4*, 100118. DOI: 10.1016/j.caeai.2022.100118

Crompton, H., & Burke, D. (2023). Artificial intelligence in higher education: The state of the field. *International Journal of Educational Technology in Higher Education*, *20*(1), 22. DOI: 10.1186/s41239-023-00392-8

Floridi, L., Cowls, J., Beltrametti, M., Chatila, R., Chazerand, P., Dignum, V., Luetge, C., Madelin, R., Pagallo, U., Rossi, F., Schafer, B., Valcke, P., & Vayena, E. (2018). A I4People an ethical framework for a good AI society: Opportunities, risks, principles, and recommendations. *Minds and Machines*, *28*(4), 689–707. DOI: 10.1007/s11023-018-9482-5 PMID: 30930541

Gustilo, L., Ong, E., & Lapinid, M. R. (2024). Algorithmically driven writing and academic integrity: Exploring educators' practices, perceptions, and policies in AI era. *International Journal for Educational Integrity*, *20*(1), 1–43. DOI: 10.1007/s40979-024-00153-8

Kamalov, F., Santandreu Calonge, D., & Gurrib, I. (2023). New era of artificial intelligence in education: Towards a sustainable multifaceted revolution. *Sustainability (Basel)*, *15*(16), 12451. DOI: 10.3390/su151612451

Kandlhofer, M., Steinbauer, G., Hirschmugl-Gaisch, S., & Huber, P. (2016). Artificial intelligence and computer science in education: From kindergarten to university, *IEEE Frontiers in Education Conference (FIE), Erie,* PA, USA, 2016, pp. 1-9, DOI: 10.1109/FIE.2016.7757570

Khairullah, S. A., Harris, S., Hadi, H. J., Sandhu, R. A., Ahmad, N., & Alshara, M. A. (2025). Implementing artificial intelligence in academic and administrative processes through responsible strategic leadership in the higher education institutions. *Frontiers in Education*, *10*, 1548104. DOI: 10.3389/feduc.2025.1548104

Khan, A., & Yasir, M. (2024). *Impact of artificial intelligence on the global economy and technology advancements in Artificial General Intelligence (AGI) Security: Smart Applications and Sustainable Technologies*. Springer Nature Singapore., DOI: 10.1007/978-981-97-3222-7_7

Kim, S. W., Kong, J. H., Lee, S. W., & Lee, S. (2022). Recent advances of artificial intelligence in manufacturing industrial sectors: A review. *International Journal of Precision Engineering and Manufacturing*, *23*(1), 111–129. DOI: 10.1007/s12541-021-00600-3

Lakhanpal, S. (2024). Augmented reality and AI: Shaping immersive learning experiences. Retrieved from: https://www.linkedin.com/pulse/augmented-reality-ai-shaping-immersivelearning-sandhya--yaekc on 13/03/2024

Lee, D., Arnold, M., Srivastava, A., Plastow, K., Strelan, P., Ploeckl, F., Lekkas, D., & Palmer, E. (2024). The impact of generative AI on higher education learning and teaching: A study of educators' perspectives. *Comput. Educ. Artif. Intell.*, *6*, 100221. DOI: 10.1016/j.caeai.2024.100221

Lozano, A., & Blanco Fontao, C. (2023). Is the education system prepared for the irruption of artificial intelligence? A study on the perceptions of students of primary education degree from a dual perspective: Current pupils and future teachers. *Education Sciences*, *13*(7), 733. DOI: 10.3390/educsci13070733

Ngai, E. W. T., Hu, Y., Wong, Y. H., Chen, Y., & Sun, X. (2021). The application of data mining techniques in financial fraud detection: A classification framework and an academic review of literature. *Decision Support Systems*, *50*(3), 559–569. DOI: 10.1016/j.dss.2010.08.006

Pandey, V. (2025). Leadership in the AI era: Navigating and shaping the future of organizational guidance. Available at *SSRN*: https://ssrn.com/abstract=5331975 or http://dx.doi.org/DOI: 10.2139/ssrn.5331975

Pogorskiy, E., & Beckmann, J. (2023). From procrastination to engagement? An experimental exploration of the effects of an adaptive virtual assistant on self-regulation in online learning. *Computers and Education: Artificial Intelligence.*, *4*, 100111. DOI: 10.1016/j.caeai.2022.100111

Rafik, M. (2023). Artificial intelligence and the changing roles in the field of higher education and scientific research. In *Artificial Intelligence in Higher Education and Scientific Research: Future Development* (pp. 35–46). Springer Nature Singapore., DOI: 10.1007/978-981-19-8641-3_3

Rahiman, H. U., & Kodikal, R. (2023). Revolutionizing education: Artificial intelligence empowered learning in higher education. *Cogent Education*, *11*(1), 2293431. Advance online publication. DOI: 10.1080/2331186X.2023.2293431

Ransbotham, S., Khodabandeh, S., Kiron, D., Candelon, F., LaFountain, B., & Chirinos, L. (2017). Reshaping business with artificial intelligence: Closing the gap between ambition and action. *MIT Sloan Management Review*.

Rashid, S., Malik, S., Abbas, F., & Khan, J. A. (2024). Pakistani students' perceptions about knowledge, use and impact of artificial intelligence (AI) on academic writing: A case study. *Journal of Computers in Education*, •••, 1–26. DOI: 10.1007/s40692-024-00338-7

Rinku, G. S. (2023). Artificial Intelligence in Sustainable Energy Industry: Status Quo, Challenges, and Opportunities. *EPRA International Journal of Multidisciplinary Research (IJMR), 9.*

Siegel, J., & Pappas, G. (2023). Morals, ethics, and the technology capabilities and limitations of automated and self-driving vehicles. *AI & Society*, *38*(1), 213–226. DOI: 10.1007/s00146-021-01277-y

Siemens, G. (2005). Connectivism: A learning theory for the digital age. *International Journal of Instructional Technology and Distance Learning*, *2*(1), 3–10. https://www.scirp.org/reference/referencespapers?referenceid=148504

Sposato, M. (2025). Artificial intelligence in educational leadership: a comprehensive taxonomy and future directions. *All Works*. 7270. https://zuscholars.zu.ac.ae/works/7270

Tsolaki, K., Vafeiadis, T., Nizamis, A., Ioannidis, D., & Tzovaras, D. (2023). Utilizing machine learning on freight transportation and logistics applications: A review. *ICT Express*, *9*(3), 284–295. DOI: 10.1016/j.icte.2022.02.001

Zawacki-Richter, O., Marín, V. I., Bond, M., & Gouverneur, F. (2019). Systematic review of research on artifcial intelligence applications in higher education–where are the educators? *International Journal of Educational Technology in Higher Education*, *16*(1), 1–27. DOI: 10.1186/s41239-019-0171-0

APPENDIX-1 INTERVIEW QUESTIONS

1. What does AI literacy mean to you, especially in the context of leadership education?
2. How do you think learning about AI can help students become more effective future leaders?
3. Which specific AI-related skills or concepts do you believe should be included in leadership programs?
4. What leadership qualities or competencies are becoming more critical because of AI integration in workplaces?
5. Do you think students in your leadership courses understand both the opportunities and challenges that come with AI? Why or why not?
6. Can you describe any strategies or methods you use to teach students about AI in leadership contexts?
7. Have you used AI tools or content in your teaching? If yes, how have they enhanced or impacted students' leadership learning or decision-making?
8. What ethical concerns or equity issues have you encountered when teaching with AI, and how have you addressed them?
9. How confident do you feel in teaching about AI's role in leadership and the workplace? What kind of training or support would strengthen your confidence?
10. What future do you envision for AI-skilled workforce leaders in the UAE or your country, especially in relation to national strategies like UAE Vision 2031?

Chapter 5
Preparing Educational Leaders for AI Literacy Through Ethical, Purpose-Driven, and Culturally Responsive Leadership

Rolla Elsaiary
http://orcid.org/0000-0001-5765-1056
Arabic Immersion Magnet School, USA

ABSTRACT

As artificial intelligence (AI) becomes integrated into instruction, assessment, communication, and school operations, educational leadership must shift from technical adoption to purpose-driven and ethical practice. This chapter argues that effective AI leadership begins with knowing one's "why," drawing on Simon Sinek's purpose-centered leadership, Brené Brown's focus on vulnerability and courage, and John C. Maxwell's influence-based model. AI literacy is defined as a holistic capacity that combines technical awareness with ethical judgment, cultural responsiveness, equity-focused thinking, and strategic clarity. The L.E.A.D. Framework (Learn, Evaluate, Apply, Develop) is presented as a guide for intentional AI leadership, supported by principles of psychological safety, engagement, and meaningful work. A dual-language, project-based learning example illustrates how human-centered leadership guides responsible AI use. The chapter concludes with practical tools and a research agenda for building ethical, equitable, and future-ready AI leadership capacity.

DOI: 10.4018/979-8-3373-4908-4.ch005

INTRODUCTION

Artificial intelligence has rapidly shifted from a specialized technological field into a mainstream component of everyday educational practice. Once limited to research laboratories or advanced computing applications, AI now appears in learning management systems, assessment platforms, adaptive tutoring tools, instructional planning assistants, translation resources, communication systems, and administrative data dashboards (Holmes & Tuomi, 2022; Luckin, 2018). The rise of generative AI, predictive analytics, and language-processing models has further accelerated integration into classroom workflows, teacher planning, and student support systems (UNESCO, 2023). As these tools become embedded in the daily operations of schools, concerns about algorithmic bias, data privacy, cultural inclusivity, transparency, and teacher agency have simultaneously grown (Benjamin, 2019; Crawford, 2021).

In this evolving landscape, educational leaders face unprecedented responsibility. They must not only adopt AI systems that shape teaching, learning, and organizational culture, but also govern them in ways that align with institutional values of equity, dignity, and shared purpose (Reich, 2020). Leadership decisions around AI, such as which tools to pilot, how to implement them, and how to evaluate their impact, have direct consequences for student identity, staff workload, family trust, and community well-being. As scholars have noted, the introduction of AI into schools raises ethical and social questions that demand strong, principled leadership (Williamson & Piattoeva, 2022).

Yet many leadership preparation programs remain anchored in a tool-centered, compliance-driven model of technology adoption. Leaders are frequently trained to implement software, ensure adherence to district policy, and monitor usage metrics rather than explore the human, ethical, cultural, and relational implications of AI (Holmes & Tuomi, 2022). This approach treats AI as a technical challenge rather than a human one. As Simon Sinek (2009) argues, effective leadership does not begin with what we do or how we execute tasks, but with why, the deeper purpose guiding action. Purpose is the anchor that ensures decisions remain coherent, trustworthy, and aligned with human flourishing rather than short-term technological efficiencies.

In this chapter, AI leadership is positioned as a fundamentally human responsibility, one that requires purpose-driven, ethical, relational, and culturally responsive practices. To lead AI adoption responsibly, educational leaders must integrate technical understanding with deeper human skills including vulnerability, transparency, cultural humility, and moral influence. The leadership philosophies of Sinek (2009), Brené Brown (2018), and John C. Maxwell (2011) converge around the idea that leadership begins with clarity of purpose, is enacted through courage and authentic relationality, and ultimately develops others to lead with integrity and influence.

These paradigms provide a conceptual foundation for a new, more holistic form of AI literacy tailored to educational leadership.

A growing body of research on employee engagement, psychological safety, and meaningful work also offers essential insights into how organizational culture shapes educational innovation. Scholars emphasize that meaningful organizational change requires three cultural conditions: strong psychological safety, high employee engagement, and a deeply shared sense of purpose (Edmondson, 2019). These elements are not peripheral to AI implementation, they are foundational. AI-related change often evokes uncertainty, fear, or vulnerability among staff, particularly when tools affect instructional autonomy, professional identity, or evaluation processes. If teachers do not feel psychologically safe to ask questions, critique AI outputs, or express confusion, AI adoption becomes coercive rather than empowering.

Therefore, integrating psychological safety, engagement, and meaning into AI leadership is not optional, it is a moral imperative. Leaders must intentionally foster environments where teachers feel supported to experiment with AI tools, identify errors or biases, and collaboratively develop best practices. This requires modeling the vulnerability Brown (2018) describes, embracing uncertainty, and creating space for collective learning. Leaders must also articulate a clear and shared purpose for AI, one that centers equity, multilingual inclusion, culturally responsive pedagogy, and the dignity of human relationships.

This chapter addresses these needs through five key goals. First, it defines AI literacy for educational leaders in a way that transcends technical proficiency, centering ethical, cultural, equity-driven, and humanizing competencies. Second, it examines why AI literacy is especially critical for leaders working in diverse, multilingual, and culturally dynamic school communities. Third, it explores foundational leadership theories, Sinek's purpose-driven leadership, Brown's vulnerability and courage, and Maxwell's people-centered influence, and connects them to AI governance. Fourth, it introduces the L.E.A.D. Framework (Learn, Evaluate, Apply, Develop), a structure for building purpose-anchored AI leadership capacity. Fifth, it illustrates these concepts through a case scenario in a dual-language, project-based learning school, highlighting the indispensable role of psychological safety, meaningful work, and teacher agency during AI implementation.

The chapter concludes with implications for leadership preparation programs, ethical governance structures, and future research directions. Ultimately, AI becomes not merely a set of tools but a catalyst for rethinking leadership, human connection, multilingual equity, and justice. When school leaders know their "why," AI can serve, rather than undermine, human dignity, cultural identity, and educational transformation.

DEFINING AI LITERACY FOR EDUCATIONAL LEADERS

Expanding the Concept of AI Literacy

Although AI literacy is increasingly discussed in K–12 and higher education, much of the existing discourse focuses narrowly on what students or teachers should know about algorithms, machine learning, or responsible data practices (Long & Magerko, 2020). While these understandings are important, they are insufficient for educational leaders whose decisions influence entire ecosystems of teaching, learning, and school governance. For leaders, AI literacy must be understood as a multidimensional construct that integrates technical fluency, ethical discernment, cultural and linguistic awareness, and strategic leadership capacity (UNESCO, 2023).

Technical fluency refers to a leader's foundational understanding of core AI concepts such as natural language processing, algorithmic training, supervised and unsupervised learning, predictive modeling, and the limitations inherent in large language models (Krumholz, 2023). Leaders do not need to become engineers; however, they must understand enough to ask critical questions about data provenance, model accuracy, hallucination risks, and systemic bias. Without this foundational comprehension, leaders are vulnerable to vendor persuasion, over-reliance on automation, or uncritical adoption of tools that undermine equity.

Ethical literacy is equally essential. Decades of research have shown that algorithms can reproduce or amplify biases embedded in training data, disproportionately affecting marginalized groups (Benjamin, 2019; Noble, 2018). In schools, biased AI can distort translation accuracy, misinterpret dialectical features, mislabel student writing, or affect predictions related to discipline, attendance, or achievement (Crawford, 2021). Leaders therefore must understand principles of fairness, transparency, privacy, accountability, and human rights. Ethical literacy includes the ability to interrogate vendor claims, demand documentation such as model cards or risk assessments, and ensure alignment with legal frameworks such as FERPA, COPPA, GDPR, and state privacy laws (Regan & Jesse, 2019).

Cultural and equity literacy is especially urgent. AI systems are not culturally neutral; they reflect the linguistic, racial, and cultural biases present in datasets and design teams (Birhane, 2021). In multilingual schools, AI translation and language-support tools can misinterpret cultural nuance, erase heritage dialects, or elevate standardized forms of language at the expense of linguistic identity (Eloundou et al., 2024). Leaders must recognize these sociolinguistic implications and ensure that AI tools affirm rather than erase students' cultural and linguistic identities. This requires specialized understanding of multilingualism, translanguaging, heritage language variation, and the complexities of dialectal representation in Arabic, including Levantine, Egyptian, Gulf, Maghrebi, and Modern Standard Arabic.

Strategic leadership literacy refers to a leader's capacity to integrate AI decisions into broader organizational missions, instructional goals, cultural commitments, and long-term visions. AI adoption cannot occur in isolation; it must be interwoven with culturally responsive pedagogy, family engagement, teacher learning communities, student agency, and ethical governance (Reich et al., 2023). Strategic literacy includes knowing when AI should be used, when it should not be used, and how to embed human oversight in all AI-mediated workflows. Leaders must treat AI not as a technological initiative but as a systems-level change that requires thoughtful communication, professional learning, and shared purpose. This systems-level perspective aligns with scholarship emphasizing that effective school leadership operates within interconnected instructional, cultural, and organizational domains (Dexter, 2011; Leithwood et al., 2020).

Together, these four dimensions, technical, ethical, cultural, and strategic, constitute a comprehensive vision of AI literacy for educational leaders. This expanded framework shifts AI literacy away from narrow notions of digital competence and toward purpose-driven, equity-centered, and human-centered leadership.

Why AI Literacy Matters for Educational Leaders

AI literacy is essential for educational leaders because AI is not a neutral tool; it is a powerful organizational force that shapes instruction, assessment, communication, relationships, and identity. Leaders must understand AI's potential to enhance personalization, support differentiation, accelerate feedback, and expand multilingual access (Luckin, 2018). At the same time, they must maintain vigilance toward risks such as algorithmic bias, privacy invasion, surveillance creep, inequitable distribution of technological resources, and the erosion of teacher professional autonomy (Williamson & Piattoeva, 2022).

AI is reshaping instructional practice in ways that require leader oversight. Adaptive learning platforms adjust pacing and content based on machine-generated interpretations of student performance, while generative AI assists with academic writing, feedback cycles, and scaffolded language tasks (Holmes & Tuomi, 2022). In multilingual settings, AI translation tools offer real-time support but often misinterpret nuances, flatten dialectical distinctions, or reinforce standardized forms of language that may misalign with students' linguistic identities. Leaders must therefore understand not only the affordances of these tools but also their cultural and pedagogical limitations. AI literacy is also fundamental to equity stewardship. Without intentional oversight, AI may perpetuate or exacerbate inequities experienced by multilingual learners, students with disabilities, and historically marginalized communities (Benjamin, 2019). Equity-focused AI leadership requires understanding how datasets, model design, and algorithmic recommendations may reflect unequal distributions of power, privilege, and cultural representation. Leaders must advocate for AI systems that reflect linguistic diversity, respect cultural identity, and uphold student dignity (UNESCO, 2023). Educational leadership research consistently demonstrates that trust, moral purpose, and equity commitments are foundational to sustainable reform (Furman, 2012; Starratt, 2004).

Moreover, AI literacy supports trust and legitimacy. School communities increasingly expect transparency around how AI tools operate, what data they collect, and how they may influence educational opportunities. If leaders cannot articulate a clear purpose or rationale for AI adoption, or if AI implementation appears disconnected from community values, stakeholders may reject or distrust the technology (Reich, 2020). Trust is earned through clarity, ethical consistency, and open communication, all of which depend on leaders' AI literacy.

Therefore, AI literacy for educational leaders is not merely a technical competency but a moral, relational, cultural, and strategic responsibility. Leaders must navigate AI's possibilities with a mindset grounded in purpose, equity, and human dignity.

AI Leadership in Educational Contexts: Expanding the Scholarly Grounding

Although this chapter establishes a strong interdisciplinary foundation, AI leadership must also be situated within emerging education-specific frameworks that address digital leadership, AI literacy, and governance in school systems. Recent scholarship and policy guidance have begun to articulate competency models and governance structures tailored to educational contexts.

UNESCO (2024) introduced an AI Competency Framework for Teachers that identifies knowledge, ethical, pedagogical, and professional dimensions required for responsible AI integration. While designed for educators, the framework implicitly calls for leaders capable of enabling institutional conditions for ethical adoption, professional learning, and equitable access. Similarly, Digital Promise's AI Literacy Framework for Primary and Secondary Education (2025) emphasizes critical evaluation of AI systems, bias awareness, and human oversight—competencies that require leader facilitation and policy alignment.

From a leadership standards perspective, the International Society for Technology in Education (ISTE, 2018) Standards for Education Leaders position digital leadership as a function of visionary planning, equity advocacy, system design, and capacity-building. These standards reinforce that digital innovation is not merely technical implementation but strategic leadership work grounded in culture, trust, and sustainability.

Governance scholarship further highlights the complexity of AI implementation in education systems. The OECD Digital Education Outlook (2023) underscores the importance of procurement transparency, bias auditing, privacy safeguards, and accountability mechanisms when deploying generative AI in schools. District-level planning guides similarly recommend phased pilots, stakeholder consultation, and ongoing impact evaluation rather than full-scale immediate adoption (Virtual Learning Leadership Alliance [VLLA], 2023).

Positioning the L.E.A.D. framework within this landscape clarifies its unique contribution. Whereas many existing models focus on teacher competencies or high-level governance principles, L.E.A.D. integrates ethical purpose, psychological safety, cultural responsiveness, and iterative organizational learning into a cohesive leadership cycle. It extends digital leadership standards by embedding vulnerability, human dignity, and linguistic equity into each implementation phase. Research on digital leadership further emphasizes that leaders must move beyond tool adoption toward systems thinking and culture-building (Sheninger, 2019), reinforcing the necessity of an ethically anchored, iterative framework.

THEORETICAL FOUNDATIONS: PURPOSE, VULNERAGE, AND INFLUENCE

Building AI-ready schools requires more than technical skill; it requires leaders who are anchored in human purpose, equipped with relational courage, and committed to the ethical development of others. Artificial intelligence introduces ambiguity, ethical risk, and cultural complexity into schooling, and leaders must navigate this landscape in ways that protect dignity, equity, and trust. For these reasons, the leadership philosophies of Simon Sinek, Brené Brown, and John C. Maxwell provide a foundational framework for understanding why AI leadership must remain deeply human. Their theories collectively frame AI leadership as a moral, relational, and developmental responsibility rather than a technical administrative task. In an era where algorithms increasingly shape learning environments, these theories remind leaders that human-centered principles, purpose, vulnerability, and influence, must guide all decisions.

Simon Sinek's "Start With Why" and the Infinite Mindset

Simon Sinek's Golden Circle model (2009) establishes that effective leadership begins with clarifying purpose, "why" we do what we do, before determining "how" and "what." This model is especially relevant to AI leadership because technological adoption without clear purpose often leads to fragmented implementation, misalignment with equity goals, and diminished teacher trust. Leaders must define why AI matters for their specific school community: whether to enhance linguistic access for multilingual learners, streamline teacher workload, personalize instruction, or strengthen culturally responsive pedagogy. When leaders articulate a compelling why, AI adoption becomes mission-driven rather than tool-driven.

A purpose-first approach prevents reactive decision-making. Schools are frequently pressured by vendors, district mandates, or trends to adopt AI tools quickly, but Sinek (2009) warns that without a clear why, organizations become inconsistent and lose credibility. In the context of education, misaligned AI adoption risks undermining core values such as human connection, cultural responsiveness, and student dignity. Purpose acts as a compass that keeps AI anchored in long-term student well-being rather than short-term efficiency metrics.

Sinek's concept of the "infinite mindset" further strengthens AI leadership. Unlike a finite mindset that focuses on immediate wins, the infinite mindset emphasizes long-term vision, continuous learning, and adaptability (Sinek, 2019). This is essential in AI contexts because AI tools evolve rapidly, produce unpredictable outputs, and require ongoing ethical vigilance. Leaders must embrace uncertainty, invest in learning cycles, and remain open to revision as evidence emerges. The infinite mindset rejects the illusion of finality, there is no "finished" state with AI, only ongoing improvement. This perspective encourages leaders to prioritize stewardship, adaptability, and sustained ethical reflection rather than compliance-driven implementation.

Together, Sinek's theories suggest that purpose and long-term thinking are not optional elements but essential anchors for responsible AI governance.

Brené Brown's Vulnerability, Courage, and Empathy

Brené Brown's research emphasizes vulnerability as a core leadership competency, describing it as the willingness to engage with uncertainty, risk, and emotional exposure (Brown, 2018). In AI leadership, vulnerability becomes indispensable because AI introduces ambiguity, ethical dilemmas, and knowledge gaps. Leaders cannot, and should not, pretend to have all the answers about complex algorithmic systems. Instead, they must openly acknowledge uncertainty, invite questions, and normalize collaborative learning.

Vulnerability also enables psychological safety, which Edmondson (1999, 2019) identifies as a critical factor in learning and innovation. When leaders model vulnerability, teachers feel safer admitting when AI outputs are confusing, biased, or culturally inaccurate, and they are more willing to critique systems that do not serve students equitably. This relational transparency ensures that potential harms are surfaced early rather than buried beneath fear or compliance culture.

AI implementation can create significant anxiety among educators. Teachers may fear automation, worry that AI will replace creative or relational aspects of their role, or feel insecure about their own technological proficiency. Brown's (2018) assertion that courage emerges from vulnerability becomes relevant here: leaders must create supportive environments where teachers' fears are acknowledged rather than dismissed. Courageous leadership may require pushing back against district pressures, pausing an AI rollout due to equity concerns, or advocating for multilingual learners when AI tools fail to represent their linguistic identities accurately.

Empathy is also essential. AI tools often fail to capture cultural nuance, emotional tone, or lived experience. Leaders grounded in empathy understand that technology can never fully replace human judgment, cultural awareness, or emotional presence. Brown's emphasis on human connection reinforces that AI must augment, not diminish, relationships.

John C. Maxwell's Theory of Influence and People Development

John C. Maxwell's leadership philosophy centers the idea that real leadership is defined by influence rather than position (Maxwell, 1998, 2011). In AI adoption, where mandates and compliance pressures are common, Maxwell's theory shifts the focus toward relational trust and authentic influence. Leaders must guide teachers, students, and families not through authority but through credibility, clarity, and shared purpose.

Maxwell's five levels of leadership provide a powerful lens for understanding AI implementation. At Level 1 (Position), leaders adopt AI because they are told to. At Level 2 (Permission), leaders build relationships that foster buy-in. At Level 3 (Production), leaders demonstrate how AI aligns with goals and improves outcomes. At Level 4 (People Development), leaders empower teachers to lead aspects of AI adoption, cultivating distributed leadership. At Level 5 (Pinnacle), leaders serve as moral exemplars influencing AI ethics across the entire district (Maxwell, 2011). This progression mirrors the developmental nature of AI leadership: influence grows as leaders support, empower, and elevate others.

Maxwell's emphasis on developing people aligns with research on engagement and meaningful work. Teachers are more likely to commit to AI innovation when they feel valued, respected, and part of a collective purpose (Harter et al., 2002; Rosso et al., 2010). When leaders invest in coaching, professional learning, and collaborative decision-making, they strengthen the psychological and emotional conditions needed for responsible AI adoption. This aligns with Elsaiary (2025), who argues that engagement and psychological safety are foundational to organizational change, especially when navigating vulnerable learning spaces.

Maxwell's focus on influence also supports ethical stewardship. AI tools can shape discipline predictions, translation accuracy, assessment patterns, and cultural representation. Leaders must influence decisions in ways that protect equity and uphold dignity, rather than allowing algorithms or vendors to dictate practice.

Integrating Purpose, Vulnerability, and Influence

When integrated, the leadership frameworks of Sinek, Brown, and Maxwell create a powerful triad for AI leadership. Purpose ensures that AI adoption supports educational missions rather than technological trends. Vulnerability ensures leaders remain open to learning, ethical reflection, and collaborative problem-solving in an unfamiliar technological landscape. Influence ensures that leaders cultivate trust, empower others, and guide their communities toward responsible, ethical AI implementation.

Together, these theories reinforce that AI leadership is fundamentally human-centered. Purpose provides direction; vulnerability builds trust and psychological safety; and influence develops collective capacity. This triad reflects the central argument of the L.E.A.D. Framework introduced in the next section: that AI decisions must be grounded in ethical purpose, relational courage, and developmental leadership in order to serve all students, especially those from multilingual, culturally diverse communities.

LEADERSHIP TENSIONS IN AI ADOPTION

AI leadership unfolds within complex and often competing pressures. Educational leaders face tensions that require ethical discernment rather than procedural compliance:

- **Innovation urgency vs. ethical deliberation** – Pressure to adopt rapidly evolving AI tools may conflict with the need for careful bias auditing and community dialogue.
- **Efficiency gains vs. professional autonomy** – AI tools can reduce workload, yet over-automation risks narrowing teacher agency.
- **Personalization vs. privacy risk** – Data-driven personalization often depends on expanded data collection.
- **Standardization vs. linguistic diversity** – Generative systems may privilege dominant dialects over culturally embedded expressions.
- **Pilot enthusiasm vs. sustainability constraints** – Initial funding may not guarantee long-term viability.

Responsible leadership requires balancing these tensions through transparent communication, phased implementation, stakeholder consultation, and principled restraint. These realities frame the necessity of a structured framework such as L.E.A.D., which embeds ethical evaluation and iterative reflection into innovation cycles. These tensions reflect broader patterns identified in school improvement research, where leaders must balance innovation with stability and moral responsibility (Leithwood et al., 2020).

THE L.E.A.D. FRAMEWORK FOR PURPOSE-DRIVEN AI LEADERSHIP

The L.E.A.D. Framework, Learn, Evaluate, Apply, Develop, provides a systematic structure for cultivating purpose-driven, ethical, and culturally responsive leadership in the age of artificial intelligence. This framework recognizes that AI adoption is not simply a technical shift but a deep organizational, cultural, and human transformation. Each stage integrates the theoretical foundations of Sinek's (2009) purpose-centered leadership, Brown's (2018) scholarship on vulnerability and courage, and Maxwell's (2011) model of leadership influence. It also aligns with the author's earlier work on psychological safety, employee engagement, and meaningful work as foundational preconditions for innovation (Elsaiary, 2025). Through these interconnected dimensions, the L.E.A.D. Framework positions AI leadership as an ethical, relational, iterative, and culturally grounded practice.

While the L.E.A.D. framework may appear structurally similar to cyclical models of change or innovation planning, its contribution lies not in sequencing implementation steps, but in re-centering ethical purpose, cultural responsiveness, and relational conditions as structural prerequisites for AI governance. Traditional change management models often emphasize urgency, stakeholder alignment, and execution momentum. By contrast, L.E.A.D. begins with deliberate ethical anchoring and sustained inquiry before movement toward scale.

Similarly, digital leadership standards, such as those articulated by ISTE (2018), identify visionary planning, equity advocacy, and capacity-building as core competencies for education leaders. These frameworks provide important benchmarks for leadership practice. However, they do not always specify how leaders should navigate the uniquely complex sociotechnical tensions introduced by artificial intelligence—particularly in multilingual, culturally dynamic environments. L.E.A.D. extends these conversations by embedding cultural-linguistic equity, psychological safety, and human dignity directly into each phase of decision-making.

Moreover, while existing AI literacy frameworks primarily define competencies for teachers and students (UNESCO, 2024; Digital Promise, 2025), fewer models articulate how leaders must structure organizational learning conditions, governance mechanisms, and reflective cycles to sustain ethical AI integration. L.E.A.D. addresses this gap by conceptualizing AI leadership not as a set of discrete skills, but as an iterative stewardship process. It integrates purpose (Sinek, 2009), vulnerability and relational courage (Brown, 2018), and developmental influence (Maxwell, 2011) into a cohesive architecture for institutional decision-making.

In this sense, L.E.A.D. does not replace existing leadership standards or change models; rather, it deepens them. It reframes AI adoption as a moral and cultural leadership responsibility—one that requires sustained reflection, participatory governance, and vigilance toward equity. By structurally embedding ethical deliberation, cultural audit, and human oversight within each phase, the framework moves beyond implementation mechanics toward principled institutional design.

4.1. Learn: Building Foundational Understanding and Purpose Alignment

Learning forms the first stage of the L.E.A.D. Framework and requires leaders to cultivate both technical and humanistic understanding of AI systems. Leaders must learn core concepts such as algorithmic logic, bias detection, data governance, and the affordances and limitations of multilingual AI tools. However, effective AI leadership must begin not with technical mastery but with clarity of purpose, why AI is relevant to the school, whom it serves, and how it aligns with equity, human dignity, and culturally responsive education. This mirrors Sinek's (2009) argument that transformational leadership begins with "why," as purpose provides coherence and safeguards against technology-driven decision-making lacking ethical grounding.

Learning in this context also requires leaders to demonstrate intellectual humility and emotional openness. Brown's (2018) work on vulnerability shows that leaders must model courage by acknowledging uncertainty, questioning their own assumptions, and inviting others into collaborative meaning-making. When leaders openly admit what they do not yet understand about AI, they create psychological safety, a condition Edmondson (2019) identifies as essential for learning and innovation. Under such conditions, teachers are more likely to experiment with new tools, voice concerns, and engage in authentic inquiry without fear of judgment.

Maxwell's (2011) emphasis on credibility and relational influence further underscores that leaders must learn in partnership with their staff. When leaders approach AI with humility and curiosity, they build trust and strengthen relational capital, which enhances their ability to influence instructional practice. Learning also includes studying the cultural implications of AI, especially in multilingual and multicultural schools where AI may inadvertently privilege dominant dialects, erase linguistic identities, or misinterpret cultural nuance. Leaders must understand how these risks intersect with equity and culturally responsive teaching.

In this stage, learning is both cognitive and relational, both technical and purpose-driven. It is the foundation upon which ethical AI adoption is built.

Evaluate: Assessing Alignment, Equity, Bias, and Risk

The Evaluate stage calls for leaders to scrutinize how AI tools align with the school's mission, values, community expectations, and equity commitments. This evaluative work requires leaders to examine issues of fairness, cultural responsiveness, linguistic accuracy, and potential unintended harm. AI systems may reproduce bias by privileging certain dialects, misinterpreting culturally embedded expressions, or reinforcing inequities in assessment or resource allocation. Recognizing these risks requires leaders to engage in ethical inquiry and community-centered decision-making.

Evaluation also depends heavily on psychological safety. Environments that support "felt permission for candor" enable honest critique, error detection, and ethical challenge. Without psychological safety, stakeholders may remain silent about problematic outputs, privacy concerns, or cultural mismatches, resulting in superficial evaluation. Edmondson (2019) similarly emphasizes that teams cannot meaningfully assess risks in environments where dissent is discouraged.

Sinek's (2009) notion of purpose again plays a central role. Leaders must ask whether a proposed AI tool advances the school's core purpose or distracts from it. This requires evaluating not only technical performance but the human implications of AI adoption: Does the tool strengthen or undermine teacher agency? Does it enhance meaningful work or reduce teaching to mechanical tasks? These questions reflect research showing that engagement and meaning are powerful drivers of educator motivation and well-being (Harter et al., 2002; Rosso et al., 2010).

Evaluation must also include ethical considerations such as data privacy, transparency, human oversight, and compliance with legal frameworks. Leaders must remain vigilant about over-reliance on automation, ensuring that human judgment remains central to decisions affecting learning, culture, and equity. Through systematic evaluation, leaders determine whether AI tools advance or conflict with their mission-driven goals.

Apply: Implementing AI Through Pilots, Collaboration, and Ethical Governance

The Apply stage moves leaders from analysis to action through structured, small-scale pilots that emphasize collaboration, agency, and ethical guardrails. Implementation must occur in environments where experimentation is encouraged and errors are treated as sources of learning rather than failure. This approach aligns with Brown's (2018) concept of vulnerability as a catalyst for growth: when teachers are free to try, fail, and learn, they engage more deeply with innovation.

Meaningful work becomes critical during implementation. Teachers must experience AI as a tool that enhances their professional identity, not one that threatens it. Research defines engagement as the emotional and cognitive energy employees invest in their work (Schaufeli et al., 2002) and shows that engagement rises when staff feel empowered, valued, and connected to purpose (Harter et al., 2002). When AI reduces administrative load, supports differentiation, or enhances creative tasks, teachers perceive the work as more meaningful, aligning with findings that meaning arises when work feels significant and connected to something larger (Rosso et al., 2010).

Maxwell's (2011) leadership model also emphasizes that influence grows when leaders invest in developing others. In this stage, leaders must support teachers through coaching, co-planning, and collaborative inquiry. Distributed leadership strengthens collective ownership and trust, which is vital for sustained innovation. Ensuring that AI implementation remains aligned with Sinek's (2009) purpose-driven framework protects against misalignment and technological drift.

Through intentional application, AI becomes not a mandate but a shared learning process grounded in collaboration and ethical reflection.

Develop: Reflecting, Iterating, Scaling, and Sustaining Ethical AI Leadership

The Develop stage focuses on reflection, iteration, refinement, and long-term sustainability. Leaders must engage teachers, students, and families in collective reflection to assess whether AI implementation upholds the school's core purpose, advances equity, and supports high-quality instruction. This requires honest examination of what worked, what failed, and what requires adjustment. Reflection aligns with Maxwell's (1998) argument that leadership growth is continuous and grounded in self-examination.

Scaling AI use must occur slowly and intentionally, ensuring that cultural responsiveness, teacher agency, and student dignity remain central. Development also includes planning for long-term capacity-building through ongoing professional development, coaching, and leadership growth pathways. Leaders must prepare future leaders, teachers, coordinators, instructional coaches, to sustain ethical AI practices beyond the initial implementation.

The concept of meaningful work again plays a significant role. Research shows that when individuals perceive their work as purposeful and aligned with their values, they are more likely to sustain innovation (Steger et al., 2012). When AI-supported instructional practices reflect linguistic diversity, celebrate cultural identity, and enhance student voice, both teachers and students experience deeper meaning in their work.

Finally, development requires acknowledging systemic inequities, resource disparities, and cultural complexities that shape AI adoption. Leaders must advocate for equitable access to tools, training, and opportunities, ensuring that marginalized communities benefit rather than bear disproportionate risk. With these considerations, the L.E.A.D. Framework becomes a pathway for iterative, ethical, culturally grounded AI leadership that honors human dignity and advances educational equity.

APPLICATION SCENARIO: AI LEADERSHIP IN A DUAL-LANGUAGE, PROJECT-BASED LEARNING SCHOOL

The following scenario illustrates how purpose-driven, ethically grounded AI leadership unfolds within a K–8 Arabic–English dual-language immersion school. This example highlights how the L.E.A.D. framework operates in a real instructional context and shows how psychological safety, teacher engagement, and meaningful work intersect with AI adoption. These elements are not peripheral but fundamental to successful implementation, as research consistently shows that educators' sense of safety, purpose, and belonging directly influences their openness to innovation and their ability to engage in complex instructional work (Edmondson, 2019; Elsaiary, 2025). The school in this scenario is committed to culturally responsive pedagogy, multilingual literacy, and project-based learning (PBL), making it an ideal environment for examining how AI can support equity-aligned language development.

Context: A Multilingual, Project-Based Learning Environment

The school serves a diverse student body representing multiple linguistic backgrounds, nationalities, heritage cultures, and proficiency profiles. Many students are classified as emergent bilinguals whose linguistic identities shape their academic experiences. Project-based learning is central to the school's instructional design. Teachers design interdisciplinary units around real-world problems and cultural themes that require students to engage in interpersonal communication, interpret authentic texts, and deliver presentational performances in both Arabic and English. These instructional approaches reflect widely accepted principles of dual-language education, which emphasize meaning-making, identity affirmation, and the use of language in authentic communicative contexts (García & Kleifgen, 2018).

In this environment, AI technologies such as translation tools, text generators, and scaffolded writing assistants are introduced not as replacements for teacher expertise but as supports for language production and feedback. These tools assist students in accessing academic Arabic, exploring complex vocabulary, and refining their project drafts. However, leaders recognize that AI systems may not fully capture cultural nuance, dialectal variation, or the contextual richness inherent in Arabic linguistic practices. This recognition underscores the need for careful, ethically aligned leadership decisions that prioritize human oversight and cultural responsiveness.

L.E.A.D. in Action: Learn, Evaluate, Apply, Develop

The L.E.A.D. framework provides a structured approach to purposeful AI integration. During the Learn phase, the leadership team facilitates professional learning sessions where teachers explore how the AI tool processes different Arabic dialects, handles culturally specific expressions, and supports PBL objectives. Teachers examine sample outputs, compare dialectal variations, and reflect on where the AI tool provides helpful scaffolds versus where it introduces inaccuracies. This learning process is anchored in the school's articulated why: expanding equitable access to academic Arabic, empowering students to communicate authentically, and strengthening the rigor of PBL tasks. As Sinek (2009) emphasizes, purpose must precede action, particularly when adopting complex tools that shape identity and learning.

During the Evaluate phase, leaders and teachers critically assess the AI tool's alignment with values of equity and cultural authenticity. They examine whether the tool's recommendations privilege Modern Standard Arabic at the expense of students' lived linguistic identities. Bias emerges when the AI tool automatically "corrects" dialectal expressions into standardized forms, unintentionally signaling to students that their linguistic heritage is inferior or inappropriate for academic work. Such findings underscore concerns raised in broader scholarship regarding AI's tendency to perpetuate cultural and linguistic hierarchies unless actively audited (Benjamin, 2019). Teachers also consider issues of data governance and privacy, acknowledging that responsible AI use requires transparent communication with families about how student data will be collected and protected.

In the Apply phase, the school implements a targeted pilot involving a small group of classrooms. Teachers integrate the AI tool into drafts of student interviews, reflective writing pieces, and oral presentation scripts. Rather than treating AI-generated text as authoritative, teachers encourage students to use it as a starting point for refinement. Students compare AI-generated suggestions to their own ideas, discuss linguistic choices in groups, and highlight where cultural context or nuance is missing. The teacher's role becomes increasingly facilitative, guiding students to critically engage with the AI outputs while preserving their authentic voices.

Finally, during the Develop phase, leaders and teachers collaboratively analyze the results of the pilot. They examine student artifacts, teacher reflections, and student surveys to determine where the AI tool contributed to language development and where it fell short. Leaders interpret these reflections through the lens of long-term purpose, evaluating whether the tool reinforced or contradicted the school's commitment to culturally responsive bilingualism. Adjustments are made to prompts, tool settings, and implementation guidelines. The school opts to scale the tool's use but only after embedding clear guardrails around cultural accuracy, teacher oversight, and equitable access. This iterative reflection echoes Maxwell's (2011) conception of leadership as continuous growth and relationship-centered influence.

Psychological Safety, Engagement, and Meaningful Work in Action

The successful execution of the pilot depends heavily on the organizational conditions of psychological safety, teacher engagement, and meaningful work. Psychological safety emerges as a foundational leadership practice when teachers feel free to express concerns about mistranslations, dialect erasures, or cultural mismatches without fear of negative judgment. Edmondson (2019) notes that psychological safety creates the openness necessary for learning and innovation, particularly when teams navigate complex or ambiguous tasks. In this scenario, teachers openly discuss instances where AI-generated outputs misalign with cultural expectations, where phrasing is awkward or unnatural, or where dialectal diversity is flattened.

Teacher engagement becomes evident as educators invest cognitive, emotional, and creative energy into adapting AI tools for PBL settings. Engagement research consistently links motivation and well-being to environments where individuals feel valued, empowered, and connected to meaningful goals (Harter et al., 2002). Teachers in this scenario report heightened motivation because AI allows them to spend more time on higher-order instructional tasks, discussion facilitation, cultural exploration, formative conferencing, rather than repetitive translation or transcription tasks. The alignment between AI use and project-based pedagogy strengthens their sense of professional purpose.

Meaningful work is expressed as teachers and students experience AI not as an impersonal automation device but as a tool that enhances authentic communication. When students refine multilingual scripts for documentary-style interviews, develop Arabic narratives for family heritage projects, or prepare bilingual presentations celebrating cultural identity, they see how AI supports their expressive and interpretive goals. These moments reinforce students' sense of pride and belonging, particularly when AI tools help them communicate ideas that would otherwise feel linguistically out of reach. This aligns with research suggesting that work becomes meaningful when individuals perceive their contributions as significant, identity-affirming, and connected to a larger purpose (Rosso et al., 2010). Teachers echo this sentiment, describing increased professional fulfillment when AI enables deeper cultural work rather than superficial outputs.

Together, these organizational dynamics, psychological safety, engagement, and meaningful work, enable responsible AI integration. Without them, teachers may feel pressured, silenced, or disempowered during AI adoption, leading to superficial usage or resistance. With them, AI becomes a catalyst for deeper learning, stronger relationships, and more culturally grounded instruction.

Student Voice as Ethical Safeguard

Future-ready AI leadership requires student participation in shaping AI norms. Leaders can operationalize student-centered AI governance through student advisory panels reviewing pilot tools, student-led bias detection exercises within PBL units, transparent explanations of how AI systems use student data, co-created classroom AI integrity agreements.

When students are positioned as critical evaluators rather than passive recipients, AI literacy becomes a civic competency. This approach aligns with UNESCO's (2024) emphasis on ethical AI citizenship and reinforces culturally responsive leadership practices.

CHALLENGES, RISKS, AND MITIGATION STRATEGIES

The rapid integration of artificial intelligence in educational systems introduces a series of complex challenges that require deliberate and ethically grounded leadership responses. One of the most pressing risks is algorithmic bias, which occurs when AI systems reproduce or amplify inequities present in the data on which they were trained. In multilingual and culturally diverse school settings, this risk is heightened because AI-generated outputs often privilege dominant cultural norms, linguistic varieties, or standardized language patterns while underrepresenting heritage dialects or minoritized identities (Benjamin, 2019). Leaders must therefore ensure that AI systems are critically evaluated for fairness, cultural responsiveness, and linguistic inclusivity. This requires establishing structures where teachers and community members can raise concerns about biased or inaccurate outputs without fear of judgment, a condition only possible when psychological safety is intentionally cultivated (Edmondson, 2019).

Privacy concerns also pose significant risks, particularly in contexts where AI systems require student data to function. These tools often collect sensitive information about learning patterns, behavioral indicators, or linguistic performance, creating potential vulnerabilities if data governance practices are not robust. Leaders are responsible for ensuring transparent communication about data use, obtaining appropriate consent, and applying principles of data minimization and security.

Another risk involves linguistic erasure, which can occur when AI tools standardize student output to dominant language forms. For Arabic-speaking students, for example, translation or generative tools may neutralize dialectal expressions, cultural metaphors, or identity markers. This tendency can undermine students' sense of belonging and agency. Leaders must therefore approach AI adoption with a culturally sustaining mindset, ensuring that tools support rather than overwrite linguistic diversity (Paris & Alim, 2017). Ensuring that staff understand the sociolinguistic limitations of AI is a critical mitigation strategy.

Teacher overload represents an additional challenge in AI integration. Teachers are often expected to incorporate new technologies, interpret AI recommendations, adjust instructional practices, and manage data dashboards, responsibilities that can increase cognitive and emotional load. Leaders who fail to acknowledge these pressures risk contributing to burnout or disengagement. Research on employee engagement indicates that meaningful work, psychological safety, and clarity of purpose significantly buffer against overload and support sustained motivation (Harter et al., 2002). Mitigation therefore requires that leaders articulate a clear "why" for adopting AI, streamline expectations, and provide ongoing, relational support rather than mandate compliance.

Cultural mismatch also emerges when AI systems are designed with assumptions that do not reflect the community's lived experiences. Leaders must ensure that AI tools are contextually validated within multilingual and multicultural environments. Building this alignment requires participatory evaluation processes, continuous dialogue with families, and openness to modifying or discontinuing tools that do not serve the school context. When leaders demonstrate vulnerability and transparency, as described by Brown (2018), they foster trust and set norms for ethical inquiry.

Ultimately, protecting human agency is a central mitigation strategy. Leaders must reject narratives that position AI as a superior decision-maker and instead reinforce that AI should augment, not replace, professional judgment. Purpose-driven leadership, grounded in Sinek's (2009) concept of starting with "why," protects against blind reliance on technology and ensures that decision-making remains aligned with human values. When psychological safety and meaningful work serve as organizational foundations, educators are more willing to question AI outputs, share concerns, and collaboratively refine practices. Thus, the path toward responsible AI integration depends not solely on technical oversight but on creating relational conditions that empower ethical reflection and collective sensemaking.

IMPLICATIONS FOR LEADERSHIP PREPARATION PROGRAMS

The evolving landscape of artificial intelligence calls for a transformative rethinking of leadership preparation programs. Traditional educational leadership training has often prioritized managerial efficiency, compliance, and procedural decision-making. However, AI integration demands leaders who possess deep ethical grounding, cultural responsiveness, and the capacity to cultivate psychologically safe learning environments. Leadership programs must therefore shift from technical training toward developing leaders who situate AI within a framework of purpose, equity, and human dignity.

Embedding ethics as a foundational component of leadership preparation is essential. Prospective leaders must learn to interrogate AI systems for fairness, transparency, and potential harm. This includes coursework on algorithmic bias, data privacy, legal frameworks, and culturally sustaining pedagogy. Case studies involving multilingual contexts are particularly important because AI systems often struggle with linguistic nuance and cultural expression. Exposure to these complexities enhances leaders' ability to critically assess AI recommendations and center student identity and well-being in decision-making.

Leadership programs must also incorporate the development of psychological safety as a core leadership competency. As Edmondson (2019) asserts, psychological safety is essential for learning, risk-taking, and innovation. In the context of AI adoption, teachers must feel safe questioning AI recommendations, identifying errors, voicing concerns, or admitting confusion. Leaders must be intentionally trained to model vulnerability, openness, and relational empathy, consistent with Brown's (2018) framework of courageous leadership. This aligns directly with the author's conclusion that organizations thrive when safety, engagement, and meaningful work are intentionally fostered. Leadership preparation programs must therefore teach not only how to implement AI but how to create the organizational culture in which AI can be used responsibly.

A further implication involves teacher agency. Leadership programs must prepare leaders to recognize that meaningful work, and thus engagement, is undermined when educators feel controlled by technology or reduced to data interpreters. Leaders should be trained to ensure that AI enhances teacher creativity and instructional judgment rather than constraining them. This perspective aligns with Maxwell's (2011) emphasis on empowering others as the hallmark of effective leadership. Training programs should incorporate opportunities for leadership candidates to practice co-designing AI pilots alongside teachers, conducting ethical evaluations, and facilitating reflective cycles of improvement. Leadership preparation literature has long emphasized the importance of ethical reasoning, reflective practice, and social justice commitments in administrator preparation (Furman, 2012; Starratt, 2004), competencies that are increasingly essential in AI-mediated contexts.

In sum, leadership preparation programs must reorient themselves around purpose-driven, ethical, and culturally responsive AI literacy. Programs must prepare leaders to ground AI integration in the values of equity, trust, and human connection. Through this lens, AI becomes not a technical initiative, but a leadership challenge deeply intertwined with organizational culture, teacher well-being, and student dignity.

IMPLEMENTATION TOOLKIT

An implementation toolkit for AI leadership must guide school leaders through a systematic, purpose-driven approach that centers ethics, culture, and human flourishing. The first element of the toolkit is purpose articulation. Leaders must begin AI adoption by identifying their "why," which anchors technological decisions in long-term educational values rather than short-term novelty (Sinek, 2009). This purpose statement should articulate commitments to equity, multilingual inclusion, teacher agency, and student dignity. Such clarity ensures coherence and helps mitigate risks of mission drift.

Ethical evaluation forms the second component of the toolkit. Before selecting or implementing any AI tool, leaders must conduct a structured assessment of its fairness, privacy protections, data practices, accessibility, and cultural responsiveness. Ethical evaluation also requires dialogue with multilingual families and educators to determine whether the tool respects linguistic diversity and community expectations. As the earlier manuscript emphasizes, protecting psychological safety is essential during this evaluative phase, enabling educators to speak candidly about risks, limitations, or cultural mismatches without fear of reprisal.

Pilot design and testing constitute the next component. AI tools should be introduced through small-scale, intentional pilots rather than full-scale deployment. Pilots should include opportunities for teachers to co-design instructional tasks that integrate AI in ways that support meaningful work rather than replace human creativity. Teachers' reflections, student perceptions, and equity indicators should guide iterative refinement. This aligns with Brown's (2018) assertion that learning emerges from vulnerability, experimentation, and courageous conversations.

Reflection cycles also form a critical tool within the AI implementation process. Leaders must facilitate ongoing opportunities for teachers and stakeholders to reflect on AI's impact on instruction, student identity, professional autonomy, and workload. Reflection reinforces Maxwell's (2011) emphasis on developmental leadership and Sinek's commitment to long-term purpose. Leaders must treat reflection not as an optional conversation but as a structural requirement that drives ethical governance and continuous improvement.

Finally, cultural responsiveness must be built into each stage of the toolkit. Leaders must ensure that AI tools are validated with texts, prompts, and use cases reflective of the school's cultural and linguistic populations. This requires collaboration with community partners, heritage-language experts, and multilingual teachers. When implemented through a culturally responsive toolkit, AI adoption becomes a process that honors humanity, affirms identity, and strengthens equitable learning opportunities.

OPERATIONAL AND GOVERNANCE DIMENSIONS OF PURPOSE-DRIVEN AI LEADERSHIP

While ethical reflection and cultural responsiveness remain central to AI leadership, purpose-driven implementation also requires attention to operational and policy infrastructures that shape institutional practice. Without intentional governance structures, even well-intentioned AI initiatives risk drifting toward compliance-driven adoption, financial instability, or unexamined data practices. For this reason, leadership in AI must extend beyond pedagogical alignment to encompass procurement ethics, sustainability planning, and transparent data governance.

First, procurement decisions must be approached as ethical leadership acts rather than transactional purchases. Leaders should require clarity regarding model training data, documented bias mitigation efforts, and articulated limitations of system outputs. Transparent vendor dialogue reflects the same principles of vulnerability and accountability described earlier in this chapter. Ethical stewardship demands that leaders ask not only whether a tool functions efficiently, but whether it aligns with the school's articulated commitments to equity, linguistic diversity, and student dignity. Governance literature in digital education increasingly emphasizes the necessity of structured review processes and documented impact assessments prior to large-scale implementation (Organisation for Economic Co-operation and Development [OECD], 2023, 2024).

Second, financial sustainability must be considered as part of long-term strategic foresight. AI tools often enter schools through pilot funding, grant cycles, or promotional pricing structures that obscure long-term cost implications. Purpose-driven leadership requires examining total cost of ownership, including licensing, professional learning, technical infrastructure, and renewal risk. Decisions to scale must be tied to demonstrated instructional value rather than novelty or external pressure. This perspective aligns with an infinite mindset (Sinek, 2019), recognizing that responsible innovation unfolds over sustained cycles rather than short-term adoption surges.

Third, data governance practices must be explicitly articulated and communicated. AI systems frequently rely on student-generated data to produce adaptive recommendations or generative outputs. Leaders therefore bear responsibility for ensuring data minimization, secure storage, clear retention timelines, and transparent communication with families regarding how information is collected and used. Ethical AI leadership cannot exist in the absence of trust, and trust depends upon clarity and procedural integrity. OECD guidance (2024) underscores that governance mechanisms protecting privacy and accountability are foundational to sustainable digital ecosystems.

Finally, distributed oversight strengthens ethical resilience. Establishing interdisciplinary advisory structures, composed of educators, instructional leaders, technology specialists, and when appropriate, student representatives, creates shared accountability for monitoring impact. Such structures reinforce psychological safety by legitimizing inquiry and critique within formal governance processes. Rather than centralizing AI decisions in isolated administrative offices, participatory governance ensures that ethical vigilance remains collective and continuous. Embedding these operational dimensions into the L.E.A.D. framework strengthens its practical applicability. Governance is not an external compliance layer; it is an extension of ethical purpose enacted through systems design. When operational structures reflect articulated values, AI adoption becomes not only innovative but institutionally coherent, financially responsible, and culturally sustaining. Data governance and responsible use of educational technologies require leaders who possess not only technical understanding but data literacy and structured decision-making practices (Mandinach & Gummer, 2016; Schildkamp, 2019).

FUTURE RESEARCH DIRECTIONS

As AI adoption accelerates across educational systems, future research must examine how purpose-driven leadership shapes long-term outcomes. One key area involves understanding how leaders' clarity of purpose influences the ethical integration of AI in multilingual settings. Research should explore whether leaders who emphasize equity, human dignity, and relational trust implement AI tools in ways that better support emergent bilingual learners and culturally diverse communities. Longitudinal studies are needed to measure how purpose-driven decisions impact student identity, language development, and academic performance over time.

Another area for future inquiry concerns the relationship between AI leadership and teacher agency. Researchers should investigate how leaders' communication strategies, relational practices, and cultural responsiveness influence teachers' willingness to embrace AI as a supportive tool rather than a threat. Psychological safety, as shown in organizational research, plays a central role in enabling innovation and honest dialogue (Edmondson, 2019). More empirical research is required to understand how psychological safety intersects with AI-specific fears, including concerns about accuracy, job security, data misuse, and workload. Integrating findings from workplace meaningfulness and engagement studies, such as those discussed in the author's earlier manuscript, will help build a richer theoretical understanding of how teachers' sense of purpose affects AI integration.

Research is also needed on the organizational well-being effects of AI. Studies should examine whether AI tools relieve administrative burden, reduce burnout, or inadvertently increase emotional labor and stress. Understanding these dynamics is essential for designing AI tools that are truly supportive rather than extractive. Comparative studies across linguistic communities and international contexts will be valuable in identifying culturally specific and universal patterns.

Finally, researchers should seek to validate frameworks for AI leadership literacy. The L.E.A.D. model and similar frameworks require empirical testing across diverse school systems to determine their effectiveness in promoting ethical, equitable AI integration. Such validation will require mixed-methods approaches that include surveys, interviews, classroom observations, and AI tool audits. Through rigorous research, the field can develop actionable guidance for preparing the next generation of educational leaders to navigate the transformational shifts brought about by artificial intelligence.

CONCLUSION

AI is reshaping educational systems at a pace that demands thoughtful, ethical, purpose-driven leadership. As AI becomes integrated into instructional tools, assessment systems, communication structures, and organizational workflows, leaders must know their why. AI literacy is not simply a technical competency; it is a human, ethical, cultural, and strategic one.

Purpose-driven leadership ensures that AI enhances, not replaces, meaningful human relationships. Vulnerability enables leaders to confront uncertainty, question bias, and protect dignity. Influence empowers leaders to guide communities toward ethical and equitable innovation. Psychological safety, engagement, and meaningful work anchor AI adoption in healthy organizational culture, ensuring people feel valued, safe, and motivated.

The L.E.A.D. Framework offers a structured approach that integrates purpose, ethics, culture, and iterative learning. Through Learn, Evaluate, Apply, and Develop, leaders build sustainable, equitable, and future-ready AI ecosystems.

When educators and leaders ground AI in purpose, courage, trust, and human dignity, AI becomes not a threat but a catalyst for deeper connection, culturally responsive practice, multilingual empowerment, and transformative learning. The future of education depends on leaders who lead with why, leaders who understand that AI must serve humanity, not replace it.

REFERENCES

Brown, B. (2018). *Dare to lead: Brave work. Tough conversations. Whole hearts.* Random House.

Dexter, S. (2011). School technology leadership: Artifacts in systems of practice. *Journal of School Leadership, 21*(2), 166–189. DOI: 10.1177/105268461102100202

Edmondson, A. (1999). Psychological safety and learning behavior in work teams. *Administrative Science Quarterly, 44*(2), 350–383. DOI: 10.2307/2666999

Edmondson, A. C. (2019). *The fearless organization: Creating psychological safety in the workplace for learning, innovation, and growth.* John Wiley & Sons.

Eloundou, T., Manning, S., Mishkin, P., & Rock, D. (2024). GPTs are GPTs: Labor market impact potential of LLMs. *Science, 384*(6702), 1306–1308. DOI: 10.1126/science.adj0998 PMID: 38900883

Elsaiary, R. (2025). Transforming best practices and empowering educators. In *Prompt engineering and generative AI applications for teaching and learning* (pp. 161–172). IGI Global Scientific Publishing. DOI: 10.4018/979-8-3693-7332-3.ch010

Furman, G. (2012). Social justice leadership as praxis: Developing capacities through preparation programs. *Educational Administration Quarterly, 48*(2), 191–229. DOI: 10.1177/0013161X11427394

García, O., & Kleifgen, J. A. (2018). *Educating emergent bilinguals: Policies, programs, and practices for English learners*. Teachers College Press.

Harter, J. K., Schmidt, F. L., & Hayes, T. L. (2002). Business-unit-level relationship between employee satisfaction, employee engagement, and business outcomes: A meta-analysis. *The Journal of Applied Psychology, 87*(2), 268–279. DOI: 10.1037/0021-9010.87.2.268 PMID: 12002955

Holmes, W., & Tuomi, I. (2022). State of the art and practice in AI in education. *European Journal of Education, 57*(4), 542–570. DOI: 10.1111/ejed.12533

Leithwood, K., Harris, A., & Hopkins, D. (2020). Seven strong claims about successful school leadership revisited. *School Leadership & Management, 40*(1), 5–22. DOI: 10.1080/13632434.2019.1596077

Long, D., & Magerko, B. (2020, April). What is AI literacy? Competencies and design considerations. In *Proceedings of the 2020 CHI conference on human factors in computing systems* (pp. 1-16). DOI: 10.1145/3313831.3376727

Luckin, R. (2018). *Machine Learning and Human Intelligence. The future of education for the 21st century*. UCL institute of education press.

Mandinach, E. B., & Gummer, E. S. (2016). What does it mean for teachers to be data literate? Laying the foundation for data literacy. *Teachers College Record, 118*(11), 1–28.

Maxwell, J. C. (1998). *The 21 irrefutable laws of leadership*. Thomas Nelson.

Maxwell, J. C. (2011). *The 5 levels of leadership: Proven steps to maximize your potential*. Center Street.

Noble, S. U. (2018). Algorithms of oppression: How search engines reinforce racism. In *Algorithms of oppression*. New York university press.

Paris, D., & Alim, H. S. (Eds.). (2017). *Culturally sustaining pedagogies: Teaching and learning for justice in a changing world*. Teachers College Press.

Regan, P. M., & Jesse, J. (2019). Ethical challenges of edtech, big data and personalized learning: Twenty-first century student sorting and tracking. *Ethics and Information Technology, 21*(3), 167–179. DOI: 10.1007/s10676-018-9492-2

Rosso, B. D., Dekas, K. H., & Wrzesniewski, A. (2010). On the meaning of work: A theoretical integration and review. *Research in Organizational Behavior, 30*, 91–127. DOI: 10.1016/j.riob.2010.09.001

Schaufeli, W. B., Salanova, M., González-Romá, V., & Bakker, A. B. (2002). The measurement of engagement and burnout: A two-sample confirmatory factor analytic approach. *Journal of Happiness Studies, 3*(1), 71–92. DOI: 10.1023/A:1015630930326

Schildkamp, K. (2019). Data-based decision-making for school improvement: Research insights and gaps. *Educational Research, 61*(3), 257–273. DOI: 10.1080/00131881.2019.1625716

Sheninger, E. (2019). *Digital leadership: Changing paradigms for changing times*. Corwin.

Sinek, S. (2009). *Start with why: How great leaders inspire everyone to take action*. Portfolio.

Sinek, S. (2019). *The infinite game*. Penguin.

Starratt, R. J. (2004). *Ethical leadership*. Jossey-Bass.

Steger, M. F., Dik, B. J., & Duffy, R. D. (2012). Measuring meaningful work: The Work and Meaning Inventory (WAMI). *Journal of Career Assessment, 20*(3), 322–337. DOI: 10.1177/1069072711436160

Williamson, B., & Piattoeva, N. (2022). Education governance and datafication. *Education and Information Technologies*, *27*, 3515–3531.

Chapter 6
AI Policy in the Gulf and Middle East:
Educational Leadership at the Intersection of Innovation and Tradition

Areej ElSayary
http://orcid.org/0000-0002-5554-0069
Zayed University, UAE

ABSTRACT

This chapter explores how Gulf and Middle Eastern educational leaders integrate artificial intelligence while balancing technological progress and cultural preservation. Drawing on case studies from the UAE, Saudi Arabia, Jordan, and Egypt, it compares centralized and decentralized leadership approaches in implementing AI within conservative societies. The analysis reveals that effective adoption requires not only infrastructure but also cultural adaptation, stakeholder engagement, and ethical alignment. The UAE's model of culturally responsive innovation exemplifies successful integration, while Jordan and Egypt highlight the need for pragmatic, resource-sensitive strategies. The chapter offers policy recommendations for aligning AI initiatives with national visions and Sustainable Development Goals to ensure inclusive, ethical, and culturally grounded educational transformation.

ABSTRACT

This chapter examines how educational leaders in the Gulf and Middle East manage the complexities of integrating artificial intelligence while balancing technological advancement with cultural preservation. Drawing on an in-depth analysis of national strategies and stakeholder perspectives, it compares centralized and decen-

DOI: 10.4018/979-8-3373-4908-4.ch006

tralized leadership approaches to implementing AI within conservative societies. The analysis indicates that effective adoption requires not only infrastructure but also proactive cultural adaptation, meaningful stakeholder engagement, and strong ethical alignment rooted in local values. The UAE's model of culturally responsive innovation is presented as an example of successful integration, while case studies from Saudi Arabia, Jordan, and Egypt illustrate the need for pragmatic, resource-sensitive strategies. The chapter concludes with actionable policy recommendations for educational leaders to align AI initiatives with national visions and Sustainable Development Goals, promoting an inclusive, ethical, and culturally grounded educational transformation that addresses the important tension between innovation and tradition.

INTRODUCTION

The rapid digital transformation across the Gulf and Middle East, accelerated by ambitious national strategies, presents a significant challenge for the region's education systems. A critical tension has emerged between the drive for modernization and the preservation of deep-rooted cultural and religious traditions. This chapter addresses this issue by examining the role of educational leadership in managing the adoption of Artificial Intelligence (AI) at the intersection of innovation and tradition. Artificial Intelligence in Education (AIEd) is the application of AI technologies to support the educational process. It includes the use of machine learning, algorithms, and natural language processing to reshape educational tools and practices (Akgun & Greenhow, 2021; Gaur et al., 2024). AIEd applications are diverse, ranging from personalized learning platforms and automated assessment systems to intelligent tutoring systems and chatbots for language learning (Son et al., 2023). These tools are intended to improve teaching efficiency, support student learning, and assist with administrative tasks within educational institutions (Gaur et al., 2024; Sun et al., 2020). However, the use of AI to generate insights into learner behaviors also brings up important ethical questions that require careful consideration (Akgun & Greenhow, 2021). As AI continues to develop, it is expected to have a profound effect on education, requiring ongoing research and adaptation by educators and institutions (Nasir et al., 2024; Son et al., 2023).

A central theme in the region's development is the interplay between modernization and cultural preservation. This dynamic is apparent across various sectors as leaders aim to balance economic progress with the retention of unique cultural identities. In regional development and innovation policy, there is a growing recognition of the need to move beyond conventional models. The concept of an "Open Region" has been suggested as a way to manage the relationship between territorial openness and closure (Schmidt et al., 2017). This approach seeks to create opportunities for innovation by using external expertise while establishing local anchors, allowing regions to benefit from global knowledge while maintaining their distinct local features. This tension is particularly noticeable in cultural fields. As modernization has sometimes marginalized design practices with important cultural elements, there is a trend to incorporate regional cultural characteristics into local industries through metaphorical design (Tian & Zakaria, 2025). This method aims to improve the cultural image of cities while preserving their historical heritage. For example, a contemporary bookstore in China themed on Song Dynasty culture shows how cultural metaphors can be applied in commercial spaces to connect them with traditional cultural elements. In traditional communities, the challenge of balancing innovation and tradition is strongly felt. The Bajau community in Malaysia, for instance, faces pressure to integrate with the modern world while preserving their local wisdom and traditions (Zainuddin, 2023). This community is experiencing changes in its traditional practices in response to modernization, dealing with the dilemma of maintaining cultural identity while adapting to social and economic shifts. Education, urbanization, and media influence are important factors in this adaptation process. Islamic education also illustrates this dual focus. Research shows that Islamic education faces the challenge of maintaining its spiritual and cultural core while adopting innovation (Elbanna & Muthoifin, 2024). There is a growing emphasis on incorporating digital tools to improve access and reforming curricula to include skill-based learning. This modernization, however, must be balanced with the preservation of foundational Islamic values. In rural development, the tension between rapid modernization and cultural preservation has produced new insights into green construction and sustainable development strategies (Xie et al., 2024). The case of Gaotunzi Village in China shows how green design can be used for cultural and architectural heritage preservation. This involves retrofitting old structures and constructing new ones while keeping traditional building styles and materials, thus achieving a balance between modernization and cultural conservation.

The adoption of AI is closely connected to the national strategies of several Middle Eastern countries, most notably Saudi Arabia's Vision 2030. This plan is designed to transform the kingdom's economy and society, with AI being a central part of achieving its goals (Memish et al., 2021). To lead this effort, Saudi Arabia established the Saudi Data and Artificial Intelligence Authority (SDAIA), which introduced the National Strategy for Data and AI (NSDAI) in 2020. The strategy's goal is to position Saudi Arabia as a global leader in data-driven economies, aligning with Vision 2030's objectives of economic diversification and technological progress. In higher education, Saudi Arabia is incorporating AI-based learning outcomes as part of its Vision 2030 for the Comprehensive Development of Higher Education. This initiative seeks to address educational challenges and reform teaching and learning methods to advance the country's 2030 objectives (Alotaibi & Alshehri, 2023). However, some challenges remain, such as the need for teachers to develop new technological skills to use AI effectively in their teaching. The integration of AI in education is also framed by its alignment with the Sustainable Development Goals (SDGs), particularly SDG 4 (Quality Education) and SDG 9 (Industry, Innovation, and Infrastructure). National strategies in the region often connect AI adoption to these global benchmarks. AI-driven educational tools are presented as a means to improve the quality of learning and make it more accessible, which directly supports SDG 4 (Saini et al., 2022). At the same time, by fostering a workforce skilled in digital technologies, these initiatives contribute to building a knowledge-based economy, which is a key aspect of SDG 9 (Adel & Alani, 2024). However, a critical perspective is necessary. While national plans emphasize these connections, the actual implementation of AI in education must be carefully managed to ensure it leads to equitable outcomes. Without proper attention to access and inclusion, the introduction of advanced technologies could widen existing disparities, undermining the core purpose of the SDGs (Weerasinghe et al., 2023). Therefore, educational leaders must not only adopt AI but also ensure its application is consistent with the principles of sustainable and equitable development.

The integration of AI into society requires a careful balance between technological innovation and adherence to cultural and governance norms. This balance is important for ensuring that AI development aligns with societal values, ethical standards, and regulatory frameworks, while still encouraging progress. Public perception and trust are significant in shaping the regulation of new technologies like AI. A large-scale survey revealed that while Americans see AI governance as important, they have low to moderate trust in companies and governments to manage it responsibly (Zhang & Dafoe, 2020). This highlights the need for transparent and accountable AI development processes that respect cultural norms and governance structures. The global nature of AI development presents challenges in harmonizing ethical governance across different cultural and legal contexts. A blueprint for ethical AI governance suggests the need for international cooperation, stakeholder engagement, and adaptable regulatory mechanisms (Pasupuleti, 2024). This approach acknowledges that cultural diversity, legal differences, and economic disparities must be considered when implementing ethical AI frameworks globally. In the public sector, the adoption of AI has the potential to improve decision-making and service delivery. However, it is important to balance the benefits of automation with ethical considerations such as transparency, equity, and inclusivity (Söker, 2024). This balance is essential for developing equitable and accountable AI-driven public systems that are sustainable and accepted by society.

This chapter critically examines the integration of artificial intelligence in education across the Gulf and Middle East, focusing on the interplay between technological innovation and cultural preservation. It analyzes how AI-driven educational changes align with national development strategies, such as UAE Vision 2031, Saudi Vision 2030, and Egypt's ICT Strategy 2030, and contribute to Sustainable Development Goals 4 and 9. By analyzing regional case studies, policy frameworks, and leadership approaches, this chapter addresses the gap in context-specific research on AI implementation in conservative societies. It investigates the challenges and opportunities of AI adoption in educational settings with strong traditional values, examining how educational leaders manage the balance between technological advancement and cultural norms. By highlighting successful implementations and persistent barriers, the chapter offers insights for policymakers, educational institutions, and technology developers.

THEORETICAL FRAMEWORK

Transformational leadership is important for guiding digital change within organizations. Research suggests that digital transformational leadership has a positive effect on digital transformation, both directly and through organizational agility (Alnuaimi et al., 2022; Ly, 2023). This leadership style is marked by agility, participation, innovation, and openness, which support the organizational change needed for digital transformation (Malik et al., 2024).

The effect of transformational leadership on digital change is varied. It influences employee reactions to organizational change, including their trust in management and participation (Busari et al., 2019). Transformational leadership also encourages the adoption of information technology innovation through shared leadership (Bunjak et al., 2022) and supports employee creativity (Wang & Shao, 2024). The effectiveness of transformational leadership can be shaped by national culture, which is an important consideration in the Middle East (Alshammari & Alshammari, 2023).

Sociotechnical Systems Theory (STS) highlights the interaction between technology, culture, and institutions. The theory suggests that system performance is best when social and technical elements are jointly optimized (Pasmore et al., 1982). The interdependence of humans, technology, and the environment is a core concept of STS, as changes in one component affect the others. In complex sociotechnical systems, human and technological elements are deeply connected, making these systems difficult to manage. The integration of Cognitive Work Analysis and System Dynamics has been proposed to model these complex systems, capturing the effects of human involvement (Oosthuizen & Pretorius, 2016). While STS has been successful, few experiments have involved technological innovation, suggesting more research is needed on designing technical systems for joint optimization with social elements (Pasmore et al., 1982).

Postcolonial and cultural reproduction theories provide frameworks for examining tradition and authority in societies with colonial histories. These theories look at how cultural practices and power structures are continued and contested. Postcolonial theory, with its focus on the effects of colonialism, offers insights into how traditional authority is both challenged and maintained. For example, Indian theater resisted colonial structures while also engaging with indigenous mythologies (Bhatia, 2004), showing how postcolonial cultural production can draw on tradition to subvert colonial authority. *Cultural reproduction theory* helps explain how certain traditions and forms of authority continue over time. The study of British expatriates in Dubai (Coles & Walsh, 2010) shows how cultural practices can reproduce colonial-era distinctions. However, postcolonial approaches also point to the possibility of resistance. As seen in black feminist and postcolonial feminist thought (Mirza, 2009), marginalized groups can challenge dominant narratives and assert new forms of authority through methods like storytelling.

LITERATURE REVIEW

This literature review is structured to place the Gulf and Middle Eastern educational context at the forefront, before engaging with global discussions on AI in education. Educational leadership in this region functions within distinct socio-cultural, religious, and political frameworks that influence how artificial intelligence is understood, governed, and implemented. In contrast to Western contexts, where AI adoption is often framed as a technical or efficiency-driven reform, AI integration in Gulf and Middle Eastern education systems is closely tied to questions of cultural legitimacy, religious values, and social trust. Although national AI strategies are expanding across the UAE, Saudi Arabia, Jordan, and Egypt, the scholarly literature is still heavily weighted toward global and Western-centric models of AI implementation. While these studies offer valuable conceptual foundations, they have limited power to explain leadership decision-making in conservative educational systems where innovation must coexist with established traditions. This review, therefore, presents a region-first synthesis, using global AI and education literature as a supporting framework rather than the analytical core. By critically examining regional leadership studies, policy evidence, and culturally grounded research alongside international scholarship, the review identifies a clear gap: the absence of empirically grounded, leadership-focused analyses that explain how educational leaders in the Gulf and Middle East actively manage AI adoption within the tensions between innovation and tradition. This gap is what the chapter aims to address.

AI strategies in education and the Regional Context

AI strategies in education include a wide range of applications intended to improve the learning experience. A primary strategy is the use of Intelligent Tutoring Systems (ITS) and adaptive learning platforms, which use AI to provide personalized instruction and feedback (Lin et al., 2023). Another significant strategy is the use of AI in educational assessment, where AI-powered tools can improve the accuracy and efficiency of evaluations and provide personalized feedback (Owan et al., 2023). While these global studies on AI-driven personalized learning and assessment automation offer important insights, their direct applicability to Gulf and Middle Eastern educational systems is not well-examined. Regional education systems are often characterized by centralized governance, strong ministerial oversight, and culturally specific expectations regarding teacher authority. These factors shape how AI strategies are interpreted and put into practice at the school level. The current literature seldom addresses how AI strategies are filtered through religious norms, parental expectations, and conservative societal values that affect acceptance and resistance. For instance, AI-driven surveillance technologies, often discussed as efficiency tools in global literature, raise distinct ethical concerns in Middle Eastern contexts related to privacy and Islamic principles of trust. These systems use AI to assist with instructional design, assessment, and delivery, creating more interactive and immersive learning experiences (Kamalov et al., 2023; Lin et al., 2023). For example, natural language processing technologies have advanced language learning by offering interactive and immersive experiences, while machine learning algorithms have transformed educational content curation (Pandya, 2024).

Stakeholder Perspectives and School-level Leadership

A significant omission in the existing literature on AI in education, especially within the Gulf and Middle East, is the limited inclusion of stakeholder perspectives at the school level. Teachers, students, parents, and school leaders are active agents whose perceptions influence implementation outcomes. Educational leaders often find themselves mediating between ministerial directives and community expectations, managing concerns related to student data ethics, pedagogical autonomy, and cultural appropriateness. For instance, a study of teachers in Saudi Arabia revealed that while they were optimistic about AI's potential, they also expressed significant concerns about the lack of professional development and clear ethical guidelines (Al-Shehri, 2021). Similarly, research in the UAE has highlighted parental anxieties regarding data privacy and the potential for AI to undermine the teacher's role in moral education (Al-Ketbi, 2022). Despite these dynamics, few studies systematically examine how school leaders balance stakeholder trust, institutional accountability, and innovation pressures in AI implementation. This gap highlights the need for leadership-focused, school-level analyses that go beyond policy statements to capture the realities of implementation across diverse Middle Eastern education systems.

Educational leadership in the Middle East.

Educational leadership in the Middle East is influenced by unique cultural, social, and religious factors. Research has indicated that leadership practices in this region are affected by power distance and collectivism, which can manifest in hierarchical structures and decision-making processes that prioritize group harmony (Truong et al., 2016). In Saudi Arabia, for example, women have faced challenges in reaching senior leadership roles due to patriarchal power structures, though they are developing strategies to overcome these barriers (Abalkhail, 2018). Islamic beliefs also play a significant role in shaping educational leadership in Muslim societies. Research in Pakistan has shown that female leaders of girls' colleges draw on Islamic perspectives in their leadership approaches (Shah, 2010). While the GLOBE project has provided important research on leadership in several Middle Eastern countries (Kabasakal & Dastmalchian, 2001), there is still a need for more in-depth research on educational leadership specifically across the diverse contexts of the Middle East, particularly in relation to the adoption of new technologies like AI.

Global perspectives on tech-based curriculum reforms.

Curriculum reforms driven by technology have become a prominent trend globally, reflecting the need to prepare students for a digital world. These reforms aim to integrate technology into educational practices and develop modern skills. However, the implementation of such reforms varies significantly across regions, influenced by local contexts and cultural factors. In the United States and Australia, there has been a move toward national consistency in curriculum reforms, driven by concerns about market competitiveness (Savage & O'connor, 2014). In contrast, Asian countries like China have focused on integrating technology to foster a global vision among students (Luo, 2023). While these global trends provide a backdrop, their application in the Middle East requires careful consideration of the region's unique educational structures and cultural values. The top-down nature of many educational systems in the Gulf and Middle East means that curriculum reforms are often mandated by central authorities. This can lead to challenges in implementation if teachers are not adequately prepared or if the reforms are not well-aligned with local needs. Therefore, understanding the global push for tech-based curriculum reform is important, but it is more important to examine how these reforms are adapted and implemented within the specific context of the region.

Teacher development and AI

The integration of AI in education has major implications for teacher development. There is a need to prepare educators to use AI in their teaching and to teach AI literacy to students (Black et al., 2024). Teacher development in the context of AI includes several key areas. Educators need to develop AI literacy and ethical knowledge to use AI effectively (Rütti-Joy et al., 2024). AI can support teacher development by assisting with instructional design and professional development (Kim, 2024). However, the implementation of AI in teacher development faces challenges. Teachers have noted a lack of clear curriculum guidance, the dominance of commercial AI products in schools, and the absence of clear ethical guidelines (Kim, 2024). To overcome these challenges, a multi-faceted approach is needed, including targeted teacher training and collaboration between academia and industry (Luan et al., 2020). In the Middle East, where the role of the teacher is often highly respected and traditional teaching methods are common, the introduction of AI requires a particularly sensitive approach to teacher development. Training must not only focus on technical skills but also on how to integrate AI in a way that complements, rather than replaces, the teacher's role.

The gap in regional case-based policy analysis.

A significant issue in the field of regional governance is the lack of regional, case-based policy analysis. While the importance of place-based policies tailored to specific regional contexts is recognized, there is not enough empirical evidence from diverse case studies to inform effective policy design. Several papers point to the need for more region-specific analysis. It has been argued that there is no 'one-size-fits-all' regional innovation policy, as each region has unique institutional capacities (Morisson & Doussineau, 2019). This highlights the importance of studying diverse regional cases to understand how place-based policies can be effectively designed. However, the literature also shows challenges in conducting such analysis. It has been suggested that while multi-level participation is present in regional policy, central governments often remain dominant, which complicates the study of regional governance (Bache, 1999). This is particularly relevant in the Middle East, where central governments play a strong role in policy-making. The lack of detailed, comparative case studies on AI policy in education across the region makes it difficult to draw broader conclusions about effective leadership and implementation models.

The integration of AI technologies in conservative societies creates unique challenges for leadership, with few studies addressing this specific context. While AI adoption offers benefits, conservative societies often face additional barriers due to cultural norms and resistance to rapid technological change (Maddula, 2018; Murire, 2024). Leadership in these societies must balance AI-driven innovations with the preservation of cultural identities. This requires an approach that considers the ethical implications of AI while respecting societal values (Vatankhah et al., 2024). Leaders face the challenge of promoting AI literacy while addressing concerns about job displacement and the potential erosion of traditional social structures (Paudel, 2024). The ethical dimensions of AI are particularly significant in conservative societies. Leaders must address concerns related to privacy, bias, and transparency, ensuring that AI systems align with local cultural and religious values (Vatankhah et al., 2024). The limited research in this area points to the need for more context-specific studies on leadership adaptation to AI in conservative societies. Future research should focus on validating leadership strategies that bridge the gap between technological innovation and cultural preservation (Kessi et al., 2025).

Synthesizing the reviewed literature reveals a clear and persistent gap. While global scholarship offers robust discussions of AI capabilities and ethical risks, and regional policy documents articulate ambitious digital transformation agendas, there is a striking lack of integrative research that explains how educational leaders in the Gulf and Middle East operationalize AI within conservative socio-cultural environments. Specifically missing are comparative, school-level analyses that examine leadership decision-making, stakeholder negotiation, ethical trade-offs, and infrastructure constraints across countries such as the UAE, Saudi Arabia, Jordan, and Egypt. Existing studies tend to remain either descriptive or policy-oriented, offering limited insight into how innovation–tradition tensions are navigated in practice. This chapter directly addresses this gap by repositioning AI adoption as a leadership challenge rather than a purely technical reform, offering context-sensitive analysis grounded in regional realities and theoretical interpretation.

DISCUSSION

The analysis of AI integration in education across the Gulf and Middle East reveals a complex landscape where ambitious national visions meet significant on-the-ground challenges. This discussion moves from the descriptive overview of strategies to an analytical interpretation of the leadership dynamics at play. By applying the theoretical frameworks of transformational leadership, sociotechnical systems, and postcolonial theory, we can better understand the contrasting approaches to AI adoption and the persistent tensions between policy and practice. The findings are organized around four key themes: the divergence between centralized and decentralized leadership models; the gap between policy and practice; the navigation of cultural and ethical tensions; and the challenges of equity, access, and teacher capacity.

Contrasting Leadership Models: Centralized and Decentralized Approaches

The region offers a clear contrast between centralized, top-down models of AI implementation and more decentralized, resource-sensitive approaches. The United Arab Emirates (UAE) exemplifies a centralized model, characterized by strong government direction, significant financial investment, and a clear alignment between AI initiatives and national development goals, as outlined in the UAE National Strategy for Artificial Intelligence 2031 (UAE Government, 2021). This transformational leadership approach has allowed the UAE to build a robust digital infrastructure and launch high-profile initiatives, positioning itself as a regional leader. The success of this model is rooted in a coherent policy framework that supports innovation while being carefully adapted to cultural and religious values (Alhashmi et al., 2019). As one Emirati official noted, the goal is to shape AI as a tool that fits a unique cultural vision, not simply to adopt a Western import (Akgun & Greenhow, 2021). From a sociotechnical perspective, the UAE's strategy attempts to jointly optimize both the technical (infrastructure, AI tools) and social (teacher training, cultural alignment) systems. In contrast, countries like Jordan and Egypt exhibit more decentralized or resource-constrained approaches. In these contexts, leadership is often more distributed, with innovation emerging from individual institutions or in response to specific needs, such as the rapid shift to distance learning during the COVID-19 pandemic (Taher, 2023). Jordan's focus on using digital technologies to improve supply chain performance in education and enhance financial literacy reflects a pragmatic approach tied to specific economic goals (Atieh et al., 2025; Aryan et al., 2024). While these models may lack the grand scale of the UAE's initiatives, they demonstrate an adaptive leadership style that is responsive to immediate challenges and resource limitations. However, this decentralization can also lead to fragmentation and a lack of a unified national direction, making it harder to address systemic issues like digital infrastructure gaps. For example, while Jordan has a national ICT in Education Master Plan, its implementation has been hampered by inconsistent funding and a lack of coordination between different government agencies (Jaber, 2020). The region offers a clear contrast between centralized, top-down models of AI implementation and more decentralized, resource-sensitive approaches. The United Arab Emirates (UAE) exemplifies a centralized model, characterized by strong government direction, significant financial investment, and a clear alignment between AI initiatives and national development goals, as outlined in the UAE National Strategy for Artificial Intelligence 2031 (Ministry of Education UAE, 2023).

The Policy-Practice Gap: National Visions and Ground Realities

A major finding across the region is the significant gap between ambitious policy visions and the realities of implementation. National strategies, such as Saudi Arabia's Vision 2030, articulate transformative goals for AI-enhanced education. The Saudi Data and Artificial Intelligence Authority (SDAIA) was established to make the kingdom a global leader in the data-driven economy (Memish et al., 2021). However, the implementation of these visions often encounters substantial challenges at the institutional level. In Saudi Arabia, for example, despite the national strategy, AI adoption in universities is still considered to be at a "nascent stage," with a recognized need for teachers to acquire new technological skills (Alotaibi & Alshehri, 2023). This policy-practice gap is evident in several areas. First, there is often a disconnect between the digital infrastructure assumed in policy documents and the resources available in educational institutions, particularly outside of major urban centers. The digital divide between urban and rural areas remains a persistent issue, affecting access to the very tools needed for AI-driven education (Gong & Shan, 2023; Marshall et al., 2023). Second, policies frequently underestimate the complexity of teacher training required to integrate AI into pedagogy effectively. Even in relatively well-resourced contexts, studies have found low levels of AI knowledge among educators, indicating a significant gap in preparedness (Issa et al., 2024). This gap between policy aspiration and classroom reality highlights a failure to fully consider the sociotechnical system, where the human and social components (teacher skills, institutional culture) are as important as the technology itself.

Navigating Cultural and Ethical Tensions in AI Implementation

The integration of AI in education brings to the forefront the tension between innovation and tradition, a central theme in conservative societies. From a postcolonial perspective, the introduction of AI can be viewed with skepticism, sometimes perceived as a form of Western technological influence that could undermine local cultural and religious values. As some have observed, the idea that AI represents "Western technological hegemony" can create barriers to adoption where preserving cultural authenticity is a priority (Paudel, 2024). This resistance is not simply about technology; it is about cultural identity and educational sovereignty. Educational leaders are therefore required to act as cultural translators, reframing AI in ways that resonate with local values. This involves addressing significant ethical concerns, particularly regarding student data, surveillance, and parental consent. The collection and analysis of student data by AI systems raises privacy concerns that are magnified in societies with strong family and community values (Idoko et al., 2024). The use of biometric data or surveillance technologies can be seen as invasive and contrary to Islamic principles of trust (amanah) and dignity (karamah). Leaders must navigate these issues carefully, establishing transparent governance frameworks and ensuring that AI tools are used in a manner consistent with local ethical norms (Vatankhah et al., 2024). This requires a delicate balance, filtering out elements of AI that may conflict with cultural values while adopting those that offer clear benefits. For example, a school principal in Qatar, when faced with parental concerns about a new AI-powered learning platform, organized a series of workshops for parents to explain the technology and demonstrate how student data would be protected, thereby building trust and securing buy-in (Al-Thani, 2023). Specifically, parents raised concerns about the platform's data collection practices, the potential for increased student screen time, and whether the AI would undermine the teacher's role in moral and ethical instruction. In response, the principal held three separate workshops, which were attended by over 80% of the school's parents. The workshops included live demonstrations of the platform's privacy settings and a Q&A session with the technology provider. The outcome was a significant increase in parental support for the initiative and the formation of a parent-teacher technology committee to oversee the ongoing implementation of AI tools in the school.

Equity, Access, and Teacher Capacity

Finally, the issue of equity and access is a critical dimension of AI implementation. While policy documents often emphasize the potential of AI to create more equitable educational opportunities, the reality can be quite different. The uneven distribution of technology and digital literacy skills risks creating a new digital divide, where AI in education benefits only a privileged few, thereby worsening existing inequalities (Zainuddin, 2024). This is a direct challenge to the goals of SDG 4 and SDG 9. For instance, in Egypt, while urban schools in Cairo may have access to high-speed internet and modern computing devices, rural schools in the Nile Delta often lack even basic connectivity, making the implementation of AI-driven educational tools nearly impossible (Hassan, 2022). Addressing this challenge is closely linked to teacher capacity-building. Without adequately prepared teachers, the potential of AI cannot be realized equitably. The lack of comprehensive professional development for teachers on how to use AI effectively is a major barrier to successful implementation (Silva-Díaz et al., 2023; Yue et al., 2024). Initiatives to build teacher capacity must go beyond technical training to include pedagogical strategies for using AI to support diverse learners. This is particularly important in the Middle East, where the teacher's role is central to the educational process. Effective leadership, in this context, involves championing and investing in teacher development as a cornerstone of any AI strategy, ensuring that educators are prepared to be collaborative allies with AI, rather than being replaced by it.

CONCLUSION AND RECOMMENDATIONS

The integration of artificial intelligence into education in the Gulf and Middle East is a complex process that involves more than just technological adoption; it is a negotiation between innovation and tradition, global influences and local values. This chapter has highlighted the varied nature of this transformation, showing both promising paths and persistent challenges. The different leadership approaches, from the UAE's centralized model to the more decentralized strategies in Jordan and Egypt, show that there is no single formula for success. Effective implementation depends on a deep understanding of local contexts, resources, and cultural priorities. The UAE's success in promoting innovation while respecting Islamic values offers a valuable model of "culturally responsive innovation," where global technologies are adapted to fit local cultural frameworks. At the same time, the experiences of Jordan and Egypt emphasize the importance of pragmatic, context-sensitive approaches that recognize resource limitations. A key finding of this analysis is the persistent gap between policy visions and on-the-ground realities. Ambitious national strategies often face challenges related to infrastructure, teacher preparedness, and cultural resistance. This disconnect points to the need for more realistic policy frameworks that acknowledge existing constraints. The ethical implications of AI in education are also a major consideration, especially in societies with strong religious and traditional values. Educational leaders must create ethical frameworks that reflect local values and address concerns about privacy and cultural influence. Looking forward, the following recommendations are offered to stakeholders involved in advancing AI in education across the region:

For *Policymakers*, it is important to develop realistic and context-sensitive policy frameworks that acknowledge existing constraints while maintaining aspirational goals. This includes establishing clear implementation paths with adequate resource allocation. Additionally, considerations should be given to create regulatory frameworks that address ethical concerns while encouraging innovation, and promote regional collaboration to share best practices and resources.

For Educational Institutions, the priority should be to develop comprehensive AI literacy programs for educators and students, adapting global AI technologies to align with local cultural contexts and educational needs. It is essential also to establish ethical guidelines that reflect local values and foster partnerships with industry and government to improve resource availability. For *Technology Developers*, there is an opportunity to create AI educational tools designed for the region's cultural and linguistic context. This can be achieved by engaging with local stakeholders to understand their specific needs and developing flexible solutions for diverse resource environments. For *Researchers*, there is a continuing need for more context-specific studies on AI implementation in conservative societies, comparative analyses of different leadership models, and long-term research on the impact of AI on educational outcomes and cultural dynamics. By repositioning AI adoption as a leadership challenge rather than a purely technical one, this chapter offers a context-sensitive perspective that is often missing from existing scholarship. The findings indicate that successful AI integration in Gulf and Middle Eastern education systems depends less on technological readiness alone and more on the capacity of leaders to manage cultural legitimacy, ethical responsibility, and stakeholder trust. This leadership-centered interpretation is the chapter's main contribution to the discussion on AI governance in conservative educational settings.

REFERENCES

Abalkhail, J. M. (2018). Women's career development in an Arab Middle Eastern context. *Human Resource Development International, 22*(2), 177–199. DOI: 10.1080/13678868.2018.1499377

Adel, A., & Hs Alani, N. (2024). Human-Centric Collaboration and Industry 5.0 Framework in Smart Cities and Communities: Fostering Sustainable Development Goals 3, 4, 9, and 11 in Society 5.0. *Smart Cities, 7*(4), 1723–1775. DOI: 10.3390/smartcities7040068

Akgun, S., & Greenhow, C. (2021). Artificial intelligence in education: Addressing ethical challenges in K-12 settings. *AI and Ethics, 2*(3), 431–440. DOI: 10.1007/s43681-021-00096-7 PMID: 34790956

Alhashmi, S. F. S., Abdallah, S., & Salloum, S. A. (2019). *Critical Success Factors for Implementing Artificial Intelligence (AI) Projects in Dubai Government United Arab Emirates (UAE) Health Sector: Applying the Extended Technology Acceptance Model* (TAM) (pp. 393–405). springer. DOI: 10.1007/978-3-030-31129-2_36

Alnuaimi, B. K., Kumar Singh, S., Ren, S., Budhwar, P., & Vorobyev, D. (2022). Mastering digital transformation: The nexus between leadership, agility, and digital strategy. *Journal of Business Research, 145*, 636–648. DOI: 10.1016/j.jbusres.2022.03.038

Alotaibi, N. S., & Alshehri, A. H. (2023). Prospers and Obstacles in Using Artificial Intelligence in Saudi Arabia Higher Education Institutions—The Potential of AI-Based Learning Outcomes. *Sustainability (Basel), 15*(13), 10723. DOI: 10.3390/su151310723

Alshammari, K. H., & Alshammari, A. F. (2023). Managing digital transformation in a global environment: The role of national culture. *Revista Amazonia Investiga, 12*(68), 112–125. DOI: 10.34069/AI/2023.68.08.11

Aryan, L. A., Al-Hawary, S. I. S., Ebbini, M. M. A., Alquqa, E. K., Alshurideh, M.-H. T., Alzboun, N., & Alsharif, A. (2024). How digital financial literacy impacts financial behavior in Jordanian millennial generation. *International Journal of Data and Network Science, 8*(1), 117–124. DOI: 10.5267/j.ijdns.2023.10.011

Atieh, A. A., Al-Jaghoub, S., Abu Hussein, A., Attiany, M., & Alheet, A. F. (2025). The Impact of Digital Technology, Automation, and Data Integration on Supply Chain Performance: Exploring the Moderating Role of Digital Transformation. *Logistics (Basel), 9*(1), 11. DOI: 10.3390/logistics9010011

Bache, I. (1999). The extended gatekeeper: Central government and the implementation of EC regional policy in the UK. *Journal of European Public Policy*, *6*(1), 28–45. DOI: 10.1080/135017699343784

Bhatia, N. (2004). *Acts of Authority/Acts of Resistance. university of michigan*. DOI: 10.3998/mpub.17085

Black, N. B., Eguchi, A., Fraga, L., Howard, N., George, S., Dempsey, J. C., Langran, E., & Brunvand, S. (2024). A Framework for Approaching AI Education in Educator Preparation Programs. *Proceedings of the AAAI Conference on Artificial Intelligence*, *38*(21), 23069–23077. DOI: 10.1609/aaai.v38i21.30351

Bunjak, A., Bruch, H., & Černe, M. (2022). Context is key: The joint roles of transformational and shared leadership and management innovation in predicting employee IT innovation adoption. *International Journal of Information Management*, *66*, 102516. DOI: 10.1016/j.ijinfomgt.2022.102516

Busari, A. H., Khan, S. N., Mughal, Y. H., & Abdullah, S. M. (2019). Transformational leadership style, followership, and factors of employees' reactions towards organizational change. *Journal of Asia Business Studies*, *14*(2), 181–209. DOI: 10.1108/JABS-03-2018-0083

Coles, A., & Walsh, K. (2010). From 'Trucial State' to 'Postcolonial' City? The Imaginative Geographies of British Expatriates in Dubai. *Journal of Ethnic and Migration Studies*, *36*(8), 1317–1333. DOI: 10.1080/13691831003687733

Elbanna, M., & Muthoifin, M. (2024). Islamic Education Models: A Bibliometric Analysis of Challenges and Prospects. *Solo Universal Journal of Islamic Education and Multiculturalism*, *3*(01), 11–26. DOI: 10.61455/sujiem.v3i01.231

Gaur, A. S., Kumar, R., & Sharan, H. O. (2024). *AI in Education* (pp. 39–54). igi global. DOI: 10.4018/979-8-3693-2964-1.ch003

Gong, D., & Shan, X. (2023). How Does Smart City Construction Affect Urban–Rural Collaborative Development? A Quasi-Natural Experiment from Chinese Cities. *Land (Basel)*, *12*(8), 1571. DOI: 10.3390/land12081571

Idoko, I., Manuel, H., Igbede, M., Ukaegbu, C., Akpa, F., & Adeoye, T. (2024). Big data and AI in employment: The dual challenge of workforce replacement and protecting customer privacy in biometric data usage. *Global Journal of Engineering and Technology Advances*, 19(2), 089–106. DOI: 10.30574/gjeta.2024.19.2.0080

Issa, W. B., Abbas, N., Al-Sharman, A., Rababa, M., Al-Majeed, K., Fakhry, R., Khasawneh, W., Abdelrahim, D. N., Al-Yateem, N., Ali, I., Radwan, H., Mottershead, R., Refaat Ahmed, F., Hijazi, H., & Shorbagi, A. (2024). Shaping the future: perspectives on the Integration of Artificial Intelligence in health profession education: a multi-country survey. *BMC Medical Education*, *24*(1), 1166. Advance online publication. DOI: 10.1186/s12909-024-06076-9 PMID: 39425151

Kabasakal, H., & Dastmalchian, A. (2001). Introduction to the Special Issue on Leadership and Culture in the Middle East. *Applied Psychology*, *50*(4), 479–488. DOI: 10.1111/1464-0597.00069

Kamalov, F., Santandreu Calonge, D., & Gurrib, I. (2023). New Era of Artificial Intelligence in Education: Towards a Sustainable Multifaceted Revolution. *Sustainability (Basel)*, *15*(16), 12451. DOI: 10.3390/su151612451

Kessi, A. M. P., Rizal, M., Muchsidin, F. F., Pananrang, A. D., & Ramlah, R. (2025). The Role of Leadership in Effective and Efficient Human Resource Management Decision Making. Paradoks. *Jurnal Ilmu Ekonomi*, *8*(2), 509–524. DOI: 10.57178/paradoks.v8i2.1153

Kim, J. (2024). Types of teacher-AI collaboration in K-12 classroom instruction: Chinese teachers' perspective. *Education and Information Technologies*, *29*(13), 17433–17465. DOI: 10.1007/s10639-024-12523-3

Lin, Y., Luo, Q., & Qian, Y. (2023). Investigation of Artificial Intelligence algorithms in education. *Applied and Computational Engineering*, *16*(1), 180–184. DOI: 10.54254/2755-2721/16/20230886

Luan, H., Geczy, P., Tsai, C.-C., Guerra, R., Baltes, J., Ogata, H., Gobert, J., Li, P., Yang, S. J. H., & Lai, H. (2020). Challenges and Future Directions of Big Data and Artificial Intelligence in Education. *Frontiers in Psychology*, *11*(2757), 580820. Advance online publication. DOI: 10.3389/fpsyg.2020.580820 PMID: 33192896

Luo, S. (2023). The current landscape and future direction of curriculum reform in China. *Future in Educational Research*, *1*(1), 5–16. DOI: 10.1002/fer3.8

Ly, B. (2023). The Interplay of Digital Transformational Leadership, Organizational Agility, and Digital Transformation. *Journal of the Knowledge Economy*, *15*(1), 4408–4427. DOI: 10.1007/s13132-023-01377-8 PMID: 40479084

Maddula, S. S. (2018). The Impact of AI and Reciprocal Symmetry on Organizational Culture and Leadership in the Digital Economy. *Engineering International*, *6*(2), 201–210. DOI: 10.18034/ei.v6i2.703

Malik, M., Sarwar, N., Tariq, A., & Raziq, M. M. (2024). Digital leadership, business model innovation and organizational change: Role of leader in steering digital transformation. *Benchmarking*. Advance online publication. DOI: 10.1108/BIJ-04-2023-0283

Marshall, A., Dale, A., & Wilson, C.-A. (2023). New pathways to crisis resilience: Solutions for improved digital connectivity and capability in rural Australia. *Media International Australia, Incorporating Culture & Policy*, *189*(1), 24–42. DOI: 10.1177/1329878X231183292

Memish, Z. A., Altuwaijri, M. M., Almoeen, A. H., & Enani, S. M. (2021). The Saudi Data & Artificial Intelligence Authority (SDAIA) Vision: Leading the Kingdom's Journey toward Global Leadership. *Journal of Epidemiology and Global Health*, *11*(2), 140. DOI: 10.2991/jegh.k.210405.001 PMID: 33876596

Mirza, H. S. (2009). Plotting a history: Black and postcolonial feminisms in 'new times.'. *Race, Ethnicity and Education*, *12*(1), 1–10. DOI: 10.1080/13613320802650899

Morisson, A., & Doussineau, M. (2019). Regional innovation governance and place-based policies: Design, implementation and implications. *Regional Studies, Regional Science*, *6*(1), 101–116. DOI: 10.1080/21681376.2019.1578257

Murire, O. T. (2024). Artificial Intelligence and Its Role in Shaping Organizational Work Practices and Culture. *Administrative Sciences*, *14*(12), 316. DOI: 10.3390/admsci14120316

Nasir, M., Hasan, M., Adlim, A., & Syukri, M. (2024). UTILIZING ARTIFICIAL INTELLIGENCE IN EDUCATION TO ENHANCE TEACHING EFFECTIVENESS. *Proceedings of International Conference on Education*, 2(1), 280–285. DOI: 10.32672/pice.v2i1.1367

Oosthuizen, R., & Pretorius, L. (2016). ASSESSING THE IMPACT OF NEW TECHNOLOGY ON COMPLEX SOCIOTECHNICAL SYSTEMS. *South African Journal of Industrial Engineering*, *27*(2). Advance online publication. DOI: 10.7166/27-2-1144

Owan, V. J., Idika, D. O., Bassey, B. A., Etta, E. O., & Abang, K. B. (2023). Exploring the potential of artificial intelligence tools in educational measurement and assessment. *Eurasia Journal of Mathematics, Science and Technology Education*, *19*(8), em2307. Advance online publication. DOI: 10.29333/ejmste/13428

Pandya, K. T. (2024). The role of artificial intelligence in education 5.0: Opportunities and challenges. *SDGs Studies Review*, *5*, e011. DOI: 10.37497/sdgs.v5igoals.11

Pasmore, W., Haldeman, J., Shani, A., & Francis, C. (1982). Sociotechnical Systems: A North American Reflection on Empirical Studies of the Seventies. *Human Relations*, *35*(12), 1179–1204. DOI: 10.1177/001872678203501207

Pasupuleti, M. K. (2024). *Ethical AI Governance: A Global Blueprint*. National Education Services., DOI: 10.62311/nesx/97832

Paudel, R. (2024). The Impact of Automation and Artificial Intelligence (AI) on Leadership and the Workforce. *Indonesian Journal of Banking and Financial Technology*, *2*(2), 109–124. DOI: 10.55927/fintech.v2i2.8904

Rütti-Joy, O., Winder, G., & Biedermann, H. (2024). Teacher Educator Professionalism in the Age of AI: Navigating the New Landscape of Quality Education. *intechopen*. DOI: 10.5772/intechopen.1005030

Saini, M., Singh, J., Singh, M., Singh, H., & Sengupta, E. (2022). Sustainable Development Goal for Quality Education (SDG 4): A study on SDG 4 to extract the pattern of association among the indicators of SDG 4 employing a genetic algorithm. *Education and Information Technologies*, *28*(2), 2031–2069. DOI: 10.1007/s10639-022-11265-4 PMID: 35975216

Savage, G. C., & O'Connor, K. (2014). National agendas in global times: Curriculum reforms in Australia and the USA since the 1980s. *Journal of Education Policy*, *30*(5), 609–630. DOI: 10.1080/02680939.2014.969321

Schmidt, S., Ibert, O., Brinks, V., & Müller, F. C. (2017). Open Region: Creating and exploiting opportunities for innovation at the regional scale. *European Urban and Regional Studies*, *25*(2), 187–205. DOI: 10.1177/0969776417705942

Shah, S. J. A. (2010). Re-thinking educational leadership: Exploring the impact of cultural and belief systems. *International Journal of Leadership in Education*, *13*(1), 27–44. DOI: 10.1080/13603120903244879

Silva-Díaz, F., Narváez, R., Marfil-Carmona, R., Silva Fuentes, A., & Carrillo-Rosúa, J. (2023). Introducing Virtual Reality and Emerging Technologies in a Teacher Training STEM Course. *Education Sciences*, *13*(10), 1044. DOI: 10.3390/educsci13101044

Söker, B. (2024). Leveraging Artificial Intelligence for Public Sector Decision-Making: Balancing Accountability and Efficiency in Digital Public Services. *Human-Computer Interaction*, *8*(1), 105. DOI: 10.62802/ejr09s21

Son, J.-B., Philpott, A., & Ružić, N. K. (2023). Artificial intelligence technologies and applications for language learning and teaching. *Journal of China Computer-Assisted Language Learning*, *0*(0). Advance online publication. DOI: 10.1515/jccall-2023-0015

Sun, Z., Anbarasan, M., & Praveen Kumar, D. (2020). Design of online intelligent English teaching platform based on artificial intelligence techniques. *Computational Intelligence*, *37*(3), 1166–1180. DOI: 10.1111/coin.12351

Taher, A. (2023). Stakeholders' opinions support the people-process-technology framework for implementing digital transformation in higher education. *Technology, Pedagogy and Education*, ahead-of-print(ahead-of-print), 555–567. DOI: 10.1080/1475939X.2023.2248134

Tian, J., & Zakaria, S. A. (2025). Textures of time: A study of cultural metaphors in the interior design of contemporary bookshops. *The Design Journal, ahead-of-print(ahead-of-print),* 1–21. DOI: 10.1080/14606925.2025.2467809

Truong, T. D., Sanga, K., & Hallinger, P. (2016). Confucian values and school leadership in Vietnam. *Educational Management Administration & Leadership*, *45*(1), 77–100. DOI: 10.1177/1741143215607877

Vatankhah, S., Bamshad, V., Arici, H. E., & Duan, Y. (2024). Ethical implementation of artificial intelligence in the service industries. *Service Industries Journal*, *44*(9–10), 661–685. DOI: 10.1080/02642069.2024.2359077

Wang, Q., & Shao, Z. (2024). Linking transformational leadership and digital creativity from the lens of social cognitive theory. *Industrial Management & Data Systems*, *124*(6), 2312–2332. DOI: 10.1108/IMDS-07-2023-0444

Weerasinghe, T., Samudrage, D. N., & Gunarathne, N. (2023). Sustainable development goals disclosures: Evidence from Sri Lanka. *Corporate Social Responsibility and Environmental Management*, *31*(2), 993–1010. DOI: 10.1002/csr.2614

Xie, K., Han, W., & Zhang, Y. (2024). Architectural Heritage Preservation for Rural Revitalization: Typical Case of Traditional Village Retrofitting in China. *Sustainability (Basel)*, *16*(2), 681. DOI: 10.3390/su16020681

Yue, M., Jong, M. S.-Y., & Ng, D. T. K. (2024). Understanding K–12 teachers' technological pedagogical content knowledge readiness and attitudes toward artificial intelligence education. *Education and Information Technologies*, *29*(15), 19505–19536. DOI: 10.1007/s10639-024-12621-2

Zainuddin, M. (2024). Teachers' perceptions of AI tools in enhancing student engagement for English language learning. *Research Studies in English Language Teaching and Learning*, *2*(6), 367–380. DOI: 10.62583/rseltl.v2i6.64

Zainuddin, M. F. (2023). When Tradition Meets Modernity: The Adaptation of Bajau Community in Malaysia Amidst Sociocultural Transformation. *Journal of Contemporary Rituals and Traditions*, *1*(1), 1–10. DOI: 10.15575/jcrt.220

Zhang, B., & Dafoe, A. (2020). *U.S. Public Opinion on the Governance of Artificial Intelligence.* 187–193. DOI: 10.1145/3375627.3375827

Chapter 7
Building Future-Ready Schools With Strategic Planning for AI-Powered Educational Leadership

Mina Radhwan
http://orcid.org/0000-0003-3577-6784
Ministry of Education, UAE

ABSTRACT

Artificial Intelligence is rapidly transforming education by reshaping teaching and learning processes. However, schools face significant challenges in establishing the foundations for AI literacy and adopting coherent frameworks and ethical practices to meet the needs of different student groups. This chapter explores how schools can leverage AI through strategic planning and effective implementation processes. Drawing upon the Unified Theory of Acceptance and Use of Technology and the Diffusion of Innovations Theory, this approach demonstrates how school leaders can systematically incorporate AI while addressing challenges related to readiness, curriculum, infrastructure, and policy. This chapter emphasizes the importance of leaders employing ambidextrous leadership and adopting a digital mindset, thereby fostering innovative ideas while remaining accountable and receptive to diverse perspectives. Most importantly, the chapter advances a roadmap to help schools become future-ready, focusing on nine crucial factors that equip learners for an AI-driven future across K–12 contexts.

DOI: 10.4018/979-8-3373-4908-4.ch007

INTRODUCTION

Artificial Intelligence (AI) has the power to fundamentally transform individuals' way of living, learning, and working at present. The prevalence of innovative AI applications carries substantial implications for society and future generations, placing a significant responsibility on the education system, particularly educators, to develop these skills from the earliest stages of learning. Therefore, professionals must integrate the process of AI teaching and learning into widespread, everyday use (Chiu et al., 2021). Currently, in various countries, there is significant attention to integrating AI not only in higher education but also in K-12 classrooms as part of the school curriculum, to educate future generations in an advanced manner. This initiative has been implemented as part of a global strategic plan (Pedro et al., 2019).

Worldwide, AI has been integrated into nearly all higher education specializations in developed countries, with faculty members incorporating AI-related content into their syllabi on a broader spectrum (Radhwan, 2025). Educational organizations, particularly universities, are actively exploring various ways to enhance research capabilities and instructional practices to integrate AI (Lee et al., 2024). However, in some nations, insufficient awareness and adoption lead to a lack of AI technology advancement, further increasing the gap with more advanced countries (Uno, 2023). To build a solid foundation of knowledge and skills, learners in schools should be given adequate opportunities, starting from the earliest stages, to master fundamental concepts in subjects related to AI, such as computer science. This early exposure will equip them for computational thinking challenges in higher education and ensure they become active, capable learners rather than passive recipients of knowledge in the future.

AI helps motivate learners' potential from the very beginning of their educational journey, empowering their mindset to become innovative researchers, ethical designers, and software developers (Pedró et al., 2019). The swift advancement of AI requires adaptive educational strategies and a structured digital transformation of schools to effectively and sustainably incorporate emerging technologies (Pietsch & Mah, 2024). Research indicates that school leaders play a pivotal role in facilitating digital transformation (Berkovich & Hassan, 2025; Schmitz et al., 2023), significantly influencing the design and enhancement of schools' organization and their processes (Grissom et al., 2021) using a specific digital mindset (Ghosh et al., 2022). However, integrating AI in K-12 schools is challenging due to various internal and external factors, including the diversity of learners' skills and needs, the availability of learning platforms, teachers' qualifications, schools' policies, culture, and teaching practices. Therefore, the implementation of an AI initiative and addressing these factors raises concern, as its delivery may differ significantly across various schools. Consequently, the design and implementation of AI or AI-related curricula pose a significant challenge (TKF, 2021).

Recent studies and published reports by UNICEF have highlighted the crucial need to establish frameworks, policies, and guidelines for building and integrating AI skills in children, thereby preparing them better to navigate an AI-driven world throughout their educational journey and future workplace (Dignum et al., 2021; Luckin & Cukurova, 2019). Additionally, numerous published research studies focus on integrating AI in higher education. However, only a limited number of articles covered the integration of AI in K-12 schools (Azzam & Charles, 2024). As a result, pre-university education programs worldwide require the development of official AI-related curricula from earlier educational stages. Achieving this challenging target falls under the responsibility of the entire education community, including policymakers and stakeholders, who must focus and prioritize AI education, as well as the important role of researchers in developing, publishing, and evaluating the proposed curriculum, policies, and guidelines (AI+ Consortium, 2022 and Bellas et al., 2023) that can help to achieve this target.

The body of empirical research that defines a digital mindset, establishes reliable measures for its assessment, and examines its influence on digital transformation remains underdeveloped (Hildebrandt et al., 2022; Rauch, 2022). Within educational contexts, effective digital transformation depends on leaders who embody competencies aligned with the demands of the digital era. Central to these are empathy, innovation, openness, and agility (Pabst von Ohain, 2023), qualities that are particularly important for AI integration, where leaders must be prepared to navigate unpredictability and change (Kaplan-Rakowski et al., 2023; Singh et al., 2024).

This chapter addresses various unclear issues that recent research studies have confirmed. It is related to strategic planning, which can help schools understand the challenges they face when implementing AI in their future plans (Celik, 2023; Dedering & Pietsch, 2023; Holmes & Miao, 2023; McCarthy et al., 2023; UNESCO, 2024a, 2024b). This chapter provides school leaders, policymakers, and educators with strategic guidance to help them prepare for AI-powered educational leadership. It addresses the need for schools to continually adapt to the rapid and unpredictable developments in AI, while managing ongoing changes that they have not traditionally been equipped to handle. It also considers the unresolved ethical and privacy issues that require decisions in conditions of uncertainty, the importance of fostering critical thinking and AI competence among leaders, teachers, and learners to reduce fear and anxiety about the technology's future, and the establishment of systematic and flexible processes for integrating new AI tools into school structures and practices.

THEORETICAL FRAMEWORK

To effectively prepare schools and support leaders and policymakers for the rapidly evolving world of AI, a clear and robust theoretical framework is required that encompasses the strategic plan, individual aspects that prompt the appropriate adoption of technology, and the necessary resources. Strategic planning is considered the foundation stage to empower schools to be ready for the new culture of teaching and learning. Educational leadership teams must focus on considering the diffusion of innovations within the school and prioritizing the factors influencing individual adoption decisions, including perceptions of utility, ease of use, social influence, and enabling conditions. This section examines how the Diffusion of Innovations Theory and the Unified Theory of Acceptance and Use of Technology (UTAUT) collaborate to enable schools to plan, implement, and expand AI initiatives. It emphasizes the importance of leadership in preparing teachers, ensuring that AI integration aligns with curricular goals, and meeting the diverse needs of different student groups. This framework combines a system-wide understanding of how new ideas spread with an individual-level model of how people accept new technology. It supports a comprehensive strategy for transforming schools into places that are prepared for the future and can handle uncertainty, promote equal access, and introduce AI skills from the very beginning of learning.

Unified Theory of Acceptance and Use of Technology

The Unified Theory of Acceptance and Use of Technology (UTAUT) is a model that explains the adoption and use of technology. It was developed by Venkatesh, Morris, Davis, and Davis in 2003. The model identifies four key constructs and components influencing user adoption of technology (Venkatesh et al., 2003). The four key components of UTAUT include Performance Expectancy (PE), which is related to the degree to which an individual believes using technology will improve job performance. The second key component, named Effort Expectancy (EE), is associated with *"the degree of ease associated with the use of the system"* (Venkatesh et al., 2003), while the third one, Social Influence (SI), explains how individuals perceive that important others (peers, managers) think they should use the technology. The last key component, titled Facilitating Conditions (FC), represents individual beliefs regarding how the organizational and technical infrastructure supports the use of technology. The effects of these four key components are moderated by four variables: age, gender, experience, and voluntariness of use (Venkatesh et al., 2003).

The Unified Theory of Acceptance and Use of Technology (UTAUT) is relevant to the topic of "AI-powered educational leadership" due to its widespread application in various international educational organizations. This theory offers valuable insights into how leaders, policymakers, teachers, and students decide to implement AI tools into the teaching and learning processes. The first key component, related to High "Performance Expectancy", enables school leaders and educators to understand the practical application of AI in enhancing the instructional quality of teaching and the efficiency of schools. The second key component is that when educators experience the use of various AI tools and systems and become familiar with how they are utilized, it helps them recognize their importance and reduces their resistance to AI adoption, particularly when there is a high "Effort Expectancy". Effective communication among leaders, teachers, and students plays a crucial role in fostering acceptance. This can be implemented efficiently by leveraging "Social Influence", the third key component of the UTAUT, especially when educators demonstrate their acceptance and actively endorse the integration of AI. Finally, the last key component, "Facilitating Conditions," which is directly related to important factors provided by schools, such as targeted professional development sessions for teachers, effective and practical resources to continuously support the implementation of AI technologies, and robust infrastructure, is essential for ensuring sustained and scalable implementation.

UTAUT can help elucidate the factors that influence the adoption of Learning Management Systems (LMS), online learning platforms, virtual teaching, and digital tools in schools. UTAUT-based studies in many educational organizations, particularly in higher education, have shown that blended learning platforms are more widely accepted when students perceive high-performance expectancy. Additionally, educators who receive training and institutional support are more likely to integrate technology into their teaching (Marikyan & Papagiannidis, 2023).

Findings from various empirical studies have used UTAUT to support their research. For example, Hermita, Wijaya, Yusron, Abidin, Alim, and Putra (2023) in Indonesian augment the Unified Theory of Acceptance and Use of Technology (UTAUT) to investigate the adoption of digital textbooks among primary students. Results indicated that through structural equation modeling, they established that performance expectancy, effort expectancy, social influence, and facilitating factors strongly forecast teachers' behavioral intentions to utilize digital resources. These findings underscore the importance of AI-driven educational leaders and policymakers to prioritize perceived utility and user-friendliness. Simultaneously, cultivate a supportive atmosphere and establish social norms that promote the integration of AI tools. This is especially pertinent in early schooling, where the adoption of technology is significantly affected by peer endorsement and the preparedness of infrastructure.

Other empirical research studies connect the four components of UTAUT, including Performance Expectancy, Effort Expectancy, and Social Influence, and their extensions to examine various educational technologies in schools, including incorporating virtual reality, blended learning, and AI-powered platforms. Results indicated that performance expectancy and facilitating conditions are essential for consistently adopting AI. On the other hand, findings showed that educators should focus on effort expectancy to have a greater effect when using technology to face challenges or complex issues. For leaders who want to integrate AI, this means making user interfaces more straightforward to use, providing targeted training, and ensuring that the technology functions effectively, which can significantly increase acceptance rates, especially among teachers new to AI technologies (Wijaya et al., 2022).

Diffusion of Innovations Theory

The Diffusion of Innovations Theory (DIT), developed by Everett Rogers in 1962, explains how new ideas, products, or technologies known as innovations can be understood across various cultures or social systems over time. This theory concentrates on highlighting the adoption of innovation. It suggests that people do not adopt new ideas all at once; instead, they undergo a process influenced by factors such as time, social context, and the availability of communication channels at different rates (Rogers, 2014). Different categories of groups will be involved in this process, including innovators, early adopters, early majority, late majority, and laggards. The process begins with the first stage of learning, which involves understanding the concept of innovation, its application, and deciding whether to continue using it. This stage helps in understanding why some innovations become widely accepted quickly, while others take longer to gain traction or fail to gain acceptance at all.

The DIT provides a framework for understanding the dissemination of innovations, explaining how innovations, such as new ideas, practices, behaviors, or technologies, can spread within and between different cultures and social systems over time. This theory is beneficial for investigating the acceptance of adopting AI in examining the interaction between innovation, communication channels, social structure, and time. The findings provide clarification on the factors that may affect the dissemination of their work throughout educational organizations globally (Frei-Landau et al., 2022). For instance, Frei-Landau et al. (2022) employed the DIT to investigate how mobile learning is adopted in teachers' teaching and learning processes, highlighting the importance of compatibility and trialability in promoting its uptake. Likewise, other researchers applied DIT to study the spread of E-learning systems in educational organizations, emphasizing the critical influence of communication channels and social systems in enabling adoption (Pinho et al., 2021). Collectively, these studies demonstrate DIT's capacity to provide a detailed understanding of innovation integration within complex systems, aligning closely with the aims of the current research.

DIT examines the interaction of innovative factors, communication channels, and social systems, making it particularly effective for studying organizational and systemic adoption processes, as observed in higher education institutions worldwide. DIT can clarify how GAI-enhanced educational technologies gain acceptance, emphasizing the importance of aligning with educational goals and effectively communicating benefits throughout the institution. This understanding can inform the development of policy frameworks that optimize the benefits of this emerging technology while mitigating its associated risks (Rogers et al., 2014).

DIT is connected to this topic because it offers a valuable framework for examining the strategic integration of AI-driven educational leadership in schools that are prepared for the future. DIT offers a structured framework for understanding how AI-enhanced tools and procedures can be adopted throughout educational systems, focusing on the roles of innovative traits, such as relative advantage, compatibility, complexity, trialability, and observability. In the context of this topic, DIT clarifies the pathways through which AI initiatives transition from initial exploration to institutionalization, emphasizing the role of leadership in shaping communication channels, cultivating digital trust, and aligning AI applications with organizational values and educational equity objectives. The current theoretical chapter is crucial for creating strategic planning roadmaps that not only facilitate the responsible use of AI but also ensure that implementation is flexible, grounded in ethics, and capable of supporting long-term changes within complex educational organizations.

Findings from several empirical studies have utilized DIT to support various research on implementing AI. For example, Yang & Li (2023) apply DIT to investigate the factors influencing AI adoption in K–12 schools. The study employed a mixed-methods approach that combined surveys and interviews. The study concluded that relative advantages, alignment with existing curricula, and the ability to experiment with the approach have a direct effect on influencing teachers' adoption intentions. The study also highlighted the importance of changing agents, including the school leadership team and technology coaches, in facilitating adoption by providing targeted and up-to-date professional development sessions regularly, aligned with practical guidance for strategic planning regarding the appropriate use of AI tools.

The research by Jin, Yan, Echeverria, Gašević, and Martinez-Maldonado (2025) is one of the first global comparative assessments of AI use and regulation across diverse educational institutions. The authors employed the Diffusion of Innovations Theory as a conceptual framework to examine official regulations and guidelines from forty educational institutions across six global regions. They analyzed how elements influencing the adoption of innovations, such as compatibility (alignment with existing teaching techniques), trialability (the safety of experimentation), and observability (the visibility of AI's impact), affected preparedness for adoption. The study found that firms utilizing proactive policy communication strategies and designating specialized leadership roles for AI governance had higher adoption maturity. Policies that explicitly addressed academic integrity, equity, transparency, and digital trust were more likely to gain acceptance from both educators and learners. The study emphasizes the importance of coordinated leadership involvement, extensive stakeholder engagement, and gradual policy implementation, offering a reproducible framework for K–12 school leaders preparing to integrate AI.

The proposed roadmap is explicitly grounded in the Unified Theory of Acceptance and Use of Technology (UTAUT) and the Diffusion of Innovations Theory (DIT). UTAUT informs individual-level readiness by emphasizing performance expectancy, effort expectancy, social influence, and facilitating conditions, while DIT explains system-level diffusion through trialability, observability, and compatibility. Together, these theories justify a phased strategic approach in which leadership decisions evolve from readiness building to institutionalization.

Figure 1. Theoretical Framework of the Strategic Planning for AI-Powered Educational Leadership

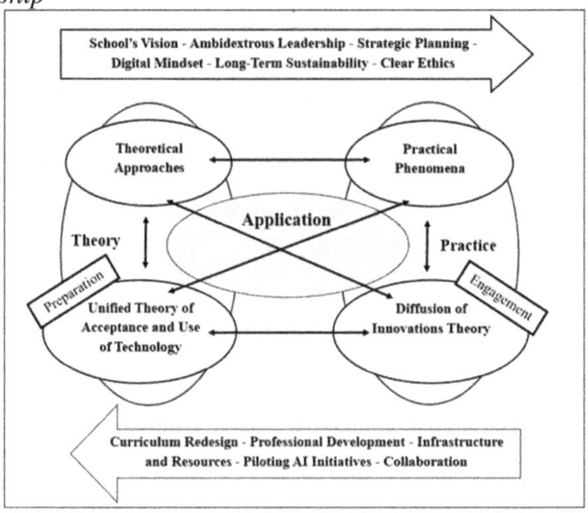

LITERATURE REVIEW

Due to significant technological advancements, nearly all educational organizations, including universities and schools, are devoting considerable attention to incorporating AI into their teaching and learning classroom environment. As AI becomes more prevalent in schools, school leaders and policymakers must reassess their current plans, policies, and strategies to ensure they align with these new technologies (Charles, 2021). Schools also face a significant issue with their AI curriculum, which lacks the necessary changes to meet the diverse needs of children of different ages in K-12 (Yang & Li, 2023). This challenge is a complicated problem because countries have different curricula and systems, which makes it challenging to develop a unified approach that everyone can use. This has also been confirmed by UNESCO (2022, p. 6), which stated, "to guide the future planning of enabling policies, the design of national curricula or institutional study programs, and implementation strategies for AI competency development.".

The implementation of this initiative has been primarily tested among middle and high school students, as their digital proficiency allows for short-term outcomes to be achieved. Students in this age group are often considered the most suitable target for active engagement within this scope. These initiatives have been mainly designed and implemented by computer scientists and AI specialists. Many authors have confirmed that secondary students may be the most suitable age group for implementing AI initiatives. For instance, Knox (2020) stated that the implementation of AI in various subjects is beneficial for this category of students in China. South Korea has offered AI courses to students since 2021 (Soohwan et al., 2020). Thereafter, India, in collaboration with IBM, introduced AI in more than 200 schools, with a particular focus on secondary students (CBSE, 2022). While these approaches demonstrate progress, a critical limitation lies in the limited involvement of secondary school educators, whose expertise and pedagogical insights are essential for designing a practical and sustainable AI curriculum (Miao et al., 2021).

Synthesis of Literature and Identified Strategic Planning Gaps

While existing studies extensively document the potential of artificial intelligence in education, the literature remains fragmented when examined through the lens of school-level strategic planning. Global research emphasizes AI readiness, ethics, and instructional innovation; however, comparatively few studies translate these insights into operational decision-making frameworks for K–12 school leaders. Leadership-focused studies tend to emphasize vision and digital mindset, yet often underplay the complexity of implementation, including staged adoption, capacity building, and evaluation mechanisms. This synthesis reveals a clear gap between conceptual leadership discourse and actionable planning logic. Addressing this gap requires an integrated framework that links adoption theory, leadership decision-making, and practical implementation processes, forming the basis for the strategic roadmap proposed in this chapter.

Ambidextrous Leadership and the Challenge of AI Integration in Schools

In the meantime, the school leadership team faces a significant challenge in maintaining an effective day-to-day routine smoothly and promoting innovations by encouraging new ideas, which are considered "opening behaviors". Simultaneously, school leaders have to ensure adherence to policies and progress tracking as "closing behaviors". In educational research studies, this duality is referred to as ambidextrous leadership, defined by the interaction of opening and closing behaviors that mitigate paradoxes, foster creativity, and facilitate digital transformation.

In educational research, a comparable function is served by the integrated leadership synthesis of instructional and transformational leadership, which enables both bottom-up creativity and systematic, top-down improvement. Ambidexterity offers a more adaptable framework for technological development than conventional educational models, as it emphasizes innovation in dynamic contexts. Findings from various empirical studies on school leaders' digital mindsets, characterized by proactive agility and empathetic perspective-taking, indicate that these mindsets have a positive influence on AI implementation and are particularly effective when paired with ambidextrous leadership. However, the published educational research studies remain limited in explicitly examining how ambidextrous leadership practices can be systematically applied to guide AI-powered transformation in K–12 schools, particularly in relation to how integrated leadership influences AI integration and how leaders' digital mindsets shape specific instructional and transformational practices (Pietsch & Mah, 2024).

A recent research study presents a meta-analysis of over 100 systematic reviews on AI in education, consolidating patterns and identifying gaps in instructional support related to teaching, learning, assessment, and stakeholder engagement. The study focused on school leaders who are responsible for integrating AI in K-12 schools. Results emphasize the role of strategic planning that extends beyond mere technical implementation. These results highlight the crucial role of leaders in developing a system and curriculum that fosters innovative ideas, encouraging students to think critically and connect these concepts to real-life applications beyond classroom discussions, all while aligning with ethical and educational standards. Moreover, leaders must focus on enhancing teachers' qualifications and skills, as well as their knowledge of student data analysis. The above results are consistent with the principles of ambidextrous leadership, which require leaders to foster experimentation and innovation while upholding responsibility and compliance simultaneously (Mustafa et al., 2024).

Balancing AI Innovation with Human-Centered Education

Schools have a significant responsibility in incorporating AI into classrooms for children of all ages. They need to make learning more dynamic and welcoming for everyone, and they must ensure that technology enhances teaching, rather than detracting from it. However, this progress comes with a price. To make schools more efficient with AI-driven technologies, they need to plan carefully, establish a strong framework to support long-term use, ensure that everyone has equal access, strike a balance between innovation and accountability, and prioritize efficiency over pedagogy. While AI can enhance the personalization of learning and simplify administrative tasks, it should never replace instructors. Instructors play a crucial role in providing emotional support to children and helping them develop socially and emotionally. New technologies and their effective use by those in charge will shape the future of education. True success lies in finding a balance between leveraging AI to enhance education and preserving the vital human relationships that make learning meaningful, ethical, and highly influential. Such an approach ensures that the digital transition strengthens schools' main mission instead of weakening it (Göçen, Bulut, & Yurdunkulu, 2025).

Moreover, another research study examines the adaptation of curricula based on various opinions from 440 educators and leaders in the era of generative AI. Results indicate that teachers predominantly augment or modify instructional information, with omissions being relatively infrequent, and that experience significantly influences adaptation methods more than school level. Currently, educational organizations are focusing on using various types of AI tools, such as ChatGPT, which are being increasingly utilized to customize and simplify content. This demonstrates how AI can assist teachers in developing flexible curricula that cater to the diverse needs of all students while still affording teachers the necessary autonomy. This aligns with other studies on curriculum adaptation, which emphasize the importance of adjusting information to meet the needs of students, institutional regulations, and classroom dynamics (Bümen & Holmqvist, 2022; Tas, 2022). Intentional adaptation has been demonstrated to improve student learning outcomes and enhance curriculum effectiveness (Kim et al., 2022). However, educators must reconcile adherence to curricular standards with the complexities of heterogeneous classrooms (Martín-Alonso et al., 2021). The findings revealed that the curriculum required revision, either through traditional means or with the aid of AI, to ensure that all types of learners were included, treated fairly, and engaged in a meaningful manner (Karataş et al., 2025).

Furthermore, a recent study highlights the importance of generating strategic plans to integrate AI that meet the diverse academic needs of different student groups. The study also focuses on providing teachers with professional development sessions, as this is a crucial factor for successful AI implementation. This involves utilizing a clear AI policy, in addition to the need for appropriate technical and human resources, such as secure platforms, mentoring, and IT support, as a critical foundation for sustainable AI use. The study emphasizes that for AI tools in classrooms to be truly safe and fair, every school district needs to adopt policies that clearly state three essentials: the ethical guidelines that will protect students, the reporting and auditing steps that guarantee everyone can see how the technology is used, and the lesson-plan links that make the tools educationally sound. Inserting these steps into district guidelines is not an abstract exercise; the school has to provide a step-by-step guide that connects budget decisions, teacher training, and governance boards in a single, coordinated action plan for the successful and responsible deployment of AI (Ng et al., 2025).

Moorhouse (2024) investigates in his study the importance of educators' and teachers' qualifications and readiness from the beginning of the academic year, particularly the newly joined staff. He emphasizes that schools must prioritize staff knowledge and understanding of the AI integration process through various practical activities and tasks. The study highlighted the adverse effects of lacking coherent guidelines or policies on the adaptation process and students' outcomes. The study's findings explained teachers' concerns regarding students' assessment data privacy. On the other hand, they believe that AI has significant potential for creating and modifying lesson planning, assessments, and resources. Therefore, the main conclusion of this study is the need for comprehensive professional development sessions that deliberately focus on generative AI. Additionally, educational organizations, particularly schools, are responsible for establishing clear frameworks to embed such language into mentoring programs and to ensure that the incorporation of AI is tethered to well-understood pedagogic principles and institutional values.

Similarly, Gouseti (2025) examines the ethical implications of AI in K-12 education, highlighting issues such as privacy, bias, students' rights, and pedagogical suitability. The study highlights the distinct vulnerabilities of young learners and advocates for ethics-based policies that promote accountability and transparency. It also suggests that teachers' moral literacy is just as critical as their technological skills, providing a compelling reason to ensure that AI is used safely in schools. The same required factors were discussed and identified by Zhu and colleagues (2025). Their study highlights the essential role of school leadership teams in establishing clear policies, providing targeted training sessions, modifying curriculum, and generating ethical standards, as well as conducting fair audits, before implementing AI in their daily tasks. Findings from the same study also focus on the crucial role of policymakers and school leaders in ensuring students' equity and rights.

From Theory and Evidence to Strategic Action

The literature and theoretical analysis demonstrate that AI integration in schools is not merely a technical challenge but a leadership and governance problem. Ethical tensions, uneven infrastructure, and teacher readiness gaps require deliberate strategic planning rather than ad hoc adoption. In response to these challenges, the following roadmap translates theoretical insights and empirical evidence into a structured, leadership-oriented planning framework designed to support sustainable and equitable AI implementation in K–12 schools.

ROADMAP FOR FUTURE-READY SCHOOLS:

Drawing on adoption theory, leadership research, and recent global policy guidance, the following roadmap operationalizes AI integration as a strategic leadership process rather than a technical initiative. Each step is analytically grounded in the Unified Theory of Acceptance and Use of Technology (UTAUT) and the Diffusion of Innovations Theory (DIT), translating evidence into decision-making actions that address governance, capacity, ethics, and sustainability.

1. Establish a Shared Vision and Governance Framework for AI

UNESCO (2024a) emphasizes that AI integration in schools must be guided by a clearly articulated vision embedded within governance and long-term strategic planning. From a DIT perspective, this alignment establishes compatibility between innovation and institutional values, while under UTAUT it strengthens social influence by signaling leadership commitment. Without explicit governance, AI adoption risks fragmentation, ethical inconsistency, and stakeholder mistrust. School leaders must therefore formalize AI use through strategic plans, ethical policies, and decision-making structures that apply coherently across curriculum, assessment, and administration.

2. Build Leadership Capacity and a Digital Mindset for Decision-Making Under Uncertainty

Pietsch and Mah (2024) argue that sustainable AI transformation depends on leaders who possess a digital mindset characterized by adaptability, ethical judgment, and strategic foresight. Leadership capacity building directly supports performance expectancy (UTAUT) by enabling leaders to recognize AI's practical value, while DIT positions leaders as change agents who shape adoption trajectories. This step addresses the leadership tension between innovation and accountability, equipping leaders to manage uncertainty without resorting to either resistance or uncritical adoption.

3. Redesign Curriculum to Embed AI Literacy, Equity, and Inclusion

UNESCO (2024b) highlights the need to embed AI literacy and computational thinking across K–12 curricula in inclusive and developmentally appropriate ways. Curriculum redesign enhances compatibility (DIT) and reduces perceived complexity (effort expectancy, UTAUT) for teachers and learners. Leadership decisions at this stage must address equity risks, ensuring that AI-supported personalization strengthens inclusion rather than amplifying existing achievement gaps or marginalizing vulnerable student groups.

4. Deliver Targeted Professional Development Focused on Pedagogy, Ethics, and Practice

Moorhouse (2024) demonstrates that teachers' confidence and pedagogical readiness are decisive factors in AI adoption. Consistent with UTAUT, professional development must strengthen effort expectancy and facilitating conditions by moving beyond tool demonstrations toward pedagogical redesign, ethical use, assessment practices, and classroom implementation realities. This step reduces resistance, mitigates change fatigue, and positions teachers as informed co-designers rather than passive adopters of AI.

5. Ensure Infrastructure Readiness and Sustainable Resource Allocation

OECD (2023) underscores that equitable AI implementation depends on secure, scalable infrastructure and realistic budgeting models. From a DIT lens, weak infrastructure undermines trialability and observability, while UTAUT highlights the necessity of facilitating conditions for sustained use. Leadership teams must confront operational trade-offs explicitly, balancing innovative ambitions with financial, technical, and human resource constraints to avoid unsustainable or inequitable adoption.

6. Pilot AI Initiatives and Evaluate Impact Before System-Wide Adoption

Yang and Li (2023) emphasize that piloting enables schools to test feasibility, surface risks, and refine practices before scaling. This step operationalizes trialability and observability (DIT), supporting evidence-based leadership decisions. Evaluation criteria should include teacher confidence, student engagement, equity of access, and instructional impact, ensuring transparency and preventing premature system-wide implementation of ineffective or ethically problematic practices.

7. Embed Ethical Oversight and Protect Human-Centered Education

Gouseti et al. (2025) stress that ethical governance must underpin all AI-related decisions in K–12 education, where learners are particularly vulnerable. Ethical oversight addresses data privacy, bias mitigation, and transparency while reinforcing the primacy of human relationships in learning. Leadership responsibility at this stage lies in operationalizing ethics through monitoring, reporting mechanisms, and decision checkpoints rather than treating ethics as a static policy statement.

8. Strengthen Stakeholder Collaboration and Distributed Responsibility

World Economic Forum (2023) highlights the importance of cross-sector and stakeholder collaboration in responsible AI adoption. Stakeholder engagement reinforces social influence (UTAUT) and strengthens communication channels critical to diffusion (DIT). Leaders should engage teachers, parents, and students as active stakeholders, ensuring that AI implementation reflects classroom realities and community expectations rather than top-down assumptions.

9. Institutionalize Continuous Review, Learning, and Adaptation

Ng et al. (2025) assert that AI integration is an ongoing process requiring continuous monitoring, policy review, and curriculum renewal. Institutionalizing adaptive mechanisms consolidates earlier roadmap steps into a sustainable leadership cycle. Guided by evidence, ethical reflection, and strategic coherence, leaders can ensure long-term resilience rather than reactive reform in response to rapid technological change.

Taken together, these nine steps address the identified gap between conceptual AI leadership discourse and school-level strategic planning by translating adoption theory and empirical evidence into an integrated, actionable framework for sustainable AI implementation in K–12 schools.

REFERENCES

AI+ Consortium. (2022). *A holistic approach to artificial intelligence (AI) curriculum for K–12 schools*. European Commission. https://ec.europa.eu/programmes/erasmus-plus/projects/

Azzam, A., & Charles, T. (2024). A review of artificial intelligence in K–12 education. *Open Journal of Applied Sciences, 14*(8), 2088–2100. DOI: 10.4236/ojapps.2024.148137

Bellas, F., Guerreiro-Santalla, S., Naya, M., & Duro, R. J. (2023). AI curriculum for European high schools: An embedded intelligence approach. *International Journal of Artificial Intelligence in Education, 33*(2), 399–426. DOI: 10.1007/s40593-022-00315-0

Berkovich, I., & Hassan, T. (2025). Principals' digital transformational leadership, teachers' commitment, and school effectiveness. *Education Inquiry, 16*(2), 177–194. DOI: 10.1080/20004508.2023.2173705

Bümen, N. T., & Holmqvist, M. (2022). Teachers' sense-making and adapting of the national curriculum: A multiple case study in Turkish and Swedish contexts. *Journal of Curriculum Studies, 54*(6), 832–851. DOI: 10.1080/00220272.2022.2121178

CBSE. (2022). *Artificial intelligence curriculum launch*. Central Board of Secondary Education. http://cbseacademic.nic.in/ai.html

Celik, I. (2023). Towards Intelligent-TPACK: Teachers' professional knowledge for ethically integrating AI-based tools into education. *Computers in Human Behavior, 138*, 107468. DOI: 10.1016/j.chb.2022.107468

Charles, T. (2021). The past, present, and future of assessment in higher education. In *The evolution of transnational education* (pp. 126–136). Routledge., DOI: 10.4324/9781003225386-13

Chiu, T. K. F., Meng, H., Chai, C. S., King, I., Wong, S., & Yam, Y. (2021). Creation and evaluation of a pre-tertiary artificial intelligence curriculum. *IEEE Transactions on Education, 65*(1), 30–39. DOI: 10.1109/TE.2021.3085878

Dedering, K., & Pietsch, M. (2023). School leader trust and collective teacher innovativeness: The mediating role of ambidextrous leadership. *Educational Review*. Advance online publication. DOI: 10.1080/00131911.2023.2195593

Dignum, V., Penagos, M., Pigmans, K., & Vosloo, S. (2021). *Policy guidance on AI for children.* UNICEF. https://www.unicef.org/globalinsight/reports/policy-guidance-ai-children

Frei-Landau, R., Muchnik-Rozanov, Y., & Avidov-Ungar, O. (2022). Using diffusion of innovation theory to conceptualize mobile-learning adoption. *Education and Information Technologies, 27*(9), 12811–12838. DOI: 10.1007/s10639-022-11148-8 PMID: 35702319

Ghosh, S., Hughes, M., Hodgkinson, I., & Hughes, P. (2022). Digital transformation of industrial businesses: A dynamic capability approach. *Technovation, 113*, 102414. DOI: 10.1016/j.technovation.2021.102414

Göçen, A., Bulut, M. A., & Yurdunkulu, A. (2025). *AI in school management: A new era of leadership*. AIEOU. https://aieou.web.ox.ac.uk/article/ai-school-management-new-era-leadership

Gouseti, A., James, F., Fallin, L., & Burden, K. (2025). The ethics of using artificial intelligence in K–12 education: A systematic literature review. *Technology, Pedagogy and Education, 34*(2), 161–182. DOI: 10.1080/1475939X.2024.2428601

Grissom, J. A., Egalite, A. J., & Lindsay, C. A. (2021). *How principals affect students and schools.* Wallace Foundation. https://www.wallacefoundation.org

Hermita, N., Wijaya, T. T., Yusron, E., Abidin, Y., Alim, J. A., & Putra, Z. H. (2023). Extending UTAUT to understand digital textbook acceptance. *Frontiers in Education, 8*, 958800. DOI: 10.3389/feduc.2023.958800

Hildebrandt, Y., Valta, M., & Beimborn, D. (2022). Quantifying the digital innovation mindset. In *Proceedings of the Computers and People Research Conference* (pp. 1–9). DOI: 10.1145/3510606.3550202

Holmes, W., & Miao, F. (2023). *Guidance for generative AI in education and research.* UNESCO. https://unesdoc.unesco.org/ark:/48223/pf0000386693

Jin, Y., Yan, L., Echeverria, V., Gašević, D., & Martinez-Maldonado, R. (2025). Generative AI adoption policies in higher education. *Computers and Education: Artificial Intelligence, 8*, 100348. DOI: 10.1016/j.caeai.2024.100348

Kaplan-Rakowski, R., Grotewold, K., Hartwick, P., & Papin, K. (2023). Teachers' perspectives on generative AI. *Journal of Interactive Learning Research, 34*(2), 313–338. DOI: 10.70725/815246mfssgp

Karataş, F., Eriçok, B., & Tanrikulu, L. (2025). AI-driven curriculum adaptation patterns. *British Educational Research Journal, 51*(1), 154–180. DOI: 10.1002/berj.4068

Kim, J., Lee, H., & Cho, Y. H. (2022). Learning design to support student–AI collaboration. *Education and Information Technologies*, *27*(5), 6069–6104. DOI: 10.1007/s10639-021-10831-6

Knox, J. (2020). Artificial intelligence and education in China. *Learning, Media and Technology*, *45*(3), 298–311. DOI: 10.1080/17439884.2020.1754236

Lee, D., Arnold, M., Srivastava, A., Plastow, K., Strelan, P., Ploeckl, F., & Palmer, E. (2024). Educators' perspectives on generative AI. *Computers and Education: Artificial Intelligence*, *6*, 100221. DOI: 10.1016/j.caeai.2024.100221

Luckin, R., & Cukurova, M. (2019). Designing educational technologies in the age of AI. *British Journal of Educational Technology*, *50*(6), 2824–2838. DOI: 10.1111/bjet.12861

Marikyan, D., & Papagiannidis, S. (2023). Unified Theory of Acceptance and Use of Technology: A review. In *TheoryHub Book*. https://open.ncl.ac.uk

Martín-Alonso, D., Sierra, E., & Blanco, N. (2021). Relationships between the curricular program and lived curriculum. *Teaching and Teacher Education*, *105*, 103433. DOI: 10.1016/j.tate.2021.103433

McCarthy, A. M., Maor, D., McConney, A., & Cavanaugh, C. (2023). Digital transformation in education. *Social Sciences & Humanities Open*, *8*(1), 100479. DOI: 10.1016/j.ssaho.2023.100479

Miao, F., Holmes, W., Huang, R., & Zhang, H. (2021). *AI and education: Guidance for policy-makers*. UNESCO. https://unesdoc.unesco.org/ark:/48223/pf0000376709

Moorhouse, B. L. (2024). Teachers' readiness for the generative AI age. *Computers and Education: Artificial Intelligence*, *6*, 100201. DOI: 10.1016/j.caeai.2024.100201

Mustafa, M. Y., Tlili, A., Lampropoulos, G., Huang, R., Jandrić, P., Zhao, J., & Saqr, M. (2024). A systematic review of AI in education literature reviews. *Smart Learning Environments*, *11*(1), 59. DOI: 10.1186/s40561-024-00350-5

Ng, D. T. K., Chan, E. K. C., & Lo, C. K. (2025). School strategies for integrating generative AI. *Computers and Education: Artificial Intelligence*, *100373*, 100373. Advance online publication. DOI: 10.1016/j.caeai.2025.100373

OECD. (2023). *Shaping digital transformation in education*. OECD Publishing., DOI: 10.1787/8f7c1e5f-

Pabst von Ohain, B. A. (2023). *Leadership for digital transformation* (Doctoral dissertation, Technische Universität München).

Pedro, F., Subosa, M., Rivas, A., & Valverde, P. (2019). *Artificial intelligence in education: Challenges and opportunities for sustainable development*. UNESCO.

Pietsch, M., & Mah, D. K. (2024). Leading the AI transformation in schools. *Educational Technology Research and Development*. Advance online publication. DOI: 10.1007/s11423-024-10439-w

Pinho, C., Franco, M., & Mendes, L. (2021). Innovation diffusion in e-learning. *Education and Information Technologies*, *26*(1), 421–440. DOI: 10.1007/s10639-020-10269-2

Radhwan, M. (2025). Opportunities, challenges, and strategies for integrating generative AI in higher education. In ElSayary, A. (Ed.), *Prompt engineering and generative AI applications for teaching and learning*. IGI Global., DOI: 10.4018/979-8-3693-7332-3.ch007

Rauch, R. (2022). *Digital mindsets: The analysis of a multidimensional construct*. Springer Nature., DOI: 10.1007/978-3-658-39753-1

Rogers, E. M. (1962). *Diffusion of innovations*. Free Press.

Rogers, E. M. (2014). *Diffusion of innovations* (5th ed.). Simon & Schuster.

Rogers, E. M., Singhal, A., & Quinlan, M. M. (2014). Diffusion of innovations. In *An integrated approach to communication theory and research* (pp. 432–448). Routledge., DOI: 10.4324/9780203710753-35

Schmitz, M. L., Antonietti, C., Consoli, T., Cattaneo, A., Gonon, P., & Petko, D. (2023). Transformational leadership for technology integration in schools. *Computers & Education*, *204*, 104880. DOI: 10.1016/j.compedu.2023.104880

Singh, N., Jain, M., Kamal, M. M., Bodhi, R., & Gupta, B. (2024). Technological paradoxes and AI implementation. *Technological Forecasting and Social Change*, *198*, 122967. DOI: 10.1016/j.techfore.2023.122967

Soohwan, K., Minjeong, L., Hyeoncheol, K., & Seonghun, K. (2020). Review on AI education for K–12. *Journal of Korean Association of Computer Education*, *23*(4), 1–11. DOI: 10.32431/KACE.2020.23.4.001

Tas, M. A. (2022). Curriculum adaptation in disadvantaged secondary schools. *Pegem Journal of Education and Instruction*, *12*(1), 10–24. DOI: 10.47750/pegegog.12.01.02

TKF, C. (. (2021). A holistic approach to AI curriculum for K–12 schools. *TechTrends*, *65*, 796–807. DOI: 10.1007/s11528-021-00637-1

UNESCO. (2022). *K–12 AI curricula: A mapping of government-endorsed AI curricula*. UNESCO. https://unesdoc.unesco.org/ark:/48223/pf0000380602

UNESCO. (2024a). *AI competency framework for students*. UNESCO Publishing., DOI: 10.54675/JKJB9835

UNESCO. (2024b). *AI competency framework for teachers*. UNESCO Publishing., DOI: 10.54675/ZJTE2084

Uno, H. B., & Umar, M. K. (2023). *Mengelola kecerdasan dalam pembelajaran*. Bumi Aksara.

Venkatesh, V., Morris, M. G., Davis, G. B., & Davis, F. D. (2003). User acceptance of information technology. *Management Information Systems Quarterly*, *27*(3), 425–478. DOI: 10.2307/30036540

Wijaya, T. T., Cao, Y., Bernard, M., Rahmadi, I. F., Lavicza, Z., & Surjono, H. D. (2022). Factors influencing microgame adoption. *Frontiers in Psychology*, *13*, 952549. DOI: 10.3389/fpsyg.2022.952549 PMID: 36160545

World Economic Forum. (2023). *Shaping the future of learning: The role of AI in education systems*. https://www.weforum.org/publications/

Yang, Z., & Li, M. (2023). Diffusion of innovation theory and AI adoption in K–12 education. *Computers & Education*, *197*, 104709. DOI: 10.1016/j.compedu.2023.104709

Zhu, H., Sun, Y., & Yang, J. (2025). Responsible AI in education. *Humanities & Social Sciences Communications*, *12*(1), 52. Advance online publication. DOI: 10.63313/SSH.9054

Chapter 8
Local Responses to Global Shifts:
AI Policy Development in a Singaporean and an East Malaysian University

Aileen Wanli Lam
http://orcid.org/0000-0002-2930-3561
National University of Singapore, Singapore

Daron Benjamin Loo
http://orcid.org/0000-0001-9203-3608
Universiti Malaysia Sabah, Malaysia

ABSTRACT

The premise of this chapter is to observe the uptake and integration of AI in higher education through the examination of relevant information from materials publicly available on the internet, comprising policy and research papers, as well as news and announcements. The contexts being examined are public universities located in Singapore and Malaysia. Based on the analysis of information, the findings indicate that Singapore is leading in terms of its efforts to ramp up AI literacy and integration in different sectors and layers of its population; meanwhile, Malaysia remains at an exploratory and nascent stage, where it is only rolling out recommendations for AI integration and collecting information about AI in education. The comparison between the two contexts shows different trajectories, though being geographically close to one another. The main contribution of this chapter is to highlight and affirm the different stages of implementation, including the opportunities and challenges faced in Asian contexts in the use of AI, especially at the university setting.

DOI: 10.4018/979-8-3373-4908-4.ch008

INTRODUCTION

Artificial Intelligence (AI) has become increasingly prevalent in industries and educational settings. Governments around the world have shown intense interest in AI advances with advocates emphasizing AI's economic, technological, social and geopolitical value (Schiff et al., 2020; Salas-Pilco, 2021; Jin et al., 2025) and framing it as inevitable and necessary. On one hand, governments are keen on utilizing AI technology for economic benefits but on the other, they understand the need to regulate potential issues related to ethics, transparency, responsibility and inclusivity (Xu et al., 2024).

In 2025, the market size in AI worldwide is projected to reach US$244.23bn and this growth is expected to continue exponentially to US$1,005.36bn in 2031 (Statista, 2025). Companies have begun upskilling their workforce in AI and Generative Artificial Intelligence (GenAI) with 29% of companies worldwide reporting doing so for over one-quarter of their workforce in 2025 (Statista, 2025). Not only is AI literacy needed for those entering specialized industries closely engaged in AI technology but also for those across diverse fields (Yang et al., 2025).

Educators have also responded to changes in the industry by accepting the pervasiveness of AI with some institutes of higher learning rolling out AI-focused programs and/or issuing policies, guidelines and support for students and staff, both academic and non-academic (Abbasi et al., 2025). These responses are often dependent on the university's stance, influenced by their history, access to resources and leadership style (Altbach, 2004). Beyond the internal context, lies a more entwined and intricate connection between the university's AI policy development and the external influences including national AI policies and their nation's technological contexts (Schiff, 2022; Frana, 2024; Lee et al., 2023) which are often influenced by the economic imperative and the argument for international competitiveness (Dai et al., 2025; Schiff, 2022; Lee, 2001). To demonstrate this complexity, this paper aims to offer a comparative view on national AI policies and technological contexts of two Asian countries - Singapore and Malaysia, and also consider local responses, namely through relevant policies, programs, and activities at the National University of Singapore (NUS) and Universiti Malaysia Sabah (UMS).

The focus on Asia is significant because of the rising influence of AI in the region. The market size in AI is predicted to reach US$76.89bn in Asia in 2025 (Statista, 2025). In fact, East Asia ranked third out of nine regions (188 countries) on the 2024 Government AI Readiness Index, at 47.59 across three pillars: Government, Technology Sector, and Data & Infrastructure. In the west, the North American region ranked first at 82.6 and the Western European region ranked second at 69.56. Singapore ranked 2nd overall in Government AI Readiness at 84.25 while Malaysia ranked 24th at 71.40 (Oxford Insights, 2025) showing the significant emphasis placed by the governments of these two countries.

LITERATURE REVIEW

Hohman (2025) conducted a global round-up of national AI policy developments of 67 countries across seven regions including Europe, North America, South America, Australia, Asia, Africa and the Middle East, and found efforts to "include legislation, national AI strategies and policies, sector-specific regulation, and voluntary guidelines". Van Berkel et al. (2020) did a systematic study of national AI policy documents across twenty-five countries and identified ten prevalent and more specific topics of discussion which include development strategy, infrastructure, private sector and public sector opportunities, data governance, ethical frameworks, education, healthcare, collaboration and research for both academic and industry perspectives. Interestingly, this study also found that geographically related countries tended to have similarities in their AI policies though there may be differing ethical focuses and argues the need for alignment of AI development to local cultures and ethical values.

Schiff (2022), in his analysis of 24 national AI policy strategies found that education is prioritised though the focus is commonly on Education for AI which is the training needed to produce highly-skilled AI talent ready for the workforce as opposed to a smaller number of AI policy strategies focusing on the use of AI for education through teaching and learning tools such as intelligent tutoring systems and argues that more policy conversations in AI for Education/ AI in Education (AIED) are needed. In fact, the integration of AIED holds the promise of student agency and educational equity through personalized learning experiences catered to the individual's needs and learning styles. The use of educational technology enhanced by AI has also been argued to strengthen instructional content, improve assessment methods, bolster interactive technologies such as virtual reality technologies and even streamline administrative processes for efficiency (Ayeni et al., 2024). In fact, GenAI tools can now create outputs such as text, images, videos, and even generate datasets. GenAI has increasingly become a focus of policy and research because of the opportunities presented though its limitations and the implications are acknowledged (Giannakos et al., 2025).

A comparison of two studies conducted by UNESCO in 2023 and 2025 shows the growing emphasis in policy making. In a study of 450 schools and universities in 2023, fewer than 10% had institutional policies or formal guidelines on the use of AI (UNESCO, 2023). However, in a 2025 survey with 400 respondents across 90 countries, 19% responded that there were formal AI policies in their institutions and 42% reported that their institutions were developing AI guiding frameworks. Around 70% of institutions in North America and Europe already had or were developing guiding frameworks. Interestingly, the interviews conducted revealed the differences in approaches. For example, some institutions choose to regulate AI use by focusing on detection while others employ a more iterative approach in consultation with students and faculty and go on to introduce AI literacy courses or redesign assessment systems (UNESCO, 2025). Most, however, were cautiously open to the integration of GenAI tools like ChatGPT in educational contexts based on a study of the policy papers of about 100 top universities in the US (Wang et al., 2024). It was also found that a significant emphasis on creating resources for educators was seen with 67.4% of universities providing resources designed for faculty and instructors while fewer resources were designed for students at 17.8% and only 14.7% offered broad guidelines for faculty, students and staff collectively. Wang et al. (2024) also emphasized the need for policies that take into account disciplinary differences. On the other hand, Dai et al.'s (2024) study on the AI policies of 30 universities in the QS top 60 Asian universities found that Asian universities were at varying stages in policy development with some policy gaps such as the exclusion of non-academic staff in policy making and a preference for traditional academic standards in academic integrity and authenticity.

To understand how AI is integrated in the academic setting, it may be worthwhile to consider Chan's (2023) AI Ecological Education Policy Framework, developed through quantitative and qualitative data from 457 students and 180 staff in Hong Kong universities. This Framework explores AI policies through three dimensions meant to reflect different stakeholders who are involved in the use of AI in education, which are the teachers, senior management and the teaching and learning and IT staff.

The three dimensions are:

(1) Pedagogical Dimension - Teachers (e.g. rethinking assessments/examinations, developing holistic competencies/ generic skills, preparation for the AI-driven workplace, encouraging a balanced approach)
(2) Governance Dimension - Senior Management (e.g. understanding and preventing academic misconduct/ethical dilemmas, addressing data privacy, transparency, accountability and security, attributing AI technologies, ensuring equitable access)
(3) Operational dimension - Teaching and Learning and IT staff (e.g. monitoring and evaluating AI implementation, training and support for teachers, staff and students)

METHOD

Data collection was done through ethnographic document analysis, where pertinent documents such as public government or industry reports, policy papers, journal articles, industry reports and press releases related to the phenomenon under investigation were consolidated and then understood in relation to their immediate relevant context (see Jacobsson, 2022). This also included the researchers' observations and lived experiences in interacting with these documents (McIntosh & Wright, 2019). Subsequently, the educational policies, programs and activities of each university were analyzed through the AI Ecological Education Policy framework (Chan, 2023), which explores three dimensions of (1) governance, (2) pedagogy and (3) operation before an analysis of leadership priorities is done.

RESULTS

To form a comprehensive understanding of how AI may be informed and how it may be integrated into education, the economic background of each country should be considered. In Table 1 below, information about the population, GDP, expenditure and economic composition for both Singapore and Malaysia are provided.

Country Information

Table 1. Country Comparison

	Singapore	Malaysia
Population	6, 111, 200 (2025)	35, 977, 838 (2025)
Annual GDP	$547, 387M (2024)	$422, 227M (2024)
GDP per capita	$90, 674 (2024)	$12, 618 (2024)
Government expenditure	14.51% of GDP (2024)	23.88% of GDP (2024)
Economic composition	Agriculture 0.03%, Industry 22.4%, Service sector 72.45% (2023)	Agriculture 7.79%, Industry 37.57%, Service sector 53.42% (2023)

Discussion

As shown in Table 1, Singapore has a smaller population at around 6 million as compared to Malaysia at around 36 million (2025) but has a higher Annual Gross

Domestic Product (GDP) and an even higher GPD per capita of $90,674 as opposed to $12,618 (2024). The Singapore government also operates a relatively smaller budget to its GDP as compared to the Malaysia government at 14.51% as compared to 23.88% (O' Neill, 2025).

The economic composition between the two countries is also different, which may explain the differing emphasis on AI implementation. Singapore has a larger service sector at 72.54% as compared to Malaysia at 53.42% (2024) while Malaysia has a larger agriculture sector than Singapore at 7.79% as compared to 0.03% (O' Neill, 2025). Singapore focuses on finance, trade, technology and high-end manufacturing (Ferenczy, 2025) while Malaysia is an export-driven economy.

In terms of the countries' focus on supporting AI infrastructure through sustainable means, Singapore has begun exploring renewable energy and sources to minimize the risk of disruption to AI-driven outputs and production. This also includes putting in mechanisms to optimize the use of and avoid wastage of energy resources in supporting AI (Islam et al., 2024). Malaysia, on the other hand, presents a different scenario as efforts have only been focused on using AI to identify key areas where energy could be better used and managed (Hasan et al., 2024).

Comparison of National Responses: AI Policies and Strategies

This next section presents information regarding Singapore and Malaysia's policy and strategies on AI use. Information was collected from public and official reports, news articles and announcements, as well as research papers.

Singapore

Singapore has had a long history in digitalizing the nation (Lee, 2024). The National computerization plan started in the 1980s with the establishment of the National Computer Board (NCB) in 1981 which focused on digitizing the economy and public sector. By 1992, the IT2000 Masterplan was introduced to guide Singapore towards becoming an intelligent island and in 1997 the nationwide broadband network (Singapore ONE network) began providing widespread internet connectivity across the nation. By 2014, the Smart Nation Program was launched for more efficiency, convenience and sustainability. It also aimed to shift the nation's focus towards data and AI. Following this, the Intelligent Nation 2015 Masterplan was launched, and the Government Technology Agency (GovTech) was formed in 2016 to develop infrastructure and implement digital solutions for the government, businesses and the citizens (GovTech, 2025). In 2017, AI Singapore was launched as a national AI research and development program which brought together the National Research foundation, the Smart Nation Digital Government Office, Economic Development

Board, Infocomm Media Development Authority, SG innovate, healthcare IT units, Singapore-based research institutions and AI startups. AI Singapore aimed to bring together Singapore-based research institutions and AI start-ups/companies to train, collaborate and develop AI products (AI Singapore, 2025a). It launched the AI Apprenticeship Program in 2018 (AI Singapore, 2025b) and planned to integrate educational resources and create online courses for school students, practitioners and citizens of all ages and in all professions (Xu et al., 2022). At the same time, universities also started offering more AI -focused courses (OpenGov, 2018; EDB Singapore 2018).

Finally, the "National AI Strategy" (NAIS) termed "Advancing our Smart Nation Journey" was introduced in 2019 and focused on foundational infrastructure and regulatory efforts. It increased research input and financial support for AI education. NAIS also looked into AI projects in sectors like municipal services, freight planning, municipal services, personalized education in schools and border clearance operations (Lee, 2024). By 2023, NAIS took on a more global outlook with the National AI strategy 2.0 termed "AI for the Public Good for Singapore and the World". NAIS2.0 focuses on three systems and ten enablers: (1) Activity Drivers - Industry, Government and Research, (2) People and Communities - Talent, Capabilities, Placemaking (3) Infrastructure and environment - Compute, Data, Trust environment, leader in thought and action. NAIS2.0 champions partnerships between industry, government and academia and works to create spaces for innovation and encourages private sector action to position Singapore globally (Smart Nation Singapore, 2025; Fercenczy, 2025). Singapore also plans to invest more than $1 billion to boost AI activities to sharpen Singapore's competitiveness (Tan, 2024; Glenn, 2025) and has committed more than $500 million through AI Singapore (Smart Nation Singapore, 2025). A large proportion of these investments would probably be directed towards international research collaborations conducted by the National University of Singapore (NUS) and Nanyang Technological University (NTU) (Lee, 2024).

Beyond this, the government encourages citizens to develop their AI skills for daily living by enhancing the Infocomm Media Development Authority (IMDA)'s Digital Skills for Life framework while firstly, working with partners to offer more GenAI programs and content, and secondly, showcasing emerging technologies that can benefit citizens across public libraries. IMDA is also working with SkillsFuture Singapore to include AI and GenAI curriculum into their training programs (Ministry of Digital Development and Information, 2025) to support Singaporeans in their development of future-ready career skills through education and training.

In schools, AI-powered tools have also been introduced to aid in personalized learning, support data generation to improve curriculum and pedagogy, and streamline administrative processes (Nanyang Technological University Singapore, 2025) which is aligned with the Ministry of Education's EdTech Masterplan 2030 and its vision - "Technology-transformed learning, to prepare students for a technology-transformed world" where one of its key implementation focus is to "empower students' learning through greater customization and personalization with EdTech" including AI-enabled EdTech tools (Ministry of Education, n.d.).

Based on how digitalization and AI have been integrated into various societal layers and sectors in Singapore, it can be seen that the nation's government is actively preparing for digitalization and widespread AI adoption/advances through education, training and development.

Malaysia

The introduction of AI into the administrative and civil sectors in Malaysia took place in the early 2020s, with guidelines being developed to steer improvement in the development of public services. This led to a roadmap in 2021, called the Malaysia National Artificial Intelligence Roadmap (AI-RMAP), which was jointly overseen by Universiti Teknologi Malaysia (UTM), PIKOM (Persatuan Industri Komputer dan Multimedia Malaysia, or the National Tech Association of Malaysia) and MOSTI (Ministry of Science, Technology and Innovation). This also involved creating a sandbox environment where new technologies and startups may be supported and tested. While this foundational work had been laid out, challenges have been reported in the quality of integration of AI into various sectors in the nation. Mahusin et al. (2024) cited limited technical expertise, weak legal frameworks for data protection, and resistance towards organizational change as factors that have contributed to this issue.

The AI-RMAP was subsequently updated in 2023, where several key points relevant to higher education were made, such as the critical importance of AI as the driving force for educational transformation, as well as a cornerstone to promote a quadruple helix collaboration between government, academia, industry, and society. Several Malaysian public universities have also been identified as key players in the promotion and development of AI in the higher education sector, namely Universiti Kebangsaan Malaysia (the National University of Malaysia), Universiti Teknologi Malaysia and Universiti Malaysia Kelantan. Through these efforts, the nation hopes to improve the ethical use of AI, especially as support in learning and assessment, as well as to raise awareness and literacy among educators and students of the potential positive impacts of AI.

Subsequently, in 2024, Malaysia released the National Guidelines on AI Governance and Ethics, again through MOSTI. In the guideline, several recommendations were made in relation to the integration of AI in higher education. For instance, the document suggests that university lecturers and students be informed on issues related to ethical dilemmas, bias mitigation, and data privacy arising from the use of AI. In conjunction with this, universities have also been urged to invest and deploy systems that would support the ethical use of AI tools, such as AI-detection capabilities, as well as internal administrative systems and bodies that would oversee decision-making in the use of AI. Besides using AI for educational purposes, the government also intends for related technologies to be used to promote the well-being of the Malaysian society, as well as to create an inclusive environment where information may be accessible to students, regardless of their background.

In 2025, efforts were made to clarify how AI should be integrated into curriculum development in higher education. This led to the drafting of program standards for universities by the Malaysian Qualifications Agency, which is a government agency that oversees the accreditation of local and international study programs offered by both public and private universities in Malaysia. So far, the working draft indicates the need for universities to ensure that Malaysian university students receive enough exposure and opportunities to develop AI literacy. The working draft also recommends that universities make use of AI technology to manage students' learning trajectories by using it to monitor their progress and offer interventions, if needed. In terms of the development of an AI ecology, the working draft suggests that universities in Malaysia look towards other institutions who have implemented and integrated AI into both administrative and teaching and learning processes; unfortunately, at this time, this working draft does not really have any concrete or specific steps for how AI should shape higher education.

While there are guidelines and policies being developed, this has not coincided with the perceptions held by the population. Artificial Intelligence Report (2024) indicated that in Malaysia, there has not been any increase in perceptions towards the relevance of AI technology and services used in everyday life. In fact, there has been a decline, not only in awareness, but also in trust and excitement about AI. This decline includes trust towards the handling of personal data by AI companies. This decline may be reflected in studies concerning the use of AI in particular industries. One example is the study of Phang et al. (2024) on the use of AI in healthcare, where the authors discuss how there is a lack of legislative oversight, ambiguous long-term plans in using AI to support healthcare, and even the lack of understanding of what constitutes ethical and acceptable use of AI-assisted analyses of information and personal data. The same study also highlighted that AI tools may not be ready to be used or tested at a large scale, given the limited data training exercises involving the Malaysian population. The negative trend associated with the use and integration of AI may also be observed through the limited research work done on it in various sectors. In searching for relevant information, many of the results indicated that research is done primarily at the university setting, where students' or lecturers' readiness and perspectives about the use and integration of AI were examined (Razak et al., 2025; Mat Yusoff et al., 2025). Studies in other sectors, however, remain few. As of 2025, when looking at the overall studies on the use and integration of AI, many remain focused on the perceived prospects and risks about the use of AI (e.g., perceived challenges in the Malaysian insurance industry, Ramachandaran et al., 2025; challenges of adoption among public relations practitioners, Ahmad et al., 2025; and understanding consumer behaviour, Ghazali et al., 2025).

Discussion

In general, both countries have put into place digital strategies and AI policies for their nations but there are differences in the robustness and operationalization of these strategies. In the Singaporean context, the use of AI may be seen as cross-sectional that involves different parties; on the Malaysian side, some efforts may be observed in the education sector, primarily universities. Nonetheless, this remains rather academic and theoretical rather than applied. Furthermore, while Singapore is currently looking at how AI may be positioned to support and boost its human and economic capital, Malaysia is still considering fundamental issues pertaining to the use of AI, such as the populations' familiarity towards AI and the ethical implications of integrating AI.

Comparison of Local Responses: University programs, policies and activities

NUS

Education For AI. NUS runs specialized AI programs such as the Bachelor of Computing in Business Artificial Intelligence System, the Bachelor of Computing in Artificial Intelligence, the Bachelor of Engineering in Robotics and Machine Intelligence as well as the Master of Computing in Artificial Intelligence, Master of Science in Artificial Intelligence and Innovation, and Master of Technology in Artificial Intelligence Systems. It also offers AI-related modules such as an Introduction to AI and Machine Learning, Foundations of Artificial Intelligence, Foundations of Machine Learning, Full-stack Software Engineering for AI solutions, AI and Machine Learning Techniques, Smart Systems and AI Governance, Generative AI and Business Applications, AI planning and decision making and AI Solutioning Capstone project (Nus Computer, n.d.; Tushara, 2025).

It also houses the NUS Artificial Intelligence Institute that drives research programs that encourage collaborations on real-world applications across "AI + X domains" such as healthcare and human potential, logistics, manufacturing and robotics, finance and economy, urban sustainability, education, humanities and social sciences, science. It also looks into AI Governance and Policy as well as Foundational AI which includes AI hardware/ software systems and AI theory (Nus Artificial Intelligence Institute, n.d). These collaborations extend to their industry partners such as IBM, Google, NEC Corporation Japan and Home Team Science and Technology Agency (Leow, 2024; Nus Artificial Intelligence Institute, n.d.).

AI for Education. NUS first introduced an Interim policy for the use of AI in Teaching and Learning in 2023 and then shared their updated AI Policy in 2024 (Nus Libraries, n.d.).

The interim AI policy (2023) stated that the university would not ban the use of AI tools among students and staff but would instead benefit from guidance regarding the proper use of technology. It reminded educators not to rely on AI detectors because of the lack of accuracy and possible biases. The policy encouraged educators to focus on testing higher order skills beyond the reach of AI, consider integrating AI into assignments and/or changing the way assessments are conducted for the testing of basic skills (e.g. supervised arrangements). Educators were given the autonomy to decide if they would allow the use of generative AI tools depending on whether it defeated or advanced the learning goals. The policy paper then addressed the students by explaining the broad principles and rationale for guidelines (i.e. need to demonstrate voice and thought, issues of plagiarism when one represents AI's output as their own; challenges with intellectual property) and provided guidelines for typical scenarios of AI tool usage (i.e. legitimate and improper use) and how they could declare their use of AI. Students were encouraged to be aware of the limitations of GenAI tools and to be responsible for their work.

The 2024 AI policy document made it clear that the university was willing to "embrace the ethical and appropriate use of AI tools among students and staff". It expanded on the 2023 policy by providing more information for educators through the explicit "Guidelines for Educators". It encouraged course developers and tutors to declare their use of AI in their courses (e.g. content creation, virtual tutors), get explicit approval for AI tools used to provide instruction (e.g. deliver and mark assignments, give feedback, answer academic queries, offer personalized learning experiences) and take the final responsibility for the quality of the courses, It also stated clearly the university's stance that a human reviewer was needed to review subjective/ open-ended assessments. The 2024 policy document also expanded on supervised assessments (i.e. those that forbade the use of AI) and reminded educators that those assessments should be conducted face-to-face under instructor supervision to ensure that students did not access AI tools because the default assumption for unsupervised assessments was that students were permitted to use AI tools as long as they acknowledged their use of AI. The document encouraged tutor-student discussion on the pros and cons of using AI tools for learning purposes (i.e. long-term learning; academic integrity) and highlighted the possibility of a digital divide.

These AI policy documents were made known to the NUS community via email and the NUS libraries website. The latter also provided AI guidelines for students through infographics on the Human-AI partnership, the limitations of AI and best practices in using AI for academic work to better inform students about generative AI usage. Beyond this, NUS also introduced an online course for new students titled "Guide to use of Generative AI tools" through their Transition to Higher Education (T.H.E) Program (NUSOne, n.d.). This course explores responsible and appropriate use of GenAI tools for learning.

Not only did the university focus on students, but it also focused on tutors. NUS rolled out AI courses for NUS academics and explained NUS' position on embracing AI, provided guidance on how educators can leverage AI for teaching and learning, and included optional courses meant to provide educators with a fundamental understanding of artificial learning and machine learning useful for teaching and research.

The Centre for Teaching, Learning and Technology also launched the NUS AI community-of-practice which hosts workshops and events such as the 'AI in Education showcase of teaching breakthroughs and new courses' and also provided AI use cases for educators to learn from via their internal portal (NUS Centre for Teaching, Learning and Technology, n.d.). In particular, the use cases showed how GenAI has been used in class to generate ideas and model how it has been used as a personal assistant, teaching assistant and analyst, and even how it has been used to create assignments. This portal also provides a list of NUS cloud-assessed AI tools that educators can tap on. This AI community-of-practice is supported by the Generative AI Team made up of various faculty members who are also part of the NUS Teaching Academy. This project team's goal is to keep up with and update educators on ways to leverage GenAI for teaching and learning, provide and vet case-studies, research and report ground sentiments, and share issues arising from the use of AI in education and at work (NUS Teaching Academy, n.d.)

Moreover, the AI Centre for Educational Technologies (AICET) which is hosted at NUS, provides technical expertise to help educators develop AI software to support pedagogy including learning management systems, feedback and assessment tools and personalized learning tools. AICET also provides pedagogical support through consultations regarding AI tool integration in teaching and can aid collaboration with software engineers to create prototypes that match pedagogical needs (AI Centre for Educational Technologies, n.d.). AICET was set up jointly by the Smart Nation and Digital Government office and the Ministry of Education and is funded by AI Singapore. It has created software such as SchoIAIstic for roleplaying scenarios in legal and nursing education (Liu, et al, 2025). SchoIAIstic is beneficial not only for students but also educators as they can create, modify and administer prompts, track learning patterns and review student interactions with AI easily.

Beyond this, NUS has also explored and created tools to support the use of AI in education. For example, NUS IT created its own in-house AI platform named AI-Know that latches on large language models (LLMS) by integrating the latest AI models from OpenAI, Google and Anthropic. It houses a suite of AI productivity tools including AI-Chat which is a chatbot with access to a large knowledge base, AI-Guide which specializes in NUS policy-related queries, AI-Draw to create images, AI-Minute to generate meeting minutes, Alca x- IT care to provide AI powered IT support and AI-create to enable staff to create AI Solutions (Nus News, 2025). AI-know is one of the NUS approved AI-tools that instructors can use whenever NUS data is involved.

With all this support and thrust towards AI for education, the university then motivates academics to embrace AI by introducing the new teaching award titled the "Annual Innovative Teaching Excellence Award" which has a subcategory that focuses on the creative and purposeful ways of using artificial intelligence.

AI for non-academic purposes. In NUS, AI tools can also be used beyond the classroom. Various centres and departments have used the AI-create function on AI-know to create AI solutions for students and staff.

For example, the NUS Centre for Future-ready Graduates has created a virtual career guidance chatbot named CFG AI-Xplore to provide students with career guidance based on their stage of study, interests and needs. This tool not only offers users advice on career options and job preparation, but it can also even recommend campus workshops, events and resources offered by the centre for their career development (Nus Centre For Future-ready Graduates, n.d.).

Another example of AI solutions would be for staff at the SingHealth Duke-NUS Academic Medical Centre. The medical centre built a custom GPT named "AskDD" using AI-create to provide academic career development guidance. It allowed users to navigate promotion and tenure policies and processes easily, and users have rated it high on usability and responsiveness (Yeo et al., 2025).

Beyond support for students and academic staff, NUS has placed an emphasis on data literacy and artificial intelligence skills for its executive and administrative staff (NUSnews, 2021). From 2020, NUS has offered the Data Literacy Program (DLP) and Artificial Intelligence Competency Program (AICP) to guide staff in understanding and applying new technologies at work. As of 2025, 4205 learners have completed the DLP basic course with others enrolled in the intermediate and advanced DLP course. Staff are also encouraged to collaborate with others on work-related projects and in 2021, over 400 projects were presented. As of 2025, 4968 learners have completed the AICC basic course with others enrolled in the intermediate course and the university is planning on rolling out the advanced course.

Discussion. As a whole, there is alignment between the National AI policy and the NUS AI policy with both placing emphasis on the adoption of AI technologies into varying contexts. Based on the AI courses offered at NUS, it can also be seen that an emphasis has been placed on preparing students to join the AI industry and/ or are equipped with the skills to use AI for education and at the workplace (i.e. the pedagogical dimension). This can be seen in the AI courses (e.g. Bachelor programs, Master programs, modules), the AI policies as well as the concerted move by the university through the Centre for Teaching, Learning and Technology and the AI Centre for Educational Technologies to encourage educators to embrace AI tools in their pedagogy. These centres are also able to provide staff training and development opportunities such as through the AI Community of practice and the consultancy for educators as well as monitor and evaluate AI implementation which is aligned with the Operational Dimension of the AI Ecological Education Policy framework (Chan, 2023)

The AI policies were also aligned with the pedagogical dimension in the framework and took on a balanced approach to AI adoption by emphasizing the competencies and skills needed in an AI-driven environment while still giving autonomy to educators to decide whether AI tools should be embedded into their courses and/or allowed in assessments depending on course learning outcomes. It also addressed the governance dimension by emphasizing accountability and attribution (i.e. AI declaration) which worked towards understanding and preventing academic misconduct.

Furthermore, AI literacy is encouraged among the executive and administrative staff through the Data Literacy Program and the Artificial Intelligence Competency Program which further strengthens the operational dimension in the framework. On top of this, NUS developed an in-house resource, AI-know, which helped address issues of data privacy and security especially when dealing with sensitive data and enhanced governance. The other functions such as AI-draw, AI-minute and AI-create which are features on AI-know create a one-stop platform to access multiple AI functions for different purposes which promotes equitable access to AI tools within the NUS community.

In all, the programs, policies and activities in NUS have shown strong intention in governance, pedagogical soundness and operational readiness.

UMS

At the moment, there are no specific guidelines produced by UMS with regards to the role and use of AI in teaching, learning, research, and even administrative processes. An Artificial Intelligence Research Unit (AIRU) was announced a decade ago in 2015; nonetheless, an Internet search for any information or activities conducted by this particular Unit yielded no results. In terms of courses offered, so far, UMS only has one course dedicated to artificial intelligence – KT24202 Artificial Intelligence – offered by the Faculty of Computing and Informatics to only its students. No information about this course such as its synopsis or objectives are publicly available on the University website or the internet. In terms of the impact that the University's staff had on AI at the global level, several researchers were identified as key contributors (in terms of work being cited).

There have been various efforts either initiated by the University (top-down), or by the various entities at the University (bottom up). In a recent top-down effort, the University had mandated that all its academic and administrative staff complete an online survey. The purpose of this survey seemed to point towards the development of AI guidelines to be used at the University. This mandatory survey was distributed by the University's Centre for E-Learning and was being carried out in collaboration with the Commonwealth of Learning, an organization based in Canada that supports development of distance education and open learning. The survey contained 31 items, ranging from perceptive items, open-ended items, and scalar items that required respondents to indicate their level of agreement. The survey was interested to know the current practices of lecturers in using AI, their knowledge of and participation in efforts in developing AI literacy at the university level, and their comments for future development of AI in teaching and learning (Universiti Malaysia Sabah, 2025c). In recent months, however, the Centre for E-Learning had experienced some redeployment of its staff and had been subsumed under the Centre for Academic Excellence and Development. Its function and responsibilities under this new management have yet to be revealed.

There are bottom-up initiatives done by various departments, faculties, and institutes at the university. These initiatives have been largely in the form of organizing conferences, such as that co-organized by the Faculty of Engineering of the University of "IEEE International Conference on Artificial Intelligence in Engineering and Technology 2025", held at the end of August 2025 at the Sabah International Convention Centre in Kota Kinabalu (IEEE Sabah Subsection, 2025).

There were also AI-related talks, such as that organized by the Department of Leadership and Talent Development of the University, entitled, "Artificial Intelligence Driving Academic Impact", which was held on the 20th of February 2025. This event was done in the form of a workshop, where educators and administrators at the University were given practical skills and knowledge about integrating AI into their work. This event was open not just to university lecturers, but also the university administrators and support staff (Universiti Malaysia Sabah, 2025b).

The AI initiatives of the University have not been bound to the higher education setting, as there have also been collaborative efforts with other local educational institutions. For instance, the University's Faculty of Computing and Informatics recently signed a Letter of Intent with Kota Kinabalu High School to embark on a collaborative effort in developing digital and Artificial Intelligence (AI) education (Universiti Malaysia Sabah, 2025a). In June 2025, the University, through the Faculty of Medicine and Health Sciences, also organized a two-day camp for 120 secondary school students that focused on healthcare and technology, including the use of AI (Sokial, 2025). Earlier in 2025, the University, in collaboration with the State's Science, Technology, and Innovation Ministry, released a statement on their plans to set up the Sabah State Artificial Intelligence Council (MAINS). At this event, the Ministry also took the opportunity to distribute about 1800 tablets to secondary school students who would be sitting for their Malaysian Examination Certificate (Sijil Peperiksaan Malaysia, SPM, or O-levels) later in the year (Dzulkifli, 2025).

Given the scarcity of information from the context of UMS, it may be worthwhile to see what other Malaysian public universities have done. Nonetheless, other Malaysian universities that have published specific guidelines on AI use remain minimal. To date, guidelines that are publicly available are those by Universiti Teknologi Malaysia and Universiti Putra Malaysia. The former had published a 17-page guideline for both undergraduate and postgraduate levels, that emphasize the use of AI to support collaboration, creativity, and critical thinking in teaching and learning; the guidelines also gave broad statements about how AI may be used for scholarly activities; and in terms of oversight, AI use was governed by at least four entities, which are the University's Center for Advancement in Digital and Flexible Education, the University Library, the ICT Center, and respective faculties. Universiti Putra Malaysia, on the other hand, published a brief guideline on how AI may be used by postgraduate students in their thesis development. This included the recognition that AI may be helpful in summarizing and proofreading, data analysis and visualization, and structuring arguments. The guideline also highlighted the important need for postgraduate students to ensure that information is both factual and accurate, even if AI was used. Students are also expected to declare and distinguish parts of their thesis that were generated or shaped by AI input or intervention. Besides the students, the guidelines also mentioned how the supervisors of the students, and their examiners have a role to play in ensuring the ethical use of AI. Both supervisors and examiners are expected to determine that the postgraduate students have an acceptable in-depth understanding of their research.

Discussion. Based on the information on the context of UMS, it may be said that AI integration in this particular context remains at the exploratory stage. Actions are only now being taken through a mandatory survey targeted at its students and staff, which reflects only the initial steps in understanding the use of AI and its possible impact on governance in the university context. Furthermore, there seems to be a disconnect between institutional support and the ambition of higher education in Malaysia in general, and the goals of the nation as outlined in its roadmaps. Nonetheless, there are some grass root efforts being spearheaded by individual staff members or faculties, either through collaboration with the immediate communities or by organizing international-level events.

Leadership Discussion. In comparing the leadership priorities of NUS and UMS, it becomes evident that NUS prioritises education for AI as well as the use of AI in education and clearly supports the three dimensions of pedagogy, governance and operations in the AI Ecological Education Policy Framework (Chan, 2023). NUS provides strong leadership, promotes shared meaning and continually supports capacity-building through the AI community-of-practice, training programmes and resources for educators and administrative staff which is aligned with Fullan's Theory of Educational Change (2006). On the other hand, UMS leadership have yet to come up with a clear plan that prioritises AI governance which can be seen through the absence of clear AI policies nor is there any clear priority in AI pedagogy, as there is only one AI course offering and little information about the teaching of AI-related skills useful for the workplace. At this time of writing, most initiatives for capacity building such as AI-related talks and conferences seem to be bottom-up initiatives by various departments, faculties or institutes at the university instead of an explicit direction from the top.

On the other hand, the NUS President actively champions discussions on AI both within and beyond the university. For example, in the opening address to 40 university leaders in ASEAN (Association of Southeast Asian Nations), he highlighted the need to have "practical considerations of large language models, adapting data management practices, capabilities, and infrastructure, to developing policies and governance that are comprehensive yet not prohibitive" (NUSnews, 2025b). He also discussed the "transformative role of artificial intelligence in shaping industries, jobs and education" while exploring the opportunities and challenges with students reading the Digital Technologies and Public policy module in NUS (LKYSPP, 2024). As a whole, the NUS leadership sets a tone that emphasises a need to consider the implications of AI throughout the university and uses the distributed leadership approach (Spillane, 2006) by encouraging shared responsibility and collaborative decision-making while empowering faculties, departments and individuals to lead in the pursuit of AI governance, pedagogy and operations. Take for example, the University Policy Workgroup responsible for the AI interim policy in 2023 and then, the updated AI Policy in Teaching and Learning in 2024. This workgroup is not made up solely of members from the provost office but is made up of academic leaders from various departments or faculties (i.e. Philosophy, Public Health, Computer Science, Biomedical Engineering, Physiology, NUS Libraries, Student conduct). Similarly, the project members of the Generative AI Team from the NUS Teaching Academy are made up of academics spread across different faculties and departments.

Beyond the concerted effort to encourage collaboration among academics from different departments, NUS also encourages leadership, responsibility and innovation within faculties, departments and members by giving educators and department heads autonomy when deciding on the use of AI. For example, distributed leadership and agency can be seen in the AI policy and guidelines for instructors encouraging educators to incorporate the use of AI when delivering courses but does not dictate an absolute need to. Similarly, the AI policy provides clear perimeters for those exploring the use of AI for assessments to provide responses, feedback and marks as well as an AI Academic Impact Assessment form that they could submit to their Head of Departments for approval instead of forbidding the use of AI entirely. It seems that the leadership is not only building capacity but working to promote and sustain AI acceptance by celebrating individual and team successes through showcases, conferences and awards (e.g. Annual Innovative Teaching Excellence Award, NUS Admin Excellence Award) to build a culture of AI awareness, motivation and innovation.

CONCLUSION

This study compared the national AI policies and strategies in Singapore and Malaysia as well as the local responses of the National University of Singapore (NUS) and Universiti Malaysia Sabah (UMS) through their programs, policies and activities relating to artificial intelligence while considering the leadership priorities of each university. This examination was guided by Chan's (2023) AI Ecological Education Policy Framework, which was useful in situating various efforts at the government and university levels and determining how they relate to each other. Overall, the study found that there was a clear national AI strategy in Singapore which was accompanied by infrastructure, regulations and investments to boost AI research and implementation. This was in tandem with the Ministry of Education's EdTech Masterplan 2030, the Infocomm Media Development Authority's Digital skills for life framework and the enhancement of career training programmes to include AI and generative AI curriculum by SkillsFuture Singapore. This may be reflective of the main economic driver for Singapore, which is largely based on the service sector (see Table 1). On the other hand, Malaysia is at an earlier stage of development but has laid the foundational work with the Malaysia National Artificial Intelligence Roadmap and the National Guidelines on AI Governance and Ethics and are working through challenges in the quality of AI integration in various sectors. The existing guidelines and policies, however, do not make clear the path forward for the industry sector, which is the main economic driver for the nation (see Table 1).

Similarly, this study compared the programs, policies and activities of NUS and UMS to understand the leadership priorities. It found that the policies and activities in NUS were robust with undergraduate and graduate programs in AI, clear policies for the use of generative AI by students and staff, training, resources and incentives for educators to work with AI and even programs and resources for administrative staff to learn about and use AI purposefully. These actions align with Fullen's Theory of Educational Change which emphasizes capacity-building and shared responsibility, and shows AI leadership in terms of governance, pedagogy and operations in the AI Ecological Education Policy Framework. On the other hand, the leadership at UMS does not seem to prioritize AI though there are efforts to work towards specific AI guidelines through their AI survey as well as efforts by entities at the university like organizing AI-related conferences and talks which shows that UMS is still at the exploratory stage.

The findings of this study are significant as it reveals differences in leadership priorities and highlights possible areas for development that could strengthen any university's approach to creating an ecosystem and environment that promotes the integration of artificial intelligence through its stakeholders, namely the students, the educators and the administrative staff. The findings of this study are also significant to those interested in the Asian context, specifically that of two neighboring countries in Southeast Asia who are at differing stages of AI adoption. Moreover, the findings reflect the need to possess an intricate understanding of different contexts found within the same region including leadership priorities. This perspective is important for researchers in ensuring that the representation of efforts and policies related to AI are not deemed to be similar, even though the outlook towards AI is predominantly positive across the globe. Having a nuanced understanding would also allow researchers to enunciate how efforts may be distinct at the implementation or grassroots level.

Limitations

This research relied on documents that were publicly available online like government policy papers, industry reports, press releases and institutional publications as well as some internal institutional documents from the researchers' home universities that they were privy to. This study may not have had access to all confidential documents, internal government or institutional documents and other unpublished reports which may affect the completeness of the analysis. Furthermore, the validity of some of the observations made in this chapter may be temporal. Given the fast-paced nature of development in AI and other related technologies, the digital landscape of both Singapore and Malaysia may be susceptible to changes in the near future.

Recommendations

We recommend that the educational policies of other universities in Singapore and Malaysia be analyzed and compared for a broader understanding of the context of each country. Other forms of public materials should also be included in future analysis, such as press releases or interviews captured in different modalities (conventional news articles or even televised or recorded news clips). Including these forms of data would provide more information about the complexities of AI integration at various levels and by different stakeholders. Furthermore, the policies of other Asian countries and universities can also be analyzed in future for a more complete understanding of the Asian context.

REFERENCES

Abbasi, B. N., Wu, Y., & Luo, Z. (2025). Exploring the impact of artificial intelligence on curriculum development in global higher education institutions. *Education and Information Technologies, 30*(1), 547–581. DOI: 10.1007/s10639-024-13113-z

Ahmad, M. K., Ismail, R. A. A., & Ganiem, L. M. (2025, May). Challenges and prospects on artificial intelligence adoption among Malaysian public relations practitioners. In *The 9th International Conference on Communication and Media (i-COME 24)* (pp. 46-52). Atlantis Press. https://doi.org/DOI: 10.2991/978-94-6463-756-4_5

AI Centre for Educational Technologies. (n.d.) *About.* Retrieved on October 1, 2025 from https://aicet.comp.nus.edu.sg/about/

Altbach, P. G. (2004). The past and future of Asian universities. In Altbach, P. G., & Umakoshi, T. (Eds.), *Asian Universities: Historical Perspectives and Contemporary Challenges* (pp. 13–32). The Johns Hopkins University Press. DOI: 10.56021/9780801880360

Ayeni, O. O., Al Hamad, N. M., Chisom, O. N., Osawaru, B., & Adewusi, O. E. (2024). AI in education: A review of personalized learning and educational technology. *GSC Advanced Research and Reviews, 18*(2), 261–271. DOI: 10.30574/gscarr.2024.18.2.0062

Chan, C. K. Y. (2023). A comprehensive AI policy education framework for university teaching and learning. *International Journal of Educational Technology in Higher Education, 20*(1), 38. Advance online publication. DOI: 10.1186/s41239-023-00408-3

Dai, Y., Lai, S., Lim, C. P., & Liu, A. (2025). University policies on generative AI in Asia: Promising practices, gaps, and future directions. *Journal of Asian Public Policy, 18*(2), 260–281. DOI: 10.1080/17516234.2024.2379070

Dzulkifli, I. (2025, January 24). Sabah state artificial intelligence council to be set up. *Daily Express.* Retrieved October 27, 2025 from https://www.dailyexpress.com.my/news/250812/sabah-state-artificial-intelligence-council-to-be-set-up/

Ferenczy, A. (2025). Hungary and AI: efforts and opportunities in comparison with Singapore. *arXiv preprint arXiv:2507.05280.*

Frana, P. L. (2024). Assessing Smart Nation Singapore as an international model for AI responsibility. *International Journal on Responsibility, 7*(1). Advance online publication. DOI: 10.62365/2576-0955.1109

Fullan, M. (2006). *Change theory: A force for school improvement (Centre for Strategic Education Seminar Series Paper No. 157)*. Centre for Strategic Education.

Ghazali, F. F., Karim, R. A., Wahid, S. D. M., & Naseri, R. N. N. (2025). Smart retail, smarter decisions: Conceptualizing the antecedents of consumer intention to use intelligent retail systems. *International Journal of Art and Design, 9*(2/SI-3), 125–135. https://doi.org/DOI: 10.24191/ijad.v9i2/SI-3.8834

Giannakos, M., Azevedo, R., Brusilovsky, P., Cukurova, M., Dimitriadis, Y., Hernandez-Leo, D., Järvelä, S., Mavrikis, M., & Rienties, B. (2025). The promise and challenges of generative AI in education. *Behaviour & Information Technology, 44*(11), 2518–2544. DOI: 10.1080/0144929X.2024.2394886

Glenn, E. (2025, May 12). AI Policy Corner: Singapore's National AI Strategy 2.0. *Montreal AI Ethics Institute.* https://montrealethics.ai/ai-policy-corner-singapores-national-ai-strategy-2-0/

Government AI Readiness Index - Oxford Insights. (2025, June 30). Oxford Insights. https://oxfordinsights.com/ai-readiness/ai-readiness-index/

GovTech. (2025, July 30). *The history of AI. Part 2: Singapore's AI journey.* Retrieved October 19, 2025 from https://www.tech.gov.sg/technews/the-history-of-ai-part-2-singapore-ai-journey/

Hasan, M. K., Ahmed, M. M., Islam, S., Kabir, S. R., Shtayat, M. B., Ahmed, F. R. A., Mahmud, M., Ahmad Nazri, M. Z., & Mohammed Babiker, N. B. (2024). Malaysia energy outlook from 1990 to 2050 for sustainability: Business-as-usual and Alternative-policy Scenarios based economic projections with AI based experiments. *Energy Strategy Reviews, 53*, 101360. Advance online publication. DOI: 10.1016/j.esr.2024.101360

Hohman, M. (2025). *Global Round-Up: National AI Policies* (p. 2). https://ccianet.org/wp-content/uploads/2025/03/2025-03-27-CCIA-Whitepaper-Global-Round-Up-National-AI-Policies-1.pdf

Jacobsson, K. (2022). Designing for the ethnographic study of documents. In Flick, U. (Ed.), *The SAGE Handbook of Qualitative Research Design* (pp. 771–784). Sage., DOI: 10.4135/9781529770278.n47

Jin, Y., Yan, L., Echeverria, V., Gašević, D., & Martinez-Maldonado, R. (2025). Generative AI in higher education: A global perspective of institutional adoption policies and guidelines. *Computers and Education: Artificial Intelligence, 8*, 100348. Advance online publication. DOI: 10.1016/j.caeai.2024.100348

Lee, A. V. Y., Koh, E., & Looi, C. K. (2023). AI in education and learning analytics in Singapore: An overview of key projects and initiatives. *Information and Technology in Education and Learning*, *3*(1), 3.1.Inv.p001. Advance online publication. DOI: 10.12937/itel.3.1.Inv.p001

Lee, J. W. (2001). Education for technology readiness: Prospects for developing countries. *Journal of Human Development*, *2*(1), 115–151. DOI: 10.1080/14649880120050

Lee, T. (2024). Artificial intelligence: Governing Singapore's smart digital journey. *Communication Research and Practice*, *10*(3), 307–315. DOI: 10.1080/22041451.2024.2346430

Leow, W. X. (2024, March 25). *Nus establishes institute to boost AI research for the public good.* The Straits Times. https://www.straitstimes.com/singapore/nus-establishes-institute-to-boost-ai-research-for-the-public-good

Liu, L., Mun, N. S., Low, K., & Leong, B. *Simulating Professional Workplaces: A Pedagogical Framework for Generative AI-Powered Role-Play for Competency-Based Education.* In AI4X 2025 International Conference.

LKYSPP. (2024, December 26). The Future of Learning and Work: Insight from Professor Tan Eng Chye's Lecture on AI. Retrieved on February 3, 2026 from https://lkyspp.nus.edu.sg/news-events/news/details/the-future-of-learning-and-work-insights-from-professor-tan-eng-chye-s-lecture-on-ai

Mahusin, N., Sallehudin, H., & Satar, N. S. M. (2024). Malaysia Public Sector Challenges Of Implementation Of Artificial Intelligence (AI). *IEEE Access : Practical Innovations, Open Solutions*, *12*, 21035–121051. DOI: 10.1109/ACCESS.2024.3448311

Malaysian Qualifications Agency. (2025). *Draft Programme Standards: Artificial Intelligence (PS: AI).* Malaysian Qualifications Agency. Retrieved October 27, 2025 from https://www.mqa.gov.my/new/document/2025/Draft%20PS%20AI%20-%2024.6.25.pdf

Mat Yusoff, S., Mohamad Marzaini, A. F., Hao, L., Zainuddin, Z., & Basal, M. H. (2025). Understanding the role of AI in Malaysian higher education curricula: An analysis of student perceptions. *Discover Computing*, *28*(1), 62. Advance online publication. DOI: 10.1007/s10791-025-09567-5

McIntosh, I., & Wright, S. (2019). Exploring what the notion of 'lived experience' offers for social policy analysis. *Journal of Social Policy*, *48*(3), 449–467. DOI: 10.1017/S0047279418000570

Ministry of Digital Development and Information. (2025, March 7). *AI Initiatives to Transform Life, Work and Business in Singapore* [Press release]. https://www.mddi.gov.sg/newsroom/ai-initiatives-to-transform-life-work-and-business-in-singapore/

Ministry of Education. (n.d.). *"Transforming Education through Technology" Masterplan 2030.* Retrieved October 30, 2025 from https://www.moe.gov.sg/education-in-sg/educational-technology-journey/edtech-masterplan

Ministry of Science. Technology and Innovation Malaysia. (2021). *Artificial Intelligence roadmap (AI-Rmap) playbook.* Putrajaya: Ministry of Science, Technology and Innovation (MOSTI). Retrieved October 27, 2025 from https://mastic.mosti.gov.my/publication/artificial-intelligence-roadmap-2021-2025/

Ministry of Science. Technology and Innovation Malaysia. (2023). *The national guidelines on artificial intelligence governance and ethics.* Putrajaya: Ministry of Science, Technology and Innovation (MOSTI). Retrieved October 27, 2025 from https://mastic.mosti.gov.my/publication/the-national-guidelines-on-ai-governance-ethics/

Nanyang Technological University Singapore. (19 May 2025). *AI Education, the Essence is People.* Retrieved on 30 October, 2025 from https://www.ntu.edu.sg/nie/news-events/news/detail/ai-education--the-essence-is-people

Nus Artificial Intelligence Institute. (n.d.). *AI + X.* Retrieved on October 1, 2025 https://ai.nus.edu.sg/research/ai-x/

Nus Centre For Future-ready Graduates. (n.d) *CFG AI-Xplore.* Retrieved on October 1, 2025 from https://nus.edu.sg/cfg/students/career-resources/cfg-ai-xplore

Nus Centre for Teaching. Learning and Technology. (n.d.) *NUS AI Community- of-Practice for Teaching and Learning.* Retrieved on October 1, 2025 from https://ctlt.nus.edu.sg/ai-community-of-practice/

Nus Computing. (n.d). *Undergraduate Programs.*Retrieved on October 1, 2025 https://www.comp.nus.edu.sg/programmes/

Nus Libraries. (n.d). *AI Guidelines for Students.* Retrieved September 10, 2025 from https://libguides.nus.edu.sg/new2nus/ai_guidelines_infographics

Nus. (n.d.) *Developing Employees for an Agile University.* Retrieved on October 1, 2025 from https://www.nus.edu.sg/inside-nus/stories/developing-employees-for-an-agile-university

Nus. (n.d.) *Empowering staff to be future-ready.* Retrieved on October 1, 2025 from https://www.nus.edu.sg/inside-nus/stories/empowering-staff-to-be-future-ready

Nus One. (n.d.). *Year One. Your journey starts here.* Retrieved October 20, 2025 from https://www.nus.edu.sg/nusone/year-one/#THE-programme

NUS Teaching Academy. (n.d) *Projects.* Retrieved on February 1, 2026 from https://www.nus.edu.sg/teachingacademy/projects/

NUSnews. (2021, November 15). *A model of lifelong learning: NUS equips staff with data literacy and artificial intelligence skills.*Retrieved on October 1, 2025 from https://news.nus.edu.sg/a-model-of-lifelong-learning-nus-equips-staff-with-data-literacy-and-artificial-intelligence-skills/

NUSnews. (2025a, May 19). *NUS IT wins Digital Achievers (Team) Award at Tech Leader Awards 2025 for groundbreaking AI-Know project.* Retrieved on October 1, 2025 from https://news.nus.edu.sg/nus-it-wins-digital-achievers-team-award-at-tech-leader-awards-2025-for-groundbreaking-ai-know-project/#:~:text=Developed%20in%2Dhouse%20by%20the,on%20Generative%20AI%20(GenAI)

NUSnews. (2025b, December 4). *(Re)invention of the human: How ASEAN universities are adapting to an AI-led future.* Retrieved on February 3, 2026 from https://news.nus.edu.sg/reinvention-of-the-human-how-asean-universities-are-adapting-to-an-ai-led-future/

O'Neill, A. (2025, June 19). *Malaysia: Share of economic sectors in the gross domestic product (GDP) from 2013 to 2023.* Statista. https://www.statista.com/statistics/318732/share-of-economic-sectors-in-the-gdp-in-malaysia/

O'Neill, A. (2025, October 7). *Ratio of government expenditure to GDP in Malaysia from 1990 to 2030.* Statista. https://www.statista.com/statistics/319126/ratio-of-government-expenditure-to-gross-domestic-product-gdp-in-malaysia/

O'Neill, A. (2025, October 8). *Ratio of government expenditure to GDP in Singapore 1990-2030.* Statista. https://www.statista.com/statistics/379453/ratio-of-government-expenditure-to-gross-domestic-product-gdp-in-singapore/#:~:text=In%202024%2C%20the%20ratio%20of,services%20produced%20during%20a%20year

OpenGov. (2018, March 2). *Singapore universities take steps to meet industry demand and prepare students for future economy.* Retrieved on September 20, 2025 from https://archive.opengovasia.com/2018/03/02/singapore-universities-take-steps-to-meet-industry-demand-and-prepare-students-for-future-economy/#

Oxford Insights. (2025). *Government AI Readiness Index 2024.* Retrieved October 10, 2025 from https://oxfordinsights.com/ai-readiness/ai-readiness-index/

Phang, K. C., Ng, T. C., Singh, S. K. G., Voo, T. C., & Alvis, W. A. (2025). Navigating Artificial Intelligence in Malaysian Healthcare: Research Developments, Ethical Dilemmas, and Governance Strategies. *Asian Bioethics Review*, *17*(3), 631–665. DOI: 10.1007/s41649-024-00314-4 PMID: 40741314

Ramachandaran, S., Mahalley, Z., Nuraini, R., & Dhar, B. K. (2025). Exploring the challenges of AI-driven business intelligence systems in the Malaysian insurance industry. *F1000 Research*, *14*(452), 452. Advance online publication. DOI: 10.12688/f1000research.163354.1 PMID: 40575004

Razak, F. Z. A., Abdullah, M. A., Ahmad, B. E., Bakar, W. H. R. B. W. A., & Misaridin, N. A. F. B. (2025). The acceptance of artificial intelligence in education among postgraduate students in Malaysia. *Education and Information Technologies*, *30*(3), 2977–2997. DOI: 10.1007/s10639-024-12916-4

Sabah Subsection, I. E. E. E. (2025). *IEEE International Conference on Artificial Intelligence in Engineering and Technology*, 26 - 28 August 2025. Sabah International Convention Centre. https://iicaiet.ieeesabah.org/

Salas-Pilco, S. Z. (2021). Comparison of national artificial intelligence (ai): Strategic policies and priorities. In Keskin, T., & Kiggins, R. D. (Eds.), *Towards an International Political economy of Artificial Intelligence* (pp. 195–217). Springer International Publishing. DOI: 10.1007/978-3-030-74420-5_9

Schiff, D. (2022). Education for AI, not AI for education: The role of education and ethics in national AI policy strategies. *International Journal of Artificial Intelligence in Education*, *32*(3), 527–563. DOI: 10.1007/s40593-021-00270-2

Schiff, D., Biddle, J., Borenstein, J., & Laas, K. (2020, February). What's next for ai ethics, policy, and governance? A global overview. *Proceedings of the AAAI/ACM Conference on AI, Ethics, and Society* (pp. 153-158). https://doi.org/DOI: 10.1145/3375627.3375804

Singapore, A. I. (2025a). *AI Singapore*. Retrieved October 19, 2025 from https://aisingapore.org/

Singapore, A. I. (2025b). *AI Apprenticeship Programme*. Retrieved October 19, 2025 from https://aiap.sg/apprenticeship/

Singapore, E. D. B. (2018, Nov 26). *Why Singapore is the premier destination for global AI investment.* Retrieved September 18, 2025 from https://www.edb.gov.sg/en/business-insights/insights/why-singapore-is-the-premier-destination-for-global-ai-investment.html

Smart Nation Singapore. (2025). *National AI Strategy. Learn how Singapore is leveraging AI and driving its adoption.* Retrieved October 15, 2025 from https://www.smartnation.gov.sg/initiatives/national-ai-strategy/

Sokial, S. (2025, June 20). UMS camp stirs rural students' interest in AI healthcare applications. *The Star*. Retrieved October 27, 2025 from https://www.thestar.com.my/news/nation/2025/06/20/ums-camp-stirs-rural-students039-interest-in-ai-healthcare-applications

Spillane, J. P. (2006). Towards a theory of leadership practice: A distributed perspective. In *Rethinking schooling* (pp. 208–242). Routledge.

Statista. (2024). *Artificial Intelligence - Asia | Statista Market forecast.* Retrieved October 10, 2025 from https://www.statista.com/outlook/tmo/artificial-intelligence/asia?srsltid=AfmBOopBdYGxM4huWyGXVGNIaI50qYw_BUsIs9e2YjOMN_2xNB4Mjthz

Statista. (2025). *Artificial Intelligence (AI) in business*. Retrieved October 10, 2025 https://www-statista-com.libproxy1.nus.edu.sg/study/133541/artificial-intelligence-ai-in-business/

Tan, A. (2024, February 19). S'pore's $1b AI boost will help sustain competitive edge in digital era, say business leaders. *The Straits Times*. https://www.straitstimes.com/business/s-pore-s-1b-ai-boost-will-help-sustain-competitive-edge-in-digital-era-say-business-leaders

Tushara, E. (2025, Jan 28). *Learning about artificial intelligence in Singapore Universities.* The Straits Times. https://www.straitstimes.com/singapore/nus-establishes-institute-to-boost-ai-research-for-the-public-good

UNESCO. (2023, June 1). *UNESCO survey: Less than 10% of schools and universities have formal guidance on AI.* Retrieved October 10, 2025, from https://www.unesco.org/en/articles/unesco-surveyless-10-schools-and-universities-have-formal-guidance-ai

UNESCO. (2025, September 2). *UNESCO survey: Two-thirds of higher education institutions have or are developing guidance on AI use.* Retrieved October 15, 2025, from https://www.unesco.org/en/articles/unesco-survey-two-thirds-higher-education-institutions-have-or-are-developing-guidance-ai-use

Universiti Malaysia Sabah. (2025b, July). *UMS, KKHS collaborate to promote next generation education in AI and digital technology* [Online announcement]. Retrieved October 27, 2025 from https://ums.edu.my/v5/banner-link/17460-ums-kkhs-collaborate-to-promote-next-generation-education-in-ai-digital-technology

University Malaysia Sabah. (2025a, February 10). Invitation to participate on artificial intelligence driving academic impact workshop. [Online Announcement]. Retrieved October 27, 2025 from https://ums.edu.my/v5/en/announcement-link-3/16677-invitation-to-participate-on-artificial-intelligence-driving-academic-impact-workshop

University Malaysia Sabah. (2025c, September 23). *Mandatory survey on artificial intelligence (AI) in teaching & learning at UMS*. [Online announcement]. Retrieved October 27, 2025 from https://ums.edu.my/v5/en/announcement-link-3/17755-mandatory-survey-on-artificial-intelligence-ai-in-teaching-learning-at-ums-sdp-points-awarded

van Berkel, N., Papachristos, E., Giachanou, A., Hosio, S., & Skov, M. B. (2020). A systematic assessment of national artificial intelligence policies: Perspectives from the Nordics and beyond. *Proceedings of the 11th nordic conference on human-computer interaction: Shaping experiences, shaping society* (pp. 1-12). https://doi.org/DOI: 10.1145/3419249.3420106

Wang, H., Dang, A., Wu, Z., & Mac, S. (2024). Generative AI in higher education: Seeing ChatGPT through universities' policies, resources, and guidelines. *Computers and Education: Artificial Intelligence*, *7*, 100326. DOI: 10.1016/j.caeai.2024.100326

Xu, J., Lee, T., & Goggin, G. (2024). AI governance in Asia: Policies, praxis and approaches. *Communication Research and Practice*, *10*(3), 275–287. DOI: 10.1080/22041451.2024.2391204

Xu, P., Dong, W., & Wang, C. (2022). Present situation and enlightenment of artificial intelligence lifelong education system in Singapore. *Journal of Autonomous Intelligence*, *5*(1), 23–33. DOI: 10.32629/jai.v5i1.499

Yang, Y., Zhang, Y., Sun, D., He, W., & Wei, Y. (2025). Navigating the landscape of AI literacy education: Insights from a decade of research (2014–2024). *Humanities & Social Sciences Communications*, *12*(1), 1–12. DOI: 10.1057/s41599-025-04583-8

Yeo, M. M., Navedo, D. D., Casey, P. J., & Tan, B. (2025). How effective is generative AI advice for the academic advancement of faculty? medRxiv, 2025-05. https://doi.org/DOI: 10.1101/2025.05.25.2532831

Chapter 9
Teachers at the Policy Frontier:
AI Integration in Education Across Europe, Asia, and Africa

Mona El Samaty
http://orcid.org/0000-0002-4019-1775
Sharjah Education Academy, UAE

Maram Al Aqra
http://orcid.org/0000-0002-1889-7659
Sharjah Education Academy, UAE

ABSTRACT

This book chapter provides a comparative analysis of how AI in Education policies in Europe, Asia and Africa influence AI implementation in the classrooms, as well as the role of teachers in this implementation. Through case studies featuring Europe's ethics-driven and teacher-autonomous models, Asia's state-led innovation and rapid capacity building, and Africa's equity-focused yet resource-constrained strategies, the chapter reveals regional differences in policy intent, governance, and classroom realities. Despite the variations, similarities include the necessity of ethical guidance, and the importance of agency and sustained professional development for teachers in order to achieve meaningful and equitable AI integration in classrooms. The chapter concludes with implications for teacher education. The chapter highlights that systemic investments in teacher capacity, context-sensitive strategies, and collaborative partnerships are essential for ensuring inclusive and ethical AI integration in classrooms.

DOI: 10.4018/979-8-3373-4908-4.ch009

INTRODUCTION

The Emerging Role of Educators in an AI-Mediated Classroom

As artificial intelligence (AI) has been embedded in education, intelligent tutoring systems and automated grading tools have been increasingly used in many schools. In this context, teachers and school leaders have become frontline decision-makers on how AI can be used in classroom practice (Michopoulou & Gan, 2025). Some have adapted their teaching strategies based on AI recommendations (Amiri et al., 2025). Others have shown professional agency, when implementing AI in education, by balancing their own judgment with automation or aligning AI tools with curriculum.

In this chapter, the term *educator* is used inclusively to refer to classroom teachers, instructional specialists, and formal leaders (e.g., principals, department heads) who are directly involved in pedagogical work. The term *teacher* specifies the classroom practitioner, while *leader* or *leadership* refers to roles with formal organizational authority and strategic responsibility for enabling others' practice. It is recognized, however, that teachers exercise leadership in their classrooms and professional communities, and that effective leaders remain grounded in pedagogical understanding

Educators' evolving role brings significant ethical and professional demands that challenge traditional educational leadership (Sposato, 2025). For example, educators can face dilemmas involving data privacy or algorithmic bias that may affect students' learning opportunities and well-being (El Samaty, 2025). They are then required to reflect on how to balance innovation with integrity, ensuring thoughtful, ethical, and equitable use of AI within their classrooms and schools. Educators must also uphold values, such as empathy, fairness, and inclusivity, in contexts increasingly shaped by non-human decision systems (Noakes et al., 2024).

Teacher agency refers to educators' capacity to make purposeful decisions, adapt their practices, and influence pedagogical and technological choices. It functions as a critical link between educational leadership and digital transformation frameworks. When school leaders intentionally foster teacher agency through supportive organizational structures, a shared instructional vision, and ongoing professional learning, teachers move beyond the role of passive technology users to become active contributors in aligning digital innovation with instructional goals. Within digital transformation frameworks, leadership that prioritizes teacher agency enables reflective experimentation, collaborative decision-making, and professional ownership among teachers (Engeness & Gamlem, 2025). Such leadership practices support more sustainable, context-responsive, and pedagogically grounded integration of digital technologies across education systems.

A Global Tri-Region Lens for AI-in-Education Policy

This chapter aims to examine how AI-in-education policies shape classroom realities across diverse global contexts. It offers a comparative analysis of Europe, Asia, and Africa to highlight how teachers navigate, interpret, and implement these policies in practice. The inclusion of Europe, Asia, and Africa is driven by the need for policy diversity and research balance. While the United States dominates much of the AI-in-education discourse, these three regions remain comparatively under-explored despite their distinct and rapidly evolving trajectories. Europe contributes mature frameworks for ethics, governance, and teacher agency; Asia offers large-scale, innovation-driven implementation models; and Africa introduces emerging blueprints grounded in equity, capacity-building, and decolonization. Examining these contrasting yet complementary contexts allows for a more globally inclusive understanding of how AI policy is framed, interpreted, and enacted within different educational systems.

It is critical to acknowledge that AI implementation is not solely directed by public policy. Private-sector EdTech companies are pivotal actors, supplying the platforms, tools, and data infrastructures that populate classrooms. Their business models, design choices, and terms of service profoundly shape the possibilities and ethical dilemmas of AI in education, making them influential, and often unregulated, co-authors of the classroom reality that policies aim to govern.

The cross-regional comparison also highlights how local economic, political, and cultural contexts shape AI integration in classrooms. Differences in infrastructure, governance, and teacher autonomy reveal how policies translate unevenly into practice. In European and Asian systems, teachers act as designers of AI-mediated pedagogy, while in African contexts, educators navigate limited access. Comparing these systems shows how institutional support and teacher leadership can ensure that AI is used as a tool for empowerment.

Building on these cross-regional insights, the chapter bridges policy design and classroom implementation through two research questions:

1. How do AI-in-education policies in Europe, Asia, and Africa influence the use and implementation of AI in classrooms?
2. How is the role of teachers evolving regarding the implementation of AI in classrooms in Europe, Asia, and Africa?

ANALYTICAL FRAMEWORK: FROM POLICY TO PRACTICE IN THE AGE OF AI

This chapter employs a policy-enactment lens, which conceptualizes educational policies as socially constructed texts that are interpreted and enacted by educators within specific institutional and cultural contexts, rather than implemented in a linear or uniform manner (Ball et al., 2012; Braun et al., 2011). This lens is used within a broader policy-to-practice framework to examine the journey of AI policies from national mandate to classroom reality (Funa & Gabay, 2024). This comparative design is informed by established methods in comparative policy analysis (Bray et al., 2014). It moves beyond a view of policy as simple implementation, instead focusing on how policies are interpreted, translated, and remade by diverse actors in specific institutional contexts. Grounded in principles of teacher agency, this framework positions educators as active policy actors who exercise professional judgment and navigate complex constraints to translate abstract policy into meaningful classroom practice (King, 2021). Viewing leadership as a distributed practice (Spillane, 2006) that is critical for successful policy enactment (Leithwood et al., 2020), the analysis understands leadership as a relational, negotiated process shaped by institutional and cultural realities.

This enactment perspective makes the model particularly appropriate for cross-regional analysis, as it shifts the focus from formal policy texts to the variable conditions of enactment, such as resources, school culture, and teacher preparedness, enabling a comparative analysis of how policy is mediated, adopted, or resisted across diverse educational systems (Coburn, 2005; Maguire et al., 2015).

Within this framework, the analysis is organized around five core dimensions, namely ethics, access, inclusion, data use, and professional development, that capture the key forces shaping AI integration in education (Al-Zahrani & Alasmari, 2024). These dimensions serve as analytical lenses to examine not only what policies prescribe but also how they are enacted, revealing the spaces for teacher agency and the site-specific challenges that arise in each region. *Ethics* deals with the moral and regulatory principles that guide responsible AI use (Borenstein & Howard, 2021). *Access* examines infrastructural foundations, such as hardware, connectivity, and digital resources, which are essential for equitable adoption of AI. *Inclusion* evaluates how policies ensure AI tools and pedagogies meet diverse learner needs and reduce disparities linked to disability, socio-economic status, or cultural background. *Data use* explores governance of student data, privacy, security, and the development of critical data literacy among educators and learners. Finally, *professional development* focuses on teacher capacity-building that extends beyond technical training to include pedagogical judgment necessary for leadership (Atenas et al., 2023). These dimensions reveal how policy environments across Europe, Asia, and

Africa empower or constrain educators as agents of ethical AI integration within the real-world dynamics of policy enactment.

MAPPING AI POLICY PATHWAYS: EUROPE, ASIA, AND AFRICA

This section examines how policies from Europe, Asia, and Africa translate national and regional ambitions into educational practice. Two policy systems were selected from each continent to capture multi-level variation. In Europe, the European Union represents the regional regulatory and ethical framework guiding member states, while Finland exemplifies localized enactment, showcasing how a teacher-driven system operationalizes EU principles through autonomy and reflective pedagogy. In Asia, China and the United Arab Emirates contrast a centralized, state-led innovation model with an innovation-driven system that emphasizes rapid capacity building and global collaboration. In Africa, Rwanda and South Africa reflect the continent's emerging diversity: Rwanda as a pioneer in ethical AI governance under resource constraints, and South Africa as a policy leader combining infrastructure investment with decolonial aims. These six cases reveal how policy interacts with governance traditions and material realities to shape AI integration and teachers' evolving roles.

Europe

European Union

1. Policy Context and Scope The Digital Education Action Plan (DEAP) (2021–2027) is a policy framework launched by the European Commission in 2021 to guide the transformation of education systems across Europe (European Commission, 2020). Developed in response to the digital acceleration triggered by COVID-19, it outlines fourteen strategic actions centered on two principles: developing a high-performing digital education ecosystem and strengthening digital skills and competencies at all levels of learning. These actions aim to create flexible, inclusive, and sustainable education systems suited to the age of technology and AI (European Commission, 2021).
2. Core Policy Focus DEAP links digital transformation and innovation with ethical practice, emphasizing that technology should serve learning rather than replace it. It aligns with broader frameworks such as the European Education Area, the 2030 Digital Compass, and the EU Artificial Intelligence Strategy (European Commission, 2021). Among its fourteen actions, Action 6 is notable for its ethical focus, providing teachers, especially those new to AI, with practical tools such as

reflection templates and classroom infographics. By fostering critical reflection on AI's role in teaching and learning, DEAP balances human judgment with digital innovation while reinforcing Europe's commitment to equity, fairness, and inclusion (European Commission, 2022).

3. Alignment with the Five Dimensions DEAP aligns closely with the five guiding dimensions of responsible digital transformation. Ethically, Action 6 sets clear standards for the use of AI, emphasizing transparency, fairness, and human oversight. In terms of Access, Action 1 strengthens connectivity and infrastructure through initiatives such as the Connecting Europe Facility and Recovery and Resilience Facility, making digital transformation more equitable and bridging the rural-urban divide. Regarding inclusion, Action 10 promotes accessibility guidelines and inclusive digital content for diverse learners (Morte-Nadal & Esteban-Navarro, 2025). On data use, Actions 6 and 11 reinforce responsible data governance through the European Education Data Space, ensuring data protection consistent with the General Data Protection Regulation. Finally, Action 9 expands the Digital Competence Framework for Educators (DigCompEdu) to boost educators' digital confidence and creativity, and professional growth. These dimensions work interdependently to form a coherent foundation for responsible digital transformation across Europe (European Commission, 2021).
4. Policy-Practice Translation DEAP's strategic vision translates into practical mechanisms, funding, and professional support for educators. For example, the Ethical Guidelines on the Use of AI and Data in Teaching and Learning provide ready-to-use resources that help teachers make informed decisions and refine teaching practices (European Commission, 2022). Funding initiatives such as the Connecting Europe Facility and Recovery and Resilience Facility expand digital infrastructure, ensuring access to devices and reliable connectivity in urban and rural schools across regions. Meanwhile, the DigCompEdu framework supports continuous professional development and fosters teachers' pedagogical and ethical competence. Teachers involved in ethics-focused professional learning across Europe report using AI-generated insights as support rather than authority. They emphasize that professional judgment is required to ensure transparency, fairness, and inclusion in classroom decisions (Mouta et al., 2025). Teachers also describe their leadership role as mediating between policy guidance and classroom realities, particularly when explaining AI-supported decisions to students (Ghamrawi et al., 2024).
5. Regional Significance While DEAP provides a unified European approach to socially and ethically responsible digital transformation, it allows for national adaptation to local priorities. Member states can tailor implementation strategies to their national priorities, while remaining aligned with shared European goals and values. Through benchmarking tools and funding mechanisms, governments

can measure progress and sustain long-term reforms. Beyond the European Union, DEAP has the potential for global relevance (European Commission, 2021). Its integration of ethics, data protection, and teacher empowerment positions it as a model for responsible digital transformation. For leaders within the EU framework, the imperative is to act as ethical stewards and system facilitators, ensuring funding and guidelines translate into equitable infrastructure and supporting cross-national professional learning communities

Finland

1. Policy Context and Scope Building on the EU's regional framework, Finland exemplifies its localized, teacher-driven enactment. Finland's national approach to AI in education is articulated through coordinated policy documents developed by the Finnish National Agency for Education (EDUFI) and the Ministry of Education and Culture (Ministry of Education and Culture, 2023). The AI Guide for Teachers, and the Policies for the Digital Transformation of Education and Training form the foundation for integrating AI across all levels of learning, from early childhood to adult and vocational education (Finnish National Agency for Education, 2024). These policies prioritize teacher autonomy, ethical responsibility, and inclusive digital transformation, reflecting Finland's broader commitment to high-quality, equitable teaching. The national framework aligns with Finland's lifelong learning and digitalization goals, ensuring that AI functions as a cross-curricular competence rather than a standalone subject for both teachers and students (Finnish National Agency for Education, 2025).
2. Core Policy Focus Finland's AI-in-education policy adopts a teacher-oriented, ethically informed strategy that empowers educators to engage with AI responsibly and creatively. The AI Guide for Teachers and related research from the University of Eastern Finland outline goals such as improving teachers' AI literacy and critical thinking, promoting ethical and transparent technology use, and ensuring that AI supports pedagogy for AI integration (University of Eastern Finland, 2024). Teacher autonomy, a cornerstone of Finland's education system, is maintained through flexible guidelines that allow adaptation to local contexts. The emphasis lies on developing reflective practitioners who can guide students in using AI for collaboration, inquiry, and problem-solving (Finnish National Agency for Education, 2024).
3. Alignment with the Five Dimensions Finland's AI policy framework is well aligned with five guiding dimensions of responsible AI enactment. In ethics, the AI Guidelines emphasize openness, justice, and human oversight consistent with both European and Finnish values (Finnish National Agency for Education, 2025). For access, the Digital Competence Framework for Education and na-

tional digitization strategies ensure equitable infrastructure and connectivity for schools across different regions (Leppänen, 2024). Inclusion is promoted through multilingual and accessible learning materials designed to meet the needs of diverse students. Regarding data use, Finnish policies uphold GDPR-compliant governance and critical data literacy for teachers and students (Finnish National Agency for Education, 2025). Finally, professional development is supported through the AI Guide for Teachers, Faktabaari's AI Literacy Frameworks (Kivinen, 2025), and national programs embedding AI ethics within teacher education. These dimensions reinforce Finland's vision of an equitable, ethical, and educator-driven digital transformation.

4. Policy-Practice Translation Finland has effectively translated policy into classroom practice through teacher training, school-based innovation, and collaborative research. The AI Guide for Teachers bridges national policy with classroom implementation, offering instructional examples, ethical reflection prompts, and lesson design tools (Finnish National Agency for Education, 2024). Projects such as Generation AI, led by the University of Helsinki and the University of Eastern Finland, embed and test AI learning modules in teacher education programs (University of Eastern Finland, 2024). Schools adopt and adapt these materials through national frameworks and micro-credential systems under the Digital Competence Framework (Leppänen, 2024). Continuous feedback loops between teachers, researchers, and policymakers ensure that Finland's AI education strategy remains both evidence-based and teacher-driven (Finnish National Agency for Education, 2024). In Finland, a qualitative interview study with digital tutors, who were primarily school principals and teachers, highlighted a significant challenge: a pervasive lack of AI knowledge among educators (Erbaş & Maksuti, 2024). in this article, Erbas and Maksuti found that teachers were acutely aware of the ethical quandaries presented by AI, such as data privacy concerns and algorithmic bias, but felt ill-equipped to address these issues effectively In their view, Finnish educators emphasize that AI must pass a *Value-Add Test* before integration. If an AI application threatens to bypass the student's own cognitive struggle or weakens the social bond between teacher and learner, it is viewed as a counterproductive intervention. By framing AI as a tool that must earn its place, Finnish leadership shifts the power dynamic so that technology is held accountable to pedagogy. This ensures that the machine supports the teacher's professional expertise rather than dictating the curriculum.
5. Regional Significance Finland's teacher-centered and ethically informed AI model has become a benchmark within Nordic and European contexts. Through collaborations with NordForsk, a funding organization under the Nordic Council of Ministers, Erasmus+ programs, and the European Commission's AI Watch, Finland's approach is recognized for balancing innovation with pedagogy (AI

Watch, 2023; NordForsk, 2024). It demonstrates how ethical governance, teacher autonomy, and continuous feedback can coexist within a national system. Globally, Finland stands as a leading example of human-centered AI integration, aligning technological advancement with lifelong learning and shared accountability between educators and policymakers (Finnish National Agency for Education, 2025; University of Eastern Finland, 2024). For Finnish school leaders, this model redefines their role as guardians of autonomy and reflective practice, where the core task is to curate a collaborative school culture that empowers teachers as pedagogical designers.

Asia

China

1. Policy Context and Scope

In contrast to European value-based models, China has adopted a centrally coordinated approach to artificial intelligence in education, led by the Ministry of Education (MOE-China) under the Smart Education initiative. This initiative, part of the broader Digital Education Strategy (2021-2025), promotes an integrated digital transformation across all educational levels, including higher education (Ministry of Education of the People's Republic of China, 2025). The overarching goal is to develop an accessible, data-driven, and innovative education system that supports China's vision of becoming a global leader in both education and AI development (State Council of the People's Republic of China, 2025). The policy emphasizes a transformation model built on strengthening digital infrastructure, renewing curricula, and improving data management. The strategy also includes comprehensive teacher training, school leadership development, and enhanced administrative governance that reflect China's top-down governance model (Knox, 2020).

2. Core Policy Focus

China's central objective is to prepare citizens for active participation in an AI-driven economy (State Council of the People's Republic of China, 2025). The national education policy emphasizes higher teaching standards, efficient governance, and the integration of AI literacy into mainstream curricula. MOE-China's Guidance on Teaching AI in Primary and Middle Schools (2024) mandates early exposure to AI concepts ensuring students acquire foundational knowledge from primary levels onward (Ministry of Education of the People's Republic of China, 2024). Complementary initiatives support teachers through intelligent tutoring systems and adaptive learning platforms to monitor student progress. Collectively, these measures establish AI as both an educational innovation and a governance tool central to China's pursuit of national competitiveness (Tlili, 2025).

3. Alignment with the Five Dimensions

China's AI-in-education framework aligns with UNESCO's *AI for Good* principles, addressing the five key dimensions of responsible AI enactment. In terms of ethics, national policies emphasize equality, transparency, and fairness (Wei & Niemi, 2023). Access has been expanded through the Smart Education Platform, which provides over 164,000 schools with high-quality digital learning resources, bridging gaps between urban and rural regions (Xinhua News Agency, 2025). Substantial investment in digital infrastructure, particularly across underdeveloped western provinces, further strengthens inclusion by reducing geographic and socio-economic disparities (State Council of the People's Republic of China, 2025). Ethical and secure data use is governed by the Personal Information Protection Law and MOE-China data regulations, ensuring accountability, security, and transparency in data management (Ministry of Education of the People's Republic of China, 2025). Additionally, professional development is prioritized through nationwide AI training programs that build teachers' technical, ethical, and pedagogical competencies for implementing intelligent education effectively (Xie & Luo, 2025).

4. Policy-Practice Translation

While based on a top-down governance system, China's AI policy framework encourages local adaptation through provincial and municipal innovation. Implementation is advanced through pilot AI classrooms, targeted teacher training workshops, and continuous expansion of the Smart Education of China ecosystem (Ministry of Education of the People's Republic of China, 2025). A notable example is the AI-TPACK project conducted in Chinese universities, which integrates AI concepts into curriculum design and assessment for pre-service teacher education programs. Teachers are also encouraged to experiment with adaptive learning technologies, while data gathered from classroom applications informs future policy development (Xie & Luo, 2025).

From the perspective of human-machine integration, the ethical responsibility of the leader is to shift the educational focus from simple knowledge transmission to the cultivation of human-knowledge, such as interpersonal empathy and ethical judgment. Highlighting this shift, Guo Yike, provost of the Hong Kong University of Science and Technology, states: "AI has disrupted education by breaking down knowledge barriers, shifting the focus from 'what to learn' to 'why learn' and 'how to apply.' The future is one of symbiosis where humans teach machines, and machines teach humans" (Zou, 2025). By embracing this partnership, educational leadership ensures that technology serves as a catalyst for deeper human inquiry rather than a replacement for it.

5. Regional Significance

China's AI-in-education policy has extended its impact regionally by exporting digital learning models and collaborating across Asia. Through partnerships with ASEAN and UNESCO's Smart Education Hub, China shares AI curricula, digital learning platforms, and teacher training resources (State Council of the People's Republic of China, 2025). While China's state-led approach contrasts with Western models that emphasize teacher autonomy, its large-scale initiatives continue to shape the global and regional dialogue on responsible and effective AI integration in education (Tlili, 2025). The leadership demand in this system is for precision implementation and data-informed adaptation, where leaders at all levels must align local practice with national goals while channelling practical feedback upward to refine central policy.

The United Arab Emirates

1. Policy Context and Scope Diverging from China's state-led scaling, the United Arab Emirates' (UAE) strategy pursues rapid capacity-building through global partnerships. The UAE's National Strategy for Artificial Intelligence 2031, developed by the UAE Artificial Intelligence Office to accelerate AI adoption across key sectors, forms the foundation of the national approach to AI (United Arab Emirates Artificial Intelligence Office, 2021). Building on this vision, the Ministry of Education's (MOE-UAE) Digital Transformation Strategy embeds AI literacy, smart-learning platforms, and data-driven systems into the national education framework (Ministry of Education-UAE, 2023). These initiatives create a cohesive ecosystem that embeds AI across K-12 and higher education, promoting students' digital competency, lifelong learning, and innovation readiness. The policies extend beyond student outcomes to encompass teacher development, curriculum innovation, and administrative efficiency. Through Vision 2031, the UAE aims to position education at the heart of its knowledge economy and establish itself as a regional leader in AI-enabled learning (United Arab Emirates Artificial Intelligence Office, 2021).
2. Core Policy Focus The main goal of the UAE's AI-in-education policy is to embed AI literacy as a core competency across all educational stages. The MOE-UAE's 2025 directive mandates AI education from early childhood, engaging students with computational thinking, ethical reasoning, and real-world AI applications (Swidan et al., 2025). Educators are recognized as catalysts for digital transformation; hence, teacher training and professional development are

central priorities (Elnagar & Ghazal, 2024). The AI 2031 Strategy promoted the creation of *AI-ready talent* through specialized academic programs and research partnerships. Beyond technical disciplines, MOE-UAE guidelines endorse AI use for personalized learning, inclusion, and smart administration. Overall, the strategy seeks to prepare learners for an AI-driven economy while embedding ethics, human values, and cultural awareness within innovation (United Arab Emirates Artificial Intelligence Office, 2021).

3. Alignment with the Five Dimensions The UAE's AI education framework embodies the five core dimensions of responsible digital transformation. Ethically, the National AI Strategy (2031) promotes transparency, fairness, and accountability in AI usage, while MOE-UAE curricula address responsible technology use (United Arab Emirates Artificial Intelligence Office, 2021; Alshamsi et al., 2025). Access is expanded through nationwide smart classrooms and equitable digital infrastructure, ensuring that every student, regardless of geographic location or economic status, engages in digital learning (Ministry of Education-UAE, 2023). Inclusion is promoted by embedding AI education across public and private educational institutions serving diverse linguistic and cultural groups. Data use follows strict privacy and ethical analytics standards under the UAE Data Protection Law (2021) (United Arab Emirates Artificial Intelligence Office, 2021). Finally, professional development remains central through teacher training programs, partnerships with AI-focused institutions, and regional digital learning centers that build educators' capacity for AI pedagogy (Elnagar & Ghazal, 2024). These initiatives form a holistic, values-driven model of AI integration in education.
4. Policy-Practice Translation The UAE applies a cohesive, innovation-driven model that connects national strategy with school-level practice. The MOE-UAE has piloted AI curricula across K-12 grade levels and introduced teacher AI training modules (Ministry of Education-UAE, 2025). The MOE's Digital Transformation Journey in Education report highlights AI-powered solutions for assessment, personalization, and administrative automation as key applications. Collaborations with UNESCO and the Regional Centre for Educational Planning further support curriculum design, teacher capacity-building, and AI ethical guidance (Elnagar & Ghazal, 2024). These measures ensure that policy vision is translated effectively into classroom practice.
5. Regional Significance The UAE's AI education initiatives position it as a regional leader in systematic AI integration from kindergarten to university (United Arab Emirates Artificial Intelligence Office, 2021). Partnerships with UNESCO, the Arab League Educational Organization, and global technology institutions establish the UAE as a hub for AI capacity-building and ethical digital transformation (Elnagar & Ghazal, 2024). Through the AI 2031 Strategy,

the UAE promotes regional and international cooperation by sharing expertise, hosting global AI summits, and providing open-access AI resources for Gulf Cooperation Council (GCC) educators. This consolidated vision positions the UAE not only as a digital innovation leader but also as a model for inclusive AI integration, influencing educational reform across the Arab region (United Arab Emirates Artificial Intelligence Office, 2021). Education leaders in the UAE model are global connectors and cultural mediators, expertly integrating external innovation with local values and ensuring rapid capacity-building is ethically and pedagogically grounded.

Africa

Rwanda

1. Policy Context and Scope Unlike the resource-rich environments of Europe and Asia, Rwanda's policy is a pioneering African framework developed under significant constraints. Rwanda's National Artificial Intelligence Policy (2023), approved by the Cabinet in April 2023, marks Africa's first comprehensive national AI framework (Republic of Rwanda, 2023). Developed by the Ministry of Information Communication Technology and Innovation (Ministry of ICT and Innovation) in collaboration with the Ministry of Education, the policy positions education as a central pillar of the nation's digital transformation under Vision 2050 framework (Republic of Rwanda, 2023; Ministry of ICT and Innovation, 2023). Its overarching goal is to leverage AI for economic growth, improve quality of life, and responsible and inclusive AI, with a specific focus on integrating AI and data science into the national curriculum from the primary school level upward.
2. Core Policy Focus The policy outlines a holistic strategy focused on human capital development and curriculum modernization for the AI era (Ministry of ICT and Innovation, 2023). A cornerstone of this effort is the creation of a dedicated Teacher Corps to lead AI integration and teacher training nationwide. The policy also institutionalizes ethics and governance, establishing a multi-sectoral AI Ethics Task Force to design data governance frameworks and ensure responsible, secure, and transparent AI use (Republic of Rwanda, 2023). Complementary investments target human capital development and technological infrastructure, including cloud services, local content creation, and connectivity, to support implementation. Distinctively in Africa, Rwanda embeds ethical governance into educational reform and aligns technological advancement with inclusive and sustainable development goals, positioning itself as a continental leader in AI in education strategies (Ministry of ICT and Innovation, 2023).

3. Alignment with the Five Dimensions Rwanda's framework strongly aligns with most of the five dimensions of digital transformation. Ethics is foregrounded through a national AI Ethics Task Force and the development of guidelines promoting responsible, transparent, and fair AI use (Ministry of ICT and Innovation, 2023). Inclusion is advanced through curriculum modernization and efforts to integrate AI education equitably across all regions and learner groups. Data use is reinforced by transparent, multi-sectoral governance protocols ensuring privacy and accountability (Republic of Rwanda, 2023). Access is addressed through planned investments and leadership innovation such as district-level device-sharing hubs and partnerships with local telecom companies to provide educational data bundles, though disparities between urban and rural schools continue to affect implementation. Finally, professional development is embedded in the Teacher Corps initiative, and the emphasis on educator capacity building and on 21 Century skills (Republic of Rwanda, 2023).
4. Policy-Practice Translation Teachers are positioned as state-supported, key implementers and co-creators of localized digital content within a system of continuous professional training. At the school level, they act as ethical mediators, embedding AI tools and digital literacy into classroom practice. However, their professional agency is partly constrained by centrally developed curriculum mandates, limited resources in rural areas, and prescribed technology frameworks, which can restrict opportunities for critical adaptation to local contexts (Republic of Rwanda, 2023).
5. Regional Significance Rwanda's policy stands out as one of the most forward-looking and comprehensive in Africa, notable for its robust, participatory development process which engaged over 120 stakeholders (Ministry of ICT and Innovation, 2023). While exemplary in its integration of ethics and teacher development, its long-term success is contingent on sustained funding, scalable teacher expertise, and equitable infrastructure, which are challenges shared across the continent's AI education environment. Leadership, in this context, requires pragmatic vision and coalition-building, where success hinges on the ability to mobilize scarce resources through partnerships and to champion incremental, context-sensitive innovation.

South Africa

1. Policy context and scope While sharing Rwanda's aspirational vision, South Africa's policy is distinctively shaped by its history of inequality and a decolonial imperative. South Africa's AI in education strategy evolved from the foundational Presidential Commission on the Fourth Industrial Revolution report (2020) and culminating in the Draft National AI Policy Plan (2024), led

by the Department of Communications and Digital Technologies (Ayandibu, 2024). The policy marks a strategic shift toward embedding AI across sectors including education, with implementation overseen by the Department of Basic Education. This policy aims to embed AI literacy into its broader Digital Learning Strategy, beginning in primary schools, thereby positioning South Africa as a continental leader (Department of Communications and Digital Technologies, 2024). A parallel objective is to address persistent equity gaps inherited from apartheid-era disparities (Presidential Commission on the Fourth Industrial Revolution, 2020).

2. Core Policy Focus The framework prioritizes major infrastructure investment, expanding school-level digital connectivity, and data centers, particularly in historically disadvantaged areas. It also focuses on skills development through academia-industry partnerships and continuous PD and upskilling programs for teachers, particularly in STEM subjects, to bridge the gap between theoretical knowledge and classroom application. Moreover, it integrates AI and computational thinking into the curriculum, introducing coding and robotics from Grades R–9, while mandating ethical reviews to detect algorithmic bias and ensure cultural and linguistic appropriateness, which are key steps toward decolonizing AI content (Department of Communications and Digital Technologies, 2024).
3. Alignment with the Five Dimensions South Africa's policy aligns closely with the access dimension through its infrastructure-first strategy, with school leaders in underserved areas often pioneering solutions like offline AI-enabled learning labs and community Wi-Fi initiatives to bridge immediate gaps. Second, through its sustainable, partnership-based teacher PD initiatives model, it directly engages the professional development dimension (Arek-Bawa & Reddy, 2022). The data-use dimension is addressed through curriculum reforms and careful governance mechanisms for responsible management of student and system data. The evolving ethics dimension is explicitly addressed through policies on algorithmic bias, data sovereignty, and culturally responsive AI. Despite these efforts, the inclusion dimension remains constrained by persistent inequalities, as many rural and under-resourced schools continue to face limited connectivity and digital access (Muyambi & Ramorola, 2025).
4. Policy-Practice Translation The policy envisions teachers as agents of change, who are expected to adopt AI tools, engage in continuous learning, and collaborate with university and industry partners to co-design educational innovations. While the vision promotes teacher agency and leadership in tech development, early research suggests that many teachers remain underprepared and resource-constrained, limiting implementation speed (Mnguni, 2025). Their potential as critical curriculum leaders is unevenly realized across provinces, with implementation largely shaped by disparities in infrastructure and institutional capacity

(Chuene & Teane, 2024). From the perspective of infrastructural equity, Teachers in South Africa often perceive AI leadership not just as a pedagogical choice, but as a struggle to ensure that students in resource-constrained environments are not left further behind by high-tech mandates. Bronagh Hammond, the Western Cape Education Department's Communications Officer expressed that "The responsibility lies upon both educator and learner to reach an equilibrium from embracing innovation and preserving the essence of human intellect... Whether it becomes a catalyst for growth or a shortcut to mediocrity depends entirely on how responsibly we choose to engage with it" (Activate, 2026).

5. Regional Significance While South Africa's policy is among the most comprehensive and ambitious in Africa, its success is entirely contingent on overcoming the digital divide as well as historic inequalities in resource distribution and ensuring sustained funding. Its clear focus on ethics and decolonization offers a valuable model for other postcolonial nations, though translating these ambitions into consistent classroom practice remains an ongoing challenge (Mnguni, 2025). South African leaders operate as equity advocates and bridge builders, tasked with navigating deep historical disparities by securing foundational resources while embedding decolonial and critical perspectives into AI integration.

DISCUSSION

Policy Influence on Classroom Implementation Across Regions

The cross-regional analysis of policy design and classroom implementation reveals shared ambitions and distinct pathways in the integration of AI in education. Addressing the first research question on the manner in which AI in education policies in Europe, Asia, and Africa influence the use and implementation of AI in classrooms, the evidence demonstrates that policy frameworks create conditions for enactment that are shaped by governance models, resource allocation, and assumptions about teacher agency. Viewing this through a policy-enactment lens (Ball et al., 2012), the translation of policy into practice is not a linear implementation but a process of contextualized interpretation and recreation by school-level actors.

In Europe, policies such as the European Union's DEAP and Finland's AI Guidelines for Teachers represent a model that deliberately creates space for professional interpretation. These velue-driven frameworks are designed for enactment through teacher agency, positioning educators as co-designers who interpret, adapt, and ethically mediate AI tools within their pedagogical contexts (Morte-Nadal & Esteban-Navarro, 2025). The European model thus exemplifies how policy can set ethical and infrastructural boundaries while trusting the situated judgment of teachers as the primary policy actors in the classroom (European Commission, 2022). A core tension in this model lies between the high ideal of teacher-led ethical reflection and the practical pressure to rapidly adopt new commercial AI tools, which can subtly erode professional autonomy (Adams et al., 2022).

In Asia, the influence of AI policy follows a different enactment logic. China's Smart Education Initiative and the United Arab Emirates' AI 2031 Strategy are examples of state-led, innovation-oriented approaches. Such policies perceive teachers as skilled implementers of a national vision, in which teacher training, curriculum design, and data infrastructure are aligned with economic and technological priorities (Xie & Luo, 2025). In the UAE, there is growing recognition of the teacher's role as a mediator of ethics and cultural identity within this digital ecosystem. For instance, through initiatives linking AI literacy with values education and professional growth, the UAE's policy demonstrates a nuanced balance between centralized coordination and human-centered purpose. In this context, the tension emerges between the drive for rapid, uniform technological implementation and the deeper, more gradual development of teacher capacity for critical ethical mediation, potentially prioritizing scale over depth (Shafee et al., 2025).

In contrast, policy frameworks of African nations such as Rwanda and South Africa are context-responsive, yet their enactment is fundamentally constrained by material realities. Rwanda's National AI Policy integrates teacher development, ethics, and equity through the creation of a national Teacher Corps and a multi-sectoral AI Ethics Task Force.

Similarly, South Africa's Draft AI Policy Plan and Digital Learning Strategy link infrastructure investment and teacher upskilling with decolonization and inclusion goals. These plans lay a strategic foundation, but their enactment is contingent on overcoming gaps in connectivity, resources, and teacher preparedness (Mnguni, 2025). The central tension is thus between ambitious, equity-focused policy aspirations and the severe material constraints on the ground, which can turn teacher agency from a design principle into a struggle for basic functionality. Teachers in these contexts are often pioneers, yet their agency is mediated by significant infrastructural and institutional limitations, showing a stark disconnect between policy ambition and the conditions for its enactment (Diallo et al., 2025).

These trajectories demonstrate a continuum of policy influence, defined by the degree of agency afforded to teachers in the enactment process. From guided interpretation in Europe, to coordinated implementation in Asia, and aspirational yet constrained mediation in Africa, each model reveals that sustainable AI integration depends less on the policy text itself and more on the supportive ecosystems that enable effective teacher-led enactment.

The Evolving Role of Teachers in AI-Enabled Classrooms

Regarding the second research question on how the role of teachers is evolving in the implementation of AI in classrooms, evidence across regions shows that AI integration in classrooms is redefining educators' professional identities across all systems. Teachers are no longer positioned as transmitters of curriculum content; their expertise now extends to encompass ethical awareness, digital literacy, and decision-making (Ghamrawi et al., 2024).

In Europe, teachers, as co-designers of AI-enabled pedagogy, exercise professional judgment when using AI to ensure transparency, inclusion, and fairness. Finnish educators, for instance, use policy tools such as the AI Guide for Teachers to design reflective learning experiences and to critically evaluate technology use in learning (Mouta et al., 2025).

In Asia, teachers occupy a more technically-oriented role, reflecting the centralized nature of governance. In China, educators implement AI-powered systems in learning under standardized protocols, in a highly regulated environment. Within this model, teachers' capacity for adaptation and feedback is increasingly valued, particularly as local schools pilot AI curricula and contribute to national databases of best practice (Tlili, 2025). In the UAE, teachers' roles blend technical competence with cultural stewardship, while professional development programs emphasize the mechanics of AI together with its responsible use in multilingual and multicultural classrooms. This approach situates teachers as both innovators and moral anchors within this rapidly digitizing education system (Noakes et al., 2024).

In African contexts, the teacher's role is expanding despite systemic challenges. Rwandan and South African educators are considered pioneers as they co-construct digital content, while incorporating ethical reflection into teaching. Their agency, however, remains influenced by infrastructural and institutional constraints (Diallo et al., 2025).

Leadership Implications and Enabling Teacher Agency

Across these diverse policy and governance contexts, several shared patterns emerge in how teachers' roles are evolving in AI-enabled classrooms. Ethics, professional development, and teacher agency consistently function as central drivers of sustainable AI integration, as reflected in initiatives such as the EU's DigCompEdu framework, Rwanda's Teacher Corps, and China's AI-TPACK programs. These initiatives increasingly emphasize critical reflection alongside technical competence, highlighting the need for teachers to exercise informed professional judgment when engaging with AI tools. At the same time, the extent to which teachers can enact these roles varies considerably, depending on local infrastructure, governance arrangements, and institutional cultures.

Building on these patterns, the successful translation of evolving teacher roles into everyday classroom practice depends largely on leadership at school and system levels. Educational leaders play a pivotal role in shaping the conditions for ethical and pedagogically grounded AI use by fostering cultures of professional trust, providing differentiated resources and sustained professional learning, and establishing collaborative structures that support teacher feedback, experimentation, and innovation. Without such leadership support, teacher agency risks remaining aspirational rather than operational, limiting the long-term impact of AI-related reforms.

IMPLICATIONS FOR LEADERSHIP AND PROFESSIONAL DEVELOPMENT

The growing presence of AI in education redefines teachers' professional identities and thus necessitates new forms of digital and pedagogical competence. For example, teachers can no longer rely on subject matter knowledge, but need to be able to read, critique, and adapt algorithmic outputs depending on learning needs and local curriculum goals (Ghamrawi et al., 2024). Teachers can acquire these competencies through PD programs, AI pedagogy labs, micro-credentials, coaching, government-led training or partnership-based initiatives, depending on their regional context (Borenstein & Howard, 2021). These teacher training programs must evolve from including simple digital skills to including courses on algorithmic bias and data privacy in order to foster critical thinking of AI's role in education (El Samaty, 2025). Through such technical and moral awareness, educators will then be able to audit AI outcomes, with deeper commitments to fairness, empathy, and inclusion.

However, sustainable AI integration and the empowerment of teacher agency are ultimately dependent on supportive leadership at the school and system levels. Principals, department heads, and district leaders are pivotal in creating the organizational conditions, such as a culture of reflective experimentation, collaborative time, and ethics, that enable teachers to enact policy effectively. Leadership development must therefore evolve to equip these leaders with specific competencies for the AI-mediated era. These include AI policy literacy to interpret national and regional directives; ethical stewardship to establish governance frameworks for data privacy and conducting equity audits for AI tools within their institutions; and distributed leadership practices to foster teacher-led innovation and build professional learning communities (Zeng et al., 2025). For principals and department heads, this also demands competencies in negotiating with EdTech vendors, interpreting data privacy implications for their school, and facilitating professional learning communities where teachers can safely critique and adapt AI-driven pedagogies.

The cross-regional analysis highlights how leadership models shape enactment. In high-autonomy systems like Finland, school leaders are already facilitators of teacher collaboration, a role that expands to include managing digital transformation. In centralized systems like China, mid-level leaders become crucial mediators who can translate top-down mandates into workable classroom practices and provide upward feedback. In resource-constrained contexts like Rwanda, district and school leaders take on the critical advocacy role of securing infrastructure and partnerships, while protecting teachers from innovation overload.

On the other hand, the implications of AI integration differ sharply across educational systems. In high-autonomy systems, professional development continues to nurture collaborative, teacher-led innovation communities, while in more centralized or resource-constrained contexts, scaffolding teacher agency can still allow room for reflection and adaptation. Moreover, international partnerships and shared knowledge networks can enable teachers and leaders to exchange insights across policy environments. In brief, the success of AI in education relies mainly on a coherent leadership-teacher nexus, where leaders create the enabling environment for teachers to interpret and adapt these technological tools to serve pedagogical and societal aims (Ghamrawi et al., 2024).

A Typology of Teacher-Leadership Synergy for AI Integration

The comparative analysis in *Table 1* reveals distinct regional patterns in how teachers enact AI policy and the specific leadership supports that enable their effectiveness. The following typology synthesizes these trends to provide a concise model for policymakers and educational leaders.

Table 1. Comparative Patterns of Teacher Agency and Leadership Support in AI Integration

Region / Policy Model	Primary Teacher Role in AI Enactment	Leadership Support Required
European (Value-Driven Autonomy)	Pedagogical Designer & Ethical Mediator Teachers interpret and adapt AI tools through reflective, pedagogical, and ethical judgment.	Foster a collaborative culture for critical reflection; protect teacher autonomy in tool selection; provide robust ethical frameworks and professional learning communities.
Asian (Centralized Innovation)	Skilled Implementer & Data Interpreter Teachers execute AI-integrated curricula with technical proficiency and use data to inform instructional adjustments.	Provide high-quality, standardized technical training; align school-level goals with the national innovation vision; create formal channels for teacher feedback to inform policy refinement.
African (Context-Responsive Aspiration)	Pioneer & Adaptive Innovator Teachers navigate significant constraints to pilot AI use, often co-creating localized content and solutions.	Advocate for and secure foundational resources (connectivity, devices); build community and industry partnerships; scaffold and celebrate incremental innovation in low-resource settings.

This model underscores that effective AI integration is not a generic process but requires leadership strategies intentionally matched to the specific teacher role predominant within a given policy and resource context.

CONCLUSION

In conclusion, this cross-regional analysis reveals that the integration of AI in education is not a uniform technological transition but is strongly shaped by the unique policy structures in each context. While Europe's value-driven frameworks prioritize teacher autonomy, Asia's centralized models emphasize rapid implementation, and Africa's aspirational strategies navigate infrastructural constraints. Despite the diversity, it was found that in all contexts, sustainable AI integration depends less on technological sophistication than on empowering teachers as ethical mediators, pedagogical designers, and local policy leaders (Mnguni, 2025). Therefore, policy ambitions alone are insufficient without systemic investment in teacher capacity, contextual adaptability, and conditions that enable educators to translate abstract mandates into equitable classroom practice.

Recommendations for Global Educational Leadership

To translate the insights from this comparative analysis into actionable strategy, the following forward-looking recommendations are proposed for educational leaders at school, system, and policy levels:

1. **Invest in Meso-Leadership Capacity:** Prioritize the development of principals, department heads, and district leaders as the critical brokers of AI policy. Professional development must move beyond technical awareness to equip them with competencies in ethical technology stewardship, strategic resource advocacy, and the facilitation of teacher-led innovation communities.
2. **Create Co-Governance Frameworks with the EdTech Sector:** Develop proactive policy and procurement standards that mandate transparency, pedagogical alignment, and equity audits for private-sector AI tools. Leaders should establish formal channels for educator feedback in EdTech development to ensure tools serve public educational values.
3. **Design Differentiated Support Systems:** Adapt support models to the dominant teacher role in each context: protecting autonomous reflection in high-agency systems, enabling effective translation and feedback in centralized systems, and fostering entrepreneurial partnership-building in resource-constrained contexts.
4. **Establish Global Peer Networks for Equitable Innovation:** Create international partnerships that connect leaders across similar resource and challenge profiles (e.g., a network for rural school principals integrating AI). These networks should focus on sharing concrete, low-cost strategies for improving access, auditing for bias, and navigating ethical dilemmas.
5. **Embed Foresight and Evaluation into Policy Cycles:** Make regular, evidence-based reviews of AI's educational impact, involving teachers and leaders in the assessment process. This will enable policies to adapt dynamically to technological change and on-the-ground realities.

Ultimately, the future of AI in education will be determined by the quality of leadership that navigates the complex interplay of policy, pedagogy, and professional agency across global contexts.

REFERENCES

Activate! (2026, January 13). *When AI replaces effort: The silent cries in South African classrooms.* https://activatechangedrivers.co.za/when-ai-replaces-effort-the-silent-cries-in-south-african-classrooms/

Adams, C., Pente, P., Lemermeyer, G., Turville, J., & Rockwell, G. (2022). Artificial intelligence and teachers' new ethical obligations. *International Journal of Information Ethics, 31*(1). Advance online publication. DOI: 10.29173/irie483

Al-Zahrani, A. M., & Alasmari, T. (2024). Exploring the impact of artificial intelligence on higher education: The dynamics of ethical, social, and educational implications. *Humanities & Social Sciences Communications, 11*(1), 1–12. DOI: 10.1057/s41599-024-03432-4

Alshamsi, S., Alshamsi, D., Mohammed, K., & El Khatib, M. (2025). Global perspectives on AI usage in the education sector: Insights from the UAE education system. *International Journal of Technology and Systems, 10*(2), 1–26. DOI: 10.47604/ijts.3221

Amiri, S. M. H., Islam, M. M., & Akter, N. (2025). Educating the future: AI's role in shaping next-generation pedagogies. *International Journal of Science and Research Archive, 15*(1), 621–636. DOI: 10.30574/ijsra.2025.15.1.1036

Arek-Bawa, O., & Reddy, S. (2022). Digital curricular transformation and fourth industrial revolution 4.0 (4IR): Deepening divides or building bridges. *E-Journal of Humanities. Arts and Social Sciences, 7*(11), 308–326. DOI: 10.38159/ehass.2022sp31124

Atenas, J., Havemann, L., & Timmermann, C. (2023). Reframing data ethics in research methods education: A pathway to critical data literacy. *International Journal of Educational Technology in Higher Education, 20*(1), 11. DOI: 10.1186/s41239-023-00380-y PMID: 36846483

Ayandibu, E. (2024). Artificial intelligence and ethical implications in South African higher education: A policy framework perspective. *International Journal of Innovative Technologies in Economy, 3*(47), 1–9. DOI: 10.31435/rsglobal_ijite/30092024/82111

Ball, S. J., Maguire, M., & Braun, A. (2012). *How schools do policy: Policy enactments in secondary schools*. Routledge.

Borenstein, J., & Howard, A. (2021). Emerging challenges in AI and the need for AI ethics education. *AI and Ethics, 1*(1), 61–65. DOI: 10.1007/s43681-020-00002-7 PMID: 38624388

Braun, A., Ball, S. J., Maguire, M., & Hoskins, K. (2011). Taking context seriously: Towards explaining policy enactments in the secondary school. *Discourse (Abingdon), 32*(4), 585–596. DOI: 10.1080/01596306.2011.601555

Bray, M., Adamson, B., & Mason, M. (Eds.). (2014). *Comparative education research: Approaches and methods* (Vol. 19). Springer. DOI: 10.1007/978-3-319-05594-7

Chuene, D. M., & Teane, F. M. (2024). Resource inadequacy as a barrier to effective curriculum implementation by life sciences teachers in South Africa. *South African Journal of Education, 44*(2), 1–10. DOI: 10.15700/saje.v44n2a2387

Coburn, C. E. (2005). Shaping teacher sensemaking: School leaders and the enactment of reading policy. *Educational Policy, 19*(3), 476–509. DOI: 10.1177/0895904805276143

Department of Communications and Digital Technologies. (2024). Draft national artificial intelligence policy plan. Pretoria: Government of South Africa. https://www.dcdt.gov.za/sa-national-ai-policy-framework/file/338-sa-national-ai-policy-framework.html

El Samaty, M. (2025). Beyond AI-Enabled Classrooms: Fostering Critical Thinking in the Age of Generative Artificial Intelligence. In ElSayary, A. (Ed.), *Prompt Engineering and Generative AI Applications for Teaching and Learning* (pp. 527–546). IGI Global Scientific Publishing., DOI: 10.4018/979-8-3693-7332-3.ch030

Elnagar, A., & Ghazal, M. (2024). *AI in the United Arab Emirates' computing, creative design and innovation K-12 curriculum: A case study*. UNESCO. https://unesdoc.unesco.org/ark:/48223/pf0000388652

Engeness, I., & Gamlem, S. M. (2025). Agency in digital education: Empowering students and teachers in technology-rich learning environments. *Education Sciences, 15*(8), 1051. DOI: 10.3390/educsci15081051

European Commission. (2020, September 30). *Digital Education Action Plan (2021–2027): Resetting education and training for the digital age* (COM (2020) 624 final). Publications Office of the European Union. https://education.ec.europa.eu/focus-topics/digital-education/action-plan

European Commission. (2021, March 9). *2030 Digital Compass: The European way for the Digital Decade* (COM(2021) 118 final). https://www.europeansources.info/record/2030-digital-compass-the-european-way-for-the-digital-decade/

European Commission. (2022). *Ethical guidelines on the use of artificial intelligence (AI) and data in teaching and learning for educators.* Publications Office of the European Union. https://education.ec.europa.eu/news/ethical-guidelines-on-the-use-of-artificial-intelligence-and-data-in-teaching-and-learning-for-educators

Finnish National Agency for Education. (2024). *AI guide for teachers.* https://www.oph.fi/en/statistics-and-publications/publications/ai-guide-teachers

Finnish National Agency for Education. (2025). *AI guidelines.* https://www.oph.fi/en/ai-guidelines

Funa, A., & Gabay, R. A. E. (2024). Policy guidelines and recommendations on AI use in teaching and learning: A meta-synthesis study. *Social Sciences & Humanities Open, 11*, 101221. Advance online publication. DOI: 10.1016/j.ssaho.2024.101221

Ghamrawi, N., Shal, T., & Ghamrawi, N. A. (2024). Exploring the impact of AI on teacher leadership: Regressing or expanding? *Education and Information Technologies, 29*(7), 8415–8433. DOI: 10.1007/s10639-023-12174-w

King, E. (2021). Translating policy into practice: Cambodian primary schoolteachers' sense- making of the Child Friendly Schools policy. *Compare: A Journal of Comparative Education, 52*(8), 1314–1331. DOI: 10.1080/03057925.2020.1866495

Kivinen, K. (2025, February 20). *AI literacy frameworks for teachers.* Faktabaari EDU. https://faktabaari.fi/edu/ai-literacy-frameworks-for-teachers/

Knox, J. (2020). Artificial intelligence and education in China. *Learning, Media and Technology, 45*(3), 298–311. DOI: 10.1080/17439884.2020.1754236

Leithwood, K., Harris, A., & Hopkins, D. (2020). Seven strong claims about successful school leadership revisited. *School Leadership & Management, 40*(1), 5–22. DOI: 10.1080/13632434.2019.1596077

Leppänen, P. (2024). *Digital competence – the Finnish framework.* https://www.erasmusplus.lv/sites/default/files/media_document/Digital%20Competence%20%E2%80%93%20the%20Finnish%20Framework.pdf

Maguire, M., Braun, A., & Ball, S. J. (2015). 'Where you stand depends on where you sit': The social construction of policy enactments in the (English) secondary school. *Discourse (Abingdon), 36*(4), 485–499. DOI: 10.1080/01596306.2014.977022

Michopoulou, K., & Gan, J. K. C. (2025). Ethical leadership in AI-enabled schools: Navigating human rights, equity, and justice in education. *European Journal of Education and Pedagogy, 6*(5), 24–33. DOI: 10.24018/ejedu.2025.6.5.988

Ministry of Education and Culture. (2023). *Finland's policies for the digitalisation of education and training until 2027*. https://dig.watch/resource/finlands-policies-for-the-digitalisation-of-education-and-training-until-2027

Ministry of Education of the People's Republic of China. (2024, December 10). *Guidance on teaching AI in primary and middle schools*. http://en.moe.gov.cn/news/press_releases/202412/t20241210_1166454.html

Ministry of Education of the People's Republic of China. (2025, April 3). *MOE outlines 2025 national strategy for digital education*. http://en.moe.gov.cn/news/press_releases/202504/t20250403_1186060.html

Ministry of Education-UAE. (2023, November 17). *Digital transformation journey in education*. https://www.moe.gov.ae/En/ImportantLinks/Pages/DigitalTransformation.aspx

Ministry of ICT and Innovation. (2023). National artificial intelligence policy. Kigali: Republic of Rwanda. https://www.minict.gov.rw/index.php?eID=dumpFile&t=f&f=67550&token=6195a53203e197efa47592f40ff4aaf24579640e

Mnguni, L. (2025). A qualitative analysis of South African pre-service life sciences teachers' behavioral intentions for integrating AI in teaching. *Journal for STEM Education Research*, *8*(2), 230–256. DOI: 10.1007/s41979-024-00128-x

Morte-Nadal, T., & Esteban-Navarro, M. Á. (2025). Recommendations for digital inclusion in the use of European digital public services. *Humanities & Social Sciences Communications*, *12*(1), 1–14. DOI: 10.1057/s41599-025-04576-7

Mouta, A., Torrecilla-Sánchez, E. M., & Pinto-Llorente, A. M. (2025). Comprehensive professional learning for teacher agency in addressing ethical challenges of AIED: Insights from educational design research. *Education and Information Technologies*, *30*(3), 3343–3387. DOI: 10.1007/s10639-024-12946-y

Muyambi, G. C., & Ramorola, M. Z. (2025). Unveiling educators' readiness to teach through Digital Media (DM): The case of South Africa. *Education and Information Technologies*, *30*(10), 13807–13834. DOI: 10.1007/s10639-024-13310-w

Noakes, S., Shell, A., Murillo, A. M., Nostrand, P. V., Ruiz, P., Cornick, S., & Karim, S. (2024). *An Ethical and Equitable Vision of AI in Education: Learning Across 28 Exploratory Projects*. Digital Promise., DOI: 10.51388/20.500.12265/232

NordForsk. (2024, May 7). *Annex 2: National AI strategies in the Nordic countries*. https://www.nordforsk.org/node/1377

Presidential Commission on the Fourth Industrial Revolution. (2020). Report of the Presidential Commission on the Fourth Industrial Revolution. Republic of South Africa. ttps://www.gov.za/sites/default/files/gcis_document/201904/42388gen209.pdf

Republic of Rwanda. (2023). Vision 2050 and national AI implementation strategy. Kigali: Government of Rwanda. https://www.minecofin.gov.rw/fileadmin/user_upload/Minecofin/Publications/REPORTS/National_Development_Planning_and_Research/Vision_2050/English-Vision_2050_Abridged_version_WEB_Final.pdf

Shafee, M., Sabri, S., Ismail, I., Abd Hamid, N., & Khushairi, N. (2025). Digital education in ASEAN: A strategic framework for sustainable growth. *International Journal of Research and Innovation in Social Science*, *9*(24), 38–43. DOI: 10.47772/IJRISS.2025.924ILEIID005

Spillane, J. P. (2006). *Distributed leadership*. Jossey-Bass.

Sposato, M. (2025). Artificial intelligence in educational leadership: A comprehensive taxonomy and future directions. *International Journal of Educational Technology in Higher Education*, *22*(1), 20. Advance online publication. DOI: 10.1186/s41239-025-00517-1

State Council of the People's Republic of China. (2025, May 13). *China advances AI curriculum to cover full basic education*. http://english.scio.gov.cn/pressroom/2025-05/13/content_117871666.html

Swidan, A., Lee, S. Y., & Romdhane, S. B. (2025). College students' use and perceptions of AI tools in the UAE: Motivations, ethical concerns and institutional guidelines. *Education Sciences*, *15*(4), 461. DOI: 10.3390/educsci15040461

Tlili, A. (2025). Artificial intelligence in higher education in China: Policy, case study, and challenges. *Revue Internationale d Éducation de Sèvres*, *HS - 4*(HS-4). Advance online publication. DOI: 10.4000/146vq

United Arab Emirates Artificial Intelligence Office. (2021). *UAE National Strategy for Artificial Intelligence 2031*. https://ai.gov.ae/wp-content/uploads/2021/07/UAE-National-Strategy-for-Artificial-Intelligence-2031.pdf

University of Eastern Finland. (2024, June 12). *AI education in Finland: Enhancing children's understanding, critical thinking and creativity through collaborative designing of AI apps*. https://www.uef.fi/en/article/ai-education-in-finland-enhancing-childrens-understanding-critical-thinking-and-creativity-through

Watch, A. I. (2021, September 1). *Finland AI Strategy Report*. European Commission. https://ai-watch.ec.europa.eu/countries/finland/finland-ai-strategy-report_en

Wei, G., & Niemi, H. (2023). Ethical guidelines for artificial intelligence-based learning: A transnational study between China and Finland. In Niemi, H., Pea, R. D., & Lu, Y. (Eds.), *AI in Learning: Designing the Future* (pp. 265–282). Springer., DOI: 10.1007/978-3-031-09687-7_16

Xie, Y., & Luo, Z. (2025). *The status quo and future of AI-TPACK for mathematics teacher education students: A case study in Chinese universities*. ArXiv. /arXiv.2503.13533DOI: 10.48550

Xinhua News Agency. (2025, May 17). *Chinese Smart Education Online Platform Surpasses* 164 Mln Registered Users. https://english.www.gov.cn/archive/statistics/202505/17/content_WS6828769cc6d0868f4e8f29e4.html

Zeng, M., Lee, K. C. S., & Abdullah, Z. (2025). The influence of school principals' digital leadership on teachers' competency in integrating artificial intelligence: A systematic thematic review. *Frontiers in Education*, *10*, 1655967. Advance online publication. DOI: 10.3389/feduc.2025.1655967

Zou, S. (2025, December 10). *Experts weigh pros and cons of AI in education.* China Daily. https://www.chinadaily.com.cn/a/202512/10/WS6938c7c7a310d6866eb2dcae.html

Chapter 10
Transforming Education Through AI:
A Global Policy Perspective

Noor Aisha
http://orcid.org/0000-0002-4306-8203
Indira Gandhi National Open University, India

Ghadah Al Murshidi
http://orcid.org/0000-0002-0230-2825
United Arab Emirates University, UAE

Badria Almurshidi
http://orcid.org/0009-0001-2784-9069
United Arab Emirates University, UAE

Ahmed Al Zaabi
General Department of Protective Security and Emergency, Dubai Police Academy, UAE

Maxwell Peprah Opoku
http://orcid.org/0000-0001-7620-0007
United Arab Emirates University, UAE

ABSTRACT

The integration of Artificial Intelligence (AI) in education has transformative potential, but its effective implementation requires robust policies in national and global contexts. The present research conducted a thematic analysis of existing policies for AI in education The study's results explain the development of effective policies, guide educators on AI use, and identify areas for further research. By exploring the potential consequences of different policy approaches, this research contributes to

DOI: 10.4018/979-8-3373-4908-4.ch010

the development of comprehensive and coordinated policies for AI in education, and bridging it with practice to equip educational leaders to bring sustainable transformation and ultimately enhancing the responsible use of AI technologies and contributing to the creation of a more equitable, inclusive, and effective education system that leverages the benefits of AI to enhance student learning outcomes and prepare future generations for success in an increasingly complex and rapidly changing world.

INTRODUCTION

The integration of Artificial Intelligence (AI) into the educational sector has the potential to revolutionize the traditional teaching and learning paradigm (Fitria, 2021). As, AI technologies become more pervasive in educational settings, they offer the capacity to enhance students' outcomes, streamline teacher efficiency and expand access to academic resources (Vieriu & Petrea, 2025; Treve, 2024; Fitria, 2021). However, the increasing prevalence of these tools necessitates a critical examination of the policies governing their implementation (Onuorah & Bosso, 2024). Robust policy frameworks are essential to ensuring that AI is deployed in a manner that fosters equity, inclusion and high-quality education for all learners (Onuorah & Bosso, 2024; Ajirotutu et al., 2024).

The development and deployment of AI in education are largely governed by national policy frameworks (NEP, 2020). By regulating technology acquisition, curriculum design and teacher preparation, these policies determine the impacts of AI on learning environments (Vieriu & Petrea, 2025; Fitria, 2021). Robust policy-making is essential to ensure that AI integration fosters positive outcomes for all stakeholders in the education system (Ajirotutu et al., 2024).

Academic discourse highlights the importance of effective governance to guarantee the responsible use of AI in educational settings (Onuorah & Bosso, 2024). Despite AI's proven potential to improve academic performance and teacher productivity, these benefits must be balanced against critical challenges (Walter, 2024; Fitria, 2021). Specifically, issues regarding data security, equity and inherent bias (Maghsoudi, et al., 2025) remain a primary concern for policymakers and educational leaders.

The opportunities and risks associated with AI in education necessitate a critical review of existing policy frameworks (Onuorah & Bosso, 2024). This study explores the dominant themes in existing AI in education policies and their implications for stakeholders. Therefore, a thematic analysis was conducted, to identify the key themes and trends in the policies for AI in education. The research objectives guiding this study are:

1. To identify the key themes in existing policies for AI in education.
2. To explore the implications of these themes for the stakeholders.

By analyzing current policies and literature, this study seeks to provide a comprehensive overview of AI's regulatory state in education. The significance of this research lies in its potential to foster more equitable, inclusive and effective education systems by informing the development of robust policy frameworks and implementation for AI in education.

LITERATURE REVIEW

In recent years, the role of AI in education has become a priority for global policymakers, driven by the recognition that these technologies can fundamentally reshape the educational experience for both students and educators (Maharishi et al., 2025). The rapid proliferation of AI in education requires policymakers to develop effective strategies that maximize technological advantages while proactively addressing associated risks (Ajirotutu et al., 2024; Kolog et al., 2022). The development of policies on AI has become a priority for many countries around the world (Li et al., 2025; Shittu et al., 2024). The policies aim to promote the development and adoption of AI (Igbinenikaro & Adewusi, 2024), while also addressing the potential risks and challenges associated with its use (Filgueiras, 2024; K. Wang et al., 2021).

Recent studies have shown that many countries are developing policies to support the integration of AI in education (Li et al., 2025; Maharishi et al., 2025; Shittu et al., 2024; NEP, 2020). The policies focus on promoting digital literacy, developing AI-related skills, and ensuring equal access to equitable and sufficient AI-powered educational resources (S. Wang, 2024; Agba et al., 2023; Kolog et al., 2022; Fitria, 2021). The European Union's Digital Education Action Plan (2021-2027) emphasizes the need for AI-powered education that is inclusive, accessible, and of high quality (Yanli & Danni, 2021).

Several countries have developed policies and strategies for AI (Li et al., 2025; Shittu et al., 2024). These policies vary in their focus and approach, but most emphasize the importance of promoting AI research and development, supporting the adoption of AI in industry, and ensuring that AI is developed and used in a responsible and ethical manner (Li et al., 2025; Shenkoya, 2023; Shittu et al., 2024; Chatterjee, 2020; Igbinenikaro & Adewusi, 2024)

Despite the growing interest in AI in education, several challenges and concerns have been raised (Filgueiras, 2024; Kolog et al., 2022; K. Wang et al., 2021). One major concern is the lack of transparency and accountability in AI decision-making processes (Shenkoya, 2023; K. Wang et al., 2021). Additionally, there are concerns about bias in AI-powered systems, which can perpetuate existing inequalities and disadvantage certain groups of students (Kolog et al., 2022; K. Wang et al., 2021). Furthermore, the integration of AI tools introduces significant concerns regarding the privacy and security of student data.

Several key policy implications for AI in education were identified. It is imperative to ensure that AI-driven systems are transparent, explainable and inherently fair (Walter, 2024; (Oluwaseun et al., 2022). Additionally, sustained professional development is required to equip educators with the competencies necessary to integrate AI effectively into their pedagogical practices. Also, policymakers must prioritize equity and inclusion (Oluwaseun et al., 2022), within policy frameworks to guarantee that all students have equitable access to AI-powered resources and opportunities (Vieriu & Petrea, 2025; Ajirotutu et al., 2024).

AI policy frameworks are increasingly multifaceted, focusing on the expansion of research, infrastructure and innovations (Shittu et al., 2024). Beyond education, the policies facilitate industrial AI adoption by offering financial support and resources for implementation (Eckhardt et al., 2021). To ensure responsible use, ethical safeguards regarding transparency and bias (Ajirotutu et al., 2024; Shenkoya, 2023) have been mandated, with a primary focus on talent acquisition through significant investment directed towards AI-centered education and professional training (Oluwaseun et al., 2022).

Developing evidence-based policies for AI in education should be a primary focus of future research (Oluwaseun et al., 2022). This includes evaluating how AI transforms learning processes and teacher roles (Vieriu & Petrea, 2025). Moreover, researcher should address the critical ethical gaps in current literature, prioritizing studies on accountability and the societal impact of AI (Shenkoya, 2023). As AI policy in education continues to evolve, global stakeholders are focused on balancing innovation with ethical safeguards. It is evident that effective governance must be grounded in transparency, accountability and equity (Shenkoya, 2023; Oluwaseun et al., 2022). This study synthesizes existing policies to provided a foundation for strategic framework for AI integration that prioritizes students' success and systemic fairness.

While AI policies are becoming more common, their effectiveness and ling-term consequences are not yet fully understood. A major limitation is the absence of comprehensive research into how these policies drive or hinder AI adoption. Additionally, more work is needed to assess the specific impacts of these regulations on diverse stakeholders for successful implementation (Oluwaseun et al., 2022).

Despite the foundational role of national and global AI policies, there is notable gap between theoretical goals and localized implementation. Research suggests that the actual integration of AI is less a product of policy mandates and more a result of institutional readiness, the influence of leadership and the unique socio-technical environments contexts of educational institutions (Bearman et al., 2023).

Research regarding AI ethics in education underscores that, the lack of robust leadership may exacerbate existing systemic inequities. These disparities may stem from the use of biased training data, the lack of transparency or black-box algorithms and the persistent digital-divide regarding infrastructure access (Williamson et al., 2023; Zawacki-Richter et al., 2019). Additionally, the teachers' adoption of AI is greatly influenced by their pedagogical values, autonomy and technological skills. Without adequate leadership guidance and training, educators may resist these tools or utilize them only at a surface level, failing to achieve deeper educational impact (Holmes et al., 2022).

While educational leaders are the primary mediators of policy, tasked with everything from ethical oversight to stakeholder engagement. Future researches on AI in education needs to focus on their perspectives. Hence, a descriptive analysis of policy is presented in this study which can further guide the future researches towards an exploration of leadership-informed implementation which is essential for the sustainable AI implementation in education.

METHODOLOGY

The development of policies on AI in education is a critical area of focus, considering the potential of AI to transform the education sector. Through employing a qualitative research approach, a comprehensive review of 15 policy documents, this research aims to identify key themes or trends and implications focused in the policies on AI in education. This study aims to contribute to this understanding by conducting a thematic analysis of policies on AI in education.

This research employed a thematic analysis approach, using a framework that categorizes policies on AI in education into six key areas: Policy and Governance, Teaching and Learning, Ethics and Responsibility, Inclusion and Accessibility, Research and Development, and Collaboration and Partnerships. By examining the policies in these areas, this study intended to provide a comprehensive understanding of the current state of AI in education and identify implications and opportunities for future growth and development.

The data have been analysed using thematic analysis approach by Braun and Clarke's (2006) thematic analysis which involves six phases: familiarizing with the data, generating initial codes, searching for themes, reviewing themes, defining and naming themes, and producing the report. This process allows researchers to systematically analyse qualitative data, identify patterns, and develop meaningful themes that capture the essence of the data.

RESULTS

The study employed an analytical framework that categorizes national policies on AI in education into six key areas or themes: Policy and Governance; Teaching and Learning; Ethics and Responsibility; Inclusion and Accessibility; Research and Development; Collaboration and Partnerships.

Theme 1: Policy and Governance

Governments are creating policies to ensure that AI is used responsibly in education. This includes developing guidelines for the development, implementation, and oversight of AI tools. The goal is to reduce administrative workload for teachers, allowing them to focus on teaching and helping students. AI can help with tasks like grading, tracking student progress, and managing school operations. By automating administrative tasks, AI can help reduce teachers' workload, allowing them to focus on teaching and helping students. For AI to be effective in education, schools need the right infrastructure and resources. This includes having reliable internet connectivity, computers, and other digital tools. It is also important to ensure that all students and teachers have equal access to these resources, regardless of their background or location. Reliable infrastructure and resources are essential for AI to be effective in education. This includes internet connectivity, computers, and other digital tools. Ensuring equal access to these resources is crucial to prevent disparities in education. Effective policy frameworks and governance are crucial for the responsible adoption of AI in education. Governments and educational institutions need to develop guidelines and regulatory frameworks that ensure the safe and effective use of AI tools. This includes establishing standards for AI use, providing funding for AI infrastructure, and ensuring internet connectivity and access. By investing in AI infrastructure and resources, educational institutions can create an environment that supports innovative teaching and learning.

Policy Frameworks and Governance: It has been the focus of governments to create rules and guidelines for using AI in education, which would focus the development, implementation, and oversight of AI in education in the context of Automation and Administrative Tasks. One key goal is to reduce the administrative workload of teachers, allowing them to focus on teaching and helping students. AI can help with tasks like grading, tracking student progress, and managing institutional operations. By automating these tasks, teachers can spend more time on what matters most, thereby providing quality education and achieving learning outcomes. The European Parliament (2021) has mentioned that "AI could have practical applications in terms of reducing the administrative work of educators and educational institutions, freeing up time for their core teaching and learning activities" (p. 7).

The OECD (2023) explains that "...governments are actively working to design, update and implement digital education policies. Most of these policies seek to harness the power of digital technologies to solve quality, equity and efficiency issues in educational systems..." (p. 373).

UNESCO (2021) remarks that-

Artificial intelligence (AI) is envisioned as a new tool to accelerate the progress towards the achievement of SDG 4. Policies and strategies for using AI in education are central to maximizing the benefits of AI and mitigating its potential risks. Fostering AI-ready policy-makers is the starting point of the policy development process (p. 50).

Therefore, it was observed that to draft policies on AI in education, emerging existing policies and best practices can be collected and analyzed, humanistic and strategic objectives can be planned, key policy components can be identified, and then implementation strategies can thereby be developed (UNESCO, 2021, p.4).

Infrastructure and Resources: For AI to be effective in education, institutions need the right infrastructure, resources and policies related to the development and maintenance of AI infrastructure in education. This includes having reliable internet connectivity, computers, and other digital tools. It is also important to ensure that all students and teachers have equal access to these resources, regardless of their background or location. Governments are continuously working to invest in these areas, but there's still a lot of work to be done. Without proper infrastructure and resources, the benefits of AI in education cannot be fully realized. In simple terms, governments are trying to create a framework that allows AI to support education, while also ensuring that everyone has access to the necessary tools and resources. This requires careful planning, investment, and implementation. Realizing the importance, the European Parliament (2021) suggested to acquire "...equal and fair access to digital technologies and high-speed connectivity ... in order to make the use of AI beneficial to the whole of society" (p. 7). While focusing on a sufficient investment for AI in education, the European Parliament (2021) remarks that "... public investment in AI in the Union has been vastly lagging behind other major economies; whereas underinvestment in AI will be likely to have an impact on the Union's competitiveness across all sectors" (p. 5). Insufficient investment in AI can compromise a region's or country's competitiveness across various sectors, as AI is a key driver of innovation and economic growth. Or, more broadly, adequate investment in AI is crucial for maintaining competitiveness and driving economic growth in today's technology-driven world. While pointing the relevance of sufficient infrastructure, the OECD (2023) mentioned that-

The implementation of digital education policies is inherently complex for at least two reasons. First, it needs to integrate activities of different domains such as the provision of digital infrastructure in schools, the production and distribution of digital materials, and teachers' professional development. (OECD, 2023, p.373).

Thus, the advent of data-driven insights has revolutionized policy planning, facilitating better decision-making. Integrating AI technology into education management systems can significantly enhance data collection and processing. This, in turn, can make education management and delivery more effective, equitable, and personalized, ultimately benefiting all stakeholders (UNESCO, 2021, p.17). So, as to develop AI-powered systems to monitor and track learning outcomes and credentials across various educational levels and locations. This involves creating platforms that facilitate skill specialization and exploring ways to utilize AI to increase access to educational credentials and qualification pathways, making it easier for individuals to pursue their educational and career goals (p.38).

Theme 2: Teaching and Learning

As AI continues to spread rapidly, it is critical for students, teachers, and educators to understand how to use it effectively. This includes understanding how to use AI to personalize learning, identify biases, and develop critical thinking skills. Teachers play a critical role in integrating AI into education. To do this successfully, they need training and support. AI can make learning more engaging and effective for students. Using AI-powered education, students can receive personalized instruction tailored to their individual needs and abilities. Governments are implementing policies to help teachers learn how to use AI tools to improve teaching and learning. It includes monitoring student progress, providing personalized instruction, and rethinking traditional teaching methods. Policies are being developed to use AI-powered education to improve student engagement, motivation, and learning outcomes. A key benefit of AI in education is personalized learning, where students receive customized educational approaches tailored to their individual needs and abilities. AI has the potential to transform teaching and learning by providing personalized learning methods, adaptive assessments, and feedback. To achieve this goal, teachers need training and support to develop their AI literacy and competence. It includes curriculum development, teacher training programs, and assessment frameworks that incorporate AI-powered tools. Teachers also need resources and incentives to develop their skills and effectively support students.

AI Literacy and Competency: For an AI-driven education, governments are implementing policies to promote AI literacy to prepare students, teachers, and educators. It requires developing the skills and knowledge needed to effectively utilize AI tools and leverage their potential to enhance learning. The aim is to equip the stakeholders with the necessary competencies to thrive in a world where AI is increasingly pervasive. In this context, UNESCO (2021) has remarked that "future learning and training systems must equip all people with core AI competencies, including understanding of how AI collects and can manipulate data, and skills to ensure safety and protection of personal data (UNESCO, 2021, p.4). However, merely providing access to digital resources is not enough; a more rigorous effort is required to bridge the gap between access to digital devices or tools and its effective use. According to OECD (2023), there is "a disparity between the availability of digital resources and their actual use, with findings indicating underutilization or ineffective application." (OECD, 2023, p.152). By prioritizing AI literacy and competency development, it can be ensured that the stakeholders are well-prepared to succeed in an AI-integrated education. According to UNESCO (2021), it is crucial to "integrate AI-related skills into school curricula and technical and vocational education and training ... to prepare students for the future, ensuring their relevance to shifting economies, labor markets and societies across all subjects and competencies" which requires to "develop courses, programmes and qualifications to provide awareness and expertise around how AI technologies work, their ethical implications, and how they should be designed" (UNESCO, 2021, p.39). Therefore, in today's digital landscape, the ability to continuously learn and adapt in AI is key to job security and career longevity. In this context the European Parliament (2021) has remarked that "... the notion of lifelong learning in AI has emerged as one of the key strategies for job security and employment in the digital era" (p. 27).

Teacher Professional Development: There is an emerging need of policies supporting teachers in integrating AI into their practice. Teachers play a vital role in integrating AI into education. To do this successfully, they need training and support. Governments are implementing policies to help teachers learn how to use AI tools in ways that enhance teaching and learning. This includes monitoring student progress, providing personalized education, and rethinking traditional teaching methods. The key is not just about using technology, but about using it in a way that improves learning outcomes. By developing teachers' digital competencies, education systems can ensure that they are using AI effectively. The OECD (2023) mentioned that the "...digital technologies in education systems are not in themselves a transformative force: they require educators who know how to use them in ways that can strengthen innovative teaching practices and improve learning outcomes" (OECD, 2023, p.180). The European Parliament (2021) support the idea that AI is "...enabling teachers to closely monitor students' progress. ... to make personalized education a reality..." (European Parliament, 2021, p.26). The growing integration of AI in education necessitates a comprehensive overhaul of the education system, including redefining teaching roles and providing retraining for educators. This transformation requires a fundamental shift in the approach of education, teaching, and teacher training (European Parliament, 2021, p.27). However, learning outcomes are determined not by technology itself, but by teachers' ability to integrate it in pedagogically effective ways. Effective technology use in education depends on teachers' skill in leveraging it to enhance learning (European Parliament, 2021, p.7). According to OECD (2023), "education systems can formalize the development of teacher digital competences…" (p.202); through a multi-faceted approach. This includes establishing and enforcing professional teacher standards, providing incentives for professional development, and creating comprehensive support structures for teachers and digital education initiatives, ultimately enhancing the effective integration of technology in educational settings (OECD, 2023). This systemic transformation should involve educators in AI development and deployment, focusing on practical applications that support their daily tasks and reinforce their essential role in education (UNESCO, 2021). Teachers need ongoing training and assistance to master AI tools, ensuring they can seamlessly integrate technology into their work. By providing comprehensive training and reliable support, educators can confidently leverage AI to enhance their teaching practices. This includes providing dependable resources and support to address any technical issues that may arise, ultimately investing in their professional development and equipping them with the necessary skills and knowledge (UNESCO, 2021).

Student Engagement and Learning Outcomes: There is a need to enhance student engagement, motivation, and learning outcomes through AI-powered education. AI can help make learning more engaging and effective for students. Policies are being developed to use AI-powered education to enhance student engagement, motivation, and learning outcomes. One of the main benefits of AI in education is personalized learning, where students receive a tailored educational approach that meets their individual needs and abilities. However, simply using digital technologies is not sufficient, what matters is that how teachers use them. Through adequate training and support, teachers can harness the power of AI to improve student learning outcomes. By harnessing the power of AI, education can become more adaptive, catering to the unique strengths, challenges, and learning styles of each student. This tailored approach enables learners to receive a more effective and engaging educational experience (European Parliament, 2021).

But, simply the mere integration of digital technologies into educational settings does not inherently lead to better learning outcomes for students (OECD, 2023), which further emphasize the importance of the intervention and training of teachers UNESCO (2021).

The application of AI in education has seen rapid expansion over the last decade, with an accelerated uptake following the pandemic-induced shift in educational landscapes (Holmes et al., 2019). Despite this growth, there is still limited understanding of impact of AI on learning outcomes and its potential to inform the science and practice of effective learning (Zawacki-Richter et al., 2019; UNESCO, 2021, p.16). Educational AI can be organized into distinct categories that address specific needs. The four key areas suggested by (Baker et al., 2019) includes managing and delivering education, facilitating learning and assessment, supporting teachers, and fostering lifelong learning. Each category has its own set of applications, and many AI solutions can bridge multiple areas, such as tutorial apps that benefit both students and educators (UNESCO, 2021, p.6).

Theme 3: Ethics and Responsibility

Ensuring that AI is used fairly, transparently, and accountably is crucial. Governments are focusing to address the ethical implications of AI in education, including preventing biases and unfair treatment. As AI becomes more prevalent in education, it is crucial to ensure that it is used in a way that is fair, transparent, and accountable. Governments are aiming to address the ethical implications of AI in education, including ensuring that AI tools do not perpetuate biases or unfair treatment of certain groups. It also includes ensuring transparency in AI decision-making, accountability for AI-driven outcomes, and responsibility for AI system design and implementation. Educational institutions also need to prioritize data protection and privacy by implementing regulations, consent mechanisms, and data security measures.

Ethics and Responsibility: Ethical implications of AI in education, including transparency, accountability, and responsibility in AI decision-making is crucial. The goal is to safeguard students' rights and well-being while using AI in education. OECD (2023) remarked that "...guidelines are essential to ensuring that AI tools are used responsibly and ethically, safeguarding against biased content generation, data privacy breaches, and unintentional reinforcement of stereotypes" (p. 4). The integration of AI in education poses significant challenges related to data privacy, security, and the potential exploitation of sensitive information, thereby putting individuals' fundamental rights at risk (European Parliament, 2021, p.37). The role of AI in education has far-reaching implications that touch on various aspects of sustainable development. Concerns arise from biases in data and algorithms, the impact of technology on teaching methods, unequal access to digital resources, and the potential infringement on children's rights and freedoms. Furthermore, AI may exacerbate existing inequalities related to socioeconomic status, location, ability, and cultural background (UNESCO, 2021, p.20). In this context, UNESCO has suggested "ROAM framework: Rights, Openness, Access and Multi-stakeholder Governance" (UNESCO, 2021, p.22), to be applied, to adopt a multifaceted strategy that integrates human rights and ethical considerations into AI-driven education initiatives. (UNESCO, 2019a).

Data Protection and Privacy: When AI is used in education, it collects and stores student data. Governments are implementing policies to protect this data and ensure that it is used responsibly. This includes respecting students' rights to privacy and ensuring that their personal data is secure. It is also important to have clear guidelines for how AI applications collect, store, and use student data. Additionally, students should have the right to human intervention if they are concerned about how AI is being used. By prioritizing safeguards and privacy rights would help create a trustworthy foundation for AI in education, allowing it to benefit students equitably. According to European Parliament (2021), upholding fundamental rights and ensuring robust data protection laws are paramount when implementing technologies like AI, which can significantly impact individual privacy (p.11). Further, OECD (2023) suggested that the nations ought to establish and share transparent directives for integrating generative AI in educational settings. By doing so, they can harness its potential to enhance instructional methods and student learning, while tackling concerns around biased algorithms, privacy, and data safeguarding.

Theme 4: Inclusion and Accessibility

AI-powered education can be a powerful tool for promoting fairness and equality in learning. Governments are creating policies to ensure that AI systems are designed and used in ways that address issues of accessibility, bias, and fairness. The goal is to make sure that all students, regardless of their background or circumstances, have access to high-quality education and opportunities to succeed. AI-powered education can promote fairness and equality in learning. Governments are creating policies to ensure that AI systems are designed and used in ways that address issues of accessibility, bias, and fairness. AI-powered education can promote equity and inclusion by providing personalized learning approaches and adaptive technologies for students with special needs. Educational institutions need to develop strategies for promoting equity and inclusion, addressing bias and fairness in AI-powered education, and ensuring accessibility for diverse student populations. By prioritizing accessibility and special needs, an inclusive learning environment can be created that supports all students.

Equity and Inclusion: AI-powered education can be a powerful tool for promoting fairness and equality in learning. Governments are creating policies to ensure that AI systems are designed and used in ways that address issues of accessibility, bias, and fairness. The goal is to make sure that all students, regardless of their background or circumstances, have access to high-quality education and opportunities to succeed. By using AI to tailor learning experiences to individual needs can be promoted for more equitable education systems and help students lead fulfilling lives. Leveraging AI and associated technologies can enhance educational approaches by facilitating the use of equitable data, personalized learning pathways, and increased access to education, while streamlining administrative processes (European Parliament, 2021, p.7). In today's world, digital access and learning are crucial components of education. Children and youth require learning experiences that prepare them for fulfilling lives, and digital technologies can play a key role in this preparation (OECD, 2023, p.373). Therefore, efforts should be made to ensure equitable access to AI-powered education for all, regardless of background or circumstance, prioritizing vulnerable populations and avoiding exacerbation of existing gaps (UNESCO, 2021, p.22).

Accessibility and Special Needs: AI can be a game-changer for students with special needs. Policies are being developed to ensure that AI-powered education is accessible to all students, including those with disabilities. For example, AI can help create customized learning plans, identify learning difficulties early on, and provide personalized support. However, it is also important to recognize that not all students have equal access to technology or learning environments. Governments are working to address these disparities and ensure that all students have the support they need to succeed, whether that is through AI-powered tools or alternative approaches. By prioritizing accessibility and inclusivity, more equitable and effective education systems can be created. The European Parliament, (2021) mentions that-

> *"AI has many applications, such as customisable approaches to learning, AI-based tutors, textbooks and course material with customised content, smart algorithms to determine best teaching methods, AI game engines, and adaptive user models in personalised learning environments (PLE) which can allow early identification of difficulties, such as dyslexia or risks of early school leaving" (European Parliament, 2021, p.26).*

OECD (2023) also explains that students' home environments vary greatly in terms of internet access, study space, and exam settings. Given these disparities, authorities should weigh the need for non-digital alternatives to ensure fairness and equity in education (OECD, 2023, p.411). AI is being harnessed to bridge educational gaps. Innovative applications include voice-assisted libraries, dyslexia screening tools, and AI-powered speech technology for individuals with communication difficulties. Virtual tools, robots, and intelligent tutoring systems are also being used to support students with diverse needs, promoting more inclusive learning environments (UNESCO, 2021, p.22).

AI is driving educational inclusion through cutting-edge tools and technologies. From voice-activated reading aids and dyslexia screeners to speech-generating devices, live captioning, and sign language apps, these innovations are expanding access to education. AI-powered robots and adaptive learning systems further support students with diverse needs, promoting more equitable learning environments (UNESCO, 2021).

Theme 5: Research and Development

Investing in research and development is essential to understand the benefits and challenges of AI in education. Governments are focusing to address the use of AI in assessment and evaluation, ensuring that it is used fairly and effectively. Governments are supporting research and development in AI-powered education to explore its potential benefits and challenges. AI is being used to create new and innovative learning tools, such as customized learning approaches and AI-based tutors. Investing in research and development is crucial to harness the potential of AI in education. It may include funding research projects, establish innovation hubs, and partner with industry partners. By exploring new assessment frameworks and methodologies, AI-powered grading systems, and evaluation of AI-driven educational outcomes, effective strategies can be developed for using AI in education. The growing use of AI in education necessitates a thorough assessment of its impact on learning outcomes, fairness, and the need for human judgment in key decisions.

Research and Development: Policymakers are promoting research and development in AI-powered education to explore its transformative potential. This involves creating innovative learning tools and gathering evidence on the effects of AI on learning outcomes. Strategic investment in research, monitoring, and collaboration among stakeholders is crucial for harnessing the benefits of AI and addressing its challenges in educational settings.

Recent technological innovations are yielding significant improvements in various academic disciplines through AI-driven solutions (European Parliament, 2021, p.7). AI is being utilized in various educational contexts, including personalized learning pathways, adaptive instructional systems, tailored educational resources, and sophisticated algorithmic approaches to optimize teaching methodologies (European Parliament, 2021, p.26). A comprehensive research framework, encompassing data collection and monitoring, is essential to inform the effective utilization of digital learning tools. International coordination and collaboration on such research initiatives would be beneficial (OECD, 2023, p. 152). Research into the applications of generative AI in teaching and learning should be promoted at a national level. Strategic partnerships among education authorities, AI developers, and researchers would yield valuable insights into the benefits and challenges of this technology (OECD, 2023, p. 273). Despite five decades of research into AI in education, its adoption in academic institutions remains limited, even in developed nations. The efficacy of AI technologies in addressing educational needs also warrants further examination about the readiness of these technologies for practical application (UNESCO, 2021, p.26). It is crucial to acknowledge the scarcity of comprehensive research on the educational implications of AI. Consequently, supporting investigations, innovative developments, and assessments of the influence of AI on learning processes and outcomes is essential (UNESCO, 2021, p.26).

Assessment and Evaluation: The increasing use of AI in assessment and evaluation necessitates the development of targeted policies. Governments and educational institutions must prioritize fairness, reliability, and transparency in AI-driven evaluations, ensuring human oversight and alternative approaches for high-stakes decisions. Effective policy frameworks will be crucial in harnessing the potential of AI to enhance educational outcomes while mitigating potential risks and biases. AI in education offers various benefits, such as improved access to knowledge and tailored learning experiences. Nonetheless, it poses challenges related to educational equity and equality. A thorough assessment of AI tools is essential to ensure their alignment with children's rights and to mitigate potential negative consequences (European Parliament, 2021, p.30). Critical assessments that significantly impact learners or educators may require human evaluation alternatives. AI-facilitated remote proctoring can enable secure and monitored assessments in remote settings (OECD, 2023, p. 411).

Theme 6: Collaboration and Partnerships

The rapid evolution of AI technology is transforming the education sector at an unprecedented rate, necessitating governments to acknowledge the significance of global collaboration and partnerships in AI-driven education. Through collective efforts, nations can exchange knowledge, best practices, and resources to facilitate the effective and responsible integration of AI. This can be achieved by sharing knowledge, conducting joint research, and establishing global standards. Furthermore, partnerships with industry partners and other stakeholders can provide valuable insights and resources for developing AI-powered education. Ultimately, by working together and developing effective policies and strategies, countries can harness the full potential of AI to revolutionize learning and teaching, addressing key aspects such as policy frameworks, infrastructure, AI literacy, teacher professional development, student engagement, ethics, equity, research, assessment, and international collaboration, to enhance education and improve learning outcomes for all students.

International Collaboration and Partnerships: The rapid evolution of AI in education underscores the importance of international collaboration and partnerships. By working together, governments, private entities, and educational institutions can share knowledge, resources, and expertise to harness the potential of AI, promote innovation, and create inclusive and effective learning environments.

Technological innovation is catalyzing a transformative shift in the education sector, impacting pedagogical approaches, institutional frameworks, and policy landscapes (European Parliament, 2021, p.26). It highlights the need for public investment and public-private partnerships to synergize efforts, drive innovation, and maximize the benefits of AI in education, culture, and audiovisual sectors (European Parliament, 2021, p.37). Governments can facilitate collaborative platforms to promote information exchange and best practice sharing on generative AI adoption in education (OECD, 2023, p. 273). In this context, OECD (2023) mentioned that "the implementation of digital education policies…require different expertise … since multi-stakeholder partnerships need to be established, managed, and monitored" (OECD, 2023, p.373). The inherent interdisciplinary nature of AI necessitates a collaborative approach to policy development, engaging stakeholders from diverse fields and sectors to ensure effective integration of AI in education (UNESCO, 2021, p.1). Maximizing the benefits of AI in education while minimizing risks demands a holistic strategy, centered on systemic planning, rigorous evaluation, and collaborative initiatives. Success is dependent upon dedicated funding, specialized research, and global partnerships (UNESCO, 2021, p.30). By addressing these aspects and working together, the potential of AI can be harnessed to enhance education and improve learning outcomes for all students. Effective policy frameworks, teacher training, ethics, inclusion, research, and collaboration are all essential components of a successful AI-powered education system.

Furthermore, the six categories identified in Table 1 provide a strategic roadmap for AI integration in education. These categories outline the specific implications for policymakers, leaders and educators, while balancing potential opportunities against inherent challenges. Policymakers are tasked with developing frameworks that safeguard equity, accessibility and quality, alongside allocating resources for infrastructure and professional development. Educators require sustained training to effectively integrate AI tools and adapt curricula for an evolving technological landscape. Ultimately, the objective is to leverage AI to cultivate an effective, efficient and equitable system that prepares students for a future defined by AI-driven innovation.

Table 1. Implications of AI in Education for policymakers, educators, and stakeholders

Implications for the use of AI in education	*Opportunities*	*Challenges*
Personalized and Adaptive Learning	Tailors learning to the individual need, increases engagement and motivation	Risk of over-reliance on AI, requires large amount of students' information
Intelligent Tutoring System (ITS)	Provides personalized support, improves learning outcomes	Potential to replicate bias, lacks human empathy
Automation of Administrative Tasks	By streamlining administrative work through automation., teachers can focus on creative and student-centered activities.	Dependence on technological tools can increase risk of data mishandling/misuse by them
Learning Analytics and Data-Driven Insights	Analyzing and harnessing learning data for better outcomes and learning improvement; Identifies students' needs, improves retention and learning outcomes	Concerns about privacy and potential for bias
Equity and Inclusion	Provides equal access and Inclusive support for learners with disabilities, language challenges, and socio-economic disadvantages	Digital divide, unequal access to technology due to lack of skills and connectivity issues
Ethical, Privacy and Governance Concerns	Promotes AI accountability and trustworthy adoption by establishing responsible AI use through trust and transparency	Openness, clear explanations, and strict data protection compliance
Teacher Roles and Professional Development	Enhances teacher capabilities with innovative resources, new tools and opportunities of training, boosting teaching qualities, competencies, leading to better student outcomes	Teacher reluctance to adapt, Resistance to new methods and inadequate teacher support and insufficient training
Lifelong and Vocational Learning	Aligns education with future workforce demands, promoting lifelong learning	Skills gap created from outdated curriculum leads to Discrepancy between education and industry needs, exacerbated by funding gaps
Immersive and Innovative Pedagogies	Enhances learning with interactive experiences, augmented reality, and adaptive technologies	Significant high-cost infrastructure investments and disparities in implementation
Global Policy and Investment Trends	Supports digital advancement and worldwide collaborative efforts	Disparities in policy adoption and investment across regions; Uneven policy implementation globally, with some regions underfunded

The policy trends analysis revealed the potential of AI in education, its implications for policymakers, educators, and stakeholders, along with associated challenges and opportunities that need to be addressed, as presented in Table 1, and have been explained as follows:

Personalized and Adaptive Learning: AI can enable tailored educational experiences by adjusting pace, content, and support to individual learners' needs, thereby increasing engagement and motivation. But over-reliance on AI can be risky as it may inhibit students' critical thinking and creativity; also, the use of various AI tools requires a large amount of students' information to work and give the desired output.

Intelligent Tutoring Systems (ITS): AI-powered tutors provide personalized style support, feedback, and adaptive practice, helping students with diverse learning styles improve learning outcomes. However, the use of AI in education can also risk biases in the results. Also, it lacks human empathy, which can lead to inadequate support for students' emotional needs.

Automation of Administrative Tasks: AI can reduce teachers' workloads by handling grading, scheduling, and routine communication, allowing educators to focus more on pedagogy. Thus, by streamlining administrative work through automation, teachers can focus on creative and student-centered activities. However, dependence on technological tools can increase the risk of data mishandling and misuse by them.

Learning Analytics and Data-Driven Insights: AI can be used to track students' progress, predict outcomes, and identify those at risk of dropping out or needing extra support. Thus, by analysing and harnessing learning data can be helpful for better outcomes and improvement in learning. AI can help identify students' needs, improve retention and learning outcomes, but it may raise concerns about their privacy and potential biases.

Equity and Inclusion: AI tools can assist learners by providing equal access and inclusive support, especially for learners with disabilities (*viz.,* text-to-speech, translation), language challenges, and socio-economic disadvantages; but there are concerns about bias, accessibility, and digital divides due to a lack of skills and connectivity issues.

Ethical, Privacy, and Governance Concerns: There is an increasing demand for policy frameworks that explicitly address data protection, algorithmic transparency, fairness and students' rights. By prioritizing transparency, stakeholders can ensure the accountability necessary for adopting trustworthy AI systems that provide broad societal benefits. Establishing rigorous guidelines and standards for responsible AI use is essential to strengthen the stakeholders' trust and fostering a culture of accountability during development and deployment. A primary challenge remains the black-box nature of AI systems, which obscures decision-making processes. Consequently, ensuring strict compliance with data protection regulations is vital to maintain user-trust and mitigating potential harm.

Teacher Roles and Professional Development: The use of AI can lead to better student outcomes by enhancing teachers' capabilities with innovative resources, new tools, and training opportunities, teaching qualities, and competencies, thus changing teachers' responsibilities towards guiding and monitoring AI systems, requiring new training and digital skills. However, teachers' reluctance to adapt, and their resistance to new approaches and inadequate support or training of teachers can be seen as a challenge in its effective implementation.

Lifelong and Vocational Learning: AI adoption in education can support reskilling and upskilling, especially in the context of labour market changes and the demand for 21st century skills, which aims to align education with the demands of the future workforce, promoting lifelong learning. As such, the skills gap created by outdated curricula can lead to a discrepancy between education and industry needs, which can be further exacerbated by funding gaps.

Immersive and Innovative Pedagogies: The integration of AI with virtual reality, augmented reality, and gamification can create engaging learning environments and enhance learning with interactive experiences through adaptive technologies. However, the significantly higher cost of infrastructure investment can create disparities in effective implementation.

Global Policy and Investment Trends: Governments and institutions support digital development and encourage collaborative efforts around the world. They are increasingly adopting AI strategies into education, although implementation levels vary, which leads to disparities in policy adoption and investment across regions, also leading to uneven policy implementation globally, with some regions receiving less funding.

DISCUSSION

The development and implementation of policies on AI in education require a comprehensive framework that addresses various aspects of AI integration (Oluwaseun et al., 2022). The categorization of themes into six categories: Policy and Governance, Teaching and Learning, Ethics and Responsibility, Inclusion and Accessibility, Research and Development, and Collaboration and Partnerships, provides a useful structure for analyzing policies. The integration of AI in education has the potential to revolutionize the way of teaching and learning (Fitria, 2021). To harness its full potential, governments are developing policies and frameworks to address various aspects of AI in education. The integration of AI in education requires a multifaceted approach that addresses various aspects, including policy, teaching and learning, ethics, inclusion, research, and collaboration. including policy frameworks, infrastructure, AI literacy, teacher professional development, student engagement, ethics, equity, research, assessment, and international collaboration (Kolog et al., 2022; Eckhardt et al., 2021).

An analytical matrix shown in Table 2 has been synthesized by undertaking the AI-in-education policy documents, mapping key recommendations across thematic domains highlighting the converging and diverging trends in AI-in-education strategies, providing insights into global priorities and approaches toward integrating AI responsibly in education systems while informing actionable educational reforms. Further, the thematic analysis has led to derive a conceptual framework presented in the Table 3.

Table 2. Analytical Matrix of Global AI-in-Education Policies: Thematic Alignment of Recommendations and Implications

S. No.	Country / Organization	Major Policy Recommendations	Alignment of Major Policy recommendations with the observed six themes	Suggested Implications of AI/Functional Areas of AI
1	UNESCO (2019b)	Promote global collaboration on AI in education; integrate AI literacy into formal curricula; emphasize teacher capacity-building; ensure ethical, inclusive, and equitable AI use; support research and development of AI tools for learning; strengthen international partnerships for AI governance.	Promote global AI policy alignment and international partnerships for governance; Integrate AI literacy into formal curricula and develop teacher capacity-building programs; Emphasize ethics, fairness, and responsible AI in education; Ensure equitable access to AI resources and accessibility for all; Support R&D of AI tools for learning and evaluate their educational impact; Strengthen digital infrastructure and protect data.	Promote AI tools for adaptive learning; Encourage ITS adoption globally; Automate routine admin tasks; Develop analytics for learning evaluation; Ensure equitable access for all; Embed ethical standards in AI; Train teachers for AI integration; Encourage continuous learning; Support innovative pedagogies; Foster international AI policy coordination.
2	UNESCO (2021)	Guide policymakers to implement AI in education responsibly; develop national AI strategies aligned with SDGs; embed ethics, privacy, and data protection into AI curricula; build teacher digital competencies; ensure equitable access to AI resources; support adaptive learning technologies and evidence-based policies.	Develop national AI strategies aligned with SDGs, promoting international collaboration and partnerships; Embed ethics, privacy, and data protection into AI curricula and ensure responsible AI deployment; Promote equitable access and inclusive learning environments for all learners; Support adaptive learning technologies, personalized learning, and evidence-based policies; Foster student AI literacy, teacher digital competence, and AI research; Ensure infrastructure for adaptive learning, data protection, and accessibility considerations	Implement personalized learning with AI; Support ITS in classrooms; Automate grading and admin workflows; Use AI-driven insights for decision-making; Promote inclusive AI adoption; Privacy, responsible AI use; Enhance teacher PD for AI; Support lifelong learning initiatives; Encourage creative pedagogical practices; Align global AI education strategies
3	OECD (2023)	Establish effective digital education ecosystems; integrate AI tools for learning analytics and personalized learning; foster teacher professional development; provide infrastructure and digital resources; monitor AI impacts on learning outcomes; encourage international research collaborations and data-driven evaluation.	Establish effective digital ecosystems with policy guidance and infrastructure to support all learners; Integrate AI for personalized and adaptive learning, promoting equity in access and accessibility; Ensure ethical AI use, data protection, and data privacy; Foster AI literacy skills, teacher professional development, and research on AI effectiveness; Encourage international collaboration, R&D for digital education, and learning analytics; Promote digital tools and platforms that support inclusive and effective learning environments.	Adaptive learning through AI; ITS deployment in classrooms; Streamline administrative tasks, Learning analytics for student outcomes; Promote equal access; Ethical use & data protection; Train educators in AI; Promote vocational learning; Foster innovative AI-enabled pedagogy; International investment in AI education.

continued on following page

Table 2. Continued

S. No.	Country / Organization	Major Policy Recommendations	Alignment of Major Policy recommendations with the observed six themes	Suggested Implications of AI/Functional Areas of AI
4	European Parliament (2021)	Recommend AI integration into schools and vocational training; emphasize transparency, accountability, and data protection; promote AI literacy and digital skills; support inclusive access for all learners; encourage ethical AI research; align national strategies with EU regulations and international partnerships.	Align national policies with EU regulations, ensuring transparency, accountability, and ethics in AI use; Promote AI literacy, digital skills, and teacher training programs in schools; Ensure data protection, privacy, and responsible AI practices in education; Provide inclusive access to AI-supported learning, prioritizing accessibility and accessibility considerations; Support research on AI impact in education, monitoring, and evaluation; Foster EU and international partnerships, collaboration, and knowledge sharing.	AI-based adaptive curricula; Promote ITS for personalized learning; Reduce administrative workload via AI; Data-driven insights for policy & practice; Inclusive AI policies; Ethics, transparency, accountability; Teacher training for AI integration; Lifelong skills and vocational programs; Innovative teaching methodologies; EU and international funding & collaboration.
5	United States (U.S. Dept. of Education, 2023)	Support responsible AI adoption in teaching and learning; provide guidance on generative AI, learning analytics, and adaptive systems; develop teacher training programs; protect student data privacy; promote research on AI effectiveness; ensure inclusive access and equity in AI-supported learning.	Infrastructure, and ethical use; Support AI adoption in teaching and learning, promoting AI literacy and teacher support programs; Protect student data, ensure ethical AI use, and prioritize data privacy; Promote equitable access, inclusion, and accessibility in AI-powered education; Research AI effectiveness, learning outcomes, and assessment methods; Foster partnerships, sharing best practices, and collaboration among stakeholders.	Personalized AI-driven instruction; ITS adoption; Automate grading & feedback; Learning analytics for performance; Equal opportunity access; Ethics & privacy standards; Teacher PD on AI tools; Support workforce upskilling; Innovative AI pedagogies; Investment in AI ed-tech.
6	United Kingdom (UK Department for Education, 2023)	Implement generative AI responsibly in classrooms; provide teacher support and training; integrate AI into digital literacy curricula; ensure data privacy and ethical AI usage; monitor impacts on learning outcomes; promote inclusive access across all school levels.	Implement responsible AI in classrooms with guidance, infrastructure, and national AI guidelines; Integrate AI into digital literacy curricula, promoting AI literacy and teacher professional development; Ensure data privacy, ethical AI use, and data protection; Provide inclusive access to AI-powered education, prioritizing accessibility; Monitor and assess AI's impact on learning outcomes, informing future development; Foster international collaboration, research, and knowledge sharing on AI in education.	AI for personalized learning; Support ITS tools; Automate admin & evaluation; Analytics for learning improvement; Inclusive access; Ethical, privacy-compliant AI; Teacher training and PD; Lifelong education; Encourage innovative pedagogy; Global AI partnerships.

continued on following page

Table 2. Continued

S. No.	Country / Organization	Major Policy Recommendations	Alignment of Major Policy recommendations with the observed six themes	Suggested Implications of AI/Functional Areas of AI
7	European Union (EC) (European Commission, 2022)	Offer ethical guidelines for AI in education; prioritize teacher awareness and professional development; ensure safe use of student data; emphasize ethical, inclusive, and accessible AI; foster international collaboration on AI tools and pedagogy; support evidence-based assessment of AI's educational impact.	Establish ethical AI guidelines and policies for education; Develop teacher capacity for AI integration and literacy; Prioritize data privacy, ethics, and responsible AI use; Promote inclusive and accessible AI-powered learning; Evaluate AI's impact on learning outcomes and effectiveness; Foster global partnerships and collaborative innovation in AI education.	Adaptive learning systems; ITS in schools; Automate reporting & administration; Data-driven educational insights; Promote equity; Ethical & responsible AI; Teacher professional development; Support lifelong and vocational learning; Innovative pedagogical approaches; EU & international AI policies.
8	Australia (Australian Government, 2023)	Establish a framework for generative AI in schools; support teacher training; integrate AI literacy into curricula; ensure ethical and responsible AI use; promote personalized learning and adaptive tools; monitor student learning outcomes; encourage research and international collaboration.	Develop and implement a national AI framework for schools; Foster AI literacy and teacher capacity in education; Prioritize ethics, responsibility, and data privacy in AI use; Ensure equitable access and accessibility to AI-powered learning; Drive innovation in personalized and adaptive learning; Strengthen international partnerships and collaboration in AI education.	Personalized AI-based learning; ITS tools in classrooms; Automate administrative tasks; Use analytics for insights; Inclusive AI access; Ethics, data protection; Teacher PD on AI tools; Lifelong learning programs; Innovative pedagogies with AI; Investment in AI education.
9	China (State Council, 2017)	Implement AI across education levels; integrate AI into curricula, vocational training, and research; enhance teacher digital competency; support ethical and responsible AI deployment; invest in infrastructure and resources; foster innovation through R&D; encourage international AI collaborations.	Develop and implement a national AI policy, integrating AI across education levels and curricula; Foster AI literacy, teacher capacity building, and curriculum-based learning; Ensure ethical deployment of AI, prioritizing ethics, responsibility, and data protection; Promote equitable access to AI-powered education, emphasizing accessibility and inclusivity; Drive R&D, innovation, and learning assessment in AI-powered education; Foster international collaboration and knowledge sharing for AI education and research.	Personalized learning via AI; Implement ITS; Automate; administrative workflow; Learning analytics for assessment; Equity in access; Ethics & privacy compliance; Teacher training & AI competency; Lifelong and vocational learning; Innovative AI pedagogies; Strategic investment & international AI collaboration.

continued on following page

Table 2. Continued

S. No.	Country / Organization	Major Policy Recommendations	Alignment of Major Policy recommendations with the observed six themes	Suggested Implications of AI/Functional Areas of AI
10	Singapore (Ministry of Education Singapore, 2023)	Introduce AI ethics framework for education; develop teacher professional development programs; implement AI literacy modules for students; promote equity and inclusion; ensure privacy and responsible AI use; support adaptive and personalized learning; monitor and evaluate AI's impact on learning.	Establish ethics framework and policy guidance for AI in education; Foster AI literacy, competency, and teacher capacity building; Ensure equity, inclusion, and accessibility in AI-powered learning; Support adaptive learning, R&D, and innovation in AI education; Evaluate learning outcomes and monitor AI's impact on education; Strengthen international partnerships for AI education and collaboration.	Adaptive learning systems; ITS integration; Automate administrative tasks; Data-driven insights; Inclusive and equitable AI; Ethical AI & data protection; Teacher PD and training; Lifelong learning initiatives; Innovative AI pedagogy; Policy alignment & international collaboration.
11	India (NITI Aayog, 2023)	Implement AI integration across education and skilling programs; build teacher capacity; ensure equitable access; develop AI literacy curricula; support research and innovation; establish ethical guidelines and data protection policies; foster collaborations with industry and academia.	Implement a national AI strategy for education, infrastructure, and resources; Build teacher capacity and AI literacy for students and educators; Ensure ethics, responsibility, and data protection in AI use; Promote equitable access and accessibility to AI-powered learning; Drive innovation, R&D, and evaluation in AI education; Strengthen industry-academia partnerships for AI education and research.	AI-supported personalized learning; ITS adoption; Admin automation; Learning analytics; Equitable access; Ethics & privacy compliance; Teacher PD & capacity-building; Lifelong & vocational learning; Innovative pedagogical approaches; Investment & collaboration in AI education.
12	UAE (Ministry of Education UAE, 2025)	Introduce AI as a curriculum subject K–12; provide teacher training and professional development; embed AI literacy, ethics, and data privacy in lessons; promote student engagement with AI projects; ensure equitable access across emirates; partner with global tech firms; encourage R&D and monitoring of AI outcomes.	Ministry-led AI curriculum roll-out, integrating AI labs, digital tools, and AI literacy; Teacher training and professional development, focusing on AI ethics and responsible AI; Embed AI ethics and data privacy in education, prioritizing responsible AI use; Ensure equitable access to AI-powered education across all emirates, promoting accessibility; Pilot R&D projects, monitoring, and evaluating outcomes to inform future development; Foster global tech partnerships for implementation, knowledge sharing, and collaboration.	Personalized learning in K–12 AI curriculum; ITS for student projects; Automate grading & admin; Analytics to monitor learning outcomes; Equitable access across emirates; Ethics & data privacy; Teacher training & PD; Lifelong & vocational learning; Innovative AI pedagogy; International tech partnerships & investment.

continued on following page

Table 2. Continued

S. No.	Country / Organization	Major Policy Recommendations	Alignment of Major Policy recommendations with the observed six themes	Suggested Implications of AI/Functional Areas of AI
13	Saudi Arabia (Ministry of Education Saudi Arabia, 2024)	Develop AI in education framework; integrate AI into school curricula; promote teacher digital competencies; ensure ethical and responsible AI use; provide infrastructure and access to digital resources; encourage research, innovation, and assessment of AI-enabled learning; collaborate with global AI initiatives.	Develop a national AI framework, providing infrastructure and resources for education; Foster teacher professional development, AI literacy, and curriculum integration; Ensure ethical AI adoption, prioritizing responsible AI, data privacy, and student engagement; Promote equitable access to digital resources, emphasizing accessibility and inclusivity; Support research, innovation, assessment, and evaluation in AI education; Foster international collaboration for AI initiatives, knowledge sharing, and global partnerships.	AI-driven personalized learning; ITS adoption; Administrative automation; Learning analytics; Equitable access; Ethics & privacy compliance; Teacher PD; Lifelong learning programs; Innovative pedagogy; Global collaboration & investment.
14	Finland (Finnish Ministry of Education, 2023)	Integrate AI education into national curricula; build teacher capacity and professional development; promote student AI literacy; ensure ethical, responsible, and inclusive AI use; provide infrastructure and resources; support R&D and monitoring; collaborate internationally for best practices.	Develop a national AI education strategy, providing infrastructure support and promoting AI literacy; Foster teacher training and professional development, focusing on AI literacy and pedagogy; Ensure ethical, responsible, and inclusive AI use, prioritizing data privacy and equitable access; Promote accessibility and inclusivity in AI-powered education; Support research, development, monitoring, and evaluation of AI in education; Collaborate internationally to share best practices, leverage expertise, and drive innovation.	Personalized AI learning tools; ITS in classrooms; Automate administrative workflow; Analytics for learning outcomes; Ensure inclusive access; Ethics & privacy; Teacher PD programs; Lifelong & vocational learning; Innovative pedagogical practices; Investment in AI education & international collaboration.
15	New Zealand (Ministry of Education New Zealand, 2023)	Implement AI education strategy in schools; provide teacher training and professional development; promote AI literacy and competency; embed ethics, privacy, and responsible AI usage; ensure equitable access; support research, innovation, and evaluation; foster partnerships at national and international levels.	Implement AI strategy in schools, infrastructure, and AI literacy; Build teacher capacity and student engagement through AI education; Prioritize ethics, responsibility, and data privacy in AI use; Ensure equitable access and accessibility to AI-powered learning; Drive innovation through research, assessment, and evaluation; Strengthen international partnerships for AI education and collaboration.	Adaptive learning AI systems; ITS adoption; Automate administrative processes; Learning analytics for student performance; Equitable access; Ethics & responsible AI; Teacher training & professional development; Lifelong learning & skills programs; Innovative AI pedagogies; Global AI policy & investment trends.

Table 3. Conceptual Framework derived from the Policies on AI in Education

Key Theme	Category	Sub-category	Implications
Policy and Governance	Policy Frameworks and Governance	- Guidelines for AI adoption - Regulatory frameworks - Standards for AI use	- Global Policy and Investment Trends - Ethical, Privacy and Governance Concerns
	Infrastructure and Resources	- Funding for AI infrastructure - Hardware and software requirements - Internet connectivity and access	
Teaching and Learning	AI Literacy and Competency	- Curriculum development - Teacher training and support - Assessment frameworks	- Personalized and Adaptive Learning - Intelligent Tutoring System (ITS) - Immersive and Innovative Pedagogies - Teacher Roles and Professional Development - Automation of Administrative Tasks
	Teacher Professional Development	- Training programs for teachers - Resources and support for teachers - Incentives for teacher development	
	Student Engagement and Learning Outcomes	- Personalized learning approaches - Adaptive assessments and feedback - Strategies for enhancing student motivation and engagement	
Ethics and Responsibility	Ethics and Responsibility	- Transparency in AI decision-making - Accountability for AI-driven outcomes - Responsibility for AI system design and implementation	- Ethical, Privacy and Governance Concerns
	Data Protection and Privacy	- Data protection regulations - Consent mechanisms for student data - Data security measures	
Inclusion and Accessibility	Equity and Inclusion	- Strategies for promoting equity and inclusion - Addressing bias and fairness in AI-powered education - Ensuring accessibility for diverse student populations	- Equity and Inclusion
	Accessibility and Special Needs	- Adaptive technologies for students with special needs - Personalized support systems - Accessibility standards for AI-powered education	
Research and Development	Research and Development	- Funding for research projects - Innovation hubs and partnerships with industry partners - Knowledge sharing and dissemination	- Learning Analytics and Data-Driven Insights - Lifelong and Vocational Learning
	Assessment and Evaluation	- New assessment frameworks and methodologies - AI-powered grading systems - Evaluation of AI-driven educational outcomes	
Collaboration and Partnerships	International Collaboration and Partnerships	- Knowledge sharing and joint research initiatives - Global standards for AI in education - Partnerships with industry partners and other stakeholders	- Teacher Roles and Professional Development - Global Policy and Investment Trends

This framework can provide a structure for analysing policies on AI in education, identifying the key areas or categories. It can be used to guide research, policy development, and implementation efforts.

Effective policy frameworks and governance structures are essential for ensuring that AI is integrated into education in a responsible and sustainable manner (Ajirotutu et al., 2024). Policies should provide clear guidelines on the development, implementation, and oversight of AI in education, including infrastructure and resource allocation (Oluwaseun et al., 2022).

The integration of AI in education has significant implications for teaching and learning (Fitria, 2021). National policies prioritize AI literacy and competency among students, teachers, and educators. Teacher professional development is critical to ensure that educators can effectively integrate AI into their practice. Moreover, policies focus on enhancing student engagement, motivation, and learning outcomes through AI-powered education (Eckhardt et al., 2021).

The use of AI in education raises important ethical considerations, including transparency, accountability, and responsibility in AI decision-making (Shenkoya, 2023). Policies address these concerns by establishing guidelines for the responsible development and use of AI in education. Data protection and privacy are also critical issues that require careful consideration (Oluwaseun et al., 2022). Policies on AI in education prioritize equity and inclusion, addressing issues of accessibility, bias, and fairness in AI-powered education. Policies also ensure that AI-powered education is accessible to students with special needs. India's NEP (2020) highlights the role of technology, including AI, in transforming education and promoting inclusivity. Research and development are critical to the effective integration of AI in education. Policies support research and development in AI-powered education, including the assessment and evaluation of AI-powered educational systems. India's NEP (2020) recommends establishing a National Research Foundation to expand research in AI. International collaboration and partnerships can play a significant role in shaping national policies on AI in education. National policies encourage collaboration and knowledge-sharing between governments, industry partners, and educational institutions (Igbinenikaro & Adewusi, 2024; Agba et al., 2023).

As, the impact of AI on education demands a multifaceted approach. Policy-makers must craft frameworks that prioritize equity, accessibility, and quality, while investing in infrastructure and training (Oluwaseun et al., 2022). Educators require continuous professional development to seamlessly integrate AI and revamp curricula for an AI-centric learning environment. Meanwhile, stakeholders must remain informed, build partnerships, and emphasize ethics. By ensuring every aspect is properly coordinated, the potential of AI can be harnessed to transform education into a more effective, efficient, and equitable system that prepares students for an AI-driven education.

Personalized and adaptive learning involves using AI to tailor educational content and experiences to students' individual needs, abilities, and learning styles. This approach can enhance student engagement, motivation, and outcomes (Eckhardt et al., 2021; Fitria, 2021). AI-powered adaptive learning systems can provide real-time feedback, adjust difficulty levels, and offer personalized learning paths, thus improving student performance and narrowing achievement gaps. Developing effective personalized learning systems requires high-quality data, sophisticated algorithms, and continuous evaluation to ensure that the systems are fair, accurate, and beneficial for all students (Vieriu & Petrea, 2025).

The Intelligent Tutoring Systems (ITS) can make use of AI to provide personalized support to students, offering them real-time feedback, guidance, and assessment. ITS can complement human teachers, providing additional support to struggling students and delivering immediate feedback, allowing teachers to focus on higher-level and more critical tasks. It is essential to ensure that ITS are designed, developed, and integrated effectively so that they meet the diverse needs of students, and maintain student engagement (Vieriu & Petrea, 2025; Treve, 2024).

Automating administrative tasks means using AI to streamline processes such as grading, data entry, and student tracking, allowing teachers to focus on teaching and mentoring. AI-based automation can reduce the workload of teachers, increase accuracy, and improve efficiency, freeing up more time for the teachers to engage in more meaningful activities (Fitria, 2021). Careful consideration of factors such as the suitability of the task for automation, data quality, and potential changes to job roles is essential to ensure that automation complements human roles rather than replacing them (Walter, 2024; Fitria, 2021).

Learning analytics uses artificial intelligence to analyse large datasets, providing valuable insights into student performance (Vieriu & Petrea, 2025; Treve, 2024). This can help educators identify areas for improvement and enhance teaching practices. AI-based learning analytics can assist teachers in identifying knowledge gaps, developing targeted interventions, and evaluating teaching effectiveness, facilitating data-driven decision-making. To effectively utilize learning analytics, it is crucial to ensure data quality, address privacy concerns, and develop robust analytics tools (Treve, 2024).

Ensuring equity and inclusion means designing AI-enabled education systems that meet the diverse needs of all students, regardless of their background, abilities, or socioeconomic status (UNESCO, 2021). AI can help identify and address learning gaps, provide personalized support, and promote accessibility, thus improving equity and inclusion in education (Vieriu & Petrea, 2025). Developing inclusive AI systems requires careful consideration of bias, fairness, and accessibility to ensure that the system does not exacerbate existing inequalities.

Concerns related to ethics, privacy, and governance include ensuring that AI-based education systems are designed and implemented in a way that respects student data, maintains transparency, and guarantees accountability (Kolog et al., 2022), thereby building trust in AI-based education systems (Shenkoya, 2023). Developing robust governance frameworks, ensuring data quality, and addressing concerns related to bias and fairness are crucial for mitigating ethical and privacy risks.

The role of teachers and their professional development involve ensuring that teachers have the necessary skills and support to effectively integrate AI-based tools into their teaching practices. AI can enhance teacher productivity, provide real-time feedback, and support professional development, enabling teachers to adapt to changing environments. Providing teachers with ongoing training, support, and resources is essential for them to effectively incorporate AI-based tools into their teaching methods (Fitria, 2021).

In the context of lifelong learning and professional development, the use of AI involves promoting continuous skills development and professional training, enabling individuals to adapt to the evolving needs of the job market (Igbinenikaro & Adewusi, 2024). AI-based learning platforms can offer personalized learning experiences, skills assessments, and career guidance, thus supporting lifelong learning and professional development. It is crucial to ensure that AI-based learning platforms are accessible, effective, and aligned with labour market needs in order to realize the full benefits of lifelong learning and professional training (Agba et al., 2023).

Engaging and innovative teaching methods using AI incorporate interactive, exciting, and immersive learning experiences that boost student motivation and enhance comprehension (Fitria, 2021). These AI-powered immersive learning experiences increase student engagement, foster deeper understanding, and develop essential skills such as critical thinking and problem-solving (Eckhardt et al., 2021). Developing effective immersive learning experiences requires careful design, development, and evaluation to ensure they meet learning objectives and are accessible to all students.

Global policy trends show that governments recognize the potential of AI in education and are investing in initiatives that promote AI adoption, innovation, and research (Igbinenikaro & Adewusi, 2024). Increased investment in AI-based education can foster innovation, improve learning outcomes, and enhance global competitiveness (Igbinenikaro & Adewusi, 2024). To realize the benefits of AI in education, it is crucial to ensure that AI-based education systems are designed to address global challenges, promote equity, and prioritize the needs of students.

Therefore, the development and implementation of policies on AI in education requires a comprehensive framework that can address various aspects of AI integration. By considering it, the policymakers can ensure that AI integration is responsible, sustainable, and effective in enhancing teaching and learning (Ajirotutu et al., 2024).

The findings across the six thematic areas reveal a consistent tension between ambitious AI policy narratives and the complex realities of educational implementation. Although, policy documents emphasize ethics, equity, and innovation, their realization depends greatly on leadership decisions related to resource allocation, professional learning, governance structures, and stakeholder trust. Educational leaders must navigate practical constraints including infrastructure disparities, system costs, data privacy risks, and teacher readiness, while balancing accountability pressures and innovation goals.

The analysis suggests that AI integration is not merely a technical upgrade but a complex organizational change process that demands strategic leadership, robust management and sound ethical judgement. Leaders play a pivotal role in interpreting policy frameworks, negotiating partnerships with technology providers, addressing resistance among educators. Crucially they must ensure that AI tools align with core pedagogical values rather than being governed by efficiency-driven metric, only. Without this leadership mediation, AI policies risk becoming purely symbolic or, worse, reinforcing existing inequalities. Consequently, these findings highlight the need to reframe AI policy implementation as a leadership challenge rather than a strictly technological or regulatory task.

CONCLUSION

This research examines the evolving landscape of AI in education policy through a six-theme analytical framework. While, these policies articulate compelling visions of ethical, inclusive and innovative education systems, their ultimate impact is dependent upon the ability of educational leaders to translate policy into practice. The analysis reveals that AI adoption is not neutral or technical process but a deeply human and organizational endeavor within the ethical standards. Consequently, educational leaders are positioned at the center of this transformation serving as policy interpreters, stewards of ethical governance, facilitators of professional learning and negotiators of complex stakeholder relationships. To support sustainable AI implementation, leaders must move beyond compliance- oriented adoption towards strategic engagement. This shift requires investing in teacher capacity, establishing transparent evaluation frameworks, addressing infrastructure disparities, access gaps and embedding ethical principles into core decision-making. Essential leadership competencies which include systems thinking, ethical reasoning, change management and collaborative governance are essential for navigating AI-driven reforms. By emphasizing educational leadership, this study aims to bridge the gap between policy and practice, thereby guiding educational leaders toward context-responsive, equitable and pedagogically grounded decisions. Thus, it positions policies not as an end in itself, but as a strategic instrument for advancing inclusive and sustainable educational transformation.

Implications

The implications of AI in education are multifaceted, presenting transformative opportunities alongside significant systemic challenges. To navigate this complexity, the role of educational leadership is paramount. Leaders must move beyond mere compliance toward strategic stewardship, ensuring that AI tools complement rather than replace human instruction. This requires an institutional commitment to ethical governance are prioritized in every implementation. Furthermore, leaders must proactively invest in teacher capacity and professional development to prevent technological overreliance and ensure that AI-driven reforms are pedagogically grounded. Ultimately, harnessing the potential of AI to create an effective and inclusive system is not a neutral technical process, but a leadership-driven endeavor. By balancing innovation with ethical oversight and human-centric teaching, stakeholders can ensure that AI serves as a strategic tool for sustainable educational transformation.

Recommendations

Based on the research findings, several strategic recommendations are proposed to ensure the responsible and effective integration of AI in education. Policymakers should formulate comprehensive frameworks that prioritize equity and provide robust investment in teacher professional development. Educators should be encouraged to integrate AI with pedagogical intentionality, maintaining rigorous data oversight while fostering critical thinking. Researchers should focus on developing standardized evaluation frameworks to mitigate algorithmic bias. Industry partners must prioritize transparency and co-design solutions alongside educators. And, within this ecosystem, educational leaders serve as pivotal mediators. They should prioritize ethical governance by establishing clear guidelines for privacy and transparency, both. Furthermore, leaders must invest in teacher capacity building through comprehensive AI literacy trainings and ensure equitable access to infrastructure for all students. Ultimately, they should promote a pedagogical shift that leverages AI to automate administrative tasks, thereby refocusing human effort on mentorship and socio-emotional support.

REFERENCES

Aayog, N. I. T. I. (2023). National Strategy for Artificial Intelligence (education and skilling sections). Government of India. https://www.niti.gov.in/sites/default/files/2023-03/National-Strategy-for-Artificial-Intelligence.pdf

Agba, M. S., Agba, G. E. M., & Obeten, A. W. (2023). Artificial intelligence and public management and governance in developed and developing market economies. Journal of Public Administration. *Policy and Governance Research.*, *1*(2), 1–14.

Ajirotutu RO, Adeyemi AB, Ifechukwu GO, Iwuanyanwu O, Ohakawa TC. Designing policy frameworks for the future: Conceptualizing the integration of green infrastructure into urban development. Journal of Urban Development Studies. 2024;2.

Baker, T., Smith, L., & Anissa, N. 2019. Educ-AI-tion Rebooted? Exploring the future of artificial intelligence in schools and colleges. London, NESTA. Available at: https://www. nesta.org.uk/report/education-rebooted (Accessed 28 March 2021).

Bearman, M., Ryan, J., & Ajjawi, R. (2023). Discourses of artificial intelligence in higher education: A critical literature review. *Higher Education, 86*(2), 369–385. DOI: 10.1007/s10734-022-00937-2

Chatterjee, S. (2020). AI strategy of India: policy framework, adoption challenges and actions for government. Transforming Government: People. *Transforming Government, 14*(5), 757–775. DOI: 10.1108/TG-05-2019-0031

Eckhardt, J., Fehr, C., & Friedrich, D. (2021). Engaging stakeholders for AI policy development: Lessons from global experiences. *Journal of Policy and Management.*, *40*(2), 221–237.

European Commission. (2022). Ethical guidelines on the use of AI and data in teaching and learning for educators. Publications Office of the European Union. https://education.ec.europa.eu/focus-topics/digital-education/action-plan/ethical-guidelines-for-educators-on-using-ai

European Parliament. (2021, April 19). *Report on artificial intelligence in education, culture and the audiovisual sector (2020/2017(INI))* (A9-0127/2021). European Parliament. https://www.europarl.europa.eu/doceo/document/A-9-2021-0127_EN.html

Filgueiras, F. (2024). Artificial intelligence and education governance. *Education, Citizenship and Social Justice, 19*(3), 349–361. DOI: 10.1177/17461979231160674

Finnish Ministry of Education. (2023). National AI strategy and education integration. Government of Finland. https://minedu.fi/en/ai-education

Fitria, T. N. (2021). Artificial Intelligence (AI) In Education: Using AI Tools for Teaching and Learning Process. Proceeding Seminar Nasional & Call for Papers. ISSN Online: 2654-6590. ISSN Cetak: 2654-5306

Holmes, W., Bialik, M., & Fadel, C. (2019). *Artificial Intelligence in Education: Promises and implications for teaching and learning*. Center for Curriculum Redesign.

Holmes, W., Porayska-Pomsta, K., Holstein, K., Sutherland, E., Baker, T., Shum, S. B., Santos, O. C., Rodrigo, M. T., Cukurova, M., Bittencourt, I. I., & Koedinger, K. R. (2022). Ethics of AI in Education: Towards a Community-Wide Framework. *International Journal of Artificial Intelligence in Education, 32*(3), 504–526. DOI: 10.1007/s40593-021-00239-1

Igbinenikaro E., & Adewusi, OA. (2024) Policy recommendations for integrating artificial intelligence into global trade agreements. International Journal of Engineering Research Updates. 2024;6(01):001-010.

Kolog, E. A., Devine, S. N., Egala, S. B., Amponsah, R., Budu, J., & Farinloye, T. (2022). Rethinking the implementation of artificial intelligence for a sustainable education in Africa: Challenges and solutions. In *Management and Information Technology in the Digital Era* (pp. 27–46). Emerald Publishing Limited. DOI: 10.1108/S1877-636120220000029003

Li, L., Wang, C., Chen, J., Sun, H., & Zhang, H. 2025. Artificial Intelligence Education Policy Analysis from International Perspective. In *Proceedings of the 2024 7th International Conference on Educational Technology Management (ICETM '24)*. Association for Computing Machinery, New York, NY, USA, 264–270. https://doi.org/DOI: 10.1145/3711403.3711448

Maghsoudi, M., Mohammadi, N., & Bakhtiari, M. (2025). Artificial intelligence and sustainable development: Public concerns and governance in developed and developing nations. *Cleaner Environmental Systems*, •••, 100340.

Ministry of Education. New Zealand. (2023). AI in schools strategy. Government of New Zealand. https://www.education.govt.nz/ai-education/

Ministry of Education. Saudi Arabia. (2024). AI in education framework. Government of Saudi Arabia. https://www.moe.gov.sa/en

Ministry of Education. Culture, Sports, Science and Technology (MEXT). (2025). Guideline for the use of generative AI in primary and secondary education (Ver. 2.0). MEXT. https://www.mext.go.jp/content/20250422-mxt_shuukyo01-000030823_001.pdf

Ministry of Education Singapore. (2023). AI in education / AI in SLS: AIEd ethics framework. Ministry of Education. https://www.learning.moe.edu.sg/ai-in-sls/responsible-ai/ai-in-education-ethics-framework/

Ministry of Education, United Arab Emirates. (2025). AI education roll-out from Kindergarten to Grade 12: UAE press release. Government of the United Arab Emirates. https://www.thenationalnews.com/news/uae/2025/05/04/sheikh-mohammed-announces-introduction-of-ai-as-curriculum-subject-in-uae-schools/

National Education Policy (NEP) 2020. National Education Policy (2020). Ministry of Human Resource Development. (2020). Government of India. https://www.education.gov.in/sites/upload_files/mhrd/files/NEP_Final_English_0.pdf

OECD. (2023). *OECD Digital Education Outlook 2023: Towards an Effective Digital Education Ecosystem*. OECD Publishing., DOI: 10.1787/c74f03de-

Oluwaseun, J., Sola, A., & Temidayo, O. (2022). Stakeholder engagement in AI policy development in Nigeria: A review. *Policy Studies Journal: the Journal of the Policy Studies Organization*, *50*(1), 115–130.

Onuorah, O. L., & Bosso, U. A. (2024). Public sector innovation in Nigeria: An explorative study of approaches, outcomes, and challenges. Journal of Public Administration. *Policy and Governance Research.*, *2*(1), 55–67.

Shenkoya, T. (2023). Can digital transformation improve transparency and accountability of public governance in Nigeria? Transforming Government: People. *Process and Policy.*, *17*(1), 54–71.

Shittu, R., Ahmadu, J., Famoti, O., Nzeako, G., Ezechi, O., Ewim, P.-M., Omokhoa, H., & Pub, A. (2024). Policy Frameworks for Artificial Intelligence Adoption: Strategies for Successful Implementation in Nigeria. *International Journal of Social Science Exceptional Research.*, *03*(6), 105–116. DOI: 10.54660/IJSSER.2024.3.6.105-116

State Council of the People's Republic of China. (2017). A new generation artificial intelligence development plan (English translation). State Council. https://www.airuniversity.af.edu/Portals/10/CASI/documents/Translations/2021-03-02%20China%27s%20New%20Generation%20Artificial%20Intelligence%20Development%20Plan-%202017.pdf

Treve, M. (2024). Integrating Artificial Intelligence in Education: Impacts on Student Learning and Innovation. *International Journal of Vocational Education and Training Research.*, *10*(2), 61–69. DOI: 10.11648/j.ijvetr.20241002.14

UK Department for Education. (2023). Generative artificial intelligence (AI) in education. GOV.UK. https://www.gov.uk/government/publications/generative-artificial-intelligence-in-education/generative-artificial-intelligence-ai-in-education

UNESCO. (2019a). Steering AI and Advanced ICTs for Knowledge Societies A Rights, Openness, Access, and Multi stakeholder Perspective. Available at: https://unesdoc. unesco.org/ark:/48223/pf0000372132

UNESCO. (2019b). Beijing consensus on artificial intelligence and education. UNESCO. https://unesdoc.unesco.org/ark:/48223/pf0000368303

UNESCO. (2021). AI and education: Guidance for policy-makers. UNESCO. https://unesdoc.unesco.org/ark:/48223/pf0000376709

U.S. Department of Education. (2023). Artificial intelligence and the future of teaching and learning. U.S. Department of Education. https://www.ed.gov/sites/ed/files/documents/ai-report/ai-report.pdf

Vieriu, A. M., & Petrea, G. (2025). The Impact of Artificial Intelligence (AI) on Students' Academic Development. *Education Sciences*, *15*(3), 343. DOI: 10.3390/educsci15030343

Walter, Y. (2024). Embracing the future of Artificial Intelligence in the classroom: The relevance of AI literacy, prompt engineering, and critical thinking in modern education. *International Journal of Educational Technology in Higher Education*, *21*(1), 15. DOI: 10.1186/s41239-024-00448-3

Wang, K., Zhao, Y., Gangadhari, R. K., & Li, Z. (2021). Analyzing the adoption challenges of the Internet of Things (IoT) and artificial intelligence (AI) for smart cities in China. *Sustainability (Basel)*, *13*(19), 10983. DOI: 10.3390/su131910983

Wang, S. Wang, Fang., Zhu, Zhen., Wang, Jingxuan., Tran, Tam., Du, Zhao, (2024). Artificial intelligence in education: A systematic literature review.Expert Systems with Applications, Volume 252, Part A,124167,ISSN 0957-4174, https://doi.org/ DOI: 10.1016/j.eswa.2024.124167

Williamson, B., Eynon, R., Knox, J., & Davies, H. (2023). Critical perspectives on AI in education: Political economy, discrimination, commercialization, governance and ethics. In du Boulay, B., Mitrovic, A., & Yacef, K. (Eds.), *The Handbook of Artificial Intelligence in Education*. Edward Elgar Publishing Ltd., DOI: 10.4337/9781800375413.00037

Yanli, Xu & Danni, Lu. (2021). Prospect of Vocational Education under the Background of Digital Age: Analysis of European Union's Digital Education Action Plan (2021-2027). 164-167. .DOI: 10.1109/IEIT53597.2021.00042

Zawacki-Richter, O., Marín, V. I., Bond, M., & Gouverneur, F. (2019). Systematic review of research on artificial intelligence applications in higher education-where are the educators? *International Journal of Educational Technology in Higher Education, 16*(1), 39. DOI: 10.1186/s41239-019-0171-0

KEY TERMS AND DEFINITIONS

Artificial Intelligence -: Artificial Intelligence (AI) refers to the development of computer systems that can perform tasks that typically require human intelligence, such as learning, problem-solving, and decision-making. AI involves creating machines that can think and act like humans, enabling them to learn, reason, and interact with their environment.

Artificial Intelligence (AI) in education-: Artificial Intelligence (AI) in education refers to the use of machine learning and other AI technologies to enhance teaching and learning, personalize education, and improve student outcomes. AI-powered tools can help automate administrative tasks, provide real-time feedback, and offer personalized learning experiences tailored to individual students' needs and abilities.

Educational policy-: An educational policy is a set of guidelines, rules, and principles that govern the operation of educational institutions, outlining the goals, objectives, and practices for teaching, learning, and administration. Educational policies aim to ensure quality, equity, and accountability in education, shaping the learning environment and outcomes for students, teachers, and the broader community.

Intelligent Tutoring Systems (ITS)-: These are AI-powered educational software that provides personalized, adaptive, and interactive learning experiences. They assess student knowledge, offer tailored instruction, and give real-time feedback, mimicking human tutors. ITS aim to enhance learning outcomes and efficiency.

Thematic analysis-: It refers to a qualitative research method used to identify, analyze, and interpret patterns and themes within a dataset. The goal of thematic analysis is to uncover underlying meanings, concepts, and ideas that emerge from the data.

Chapter 11
Data-Informed, Not Data-Driven:
Leadership Practices for Responsible AI Integration in K-12 Schools

Karim Ragab
http://orcid.org/0000-0003-1337-3562
Al Ittihad Private School – Mamzar, UAE

ABSTRACT

As artificial intelligence tools increasingly shape instructional delivery, student monitoring, and administrative operations in K–12 education, school leaders must navigate the fine line between leveraging data for insight and over-relying on algorithmic outputs. This chapter critically examines the evolving role of educational leaders in Gulf and Middle Eastern school systems, where ambitious national AI strategies intersect with traditional education governance and cultural expectations. It argues for a data-informed leadership model, one that integrates AI-generated insights into human-centered, pedagogically sound decision-making processes. The chapter unpacks the risks of data determinism, including eroded teacher agency, student dehumanization, and biased performance metrics. It introduces actionable strategies and transparency frameworks that restore judgment, context, and trust to leadership practices. The chapter positions AI not as a substitute for educational vision but as a tool that must be curated, interpreted, and ethically managed by reflective school leaders.

DOI: 10.4018/979-8-3373-4908-4.ch011

INTRODUCTION

The rapid integration of Artificial Intelligence (AI) is reshaping K-12 education globally, transforming instruction, student assessment, and administrative systems. The promise of AI-powered tools to deliver personalized learning paths (Onesi-Ozigagun et al., 2024), facilitate collaborative learning (Adeleye et al., 2024), and provide real-time feedback (Lin et al., 2023) has captured the attention of policymakers and educators worldwide. In administration, AI is optimizing processes from enrollment to resource allocation, promising new efficiencies for educational institutions (Onesi-Ozigagun et al., 2024). However, this technological shift presents unique and complex challenges for educational leaders, particularly in the Gulf and Middle Eastern contexts. In this region, ambitious national AI strategies create a powerful imperative for digital transformation in schools. These top-down innovation mandates intersect with deeply rooted cultural values, traditional pedagogical approaches, and established governance structures, creating a landscape of significant tension and opportunity for school leaders. This chapter argues that the prevailing discourse of "data-driven" leadership, which prioritizes algorithmic outputs, is ill-suited to this complex environment. Instead, it proposes a "data-informed" model that empowers school leaders to integrate AI-generated insights within a framework of human-centered, pedagogically sound, and culturally responsive professional judgment. This approach is critical for ensuring that AI serves as a tool for augmenting educational practice, rather than a deterministic force that erodes teacher agency and undermines the core values of education. While the potential for AI to enhance education is significant, with projections of substantial market growth (Thomas, 2024), its responsible integration requires navigating persistent challenges, including data privacy concerns, algorithmic bias, the need for teacher training (Onesi-Ozigagun et al., 2024), and the broader ethical, legal, and social implications of its use (Thomas, 2024).

Policy and Cultural Contexts in the Gulf and Middle East

The Gulf Cooperation Council (GCC) countries have emerged as global leaders in articulating ambitious national AI strategies, positioning artificial intelligence as a cornerstone of economic diversification and knowledge-based development. The United Arab Emirates (UAE) has taken a pioneering step by appointing a State Minister for Artificial Intelligence, making it the first country in the world to do so (Halaweh, 2018), signaling a strong governmental commitment to embracing AI at the highest policy levels and leading to a new generation of digital government referred to as "Gov. 3.0". However, this policy-level enthusiasm for AI must be understood within the context of the region's broader development trajectory.

While Qatar and the UAE have been assessed on their progress towards becoming knowledge-based economies (Parcero & Ryan, 2016), both countries were found to lag behind knowledge economy leaders, particularly in the innovation pillar. This gap between policy ambition and implementation capacity presents a critical challenge for educational leaders tasked with translating national AI mandates into school-level practice. The United Arab Emirates (UAE) has taken a pioneering step by appointing a State Minister for Artificial Intelligence, making it the first country in the world to do so (Halaweh, 2018). This move indicates a strong commitment to embracing AI at the governmental level, leading to a new generation of digital government referred to as "Gov. 3.0". The UAE's decision to embrace AI is expected to have positive impacts on society, including businesses, organizations, and individuals, as well as on the AI industry itself. While not explicitly mentioned in the context, it's worth noting that Qatar and the UAE have been assessed on their progress towards becoming knowledge-based economies (Parcero & Ryan, 2016). The assessment used a framework that included information and communication technology, education, innovation, and economy and regime. The results showed that the UAE ranked slightly better than the median of the 19 compared countries, while Qatar ranked somewhat below. Both countries were found to lag behind knowledge economy leaders, particularly in the innovation pillar. While comprehensive information on national AI strategies for all GCC countries is not provided, the UAE's appointment of an AI minister demonstrates a clear commitment to AI development at the national level. The assessment of knowledge-based economies suggests that there is room for improvement in innovation and technology adoption in both the UAE and Qatar, which likely extends to their AI strategies as well. Further research would be needed to provide a more complete picture of AI strategies across the GCC region.

Cultural values and governance structures in education

AI strategies in education are significantly influenced by cultural values and governance structures, as evidenced by various studies across different regions. In Nordic countries, national AI policies emphasize cultural values of trust, transparency, and openness. These policies support AI development through clear information security, AI literacy education, and open data initiatives (Robinson, 2020). This approach reinforces societal values while implementing AI technologies, highlighting the importance of citizen involvement and education to prevent alienation. Contrastingly, global perspectives on AI governance reveal challenges due to cultural differences. The human rights approach to AI governance, intended as a universal framework, may not be straightforwardly applicable in non-Western contexts (Wong, 2020). This underscores the need for considering cultural diversity in developing ethical AI governance strategies.

In conclusion, effective AI strategies in education require a balance between technological innovation and cultural sensitivity. The Beijing Consensus on AI in education emphasizes the need for new governance practices that address both the potential benefits and risks of AI adoption (Filgueiras, 2023). Furthermore, establishing an ethical AI environment in higher education demands comprehensive efforts across policy regulation, governance, and education, with a focus on interdisciplinary collaboration to address complexities such as AI bias (Barnes & Hutson, 2024). As AI continues to transform education, it is crucial to develop adaptive governance frameworks that align with cultural values while promoting responsible and equitable use of AI technologies. In Gulf and Middle Eastern educational contexts specifically, the integration of AI must account for distinctive governance structures and cultural values. Educational systems in the region often reflect centralized governance models, where policy decisions are made at the national or ministerial level and cascaded to schools with limited local autonomy. This hierarchical structure can facilitate rapid, system-wide adoption of AI initiatives but may also constrain the professional autonomy and contextual adaptation that are essential for effective implementation. Furthermore, cultural values emphasizing collective well-being, respect for authority, and the preservation of Islamic principles and Arabic language and culture shape how AI is perceived and adopted in educational settings. Leaders must therefore navigate the tension between responding to top-down national mandates for AI adoption and respecting the cultural and pedagogical values that define their school communities. This requires not simply importing AI governance frameworks from Western contexts but developing regionally grounded approaches that honor local values while achieving the innovation goals articulated in national development plans.

Tensions between innovation imperatives and traditional pedagogies

The integration of AI in education presents significant tensions between innovation imperatives and traditional pedagogies. While AI offers transformative potential for personalized learning and creative problem-solving, it challenges established teaching practices and raises ethical concerns. AI technologies like ChatGPT are reshaping teacher roles and pedagogical approaches in fields such as English Language Teaching (ELT). Teachers are shifting from traditional methodologies to more facilitative roles, emphasizing active learning models like blended, collaborative, and project-based learning (Baskara, 2023). However, this transition creates tensions, particularly in East Asian contexts where traditional transmission models of learning still dominate despite policy initiatives for ICT integration and educational reform (Richards, 2004). Similarly, in Gulf educational contexts, the tension between innovation imperatives and traditional pedagogies is particularly acute. National AI strategies emphasize student-centered, personalized learning models that contrast with established pedagogical practices that prioritize direct instruction and collective learning experiences. In many Gulf schools, particularly those serving local Arab populations, there is a strong cultural emphasis on the teacher as the authority figure and knowledge transmitter. The introduction of AI systems that promote student autonomy and self-directed learning can therefore create friction with both teacher professional identity and parental expectations about the role of formal education. School leaders must navigate this tension thoughtfully, finding ways to leverage AI's personalization capabilities while preserving the teacher-centered, collectively oriented pedagogical approaches that are culturally valued. The implementation of AI in education faces several contradictions. These include technological challenges like interface complexity and infrastructure limitations, conflicts with professional identity, reduced pedagogical flexibility, and organizational issues such as inadequate support systems and unclear policies (Zha et al., 2025). Additionally, there are ethical tensions related to fairness, transparency, privacy, and human rights in AI adoption (Madan & Ashok, 2022). These contradictions can be culturally and politically challenging to confront but should be viewed as motors for change rather than threats to AI implementation (Keegan et al., 2022). While AI presents opportunities to enhance curricula, address resource scarcity, and provide personalized learning experiences (Sharma et al., 2024), its integration requires a careful balance between leveraging technology and retaining essential human elements of teaching (Kovalenko & Baranivska, 2024). Success in AI integration demands a holistic approach that addresses both technological and human factors, emphasizing the need for robust infrastructure, teacher training, and alignment with curricular goals (Henriksen et al., 2024; Kearney et al., 2018). As the debate continues, it is crucial to re-evaluate the nature of learning and the purpose of education, shifting focus towards critical thinking, analytical skills, and creativity in the AI era (Weidmann, 2024).

The Risks of Data Determinism in School Leadership

AI-generated metrics and dashboards have become increasingly prevalent in decision-making processes across various industries. While these tools offer valuable insights and efficiency, there is a growing concern about overdependence on them (Abdulrahman, 2024; Zhai et al., 2024). This overreliance can lead to a decrease in critical thinking skills and analytical reasoning abilities among users (Zhai et al., 2024). Interestingly, the type of decision-making task (e.g., increasing vs. decreasing prices) can have an even greater influence on reliance than the presence of AI explanations (Scharowski et al., 2023). This challenges the presumed importance of transparency in AI systems and highlights the need to consider other factors in human decision-making, such as potential heuristics and biases. To mitigate the risks of overdependence, it is crucial to strike a balance between leveraging AI capabilities and maintaining human agency (Abdulrahman, 2024). Implementing human-centered explanations, such as feature importance and counterfactuals, can help increase trust and reliance on AI systems while encouraging users to review AI suggestions more analytically (Lee & Chew, 2023). Additionally, fostering a mindful integration of AI that upholds human expertise and critical thinking is essential for achieving optimal results in decision-making processes (Abdulrahman, 2024).

The integration of AI in education raises concerns about the potential erosion of teacher professional judgment and agency. While AI technologies offer benefits in terms of efficiency and data-driven decision-making, they also present challenges to teachers' autonomy and professional expertise. Research indicates that AI implementation in education can lead to a reduction in human interaction and weaken the use of professional judgment (Coşkun et al., 2024). This is particularly concerning as nursing, and by extension teaching, is fundamentally based on human interactions. The control exerted by policymakers and educational leaders through AI systems can restrict teachers' agency in various aspects of their professional learning and practice (Nezhad & Stolz, 2024). Additionally, there are serious concerns about AI's reliability and ethical implications in educational settings (Coşkun et al., 2024). However, it's important to note that AI can also be viewed as a supportive tool that enhances, rather than replaces, teacher expertise. The key lies in striking a balance between leveraging AI's potential to enrich learning experiences and addressing the challenges posed by its misuse (Alasgarova & Rzayev, 2024). To mitigate the erosion of professional judgment, it is crucial to foster AI literacy and AI-related ethical knowledge among teacher educators (Rütti-Joy et al., 2024). This approach can help ensure that AI integration in education is ethical and effective, preserving teacher agency while benefiting from technological advancements. While AI poses challenges to teacher professional judgment and agency, its integration in education should be carefully managed to complement rather than diminish human skills (Watkins & Barak-Medina, 2024). By promoting AI literacy, addressing ethical concerns, and maintaining a focus on human interaction and professional expertise, educators can harness the benefits of AI while preserving their essential role in the teaching and learning process.

Algorithmic bias in AI systems can lead to the marginalization of certain student groups, perpetuating existing inequalities in education. Multiple studies have highlighted concerns about AI systems replicating biases present in their training data, potentially disadvantaging underrepresented or marginalized groups (Aquino,

2023; Peters, 2022). This bias can manifest in various forms, including data-related, algorithmic, and user-interaction biases, which undermine fairness in AI-driven educational applications (Chinta et al., 2024). Interestingly, while most stakeholders agree that bias is a problem in healthcare AI, some argue that the benefits of AI outweigh any harms arising from bias (Aquino et al., 2023). This divergence in views extends to strategies for mitigating bias and the inclusion or exclusion of sociocultural identifiers in AI development. In the context of education, the integration of AI has transformative potential but also raises significant ethical concerns regarding validity, reliability, transparency, fairness, and equity (Bulut & Beiting-Parrish, 2024). To address these challenges, interdisciplinary collaboration and tailored stakeholder engagement activities are crucial (Aquino et al., 2023). Speculative and liberatory design thinking can help developers better understand the educational and personal contexts of underrepresented groups (Gaskins, 2022). Additionally, initiatives focused on ethical AI development and responsible AI governance can mitigate the negative impacts of AI on inequality by promoting fairness, transparency, and accountability in algorithmic decision-making processes (Farahani & Ghasemi, 2024). Ultimately, addressing real-world disparities and promoting inclusivity and diversity within education and AI development are essential steps towards creating more equitable AI applications in education (Lin et al., 2024; Zajko, 2021).

AI-powered surveillance and predictive systems in education raise significant ethical concerns regarding student dehumanization. These technologies, while offering potential benefits for personalized learning and administrative efficiency, also pose risks to student privacy, autonomy, and well-being. The use of AI in surveillance goes beyond mere data collection, extending to problematic purposes that may infringe on students' rights (Müller, 2021). Automated decision support systems and predictive analytics operate on data to produce outputs, which can lead to opacity and bias in educational decision-making (Müller, 2021). This lack of transparency and potential for algorithmic discrimination can contribute to the dehumanization of students, reducing them to data points rather than individuals with unique needs and circumstances.

Facial recognition systems used to generate insights about learners' behaviors (Akgun & Greenhow, 2021) and AI-driven assessment tools (Gaur et al., 2024) further exemplify the potential for dehumanization through surveillance. While these technologies aim to support learning experiences, they also raise ethical challenges regarding data privacy and the potential exacerbation of educational inequalities (Gaur et al., 2024). The intricate autonomy of AI systems and difficulties in comprehending and interpreting algorithmic outcomes (Abdelaal & Sawy, 2024) can lead to a disconnect between educators and students, potentially undermining the human element of education. To mitigate these risks, it is crucial to implement balanced policies and practices that focus on developing students' AI competencies alongside critical thinking abilities (Bai, 2024). Educators and policymakers must prioritize transparency, accountability, and ethical considerations in AI implementation to ensure that these technologies augment human capabilities rather than replace them. By addressing the ethical challenges and dilemmas of using AI in education (Akgun & Greenhow, 2021) and fostering a comprehensive understanding of AI ethics among educators and students, we can work towards a more equitable and humanizing approach to AI integration in educational settings.

Although the risks of data determinism are significant, they are not the only barriers to responsible AI integration in Gulf schools. Educational leaders in the region face a constellation of practical challenges that shape their capacity to implement data-informed leadership practices. Infrastructure disparities remain a significant concern; while some private schools in major urban centers have robust technological infrastructure, many public schools and schools in smaller cities face limitations in internet connectivity, device availability, and technical support capacity. These disparities create equity challenges, as schools with greater resources can more readily adopt sophisticated AI systems, potentially widening the gap between well-resourced and under-resourced institutions. Additionally, the multilingual and multicultural composition of Gulf school populations presents specific challenges for AI tool selection and implementation. Many Gulf schools serve diverse student populations, including local Arab citizens, Arab expatriates from across the region, and non-Arab expatriates from South Asia, Southeast Asia, Europe, and beyond. AI tools designed primarily for English-language contexts may not adequately support Arabic language instruction or may contain cultural assumptions that are not appropriate for the region's diverse communities. Furthermore, the cost and sustainability of AI initiatives require careful financial planning. While initial adoption may be supported by government grants or short-term funding, leaders must develop long-term financial strategies to ensure the sustainability of these initiatives within their school budgets. Finally, the rapid pace of technological change and the proliferation of AI vendors create challenges for vendor selection and management. School leaders must develop the capacity to evaluate AI tools critically, assessing not only their technical capabilities but also their alignment with pedagogical goals, cultural values, and ethical standards.

REDEFINING LEADERSHIP: THE DATA-INFORMED MODEL

Core principles: reflection, context, pedagogy-first, human judgment

For school leaders in Gulf and Middle Eastern contexts, the integration of AI requires adherence to four core principles that ensure its effective and ethical use while honoring local cultural values and pedagogical traditions. These principles, reflection, context, pedagogy-first approach, and human judgment, provide a framework for translating national AI mandates into school-level practice that is both educationally sound and culturally responsive. Reflection is crucial when implementing AI in educational settings. Students leveraging AI tools as brainstorming partners, co-writers, and co-readers demonstrate the importance of meta-reflective practices (Aure & Cuenca, 2024). This approach not only enhances research efficiency and comprehension but also promotes responsible AI usage and develops students' self-awareness and critical thinking skills. Context plays a vital role in AI implementation. The Safe AI in Education principles emphasize the need for AI to align with institutional strategies and adhere to didactic practices (Peñalvo et al., 2024). Similarly, the analogy-based pedagogical approach for teaching AI in K-12 education highlights the importance of age-appropriate, child-friendly methods that consider the learners' context (Dai et al., 2023). A pedagogy-first approach is essential when integrating AI into education. The intersection of AI and critical pedagogy (Sari et al., 2024) and the use of AI to enhance students' critical thinking skills in project-based service-learning (Kimmel, 2024)demonstrate the importance of prioritizing pedagogical goals. Education 6.0 vision further emphasizes personalized learning experiences and adaptive pedagogy enabled by AI (Moleka, 2023). Human judgment remains paramount in AI-enhanced education. The need for human oversight to maintain ethical principles is emphasized (Tariq, 2024), particularly in critical decision-making processes. Additionally, the importance of preserving humanistic values and ensuring a balanced, ethical, and inclusive educational environment is stressed when integrating AI with constructivist pedagogy (Grubaugh et al., 2023). While AI offers transformative potential in education, its successful implementation hinges on adhering to these core principles. By prioritizing reflection, considering context, putting pedagogy first, and maintaining human judgment, educators can harness AI's benefits while mitigating potential risks and ensuring a holistic, ethical approach to learning.

Key shifts in mindset and practice from reactive to interpretive leadership

The shift towards data-informed leadership in Gulf school contexts involves three interconnected transformations in how leaders approach their roles. First, leaders must develop what might be called a 'reflective technological mindset', being proactive and forward-thinking about AI's potential while maintaining a critical, questioning stance toward algorithmic outputs. This involves being adaptable and able to understand diverse perspectives as AI transforms school processes (Pietsch & Mah, 2024), while also developing the ethical and moral discernment to guide AI systems toward responsible outcomes (Smith & Green, 2018). In Gulf schools, where hierarchical leadership structures have traditionally predominated, this shift requires leaders to move from simply implementing top-down directives to actively interpreting and adapting AI initiatives to fit their school's specific cultural and pedagogical context.

Second, leaders must learn to manage what might be called 'hybrid ecosystems'—balancing the capabilities of AI systems with the irreplaceable expertise and judgment of human educators. This requires developing new communication standards and supervision approaches that honor both technological tools and human relationships (Smith & Green, 2018; Sposato, 2024). In practice, this might mean that while an AI system provides data on student learning gaps, the teacher's professional judgment about the causes of those gaps and the most appropriate interventions remains paramount.

Third, leaders must cultivate what we might term 'interpretive leadership'—the capacity to make meaning from data and to translate strategic vision into operational practice. This involves leveraging AI as a strategic partner rather than simply as a tool for efficiency (Edilia & Larasati, 2023). For a school leader in Riyadh, this might mean using AI-generated data on student attendance patterns not simply to enforce compliance but to understand the underlying factors affecting attendance and to design culturally appropriate interventions that address root causes.

Empowering school leaders to ask *why* and *how*, not just *what*

AI has the potential to transform education by empowering school leaders to focus on the "why" and "how" of learning, rather than just the "what." This shift allows for a more strategic and holistic approach to education management and decision-making. AI can assist school leaders in analyzing large amounts of data to identify trends, patterns, and areas for improvement in student performance and school operations (Tarisayi, 2024). By automating administrative tasks and streamlining processes, AI frees up time for leaders to concentrate on higher-level thinking and strategic planning (Seo et al., 2024; Tarisayi, 2024). For example, AI-powered chatbots can handle routine inquiries, allowing leaders to focus on more complex issues and long-term goals.

Interestingly, while AI offers numerous benefits, it also presents challenges. The implementation of AI in education requires careful consideration of ethical, cultural, and resource-related issues (Tarisayi, 2024). Additionally, there may be resistance to change among employees, highlighting the need for effective leadership in managing AI-induced transformations (Frick et al., 2021). AI empowers school leaders by providing them with tools to make data-driven decisions, automate routine tasks, and personalize learning experiences. This allows leaders to shift their focus from the "what" of education to the 'why' and 'how,' fostering innovation and improvement in educational practices. However, successful integration of AI requires addressing challenges and ensuring responsible adoption to maximize its potential in enhancing education. Although this shift toward asking 'why' and 'how' is conceptually sound, it faces particular challenges in Gulf educational contexts. The hierarchical governance structures that characterize many Gulf school systems may limit leaders' autonomy to ask critical questions about top-down AI mandates. Additionally, the rapid pace of technological change and the pressure to demonstrate alignment with national AI strategies can create urgency that discourages the reflective, questioning stance that data-informed leadership requires. Furthermore, the diversity of stakeholder perspectives in Gulf schools, including local citizens, Arab expatriates, non-Arab expatriates, and families with varying expectations about the role of technology in education, requires leaders to facilitate complex conversations about the 'why' and 'how' of AI integration. This requires not only the time and space for reflection but also the cultural competence and communication skills to navigate diverse perspectives. Nevertheless, by creating structures and processes that support this reflective questioning, such as regular data review meetings that bring together teachers, parents, and administrators, leaders can cultivate the interpretive leadership practices essential for responsible AI integration. The data-informed leadership model presented in this section provides a conceptual framework for responsible AI integration in K-12 education. For school leaders in Gulf and Middle Eastern contexts, this model offers a pathway to navigate the tension between national innovation mandates and the preservation of cultural and pedagogical values. By adhering to the core principles of reflection, context, pedagogy-first thinking, and human judgment, and by cultivating the interpretive leadership capacities described above, leaders can ensure that AI serves their school's educational mission rather than reshaping that mission according to technological imperatives. The following section translates this conceptual framework into a practical, phased implementation roadmap that Gulf school leaders can adapt to their specific institutional contexts.

STRATEGIC FRAMEWORKS FOR ETHICAL AI INTEGRATION

Data Ethics Checkpoints

For school leaders in Gulf schools, implementing data-informed AI integration requires establishing clear ethical checkpoints throughout the AI lifecycle, from initial tool selection through ongoing monitoring and evaluation. These checkpoints serve as structured moments for critical reflection, allowing leaders and their teams to pause and ask essential questions about whether an AI tool or data-driven decision aligns with the school's educational mission, cultural values, and ethical commitments. Rather than treating AI systems as black boxes that generate objective truth, ethical checkpoints position school leaders as active interpreters and stewards of technology, ensuring that algorithmic outputs are subjected to the same rigorous scrutiny as any other source of evidence. During the data collection and preparation phase, ethical considerations arise regarding data quality, bias, and privacy. As noted in Guan et al. (2022), "incomplete data" is a major source of ethical risks in AI decision-making. Organizations must carefully evaluate data sources, obtain proper consent, and implement robust data governance practices to mitigate these risks (Li, 2024). Additionally, addressing bias in AI algorithms is crucial to prevent discriminatory outcomes (Božić, 2023). The model development and deployment stages present further ethical challenges. Yu et al. (2018) highlight the importance of "individual ethical decision frameworks" and "collective ethical decision frameworks" in AI governance. These frameworks should guide the design and implementation of AI systems to ensure they align with ethical principles. Transparency and interpretability of AI models are also critical factors, as emphasized in Gupta (2023), which states the need for "transparency measures" to foster accountability. Ethical reflection is necessary throughout the AI lifecycle to address potential risks and ensure responsible AI deployment. Key checkpoints include data collection and preparation, model development, deployment, and ongoing monitoring. By implementing robust ethical frameworks and governance models, as suggested in Brendel et al. (2021)'s EMMA framework, organizations can navigate the complex ethical landscape of AI decision-making and build trust in their AI systems.

Collaborative Data Review Teams

AI-driven collaborative data review teams that bring together diverse roles can provide holistic interpretations of complex datasets, enhancing decision-making and insights across industries. These cross-functional teams leverage the complementary strengths of human expertise and AI capabilities to analyze data from multiple perspectives (Schleiger et al., 2024).

In healthcare, collaborative AI initiatives have enabled studies across clinical specialties by democratizing access to unstructured health information and AI/ML tools. This approach has fostered closer collaborations between clinicians, scientists, and administrators, advancing institution-level learning health systems (Luo et al., 2024). Similarly, in manufacturing, finance, retail, transportation, and construction, cross-functional teams comprising AI specialists, domain experts, and managers are crucial for the seamless integration of advanced AI systems like ChatGPT. These teams optimize processes, enhance decision-making, and drive innovation by combining diverse expertise (Rane, 2023). However, integrating AI into human teams poses challenges. Human-AI teams (HATs) often experience reduced coordination, communication, and trust compared to all-human teams. Trust in AI teammates tends to decline over time due to initial overestimation of capabilities, potentially impairing teamwork (Schmutz et al., 2024). To address these issues, research has identified four consistent team roles for AI-based teammates: coordinator, creator, perfectionist, and doer. Understanding these roles can help in better designing hybrid human-AI teams and managing team dynamics (Siemon, 2022). While AI-driven collaborative data review teams offer significant potential for holistic data interpretation and improved decision-making, their success depends on effectively addressing the challenges of human-AI collaboration. Interdisciplinary conferences and educational initiatives play a crucial role in fostering the necessary cross-disciplinary exchange and advancing AI literacy to realize the full potential of these collaborative teams (Allen & Kendeou, 2023; Patel et al., 2024). Although the research on collaborative data review teams comes primarily from healthcare and corporate contexts, the principles are directly applicable to K-12 schools. In Gulf educational settings, establishing a Collaborative Data Review Team can be particularly powerful for building shared understanding and addressing the diverse perspectives that characterize multicultural school communities. A typical school-based Collaborative Data Review Team might include: the school leader or assistant principal; lead teachers from different grade levels or subject areas; a teacher representative from the school's support services (e.g., special education, English language support); a parent representative; and, where possible, a student representative. The team meets regularly, perhaps monthly, to review data related to a specific area of focus, such as student literacy development, attendance patterns, or the implementation of a new AI-powered tool. For example, a school in Dubai implementing an AI-powered math tutoring system might establish a Collaborative Data Review Team to examine data on student performance, engagement, and learning gains. The team would include math teachers, who can speak to how students are responding to the system in the classroom; a special education specialist, who can assess whether the system is appropriately supporting students with learning differences; a parent representative, who can share family perspectives on the tool; and a student representative, who can offer insights into the user experience. By bringing these diverse perspectives together, the team can identify both successes and challenges that would be invisible in a top-down data dashboard. For instance, the team might discover that while the system is improving overall math scores, it is less effective for students whose primary language is Arabic, or that some students are becoming overly dependent on the system's hints rather than developing problem-solving strategies. These insights allow the school to adapt its use of the tool rather than accepting its outputs uncritically. A key challenge in Gulf schools is the hierarchical governance structures that can limit open dialogue. Establishing a Collaborative Data Review Team requires leaders to create psychological safety, ensuring that teachers, parents, and students feel comfortable sharing honest perspectives, including concerns about AI tools or data-driven decisions. This may require explicit norms about respectful disagreement and a commitment from leaders to genuinely consider diverse viewpoints rather than simply seeking validation for predetermined decisions.

Transparency and Communication Protocols

AI transparency and communication protocols for sharing data logic and limitations with stakeholders are crucial aspects of responsible AI development and implementation. Several key factors emerge from the available research: Transparency in AI encompasses multiple facets, including explainability (XAI), mediation of AI system functionality, literacy, and legal frameworks (Larsson et al., 2023). Explainable AI techniques are essential for building trust and understanding among stakeholders, but they have limitations and are not mandated by regulations like the EU AI Act (Panigutti et al., 2023). Instead, the focus is on transparency through documentation and human oversight. Organizational readiness for data sharing is influenced by motivation and capabilities (Youssef et al., 2023). Cross-sector collaboration is identified as a key strategy to overcome barriers in accessing health data for AI development. External incentives may boost organizational motivation and facilitate sustainable data flow for AI development.

Communication of scientific uncertainties by federal agencies plays a crucial role in explaining risks and uncertainties to stakeholders (Phutane, 2023). Agencies use personalized examples to explain uncertainties that are difficult to quantify, particularly in areas of ownership, safety, and transparency. They also seek public input to gather additional data and derive consensus on issues with moral implications. Effective AI transparency and communication protocols require a multifaceted approach. This includes developing explainable AI techniques, fostering cross-sector collaboration, providing clear documentation, ensuring human oversight, and effectively communicating uncertainties to stakeholders. By addressing these aspects, organizations can build trust, improve stakeholder understanding, and promote responsible AI development and implementation.

Aligning with child protection, privacy, and equity standards

AI systems in education must align with child protection, privacy, and equity standards to ensure safe and ethical implementation. The integration of AI technologies in educational settings raises several critical concerns that need to be addressed through a comprehensive approach combining technological innovation, ethical guidelines, and regulatory frameworks. A manifesto outlining seven core principles for safe AI in education emphasizes the protection of student data, alignment with institutional strategies, and ethical transparency (Peñalvo et al., 2024). These principles are designed to guide the deployment of AI technologies in educational settings, addressing potential risks such as privacy violations and misuse. The implementation of Smart Learning Applications (SLApps) integrates AI into existing institutional technological ecosystems, enabling secure, role-adaptive, and course-specific learning experiences (Peñalvo et al., 2024). While AI holds tremendous potential for promoting equity and access to STEM education, particularly for students with disabilities, ethical concerns such as algorithmic bias and data privacy risks require critical attention (Kohnke & Zaugg, 2025). Aligning AI tools with Universal Design for Learning (UDL) principles can help personalize learning, improve accessibility, and close achievement gaps in STEM content areas. However, further research is needed to refine AI tools and ensure they meet the diverse needs of students with disabilities while promoting equity rather than exacerbating disparities (Kohnke & Zaugg, 2025). To address privacy concerns, organizations must implement robust data security measures such as encryption, anonymization, and access controls, while also prioritizing transparency and accountability in AI-driven decision-making processes (Singhal, 2024). Emerging trends in privacy-preserving techniques, such as federated learning and differential privacy, offer promising solutions for balancing innovation with patient rights and regulatory requirements (Singhal, 2024; Zhu & Yu, 2019). By adopting strategic management practices, including robust governance models and continuous monitoring, organizations can optimize the effectiveness of AI-driven systems while ensuring compliance with child protection, privacy, and equity standards (Mbah & Evelyn, 2024).

IMPLEMENTATION ROADMAP FOR SCHOOLS

The integration of AI technologies in K-12 education requires a thoughtful, phased approach that balances innovation with ethical considerations and cultural sensitivities. This section outlines a comprehensive implementation roadmap for school leaders in Gulf and Middle Eastern contexts, providing a structured pathway toward responsible AI adoption that remains data-informed rather than data-driven.

Phase 1: Foundation Building and Capacity Development

The journey toward effective AI integration begins with establishing robust foundations. School leaders must first conduct a thorough assessment of their institutional readiness, examining existing technological infrastructure, staff capabilities, and organizational culture. This assessment should not merely focus on technical aspects but should equally consider the school's ethical preparedness and alignment with cultural values. In Gulf contexts, where traditional pedagogical approaches often coexist with ambitious technological aspirations, this initial assessment becomes particularly crucial. Professional development represents the cornerstone of successful AI implementation. Rather than approaching training as a one-time event, school leaders should establish continuous learning pathways that evolve alongside technological advancements. These pathways should encompass technical skills development while emphasizing ethical considerations, critical data literacy, and pedagogical integration. As noted by Henriksen et al. (2024), success in AI integration demands a holistic approach addressing both technological and human factors. In practice, this might involve creating professional learning communities where educators can collaboratively explore AI applications, share experiences, and develop context-appropriate implementation strategies. Concurrent with professional development, school leaders must establish clear governance frameworks that delineate roles, responsibilities, and decision-making processes related to AI adoption. These frameworks should explicitly articulate the primacy of human judgment in educational decisions while clarifying how AI-generated insights will inform, rather than dictate, these decisions. Given the UAE's pioneering role in governmental AI adoption (Halaweh, 2018), educational institutions in the region have an opportunity to develop governance models that balance technological innovation with cultural values and educational priorities.

Phase 2: Pilot Implementation and Ethical Guardians

With foundations established, schools can proceed to pilot implementation, selecting specific AI applications that address identified institutional needs while aligning with educational values. These pilots should be approached as learning opportunities rather than performance evaluations, creating safe spaces for experimentation, reflection, and adaptation. School leaders should prioritize applications that augment rather than replace human capabilities, reinforcing the complementary relationship between AI and educational expertise.

Throughout pilot implementation, ethical guardrails must be systematically embedded into operational processes. Drawing on the chapter's earlier discussion of data determinism risks, schools should establish "data ethics checkpoints," structured moments of reflection where AI-generated insights are critically examined before informing decisions. These checkpoints might include questions such as: Does this data reflect our diverse student population? What contextual factors might the algorithm be missing? How might the implementation of these recommendations affect marginalized students? By institutionalizing these reflective practices, schools can mitigate the risks of algorithmic bias and maintain the centrality of human judgment. Transparency mechanisms represent another critical ethical guardrail. School leaders should develop clear communication protocols that explain how AI systems are being used, what data is being collected, and how this information informs educational decisions. These protocols should be culturally sensitive, acknowledging potential concerns about surveillance and privacy that may be particularly salient in Middle Eastern contexts. By proactively addressing these concerns, schools can build trust among stakeholders and create conditions for responsible AI adoption.

Phase 3: Scaled Implementation and Continuous Improvement

As pilot initiatives demonstrate value and ethical guardrails prove effective, schools can gradually scale implementation across additional domains and departments. This scaling should be guided by a systematic evaluation of both technical performance and human experience, ensuring that AI systems genuinely enhance educational processes rather than merely adding technological complexity. School leaders should establish multidimensional evaluation frameworks that assess impacts on student learning, teacher agency, administrative efficiency, and ethical alignment. Collaborative data review teams represent a powerful mechanism for continuous improvement during scaled implementation. These cross-functional teams—comprising administrators, teachers, data specialists, and potentially student representatives—should regularly examine AI-generated insights, contextualizing them within broader educational understandings and identifying potential biases or limitations. In Gulf educational contexts, where hierarchical structures often predominate, these collaborative teams can serve the dual purpose of improving AI implementation while fostering more distributed leadership approaches. Knowledge-sharing networks extend the continuous improvement process beyond individual institutions. School leaders should establish mechanisms for exchanging experiences, challenges, and innovations with peer institutions, creating communities of practice focused on responsible AI adoption. These networks might operate at regional levels, connecting educational institutions across Gulf countries that share similar cultural contexts and technological aspirations. By collectively navigating the complexities of AI integration, schools can accelerate learning while developing regionally appropriate implementation models.

Phase 4: Systemic Integration and Cultural Adaptation

The final phase involves moving beyond isolated AI applications toward systemic integration, where data-informed approaches become embedded in institutional culture and operational processes. This integration requires careful attention to cultural adaptation, ensuring that AI implementation respects and reinforces valued educational traditions while enabling meaningful innovation. As Wong (2020) notes, frameworks for AI governance cannot be straightforwardly applied across different cultural contexts but must be adapted to local values and priorities. In Gulf and Middle Eastern educational contexts, this cultural adaptation might involve reconciling AI-enabled personalized learning with traditional pedagogical approaches that emphasize collective learning experiences and teacher authority. Rather than positioning these as opposing forces, school leaders can facilitate dialogues that identify complementarities and creative syntheses. For example, AI systems might provide personalized practice opportunities while preserving teacher-led collective instruction for concept development and cultural transmission. Leadership development represents the capstone of systemic integration. As AI becomes increasingly embedded in educational processes, school leaders must cultivate new capabilities that blend technological understanding with ethical discernment and cultural sensitivity. Professional development for leaders should emphasize their role as ethical stewards of technology, responsible for ensuring that AI serves educational values rather than reshaping those values according to technological imperatives. In Gulf contexts, where educational leadership often carries significant cultural authority, this ethical stewardship takes on particular importance.

Implementation Considerations for Gulf and Middle Eastern Contexts

Several contextual factors warrant special consideration when implementing this roadmap in Gulf and Middle Eastern educational settings. First, the region's ambitious national AI strategies create both opportunities and pressures for educational institutions. School leaders must navigate these dynamics thoughtfully, leveraging governmental support while maintaining focus on educational priorities rather than technological adoption for its own sake. Second, cultural values regarding authority, privacy, and educational purpose significantly shape AI implementation. For example, data collection practices that might be readily accepted in Western contexts may require additional justification and safeguards in settings where privacy concerns are culturally heightened. Similarly, AI applications that distribute decision-making authority may require careful introduction in contexts where hierarchical leadership is culturally expected. Third, the region's linguistic and cultural diversity presents both challenges and opportunities for AI implementation. School leaders must ensure that AI systems adequately support Arabic language instruction and content, while also addressing the needs of expatriate communities that form significant portions of many Gulf educational systems. This diversity creates opportunities for developing AI applications that support multilingual learning environments and cross-cultural understanding. Finally, the rapid pace of technological and economic change in Gulf countries creates a dynamic implementation context. School leaders must balance immediate adoption pressures with sustainable, thoughtful implementation approaches. By emphasizing capacity building and ethical foundations, schools can develop the adaptive capabilities needed to navigate ongoing technological evolution while maintaining educational integrity. In conclusion, this implementation roadmap provides a structured yet flexible pathway toward responsible AI integration in K-12 education. By emphasizing foundation building, ethical guardrails, continuous improvement, and cultural adaptation, school leaders can harness AI's potential while avoiding the pitfalls of data determinism. Throughout implementation, the guiding principle remains consistent: AI systems should inform rather than drive educational decisions, preserving the essential role of human judgment, ethical discernment, and cultural sensitivity in shaping educational experiences.

CONCLUSION

The integration of artificial intelligence in K-12 education represents both a profound opportunity and a significant responsibility for school leaders, particularly in Gulf and Middle Eastern contexts where technological ambition intersects with traditional educational values. Throughout this chapter, we have examined the critical distinction between data-driven and data-informed leadership approaches, arguing that the latter provides a more balanced, ethical, and ultimately effective framework for educational decision-making in the AI era. The risks of data determinism, including eroded teacher agency, student dehumanization, and biased performance metrics, are not merely theoretical concerns but emerging realities that demand thoughtful leadership responses. As AI-generated metrics and dashboards become increasingly sophisticated and ubiquitous, the temptation to defer to algorithmic recommendations grows stronger. Yet, as our analysis has demonstrated, this deference comes at a significant cost: the diminishment of professional judgment, the narrowing of educational vision, and the potential reinforcement of existing inequities. The data-informed leadership model presented in this chapter offers an alternative path forward, one that positions AI as a valuable tool within a broader ecosystem of educational insight and decision-making. By implementing strategies such as data ethics checkpoints, collaborative data review teams, and transparency frameworks, school leaders can harness AI's analytical capabilities while preserving the essential human elements of educational leadership: judgment, context-sensitivity, ethical discernment, and cultural responsiveness. The implementation roadmap outlined in the previous section provides a structured approach to realizing this vision, guiding schools through the complex journey from initial capacity building to systemic integration. This roadmap acknowledges the unique contextual factors of Gulf and Middle Eastern educational settings, including ambitious national AI strategies, cultural values regarding authority and privacy, linguistic and cultural diversity, and rapid technological change. By attending to these contextual factors, school leaders can develop implementation approaches that are both technically sound and culturally appropriate.

Looking forward, the evolution of AI in education will continue to present new challenges and opportunities for school leaders. Emerging technologies such as generative AI, predictive analytics, and immersive learning environments will further blur the boundaries between human and machine capabilities, raising new questions about educational purpose, pedagogical approach, and leadership responsibility. In this evolving landscape, the principles of data-informed leadership will become even more essential, providing an ethical compass for navigating increasingly complex technological terrain. For educational leaders in Gulf and Middle Eastern contexts, this navigation requires particular attention to the intersection of technological innovation and cultural values. As these societies pursue ambitious visions of knowledge-based economies and technological leadership, educational institutions play a crucial role in developing human capabilities that blend technical expertise with ethical discernment and cultural understanding. By modeling data-informed leadership approaches, school leaders can demonstrate how technological advancement can occur in harmony with, rather than at the expense of, valued cultural traditions and educational priorities. The future of education in the AI era will be shaped not primarily by technological capabilities but by the wisdom with which these capabilities are deployed. This wisdom resides not in algorithms but in human communities, teachers, leaders, students, and families, who collectively determine how technology will serve educational purposes. By positioning themselves as facilitators of these collective determinations rather than mere implementers of technological systems, school leaders can ensure that AI enhances rather than diminishes the human dimensions of education. The promise of AI in education lies not in automation but in augmentation—the enhancement of human capabilities, the expansion of educational possibilities, and the enrichment of learning experiences. Realizing this promise requires leadership that is simultaneously forward-looking and deeply grounded, technologically informed and humanistically oriented, globally aware and culturally responsive. By embracing data-informed rather than data-driven approaches, school leaders can navigate the complexities of AI integration while preserving the essential human core of educational practice. As Gulf and Middle Eastern societies continue their ambitious journeys toward technological advancement and educational excellence, the leadership practices described in this chapter offer a pathway that honors both innovation and tradition, embracing technological possibilities while remaining firmly anchored in human values and educational purpose. In this balanced approach lies the true potential of AI in education: not as a replacement for human judgment but as a powerful tool for expanding human capability and enriching the educational experiences of all learners.

REFERENCES

Abdelaal, N., & Al Sawy, I. (2024). Perceptions, challenges, and prospects: University professors' use of artificial intelligence in education. *Australian Journal of Applied Linguistics*, *7*(1), 1–24. DOI: 10.29140/ajal.v7n1.1309

Abdulrahman, M. (2024). Balancing Act: Exploring the Interplay Between Human Judgment and Artificial Intelligence in Problem-solving, Creativity, and Decision-making. *IgMin Research*, *2*(3), 145–158. DOI: 10.61927/igmin158

Adeleye, O., Eden, C., & Adeniyi, I. (2024). Innovative teaching methodologies in the era of artificial intelligence: A review of inclusive educational practices. World Journal of Advanced Engineering Technology and Sciences, 11(2), 069–079. DOI: 10.30574/wjaets.2024.11.2.0091

Akgun, S., & Greenhow, C. (2021). Artificial intelligence in education: Addressing ethical challenges in K-12 settings. *AI and Ethics*, *2*(3), 431–440. DOI: 10.1007/s43681-021-00096-7 PMID: 34790956

Alasgarova, R., & Rzayev, J. (2024). The Role of Artificial Intelligence in Shaping High School Students' Motivation. *International Journal of Technology in Education and Science*, *8*(2), 311–324. DOI: 10.46328/ijtes.553

Allen, L. K., & Kendeou, P. (2023). ED-AI Lit: An Interdisciplinary Framework for AI Literacy in Education. *Policy Insights from the Behavioral and Brain Sciences*, *11*(1), 3–10. DOI: 10.1177/23727322231220339

Aquino, Y. S. J. (2023). Making decisions: Bias in artificial intelligence and data-driven diagnostic tools. *Australian Journal of General Practice*, *52*(7), 439–442. DOI: 10.31128/AJGP-12-22-6630 PMID: 37423238

Aquino, Y. S. J., Carter, S. M., Houssami, N., Braunack-Mayer, A., Win, K. T., Degeling, C., Wang, L., & Rogers, W. A. (2023). Practical, epistemic and normative implications of algorithmic bias in healthcare artificial intelligence: A qualitative study of multidisciplinary expert perspectives. *Journal of Medical Ethics*, *47*, jme-108850. DOI: 10.1136/jme-2022-108850 PMID: 36823101

Aure, P. A., & Cuenca, O. (2024). Fostering social-emotional learning through human-centered use of generative AI in business research education: An insider case study. Journal of Research in Innovative Teaching &amp. *Learning*, *17*(2), 168–181. DOI: 10.1108/JRIT-03-2024-0076

Bai, X. (2024). THE ROLE AND CHALLENGES OF ARTIFICIAL INTELLIGENCE IN INFORMATION TECHNOLOGY EDUCATION. *Pacific International Journal, 7*(1), 86–92. DOI: 10.55014/pij.v7i1.524

Barnes, E., & Hutson, J. (2024). Navigating the ethical terrain of AI in higher education: Strategies for mitigating bias and promoting fairness. *Forum for Education Studies, 2*(2), 1229. DOI: 10.59400/fes.v2i2.1229

Baskara, F. R. (2023). AI-Driven Dynamics: ChatGPT Transforming ELT Teacher-Student Interactions. Lensa: Kajian Kebahasaan, Kesusastraan. *Dan Budaya, 13*(2), 261. DOI: 10.26714/lensa.13.2.2023.261-275

Božić, V. (2023). Integrated Risk Management and Artificial Intelligence in Hospital. *Journal of AI, 7*(1), 63–80. DOI: 10.61969/jai.1329224

Brendel, A. B., Mirbabaie, M., Hofeditz, L., & Lembcke, T.-B. (2021). Ethical Management of Artificial Intelligence. *Sustainability (Basel), 13*(4), 1974. DOI: 10.3390/su13041974

Bulut, O., & Beiting-Parrish, M. (2024). The Rise of Artificial Intelligence in Educational Measurement: Opportunities and Ethical Challenges. *Chinese/English Journal of Educational Measurement and Evaluation, 5*(3). Advance online publication. DOI: 10.59863/MIQL7785

Chinta, S., Wang, Z., Yin, Z., Hoang, N., Gonzalez, M., Quy, T., & Zhang, W. (2024). FairAIED: Navigating Fairness, Bias, and Ethics in Educational AI Applications. / arxiv.2407.18745DOI: 10.48550

Coşkun, A. B., Kenner, C., & Elmaoğlu, E. (2024). Neonatal Intensive Care Nurses' Perceptions of Artificial Intelligence: A Qualitative Study on Discharge Education and Family Counseling. *The Journal of Perinatal & Neonatal Nursing*. Advance online publication. DOI: 10.1097/JPN.0000000000000904 PMID: 39740134

Dai, Y., Dai, D., Lin, Z., Liu, A., & Wang, W. (2023). Effect of an Analogy-Based Approach of Artificial Intelligence Pedagogy in Upper Primary Schools. *Journal of Educational Computing Research, 61*(8), 1695–1722. DOI: 10.1177/07356331231201342

Edilia, S., & Larasati, N. D. (2023). Innovative Approaches in Business Development Strategies Through Artificial Intelligence Technology. [ITSDI]. *IAIC Transactions on Sustainable Digital Innovation, 5*(1), 84–90. DOI: 10.34306/itsdi.v5i1.612

Filgueiras, F. (2023). Artificial intelligence and education governance. *Education, Citizenship and Social Justice, 19*(3), 349–361. DOI: 10.1177/17461979231160674

Frick, N. R. J., Mirbabaie, M., Stieglitz, S., & Salomon, J. (2021). Maneuvering through the stormy seas of digital transformation: The impact of empowering leadership on the AI readiness of enterprises. *Journal of Decision Systems*, *30*(2–3), 235–258. DOI: 10.1080/12460125.2020.1870065

García Peñalvo, F. J., Pereira, J., Casany, M. J., & Alier, M. (2024). Safe, Transparent, and Ethical Artificial Intelligence. IJERI. *International Journal of Educational Research and Innovation*, *22*(22), 1–21. DOI: 10.46661/ijeri.11036

Gaskins, N. (2022). Interrogating Algorithmic Bias: From Speculative Fiction to Liberatory Design. *TechTrends*, *67*(3), 417–425. DOI: 10.1007/s11528-022-00783-0 PMID: 36160677

Gaur, A. S., Kumar, R., & Sharan, H. O. (2024). AI in Education (pp. 39–54). igi global. DOI: 10.4018/979-8-3693-2964-1.ch003

Grubaugh, S., Deever, D., & Levitt, G. (2023). Harnessing AI to Power Constructivist Learning: An Evolution in Educational Methodologies. *EIKI Journal of Effective Teaching Methods*, *1*(3). Advance online publication. DOI: 10.59652/jetm.v1i3.43

Guan, H., Zhao, A., & Dong, L. (2022). Ethical Risk Factors and Mechanisms in Artificial Intelligence Decision Making. *Behavioral Sciences (Basel, Switzerland)*, *12*(9), 343. DOI: 10.3390/bs12090343 PMID: 36135147

Gupta, N. (2023). Artificial Intelligence Ethics and Fairness: A study to address bias and fairness issues in AI systems, and the ethical implications of AI applications. *Revista Review Index Journal of Multidisciplinary*, *3*(2), 24–35. DOI: 10.31305/rrijm2023.v03.n02.004

Halaweh, M. (2018). Viewpoint: Artificial Intelligence Government (Gov. 3.0): The UAE Leading Model. *Journal of Artificial Intelligence Research*, *62*, 269–272. DOI: 10.1613/jair.1.11210

Henriksen, D., Mishra, P., & Stern, R. (2024). Creative Learning for Sustainability in a World of AI: Action, Mindset, Values. *Sustainability (Basel)*, *16*(11), 4451. DOI: 10.3390/su16114451

Kearney, M., Schuck, S., & Burden, K. (2018). Disrupting Education Using Smart Mobile Pedagogies (pp. 139–157). springer. DOI: 10.1007/978-3-030-01551-0_7

Keegan, B. J., Dennehy, D., & Naudé, P. (2022). Implementing Artificial Intelligence in Traditional B2B Marketing Practices: An Activity Theory Perspective. *Information Systems Frontiers*, *26*(3), 1025–1039. DOI: 10.1007/s10796-022-10294-1 PMID: 35637917

Kimmel, S. (2024). AI Facilitated Critical Thinking in an Undergraduate Project Based Service-Learning Course. *Journal of Behavioral and Applied Management, 24*(2). Advance online publication. DOI: 10.21818/001c.122149

Kohnke, S., & Zaugg, T. (2025). Artificial Intelligence: An Untapped Opportunity for Equity and Access in STEM Education. *Education Sciences, 15*(1), 68. DOI: 10.3390/educsci15010068

Kovalenko, I., & Baranivska, N. (2024). INTEGRATING ARTIFICIAL INTELLIGENCE IN ENGLISH LANGUAGE TEACHING: EXPLORING THE POTENTIAL AND CHALLENGES OF AI TOOLS IN ENHANCING LANGUAGE LEARNING OUTCOMES AND PERSONALIZED EDUCATION. European Socio-Legal &amp. *Humanitarian Studies, 1*, 86–95. DOI: 10.61345/2734-8873.2024.1.9

Larsson, S., Högberg, C., Haresamudram, K., Nyström, A., Lao, Y., & Söderlund, K. (2023). Four facets of AI transparency (pp. 445–455). edward elgar. DOI: 10.4337/9781803928562.00047

Lee, M. H., & Chew, C. J. (2023). Understanding the Effect of Counterfactual Explanations on Trust and Reliance on AI for Human-AI Collaborative Clinical Decision Making. Proceedings of the ACM on Human-Computer Interaction, 7(CSCW2), 1–22. DOI: 10.1145/3610218

Li, Z. (2024). AI Ethics and Transparency in Operations Management: How Governance Mechanisms Can Reduce Data Bias and Privacy Risks. Journal of Applied Economics and Policy Studies. DOI: 10.54254/2977-5701/13/2024130

Lin, S., Levy, A., Pandit, S., Shoja, M. M., & Tritsch, T. (2024). What Goes In, Must Come Out: Generative Artificial Intelligence Does Not Present Algorithmic Bias Across Race and Gender in Medical Residency Specialties. *Cureus, 16*(2). Advance online publication. DOI: 10.7759/cureus.54448 PMID: 38510858

Lin, Y., Luo, Q., & Qian, Y. (2023). Investigation of Artificial Intelligence algorithms in education. *Applied and Computational Engineering, 16*(1), 180–184. DOI: 10.54254/2755-2721/16/20230886

Luo, Y., Mithal, L. B., Shah, S. J., Markl, M., Chisholm, R. L., Wunderink, R. G., Mao, C., Carson, M., Fang, D., Wehbe, F., Adams, J., Holmes, K., D'Aquila, R. T., Naidech, A., Kho, A., Green, M., Yue, F., Sanchez-Pinto, L. N., Dresden, S., & Ahmad, F. S. (2024). Northwestern University resource and education development initiatives to advance collaborative artificial intelligence across the learning health system. *Learning Health Systems, 8*(3), e10417. Advance online publication. DOI: 10.1002/lrh2.10417 PMID: 39036530

Madan, R., & Ashok, M. (2022). AI adoption and diffusion in public administration: A systematic literature review and future research agenda. *Government Information Quarterly*, *40*(1), 101774. DOI: 10.1016/j.giq.2022.101774

Mbah, G., & Evelyn, A.Geraldine O MbahAchudume Nkechi Evelyn. (2024). AI-powered cybersecurity: Strategic approaches to mitigate risk and safeguard data privacy. *World Journal of Advanced Research and Reviews*, *24*(3), 310–327. DOI: 10.30574/wjarr.2024.24.3.3695

Mohammad Nezhad, P., & Stolz, S. A. (2024). Unveiling teachers' professional agency and decision-making in professional learning: the illusion of choice. Professional Development in Education, ahead-of-print(ahead-of-print), 1–21. DOI: 10.1080/19415257.2024.2349058

Moleka, P. (2023). Exploring the Role of Artificial Intelligence in Education 6.0: Enhancing Personalized Learning and Adaptive Pedagogy. mdpi ag. DOI: 10.20944/preprints202309.0562.v1

Müller, V. C. (2021). Ethics of artificial intelligence 1 (pp. 122–137). routledge. DOI: 10.4324/9780429198533-9

Onesi-Ozigagun, O., Ololade, Y., Eyo-Udo, N., & Ogundipe, D. (2024). REVOLUTIONIZING EDUCATION THROUGH AI: A COMPREHENSIVE REVIEW OF ENHANCING LEARNING EXPERIENCES. *International Journal of Applied Research in Social Sciences*, *6*(4), 589–607. DOI: 10.51594/ijarss.v6i4.1011

Panigutti, C., Gomez, E., Hupont, I., Hamon, R., Junklewitz, H., Sanchez, I., Soler Garrido, J., Scalzo, S., Mazzini, G., Fernandez Llorca, D., & Fano Yela, D. (2023). The role of explainable AI in the context of the AI Act. 1139–1150. DOI: 10.1145/3593013.3594069

Parcero, O. J., & Ryan, J. C. (2016). Becoming a Knowledge Economy: The Case of Qatar, UAE, and 17 Benchmark Countries. *Journal of the Knowledge Economy*, *8*(4), 1146–1173. DOI: 10.1007/s13132-016-0355-y

Patel, A. U., Esper, R., Maeser, N., Maeser, D., & Gu, Q. (2024). The Crucial Role of Interdisciplinary Conferences in Advancing Explainable AI in Healthcare. *BioMedInformatics*, *4*(2), 1363–1383. DOI: 10.3390/biomedinformatics4020075

Peters, U. (2022). Algorithmic Political Bias in Artificial Intelligence Systems. Philosophy &amp. *Technology*, *35*(2), 25. Advance online publication. DOI: 10.1007/s13347-022-00512-8 PMID: 35378902

Phutane, A. S. (2023). Communication of Uncertainty in AI Regulations. *Community Change*, *4*(2), 3. DOI: 10.21061/cc.v4i2.a.50

Pietsch, M., & Mah, D.-K. (2024). Leading the AI transformation in schools: It starts with a digital mindset. *Educational Technology Research and Development, 73*(2), 1043–1069. Advance online publication. DOI: 10.1007/s11423-024-10439-w

Rane, N. L. (2023). Multidisciplinary collaboration: key players in successful implementation of ChatGPT and similar generative artificial intelligence in manufacturing, finance, retail, transportation, and construction industry. center for open science. DOI: 10.31219/osf.io/npm3d

Richards, C. (2004). From old to new learning: global imperatives, exemplary Asian dilemmas and ICT as a key to cultural change in education. Globalisation, Societies and Education, 2(3), 337–353. DOI: 10.1080/1476772042000252470

Robinson, S. C. (2020). Trust, transparency, and openness: How inclusion of cultural values shapes Nordic national public policy strategies for artificial intelligence (AI). *Technology in Society, 63*, 101421. DOI: 10.1016/j.techsoc.2020.101421

Rütti-Joy, O., Winder, G., & Biedermann, H. (2024). Teacher Educator Professionalism in the Age of AI: Navigating the New Landscape of Quality Education. intechopen. DOI: 10.5772/intechopen.1005030

Sari, T., Bozkurt, A., & Nayír, F. (2024). Reimagining education: Bridging artificial intelligence, transhumanism, and critical pedagogy. *Journal of Educational Technology and Online Learning, 7*(1), 102–115. DOI: 10.31681/jetol.1308022

Scharowski, N., Brühlmann, F., Perrig, S. A. C., Svab, M., & Opwis, K. (2023). Exploring the effects of human-centered AI explanations on trust and reliance. *Frontiers of Computer Science, 5*, 1151150. Advance online publication. DOI: 10.3389/fcomp.2023.1151150

Schleiger, E., Mason, C., Naughtin, C., Reeson, A., & Paris, C. (2024). Collaborative Intelligence: A Scoping Review Of Current Applications. *Applied Artificial Intelligence, 38*(1), 2327890. Advance online publication. DOI: 10.1080/08839514.2024.2327890

Schmutz, J. B., Outland, N., Kerstan, S., Georganta, E., & Ulfert, A.-S. (2024). AI-teaming: Redefining collaboration in the digital era. *Current Opinion in Psychology, 58*, 101837. DOI: 10.1016/j.copsyc.2024.101837 PMID: 39024969

Seo, K., Yoo, M., Dodson, S., & Jin, S.-H. (2024). Augmented teachers: K–12 teachers' needs for artificial intelligence's complementary role in personalized learning. Journal of Research on Technology in Education, ahead-of-print(ahead-of-print), 1–18. DOI: 10.1080/15391523.2024.2330525

Shahvaroughi Farahani, M., & Ghasemi, G. (2024). *Artificial Intelligence and Inequality: Challenges and Opportunities*. Qeios., DOI: 10.32388/7HWUZ2

Sharma, D. M., Verma, R., Boopathi, S., Uma Maheswari, B., Venkata Ramana, K., & Jothilakshmi, R. (2024). Integrating Generative AI Into K-12 Curriculums and Pedagogies in India (pp. 133–161). igi global. DOI: 10.4018/979-8-3693-0487-7.ch006

Siemon, D. (2022). Elaborating Team Roles for Artificial Intelligence-based Teammates in Human-AI Collaboration. *Group Decision and Negotiation*, *31*(5), 871–912. DOI: 10.1007/s10726-022-09792-z

Singhal, S. (2024). Data Privacy, Compliance, and Security Including AI ML (pp. 111–126). igi global. DOI: 10.4018/979-8-3693-2909-2.ch009

Smith, A. M., & Green, M. (2018). Artificial Intelligence and the Role of Leadership. *Journal of Leadership Studies*, *12*(3), 85–87. DOI: 10.1002/jls.21605

Sposato, M. (2024). Leadership training and development in the age of artificial intelligence. *Development and Learning in Organizations*, *38*(4), 4–7. DOI: 10.1108/DLO-12-2023-0256

Tariq, M. U. (2024). Navigating the Ethical Frontier-Human Oversight in AI-Driven Decision-Making System (pp. 425–448). igi global. DOI: 10.4018/979-8-3693-6230-3.ch013

Tarisayi, K. S. (2024). Strategic leadership for responsible artificial intelligence adoption in higher education. *CTE Workshop Proceedings*, 11, 4–14. DOI: 10.55056/cte.616

Thomas, T. (2024). The Role of Artificial Intelligence in Formal and Informal Education for Students. *International Journal for Research in Applied Science and Engineering Technology*, *12*(3), 69–71. DOI: 10.22214/ijraset.2024.58738

Watkins, R., & Barak-Medina, E. (2024). AI's Influence on Human Creative Agency. Creativity Research Journal, ahead-of-print(ahead-of-print). DOI: 10.1080/10400419.2024.2437264

Weidmann, A. E. (2024). Artificial intelligence in academic writing and clinical pharmacy education: Consequences and opportunities. *International Journal of Clinical Pharmacy*, *46*(3), 751–754. DOI: 10.1007/s11096-024-01705-1 PMID: 38472596

Wong, P.-H. (2020). Cultural Differences as Excuses? Human Rights and Cultural Values in Global Ethics and Governance of AI. Philosophy &amp. *Philosophy & Technology*, *33*(4), 705–715. DOI: 10.1007/s13347-020-00413-8

Youssef, A., Ng, M. Y., Long, J., Hernandez-Boussard, T., Shah, N., Miner, A., Larson, D., & Langlotz, C. P. (2023). Organizational Factors in Clinical Data Sharing for Artificial Intelligence in Health Care. *JAMA Network Open*, *6*(12), e2348422. DOI: 10.1001/jamanetworkopen.2023.48422 PMID: 38113040

Yu, H., Miao, C., Leung, C., Lesser, V. R., Yang, Q., & Shen, Z. (2018). Building Ethics into Artificial Intelligence. 5527–5533. DOI: 10.24963/ijcai.2018/779

Zajko, M. (2021). Conservative AI and social inequality: Conceptualizing alternatives to bias through social theory. AI &amp. *AI & Society*, *36*(3), 1047–1056. DOI: 10.1007/s00146-021-01153-9

Zha, H., Li, W., Wang, W., & Xiao, J. (2025). The Paradox of AI Empowerment in Primary School Physical Education: Why Technology May Hinder, Not Help, Teaching Efficiency. *Behavioral Sciences (Basel, Switzerland)*, *15*(2), 240. DOI: 10.3390/bs15020240 PMID: 40001871

Zhai, C., Wibowo, S., & Li, L. D. (2024). The effects of over-reliance on AI dialogue systems on students' cognitive abilities: A systematic review. *Smart Learning Environments*, *11*(1), 28. Advance online publication. DOI: 10.1186/s40561-024-00316-7

Zhu, T., & Yu, P. S. (2019). Applying Differential Privacy Mechanism in Artificial Intelligence. 1601–1609. DOI: 10.1109/ICDCS.2019.00159

Chapter 12
Evaluated by Machines: Leadership and Fairness in the Age of Algorithmic Learning Analysis

Enrio Moch
http://orcid.org/0009-0005-4722-0961
GrandEdu Research School, Germany

Tobias Oberdieck
http://orcid.org/0009-0002-2017-4991
GrandEdu GmbH, Germany

ABSTRACT

This chapter critically examines how leadership and fairness are reconfigured under the conditions of algorithmic learning analytics. Based on discourse theory, information ethics, and the concept of epistemic injustice, it analyses how educational judgment is delegated to data-driven systems that create new normative tensions. The Subjective Dynamic Decision Model (SDDM) serves as a heuristic framework for understanding decision-making under radical uncertainty in educational leadership. Case studies of Civitas Learning, JISC Early Alert, and Smart Learning Platforms illustrate how algorithmic systems reproduce power relations instead of representing them neutrally. The chapter argues that algorithmic evaluation transforms governance practices and challenges conventional ideas of transparency, responsibility, and justice. It concludes that only a reflexive leadership practice can ensure ethical and legitimate use of algorithmic systems in education. This approach highlights the necessity for institutions to align technological innovation with participatory governance.

DOI: 10.4018/979-8-3373-4908-4.ch012

1.1 INTRODUCTION

The digital transformation not only reshapes technological infrastructures but also challenges the epistemic and normative foundations of educational practice (Williamson, 2017). Initially designed to improve efficiency, learning analytics are increasingly evolving into instruments of institutional control that condense behavioural data, institutional norms, and power relations (Prinsloo & Slade, 2017; Knox, 2017). Such systems alter the epistemic fabric of academic judgment by standardising assessments, predicting behaviour, and embedding these predictions into digital infrastructures (Fricker, 2007; Tsai & Gasevic, 2017). Their impact extends beyond technical precision: they construct 'truths' about performance and belonging, often detached from discursive negotiation processes or social contexts (Williamson, 2017).

This development raises fundamental questions: Who bears responsibility for educational decisions when systems generate predictions (Williamson, 2017)? What understanding of equity underpins data-driven assessments (Fricker, 2007; Tsai & Gasevic, 2017)? And how can leadership responsibility be maintained when pedagogical judgment is replaced by algorithmic recommendations (Knox, 2017; Prinsloo & Slade, 2017)?

This chapter aims to systematically analyse the reconfiguration of pedagogical authority under conditions of machine-driven evaluation (Williamson, 2017). The focus is not on the technical functioning of individual systems but on the transformation of institutional roles, assessment practices, and normative standards (Knox, 2017). It starts from the thesis that algorithmic control creates a new form of digital governmentality in which the subject is no longer addressed but calculated in advance (Beer, 2019).

The analysis focuses on three levels: first, the technical evaluation rationality of algorithmic systems (Williamson, 2017); second, the reorganisation of institutional leadership in the context of data-driven performance management (Knox, 2017; Tsai & Gasevic, 2017); and third, the normative transformation of understandings of justice in the tension between transparency, efficiency, and participation (Fricker, 2007; Floridi, 2013). The theoretical basis of the analysis combines power-theoretical, information-ethical, and epistemological approaches. Foucault's concept of governmentality is employed to examine algorithmic control logics, particularly governance practices in the sense of a 'governmentality of algorithms' (Beer, 2019; Rouvroy & Berns, 2013). Floridi's information ethics enables an assessment of the moral quality of data-driven systems within the infosphere (Floridi, 2013). Fricker's theory of epistemic injustice addresses distortions of judgment caused by structural knowledge asymmetries (Fricker, 2007). Additionally, Jasanoff's concept of sociotechnical imaginaries is applied to analyse institutional models of algorithmic educational control (Jasanoff & Kim, 2009; 2015).

A central component of the analysis is the Subjective Dynamic Decision Model (SDDM) (Moch, 2025). This model does not conceptualise decision-making as rational optimisation but as a subjectively shaped, heuristically guided, and iterative learning process. Decisions under radical uncertainty are based on subjectively interpreted information, individual beliefs, and expectations, and are updated through adaptive decision thresholds. A metacognitive uncertainty parameter enables managers to act in a context-sensitive and reflexive way. The SDDM was specifically developed and empirically validated in the context of educational leadership (Moch, 2024; 2025). Case studies of algorithmic guidance systems in diverse geocultural contexts illustrate its application, including Civitas Learning in the United States, the JISC Early Alert system in the United Kingdom, and Smart Learning Platforms in the United Arab Emirates.

This chapter does not reject technology per se but offers a critique of its unlimited and uncontrolled application, informed by structural theory (Williamson, 2017). It advocates a context-sensitive management practice grounded in transparency, accountability, and ethical coherence (Floridi, 2013; Knox, 2017). Historically, delegating evaluation functions to technical systems is not new: performance metrics were already introduced in the 1990s, replacing qualitative judgments with quantitative indicators (Power, 1999). What is new, however, is the epistemic scope of algorithmic procedures: they predict behaviour, structure options, and intervene in real time (Beer, 2019; Rouvroy & Berns, 2013). This shifts evaluation from didactic reflection to preventive control (Williamson, 2017).

Traditional forms of pedagogical evaluation were rooted in personal observation, peer discussion, and individual judgment, reflecting social and biographical contexts (Fricker, 2007; Power, 1999). By contrast, algorithmic systems operate through statistical correlations derived from historical data. Evaluative practice becomes externalised; subjective judgments are replaced by seemingly objective calculations (Knox, 2017). Learners are addressed through their predicted behaviour, creating epistemic reversals: understanding transforms into behavioural probability (Beer, 2019). This generates tensions between principles of educational ethics and data-driven control objectives (Floridi, 2013; Tsai & Gasevic, 2017).

Another problem lies in the invisibility of algorithmic assessment systems: they appear technically neutral because they are coded in metrics and automated processes, yet their normative premises remain hidden (Rouvroy & Berns, 2013). The negotiation of pedagogical norms shifts from public discourse to the technical sphere (Williamson, 2017). Furthermore, a democratic legitimacy deficit emerges: many systems are implemented through internal administrative decisions or external providers without the deliberative participation of teachers or students. Their reach is often disproportionate to institutional transparency (Knox, 2017).

This chapter advocates a redefinition of institutional responsibility. What is required is a reflexive leadership practice that critically categorises the normative, epistemic, and social consequences of algorithmic evaluation. Responsibility does not reside in the mere implementation of technology but in the active shaping of participation and justice (Fricker, 2007; Floridi, 2013).

1.2 THEORETICAL BACKGROUND / STATE OF RESEARCH

1.2.1 Governmentality and Algorithmic Control

Michel Foucault's theory of governmentality provides a power-analytical lens for interpreting algorithmic assessment systems not merely as technical instruments but as expressions of transformed control rationality within the education system (Foucault, 2004; Rouvroy & Berns, 2013). Governmentality refers to the historically variable practices through which subjects are guided to act not by coercion but through orders of knowledge, normative expectations, and institutional arrangements (Foucault, 2004). In digitally networked educational systems, this form of power no longer manifests primarily through disciplinary procedures but through data-mediated forms of prospective subjectivation (Williamson, 2017; Beer, 2019). Algorithmic evaluation systems classify, select, and predict based on aggregated data; they not only record behaviour but also technically pre-structure future behaviour (Rouvroy & Berns, 2013; Knox, 2017).

In this context, learning analytics establishes a new logic of 'behaviour-based pre-regulation': decision-making processes are no longer grounded in retrospective assessments but in algorithmically generated risk scores, performance forecasts, and retention probabilities (Tsai & Gasevic, 2017; Williamson, 2017). These assessments intervene deeply in didactic processes by determining what is deemed conducive to learning, risky, or in need of support not through pedagogical discourse but through technical modelling (Knox, 2017). As a result, normative decisions are decontextualised; epistemic standards are fixed by computational technologies, and pedagogical judgment is transferred to automated classification processes (Fricker, 2007).

Foucault's analysis of 'governing through truth' demonstrates that modern power is not only repressive but also operates through the production of epistemic regimes (Foucault, 2004). In algorithmic education systems, this 'truth' is operationalised through data: statistical frequencies replace individual reasoning, and pattern recognition substitutes pedagogical interpretation (Beer, 2019). This creates a new form of digital governmentality that is governed not by visibility but by prediction and correlation (Rouvroy & Berns, 2013). Learners are not sanctioned for violating norms but are steered into predicted pathways by algorithmic cues (Knox, 2017). This power is not spectacular but microphysical embedded in dashboards, warning signals, and automated tutor suggestions. It appears neutral because it is technically mediated, yet it standardises based on past-oriented models (Beer, 2019). Governmentality is thus linked to digital reproduction mechanisms that do not challenge existing inequalities but instead perpetuate them algorithmically (Williamson, 2017; Fricker, 2007). The challenge, therefore, is not to expose overt authoritarian control but to reconstruct a subtle, codified power that structures action through technical expectations (Rouvroy & Berns, 2013).

1.2.2 Information Ethics and Algorithmic Responsibility

While the Subjective Dynamic Decision Model (SDDM) provides a heuristic structure for decision-making under algorithmic uncertainty, its relevance for educational leadership becomes clearer when explicitly linked to established leadership theories. The following section situates the SDDM within prominent leadership perspectives to clarify its applied significance for institutional practice. Luciano Floridi's concept of information ethics adds a normative dimension to the discussion of algorithmic systems that is not limited to human actors. The starting point is the view that informational environments have their own moral relevance and that not only humans but also information-processing structures can bear responsibility in them. Information ethics aims to minimise moral damage, ensure the integrity of information-based actors and place the handling of digital reality on a well-founded normative foundation (Floridi, 2013).

In the field of education, this perspective becomes particularly relevant where algorithmic systems make epistemic decisions, for example in the classification of learning behaviour, the assessment of potential for success or the derivation of pedagogical interventions. Floridi argues in favour of evaluating such systems not only in terms of functional efficiency, but also on the basis of their moral impact: Which information rights are violated? What epistemic autonomy is restricted? What potential for harm is externalised?

The concept of "infraethical design" is central to this. Floridi uses this term to describe the structural conditions under which ethical behaviour can develop in digital systems in the first place. An evaluation system that cannot be verified, explained or contradicted not only violates the principles of transparency, but also the ethical self-determination of those affected. Information ethics therefore calls for the reconfiguration of control architectures along normative criteria such as reversibility, context appropriateness and epistemic honesty (Floridi, 2013).

For the higher education context, this results in a dual responsibility: on the one hand, educational institutions must ensure that their algorithmic instruments do not systematically distort, discriminate or disempower. On the other hand, it is the responsibility of the management level to actively reflect on the moral quality of these systems and to intervene in a regulatory manner where informational asymmetries arise. The ethics of digital assessment is not a subordinate add-on, but a constitutive condition for legitimate educational control.

Floridi's approach thus enables a shift in perspective: not only the pedagogical result, but the structural prerequisite of data-based decisions becomes the ethical touchstone. The goal is not the perfection of the algorithm, but the moral coherence of the environment in which it operates.

1.2.3 Epistemic Injustice

From the perspective of ethical leadership, the SDDM foregrounds responsibility, justification, and accountability as core elements of leadership practice. Ethical leadership emphasises that decisions must be normatively defensible and oriented towards fairness, autonomy, and justice rather than mere efficiency.

The SDDM operationalises this perspective by requiring leaders to explicitly reflect on norm consistency and role responsibility when acting on algorithmic recommendations. Instead of delegating moral judgement to systems, leadership is understood as the active appropriation of responsibility for decisions and their consequences. Miranda Fricker's idea of *epistemic injustice* opens up an important but often overlooked aspect of algorithmic evaluation: who is trusted as a source of knowledge and who is not (Fricker, 2007). Fricker makes a clear distinction between two forms. *Testimonial injustice* means that someone's statement is unfairly devalued because of prejudice. *Hermeneutical injustice* happens when people cannot explain their experiences properly because the right words or concepts are missing (Fricker, 2007).

Both ideas matter in the world of algorithmic assessments. Many systems carry hidden assumptions about which behaviours help learning, which seem risky, and which do not fit the norm. Students rarely get a chance to challenge these labels (Knox, 2017; Williamson, 2017). They are watched but have no voice (Fricker, 2007). Turning social experiences into numbers can itself be a form of hermeneutical injustice. It narrows what teachers and students can talk about (Beer, 2019). If something cannot be turned into data, it simply does not appear and what is invisible cannot be questioned (Rouvroy & Berns, 2013). This often hits students with non-traditional paths especially hard: those with breaks in their learning, changes in context, or less typical progressions (Tsai & Gasevic, 2017).

Fricker's concept helps to see algorithmic systems for what they also are: structures that decide whose voice counts and whose does not (Fricker, 2007; Rouvroy & Berns, 2013). Universities that use these systems take on an *epistemic responsibility*. They have to make sure that judgement is not narrowed by blind spots in the system or fixed by technical models alone (Williamson, 2017).

1.2.4 Surveillance Capitalism and Data Utilisation

With her theory of *surveillance capitalism*, Shoshana Zuboff highlights the economic forces behind data-driven evaluation systems. She sees digital platforms as tools for extracting "behavioural surplus" from aspects of human activity that go beyond what users originally intended to share. This surplus is captured by algorithms, analysed, and then used commercially to predict and shape future behaviour (Zuboff, 2019).

In higher education, this has clear implications. Here too, data-heavy systems often serve not only educational goals but also economic ones. Many learning analytics platforms are created and run by private companies that process student data with unclear ownership rules, non-transparent models, and sometimes vague commercial interests. Universities act as data suppliers but often lack a clear plan for who controls the data, who profits from it, or how it might be reused (Zuboff, 2019; Couldry & Mejias, 2019).

Zuboff's work shows that algorithmic governance is never just about technical design or educational fairness it is also shaped by economic and political interests. That is why governance must go further than simple standards for transparency or data protection. Institutions need rules that ensure not only that systems work but that they are politically regulated, institutionally accountable, and ethically justified (Zuboff, 2019).

One idea in particular *behaviour modification* becomes especially sensitive in the university setting. Predictive systems are never neutral. They create expectations, steer attention, and shape what and how students learn. In doing so, they directly affect educational paths and life chances. If all this happens under conditions of economic intransparency, a university can quietly shift from being an educational community to a data-driven business platform (Zuboff, 2019; Couldry & Mejias, 2019).

Zuboff's perspective adds an essential point: algorithmic systems are not just practical tools they are embedded in infrastructures driven by commercial logic rather than educational values. Universities that want to act responsibly must recognise this tension and avoid handing over decisions about students' learning to models whose main goal is not education but the profitable prediction of behaviour (Zuboff, 2019).

1.2.5 Sociotechnical Imaginaries and Educational Governance

Sheila Jasanoff's concept of *sociotechnical imaginaries* describes the symbolic orders through which societies picture their technological future always linked to ideas of community, progress, and institutional legitimacy (Jasanoff & Kim, 2009). These imaginaries are more than stories; they shape political decisions, regulatory frameworks, and the actual design of technologies (Jasanoff & Kim, 2015). They also define what seems desirable, realistic, or legitimate including in education (Williamson, 2017).

In university management today, such imaginaries can be seen clearly. The belief in data-driven optimisation of learning, in predicting student success, or in automatically distributing resources is rooted in deep-seated myths of progress (Williamson, 2017; Prinsloo, 2020). Algorithmic systems do not just appear as neutral tools they act as symbols of a new order: efficient, evidence-based, and rational (Prinsloo, 2020).

These imaginaries have a strong normative effect. They shape what people expect from technology and what kinds of teaching, leadership, or responsibility are seen as modern or legitimate (Jasanoff & Kim, 2015). Those who question or resist data-based systems can find themselves labelled as out of step with this vision of modernity and even as a threat to the institution's future (Williamson, 2017). In this sense, algorithmic control often draws its legitimacy less from what it achieves in practice and more from how well it fits a dominant image of the future (Prinsloo, 2020).

Jasanoff's concept helps reveal this: algorithmic systems are not only practical tools but also reflect how institutions describe themselves (Jasanoff & Kim, 2015). Universities that use these systems change more than their workflows; they reshape their identity as data-driven organisations (Williamson, 2017). For leaders, this means a special task: making these imaginaries visible, questioning them critically, and designing technology not just to match a vision, but to follow principles like justice, accountability, and diversity (Jasanoff & Kim, 2015; Prinsloo, 2020).

1.3 METHODOLOGY AND ANALYTICAL PERSPECTIVE

This study follows a conceptual and theory-led approach. It does not treat algorithmic assessment systems as mere technical tools. Instead, it sees them as expressions and amplifiers of deep changes in how knowledge, power, and norms take shape in higher education (Williamson, 2017; Prinsloo, 2020). No primary data was collected. Instead, the work relies on structural theory to ask under what conditions algorithmic control gains epistemic legitimacy, how it becomes embedded, and how it produces normative effects (Foucault, 2004; Jasanoff & Kim, 2015). The basic assumption is simple: data-based control is never neutral. It codifies and reinforces existing power structures and ways of knowing (Fricker, 2007; Rouvroy & Berns, 2013).

This shapes a method that does not just measure technical functions. It looks behind them. It tries to trace how these systems carry symbolic meanings, shape norms, and influence institutions (Jasanoff & Kim, 2015). Discourse analysis and epistemology play a key role here. The work draws on thinkers like Foucault, Fricker, Jasanoff, Kim and Floridi (Floridi, 2013). In addition, it brings in a model perspective: the Subjective Dynamic Decision Model (SDDM) developed by Moch (2024).

The SDDM shows how decision-making under radical uncertainty can be better understood. Instead of seeing decisions as pure optimisation, it sees them as heuristic and reflexive learning steps. Two aspects are central: adaptive thresholds and a metacognitive uncertainty parameter (μ). Together, these help capture how people interpret situations, adjust expectations, and weigh up risks in practice (Moch, 2024). So leadership responsibility is not fixed once and for all. It is something that has to be negotiated again and again, especially when decisions rely on digital tools (Moch, 2024).

The analysis uses three levels to approach this topic:

1. **discourse-analytical reconstruction of algorithmic evaluation systems**

Algorithmic tools can be seen as part of a broader educational setup that pushes towards subject formation, standardisation, and forward-looking control (Foucault, 2004; Williamson, 2017). Metrics for assessment, risk scores, and performance indicators do not just appear as neutral outputs. They act as discursive devices that create and fix certain educational realities for example by labelling some students as “at risk” or by sorting them into pre-set learning paths (Knox, 2017; Prinsloo & Slade, 2017).

2. **institutional theoretical analysis of leadership logics**

The core question here is how decision-making power, lines of accountability, and responsibility structures change when algorithms get involved (Williamson, 2017; Prinsloo & Slade, 2017). University governance is no longer just about professional judgement grounded in ethics. More and more, it runs on data. Dashboards, KPIs, and early warning systems now guide decisions (Knox, 2017). The analysis shows how this can push responsibility outward, make legitimacy feel mechanical, and hand over parts of pedagogical freedom to automated processes (Rouvroy & Berns, 2013; Fricker, 2007).

3 Normative-ethical reflection on algorithmic infrastructure

This study takes a theory-driven, conceptual angle. It does not treat algorithmic assessment tools as neutral technical devices but sees them as part of deeper shifts in knowledge, in how institutions work, and in what is seen as fair or legitimate in higher education (Williamson, 2017; Prinsloo, 2020). There is no primary data collection here. Instead, the study relies on ideas from structural theory to ask under which conditions algorithmic control gets its epistemic and institutional legitimacy and how it produces real normative effects (Foucault, 2004; Jasanoff & Kim, 2015). The main assumption is simple: data-based control is never neutral. It encodes power and ways of knowing that already exist and pushes them forward (Fricker, 2007; Rouvroy & Berns, 2013).

This shapes the method. The systems are not broken down to pure tech specs instead, their symbolic meanings, the norms behind them, and their impact on institutions are traced (Jasanoff & Kim, 2015). The study uses discourse analysis and epistemology as its backbone, inspired by thinkers like Foucault, Fricker,Kim, Jasanoff and Floridi (Floridi, 2013). Added to this is a model perspective: the Subjective Dynamic Decision Model (SDDM) by Moch (2024).

The SDDM shows that decision-making under radical uncertainty is not about perfect rational steps. It is a learning process, guided by heuristics and reflection. At its centre are adaptive thresholds and a metacognitive uncertainty factor (μ). These help to capture how people read situations, shift their expectations, or weigh risks (Moch, 2024). Leadership, in this light, is not a static norm it is a moving target, shaped by context and changing conditions (Moch, 2024).

To make sense of this, the study works on three levels: it links theory with real cases, focuses on structural patterns, and always asks what this means for fairness and responsibility.

1.4 ANALYSIS AND RESULTS

1.4.1 Technological Rationality of Assessment

Algorithmic evaluation systems operate on the basis of specific technical rationalities that have a structuring effect rather than merely depicting (Williamson, 2017; Beer, 2019, Oberdieck & Moch, 2024). They construct realities by translating educational processes into arithmetic operations, probabilities and risk profiles (Knox,

2017). The central characteristic of this rationality is the substitution of pedagogical judgement with probabilistic modelling (Prinsloo & Slade, 2017).

Predictive metrics such as "student at risk scores", "engagement indices" or "dropout predictions", which are based on the evaluation of historical data, are at the centre of this (Williamson, 2017). These metrics suggest objectivity by quantifying and aggregating individual trajectories. However, this objectivity is structurally selective: the training data used reflects institutional assumptions, historical inequalities and performance-oriented evaluation logics (Fricker, 2007; Rouvroy & Berns, 2013).

The technical rationality of assessment shifts the focus from didactic reflection to operational intervention. Systems such as Civitas Learning generate recommendations for action based on algorithmic predictions, for example through colour-coded risk levels or automated contact suggestions (Prinsloo & Slade, 2017).

A central problem lies in the formalisation of complex educational processes: Contextual, biographical or cultural factors are only taken into account if they are quantifiable and compatible with the system (Knox, 2017). This leads to systematic marginalisation: Learners with atypical life courses, unstable learning paths or non-standardised interaction patterns fall out of the models or are marked as "anomalies" (Fricker, 2007).

Moreover, the assessment is carried out without any didactic link. While teachers have to justify, contextualise and take responsibility for their judgements, algorithmic systems act as black boxes: the basis for decisions is usually not comprehensible, the model logic remains proprietary and there is hardly any possibility of contradiction (Rouvroy & Berns, 2013).

In addition, algorithmic valuations have a performative effect. The assignment of a risk profile not only influences the institutional intervention, but also the self-perception of those affected (Beer, 2019; Prinsloo & Slade, 2017).

1.4.2 Institutional Forms of Control

The spread of algorithmic assessment systems changes more than just how teachers grade it reshapes how universities think about leadership and management (Williamson, 2017). Governance in higher education is shifting away from decisions grounded in professional ethics and towards performance models where algorithmic scores and metrics drive what happens (Knox, 2017). This shift influences what responsibility means and how decisions are actually made (Prinsloo & Slade, 2017).

At the centre of this new logic lies the outsourcing of judgement. What used to rely on experience, context, and conversations across disciplines is now often delegated to systems that produce probabilities and standardised action plans (Prinsloo & Slade, 2017). Dashboards, risk scores, and KPIs replace collegial debate. The management's epistemic authority does not grow it gets repackaged in technical form (Rouvroy & Berns, 2013).

This kind of governance builds a new kind of rationality: university leadership no longer means balancing different educational needs but optimising institutional targets (Williamson, 2017). Success becomes a matter of lowering dropout rates or boosting retention and efficiency not whether each individual decision is fair or appropriate (Knox, 2017).

A core problem here is the question of responsibility. When a system makes suggestions but humans rubber-stamp them, a gap opens up. Those responsible point to the data but often cannot see how the model really works or what blind spots it may contain (Fricker, 2007; Prinsloo & Slade, 2017). That makes accountability harder and weakens ethical judgement (Floridi, 2013).

Data-driven governance also blurs roles. Teachers start to look less like pedagogical guides and more like data suppliers (Williamson, 2017). Their work is measured in clicks, feedback speed, or completion rates (Knox, 2017). University leaders act as interpreters of data patterns rather than as moderators of real discussion (Beer, 2019).

Often, this shift stays hidden. Introducing such systems is framed as an efficiency measure, not a political choice (Rouvroy & Berns, 2013). But a real change is happening: universities are turning from places of debate and learning into data-driven organisations run by model logic (Williamson, 2017). That is not automatically wrong but it needs explanation and clear rules (Floridi, 2013).

So the question for responsible university leadership is not whether to use algorithms but how to shape their role (Prinsloo & Slade, 2017). Clear processes, real lines of accountability, and a line between what data can do and where human judgement still matters are crucial (Fricker, 2007; Floridi, 2013). Only when managers reflect on the assumptions, values, and institutional effects behind these systems can they truly act responsibly under digital conditions (Williamson, 2017).

1.4.3 Normative Reconstruction of Fairness

Bringing algorithmic assessment systems into higher education does more than just change how performance is measured it also shifts what fairness actually means (Williamson, 2017; Tsai & Gasevic, 2017). Traditionally, fairness in education was tied to equal opportunities, context awareness, and a sense of procedural justice. Now, much of this is turning into internal optimisation goals (Fricker, 2007). Fairness is no longer discussed in open dialogue; instead, it gets built into systems in ways that can have far-reaching effects (Floridi, 2013; Rouvroy & Berns, 2013).

In technical debates, fairness shows up mostly as something that can be formalised. Metrics like "equalised odds", "demographic parity", or "predictive parity" aim for statistical balance across different groups (Barocas, Hardt, & Narayanan, 2019).

Technical Note on Algorithmic bias and Mitigation

Algorithmic bias in educational assessment rarely stems from a single "biased algorithm" but typically emerges from the interaction of data, modelling choices, and institutional practice. A first source is data bias: historical datasets reflect earlier selection practices, unequal access to resources, and uneven representation of student groups, which can lead to systematically distorted predictions. A second source lies in label and measurement bias, for instance when proxies such as platform activity or attendance are treated as indicators of motivation or ability, even though they may correlate with socioeconomic constraints. Third, model and optimisation bias can occur when models are tuned for overall accuracy or retention outcomes, thereby shifting error burdens to specific subgroups. Finally, feedback-loop effects arise when interventions based on risk scores change subsequent behaviour and data generation, stabilising the very patterns the system predicts.

Common mitigation approaches include pre-processing (data balancing, improved sampling, removal of problematic proxies), in-processing (fairness constraints during training), and post-processing (threshold adjustments or calibrated decision rules). In institutional settings, these technical measures are typically complemented by fairness audits, subgroup performance monitoring, documentation of data provenance and modelling assumptions, and procedures for human review. However, such controls remain limited if they are not embedded in governance: auditing requires authority, contestability, and accountability structures. Therefore, fairness cannot be treated as a purely statistical property of models but must remain a leadership responsibility grounded in participation, transparency, and the possibility of revision.

This mathematical version of fairness is useful but by itself, it falls short. It tends to overlook structural inequalities, individual circumstances, and intersectional factors that shape real student experiences (Fricker, 2007; Tsai & Gasevic, 2017). So, the standards these systems use are not automatically unjust, but they are too narrow for the complexity they claim to handle (Williamson, 2017).

One big problem is that educational justice risks shrinking to a question of whether numbers balance out. What seems statistically fair can easily ignore discrimination patterns or breaks in a student's life story (Knox, 2017). A student with a non-linear path, a migration background, or mental health struggles is not harmed because the system is "malicious" but because the system simply cannot see them (Fricker, 2007).

Another tension comes up when fairness shifts from something negotiated in context to something pre-programmed. Justice used to mean open, flexible dialogue about what is comparable and what isn't. Now, a system defines what counts as "equal", which differences matter, and when fairness is supposedly reached (Williamson, 2017; Floridi, 2013). Students and teachers rarely get a say in this there is no real space to challenge it or renegotiate what fairness should mean (Tsai &

Gasevic, 2017). Fairness gets stripped of its political edge and turned into just another design setting (Rouvroy & Berns, 2013).

All of this creates serious normative tensions. On the one hand, the idea of fair treatment becomes functional: it serves the model's output, not social reality (Barocas et al., 2019; Fricker, 2007). On the other hand, questions of justice are baked into algorithms long before they are debated in practice (Williamson, 2017). Standards that used to belong to teachers and pedagogy now sit inside code (Knox, 2017).

University leaders have to push back against this drift. Fairness can't just be a system variable it must stay an intersubjective claim, something that invites participation, context sensitivity, and actual discussion (Fricker, 2007; Floridi, 2013). Institutions need processes that go beyond distributing scores evenly. They need spaces for reflection, so people can test, question, and adjust what fairness means in each context (Tsai & Gasevic, 2017). In the end, assessments have to be verifiable, normatively clear, and open to revision not just technically efficient (Williamson, 2017).

1.4.4 International Comparative Perspective

The rise of algorithmic assessment systems looks different around the world. Institutions, norms, and political conditions shape how these tools get introduced there is no single blueprint (Williamson, 2017; Tsai & Gasevic, 2017). A closer look shows that algorithmic governance is far from uniform. Instead, it reflects local imaginaries, governance styles, and ideas of what makes decisions legitimate (Beer, 2019; Rouvroy & Berns, 2013).

In the United States, market logic sets the tone. Systems like Civitas Learning or EAB Navigate are closely tied to strategic management in universities. They help identify risks, manage retention, and optimise performance (Williamson, 2017). Most of the technical backbone comes from private companies that earn money through data-based consulting and continuous service packages (Beer, 2019). Fairness is mainly framed as statistical balance, and deeper ethical questions tend to stay inside institutional walls (Barocas, Hardt, & Narayanan, 2019).

The UK takes a more regulated path. Projects like the JISC Early Alert System offer risk-based support and prevention, but they are embedded in clear data governance structures (Knox, 2017; Williamson, 2017). Universities are expected to make student progress measurable and feed key figures into quality assurance systems. There is more talk of fairness but even here, the debate rarely goes beyond technical equity measures (Tsai & Gasevic, 2017).

In contrast, the United Arab Emirates positions itself as an eager adopter of tech solutions in education. Smart Learning and AI University Platforms combine AI-driven assessments, learning path models, and behavioural tracking in a centralised system (Williamson, 2017). These tools are part of national digital strategies and rarely opened up for public debate (Rouvroy & Berns, 2013). Fairness, participation, and contextual awareness mostly fade into the background (Beer, 2019).

These three examples show that algorithmic evaluation systems may look different, but they always put new demands on leadership (Tsai & Gasevic, 2017). In the US, efficiency takes priority. In the UK, it's about quality assurance. In the UAE, it's all about technological ambition. Yet in all three, the ethical framework is still thin (Williamson, 2017). For responsible university leadership, copying an international best practice is not enough. Evaluation logics are shaped by culture, institutions, and politics. That means leaders have to take local realities, participation, and clear value goals seriously (Rouvroy & Berns, 2013).

1.5 PRACTICAL CASES AND LEADERSHIP RESPONSIBILITY

A normative critique of algorithmic assessment systems is not enough on paper it only comes alive when tested against real cases (Williamson, 2017; Knox, 2017). It is in everyday institutional practice that data-driven tools show their epistemic power, create tensions between teaching judgement and technical rules, and put leadership to the test (Rouvroy & Berns, 2013). This chapter looks at three international examples Civitas Learning (USA), JISC Early Alert (UK), and Smart Learning Platforms (UAE)and asks how they are embedded in governance structures and what ethical demands they place on higher education leaders (Tsai & Gasevic, 2017; Williamson, 2017).

The Subjective Dynamic Decision Model (SDDM) provides a way to unpack this in a structured way (Moch, 2024). It shows how leaders can adapt their decision-making heuristics when they face uncertainty, shifting expectations, and new information (Moch, 2024). In practice, this means that decision-makers using tools like Civitas or JISC Early Alert must constantly revisit their thresholds for what they see as risk and adjust how they act not just once, but through ongoing learning and feedback (Moch, 2024).

Seen this way, the SDDM helps map out typical leadership dilemmas that come with algorithmic systems in education. At the same time, it points to practical steps for dealing with them and thinking through their normative side (Rouvroy & Berns, 2013; Williamson, 2017).

1.5.1 Civitas Learning (USA): Commercial Forecasting and Performative Norm Setting

Civitas Learning is one of the most widely used predictive analytics systems in US higher education (Williamson, 2017; Tsai & Gasevic, 2017). The platform combines different types of data such as course histories, demographic information and digital activity patterns to generate individual risk profiles for students (Prinsloo & Slade, 2017; Knox, 2017). These "Likelihood to Succeed" scores are presented to academic advisors and teaching staff, often through colour-coded dashboards or standardised suggestions for possible interventions (Williamson, 2017). The goal is to identify students at risk early on and to allocate support more effectively (Tsai & Gasevic, 2017). This is meant to make resource management more targeted and data-based.

However, the Civitas system is proprietary. The detailed model structure, its weightings and the training data are not transparent to the universities that use it (Rouvroy & Berns, 2013; Knox, 2017). Institutions see the final scores and visualisations but cannot fully trace how these are produced. This limited insight creates a dilemma for managers: they have to act on the system's signals without knowing exactly how reliable they are (Fricker, 2007).

The Subjective Dynamic Decision Model (SDDM) helps to describe what this means for leadership in practice (Moch, 2024). Four points illustrate this:

Context sensitivity. The data basis does not include factors like students' employment, caring duties or personal crises. These gaps can lead to systematic misjudgements (Fricker, 2007; Williamson, 2017). Management should make sure that manual corrections and individual checks remain possible.

Consistency of standards. The system defines success mainly through retention rates and GPA. Broader educational aims such as inclusion or individual development are not part of this logic (Knox, 2017). It is therefore important for institutions to clarify and uphold their own values (Floridi, 2013).

Risk transparency. Information about error margins or potential bias is not always available or only on request (Rouvroy & Berns, 2013). Universities should openly communicate what risks exist and how they deal with misclassifications.

Role responsibility. Decisions based on system suggestions should not become automatic routines (Prinsloo & Slade, 2017). Each intervention needs its own ethical reasoning (Fricker, 2007). Leadership therefore means interpreting system output carefully, relating it to the local context and not giving up pedagogical judgement (Moch, 2024).

1.5.2 JISC Early Alert (UK): Regulated Early Intervention With Gaps In Participation

The British framework JISC Early Alert is used by many universities in the UK as a tool to promote academic success through early intervention (Knox, 2017; Williamson, 2017). It works on an open-source basis that allows universities to adapt the system to their specific needs. It combines structured data analyses for example, enrolment patterns, participation rates and submission frequency with individual educational advice (Tsai & Gasevic, 2017). Technically, the system is seen as mature and normatively well-justified, but it makes high demands on how institutions organise its implementation (Williamson, 2017).

Integration mostly happens through internal quality assurance processes linked to key performance indicators (KPIs) and strategic management goals (Knox, 2017). While there are occasional participatory formats for system design, there is no systematic process for democratic negotiation (Rouvroy & Berns, 2013). In practice, this means that universities use a configurable tool but do not always secure its normative basis through open discussion. As a result, pedagogical and ethical debates about assessment, intervention or responsibility can remain marginal (Fricker, 2007).

From the perspective of the Subjective Dynamic Decision Model (SDDM), four points stand out (Moch, 2024):

Context sensitivity. Although the system is flexible, how well it fits the local context depends strongly on each university's commitment and expertise (Knox, 2017). Leaders should make sure that data models do not overlook important social or structural differences (Fricker, 2007).

Norm consistency. JISC's stated aim is to support rather than to select. In practice, however, there is a risk that it shifts towards administrative performance management (Williamson, 2017). Management needs to be aware of this risk and counteract it where necessary (Floridi, 2013).

Risk transparency. False positives and biases can occur but are not always clearly documented (Tsai & Gasevic, 2017). As Ananny and Crawford (2018) note, technical transparency alone is not enough if the broader social and political context is ignored. Here, management has to take an active role in risk monitoring and should also hold system providers to account (Rouvroy & Berns, 2013).

Role responsibility. If decisions are based on system output, institutions must ensure that students have options to appeal, ask for review or receive personal advice (Knox, 2017). Technology cannot replace direct pedagogical communication (Fricker, 2007; Moch, 2024).

1.5.3 Smart Learning Platforms (UAE): total Digitalisation Without Deliberation

In the United Arab Emirates, Smart Learning Platforms are part of a broad digitalisation strategy that combines AI-supported assessment, real-time monitoring and automated feedback (Williamson, 2017). The system is fully centralised: teaching behaviour, learning activity and student interactions are continuously recorded and matched against standardised development targets (Beer, 2019; Tsai & Gasevic, 2017). Control does not happen through counselling or dialogue, but follows fixed algorithmic pathways (Rouvroy & Berns, 2013).

Participation is not foreseen in this model. Neither students nor teachers have any influence on how the systems are designed or adjusted (Fricker, 2007). Decisions are made according to the model's settings, not through pedagogical discussion. While technically efficient, the systems remain normatively disconnected from broader educational debates (Floridi, 2013).

The Subjective Dynamic Decision Model (SDDM) helps highlight where this creates challenges for leadership (Moch, 2024).

Context sensitivity. The system does not take the social context into account at all. University leaders should build in manual review options, hardship provisions or clear escalation paths to deal with exceptional cases (Williamson, 2017).

Norm consistency. Education here is mainly defined as performance improvement. It is important for leadership to define and protect alternative values, even if these are not rewarded by the system (Floridi, 2013).

Risk transparency. Decisions such as cutting funding or redirecting study paths can have serious consequences, but these are often not addressed at the institutional level (Rouvroy & Berns, 2013). Management should make the social costs of such interventions visible and discuss them openly (Fricker, 2007).

Role responsibility. In a strongly centralised system, leadership is not just about implementation but about setting clear boundaries. If no one intervenes, technocratic control becomes the default and those in charge bear responsibility for that (Rouvroy & Berns, 2013; Moch, 2024).

Conclusion. Ethics in this context begins with leadership. The analysis shows that responsibility in algorithmic environments is not an optional extra but must be an institutional core task (Floridi, 2013; Fricker, 2007). Systems like Civitas, JISC or Smart Learning do not exist outside decision-making chains they work through them and shape them by setting new norms (Williamson, 2017). The SDDM provides a practical tool to structure this responsibility systematically (Moch, 2024). It translates basic ethical principles into concrete perspectives for action and underlines that leadership starts where the system stops (Rouvroy & Berns, 2013).

1.6 DISCUSSION

1.6.1 Normative Dilemmas and Epistemic Opacity

Algorithmic assessment systems do not only pose technical questions. They create structural dilemmas that affect the normative basis of pedagogical practice (Williamson, 2017; Rouvroy & Berns, 2013). Concepts like judgement, fairness and responsibility are not openly contradicted, but gradually replaced (Fricker, 2007). The core issue is less how well a system works than which epistemic and institutional foundations it undermines (Floridi, 2013).

First dilemma: Relativisation of judgement. In traditional contexts, judgement is dialogical and reflexive (Fricker, 2007). Algorithmic systems produce probability scores from past data without regard for individual or situational aspects (Williamson, 2017). Judgement becomes categorisation. Subjectivity is reduced to a prediction (Rouvroy & Berns, 2013).

Second dilemma: Opacity. Decisions depend on model structures, weightings and training data that remain closed to users (Knox, 2017). Even with explainable systems, there is an asymmetry: the system calculates, but does not really clarify (Rouvroy & Berns, 2013). Management must justify results without being able to verify them (Fricker, 2007). Responsibility exists formally, but loses content (Floridi, 2013).

Third dilemma: Performativity. Systems produce effects by making categories like "at risk" actionable (Beer, 2019). Labels influence behaviour, self-perception and interaction (Williamson, 2017). Standardised classifications can reinforce inequalities (Fricker, 2007).

Fourth dilemma: Shift of control. This dilemma illustrates how system outputs increasingly structure decisions while responsibility formally remains human (Prinsloo & Slade, 2017; Rouvroy & Berns, 2013).

Table 1. Translating algorithmic dilemmas into leadership responsibility (SDDM)

Algorithmic dilemma	**Core leadership question**	**SDDM dimension**
Context-blind risk modelling	What relevant contextual factors are not represented in the data and how can they be considered in the decision?	Context sensitivity
KPI-driven optimization	Are algorithmic recommendations aligned with the institution's educational values and ethical commitments?	Norm consistency
Opaque predictions and uncertainty	How are uncertainty, error margins, and potential bias communicated and addressed?	Risk transparency
Automation of interventions	Who is accountable for decisions based on system outputs and how is responsibility retained?	Role responsibility

These dilemmas are structural. They cannot be resolved through technical adjustments alone, but require institutional, normative and epistemic answers (Floridi, 2013; Williamson, 2017).

The Subjective Dynamic Decision Model (SDDM) offers an approach for describing this leadership task (Moch, 2025). It understands decision-making under uncertainty as reflexive, with thresholds, subjective perception and expectations as variables (Moch, 2025). The goal is to secure the ability to make justified judgements institutionally and systematically (Fricker, 2007). This needs review structures, context sensitivity, transparency and models that must be justified (Floridi, 2013). Leadership responsibility starts where the system reaches its epistemic limit (Williamson, 2017).

1.6.2 Governance Models and Design Principles

From a distributed leadership perspective, the governance of algorithmic assessment systems cannot be reduced to individual managerial authority. Leadership emerges through the coordinated interaction of roles, responsibilities, and institutional arrangements that structure how algorithmic recommendations are interpreted, challenged, and enacted.

In this sense, the Subjective Dynamic Decision Model (SDDM) complements distributed leadership by making role responsibility and context sensitivity explicit decision dimensions. It enables institutions to clarify who is authorised to interpret system outputs, who may contest them, and how responsibility is shared without being dissolved across technical infrastructures.

The ethical and epistemic dilemmas of algorithmic evaluation do not require selective readjustment, but rather an institutional framework that structurally safeguards responsibility, transparency and auditability (Williamson, 2017; Rouvroy & Berns, 2013). This framing is not created through technology optimisation, but through governance: through the totality of rules, procedures and responsibilities that make algorithmic systems controllable, accountable and educationally ethical (Floridi, 2013). Governance does not replace technology; it enables its responsible integration (Fricker, 2007).

A viable model of algorithmic university governance must fulfil four central functions: epistemic transparency, normative feedback, participatory legitimation and adaptive control (Williamson, 2017; Knox, 2017).

Epistemic transparency means that algorithmic decisions are comprehensible in terms of their mechanisms of action (Knox, 2017). Universities must disclose which systems are used, the database on which they operate, how their models were trained and which decision criteria are applied (Tsai & Gasevic, 2017). The aim is not to disclose source code, but to communicate systemic limits, uncertainties and interdependencies in an understandable way (Floridi, 2013).

Normative feedback requires that systems are not only used functionally, but also in a value-oriented manner. The central question is not: What can the system achieve? What values does it institutionally carry? (Fricker, 2007). Universities must define which ethical guidelines apply to assessment, such as participation, reversibility and developmental justice, and ensure that the systems used meet these standards (Floridi, 2013).

Participatory legitimisation refers to the inclusion of all relevant status groups in the selection, implementation and evaluation of algorithmic systems (Knox, 2017; Williamson, 2017). Governance is thus not technocratic, but deliberative. Where systems are introduced without participation, the result is not legitimacy, but structural disenfranchisement (Rouvroy & Berns, 2013).

The UNESCO Recommendation (2021) also emphasises that educational institutions worldwide have a special responsibility for the ethical design of algorithmic systems. It calls on institutions to ensure human rights, participation, transparency and auditability in all AI applications in order to avoid discrimination and ensure institutional legitimacy (UNESCO, 2021).

Finally, adaptive control refers to the institution's ability to react flexibly to unexpected effects, systemic undesirable developments and new findings. Algorithms learn. Institutions must do the same (Williamson, 2017). Governance therefore includes continuous monitoring, ethical audits and review procedures (Floridi, 2013). The implementation of learning analytics requires universities not only to optimise technical efficiency, but also to create the institutional conditions for fair and comprehensible decision-making processes. The EU AI Act (European Parliament & Council, 2024) defines harmonised rules for the use of AI systems across Europe for the first time and emphasises risk-based governance, transparency obligations and the protection of fundamental rights. Universities that use learning analytics tools must therefore adhere to this framework and establish comparable procedures for the evaluation, monitoring and auditability of algorithmic systems. These four principles are not abstract idealisms, but concrete requirements for university management. Those who use algorithmic systems must create institutional structures that make their effects comprehensible, controllable and correctable (Knox, 2017). Proprietary lack of transparency must not be a reason to relinquish responsibility: Governance begins with contract design and extends to implementation and the evaluation of long-term effects (Williamson, 2017).

At the same time, governance is not a regime of mistrust. It is an enabling framework for equitable, accountable and learner-centred assessment (Fricker, 2007). Well-designed systems can improve access to education, promote social participation and support individual development if they are designed in such a way that they fulfil normative, epistemic and participatory requirements (Floridi, 2013). Governance is therefore not a denial of technology but an educational ethical necessity (Rouvroy & Berns, 2013).

1.6.3 Leadership Model: SDDM - Subjective Dynamic Decision Model

From the perspective of transformational leadership, algorithmic governance poses the risk that leadership becomes confined to performance optimisation and compliance with data-driven indicators. Transformational leadership, by contrast, emphasises value orientation, sense-making, and the articulation of shared institutional purposes beyond technical efficiency.

The SDDM addresses this challenge by linking decision-making explicitly to norm consistency and risk transparency, thereby reconnecting algorithmic evaluation with institutional values and educational goals. Leadership is thus understood not as alignment with system outputs, but as the capacity to interpret, question, and reframe them in accordance with normative commitments.

The Subjective Dynamic Decision Model (SDDM) was introduced in this thesis as a structuring heuristic for leadership responsibility under algorithmic conditions (Moch, 2025). It addresses the void created by data-based evaluation systems in institutional decision-making culture: the lack of reasoned judgement in an environment of standardised predictive logic (Williamson, 2017; Fricker, 2007). SDDM does not provide a mechanistic decision-making routine, but rather a reflexive orientation framework that is context-sensitive, role-conscious, risk-oriented and norm-based (Floridi, 2013). Four interlinked decision-making dimensions are at the centre of the model: Context sensitivity, norm consistency, risk transparency and role responsibility (Moch, 2025). These dimensions are not sequential steps, but complementary axes of reflection along which management decisions under algorithmic uncertainty can be systematically analysed (Fricker, 2007; Rouvroy & Berns, 2013).

Context sensitivity requires the systematic consideration of individual, social and institutional framework conditions. Leadership responsibility here means recognising whether an algorithmic proposal operates in a context-blind manner and whether this results in unfair or inadequate consequences (Fricker, 2007; Tsai & Gasevic, 2017).

Norm consistency requires a critical examination of whether an algorithm-based decision is compatible with the fundamental ethical values of the institution (Floridi, 2013). Is the assessment in line with principles such as fairness, revisability and autonomy? Or is it subordinated to these through functional efficiency? Leadership here means Linking systems back to values, not the other way round (Rouvroy & Berns, 2013).

Risk transparency means communicating probabilities as probabilities to those affected, decision-making bodies and the public (Knox, 2017; Tsai & Gasevic, 2017). University management must not rely on the apparent objectivity of algorithmic scores, but must explicitly address uncertainties (Williamson, 2017).

Finally, *role responsibility* emphasises that no decision can be delegated to a system. Leaders act on behalf of the organisation, they represent its norms and must be accountable for all decisions based on system recommendations (Prinsloo & Slade, 2017; Fricker, 2007). "This is what the system recommended" is no substitute for ethical justification (Floridi, 2013).

SDDM does not operate without preconditions. It presupposes structural conditions of the organisation: transparency about system logic, access to alternatives, participatory involvement of those affected and institutional time for reasoned reflection (Rouvroy & Berns, 2013). Where these prerequisites are lacking, it is not the model that fails but institutional responsibility (Moch, 2025).

The potential of the SDDM lies in its operational connectivity. It can be transferred into guidelines, integrated into training formats and anchored in decision-making bodies (Williamson, 2017). It does not force a particular decision, but it does demand well-founded responsibility. In a digital educational landscape where systems increasingly prepare but do not justify judgements, this is not a pedagogical ideal but a structural necessity (Fricker, 2007; Floridi, 2013).

Leadership responsibility does not begin with the system, but with the decision on how to deal with systems (Rouvroy & Berns, 2013). SDDM shifts the focus away from the question "What can the system do?" to "What do I want to be responsible for?" and thus offers an ethically viable framework for leadership decisions in the age of algorithmic evaluation (Moch, 2025).

1.7 CONCLUSION AND IMPLICATIONS

The present study has shown that algorithmic assessment systems in the higher education context are not neutral tools, but deeply intervene in the normative, epistemic and institutional structures of pedagogical practice (Williamson, 2017; Rouvroy & Berns, 2013). They not only change what is assessed, but also how assessments are made, by whom and on what basis (Fricker, 2007). This transformation affects all levels of higher education organisation, from didactic interaction to administrative control and strategic management (Knox, 2017).

The analysis of the Civitas Learning, JISC Early Alert and Smart Learning Platforms systems has provided examples of how algorithmic control manifests itself in different governance contexts (Williamson, 2017). Together, these examples show that Algorithmic evaluation is not a homogeneous phenomenon but one that requires leadership everywhere (Prinsloo & Slade, 2017).

Central to this is the realisation that algorithmic systems do not merely process data, but generate interpretative power. They influence what is considered a risk, what counts as success and when intervention appears legitimate (Beer, 2019; Tsai & Gasevic, 2017). The assessment is decontextualised, condensed, standardised and thus gains institutional authority. This authority requires explanation and cannot be taken for granted (Fricker, 2007). University management is thus at the centre of a field of tension between efficiency demands, normative uncertainty and growing accountability pressure (Williamson, 2017).

This situation gives rise to a new understanding of leadership: not as linear control, but as the shaping of normative areas of tension (Rouvroy & Berns, 2013). Responsibility shifts from the mere selection of suitable systems to the creation of institutional structures that recontextualise judgement, enable accountability and systematically anchor ethical reflection (Floridi, 2013).

The Subjective Dynamic Decision Model (SDDM), which was introduced and applied in this thesis, provides a viable orientation framework for this task (Moch, 2025). It functions as an institutional infrastructure for judgement. The four decision-making dimensions of context sensitivity, norm consistency, risk transparency and role responsibility require managers to consciously position themselves (Fricker, 2007; Floridi, 2013). The model does not allow decisions to be "passed on" to systems, but requires them to actively engage with institutional validity claims (Williamson, 2017).

Leadership responsibility does not begin with the technical implementation, but with the decision as to which image of humanity and which understanding of justice should characterise a university (Fricker, 2007). Algorithmic access to learning progressions, interactions and behavioural data is not illegitimate per se, but the assumption that valid assessments can be automatically derived from them is (Rouvroy & Berns, 2013). Leadership therefore means redrawing the line between technical plausibility and pedagogical judgement and making this line explainable, justifiable and revisable. As Biesta (2010) emphasises, good education is only possible where judgement is not reduced to standardised outputs, but remains an ethical-political practice (Biesta, 2010).

As a result, it can be stated: Algorithmic systems are not neutral but also not necessarily unjust (Williamson, 2017). Their fairness is not a system attribute, but the result of institutional behaviour (Fricker, 2007). Universities that use algorithmic assessment face not only a technical but also a political decision: Which control logic do they want to institutionalise and with which normative consequences (Rouvroy & Berns, 2013)?

This responsibility cannot be delegated. It begins with the selection of the system, continues with its application and ends with the willingness to recognise system boundaries, allow divergent judgements and be able to justify evaluation decisions (Knox, 2017). It is this culture of responsibility that becomes a condition of educational ethics legitimisation in times of algorithmic control (Floridi, 2013).

Conclusion: It is not technology that decides on justice, but leadership. It is not the system that creates legitimacy, but the institution that is responsible for it (Williamson, 2017). Beyond the theoretical perspective, this work shows that the application of the Subjective Dynamic Decision Model (SDDM) enables a precise and realistic analysis of leadership responsibility under conditions of algorithmic uncertainty (Moch, 2025). The integration of subjective decision states, heuristic thresholds and metacognitive reflection processes represents a substantial methodological innovation (Fricker, 2007; Floridi, 2013). The model opens up new perspectives both for scientific analyses and for the practical design of responsible leadership in algorithmic educational systems (Williamson, 2017).

1.8 LIMITATIONS AND OUTLOOK

This work is positioned at the interface between educational ethics theory, institutional leadership research and technology-reflective analyses of algorithmic systems (Williamson, 2017; Floridi, 2013). Its aim was to visualise the structural and normative areas of tension that arise from the use of data-based assessment systems in the higher education context (Fricker, 2007). An explicitly conceptual approach was chosen, which is based on theory-based argumentation, systematic reflection and exemplary case reconstruction (Rouvroy & Berns, 2013).

Firstly, a deliberate methodological limitation lies in the absence of empirical primary data. The study dispenses with interviews, observations or statistical analyses. Instead, publicly available information, scientific literature and exemplary case descriptions were used as a basis (Knox, 2017). This decision allows for analytical depth, but limits the informative value with regard to organisational micro-processes, institutional logic and subjective patterns of interpretation (Tsai & Gasevic, 2017).

Secondly, the selection of case studies is selective and orientated towards conceptual contrasts rather than global representativeness (Williamson, 2017). Civitas Learning, JISC Early Alert and the Smart Learning Platforms stand for different ideal types of algorithmic control (Beer, 2019), but only represent a section of global practice. The Global South, postcolonial educational spaces or transnational platform universities were not included (Floridi, 2013).

Thirdly, the work follows a normative-theoretical approach that is deliberately not intended to improve the system, but rather to reflect on leadership (Fricker, 2007). It makes no claim to completeness in the sense of data ethics testing standards, legal evaluation standards or technical validation (Rouvroy & Berns, 2013). Rather, it is about critically reconstructing the institutional preconditions of justice-oriented evaluation in the age of automated decision-making with a focus on responsibility, judgement and leadership (Williamson, 2017).

Fourthly, the proposed leadership model (SDDM) is heuristic and discursive (Moch, 2025). It does not claim to be equally applicable or operationalisable for all contexts (Fricker, 2007). Rather, it aims to open up spaces for reflection, make ethical decision-making dimensions explicit and enable leadership as a responsible practice under conditions of algorithmic intransparency and predictive control (Floridi, 2013). In this openness lies strength but also limitation (Rouvroy & Berns, 2013).

These limitations also open up productive opportunities for further research: Firstly, the SDDM model should be empirically tested, for example through case analyses in universities, participatory development projects or teaching formats on ethical leadership in digital transformation (Knox, 2017). Secondly, there is a need for quantitative and qualitative studies on the impact of algorithmic assessment on students, teachers and counsellors, including from the perspective of epistemic inequality (Fricker, 2007; Tsai & Gasevic, 2017). Thirdly, a more in-depth interdisciplinary perspective is desirable: the combination of governance theory, sociology of technology, philosophy of education and informatics ethics can contribute to not only critically reflecting on algorithmic governance, but also to making it institutionally designable (Rouvroy & Berns, 2013; Floridi, 2013). Fourthly, the international dimension must be taken into account: Education systems differ not only legally and organisationally, but also in their normative framing of assessment, legitimacy and participation (Williamson, 2017).

1.9 POWER, RESPONSIBILITY AND LEGITIMACY IN ALGORITHMIC EDUCATIONAL PRACTICE

1.9.1 Algorithmic power: Control Without Command

Algorithmic systems not only change institutional processes, but also fundamentally shift how power is exercised in the educational space (Williamson, 2017; Rouvroy & Berns, 2013). This shift is neither overtly repressive nor explicitly hierarchical. Rather, it operates in a mode of behaviour control through data aggregation, predictive metrics and automated feedback (Beer, 2019). What Michel Foucault described as "governmentality" takes on a new form under algorithmic conditions: Power by prediction not by decree (Foucault, 2004; Rouvroy & Berns, 2013).

Foucault's concept refers to a specific form of exercising power that is not based on prohibition or obedience, but on the creation of spaces of possibility (Foucault, 2004). It is governed through knowledge production, standardisation, monitoring and self-control (Williamson, 2017). This is exactly what algorithmic evaluation systems do: they define what is considered "successful", mark deviations, structure intervention paths and thus intervene preventively in pedagogical action even before it has been consciously reflected upon (Knox, 2017).

This is exemplified by the "risk scoring" logic of Civitas Learning. Students are algorithmically risk-assessed based on historical behavioural data. Teachers and counsellors receive recommendations for action derived from this, which are often not perceived as an option but as an implicit obligation (Prinsloo & Slade, 2017; Williamson, 2017). A subtle form of algorithmic power emerges: it does not work through authority, but indirectly but profoundly through infrastructure (Beer, 2019).

Shoshana Zuboff has described this mechanism as the core of "surveillance capitalism": the systematic economisation of behavioural data as a basis for control, prediction and behaviour extraction (Zuboff, 2019). In educational institutions, access to data ranging from study histories and platform activity to library use becomes a vehicle of institutional control (Williamson, 2017). The individuals concerned often do not realise that they are being monitored, let alone what the consequences are (Fricker, 2007).

This type of power is controversial because it is depersonalised. It has no concrete counterpart, no explicit order, no obvious causation (Rouvroy & Berns, 2013). Intervention does not appear as a decision, but as a system reaction. As a result, the visibility of interventions decreases and with it the possibility of criticism (Zuboff, 2019). When measures are algorithmically legitimised, resistance is delegitimised as irrational: The system supposedly "knows" better what is useful (Fricker, 2007).

University administrations that implement such systems find themselves in an ambivalent balance of power. On the one hand, they gain new control options based on seemingly objective data, evidence-based risk profiles and automated evaluation (Williamson, 2017). On the other hand, they are subjecting themselves to a logic that is increasingly beyond their pedagogical control (Knox, 2017). Power is shifting: away from conscious decision-making and towards invisible infrastructure in the configuration of data, models and access points (Beer, 2019).

This shift calls into question traditional notions of leadership responsibility. When systems pre-structure behaviour, institutional decision-making is marginalised. New forms of power emerge without a corresponding increase in responsibility - a decoupling that shakes the foundations of educational ethics legitimisation (Floridi,

2013). Those who no longer make decisions cannot be held responsible. And those who no longer act visibly evade accountability (Fricker, 2007).

It is therefore not enough to analyse algorithmic systems technically. Their effect unfolds institutionally as a new configuration of the relationship between knowledge, control and legitimacy (Rouvroy & Berns, 2013). Today, power no longer works (only) through coercion, but through prediction, inference and system architecture (Williamson, 2017). Those who want to lead must not assume this power, but recognise it, disclose it and contain it normatively (Floridi, 2013).

1.9.2 Responsibility Under Conditions of Delegation

With the introduction of algorithmic assessment systems, not only the epistemic centre of pedagogical judgement is shifting, but also the structure of institutional responsibility (Williamson, 2017; Rouvroy & Berns, 2013). Decisions are increasingly no longer made by individuals, but prepared, recommended or automated by systems (Knox, 2017). This delegation creates a new area of tension: responsibility remains formal, but is practically withdrawn (Fricker, 2007).

In traditional management processes, accountability was relatively clearly regulated: Whoever evaluates bears responsibility for the evaluation (Floridi, 2013). In data-based system architectures, however, this relationship is blurred. Recommendations are derived from complex models, decisions are made based on scores or system instructions, and managers often act in the mode of "assured execution" (Prinsloo & Slade, 2017). The more the process is mechanised, the greater the responsibility gap becomes institutionally, epistemically and ethically (Rouvroy & Berns, 2013).

Responsibility requires not only decision-making power, but also the possibility of justification, accountability and normative accountability (Fricker, 2007). A system output that is not understood cannot be justified (Williamson, 2017). Those who rely on algorithmic metrics without being able to plausibly explain how they come about are not acting responsibly, but rather reproducing systemic authority without critical appropriation (Rouvroy & Berns, 2013).

This constellation becomes particularly explosive when errors occur: Who is liable for disadvantage due to algorithmic risk attribution? Who is responsible for systematic discrimination due to unbalanced training data? And who justifies why certain interventions are made or not made? Algorithmic delegation promises objectivity, but creates invisibility (Zuboff, 2019). No one has explicitly decided, but everyone acts as if a decision has been made (Beer, 2019).

This decoupling can only be institutionally compensated for by new responsibility structures. Universities not only need technology, but also governance in the form of auditing bodies, accountability and comprehensible decision-making protocols (Williamson, 2017). What is needed are not only efficiency evaluations, but also ethical spaces for reflection that scrutinise systemic action for justice, transparency and pedagogical appropriateness (Floridi, 2013).

Individual responsibility also needs to be rethought. Anyone who adopts an algorithmic recommendation does not automatically bear its legitimacy unless the decision has been scrutinised, justified and made transparent (Prinsloo & Slade, 2017). This results in the need for a new culture of accountability: one that does not follow system outputs, but rather contextualises, classifies and compares them with ethical standards (Fricker, 2007). Leaders do not need deep systems knowledge, but they do need criteria to recognise when algorithmic logic is pedagogically inadequate (Williamson, 2017).

The Subjective Dynamic Decision Model (SDDM) offers a structuring heuristic for this challenge (Moch, 2025). It dispenses with the illusion of complete control, but defines standards for justified responsibility under conditions of uncertainty (Fricker, 2007; Floridi, 2013, Biesta, 2010). SDDM does not demand the rejection of technical systems; it requires that every system recommendation is actively made as a personal decision (Rouvroy & Berns, 2013). In this model, responsibility is not understood as a property, but as an act of appropriation: the conscious will to take responsibility for consequences that result from algorithmically supported processes (Moch, 2025).

This appropriation becomes all the more necessary the more complex and non-transparent systems become (Williamson, 2017). At a time when not only processes but also judgements are being automated, responsibility is becoming a scarce resource for institutional capacity to act (Fricker, 2007). It must not be displaced by technology - it must be reorganised through leadership (Floridi, 2013).

1.9.3 Legitimacy Problems of Digital Control

The spread of algorithmic control in educational institutions not only raises the question of efficiency and fairness, but also fundamentally of legitimacy (Williamson, 2017; Rouvroy & Berns, 2013). This means more than formal compliance with rules; it refers to the recognition of institutional decisions as justified by those who are affected by them (Fricker, 2007). Under the conditions of data-based evaluation systems, this recognition is increasingly coming under pressure (Knox, 2017).

This is because algorithmic systems not only change decision-making processes, but also the reference points of legitimacy themselves. In traditional contexts, legitimacy was based on deliberative negotiation, argumentative traceability and verifiable accountability (Floridi, 2013). As Biesta (2010) points out, good education requires ethical and political judgement that cannot be reduced to standardised outputs (Biesta, 2010). Educational judgements were embedded in professional discourses, explicit criteria and institutionally validated procedures (Williamson,

2017). With the introduction of automated systems, this framework is shifting: Decisions no longer refer to normative reasons, but to implicit modelling assumptions and statistical correlations (Beer, 2019)

Three structural legitimacy deficits arise:

Participation deficits: Affected stakeholders are rarely involved in the selection, development or adaptation of systems (Knox, 2017; Prinsloo & Slade, 2017). Governance is formally institutionalised but actually withdrawn (Rouvroy & Berns, 2013). Where participation is missing, the basis for legitimate recognition is also missing (Fricker, 2007).

Lack of transparency: The evaluation logic often remains unclear (Tsai & Gasevic, 2017). Legitimacy requires epistemic accessibility: Those who evaluate must be able to explain how and why they evaluate (Floridi, 2013). Otherwise, the result is a system that is operationally efficient but epistemically illegitimate (Williamson, 2017). As Ananny and Crawford (2018) show, the ideal of complete transparency often remains unattainable, as algorithmic responsibility can only seemingly be explained without contextualisation and socio-technical embedding (Ananny & Crawford, 2018).

Power asymmetries: Imbalances arise between management, professionals and providers (Beer, 2019; Rouvroy & Berns, 2013). Legitimacy requires normative equivalence (Fricker, 2007).

The consequences: Students experience assessment as system output, teachers lose confidence in their power of judgement, leaders delegate normative responsibility (Knox, 2017; Williamson, 2017). Legitimacy is replaced by performance, responsibility by process conformity (Beer, 2019).

In order to correct this development, institutional backing is needed: participatory governance, ethical evaluation and democratic control (Rouvroy & Berns, 2013). Universities must create spaces in which evaluation logics are publicly negotiated, not shielded, but discursively (Knox, 2017; Floridi, 2013). As Ananny and Crawford (2018) show, technical transparency remains ineffective if it is not complemented by contextual negotiation processes, as disclosure without embedding in institutional discourses does not create actual accountability (Ananny & Crawford, 2018). Legitimacy is not a property of technology, but a communicative achievement (Fricker, 2007).

1.9.4 Critical Digital Education: Perspectives for a Just Institution

In the face of profound transformation, data-based governance must be embedded in a broader educational theory horizon (Williamson, 2017). Critical digital education is not a blanket critique of technology, but a normative practice of reflection

(Fricker, 2007; Knox, 2017). It combines feasibility with justice (Floridi, 2013), designs systems, problematises effects and understands leadership as normative navigation (Rouvroy & Berns, 2013).

The recovery of pedagogical judgement is central: systems must be understood, questioned and held accountable (Williamson, 2017). Critical education does not ask whether scores are technically correct, but whether they can be ethically justified (Fricker, 2007).

Four institutional perspectives:

Governance ethics: systems must not be introduced without clarified responsibility. The SDDM offers a viable heuristic for this (Moch, 2025).

Institutionalised participation: Legitimacy requires co-decision-making at a structural level (Knox, 2017).

Leadership competence in educational ethics: Leaders must recognise normative conflicts of objectives, understand system boundaries and make responsible trade-offs (Floridi, 2013).

Critical faculties as cultural practice: Institutions must create spaces to problematise governance and make it revisable (Rouvroy & Berns, 2013).

In essence, it is about reconnecting the pedagogical idea to the culture of responsibility of the digital present: justice requires the ability to decide against system logic when it is normatively necessary (Williamson, 2017).

REFERENCES

Ananny, M., & Crawford, K. (2018). Seeing without knowing: Limitations of the transparency ideal and its application to algorithmic accountability. *New Media & Society*, *20*(3), 973–989. DOI: 10.1177/1461444816676645

Barocas, S., Hardt, M., & Narayanan, A. (2019). Fairness and Machine Learning. Cambridge, MA: fairmlbook.org.

Beer, D. (2019). *The Data Gaze: Capitalism, Power and Perception*. SAGE. DOI: 10.4135/9781526463210

Biesta, G. (2010). *Good Education in an Age of Measurement: Ethics, Politics, Democracy*. Routledge.

Couldry, N., & Mejias, U. A. (2019). *The Costs of Connection: How Data Is Colonising Human Life and Appropriating It for Capitalism*. Stanford University Press.

European Parliament & Council. (2024). Regulation (EU) 2024/1123 of the European Parliament and of the Council of 22 May 2024 laying down harmonised rules on Artificial Intelligence (Artificial Intelligence Act) and amending certain Union legislative acts. *Official Journal of the European Union, L, 204*, 1–125.

Floridi, L. (2013). *The Ethics of Information*. Oxford University Press. DOI: 10.1093/acprof:oso/9780199641321.001.0001

Foucault, M. (2004). *Sécurité, territoire, population: Cours au Collège de France (1977-1978)*. Gallimard/Seuil.

Fricker, M. (2007). *Epistemic Injustice: Power and the Ethics of Knowing*. Oxford University Press. DOI: 10.1093/acprof:oso/9780198237907.001.0001

Jasanoff, S., & Kim, S.-H. (2009). Containing the atom: Sociotechnical imaginaries and nuclear power in the United States and South Korea. *Minerva*, *47*(2), 119–146. DOI: 10.1007/s11024-009-9124-4

Jasanoff, S., & Kim, S.-H. (Eds.). (2015). *Dreamscapes of modernity: Sociotechnical imaginaries and the fabrication of power*. University of Chicago Press. DOI: 10.7208/chicago/9780226276663.001.0001

Knox, J. (2017). Data power in education: Exploring critical awareness with the 'Learning Analytics Report Card'. *Television & New Media*, *18*(8), 734–752. DOI: 10.1177/1527476417690029

Moch, E. (2025). Extending the Subjective Dynamic Decision Model: A Heuristic and Meta-Cognitive Framework for Strategic Adaptation. *East African Journal of Interdisciplinary Studies*, *8*(1), 315–328. DOI: 10.37284/eajis.8.1.3022

Oberdieck, T., & Moch, E. (2024). Lifelong Learning with Artificial Intelligence: Potentials, Challenges and Future Perspectives. *International Journal of Advanced Research*, *12*(6), 545–555. DOI: 10.21474/IJAR01/18915

Power, M. (1999). *The audit society: Rituals of verification*. Oxford University Press. DOI: 10.1093/acprof:oso/9780198296034.001.0001

Prinsloo, P. (2020). Data frontiers and frontiers of power in (higher) education: A view of/from the Global South. *Teaching in Higher Education*, *25*(4), 366–383. DOI: 10.1080/13562517.2020.1723537

Prinsloo, P., & Slade, S. (2017). An elephant in the learning analytics room: The obligation to act. *EDUCAUSE Review*, *52*(4), 51–61. DOI: 10.1145/3027385.3027406

Rouvroy, A., & Berns, T. (2013). Gouvernance algorithmique et perspectives d'émancipation. *Reseaux (London)*, *177*(1), 163–196.

Tsai, Y.-S., & Gasevic, D. (2017). Learning analytics in higher education—Challenges and policies: A review of eight learning analytics policies. In *Proceedings of the Seventh International Learning Analytics & Knowledge Conference (LAK '17)* (pp. 233–242). Association for Computing Machinery. DOI: 10.1145/3027385.3027400

UNESCO. (2021). Recommendation on the ethics of artificial intelligence. https://unesdoc.unesco.org/ark:/48223/pf0000380455

Williamson, B. (2017). *Big Data in Education: The Digital Future of Learning, Policy and Practice*. SAGE. DOI: 10.4135/9781529714920

Zuboff, S. (2019). *The Age of Surveillance Capitalism: The Fight for a Human Future at the New Frontier of Power*. Profile Books.

KEY TERMS AND DEFINITIONS

Algorithmic bias: Systematic distortions in algorithmic decision-making processes that arise from data, modelling or training procedures and can reproduce existing inequalities.

Algorithmic Evaluation: Automated assessment procedures based on computational models to generate judgements or predictions about learners; often used for performance monitoring and early intervention.

Datafication: Transformation of human behaviour, experience and decision-making into digital, algorithmically analysable data formats.

Educational leadership: Strategic and ethically and pedagogically responsible management of educational institutions, including the considered use of digital tools.

Epistemic Injustice: Violation of the epistemic rights of individuals or groups, for example through exclusion from knowledge production or a lack of transparency in algorithmic evaluation criteria.

Fairness: Normative principle of fair assessment that includes equal opportunities, context sensitivity and transparent decision-making processes, increasingly redefined technically by algorithmic models.

Governmentality: Concept developed by Michel Foucault to analyse the rationalities and techniques of exercising power extended to algorithmic control in the education sector.

Information ethics: Philosophical framework for evaluating the moral implications of data processing and digital systems, particularly in terms of respecting information-based forms of existence.

Learning Analytics: Collection, evaluation and reporting of learning data with the aim of better understanding and optimising learning processes and learning environments.

Reflexive leadership: Leadership approach that not only uses algorithmic control instruments administratively, but also critically scrutinises and actively shapes their epistemic, normative and social implications

Chapter 13
From Data To Decisions: Cultivating AI-Driven Leadership For Pedagogical Transformation

Tendai Charles
http://orcid.org/0000-0002-0253-5960
The British University in Dubai, UAE

Abdulai Abukari
The British University in Dubai, UAE

Hend Al Mazmi
The British University in Dubai, UAE

ABSTRACT

This chapter examines the emergence of AI-driven pedagogical leadership as a critical response to the challenges and opportunities posed by the integration of artificial intelligence in education. Set against the backdrop of increasingly data-intensive digital ecosystems, it argues that effective leadership must move beyond technological adoption to cultivate the capacity for ethical, inclusive and contextually grounded decision-making. Drawing on theories of distributed leadership, sensemaking and data use, the chapter explores how AI tools can support strategic planning, staff development and resource allocation. It critically analyses ethical concerns, risks of technocentrism and the erosion of teacher autonomy, while highlighting persistent data literacy and infrastructure gaps. The chapter concludes by proposing models for capacity building and strategic recommendations for embedding AI within continuous improvement cycles.

DOI: 10.4018/979-8-3373-4908-4.ch013

INTRODUCTION

The twenty-first century has seen an unprecedented expansion in the quantity of digital data produced by schools and universities. Learning management systems (LMS), student information systems, digital assessment platforms and virtual classrooms generate massive datasets describing learners' activities, interactions and outcomes. Meanwhile, advances in artificial intelligence (AI) and machine-learning algorithms promise to transform these digital traces into actionable insights that can support more responsive and personalised educational practices (Azzam & Charles, 2025). Recent reports indicate that AI has moved from merely a speculative possibility to routine presence; for example, in 2022 the EDUCAUSE Horizon Report identified AI for learning analytics and AI for learning tools as among the most disruptive technologies for teaching and learning (Zhu et al., 2025). Another international review of AI in higher education noted that the field has shifted from experimental prototypes toward mainstream adoption of predictive models, AI-enhanced tutors, automated assessment tools and learning dashboards (Crompton & Burke, 2023). Schools and universities now operate in what Pei et al. (2024) describe as data-intensive "digital ecosystems", where teachers, administrators and learners constantly interact with algorithmic systems.

Yet the proliferation of AI systems does not automatically yield better decision-making. Educational institutions often suffer from data abundance but insight scarcity. Even when predictive analytics and dashboards provide real-time information, leaders may lack the conceptual frameworks, data-literacy skills or ethical guidelines to interpret the output and turn it into meaningful pedagogical actions. The result is a widening gap between technical capability and human judgment. Research on digital academic leadership (or what some refer to as 'digital leadership' or 'e-leadership' – see Ghamrawi and Tamim, 2023; Bowden et al. 2023, Yuting et al., 2025) in Chinese universities illustrates this gap. For example, Jing et al. (2025) argue that although administrators possess "technology awareness" and receive regular briefings about emerging tools, they often struggle to translate abstract concepts such as the Metaverse (Abukhalaf et al., 2024) into concrete innovations for teaching and research. Interviews revealed significant frustration with fragmented infrastructures and siloed data, leading some leaders to describe their campuses as "innovation islands" where digital initiatives fail to communicate. The same study reported persistent skills shortages; even progressive institutions outsourced half of their advanced analytics work because internal staff lacked the necessary expertise (Jing et al., 2025). Furthermore, it is important to note that although digital leadership has been widely examined across professional sectors (including business), scholarship that specifically theorises AI-driven pedagogical leadership in education (particularly the leadership work of translating algorithmic outputs into context-sensitive instructional improvement) remains emergent. This gap reinforces the need to examine not only AI tools, but also the organisational learning processes, professional agency, and ethical safeguards through which such tools are enacted in educational settings.

Interpreting AI implementation as an organisational change process helps explain why technical capability often outpaces pedagogical uptake. AI adoption typically requires shifts in routines (data collection and cycles of inquiry), roles (e.g. data coaches, analytics specialists), and norms (e.g. openness to evidence and experimentation). Such shifts can produce resistance—particularly when AI is perceived as surveillance or as misaligned with professional values—and therefore demand deliberate culture-building, capacity development, and sustained coordination across units (Jing et al., 2025; Ni ă & Gu u, 2023). In distributed leadership terms, these change processes are mediated not only by senior leaders, but also by middle leaders (e.g. heads of department, grade-level coordinators, programme directors) who translate strategy into practice and organise collective sensemaking around AI outputs.

At the same time, responsible AI-driven leadership requires engagement with critical perspectives on data-driven decision-making. Data-intensive governance can unintentionally narrow educational purposes by privileging what is measurable, reinforcing audit-oriented compliance, and obscuring contextual or relational dimensions of learning. Moreover, predictions and classifications may amplify inequities when models embed historical bias or when access to data infrastructures is uneven (Zhu et al., 2025). Within schools, these dynamics may manifest as technocentrism or erosion of professional autonomy and trust (Duan & Zhao, 2024). A balanced leadership stance therefore treats AI outputs as provisional evidence to be interpreted alongside contextual knowledge, practitioner expertise and ethical deliberation (Charles & Papadaki, 2025).

These challenges suggest that the future of educational innovation lies not in technology alone but in *AI-driven pedagogical leadership*, a form of leadership in which administrators and instructional leaders harness AI-generated insights to make evidence-informed decisions about curriculum, resource allocation, professional development and student support. This chapter argues that AI-driven pedagogical leadership is necessary to navigate the complex intersection of data, technology and human judgment. Ultimately, the objective of this chapter is to discuss three interrelated issues:

- How AI tools (particularly predictive analytics, adaptive learning systems and dashboards) could support strategic decision-making across different levels of educational leadership;
- Opportunities and tensions that could arise when AI is integrated into school and university governance;

- Potential models, competencies and institutional conditions that are needed to cultivate AI-driven leadership that is ethical, inclusive and contextually responsive.

Across these objectives, particular attention is given to the agency of teachers and students and to the mediating role of middle leaders. AI-driven pedagogical leadership is treated as a participatory endeavour in which end-users co-design tools (e.g. dashboards) and contribute to governance through transparent decision rules, opportunities to question or contest outputs, and collaborative data inquiry (Pei et al., 2024; Sandoval-Ríos et al., 2025).

The chapter adopts a conceptual-analytical approach informed by three theoretical perspectives: (1) distributed leadership, which emphasises shared decision-making across multiple actors rather than top-down control; (2) sensemaking, which focuses on how individuals and groups interpret complex information in order to construct shared meaning; and (3) data use theories, which examine how educators collect, analyse and act upon data within specific contexts. However, it is essential to note that whilst research into AI in education is quite a complex undertaking due to the fast-evolving nature of technology and AI especially, the view of AI in the context of educational leadership adds another layer of complexity. Although the classic works on the selected theories are arguably outdated in a post-digital world, recent empirical studies reinforce their relevance to digital transformation.

For example, research on digital transformation and leadership in higher education highlights that transformational leadership — an approach that fosters shared vision and collective agency — is central to building institutional digital competencies (Ni ă & Gu u, 2023). Distributed decision-making is necessary because AI systems redistribute authority and information across roles, requiring collaborative structures rather than heroic individual leaders. Furthermore, sensemaking is critical when algorithms generate predictions and recommendations that are difficult to interpret; put simply, data do not speak for themselves but acquire meaning through organised interpretation.

These lenses operate as organising threads throughout the chapter. Distributed leadership is used to examine how AI redistributes expertise and authority across senior, middle and frontline roles; sensemaking is used to explicate how leadership teams interpret algorithmic outputs and negotiate shared meaning; and data use theories frame AI within iterative cycles of inquiry, action, reflection and revision. Complementing these perspectives, an organisational learning orientation is employed to conceptualise AI adoption as a sustained capability-building process, one that requires attention to professional learning, feedback loops, and institutional routines for improvement rather than one-off technology deployments (Ni ă & Gu u, 2023; Jing et al., 2025).

Data use theories remind leaders that data-based decisions must be embedded in cycles of inquiry, action, reflection and revision, rather than used as static "facts". In line with these perspectives, this chapter first reviews the role of AI in school decision-making and then examines the opportunities and tensions that accompany AI integration. It proposes capacity-building models for cultivating AI-driven leadership, drawing on case studies from diverse educational contexts. Finally, it outlines future directions and strategic recommendations for policymakers, practitioners and researchers.

THE ROLE OF AI IN SCHOOL DECISION-MAKING

Any attempt to discuss the role of AI in school decision-making invariably touches multiple dimensions of practice, as AI-enabled systems increasingly shape teaching, assessment, learner support and organisational operations. While a range of classifications of AI use in educational leadership has been proposed (Kuleto et al., 2021; Sposato, 2025), the discussion below foregrounds three leadership-relevant areas: (1) predictive analytics for student outcomes and wellbeing; (2) learning management systems and learning analytics dashboards that enable real-time feedback; and (3) AI-enhanced staff development and performance monitoring.

Predictive analytics for student outcomes and wellbeing

One of the most widely discussed uses of AI in education is predictive analytics, where machine-learning models identify patterns that predict future events such as course completion, dropout, academic performance or wellbeing. A recent study by Gonzalez-Nucamendi et al. (2023) developed predictive models to identify first-year university students at risk of dropping out. Using Random Forest and Gradient Boosting algorithms on demographic data, entrance exam scores, continuous assessment grades and scholarship status, the researchers achieved high accuracy in predicting dropout. Importantly, they found that early identification during the first weeks of the term allows institutions to implement timely interventions. Similarly, research on the use of AI in K-12 school systems are also adopting early warning systems that combine attendance records, behavioural data and formative assessments to flag at-risk learners. For example, a recent study introduced an early-warning system that uses dynamic time intervals and AI to determine the optimal timing for interventions (Bañeres et al., 2023). Unlike static models that generate predictions but offer little guidance on when to act, this system recommended intervention windows that reduced dropout rates, illustrating the value of combining prediction with decision support.

Beyond dropout risk, predictive analytics can inform student wellbeing and resource allocation. For instance, academic advisors can use models to identify students who are likely to experience stress or disengagement based on patterns of LMS activity. Data on attendance, participation and performance can signal emerging mental health concerns, enabling targeted counselling. However, the quality of predictions depends on data quality and algorithmic design. In the dropout study, variables such as scholarship status and entrance exam scores were influential predictors (Gonzalez-Nucamendi et al., 2023), underscoring that predictions often reflect existing social inequalities. Educators must therefore interpret risk flags critically, consider contextual factors and avoid deterministic labelling of students.

From a leadership standpoint, the most consequential design decision is how risk information is translated into supportive action. Effective implementation typically involves a distributed response: analytics or data teams validate alerts, middle leaders coordinate instructional adjustments within departments or grade teams, and learner support staff engage students in ways that preserve dignity and agency. Interpreted through a sensemaking lens, predictions become meaningful only through collective interpretation, triangulation with professional judgement, and ethically guided decision-making.

Learning management systems and real-time feedback loops

While predictive models aim to forecast future outcomes, LMSs and learning analytics dashboards provide real-time feedback on current learning processes. Recent research emphasises that dashboards are not mere information displays, but socio-technical tools designed to scaffold reflection and decision-making. An example of this was presented in a case study by Pei et al. (2024), who described LearningViz, an interactive dashboard that helps instructors identify, analyse and close performance gaps among student groups. LearningViz includes three modules (1) a Student Overall Performance Analysis module, (2) a Student Group Performance Analysis module and (3) a Final Exam Item Analysis module — that collectively allow instructors to explore weekly performance patterns, identify assessments that contribute most to achievement gaps and evaluate the quality of exam questions. The design follows a user-centred approach, incorporating data visualisation and domain expert input so that teachers without advanced analytics skills can make sense of data. Findings from the study underscore that such dashboards support instructors in detecting performance gaps, investigating contributing factors, evaluating assessment quality and implementing targeted instructional strategies.

Dashboards can also empower learners by promoting self-regulation. A systematic overview of learning analytics dashboards reported that these systems visualise time spent on tasks, access to resources and performance progression, enabling comparisons and fostering motivation (Masiello et al., 2024). The review noted that the COVID-19 pandemic accelerated adoption, with dashboards becoming integral assessment instruments in higher education due to their ability to provide real-time data on study progress and group performance. However, most dashboards offer descriptive analytics rather than advanced predictive capabilities. Many current systems identify at-risk students but lack interpretative or actionable advice, highlighting the need for dashboards that integrate predictive models with explanation and recommendation features. Crucially, a human-centred design is important to ensure dashboards augment, rather than overwhelm, teachers and students.

Participatory design can strengthen these systems by ensuring that teachers and students can interrogate what is being measured, how indicators are constructed, and what actions are considered legitimate responses. In practical terms, this entails involving end-users in dashboard co-design, providing accessible explanations for visualisations and alerts, and creating avenues for feedback or contestation when analytics are misleading (Pei et al., 2024; Masiello et al., 2024).

AI-enhanced staff development and performance monitoring

AI is increasingly being used to support teacher professional development and performance evaluation (Charles, 2025). Video analytics, natural language processing and large language models (LLMs) can capture classroom interactions, provide feedback on pedagogy and generate recommendations for improvement (Charles & Hill, 2025). Lee et al. (2024) presented a GPT-4 vision-powered observational assessment system that automatically analyses classroom videos to evaluate teachers' instructional behaviours. The system detects features such as questioning strategies, wait time, use of multimedia and classroom management, offering detailed feedback reports that would be impractical to generate manually. The authors argue that teacher analytics, situated at the intersection of learning assessment and data analytics, empowers educators to refine teaching based on concrete evidence. Nevertheless, they caution that AI should not replace human judgment; observational assessments remain contextual and value-laden, and ethical considerations around privacy and consent must guide deployment. In leadership terms, the key challenge is ensuring that AI-supported observation and feedback functions as a developmental resource rather than a compliance mechanism. Middle leaders (e.g., instructional coaches, heads of department) can play a critical mediating role by facilitating reflective dialogue around AI feedback, contextualising recommendations, and safeguarding consent and professional agency (Lee et al., 2024; Charles, 2025).

Other AI applications aim to reduce administrative workload and support professional growth. For instance, AI-driven tools can automatically transcribe and code teacher reflections, match instructors with relevant professional development resources and facilitate peer feedback. Duan & Zhao (2024) examined the effects of AI-powered applications on teachers' perceived autonomy, professional development and digital burnout. The study found that AI tools improved teachers' sense of agency and professional growth by streamlining routine tasks, providing personalised recommendations and fostering communities of practice. Notably, the integration of AI reduced digital burnout by automating repetitive duties and enabling teachers to focus on high-value pedagogical activities. Such findings suggest that AI can support, rather than undermine, teacher autonomy when designed to augment human expertise (Charles et al., 2025).

Taxonomies of AI applications in educational leadership

Understanding the diversity of AI applications is essential for leaders to make informed choices. Sposato (2025) developed a comprehensive taxonomy of AI uses in educational leadership. The taxonomy identified ten domains, including administrative efficiency, personalised learning, decision support, resource optimisation, community engagement and ethical governance (*see* Table 1). The authors observed that AI integration in education requires balancing technological advancement with outcomes, ethics and resource constraints. They emphasised that the promise of AI is inseparable from concerns about privacy, equity and agency; as such, leaders must adopt a balanced approach that addresses ethical and equity issues rather than pursuing AI for its own sake. The taxonomy serves as a conceptual map for leaders to align AI initiatives with institutional goals and ethical guidelines.

In sum, AI tools can support educational decision-making at multiple levels—predicting future outcomes, providing real-time feedback and enhancing staff development. However, the potential benefits depend on leaders' capacity to interpret AI outputs, integrate them into pedagogical and organisational processes and address ethical considerations. Across these AI applications, the decisive variable is not the sophistication of the technology but the quality of leadership practice around interpretation, participation and governance. For example, leaders need to (a) establish distributed routines for interpreting analytics; (b) protect teacher and student agency through participatory design and transparent decision rules; and (c) ensure ethical safeguards (privacy, fairness and accountability) are embedded from the outset.

Table 1. Taxonomy of AI applications in educational leadership (adapted from Sposato, 2025)

Domain	Definition	Examples
Administrative Efficiency	Use of AI to streamline institutional operations, reduce manual workload, and optimise resource management	Automated timetable generation; AI-assisted scheduling; predictive maintenance for facilities
Personalised Learning	Tailoring learning experiences to individual student needs through adaptive systems and real-time analytics	AI-driven adaptive learning platforms; personalised learning pathways; automated feedback systems
Decision Support	Providing leaders with data-driven insights to inform policy, strategic planning, and operational choices	Predictive analytics for enrolment forecasting; risk identification dashboards; AI-assisted budget allocation tools
Resource Optimisation	Allocating financial, human, and physical resources more effectively based on predictive modelling and usage data	AI models for staff deployment; library resource recommendation systems; energy consumption optimisation
Community Engagement	Enhancing communication and collaboration between institutions and stakeholders using AI-enabled platforms	Chatbots for parent–school communication; AI-driven social media sentiment analysis; community feedback portals
Ethical Governance	Establishing policies and systems to ensure responsible, transparent, and equitable AI use in education	AI ethics committees; algorithmic bias audits; compliance monitoring tools
Data-Driven Curriculum Design	Informing curriculum development with data on student performance, labour market trends, and emerging skills needs	AI analysis of graduate employability data; skills-gap forecasting; automated curriculum alignment tools
Learner Support Services	Using AI to enhance academic advising, career counselling, and wellbeing interventions	Virtual academic advisors; AI-powered mental health chatbots; predictive models for identifying at-risk students
Professional Development	Supporting educator growth and performance through AI-assisted feedback, analytics, and training recommendations	AI analysis of teaching videos; personalised CPD pathways; automated reflective practice summaries
Monitoring and Evaluation	Employing AI to track institutional performance, programme outcomes, and strategic goal attainment	AI-assisted programme evaluation; real-time KPI dashboards; automated accreditation reporting tools

OPPORTUNITIES AND TENSIONS

From data abundance to strategic insight

One of the promises of AI is turning vast amounts of data into actionable knowledge. Dashboards like LearningViz enable instructors to examine performance patterns and tailor instruction (Pei et al., 2024), while predictive models identify at-risk students early (Gonzalez-Nucamendi et al., 2023). When properly integrated, these tools can support more equitable and personalised learning experiences. For instance, a data-driven leadership review by Chigbu & Makapela (2025) emphasised that integrating data analytics in higher education can improve institutional efficacy, align curricula with labour market demands and strengthen student outcomes. AI can also support inclusive transformation by highlighting disparities across demographic groups and enabling targeted interventions (Charles & Alshamsi, 2025).

However, moving from data abundance to strategic insight is challenging. A Chinese digital leadership study found that despite regular technology briefings, leaders struggled to translate knowledge about emerging AI tools into practical pedagogical innovations (Jing et al., 2025). Fragmented data infrastructures and siloed systems impede cross-unit collaboration. Even when dashboards exist, they may provide descriptive statistics without guidance on how to act (Masiello et al., 2024). Leaders must therefore cultivate data literacy—the ability to access, interpret, act on and communicate data. A recent systematic review of data literacy training programmes found that structured decision-making models, authentic contexts, collaborative learning and long-term follow-up improved teachers' self-efficacy and knowledge (Sandoval-Ríos et al., 2025). Yet the review also noted that most programmes emphasised data analysis over instructional application, leaving a gap in explicit decision-making skills.

AI adoption as organisational change: resistance, culture and capacity

AI integration should therefore be approached as a socio-technical change initiative rather than as a procurement exercise. Leaders must anticipate resistance (e.g., concerns about surveillance, workload, or loss of professional discretion) and actively shape organisational culture through dialogue, professional learning, and visible alignment between AI use and educational values. Evidence from digital academic leadership in China illustrates how fragmented infrastructures and bureaucratic hierarchies can inhibit change, while digital taskforces and coordinated resource strategies can support it (Jing et al., 2025).

Distributed leadership provides a practical change mechanism: senior leaders articulate purpose and allocate resources, while middle leaders translate strategy into departmental routines and facilitate teacher-led inquiry cycles. When teachers and students are treated as co-constructors (rather than passive recipients) AI tools such as dashboards are more likely to be interpreted as supports for learning rather than as external controls (Pei et al., 2024; Sandoval-Ríos et al., 2025).

Critical perspectives on data-driven leadership

Analytical balance is also necessary because data-driven leadership is not value-neutral. Data can privilege what is measurable, encourage short-term performance optimisation, and inadvertently reproduce inequities when datasets reflect structural disadvantage (Zhu et al., 2025). Moreover, when analytics become associated with monitoring and evaluation, educators may experience metric pressure and reduced autonomy, potentially undermining the professional trust that distributed leadership seeks to cultivate (Duan & Zhao, 2024). Ethical leadership in technology integration therefore requires explicit deliberation about the purposes of data use, the limits of prediction, and the conditions under which stakeholders can contest algorithmic outputs (Charles & Papadaki, 2025).

Ethical challenges: bias, opacity and privacy

Although AI promises efficiency and personalisation, it raises significant ethical concerns (Charles & Papadaki, 2025). Zhu et al.'s (2025) systematic review on responsible AI in education identified three dimensions of ethical risk: technology, education and society. Technological risks include privacy invasion, data leakage, algorithmic bias, black-box algorithms and algorithmic error. Education-related risks involve homogenised teaching, teacher deprofessionalisation, deviation from educational goals and alienation of the teacher–student relationship. Societal risks encompass exacerbation of the digital divide, absence of accountability and conflicts of interest. The review noted that AI's application in education can introduce unfairness and lack transparency. For example, algorithmic bias may embed historical inequities into recommendations, while opaque "black box" models make it difficult for stakeholders to understand how predictions are generated. Also, data leaks can compromise students' sensitive information.

Notably, several international organisations have responded to these challenges by issuing ethical guidelines. Such as UNESCO's 'AI and Education: Guidance for policymakers', which highlights issues around data and algorithms, inclusion, privacy and equity, stressing the need for human agency and fairness. Also, the European Commission's 'Ethical guidelines on the use of AI and data in teaching and learning' emphasises human agency, fairness, humanity and justified choice. Furthermore, the U.S. Department of Education has similarly underlined the importance of data privacy and security. These guidelines align with the ethical principle that AI should augment human judgment rather than replace it. In practice, leaders must ensure transparent algorithms, protect data privacy, mitigate biases and establish accountability mechanisms.

One actionable way to move from principles to practice is to institute routine algorithmic bias audits. Rather than treating fairness as an abstract aspiration, leaders can require that predictive models be evaluated across demographic groups, that error patterns be documented, and that decision thresholds be reviewed with educators who understand local context. Importantly, bias auditing is not a one-time technical check: it is a governance routine that combines statistical testing with professional judgement, stakeholder voice, and a clear process for remediation and appeal (Zhu et al., 2025). The capacity-building section below outlines a practical workflow for such audits.

Risks of technocentrism and erosion of teacher autonomy

The integration of AI into educational decision-making can provoke technocentrism (the belief that technology alone will solve educational problems) and erode teacher autonomy. Research on teacher analytics warns that while AI-powered observational assessments provide detailed feedback, they should not be used as mechanistic tools that determine teacher competence (Lee et al., 2024). Teachers may feel surveilled or reduced to numerical scores. Similarly, in a study on AI applications and teacher autonomy, Duan & Zhao (2024) found that although AI tools can enhance professional development and reduce digital burnout, they may also create dependence on algorithmic recommendations. To preserve autonomy, AI systems must be designed to support teachers' professional judgment rather than dictate it.

Another risk is the misinterpretation of AI outputs, leading to overreliance on machine recommendations. The early-warning dropout study emphasised that predictions should be used as guidance rather than definitive labels; early detection should prompt conversation and support, not automatic remedial measures (Gonzalez-Nucamendi et al., 2023). Overreliance on AI can also obscure the importance of contextual factors and qualitative knowledge. For example, the Chinese digital leadership study revealed that leaders often received technology briefings but lacked deep understanding of local instructional needs, leading to superficial adoption of trendy tools (Jing et al., 2025). Balanced leadership requires critical engagement with AI outputs, consideration of local context and ethical reflection.

Data literacy gaps and capacity deficits

Evidently, a recurring theme across all these studies is the gap between data availability and leaders' capacity to use data effectively. Leaders often face a lack of formal regulations and ethical guidelines to govern digital practices. High investment costs and limited funding further constrain digital initiatives. Organisational barriers, such as bureaucratic hierarchies, "innovation islands" and skill shortages, hinder agile decision-making. Data and technological bottlenecks include fragmented data ownership, inconsistent governance frameworks and delayed data synchronisation. These challenges point to the need for systemic capacity building, including developing hybrid professionals who can bridge pedagogical priorities and technical implementations.

The tensions above indicate that AI adoption succeeds when leaders treat analytics as a sensemaking resource embedded in organisational learning, not as a substitute for professional judgement. Accordingly, leaders should (i) invest in data/AI literacy and interpretability; (ii) build participatory governance that includes teacher and student voice; (iii) support middle leaders as translators and conveners; and (iv) institutionalise ethical routines such as privacy checks and bias audits.

CULTIVATING AI-DRIVEN LEADERSHIP THROUGH CAPACITY-BUILDING

The evidence reviewed in this chapter underscores the importance of developing institutional capacity for AI-driven leadership. Capacity building encompasses digital and data literacy, ethical governance, cross-functional collaboration and supportive professional development. This section proposes models and strategies for cultivating AI-driven leadership, drawing on empirical findings and theoretical insights.

Developing AI and data literacy

To begin with, it is clear that the foundation of AI-driven leadership is literacy in data and AI. Leaders must be able to access, interpret, act on and communicate data. Sandoval-Ríos et al.'s (2025) systematic review on data literacy training emphasised that programmes integrating structured decision-making models, authentic contexts and collaborative learning produce significant improvements in teachers' self-efficacy and knowledge. Real-world data applications and structured instructional support had the greatest impact on participants' confidence and ability to use data for pedagogical decisions. To address the gap between analysis and action, training should explicitly integrate decision-making exercises where participants apply data to case studies and reflect on outcomes. Long-term follow-up ensures that skills are retained and embedded in practice.

Capacity building must also include basic AI concepts, model interpretability and ethical awareness. Leaders should understand common algorithmic techniques (e.g., decision trees, random forests, neural networks), their strengths and limitations, and how to interrogate model outputs. They should also be trained in interpretability tools to explain predictions to stakeholders. Ethical considerations (i.e. privacy, fairness, transparency and accountability) should be embedded in every training module. Professional development may adopt a blended approach combining online tutorials, workshops, mentoring and peer learning communities. Importantly, training should be interdisciplinary: technologists and data scientists can collaborate with educational researchers and ethicists to design programs that are contextually relevant and value-sensitive.

Ethical data governance and stakeholder engagement

Ethical governance requires clear policies on data collection, storage, analysis and sharing. Institutions should establish data governance committees comprising educators, technologists, students, parents and community representatives. These committees can oversee data inventories, set access protocols and assess algorithmic fairness. Additionally, privacy should be protected through secure data infrastructures, anonymisation and explicit consent. To address algorithmic bias, committees should regularly audit models for disparate impact across demographic groups and adjust them accordingly. These proposals are supported by Zhu et al.'s (2025) systematic review on responsible AI, as they emphasised the need for strategies spanning technology, education and society to mitigate risks such as privacy invasion and algorithmic bias.

To operationalise ethical governance in schools and universities, leaders can formalise a cross-functional data governance and AI oversight team with clear roles, decision rights and documentation routines. Such a structure reinforces distributed leadership by ensuring that ethical and pedagogical considerations are not subordinated to purely technical criteria, and by creating regular forums for collective sensemaking about AI outputs.

- Executive sponsor (e.g., principal/vice-president): sets purpose, allocates resources and ensures alignment with educational values.
- Data protection and privacy lead: oversees consent, retention, access control and security protocols.
- Analytics lead (IT/data science): documents data provenance, model design choices, performance limits and update schedules.
- Pedagogical lead (middle leader—e.g., head of department/teaching and learning lead): translates outputs into instructional inquiry and supports interpretability for teachers.
- Teacher and student representatives: provide end-user perspectives, identify unintended consequences and participate in reviewing indicators and decision rules.

- Community/parent representative (where appropriate): strengthens legitimacy and trust, particularly when analytics affect learner support decisions. The team's remit can include approving AI use-cases, maintaining a data inventory, reviewing dashboard indicators, agreeing on escalation pathways for alerts, and maintaining an appeal process for stakeholders affected by algorithmic recommendations (Charles & Papadaki, 2025).

As an illustrative workflow, a bias-audit routine for predictive models could:

1. Clarify the educational purpose of the model (e.g., early-warning alerts) and define the decisions it will and will not automate.
2. Audit training data for representativeness, missingness and potential proxy variables that may encode structural inequities.
3. Evaluate model performance disaggregated by key groups (e.g., gender, socioeconomic status) and compare false-positive and false-negative rates.
4. Conduct a 'reasonableness review' of predictors with educators and counsellors to identify features that could be ethically problematic or contextually misleading.
5. Decide mitigation actions (e.g., revising features, reweighting data, adjusting thresholds, adding human review checkpoints, or enhancing explanations).
6. Communicate transparently through plain-language documentation (e.g., model purpose, limitations, confidence, and acceptable uses) and provide routes for challenge and appeal.
7. Monitor and re-audit routinely; track downstream effects of interventions to avoid self-fulfilling prophecies and to refine both the model and the support strategies (Zhu et al., 2025).

Another important matter is that stakeholder engagement is essential for legitimacy and trust. Teachers and students should participate in discussions about how data will be used and how AI systems influence their work and learning. Transparent communication about the capabilities and limitations of AI fosters informed consent and prevents misconceptions. Now, although ethical guidelines such as UNESCO's AI and Education report and the European Commission's framework provide starting points, but local adaptations are necessary. Leaders should also consider cultural differences when introducing AI tools; for example, collectivist cultures may require broader consultation and consensus, as illustrated in the Chinese digital leadership study where cross-unit collaboration was critical for resource alignment (Jing et al., 2025).

Professional development and cross-functional collaboration

AI-driven leadership thrives in collaborative environments where technologists, educators, data scientists and administrators work together. Cross-functional teams can co-design dashboards, develop predictive models and interpret results. LearningViz exemplifies this approach: the platform's design involved collaboration among experts in teaching excellence, computer science, psychology and educational technology (Pei et al., 2024). Such interdisciplinary collaboration ensures that dashboards address pedagogical needs and are accessible to non-experts. Similarly, digital academic leadership in China was supported by "digital taskforces" that brought together IT staff, deans and library directors to coordinate resources across departments (Jing et al., 2025). Building institutional capacity therefore requires structures that facilitate ongoing collaboration and knowledge sharing.

Professional development should also emphasise mentoring and coaching (Charles, 2025). Veteran leaders who successfully use AI can mentor peers through communities of practice. Peer learning sessions where leaders share experiences, challenges and solutions foster a culture of continuous improvement. Additionally, institutions can create innovation labs where staff experiment with AI tools in low-risk settings and reflect on their pedagogical implications. This aligns with the idea of distributed leadership, where leadership is enacted collectively through networked relations rather than vested in a single leader.

To translate the sensemaking lens into actionable leadership practice, leadership teams can adopt a brief protocol for interpreting AI outputs before implementing interventions. The purpose is to slow decision-making enough to surface assumptions, triangulate evidence and preserve professional and learner agency. For example, a weekly 30-minute 'data huddle' brings together the principal (sponsor), an analytics lead, a head of department (middle leader), a classroom teacher, a student support lead and a student representative. The team reviews an early-warning list generated from LMS activity and a dashboard showing an emerging performance gap in a gateway module (Gonzalez-Nucamendi et al., 2023; Pei et al., 2024). Rather than acting on alerts immediately, the team uses the protocol below to construct a shared interpretation and agree on proportionate, supportive actions.

1. Clarify the decision question: What problem are we trying to solve, and what would count as improvement?
2. Validate the signal: What data sources feed the alert? Are there missing data, anomalies, or recent assessment changes?
3. Disaggregate and contextualise: Which groups are most affected, and what contextual factors (timetable, language, workload) might explain patterns?

4. Generate and test hypotheses: Combine analytics with teacher observations and student voice; identify plausible causes.
5. Decide actions with agency safeguards: Choose interventions that invite student participation and avoid deficit labelling; specify who owns each action.
6. Communicate transparently: Explain to teachers and students what the data indicate, what they do not indicate, and how decisions were reached.
7. Review impact and learn: Revisit the data after a defined period, reflect on outcomes, and refine both practice and the model. Such structured routines align with evidence that decision-making models, authentic contexts and collaborative learning strengthen educators' data literacy, confidence and capacity to translate analysis into action (Sandoval-Ríos et al., 2025).

Building institutional infrastructure and policy alignment

Capacity building extends beyond individual skills to organisational infrastructure. Institutions must invest in integrated data platforms that break down silos and enable real-time synchronisation. Moreover, policies should align digital transformation with institutional missions; digital initiatives should be prioritised not by novelty but by their potential to enhance learning, equity and inclusion. The data-driven leadership review by Chigbu & Makapela (2025) proposed aligning data analytics with sustainable development goals (SDGs), emphasising that data-driven decisions should promote inclusivity and social justice. Essentially, leaders should therefore develop strategic plans that link AI initiatives to broader institutional and societal goals, ensuring that technological investments are purposeful and value-driven. Fundamentally, capacity-building is most effective when leaders treat AI as a learning system—developing people, routines and governance alongside tools. The case studies that follow illustrate how these capacity-building principles and ethical safeguards are enacted across diverse institutional contexts.

CASE STUDIES

In order to provide illustrative examples of the points addressed in this chapter so far, we now present five short case studies from around the world.

Each case is presented as a leadership vignette rather than as a purely technical example. In line with the chapter's organising lenses—distributed leadership, sensemaking and data use theories—the analysis highlights the leadership behaviours, mediating roles (particularly middle leaders) and governance routines required to translate AI outputs into context-sensitive pedagogical action.

Case Study 1: Predictive Analytics for Early Intervention in Higher Education

The first case study illustrates how predictive analytics can inform early intervention strategies aimed at reducing dropout in higher education. Gonzalez-Nucamendi et al. (2023) developed a machine-learning framework to identify first-year students at risk, demonstrating the value of early identification within the opening weeks of a term. From a leadership perspective, the salient lesson is the design of a supportive response system: risk flags are used to trigger advisor outreach and coordinated support (e.g., tutoring, counselling and financial aid), with clear safeguards against deterministic labelling. The case also underscores governance requirements—data quality management, regular model updating, and careful attention to how predictors (e.g., scholarship status) may reflect structural inequalities that shape both risk identification and intervention priorities. Leadership behaviours and decisions illustrated include:

- Establishing a cross-functional early-intervention team (advising, teaching, student support and analytics) to interpret alerts and coordinate action.
- Positioning middle leaders to translate risk information into department-level instructional adjustments and follow-up.
- Embedding ethical safeguards—such as bias-aware review of predictors and an emphasis on supportive, non-punitive outreach—within the intervention protocol.

Case Study 2: AI-Enabled Dashboards for Instructional Planning

The second case study focuses on LearningViz, an interactive dashboard designed to help instructors identify and address performance gaps in a mastery-based course (Pei et al., 2024). The leadership significance lies in the user-centred, interdisciplinary design process, which enabled instructors without advanced analytics expertise to examine weekly patterns, group disparities and assessment quality. Interpreted through distributed leadership, the dashboard functions as a boundary object that supports shared inquiry across teachers, middle leaders and learning designers. The case also illustrates sensemaking in action: visualisations are used to generate and test hypotheses about teaching and assessment, leading to targeted instructional responses rather than merely descriptive reporting. Leadership behaviours and decisions illustrated include:

- Co-designing analytics tools with end-users (teachers and, where appropriate, students) to ensure indicators are meaningful and actionable.
- Using middle leaders to convene regular 'data huddles' that translate dashboard patterns into instructional experiments and support strategies.
- Embedding dashboard use within cycles of inquiry, action and reflection rather than treating analytics as static performance reporting.

Case Study 3: Digital Academic Leadership in Chinese Higher Education

The third case study examines digital academic leadership (DAL) in Chinese universities, highlighting how leaders perceive and enact digital transformation (Jing et al., 2025). The study identifies four interrelated DAL dimensions—digital strategic foresight, digital resource coordination, technology awareness and digital culture building—each of which involves leadership work of aligning vision, infrastructure and organisational norms. The findings indicate that while leaders actively scan emerging technologies through partnerships, translating awareness into pedagogical innovation can be constrained by budgeting cycles and organisational fragmentation. Where cross-unit digital taskforces were established, leaders were better able to consolidate platforms and coordinate resources—an example of distributed leadership enabling system-level change (Jing et al., 2025).

The study also highlighted persistent barriers: limited ethical regulation and governance for data/AI use, high costs and unequal funding, bureaucratic hierarchies that inhibit collaboration, fragmented data ownership and delayed synchronisation that undermines trust in analytics, and expertise gaps that force outsourcing of advanced analytics work (Jing et al., 2025). Viewed through a sensemaking lens, these conditions impede shared interpretation and coordinated action, reinforcing the need for integrated infrastructures, clear governance routines and sustained capacity building. Leadership behaviours and decisions illustrated include:

- Creating cross-unit digital taskforces to coordinate platforms, data governance and resource allocation across departments.
- Using middle leaders to broker between institutional strategy and local teaching/research practices, enabling context-sensitive implementation.
- Addressing 'analytical mistrust' through integrated data infrastructures, transparent governance routines and investment in internal analytics capability.

Case Study 4: Teacher Analytics Using GPT-4 Vision

The fourth case study demonstrates teacher analytics using large multimodal models to generate automated observational feedback from classroom video (Lee et al., 2024). The leadership significance lies in using AI to augment professional learning at scale—providing timely, consistent feedback on instructional practices—while maintaining clear safeguards around consent, privacy and purpose. Interpreted through distributed leadership, the most responsible implementation positions middle leaders and instructional coaches as facilitators of reflective dialogue, ensuring AI feedback informs professional growth conversations rather than punitive performance management. Leadership behaviours and decisions illustrated include:

- Establishing clear consent, privacy and purpose statements so that video-based analytics function as professional learning rather than surveillance.
- Embedding AI feedback within coaching cycles led by middle leaders or instructional coaches who contextualise recommendations.
- Treating AI-generated observations as prompts for sensemaking—triangulated with teacher reflection and contextual knowledge—rather than as definitive judgements.

Case Study 5: Data-Driven Leadership for Sustainable Development in Higher Education

The fifth case study draws on a systematic literature review of data-driven leadership and sustainability in higher education (Chigbu & Makapela, 2025). The review proposes that analytics-informed leadership can advance sustainable development goals (SDGs) by strengthening curriculum relevance, resource allocation and student support while promoting equity and inclusion. From a leadership standpoint, the case illustrates the importance of aligning AI and data initiatives with broader societal purposes rather than narrowing attention to short-term performance metrics. It also underscores that data-driven leadership is most credible when accompanied by explicit equity commitments and organisational learning routines that evaluate both intended outcomes and unintended consequences. Leadership behaviours and decisions illustrated include:

- Framing AI and analytics as instruments for mission-driven improvement (including equity and SDG-aligned goals) rather than as ends in themselves.
- Using disaggregated data to identify inclusion gaps and to guide targeted, context-sensitive interventions.

- Institutionalising reflection and evaluation routines that track both benefits and unintended consequences of data-driven initiatives.

Table 2. Cross-case synthesis of opportunities, risks and leadership responses

Case / context	AI-enabled focus	Key opportunity	Key risk / tension	Leadership response
Case 1: Higher education early-warning (dropout) (Gonzalez-Nucamendi et al., 2023)	Added organisational change and organisational learning framing in the Introduction and theoretical framing; inserted new discussion on AI adoption as socio-technical organisational change (resistance, culture and capacity-building) and added a critical/sceptical perspective on data-driven leadership to strengthen analytical balance, while keeping the existing reference base unchanged.	Earlier, better-targeted learner support and resource allocation	Deficit labelling; biased predictions reflecting structural inequalities	Cross-functional intervention routines; middle leaders translate alerts into instructional/support actions; bias-aware review and supportive outreach
Case 2: LearningViz dashboard (Pei et al., 2024)	Strengthened teacher and student agency by adding explicit discussion of participatory design, data literacy and stakeholder oversight; foregrounded middle leaders as critical mediators throughout; added a practice-oriented leadership-team sensemaking protocol/ scenario; and expanded algorithmic bias auditing (including practical audit routines and decision safeguards).	Real-time insight into performance gaps and assessment quality	Data overload; misinterpretation; narrowing attention to visible metrics	Participatory co-design; regular 'data huddles' for collective interpretation; use within inquiry cycles rather than static reporting
Case 3: Digital academic leadership in China (Jing et al., 2025)	Revised the case studies to make the leadership behaviours and decisions explicit (including distributed roles, governance moves and sensemaking routines) and added a synthesising visual (Table 2) comparing opportunities, risks and leadership responses across cases/ contexts.	Platform consolidation, resource alignment and digital culture building	Siloed data and 'innovation islands'; governance gaps; skills shortages	Digital taskforces and shared decision rights; integrated infrastructures; sustained capacity building and culture work

continued on following page

Table 2. Continued

Case / context	AI-enabled focus	Key opportunity	Key risk / tension	Leadership response
Case 4: Teacher analytics with GPT-4 vision (Lee et al., 2024)	Applied the theoretical lenses (distributed leadership and sensemaking) more explicitly in the analysis of case studies and in the recommendations; streamlined case descriptions to reduce technical detail and maintain emphasis on the central leadership argument, improving overall coherence.	Scalable formative feedback to support professional learning	Surveillance concerns; privacy risks; erosion of autonomy	Consent and purpose governance; middle leaders facilitate coaching and sensemaking; AI outputs treated as prompts, not verdicts
Case 5: Data-driven leadership for SDGs (Chigbu & Makapela, 2025)	Added operational detail to the capacity-building recommendations by providing an illustrative data governance and AI oversight team model and a step-by-step bias-audit workflow; embedded examples and links to cases within thematic sections and added explicit sensemaking/distributed leadership enactments.	Mission-driven improvement linked to equity and societal goals	Managerialism; overemphasis on performance metrics; neglected unintended consequences	Align AI/data use with values and SDG goals; equity-focused monitoring; reflective evaluation loops and stakeholder engagement

As Table 2 demonstrates, across these cases, the 'AI' in AI-driven pedagogical leadership is less a single tool than an institutional capability. What differentiates effective practice is the presence of distributed leadership structures (including empowered middle leaders), deliberate sensemaking routines for interpreting analytics, and ethical governance mechanisms that protect agency and fairness. The future directions that follow therefore emphasise institutionalising continuous improvement cycles, strengthening hybrid intelligence, and developing policy frameworks that support responsible, human-centred AI adoption.

FUTURE DIRECTIONS AND STRATEGIC RECOMMENDATIONS

Embedding AI in continuous improvement cycles

To harness AI's potential sustainably, leaders should integrate AI tools into continuous improvement cycles. Such cycles involve iterative stages such as data collection, analysis, interpretation, action and reflection. Predictive analytics can flag students at risk or identify teaching strategies that yield high engagement (Gonzalez-

Nucamendi et al., 2023); dashboards can provide real-time feedback on implementation (Pei et al., 2024); and teacher analytics can inform professional development (Lee et al., 2024). However, the cycle must also include human sensemaking and judgement. After analysing AI outputs, teams should reflect on contextual factors, discuss ethical implications and decide on interventions. Reflection should inform subsequent data collection and model refinement. Embedding AI in improvement cycles fosters a culture of inquiry and adaptability and mitigates the risk of static or decontextualised use of AI. From a distributed leadership standpoint, these cycles function best when responsibility for interpretation and action is shared: middle leaders convene local inquiry, teachers and students contribute contextual evidence, and senior leaders provide resources and ensure ethical governance.

Preparing leaders for hybrid intelligence environments

'Hybrid intelligence' refers to systems where humans and AI collaborate, each contributing distinct strengths. In education, hybrid intelligence entails combining AI's analytical power with human empathy, ethical reasoning and contextual knowledge. Preparing leaders for hybrid environments involves developing competencies in collaboration, interpretation and ethical judgment. Leaders should be trained to interrogate AI predictions, identify biases and communicate insights clearly. They should also cultivate distributed leadership structures that empower teachers, students and technologists to share responsibility for AI integration. Hybrid intelligence requires sensemaking across different knowledge domains and coordination across organisational levels. Encouraging reflective practice, collaborative problem solving and participatory design can strengthen hybrid intelligence. Practically, hybrid intelligence in education depends on structured sensemaking: leaders must create forums where algorithmic recommendations are interrogated, explained and ethically weighed alongside professional judgement and student voice.

Developing national frameworks and policy guidelines

Policy frameworks at the national and regional levels are critical for scaling AI-driven leadership. These frameworks should articulate principles of fairness, transparency, accountability and inclusivity, drawing on international guidelines such as UNESCO's AI and Education and the European Commission's ethical guidelines (Zhu et al., 2025). They should provide standards for data quality, algorithmic transparency and user consent, and establish mechanisms for auditing and redress. National frameworks can also outline qualifications and competencies for AI-driven leaders, ensuring that training programmes align with professional standards. In contexts like the United Arab Emirates, national AI strategies and digital transformation plans should explicitly address educational leadership, encouraging universities and schools to adopt ethical AI tools and invest in capacity building. Such frameworks can also encourage operational practices—such as mandatory privacy impact assessments, routine bias auditing, and transparent documentation of model purpose and limitations—that enable responsible use beyond aspirational principles.

Fostering international collaboration and research

AI in education is a global phenomenon, and cross-national collaboration can accelerate learning and innovation. Comparative studies across contexts—such as the digital academic leadership research in China (Jing et al., 2025), early-warning systems in Latin America (Gonzalez-Nucamendi et al., 2023), learning analytics dashboards in the United States (Pei et al., 2024) and sustainability-oriented data leadership in Europe (Chigbu & Makapela, 2025) — reveal both universal challenges and context-specific solutions. International organisations can convene forums for sharing best practices, developing common ethical standards and coordinating research agendas. Collaborative networks can also support capacity building in low-resource contexts, ensuring that AI benefits do not exacerbate global educational inequalities.

CONCLUSION

This chapter has argued that the future of educational innovation lies in cultivating AI-driven pedagogical leadership, where leaders harness AI tools — predictive analytics, adaptive learning systems, dashboards and teacher analytics — to inform and transform decision-making. AI offers significant opportunities to personalise learning, identify risk early, enhance teacher development and optimise resources (Pei et al., 2024). However, these opportunities are accompanied by ethical challenges (Zhu et al., 2025), risks of technocentrism and erosion of teacher autonomy (Duan & Zhao, 2024), and persistent capacity gaps (Jing et al., 2025). Effective AI integration therefore requires leaders to develop data and AI literacy, establish ethical governance structures, foster cross-functional collaboration, invest in infrastructural alignment and embrace distributed leadership and sensemaking frameworks. Framed as organisational change, AI integration depends on culture-building, capacity development and the mediating work of middle leaders who translate strategy into pedagogical routines (Ni ă & Gu u, 2023; Jing et al., 2025).

The case studies presented illustrate how AI can be used to support early interventions, instructional planning, digital transformation, teacher development and sustainability. From predictive models that enable timely support for at-risk students (Gonzalez-Nucamendi et al., 2023) to dashboards that empower instructors to address achievement gaps (Pei et al., 2024), and from digital academic leadership in Chinese universities (Jing et al., 2025) to teacher analytics using GPT-4 vision (Lee et al., 2024), these examples demonstrate both the promise and the complexity of AI-driven leadership. They reveal that technology alone does not drive change; rather, change emerges when human leaders interpret, adapt and act on data ethically and thoughtfully.

Ultimately, AI-driven pedagogical leadership must be grounded in human values, collaborative intelligence and strategic foresight. Leaders must act as translators who turn data points into pedagogical insight, balancing algorithmic recommendations with local context and professional judgment. By cultivating AI-driven leadership, educational institutions can navigate the rapidly evolving digital landscape, promote equity and inclusion, and prepare learners for a world where data and AI are integral to knowledge creation and social participation. Operationally, this entails participatory design and oversight that protects teacher and student agency, transparent decision rules, and routine bias auditing and review processes that keep fairness and accountability visible in everyday practice (Pei et al., 2024; Zhu et al., 2025).

REFERENCES

Abukhalaf, S., Charles, T., & Hill, C. (2024). The Metaverse as a Virtual Learning Space: Perceptions from the UAE. *Journal of Ecohumanism*, *3*(5), 1037–1052. DOI: 10.62754/joe.v3i5.3954

Azzam, A., & Charles, T. (2025). K-12 STEM Teachers' Experiences with Artificial Intelligence. *TEM Journal, 14*(1), 463. https://doi.org/DOI: 10.18421/TEM141-41

Bañeres, D., Rodríguez-González, M. E., Guerrero-Roldán, A. E., & Cortadas, P. (2023). An early warning system to identify and intervene online dropout learners. *International Journal of Educational Technology in Higher Education*, *20*(1), 3. DOI: 10.1186/s41239-022-00371-5

Bowden, A. B., Danks, A., Rodriguez, V., Yang, H., & Davis, R. (2023). Examining State and District Policy and Resource Allocation to Support Digital Learning. *Peabody Journal of Education*, *98*(1), 6–25. DOI: 10.1080/0161956X.2023.2160105

Charles, T. (2025). AI in Professional Development for English Language Teachers. In Ali, M., Anwar, M., Fazal, S., & Ayyaz, S. (Eds.), *AI Applications for English Language Learning* (pp. 73–92). IGI Global., DOI: 10.4018/979-8-3693-9077-1.ch004

Charles, T., & Alshamsi, A. (2025). Navigating Challenges in Technology Integration for Inclusive Classrooms: Insights for Pre-Service Teachers. In Ajani, O. (Ed.), *Empowering Pre-Service Teachers to Enhance Inclusive Education Through Technology* (pp. 87–126). IGI Global., DOI: 10.4018/979-8-3693-8759-7.ch004

Charles, T., & Hill, C. (2025). Micro-Credentials and AI in Higher Education: Transforming Professional Development. In ElSayary, A. (Ed.), *Prompt Engineering and Generative AI Applications for Teaching and Learning* (pp. 1–14). IGI Global., DOI: 10.4018/979-8-3693-7332-3.ch001

Charles, T., & Papadaki, M. (2025). Ethical Leadership in Technology Integration and Digital Education. In Soles, B., & Meyerott, T. (Eds.), *Diverse Leadership Perspectives in Education: From K-12 to Higher Education* (pp. 437–454). IGI Global., DOI: 10.4018/979-8-3693-6115-3.ch016

Charles, T., Zoelfakar, S., & Sebastian, S. (2025). Micro-Credentials in Vocational and Professional Training. In Durak, G., & Cankaya, S. (Eds.), *Integrating Micro-Credentials With AI in Open Education* (pp. 217–250). IGI Global., DOI: 10.4018/979-8-3693-5488-9.ch010

Chigbu, B. I., & Makapela, S. L. (2025). Data-driven leadership in higher education: Advancing sustainable development goals and inclusive transformation. *Sustainability (Basel), 17*(7), 3116. DOI: 10.3390/su17073116

Crompton, H., & Burke, D. (2023). Artificial intelligence in higher education: The state of the field. *International Journal of Educational Technology in Higher Education, 20*(1), 22. DOI: 10.1186/s41239-023-00392-8

Duan, H., & Zhao, W. (2024). The effects of educational artificial intelligence-powered applications on teachers' perceived autonomy, professional development for online teaching, and digital burnout. *International Review of Research in Open and Distance Learning, 25*(3), 57–76. DOI: 10.19173/irrodl.v25i3.7659

Ghamrawi, N., & Tamim, M., R. (. (2023). A typology for digital leadership in higher education: The case of a large-scale mobile technology initiative (using tablets). *Education and Information Technologies, 28*(6), 7089–7110. DOI: 10.1007/s10639-022-11483-w PMID: 36465422

Gonzalez-Nucamendi, A., Noguez, J., Neri, L., Robledo-Rella, V., & García-Castelán, R. M. G. (2023). Predictive analytics study to determine undergraduate students at risk of dropout. In *Frontiers in Education* (Vol. 8, p. 1244686). Frontiers Media SA. https://doi.org/DOI: 10.3389/feduc.2023.1244686

Jing, M., Guo, Z., Wu, X., Yang, Z., & Wang, X. (2025). Higher education digital academic leadership: Perceptions and practices from Chinese University Leaders. *Education Sciences, 15*(5), 606. DOI: 10.3390/educsci15050606

Kuleto, V., Ilić, M., Dumangiu, M., Ranković, M., Martins, O. M. D., Păun, D., & Mihoreanu, L. (2021). Exploring Opportunities and Challenges of Artificial Intelligence and Machine Learning in Higher Education Institutions. *Sustainability (Basel), 13*(18), 10424. Advance online publication. DOI: 10.3390/su131810424

Lee, U., Jeong, Y., Koh, J., Byun, G., Lee, Y., Lee, H., Eun, S., Moon, J., Lim, C., & Kim, H. (2024). I see you: Teacher analytics with GPT-4 vision-powered observational assessment. *Smart Learning Environments, 11*(1), 48. DOI: 10.1186/s40561-024-00335-4

Masiello, I., Mohseni, Z., Palma, F., Nordmark, S., Augustsson, H., & Rundquist, R. (2024). A current overview of the use of learning analytics dashboards. *Education Sciences, 14*(1), 82. DOI: 10.3390/educsci14010082

Ni ă, V., & Gu u, I. (2023). The role of leadership and digital transformation in higher education students' work engagement. *International Journal of Environmental Research and Public Health, 20*(6), 5124. DOI: 10.3390/ijerph20065124 PMID: 36982029

Pei, B., Cheng, Y., Ambrose, A., Dziadula, E., Xing, W., & Lu, J. (2024). LearningViz: A dashboard for visualizing, analyzing and closing learning performance gaps—a case study approach. *Smart Learning Environments, 11*(1), 56. DOI: 10.1186/s40561-024-00346-1

Sandoval-Ríos, F., Gajardo-Poblete, C., & López-Núñez, J. A. (2025). Role of data literacy training for decision-making in teaching practice: a systematic review. In *Frontiers in Education* (Vol. 10, p. 1485821). Frontiers Media SA. https://doi.org/ DOI: 10.3389/feduc.2025.1485821

Sposato, M. (2025). Artificial intelligence in educational leadership: A comprehensive taxonomy and future directions. *International Journal of Educational Technology in Higher Education, 22*(1), 20. DOI: 10.1186/s41239-025-00517-1

Yuting, Z., Adams, D., & Lee, K. C. S. (2025). A systematic review of E-leadership and its effects on student learning in higher education. *Management in Education, 39*(2), 78–88. DOI: 10.1177/08920206221111668

Zhu, H., Sun, Y., & Yang, J. (2025). Towards responsible artificial intelligence in education: A systematic review on identifying and mitigating ethical risks. *Humanities & Social Sciences Communications, 12*(1), 1–14. DOI: 10.1057/s41599-025-05252-6

Chapter 14
Hybrid School Models: Blending Human and Machine Intelligence in Leadership

Satya Subrahmanyam
http://orcid.org/0000-0003-0441-2742
Holy Spirit University of Kaslik, Lebanon

Nada Sarkis
http://orcid.org/0000-0003-3397-1201
Holy Spirit University of Kaslik, Lebanon

ABSTRACT

This chapter examines the integration of artificial intelligence (AI) into educational leadership through hybrid school models that unite human and machine intelligence. It explores how AI-enhanced tools support data-driven decision-making, operational efficiency, and personalized learning, while human leaders provide empathy, ethics, and strategic vision. Grounded in sociotechnical systems theory and augmented intelligence, the chapter analyzes enabling infrastructures like adaptive learning platforms and AI dashboards. Drawing on global case studies, it highlights both benefits and challenges—such as algorithmic bias and digital equity—emphasizing the need for ethical governance, professional development, and stakeholder trust. Ultimately, it envisions a future where hybrid leadership models foster inclusive, responsive, and future-ready schools.

DOI: 10.4018/979-8-3373-4908-4.ch014

1. INTRODUCTION

1.1 AI-Driven Transformation in Educational Leadership

The leadership of education is changing radically due to the development of artificial intelligence (AI) and other technologies based on data. AI is no longer used in experiments but has become integrated into basic educational functions like student evaluation, resource distribution, curriculum development, and institutional leadership. In this regard, educational leaders are no longer merely pedagogical visionaries or administrative coordinators, but more and more of them are being called upon to play the strategic stewardship role of sociotechnical systems. According to recent research, the use of AI-powered tools can assist leaders with the accuracy of decisions, predictive insights, and evidence-based leadership practices (Sposato, 2025). Such a transformation also will require re-evaluation of leadership roles, responsibilities, and competencies, especially regarding the area of ethics, accountability, and decisions that are human-centered.

The increased pace of the digital transformation after the COVID-19 pandemic has only increased the necessity to have adaptive and resilient leadership models. School leaders are now to deal with uncertainty, complexity and rapid change, and continuity of learning and institutional stability. Artificial intelligence (AI) change is therefore not a technological change but a kind of structural rearrangement of educational leadership practice where data-driven wisdom is seen as a complement but not an alternative to professional judgment (Berkovich, 2025).

1.2 Rationale for Hybrid School Models in the Post-Digital Era

The hybrid school models were the strategic reaction to the restrictions of the traditional school system and the totally online school system. Hybrid models combine in-person teaching with online platforms, learning analytics, and AI-based products to assist in personalized and adaptable paths to learning. Such models are also becoming less of an option and more of a necessity in the post-digital education age of technology that is not something new but a matter of course (Raptis et al., 2025). Hybrid schooling provides institutions with the ability to serve various needs of learners, improve the continuity of instruction, and use data to achieve continuous improvement.

As a leadership concept, hybrid models allow redesigning the organizational framework and educational practices and maintaining the relational and social aspects of education. The studies have revealed that well guided hybrid systems have the potential to enhance teacher autonomy, student engagement, and institutional responsiveness (Zeng et al., 2025). Hybrid schooling is also very heavily reliant on leadership capacity in order to balance technology integration with pedagogical values, equity considerations, and long-term institutional goals.

1.3 Convergence of Human Judgment and Machine Intelligence

The intersection of human judgment and machine intelligence is the most critical element of AI-enabled educational leadership. Artificial intelligence (AI) systems are efficient in terms of processing massive amounts of data, revealing trends, and providing insights into the future, and human leaders, in turn, add contextual know-how, moral reasoning, and emotional intelligence to decision-making. Such convergence is a movement towards augmented leadership, in which AI is a cognitive support system, instead of the human agency replacement (Li, 2025).

As educational leaders continue to depend on AI-based dashboards, predictive analytics, and decision-support systems to inform policy decisions and operational strategies. However, it is the human factor that is, finally, responsible to interpret, to align values and render morally accountable. The researchers state that this human-Artificial intelligence collaboration should be carefully planned so that it ensures a transparent, fair, and inclusive process, especially in the case of high-stakes educational decisions that may impact students and personnel (Sposato, 2025). As a result, the effectiveness of leadership in the AI age lies in the possibility to critically analyze the product of the algorithms and combine it with professional knowledge and organizational principles.

1.4 Chapter Objectives, Scope, and Structure

This chapter is expected to accomplish three main purposes. To begin with, it aims at contextualizing AI-based change in the current educational leadership and showcasing the way new technologies are transforming the current leadership practices and expectations. Second, it explores the justification of the hybrid type of school in the post-digital period in terms of its strategic utility in terms of resilience, innovation, and equity. Third, it theorizes the meeting of human judgment and machine intelligence, providing a theoretical context in the interpretation of AI-enhanced leadership in educational institutions.

The chapter is written in the context of K-12 and higher education and is based on recent empirical studies, systematic reviews, and conceptual frameworks published in the past two years. Ethical considerations, leadership competencies, and institutional readiness are discussed in the course of it. Structurally, the chapter moves towards theoretical premises on to applied models of leadership as well as illustrative examples and ends with practical implications and recommendations on how educational leaders will manage AI-enabled and hybrid learning spaces.

2. CONCEPTUAL FOUNDATIONS OF HYBRID SCHOOL MODELS

The theoretical premises of hybrid school paradigms lie deep in the changing nature of educational leadership in the conditions of intensive technological development. Conventionally, school leadership has been largely humanistic in nature with reliance on professional judgment, experiential knowledge and interpersonal influence to make decisions and shape organizational development. Although these qualities cannot be replaced, the growing access to data, learning analytics, and artificial intelligence (AI) systems has changed the leadership expectations. The modern educational leadership is increasingly moving in the direction of AI-enhanced models, where computer-based systems are used to help the leader decode more complicated information and predict trends and act proactively to the challenges posed by an institution (Subrahmanyam, 2025). This change is an indication of a larger shift toward a leadership style that is not guided by intuition but empowers evidence and supports it through a dramatically greater system.

2.1 Evolution from Human-Centric to AI-Augmented Leadership

School leadership development could be perceived as continuation instead of substitution of human authority. Early digital leadership was concerned with adoption of technology and management of infrastructure, and AI-augmented leadership is concerned with intelligent decision support systems, predictive analytics, and adaptive systems. It is shown that the AI tools currently help leaders in their enrollment prediction, identification of student risk, teacher performance analysis, and optimization of resources (Subrahmanyam et al., 2024). They can be best utilized where they are integrated into leadership models that maintain a sense of ethical rationale, situational knowledge, and trust.

Table 1. Evolution of School Leadership Models

Dimension	Human-Centric Leadership	AI-Augmented Leadership
Decision basis	Experience and professional judgment	Data-informed and predictive insights
Role of technology	Administrative support	Strategic decision augmentation
Accountability	Primarily human	Human with algorithmic support
Ethical responsibility	Implicit	Explicit and governance-driven

2.2 Defining Hybrid Intelligence in Educational Contexts

In this changing leadership paradigm, the concept of hybrid intelligence has become very prominent. Hybrid intelligence happens to be the deliberate merger of human cognitive, emotional, and ethical astuteness with machine intelligence to advance the quality of decisions and business efficacy. Hybrid intelligence can be used in educational settings to help a leader improve their coping with complexity by balancing the computational capabilities of AI and human interpretive and moral reasoning (Li, 2025). This methodology recognizes that although AI systems are very effective in pattern recognition and processing large amounts of data, they will be contextually insensitive, value blind and socially unaware, which is not desirable in educational settings where diversity and equity matters are highly relevant and developmental objectives are greatly valued.

Hybrid intelligence is therefore a conceptual support of hybrid school models. It allows leaders to create technologically sophisticated, but pedagogically based, learning environments where AI applications would not be isolated products of operational efficiency, but instead in service to the value of education.

2.3 Automation, Augmentation, and Collaboration

An important difference in the discourse of hybrid leadership is that of automation, augmentation, and collaboration. Automation is the process of assigning mundane or repetitive tasks to the machines completely, e.g. creating a timetable or recording attendance. Augmentation is when AI systems augment human decisions with information or advice, and collaboration is when there is a stronger interaction between humans and AI systems, where co-creation of solutions is produced (Zeng et al., 2025). The failure to comprehend these differences may result in under-use of technology or hostility towards the use of technology.

Table 2. Distinction Between Automation, Augmentation, and Collaboration

Concept	Description	Leadership Implication
Automation	Tasks performed entirely by AI	Efficiency-focused leadership
Augmentation	AI supports human decisions	Evidence-informed leadership
Collaboration	Human–AI co-decision processes	Strategic and adaptive leadership

The models of the hybrid schools are mostly performed in the augmentation and collaboration areas, with the leadership agency kept at the center, and technology as a facilitator, not a regulation.

2.4 Systems Thinking and Socio-Technical Perspectives

It is also important to have a socio-technical and systems thinking approach in understanding hybrid school leadership. Schools are complex adaptive systems whereby technology, people, policies and culture dynamically interact. The socio-technical theory stresses that technological innovation cannot exist outside the social organizations, professional norms and institutional values (Raptis et al., 2025). In this way, hybrid leadership implies adapting technical systems to human practices so that the introduction of AI can improve but not destroy educational systems.

Systems thinking implies that leaders should think of AI as one of the components of a network that impacts teaching, learning, governance, and relationships with stakeholders. This methodology supports the demand of whole leadership strategies to incorporate technological design, capacity building, and ethical governance. Therefore, hybrid school designs rise as a new type of teaching not only in the form of blended instructions but an organizational structure in which human and machine intelligence are carefully coordinated to provide sustainable educational change.

3. HUMAN INTELLIGENCE IN EDUCATIONAL LEADERSHIP

3.1 Cognitive, Emotional, Ethical, and Relational Dimensions of Leadership

The area of effective educational leadership is based on human intelligence, especially in the situation where there are uncertainty, diversity, and moral responsibility. In its most basic sense, leadership intelligence involves set of cognitive abilities, including sense-making, strategic thinking, problem solving; emotional abilities, including empathy, self-control and motivation; ethical abilities, including value-based and fair reasoning; and relational abilities, including trust-building and collaboration. In modern leadership research, the two dimensions have been highlighted as highly interdependent and play a role in how leaders are perceived to interpret information, act upon stakeholders, and influence institutional change (Northouse, 2021). Emotional and ethical intelligence are particularly relevant in educational environments, where leadership choice has a direct impact on the development and well-being of learners, which supports the human-centered culture of leadership.

Human leaders, unlike algorithmic systems, have the capability to read social cues, negotiate meaning, and change behavior to subtle interpersonal situations. These attributes are essential in schools which are not technical organizations but social organizations. By way of this, human intelligence offers the interpretive and moral foundation that is required to enable responsible leadership in the education sector.

3.2 Professional Judgment, Contextual Reasoning, and Moral Agency

Educational leadership is characterized by professional judgment which is the capacity of leaders to be able to synthesize experience, evidence, and values in the quest to make decisions. Contextual reasoning enables the leaders to understand data and policies within the norms of the culture, the expectations of the community, and the history of the institution. Moral agency also makes human agency leadership stand out because it allows leaders to be responsible on the decisions, make ethical justifications and be answerable to the stakeholders (Argyropoulou & Lintzerakou, 2025). Such abilities are especially important in complicated and uncertain circumstances where a set of rules cannot work out.

According to recent studies, we have entered the era when the effectiveness of leadership is determined by the ability to critically interpret the facts instead of directly implementing them (Berkovich, 2025). This requires human leaders to evaluate the applicability, constraints and consequences of data and strike a balance between quantitative and qualitative knowledge. The moral agency makes sure that the choices of leaders are not out of step with the values of education like equity, inclusion and student welfare - all aspects of education that cannot be entirely programmed into the algorithms.

3.3 Limitations of Exclusively Human-Centered Leadership in Complex Systems

Although human intelligence is unavoidable, dependence on entirely human centered leadership exhibits shortcomings in the ever more complicated education systems. Schools are currently functioning in networks of policies, technologies, accountability practices, and diverse needs of learners. The volume and rate of data creation is many times beyond the capacities of human cognition and leaders struggle to see patterns, predict threats, or act ahead of the game without technology (Sposato, 2025). Human decision-making may also be limited by cognitive overload, limited rationality and bias, especially when faced with conditions of time and uncertainty.

Human leadership might have challenges in finding consistency and scalability at large or distributed educational systems. According to the research in the field of systems leadership, complex tasks need the tools that can facilitate holistic analysis and longitudinal monitoring, which AI and analytics can perform with great benefits (Raptis et al., 2025). These restrictions do not reduce the worth of human leadership but just point to the necessity of complimentary types of intelligence that can enhance human capacity within complex environments.

3.4 Leadership Competencies Essential for Hybrid Environments

The interplay of human and machine intelligence that entails human and machine intelligence interacting in the same space requires a broader range of leadership skills. In addition to conventional teaching and relationship skills, leaders will have to acquire digital literacy, ability to interpret data, and awareness of ethical issues concerning the use of AI. Digital leadership competence entails the awareness of the functioning of AI systems, their limitations, and informed decision-making on whether to adopt them and to govern them (Zeng et al., 2025). Ethical competence is also important since leaders have to deal with problems of data privacy, algorithm biases and transparency.

Other vital competencies in a hybrid situation are adaptive capacity and learning orientation. Leaders have to be ready to constantly learn and explore new tools, as well as assist staff in the technological changeover. Notably, attention should still be given to relational and emotional intelligence which will allow leaders to mediate change and help establish trust and a culture of collaboration between human actors and technological systems. Hybrid leadership is therefore not a revolution of human intelligence but the evolution of the same- where cognitive capacity, emotional capacity and ethical capacity is enhanced by intelligent incorporation with intelligent technologies.

4. MACHINE INTELLIGENCE IN SCHOOL LEADERSHIP

4.1 AI Applications in Educational Administration and Governance

The intelligence of machine has gradually become entrenched within the administrative and governance roles of schools and how leaders handle resources, track performance and hold schools accountable. Application of AI is now widely applied in fields like student enrollments management, scheduling, budget, compliance reporting, and quality assurance. Such systems help school leaders to work with significant amounts of administrative data in a more efficient way and minimize the number of people working manually and enhance the accuracy of the operations (Sposato, 2025). On the governing level, AI tools help in evidenced-based policy-making because they accumulate institutional data and coordinate it with regulatory and strategic goals. Consequently, focus on leadership can be changed to strategic planning and pedagogical leadership as opposed to daily administration.

Notably, AI-powered governance is not something that will remove human control. Rather, it brings about new types of collective responsibility, in which leaders should make sure that algorithmic systems do not conflict with the values of the institutions, the law, or moral principles. The reframing of the role of machine intelligence as an infrastructural element of leadership and not an independent decision-maker.

4.2 Predictive Analytics, Decision-Support Systems, and Adaptive Planning

Predictive analytics and decision support systems are one of the most noticeable changes towards which machine intelligence applied in school leadership. Predictive models enable leaders to foresee trends like student dropout rates, teacher turnover, changes in enrolments and resource requirements. These systems would increase the ability of leaders to make proactive and adaptive plans because they can easily reveal patterns that are not obvious to human decision-makers (Subrahmanyam, 2024). Predictive analytics may drive early interventions on at-risk students or staffing based on the anticipated changes in enrolment.

Decision-support systems combine results of various data sources and deliver actionable information in form of simulations, alerts, or recommendations. These systems do not supplant the judgment of leadership but offer systematic contributions that will help them make better and more timely decisions. In active learning systems, dynamic planning enabled by AI can enable schools to react more efficiently to uncertainty, policy changes, and external shocks, which strengthens the organizational resilience (Raptis et al., 2025).

4.3 Role of Generative AI, Learning Analytics, and Intelligent Dashboards

The recent developments in generative AI have broadened the area of machine intelligence in school leadership. Generative AI systems are useful to help leaders write policy documents, summarize institutional reports, create communication resources, and professional development materials. In a responsible manner, these tools can improve productivity and the clarity of communication and allow the leader to concentrate on relational and strategic activities (Zeng et al., 2025). They should also be governed carefully so that they are not overused, or the outputs of AI are embraced blindly.

Intelligent dashboards and learning analytics serve as a complement to one another through the translation of difficult data to understandable visual information. Dashboards are made with real-time information about student performance, attendance, and teacher interaction and resource use, which allows leaders to check the health of their institutions in a single glance (Li, 2025). These tools contribute to the continuous improvement process by rendering the performance trends visible and helping leadership teams to have a data-driven conversation. Collectively, the combination of generative AI, analytics, and dashboards represents a systemic ecosystem of machine intelligence that improves the level of awareness and responsiveness about leadership.

4.4 Capabilities and Constraints of Machine Intelligence in Leadership Contexts

Even with its increasing influence, machine intelligence has some inherent limitations that provide it with little ability to act independently in leadership situations. AI systems are good at recognizing patterns, scaling, and speed, but they do not understand the context, make moral judgements, and are not sensitive to emotions. They work with past information and pre-established goals that can be biased or incapable of considering the changes in social and cultural dynamics (Bhardwaj, 2025). Therefore, AI generated suggestions must be critically interpreted by humans to prevent unintended consequences, especially in making high stakes decisions about education.

Machine intelligence relies on the quality of data, system design, and governance structures. Unfinished or incomplete data may produce false results, which strengthen injustices instead of combating them. The issue of data privacy, transparency, and accountability also comes with ethical issues that limit the independent utilization of AI in school leadership (Berkovich, 2025). The limitations highlight the significance of bringing machine intelligence in as an aiding but not as a replacing force.

Figure 1. Machine Intelligence in School Leadership

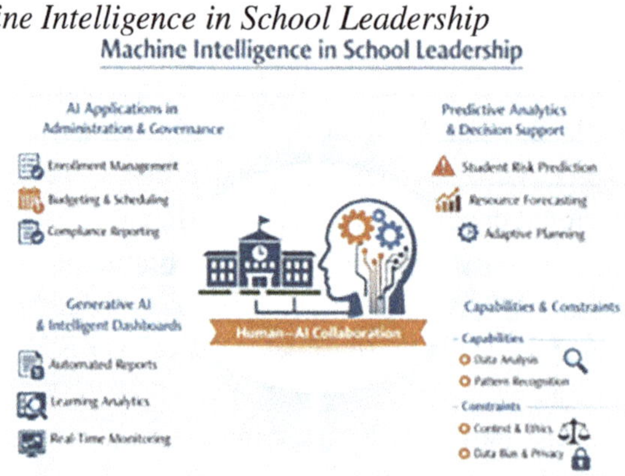

Machine intelligence can be used to enhance human thinking ability, which is the main strength of hybrid leadership models, and is not used to substitute human judgment. Effective school leadership would then be the result of a measured combination of the machine possibilities and human intelligence when leaders still have the interpretive powers, morality, and relationships agency. Machine intelligence is the most useful in case it is entrenched in a larger context of leadership that upholds educational values, contextual awareness, and shared responsibility.

5. DESIGNING HYBRID LEADERSHIP ARCHITECTURES IN SCHOOLS

The fast adoption of artificial intelligence (AI) in schools is transforming the leadership, governing, and management of schools. Instead of overtaking human leadership, AI is becoming more of a complementary factor that will enhance decision-making, coordination and strategic visioning. The development of hybrid leadership structures in the school thus involves a conscious convergence of human judgment, moral accountability, and machine intelligence in order to improve the effectiveness of the institutions without sacrificing the primary human principles of schooling.

5.1 Human–AI Interaction Models for School Leadership

The concept of hybrid leadership in schools is based on the effective models of human-AI interaction, where AI systems are the means of support, but not the decision-makers. School leaders keep their agency in strategic and moral decisions, whereas AI adds analytical skills like foresight and predictive ideas, trends, and surveillance in such models. According to research, human-in-the-loop systems are crucial and guarantee that AI outputs are decoded, verified, and contextualized by educational leaders (Shrestha et al., 2019). The use of AI-based dashboards may be able to deliver principals early warning of student disengagement or teacher workload imbalance, but the final interventions have to be based on contextual knowledge, empathy, and professional judgment. Such co-working results in developing confidence in AI systems and countering the risks linked to automation bias.

5.2 Decision-Making Frameworks Integrating Human Oversight and AI Insights

The architectures of effective hybrid leadership are based on the frameworks of decision-making that combine AI generated information with human control. These systems usually integrate both ethical and pedagogical and analytical data. Big data can be used to facilitate evidence-based decision-making because AI can be used to process substantial amounts of data concerning attendance, learning outcomes, and resource use. Yet, researchers warn that algorithmic recommendation must not be perceived as neutral or flawless, and it might have biases or incomplete data (Williamson and Eynon, 2020). In turn, hybrid structures focus on transparency, explainability, and accountability by allowing school leaders to question AI outputs with criticality. Having decision protocols, which involve justification, consultation with peers, and human validation, can be useful in ensuring that AI-informed decisions are consistent with the institutional values and equity objectives.

5.3 Distributed Leadership Supported by Intelligent Systems

Distributed leadership models are also supported by hybrid leadership architectures that allow increasing the extent of participation in the decision making process. The technology of intelligent systems helps in cooperation between the principals, departmental heads, teachers and administrative personnel as it offers common access to information and knowledge. As an example, AI-assisted platforms can be used to assist instructional leaders determine the need of professional development within departments and teachers can apply analytics to change instructional approaches in a collaborative way. This is technological mediation sustaining a transition between hierarchical leadership and network and participatory forms of governance (Subrahmanyam, 2025). With a reduced amount of information asymmetries, improved coordination, AI will allow allocating leadership roles to distribute them more efficiently among the school members to promote collective ownership and organizational learning.

5.4 Organizational Redesign for Hybrid Governance Structures

The adoption of hybrid leadership means that the organization needs to be redesigned with new roles, workflows, and governance mechanisms. To prevent risks of data privacy invasion, schools should formulate policies to outline the extent of AI application, specify the rights of decisions, and provide ethical protection. It may require new functions, like data stewards or AI coordinators, to control the quality of data, system integrity and adherence to privacy policies. The leadership development initiatives should be re-focused to develop data literacy and algorithmic awareness, ethical competence in school leaders (Akgun & Greenhow, 2022). Iterative feedback loop should also be enabled by organizational structures, where leaders must evaluate the effect of AI-supported decisions and adjust the practices as time goes by. This adaptive governance is important in order to make sure that the hybrid leadership is sensitive to changing needs in education and social expectations.

Figure 2. Designing Hybrid Leadership Architectures in Schools

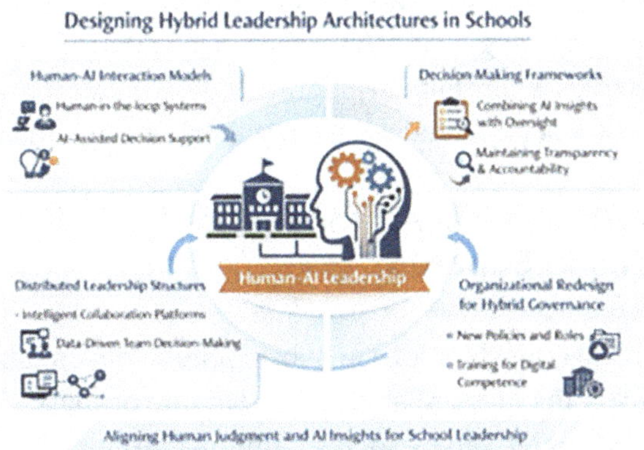

The need to develop hybrid leadership formations in schools is one of the strategic responses to the expanding role of AI in education. Through the combination of the human-AI interaction models, effective decision-making systems, distributed leadership, and restructured forms of governance, schools will be able to embrace the analytical capabilities of AI and preserve human values and professional autonomy. Hybrid leadership is not a technology but an institutional and moral adherence to apply intelligence, human and artificial, to serve educational excellence.

6. POLICY AND ETHICAL DIMENSIONS OF HYBRID SCHOOL LEADERSHIP

6.1 Governance, Accountability, and Transparency in AI-Assisted Leadership

Having introduced artificial intelligence to the school leadership changes the very framework of governance, bringing up the essential issues of accountability and transparency. In hybrid school leadership model, the prerogative of making decisions is no longer confined to the human leaders but is meditated by the algorithmic system that produces recommendations, forecasts and performance indicators. This transition requires powerful governance systems that will keep decisions that have been achieved with the help of AI explainable, auditable, and consistent with educational values. The issue of transparency is especially crucial in the school setting, where parties such as teachers, parents, students and regulators should get acquainted with how evidence-based information affects the policy of admissions, resource distribution, student evaluation and employee evaluation. Current literature highlights the fact that absent responsibility structures, AI systems are likely to blur responsibility and introduce what has been described as the accountability gap in algorithmic governance (Yang & Li, 2020; Wirtz et al., 2020). Hybrid leadership thus entails having strict roles where human judgment can override the algorithmic advice and accountability of leaders to the results obtained through the assistance of AI.

6.2 Ethical Leadership, Algorithmic Bias, and Data Justice in Schools

The focus of ethical considerations in hybrid school leadership is on algorithmic bias, and data justice. Education-related AI systems are primarily based on previous data, which can be characterized by social, cultural, and economic disparities existing today. The use of such data blindly can be relied upon to increase bias based on socioeconomic status, gender, ethnicity, or disability, weakening the objectives of equity and inclusion in education. Ethical leadership in hybrid settings entails not merely knowledge of these dangers, but also active approaches to alleviating them by means of bias audits, encompassing data practices that are inclusive, and ethical review committees (Williamson & Eynon, 2020). Data justice also goes further to apply ethical responsibility by underlining the recipient of data-driven decision-making and those who may be sidelined by it. Leaders of the school have to make sure that data gathering, and analytics is aligned to the pedagogical betterment and student well-being but not to monitoring or managerial oversight. It is becoming a growing consensus among scholars that ethical AI in education should be based on human-centered values, and leaders should be moral agents who critically question the results of algorithms and not follow them (Holmes et al., 2019).

6.3 Policy Frameworks Supporting Responsible AI Adoption in Education

Online leadership requires harmonized policy frameworks that can inform relevant AI implementation at institutional and systemic levels. UNESCO and the OECD have issued normative issues that focus on human monitoring, inclusivity and sustainability of AI implementation in education. The Recommendation of the Ethics of Artificial Intelligence by UNESCO points at education as one of the key areas where AI should improve human decision-making and professional autonomy, not substitute them (UNESCO, 2021). On the national and institutional level, policy attention has shifted towards data management, ethical acquisition of AI technology, professional learning of school leaders, and mobilization of school leaders and communities in making decisions. These models acknowledge that leadership capability is a major factor in effective and ethical implementation of AI. A lack of supportive policies can lead school leaders to a more disjointed approach, solutions based on vendors, or compliance-oriented approaches which do not take advantage of the transformative potential of AI (Selwyn, 2022).

6.4 Regulatory Implications for School Systems and Ministries of Education

The emergence of mixed forms of leadership also has great regulatory consequences to school systems and education ministries. Regulators have a role to strike a balance between innovation and protection, whereby the use of AI in schools adheres to the provisions of data protection laws, child rights conventions, as well as new AI regulatory provisions. Such events as the Artificial Intelligence Act of the European Union are indicators of a shift towards risk-based regulation, according to which educational AI systems might be scrutinized more thoroughly because they affect the life chances of learners (Veale & Borgesius, 2021). In the case of ministries of education, this regulatory environment demands new AI literacy, oversight as well as intersectoral coordination capabilities. The hybrid school leadership therefore functions in a multi-level governance setting, in which the school leaders have to tune the institutional practices in accordance with national regulations and international standards. This is highlighted by the policy and ethical aspects of the leadership of hybrids school, which reveal that technological development in education does not represent a technical issue, but a highly normative issue, which requires strategic, ethical, and socially responsible leadership.

7. IMPLEMENTATION CHALLENGES AND CHANGE MANAGEMENT

7.1 Cultural Resistance and Trust in AI-Mediated Leadership

Cultural resistance by the educators and administrators is one of the biggest challenges in the implementation of hybrid school leadership models. Schools are highly value-oriented organizations in which trust, professional autonomy, and relational leadership are the primary aspects of daily practice. The use of AI-mediated decision-making can be viewed as the menace to professional judgment with the threat of surveillance, dehumanization, or control loss. Research shows that the opposition to technologies is not always due to resistance to technology as such but is rooted in the fear of the way AI technologies are deployed and regulated (Selwyn, 2022). The application of AI tools without any meaningful consultation, transparency, can decrease trust and increase skepticism. Successful change management then needs leaders to position AI as an empowering tool instead of a managerial tool to highlight that it is a supporting tool and not a tool that replaces human experience. The elements that are important to inspire trust in AI-enhanced leadership are open communication, moral commitments, and collaborative execution procedures.

7.2 Capacity Building, Digital Literacy, and Leadership Upskilling

The ability to perceive and critically interact with AI technologies is crucial to the successful implementation of hybrid leadership models by school leaders. The concept of digital literacy is no longer confined to a simple technological adequacy, but it goes further to include data comprehension, algorithmic consciousness, and moral argumentation. It is found in the literature that another alarming development is the emergence of the skills gap among educational leaders, most of whom lack access to the concept of AI and analytics-based decision-making (Akgun & Greenhow, 2022). To fill this gap, there should be a systematic leadership development process with the aim of AI literacy, data-driven leadership, and ethical governance. Continuous upskilling can be encouraged with the help of professional learning communities, mentoring, and cross-sector collaboration with technology specialists. Notably, capacity building should also be spread to teachers and middle leaders to promote consistent organizational learning. The problem is that without proper investment in human capability, AI tools will become either underused or misused, which will compromise the benefits they can bring.

7.3 Infrastructure, Data Readiness, and Interoperability Challenges

In addition to human constraints, there are technical and infrastructural constraints that are a significant hindrance to the implementation. The school systems have disjointed digital infrastructures, old systems and data standards that are inconsistent in many school systems. The truth of effective hybrid leadership is based on high-quality interoperable data to draw meaningful insights. The obstacles to use AI in education are likely to be data silos, ineffective data management, and inadequate analytical tools (Williamson & Eynon, 2020). Inequality in infrastructure between schools, especially between urban and rural or well-equipped and under-equipped settings. brings up the issue of digital inequality. The leaders thus need to resolve the data preparation problems such as quality, security, and integration of data as a subset of overall change plans. Interoperable platform and shared data standard investments are also necessary to allow AI-supported scale leadership and stay within the privacy and protection laws.

7.4 Managing Risk, Uncertainty, and Unintended Consequences

The process of AI implementation in the field of school leadership is fraught with considerable risks and uncertainties. The AI systems can make incorrect predictions, enhance the level of existing bias, or make them over-rely on quantitative metrics at the cost of qualitative judgments. These undesired effects may have a detrimental impact on decision-making, equity, and trust in school communities. Experts warn of so-called automation bias, when leaders give too much precedence to algorithmic advice, especially in conditions of complexity or time constraints (Shrestha et al., 2019). Sound change management thus involves sound risk management techniques such as pilot testing, constant surveillance and feedback. Ethical impact assessment and scenario planning may assist leaders to foresee the possible harms and implement changes in advance. Notably, uncertainty must not be underestimated but instead seen as part of the new reality; a more adaptable style of leadership, which values learning and reflection and focuses on flexibility, is more appropriate in dealing with the complexity of AI. Schools can reduce risks but introduce innovation by integrating reflexivity and accountability into the implementation processes.

8. CASE ILLUSTRATIONS AND EMERGING PRACTICES

8.1 Examples of Hybrid Leadership Models in K–12 and Higher Education

In education, both K-12 and higher education, there are starting to be hybrid models of leadership that show how leaders cope with human-AI collaboration. Berkovich, a global survey of school leaders in the K-12 sector concluded that about one-half of school leaders were in the early majority phase of generative AI (GenAI) tool adoption, especially in instructional leadership activities of planning, assessment, and communication (Berkovich, 2025). This empirical study explains the initial adoption of AI-mediated leadership practices in which principals and department heads incorporate AI knowledge in managerial and instructional spheres instead of basing their decisions exclusively on the old instincts or experience. Also, in the field of higher education, AI-based intelligent assistants to tailor adaptive learning routines present an example of how academic institutions can develop hybrid leadership structures that can guide faculty and students in real time (Sajja et al., 2024). These systems supplement the human faculty by alleviating cognitive load and allowing customized pedagogical plans. These instances show that hybrid leadership is not something of the future in its abstract form but instead the new form of leadership which involves human beings collaborating with AI systems on purpose.

8.2 Comparative Insights from Global and Cross-Cultural Contexts

Cross-cultural comparisons also outline the fact that hybrid leadership practices have to be sensitive to the local educational cultures, infrastructures, and policy environments. A school leadership study of integrating digital and AI technologies into Cyprus found that leaders perceived that digital technologies could be used to create better communication levels and administrative efficiency, although there was a lack of awareness regarding the limitations associated with the infrastructure and specific training (Kafa, 2025). The case of Cyprus highlights the fact that hybrid leadership cannot be brought to the market in the retail assembly; it must be adjusted to the context that involves identification of the available capabilities and limitations in school ecosystems. Similarly, the literature in rural K-12 STEM education in various states of the U.S. demonstrates the disparity in the perceptions of leaders regarding AI adoption: rural leaders encountered distinctive issues affecting their geographic location, shortage of resources, and professional support systems (Kim & Wargo, 2025). Such insights stress the fact that hybrid leadership practices are different not only by the level of education but also by cultural and socio-economic conditions and as such ought to be localized to work.

8.3 Insights Gained from Early Adopters and Pilot Initiatives

Proactive AI-assisted leadership adopters offer useful real-life lessons related to approaches, challenges, and advantages. In Israel, a study by Berkovich showed that most school leaders were employing generative AI to supplement instructional leadership, implying that early adopters of AI technology view the technology as improving productivity and creativity instead of a danger to professional autonomy (Berkovich, 2025). These leaders frequently took a step-by-step method where they would start with less risky managerial assignments and move on to instructional uses. Another example is intelligent tutoring systems (ITS) in Qatar which show that teachers employing AI to enhance adaptive and personalized learning have a positive attitude but also raise issues regarding ethical concerns and data usage (Alkubaisi, 2025). These pilot projects show that effective hybrid leadership requires repetitive learning, teacher buy-in, moral deliberation, and continuous crystallization as opposed to hasty growth.

8.4 Indicators of Effectiveness and Sustainability

The evaluation of the effectiveness and sustainability of the hybrid leadership practices would not be done without both qualitative and quantitative indicators. The initial research indicates that the efficiency of administration, enhanced data-driven decision-making, and professional growth are associated with success. The school leaders who have implemented AI to analyse and predict trends note that they spend less time on mundane tasks and more time on more strategic leadership operations (Nyakora & Monda, 2025). Hybrid human-AI tutoring models, particularly in adaptive learning, are found to assist students in gaining proficiency, especially lower-achieving students, which is a promising sign of fair impact given the optimal application of AI (Thomas et al., 2023). Continuity of leadership, professional capability, and infrastructure preparedness are also factors the contribution of sustainability: schools that have robust training programs and interoperable data systems are in a better position to continue with hybrid leadership practices in the long term.

When considering sustainability, one should be aware of possible pitfalls, including the variation in digital literacy among the employees, disproportionate access to resources, and ethical issues of algorithmic bias and data privacy. The presence of governance protocols, transparency in AI use, and stakeholder feedback mechanisms is also an indicator. At its finest, hybrid leadership is not an accomplishment but a continuous leadership process that is continuously evaluated, adapted and ethically managed.

9. IMPLICATIONS FOR EDUCATIONAL POLICY AND PRACTICE

9.1 Rethinking Leadership Standards and Competency Frameworks

The emergence of AI and hybrid leadership styles compel educational policy-makers and practitioners to redefine the conventional leadership norms and competency models. Traditional leadership criteria, which focus on teaching, managing resources, and building relationships with communities, are no longer applicable in situations in which leaders have to process information, regulate the application of AI, and support technology-enhanced innovation. The integration of AI in the field of education has been studied empirically, and the researchers identify developing skills, including digital mindset, ethical thinking, and data literacy, as key to successful leadership in the age of AI (Raptis et al., 2024). The leadership models need to be broadened at these areas, and the future and existing leaders should be ready to lead amalgamated organizations in which human intelligence and machine intelligence could collaborate. As an illustration, the 5C's model (Catalyst, Curator, Champion, Cultivator, Connector) offers systematic information about how leaders can implement AI integration in a responsible and strategic manner in schools (Ghamrawi & Ghamrawi, 2025).

More importantly, AI literacy, ethical governance, and data interpretation should be incorporated into the education leadership preparation programs. In their absence, leaders might not have the ability to transform technological opportunity into long-term educational gains and might be poorly prepared to guide digital shifts that put students in charge and focus on equity.

9.2 Institutional Strategies for Scaling Hybrid School Models

The hybrid school leadership models cannot be scaled to districts and institutions without coherent institutional approaches and not isolated pilot projects. A number of studies emphasize the significance of comprehensive policy alignment and professional growth and governance frameworks that enable the responsible use of AI (Ghimire & Edwards, 2024). In institutions, there should be articulate AI governance policies, such as ethical principles, data protection, and human oversight roles. Governance memos must be malleable and dynamic so that the schools can respond to changed technological and pedagogical sceneries.

Practically, scaling hybrid leadership also comes with the creation of leadership pipelines, which strategically nurture the competencies of adaptive thinking, technology strategy, and collaborative problem solving. According to literature on equity-oriented leadership, university-district partnerships can foster leadership pipelines, which focuses leadership to be inclusive and being data-driven in decision-making at the earliest levels in the development of the professional (Thessin et al., 2024). These pipelines assist in the provision of leaders with the values, as well as technical abilities, they need to govern the hybrid organizational models at scale.

9.3 Impacts on Equity, Inclusion, and Educational Outcomes

There are far-reaching consequences of the implementation of AI in the leadership and practice of schools in terms of equity and inclusion. Individualized learning journeys, adaptive testing, and immediate feedback can be facilitated by AI tools, and achievement disparities in students with a wide range of learning requirements might be reduced (Toyokawa et al., 2023; OECD, 2024). Studies on inclusive education prove that adaptive learning systems based on AI can be applied to learners with disabilities and linguistic diversity due to the ability to adapt to individual learning patterns (OECD, 2024; Toyokawa et al., 2023). With careful implementation of such technologies, they facilitate engagement and access in a manner traditional practices cannot.

The positive aspects of AI are conditional on the need to fix systemic challenges, including digital inequity, lack of adequate infrastructure, and disproportional access to training. In the absence of policy measures that would provide equal access to technology and capacity building among educators, AI adoption will only support the status quo (Alfaleh, 2026). Ethical leadership studies highlight that equity, rather than diversity efforts, should be the foundation of true inclusion and that leaders should be the agents of reducing algorithmic bias and making decisions participatively (Sreeram et al., 2025). Based on this, the policy and practice have to focus on not only fair infrastructure but also inclusive methods that include all involved stakeholders, including those who represent historically marginalised communities.

9.4 Aligning Leadership Innovation with System-Level Reform

The spread of hybrid leadership models cannot take place without more general reforms at the system level. The policies should link school level innovation to the district and national objectives in the educational systems. An AI application taxonomy in educational leadership demonstrates areas of AI in governance, compliance, and policy formulation, which means that AI is overlapping strategic planning and systemic governance (Sposato, 2025). This compatibility implies that leadership innovation is to be incorporated into strategic planning on digital transformation, budgetary allocations and education priorities.

The necessity to ensure ethical, transparent, and accountable use of AI in education is supported by national and global policy guidelines like the Recommendation on the Ethics of Artificial Intelligence released by UNESCO that offers a global normative framework that can be modified by local policymakers (UNESCO, 2021). Intersectoral cooperation, such as alliances such as the Digital Education Council, also contributes to aligning policy and practice by uniting stakeholders who are concerned with responsible use and management of AI (Digital Education Council, 2024). The combination of innovative leadership and systemic reforms is necessary to make sure that the hybrid models are sustainable, can be extended, and can contribute to the equitable educational results in various settings.

10. FUTURE DIRECTIONS AND RESEARCH AGENDA

10.1 Evolving Roles of School Leaders in AI-Enhanced Ecosystems

The role of school leaders is constantly changing as the influence of artificial intelligence (AI) in the education system increases. The contemporary definition of the leader is not simply to control people and resources but only to have to navigate their intricate AI-driven ecosystems where data, morality, and human judgment intersect. The available empirical findings indicate that AI is transforming the practice of leadership as it provides more accurate and effective decision-making support, especially in instructional leadership and strategic planning (Subrahmanyam & Baz, 2025).

In this regard, school leaders are becoming more of coordinators of composite intelligence blending human capabilities like moral thinking and interpersonal insights with the analytical abilities of AI. This change in the evolution of roles has consequences on the identity of leadership and professional expectations. Leaders who welcome AI could become strategic interluders of technology and pedagogy, and those who are opposed to it could find it hard to adapt to the changes in the organization (Sposato, 2025). Further studies are therefore necessary to understand how leadership personas evolve in AI-intensive learning systems, such as the shifting expectations of stakeholders, the influence of autonomy on leaders and the limits of human-machine partnerships.

10.2 Hybrid Intelligence and the Future of Educational Governance

A model where human intelligence works with machine intelligence is the hybrid intelligence that is going to transform the governance of education. As opposed to autonomous systems making decisions on their own, hybrid intelligence aids human leaders in deriving meaning of complex datasets, predicting trends, and developing policy responses to contexts. The emergence of elaborate taxonomies and conceptual frameworks in the recent literature demonstrates the relevance of implementing AI applications in the leadership field in terms of governance, compliance, and strategic planning (Sposato, 2025). These frameworks are capable of informing governance reforms that incorporate AI tools without neglecting ethical stewardship, accountability and transparency. International bodies such as UNESCO have introduced joint research projects with specific aims of investigating what AI can do to assist educational governance and in a fair and responsible way (UNESCO, 2025). These activities are leading towards a situation where educational governance integrates data intensive planning with normative promises of inclusion, fairness and quality of education. The vision will be realized when longitudinal research studies are conducted to test the effectiveness of hybrid intelligence models in various educational systems.

10.3 Key Research Gaps and Methodological Considerations

Although the topic has increased attention, there are still major gaps in the research regarding AI in educational leadership. Detailed reviews indicate the scarcity of longitudinal research that evaluates the future influence of AI incorporation on academic achievements and academic performance (Sposato, 2025). A lot of literature is presented as a cross-sectional snapshot of adoption and perception but lacks a systemic change. A second gap is around culturally responsive frames of hybrid leadership; the vast majority of them have been made in the West and might not be easily applicable to other educational cultures or policy settings (Sposato, 2025). In the future, methodological research should be balanced in the quantity and qualitative methods. Suggestions AI-based analytics provide the possibility of analysing large amounts of data (e.g., predictive modelling of student outcomes), but to comprehend what the life of leaders, teachers, and learners in the AI ecosystems is like, qualitative research is needed. Mixed-methods designs, participatory action research, and design-based implementation research could give sound contributions to both the technical and human aspects of hybrid leadership. One should focus the ethical frameworks in research that directly speak about algorithmic bias, data justice, and human-AI trust.

10.4 Strategic Pathways Toward Resilient and Adaptive School Systems

The strategic pathways between policy, practice, and research required to develop adaptive and resilient school systems able to utilize hybrid intelligence. There is an interest in policy actors, such as ministries of education, and international organisations such as the Digital Education Council, in the development and implementation of responsible adoption of AI policies that include infrastructure preparedness, ethical governance, and workforce development (Digital Education Council, 2024). School districts can encourage AI literacy and data fluency among leaders and teachers at the practice level by fostering professional learning ecosystems. The latest research promotes the idea of incorporating AI competency training into leadership development courses with a focus on human-centered strategic thinking, ethical management, and reflective practice (Subrahmanyam, 2025). These programs are able to produce leaders who are able to guide institutions towards technological change without sacrificing relational and pedagogical priorities. Equity and access should also be taken into account during strategic planning; AI systems tend to reproduce the existing structure of disparities without special measures and designed to decrease the biases and promote an inclusive result. Therefore, the ways to become resilient are not just about investment in technology but also governance changes that incorporate the ongoing assessment, consultation with stakeholders and ethical responsibility.

The future of educational leadership in AI-enhanced ecosystems is typified by the growth of roles, novel forms of governance, frontiers in the methodological domain, and strategic needs. Studies should go further beyond descriptive adoption literature and look at longitudinal effects, culturally sensitive practices, and hybrid intelligence systems that pre-empt ethical and human-centric leadership. With the priorities of the policy and practice being aligned with the research agenda, the field can contribute to resilient and adaptive education systems that can realize the potential of AI without harming the fundamental purpose of equitable learning.

11. CONCLUSION

The introduction of hybrid intelligence in educational leadership exemplifies a paradigm shift in the school governance, leadership, and management, as of how the school should be managed. Throughout the previous chapters of this book, it has been indicated that the intersection between human judgment and AI functionality is the main challenge to be attempted in the case of successful leadership in AI-enhanced ecosystems, where both ethical and relational competence and technological fluency are essential. The contextual reasoning, moral agency and building trust in human intelligence are still invaluable, whereas the analytical rigor, predictive and decision-support capabilities are offered by machine intelligence. The combination of both of them creates a hybrid model of leadership, which can help to tackle any complicated issues within K-12 education and higher education.

Theoretically, hybrid intelligence systems will enhance the conventional models of leadership by replacing AI as an instrument with a partner, and thus, re-evaluate the ways of leadership skills and the system of governance. The policy implications are the necessity to have moral norms, data management, and systemic approaches to ensure fair accessibility and reduce algorithmic bias. In practice, leaders will have to be involved in lifelong learning, develop a sense of trust in AI systems, and redesign organizational processes to use hybrid intelligence to their advantage.

The revolution of educational leadership that has occurred under hybrid intelligence is not simply technological but is rather human oriented. It provides a chance to improve decision-making, foster inclusivity, and create adaptive and resilient educational systems that are able to react to current changes in the learning environment of the 21 st century.

REFERENCES

Akgun, S., & Greenhow, C. (2022). Artificial intelligence in education: Addressing ethical challenges in K-12 settings. *AI and Ethics*, *2*(3), 431–440. DOI: 10.1007/s43681-021-00096-7 PMID: 34790956

Alfaleh, M. (2026). Sustainable AI-Driven Assessment in Higher Education: A systematic review of fairness, transparency, pedagogical innovation, and governance. *Sustainability (Basel)*, *18*(2), 785. DOI: 10.3390/su18020785

Alkubaisi, M. (2025). Optimising adaptive learning: A case study of Intelligent Tutoring Systems in schools in Qatar, using the Activity-Oriented Design Method. *Studies in Technology Enhanced Learning*, *4*(3). Advance online publication. DOI: 10.21428/8c225f6e.d3eae020

Argyropoulou, E., & Lintzerakou, E. E. (2025). Contextual factors and their impact on ethical leadership in educational settings. *Administrative Sciences*, *15*(1), 23. DOI: 10.3390/admsci15010023

Berkovich, I. (2025). The rise of AI-assisted instructional leadership: Empirical survey of generative AI integration in school leadership and management work. *Frontiers in Education*, *10*, 1643023. Advance online publication. DOI: 10.3389/feduc.2025.1643023

Bhardwaj, A. (2025). Artificial intelligence and the limits of reason: A framework for responsible use in public and private sectors. *Humanities & Social Sciences Communications*, *12*(1), 1565. Advance online publication. DOI: 10.1057/s41599-025-05749-0

Digital Education Council. (2024). *Digital Education Council overview*. https://www.digitaleducationcouncil.com/post/digital-education-council-global-ai-student-survey-2024

Ghamrawi, N. A., & Ghamrawi, N. (2025). Effective school leadership enactment of GAI: A 5C's framework for integration. *Frontiers in Education*, *10*, 1561414. Advance online publication. DOI: 10.3389/feduc.2025.1561414

Ghimire, A., & Edwards, J. (2024). From guidelines to governance: A study of AI policies in education. *arXiv*. https://doi.org//arXiv.2403.15601DOI: 10.1007/978-3-031-64312-5_36

Holmes, W., Bialik, M., & Fadel, C. (2019). *Artificial intelligence in education: Promises and implications for teaching and learning*. Center for Curriculum Redesign. https://curriculumredesign.org/wp-content/uploads/AIED-Book-Excerpt-CCR.pdf

Kafa, A. (2025). Exploring integration aspects of school leadership in the context of digitalization and artificial intelligence. *International Journal of Educational Management, 39*(8), 98–115. DOI: 10.1108/IJEM-11-2024-0703

Kim, J., & Wargo, E. (2025). Empowering educational leaders for AI integration in rural STEM education: Challenges and strategies. *Frontiers in Education, 10*, 1567698. Advance online publication. DOI: 10.3389/feduc.2025.1567698

Li, S. (2025). Human-Centered AI in Educational Leadership: Implications for Students' Academic Empowerment in a Music College in Inner Mongolia. *Journal of Education and Educational Research, 16*(2), 85–91. DOI: 10.54097/a4eywq15

Northouse, P. G. (2021). *Leadership: Theory and practice* (9th ed.). Sage Publications.

Nyakora, M., & Monda, D. (2025). Developing AI literacy as a core competency for future leaders. *International Journal of Research and Innovation in Social Science, 9*(14), 1723–1726. DOI: 10.47772/IJRISS.2025.914MG00129

Organisation for Economic Co-operation and Development. (2024). *The potential impact of artificial intelligence on equity and inclusion in education* (Working Paper No. EDU/WKP(2024)15). OECD Publishing. https://www.oecd.org/education/the-potential-impact-of-ai-on-equity-and-inclusion-in-education_0d7e9e00.htm

Raptis, N., Psyrras, N., Konstantinidi, N. P., & Koutsourai, S. A. (2025). Distributed leadership, new technologies and teachers' digital competence in the post-COVID era. *European Journal of Education and Pedagogy, 6*(2), 29–37. DOI: 10.24018/ejedu.2025.6.2.904

Raptis, N., Psyrras, N., Koutsourai, S.-E., & Konstantinidi, P. (2024). Examining the role of school leadership in the digital advancement of educational organizations. *European Journal of Education and Pedagogy, 5*(2), 817. Advance online publication. DOI: 10.24018/ejedu.2024.5.2.817

Sajja, R., Sermet, Y., Cikmaz, M., Cwiertny, D., & Demir, I. (2024). Artificial Intelligence-Enabled Intelligent Assistant for Personalized and Adaptive Learning in Higher Education. *Information (Basel), 15*(10), 596. DOI: 10.3390/info15100596

Selwyn, N. (2022). *Education and technology: Key issues and debates* (3rd ed.). Bloomsbury Academic. DOI: 10.5040/9781350145573

Shrestha, Y. R., Ben-Menahem, S. M., & von Krogh, G. (2019). Organizational decision-making structures in the age of artificial intelligence. *California Management Review, 61*(4), 66–83. DOI: 10.1177/0008125619862257

Sposato, M. (2025). Artificial intelligence in educational leadership: A comprehensive taxonomy and future directions. *International Journal of Educational Technology in Higher Education, 22*(1), 20. DOI: 10.1186/s41239-025-00517-1

Sreeram, A., Mehra, R., Parashar, K., Rao, B. U., Mohapatra, C. K., Jabbar, M. A., & Malagi, V. (2025). Ethical leadership in managing AI-integrated library environments. *Indian Journal of Information Sources and Services, 15*(3), 131–139. DOI: 10.51983/ijiss-2025.IJISS.15.3.15

Subrahmanyam, S. (2024). Role of data analytics and big data in operational decision-making and performance improvement. In Martínez-Falcó, J., Sánchez-García, E., Marco-Lajara, B., & Visser, G. (Eds.), *Convergence of technology and operations management in modern businesses* (pp. 105–140). IGI Global Scientific Publishing., DOI: 10.4018/979-8-3693-6200-6.ch003

Subrahmanyam, S. (2025). AI-Driven Leadership in the Modern Era for Revolutionizing Next-Generation Strategies: Organizational Impacts and Future Development. In Agnihotri, A., & Balusamy, B. (Eds.), *Leadership Paradigms and the Impact of Technology* (pp. 61–86). IGI Global Scientific Publishing., DOI: 10.4018/979-8-3693-7175-6.ch003

Subrahmanyam, S. (2025). Open Educational Resources and Their Impact on Curriculum Flexibility and Accessibility. In Cruz, M., Queirós, R., & Mascarenhas, D. (Eds.), *Building Teaching Competencies for AI-Driven and Inclusive Learning* (pp. 69–102). IGI Global Scientific Publishing., DOI: 10.4018/979-8-3373-7729-2.ch002

Subrahmanyam, S. (2025). Using AI-Driven Analysis for Training and Leadership Growth. In Mrabet, J., Boudagga, S., Sharma, R., & Bansal, R. (Eds.), *Harnessing Emotion AI for Customer Support and Employee Wellbeing* (pp. 321–352). IGI Global Scientific Publishing., DOI: 10.4018/979-8-3373-3658-9.ch013

Subrahmanyam, S., Azoury, N., & Sarkis, N. (2024). AI and Business Planning: Revolutionizing Forecasting and Resource Allocation. *2024 International Conference on Advances in Computing, Communication and Applied Informatics (ACCAI)*, Chennai, India, 2024, pp. 1-6. https://doi.org/DOI: 10.1109/ACCAI61061.2024.10601728

Subrahmanyam, S., & Baz, B. E. (2025). AI and Diversity: Ensuring Fairness in Automated Decision-Making. In El Imrani, O. (Ed.), *Navigating Responsible Business Practices Through Ethical AI* (pp. 19–50). IGI Global Scientific Publishing., DOI: 10.4018/979-8-3373-3104-1.ch002

Thessin, R. A., Tekleselassie, A. A., Trimmer, L. B., Shepard, S. D., & Clayton, J. K. (2024). Leveraging a candidate assessment system to develop an equity-centered school leadership pipeline through a university–district partnership. *Education Sciences*, *14*(12), 1408. DOI: 10.3390/educsci14121408

Thomas, D. R., Lin, J., Gatz, E., Gurung, A., Gupta, S., Norberg, K., Fancsali, S. E., Aleven, V., Branstetter, L., Brunskill, E., & Koedinger, K. R. (2023). Improving student learning with hybrid human-AI tutoring: A three-study quasi-experimental investigation (arXiv:2312.11274). arXiv. https://doi.org//arXiv.2312.11274DOI: 10.48550

UNESCO. (2021). *Recommendation on the ethics of artificial intelligence*. UNESCO Publishing. https://unesdoc.unesco.org/ark:/48223/pf0000377897

UNESCO International Institute for Educational Planning. (2025). *Artificial intelligence and planning the future of education*. UNESCO. https://www.iiep.unesco.org/en/articles/artificial-intelligence-and-planning-future-education

Veale, M., & Zuiderveen Borgesius, F. (2021). Demystifying the draft EU Artificial Intelligence Act: Analysing the good, the bad, and the unclear elements of the proposed approach. *Computer Law Review International*, *22*(4), 97–112. DOI: 10.9785/cri-2021-220402

Williamson, B., & Eynon, R. (2020). Historical threads, missing links, and future directions in AI in education. *Learning, Media and Technology*, *45*(3), 223–235. DOI: 10.1080/17439884.2020.1798995

Yang, N., & Li, T. (2020). How stakeholders' data literacy contributes to student success in higher education: A goal-oriented analysis. *International Journal of Educational Technology in Higher Education*, *17*(1), 41. Advance online publication. DOI: 10.1186/s41239-020-00220-3

Zeng, M., Cheah, K. S. L., & Abdullah, Z. (2025). The influence of school principals' digital leadership on teachers' competency in integrating artificial intelligence: A systematic thematic review. *Frontiers in Education*, *10*, 1655967. DOI: 10.3389/feduc.2025.1655967

KEY TERMS AND DEFINITIONS

Adaptive Leadership: A leadership style that emphasizes flexibility, learning, and responsiveness in complex environments, leveraging AI to anticipate challenges, monitor outcomes, and adjust strategies dynamically.

AI-Augmented Leadership: Leadership practices where artificial intelligence tools enhance human decision-making, rather than replacing it, through predictive analytics, automated reporting, scenario modeling, and data-informed recommendations.

Algorithmic Bias: The occurrence of systematic errors in AI outputs that reflect underlying biases in data or design, potentially leading to unfair or inequitable outcomes in school decisions if not carefully monitored.

Decision-Support System (DSS): A software system that collects, processes, and visualizes data to aid school leaders in making informed, evidence-based decisions, often incorporating predictive modeling and scenario analysis.

Distributed Leadership: A leadership approach in which responsibilities and decision-making authority are shared across multiple actors, often facilitated by AI systems that provide timely insights and coordination among school teams.

Ethical AI in Education: The practice of implementing artificial intelligence in schools responsibly, ensuring fairness, transparency, accountability, avoidance of algorithmic bias, and alignment with educational values and student rights.

Human Oversight: The concept that human leaders retain ultimate authority and accountability for decisions, even when AI provides recommendations or performs analytical tasks, ensuring moral and contextual judgment guides action.

Hybrid Intelligence: The synergistic combination of human and machine capabilities, where cognitive, ethical, and emotional strengths of humans complement the computational power, data processing, and predictive capabilities of AI in decision-making.

Hybrid School Model: A school leadership framework that integrates human judgment, expertise, and relational skills with machine intelligence (e.g., AI-driven analytics, dashboards, and decision-support systems) to enhance governance, instructional quality, and organizational performance.

Socio-Technical Systems: An analytical perspective that views schools as integrated human and technological systems, emphasizing the interactions between people, processes, and AI-enabled tools in achieving organizational goals.

Chapter 15
AI's Role in Fostering Student Motivation and Retention

Nikitaben Randipsinh Chhasatiya
http://orcid.org/0009-0006-7629-6452
Indukaka Ipcowala Institute of Management, Charusat, India

Reshma Gunaji Sable
http://orcid.org/0000-0002-4119-2761
Indukaka Ipcowala Institute of Management, Charusat, India

S. Subhashree
http://orcid.org/0000-0002-1672-7437
Indukaka Ipcowala Institute of Management, Charusat, India

Foram Pathak
http://orcid.org/0000-0003-4219-0992
Indukaka Ipcowala Institute of Management, Charusat, India

Dhartiben Neelkumar Patel
Indukaka Ipcowala Institute of Management, Charusat, India

Sumetha Madhu
http://orcid.org/0009-0001-5707-9384
Indukaka Ipcowala Institute of Management, Charusat, India

Khushboo Bhatt
http://orcid.org/0000-0002-2192-6369
Indukaka Ipcowala Institute of Management, Charusat, India

ABSTRACT

This study investigates the relationship between artificial intelligence (AI) and student motivation and engagement. It does this by examining how cognitive factors, psychology and emotional factors affect student motivation in the classroom. This has been done by conducting a review of existing literature and previous studies involving students in tertiary institutions in the modern classroom, especially those engaged in remote learning and in classes with large populations. These have

DOI: 10.4018/979-8-3373-4908-4.ch015

shown improvement in the learning experience, including motivation, confidence and self-esteem, through AI capabilities such as predictive analytics, adaptive learning, intelligent tutoring systems and affective computing. Studies show that thrugh the adaptive capacity of AI, learning complexity can be adjusted easily to suit the individual learner, promoting competence and confidence. AI can also provide constructive non-judgmental feedback to improve learner confidence, as well as motivational prompts for encouragement. AI also enables the learner autonomy over the learning process, where they control the pace and difficulty of the work, with instantaneous feedback, making learning interactive to promote connection using virtual assistants, simulating student-teacher interactions. This satisfies the requirements that the Self-Determination Theory highlights for building intrinsic motivation; autonomy, competence and relatedness. These findings highlight the potential of AI to transform higher education, where AI can be used to promote accessibility to quality education, reduce cognitive load on educators and create a customized learner experience for each student. This can however only be successfully implemented when partnership is fostered between AI and human educators while ethical concerns are addressed to protect data privacy and prevent bias while preserving human connection that is necessary for a learner's holistic development.

1. INTRODUCTION

Motivation in the classroom can be measured in different ways, one of them being in the level of participation among students in class. The level of participation usually indicates the level of retention of students in schools, with studies showing demotivation rates being as high as 40% in students in higher education (Kuh 2009, Tinto, 2017). Participation usually falls to a small number of students while the rest remain detached from class activities. While it may seem like a minute issue, motivation levels are reliable indicators for drop-out rates, often being an impeding factor to student achievement.

Demotivation has a myriad of causes. In today's age of remote learning and large class populations, many students end up lost within the crowd, with the contact between the educator and the students increasingly limited (Hart, 2012). Furthermore, educational content tends to lag behind technological and real-world progress, hence its usefulness is often undermined. This is in addition to the high demands of higher education on a student's mental faculties, and a resulting lowering of their sense of usefulness and importance in the classroom. Many higher institutions however still use conventional means of teaching, which often fail to address the current types of challenges that students face in their learning journey and therefore motivation goes unaddressed.

The ability of computer systems to mimic human intelligence and perform functions associated with it is called Artificial Intelligence. This intelligence simulates human learning and comprehension, allowing computational systems to undertake tasks like image analysis, logical thinking, speech recognition and creativity. While previously these functions have been used to drive automation, now they are applicable in a variety of industries including education. Through data-backed algorithms, AI tools can instantaneously adapt to learning needs and preferences to suit the learning capacity of the student. Individual students also benefit from one-on-one tutoring by Intelligent Tutoring Systems (ITS), which caters to the mastery level of students and their behavioural patterns (Luckin et al., 2016; Holmes et al., 2019).

AI-powered assessment tools also provide instantaneous feedback, identify learning gaps and recommend relevant solutions; capabilities which traditional teaching methods are limited in.

Despite its capabilities in promoting learning, AI's capacity in handling obstacles like motivation and engagement are immense. The traditional teaching methods rely on uniform delivery of classroom material, catering to the average student while the variabilities of students needs are often unaddressed. This includes motivation, and goes against the recommendations of motivational theories such as self-determination theories, which highlight competence, relatedness and autonomy as key psychological needs (Deci & Ryan, 2000). Through AI, these needs can be met by engaging the adaptability capabilities of AI through customization, such as through adapting material to the difficulty level of students in order reduce boredom and frustration, hence reducing demotivation (*Fredericks, Blumenfeld, & Paris, 2004*).

To increase student retention, educational systems can engage with AI predictive analytics, which analyses student performance, providing insight into trends that can identify shortfalls in learning or motivation. This has been used by various institutions such Georgia State University, with a marked improvement in student retention and graduation numbers (Siemens & Long, 2011). AI systems can also be used to identify demotivation through changing emotional states, using affective computing. This is through facial expressions, response times and typing biometrics, which the AI systems respond to appropriately through motivational prompts (Chen et al., 2020). Therefore, demotivation is reduced, by providing timely interventions that can change the trajectory of student performance.

AI tools can be used to make learning more accessible to marginalized students. For many students, access to education is difficult as a result of disabilities such as hearing and speech impediments and language barriers. AI tools provide speech-to-text and translation capabilities which enable learning among such students as well. Through this, student retention is improved as these students are able to actively participate in learning (*Zawacki-Richter et al., 2019*). All students are therefore catered for, promoting inclusivity in learning.

This chapter discusses student motivation and its impact on success rates in learning. It argues for the partnership between teachers and AI systems in schools in order to achieve optimum results in learning. This is because AI has the capacity to fill in the gaps that are left behind by both remote learning and traditional classroom dynamics. AI is capable of providing the individualized attention that students need in order to thrive in their learning while providing emotional support.

With many schools facing challenges in retaining student engagement and numbers, AI is being considered as a valid option to solve this due to its capacity to customize information, automate tasks and its data analytics. However, studies have shown that AI by itself cannot solve challenges in motivation. Its success highly ties to how educational leaders manage its implementation, including prior planning and regulation (Luckin et al., 2016; Williamson & Eynon, 2020).

Under the self-determination theory, students' motivation in their educational journey is highly influenced by their level of control, proficiency and human connection (Deci & Ryan, 2000). Without proper management of AI tools, factoring in ethics and teaching methods, they may end up undermining these requirements instead of providing solutions. The priority therefore must not just be integration of AI into educational structures but responsible adoption, where AI centers student needs.

The following sections detail theories of motivation and their application to AI use. This is through application of AI capabilities that improve the educational experience such as adaptation and AI analytics. It discusses opportunities for AI to transform the landscape of student retention in order to promote outcomes in education. This improves learner retention and teaches students to be drivers in their own educational journey.

2. LEADERSHIP FRAMEWORK FOR SUSTAINABLE AI INTEGRATION

Through the following framework, the role of leadership in harmonizing AI integration and motivation for students is demonstrated. It demonstrates that for optimum student motivation, indirect leadership decisions have more effect than the AI tools themselves. This is through strategic leadership decisions, goal-oriented implementation, continuous audits, ethical entrenchment and capacity building. These structures ensure that the requirements of proficiency, autonomy and human connection are maintained to maximize the returns on integration (Deci & Ryan, 2000; Holmes et al., 2019; Williamson & Eynon, 2020).

Figure 1. The Mechanics of Motivation: Customized Learning

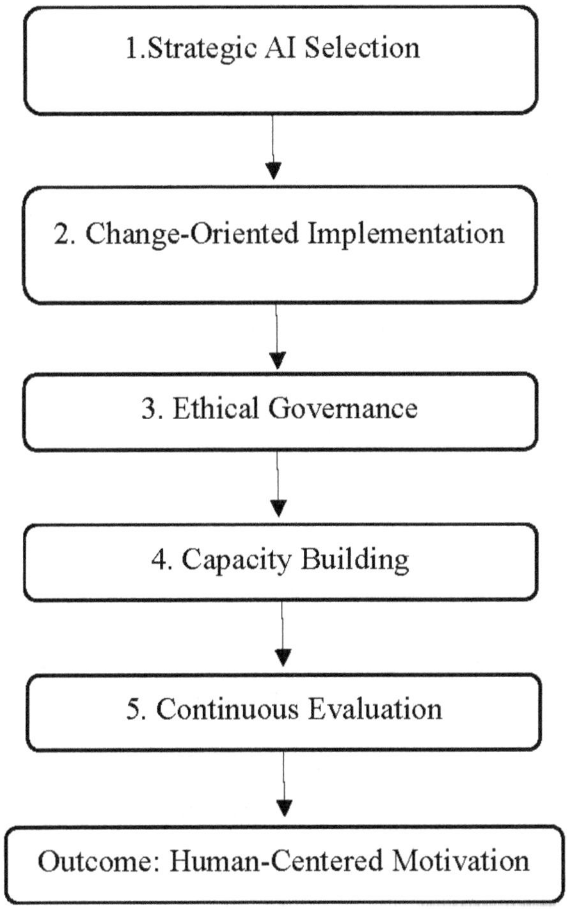

Source: Luckin et al. (2016), Intelligence Unleashed: An Argument for AI in Education.

2.1 AI-Driven Customized Learning

Conventional methods of teaching involve lecture-style delivery of educational content, which caters for the approximate needs of the average student. This means however that many students are disadvantaged as they require more personal guidance. This is where customized learning comes in, which analyzes the student's needs, including the gaps in their learning, performance patterns and weaknesses in the classroom to tailor content and learning exercises as needed and predict their future performance *(Decisive, 2023; Reiber, 2022)*. In this way, their learning experience can be customized to meet their needs and address gaps in learning flexibly (Ames, 2021; *Raza, 2023).*

Since it is interacting with the student directly, AI is able to conduct continuous assessment on student performance. It therefore collects data continuously and accurately addresses their gaps in comprehension and provide guidance. It can brainstorm directly with the student as a human teacher would with the advantage that it does not get tired and is always available. It can also detect disengagement in the student and address it, therefore promotes their learning. This promotes an interactive learning experience that improves learning outcomes.

AI provides flexible learning tools that can adapt to every student's needs, providing instantaneous feedback and varying the rate of content provision in line with student's mastery and attention. While this promotes practice with a quick feedback loop, regulation is required to prevent over-dependence on AI tools and promote student autonomy. This can be achieved by choosing the right AI tools and the best strategy to optimize on benefits of customization while avoiding such pitfalls as overreliance (Holmes et al., 2019).

Adaptive AI tools include *Dreambox Learning* and *Knewton Alta*, which adjust learning pace and difficulty of learning material according to the learner's comprehension. *Coursera* and *Duolingo* also use adaptation methods to promote learning.

Their success in promoting learning demonstrates the capacity for AI systems to improve learning outcome through customization, therefore promoting continuous engagement (Nosenko, 2020; DreamBox Learning, n.d.).

Personalization is a unique capability of AI, providing students with focused attention than human facilitators are unable. This involves tailoring of learning material and learning processes to suit each learner's needs and learning trajectory. Enabled by AI's adaptability, a student's learning needs can be continuously met through data analytics, enabled by continuous engagement with the AI. This promotes higher retention rates, motivation and deeper engagement with learning material.

AI can process variable datasets on behaviour, performance and cognition to gauge learning gaps and user's strengths. Through this, it can tailor the learning pace and content for the student, as well as their preferences and provide personalized lesson structure and difficulty levels, providing immediate feedback. They can also use this data to predict the student's future learning trajectory in order to avoid overwhelming the student with difficult material or lose them from oversimplification (Li & Liu, 2020). Through this continuous adaptation to the student's needs, they can remain motivated in learning.

Personalization is demonstrated within Intelligent Tutoring Systems (ITS) such as Knewton, ALEKS, and Carnegie Learning's MATHia. Through continuous use, they engage machine learning to diagnose misconceptions, encourage repetitive practice to reinforce mastery of material and provide targeted hints to encourage the learner. When used in conjunction with teachers, ITS's have been demonstrated to enable learning similar to human teachers (Luckin et al, 2016). In addition, AI systems enable students to discover the best learning methods for themselves, therefore promoting autonomy and self-discipline.

Individualized learning also encompasses emotional regulation that AI can personalize. Emotions are detected through facial recognition and keyboard analysis, enabling AI to identify tedium, frustration and enthusiasm. The lesson plan, pace and tone can then be adapted to maximize engagement (Holmes et al, 2019). Through affective personalization, the emotional needs of the students can also be addressed to produce better learning outcomes.

Customization goes beyond lesson plans and emotional regulation to also promote the learning goals of the student. Data analytics AI can provide recommendations on courses, real-world simulations and interdisciplinary projects that suit the student's goals in learning and career progression. They can also recommend students to a diverse range of options to promote critical thinking and exploration, encouraging students to take an active part in their own learning (Bayly-Castaneda et al., 2024).

Needs of accessibility and inclusivity can also be met using personalized AI. Various AI tools paired with machine learning enable the learner to access learning material regardless of the background, disability or language barrier. This is through functions such as speech-to-text and translation. When their unique barriers are eliminated, engagement in the learning process is improved as found by (*Zawacki-Richter et al., 2019).*

Despite all the benefits AI presents, it is important to consider the ethical concerns that it raises. It is imperative that AI integration in the classroom is co-regulated by human facilitators, therefore, becomes a co-facilitator as the human needs of the students in moral development, ethical oversight remains critical to their development. AI should not be a replacement for teachers but a partner to bridge gaps and facilitate optimized learning.

In conclusion, it is clear that AI presents a revolutionary opportunity for learning, where the student's needs are central in all decisions. Personalization in AI is an important feature towards this goal. However, ethical concerns of AI are still critical in engagement in AI. So are the aspects of human connection that human facilitators invariably provide. Therefore, it is imperative to continue fostering human-AI collaboration in the classroom to promote the goal of education.

2.2 Fostering Educational Opportunities

To promote motivation, AI can keep the learner engaged by incorporating their personal interests, career goals and learning preferences with their learning activities. This curated experience is enabled by machine learning. These AI systems analyze the students' behaviour and tendencies to predict what they engage with best and curate the learning experience (Gómez Martínez et al., 2023). This creates content that is meaningfully useful to the learner and which they can engage with best.

With tailored learning comes a broader range of opportunity for a broad range of students, where they can receive tailored support. While implementing this, stakeholders must be intentional in targeting areas of inequality to improve accessibility without which they can be exacerbated (Selwyn, 2019). Appropriate strategy must be employed in order to allocate tools and resources inclusively.

AI can be used to ground theoretical concepts to their real-world parallels, bringing the learning material from abstract to practical. AI can for example create simulations to demonstrate concepts, such as AI-generated renewable energy systems to demonstrate thermodynamics for engineering students, AI-generated case studies for a business student. Through eliminating abstractions, students can engage more deeply with the material and understand better.

AI can also encourage creativity through open-ended prompts, interdisciplinary challenges and studies that require problem-solving and teamwork. By engaging critical thinking, this has been shown to improve comprehension of learning content, which promotes participation in the learning process, improving student retention and fulfillment (Wei et al., 2025). Conventional teaching methods utilize standardized teaching content in order to apply to the widest range of student needs. This fails however to consider the individual needs of the student, as some students may need more support and end up lagging behind their peers. AI can fill this gap, providing attention to individual students while mitigating their attention spans to keep engagement. They can also tailor content that supports the student's goals, both career-wise and in their education (Aline Smadi et al., 2025). This supports motivation and student retention.

By engaging with AI tools, the student's patterns and tendencies can be analyzed and their content thus tailored towards them. AI makes learning interesting by using different modes of learning including speech and text, providing simulations to demonstrate concepts. It can also include the interests of the students in learning material, therefore enabling learning to include optimal difficulty that is engaging to students to avoid frustration and oversimplification which reduces interest in learning (Du Plooy & van der Merwe, 2024). Learning becomes interesting and therefore engagement is increased.

To improve understanding of the material, AI can demonstrate concepts such as provide examples of industry trends. These have been used by *LinkedIn Learning* and *Skillsets* by *Coursera* to provide real-world examples of theories *(Zawacki-Richter et al., 2019)*. Through this, the practical applications of concepts are demonstrated, removing them from abstract theories to applicable methods, making them relevant to the student.

AI can also promote creativity and teamwork in the classroom. As rote memorization has been shown to yield less results in learning, teamwork through interdisciplinary collaboration has been recognized to promote better learning outcomes. AI is useful here in promoting critical thinking by supporting group projects. This is through AI simulations that demonstrate processes such as sustainable business practices. This has been shown to improve comprehension, making learning interesting and improving participation (Lee & Martin, 2023).

Career counselling is an important part of the educational journey. AI support can promote the career goals of students through recommending relevant courses that can improve performance or access to opportunities. This also includes certifications that it can recommend, enabling students to actively think about their career trajectory and take steps towards their goals (Chen et al, 2020). This also improves motivation and student retention.

The adaptive ability of AI also enables AI systems to cater for a diverse range of needs, including disability, language differences and geographical location. Students from remote areas can access AI assistance. This enables them to be active participants in the learning process, since barriers to learning are reduced, promoting equity in the education system, globalization and personalization of education (Holmes et al., 2019).

As explained above, AI provides a wide range of opportunity to improve the educational experience in a range of different ways. Its adaptability, capacity for personalization and accessibility enables improvement to education prospects, aiding in the holistic development of the student. It promotes active engagement in learning materials through removing abstractions, to enable meaningful engagement that supports motivation and increasing memory and student retention and meets the needs and ambitions of students.

2.3 Improving Internal Motivation

Competence, autonomy and relatedness are identified as key drivers of motivation (Deci & Ryan, 2000) under the Self-Determination Theory. They emphasize motivation as driven psychologically, not by external push but as a product of internal investment in progress, As stated above, a student's personal investment in their own educational journey determines whether they succeed or not. AI has been shown to be an important factor that can support this journey.

The efficacy of AI tools is hinged on the structure and application of feedback received. When used to support the learning process and improve proficiency they can promote competence. However, when they are used for surveillance they undermine student autonomy (Deci & Ryan, 2000; Williamson & Eynon, 2020). Application and study design therefore depends on the strategy of educational leaders, which can either promote or hinder motivation.

This ensures students are not passive, but take charge of their learning process and outcome. With a sense of control and accountability in themselves, they are able to get better results. AI supports this through customized learning tools such as dashboards that show progress and support the goals that they have set. AI simulations, which demonstrate concepts also promote understanding. All this supports the three aspects of the Self-Determination Theory, promoting competence, autonomy and relatedness.

Affective AI systems further detect lags in concentration through identifying frustration and boredom, tracking visual and behavioural identifiers and responding accordingly to improve focus. This is especially essential in distance learning where the student is often isolated from the learning environment with no educators to detect changes in concentration.

With adaptability of AI, continuous learning can be supported on a lifelong path. Students are supported in their efforts when intrinsic motivators are reinforced, fulfilling the requirements of the Self-Determination Theory of autonomy, competence and relatedness. This provides a revolutionary opportunity for learners to be active drivers of their own ambitions and education to become fulfilling and purposeful *(U.S. Department of Education,2023).*

3. IMMERSIVE AND INTERACTIVE LEARNING

3.1 Utilizing AI Resources

AI tools can improve participation through interactive models such as simulations. Without proper design however, this can become a distraction rather than a learning tool. Education leaders must therefore consider this in order to promote learning and not hinder it (Holmes et al., 2019).

Active and participatory methods of learning are key in facilitating a deep understanding of course content. AI technologies have supported active and creative learning in many ways, transforming the educational experience with gamification, virtual laboratories and AI-generated simulations to provide. This is a departure from the lecture model that encourages passive learning. AI tools utilize data-back methods for cognitive development, promoting customized learning experiences that meet the needs of individual students and promote their investment in the material (Lee & Martin, 2023).

Project-based learning is therefore key in the student development. With AI, this can be actioned through AI-generated simulations and virtual labs that have the advantage of safety. Examples include *Labster*, which enables science simulations, and *MATLAB* Simulink for engineering powered by AI. Students can create models, phenomena, test theories and observe the results. This promotes participation, comprehension and retention of course content through practice for students.

These practical benefits are also compounded by the motivational functions that AI systems provide. Interaction with AI systems enables them to learn the student's learning tendencies, creating a pattern of behaviour which can be modified through motivational prompts for the student, adjustment of difficulty and gamification methods to promote healthy competition through leaderboards, point systems and badges. Through healthy teamwork and competition while engaging critical thinking to solve problems, students are motivated to master content and thereby develop skills that benefit them in education and in other areas. This includes collaboration, endurance and persistence. These qualities promote the psychological development of the student, fostering intrinsic motivation (Lee & Martin, 2023).

AI provides robust opportunities for innovation in education, with a diverse range of resources that promote student participation, comprehension of content and continuous learning. Utilizing AI resources such as ITS's, personalized learning tools, chatbots and virtual assistant's presents chances for better learning experiences which are collaborative and individualized (Holmes et al., 2021). Therefore, these resources enable an all-rounded learning experience.

A key characteristic of AI resources is their adaptability and capacity for interaction, compared to traditional textbooks and learning materials. AI tools are however responsive to student's capabilities. They can examine learner behaviour, performance and interests and respond with changes in presentation, pace and content to suit (Baker & Smith, 2019). Coursera and Khan

Academy, for example, have used AI to analyse student performance and recommend tailored content and supplementary material. The learner's journey is therefore maintained at optimal difficulty to enable long-time engagement while producing the best results.

AI also engages in interactive methods such as gamification and virtual immersion. This is through Virtual Reality (VR) and augmented reality (AR), where virtual classrooms are used to simulate phenomena and concepts for observation (Luckin, 2018). Game techniques are also employed such as tracking progress, instantaneous feedback and healthy competition to maintain focus in learning (Mousavinasab et al., 2021). Through satisfying requirements of the Self-

Determination Theory, these AI resources help boost motivation. AI resources further promote the emotional well-being of users by analyzing their behaviour through facial expression and changing patterns of interaction, which they adapt to accordingly. This includes increasing difficulty of challenges when confidence is high and providing encouragement when the student is disheartened (D'Mello et al., 2017). This improves the student's motivation and also promotes a sense of connection, mirroring human facilitators.

AI resources have an advantage in accessibility. As long as internet access is available, users can access chatbots such as IBM Watson Education and ChatGPT, unlike human teachers who are only available on the teaching schedule. They can be used when the student is away from the classroom, offering additional assistance on *demand (Zawacki-Richter et al., 2019).* This improves learning outcomes.

Partnership between AI and human educators is however still imperative in promoting ethics. There are many ethical concerns that AI drives, including over-reliance on the AI tools. Teachers are importance to promote moral guidance and to curb that arises from historical data. They therefore guide the students to build resilience and critical thinking and problem-solving (Holmes et al., 2021).

AI resources support motivation by promoting the three pillars of the Self-Determination Theory as stated above. This has the opportunity to yield better educational outcomes for students once paired with human oversight. The education sector therefore stands to gain by employing AI to fill these gaps, promoting better educational outcomes.

3.2 AI Chatbots and Virtual Assistants

Large class populations and remote learning have limited the attention that a teacher can give to students at a time, which has been important in addressing learning gaps in the past. In the absence of this attention, AI chatbots and virtual assistants can play this role, providing clarification for concepts in place of the teacher. Since they are also accessible at any time and place, the student is able to learn conveniently on and off campus (Labadze et al., 2023). This is important in supporting the student's progress.

These are efficient and convenient as they remove a barrier to information, providing convenient support on demand with no need for human interaction for anxious students (Ferguson, 2012). Overdependence on them however risks loss of valuable social skills that come from human interaction. Guard-rails must be implemented by leaders to prevent overreliance.

A successful application includes *Jill Watson,* an AI assistant from Georgia Tech. It provides supplementary support to students just like a teacher would; clarifying theories, explaining topics and offering guidance for students. It employs natural language processing to mimic human teachers and in this way supports the students.

Studies have shown that continuous feedback supports better learning outcomes, which AI teaching assistants provide (Chiu et al., 2023). This is through increasing their confidence level in handling difficult concepts such as programming syntax and mathematical equations, which a teaching assistant is able to break down and explain bit by bit. By detecting signs of boredom or frustration, the AI can also provide motivational prompts and recommend additional material, which supports learning, fosters resilience and emotional connection.

Through natural language processing (NLP) machine learning (ML), and deep learning algorithms, AI assistants and chatbots can mimic human interactions, simulating a user experience that is similar to student-teacher interactions. Therefore, the student is able to get all the benefits of understanding the course material with the added advantage of round-the-clock accessibility *(*Mageira et al., 2022*)*. This democratizes the learning experience and improves learning outcomes.

Roles traditionally requiring teachers such as explaining complex course content, answering factual questions and facilitating quizzes and assignments can be handled by AI chatbots such as *IBM Watson Assistant*, *ChatGPT* and *Google Bard*. Due to their accessibility advantages and the wealth of information they hold, they fill in the gap that may be left by educators, especially in remote learning. They therefore promote motivation and retention for student by being an accessible source of support (Labadze et al., 2023*)*.

With the adaptability of AI, chatbots are able to tailor the learning experience towards the students' individual needs. Previous engagement with the AI provide data on the student's performance patterns, strengths and weaknesses, enabling appropriate response with simpler prompts or more challenging exercises *(Zawacki-Richter et al., 2019)*. This promotes learning across a diverse variety of student backgrounds, where their unique requirements are met.

Affective AI chatbots also have the added advantage of being able to detect a lag in concentration or emotional dysregulation such as frustration. Through affective computing, they can pinpoint changes in the emotional states of the user, to respond with encouragement or provide emotional support *(*D'Mello & Graesser, 2015*)*. This reduces anxiety and increases the motivation of the students as they learn. With the tendency of remote or online learning to produce isolation in students, this is particularly useful in supporting a student's learning experience.

Through automation, AI chatbots can provide additional support to educators, who often undertake administrative tasks. Things such as grading, routine questions and scheduling can be automated to reduce the burden on the educators *(Gonzalez-Calero et al., 2023)*. Therefore, educators have more time to allocate towards creative pursuits, student guidance and to their research work. The data collected from the use of chatbots is additionally useful in designing curricula and teaching methods.

Partnership is however emphasized in AI use in the classroom, whereby the educator takes on the oversight role on AI insights, training the students on the appropriate use of AI while considering the ethical concerns and ensuring accuracy in information. Algorithmic bias and overreliance on

AI can produce bias in students while hindering their critical thinking capacity and spreading misinformation (Holmes et al., 2021). Furthermore, data protection should be an imperative concern when implementing AI systems in the education sector. The human touch must not be lost, therefore, in ensuring that AI is used with appropriate safeguards.

AI chatbots and virtual assistants play a transformative role in the changing educational landscape. They offer accessibility, inclusivity, personalized learning and are able to relieve routine and repetitive tasks. With human supervision, they have the potential to promote learning and solve many challenges in the educational sector.

3.3 Promoting Participation

While active tools such as game elements and prompts can increase student engagement, these extraneous methods may not support intrinsic interest. Designers of educational tools must invest in learning strategies and tools that promote educational goals long-term (Deci & Ryan, 2000).

As previously explained, a dynamic learning environment is key in fostering comprehension, developing resilience in the learning process and promoting retention of learners. Teamwork and active involvement in class activities is therefore a key part of this. This is through live analysis of teamwork dynamics, within which recommends strategies to boost motivation, provide instantaneous feedback with indicators of participation such as frequency of involvement, time spent on tasks and patterns of interaction within the group (Holen & Sortland, 2022). Therefore, focus in maintained in the group projects, which improves learning.

Analytics also enable AI to form optimum teams for maximized collaboration and engagement. Considering every team member's strengths and weakness, AI can recommend complementary team make-up that promote effective teamwork during class projects, drawing from real-world analytics on workplace dynamics. The teams can develop their collaborative skills, problem- solving and effective communication. With active participation assisted by AI, the team draws maximum benefits from the team project.

Continuous feedback further supports autonomy in the learning experience and teaches accountability and independence. Gamification methods such as progress tracking and dashboards promote visual tracking of progress and healthy competition, where students can track their progress towards their goals. This active investment in the learning journey facilitates independence and resilience in students as active participants in their own success, which promotes retention and advancement. Contrinto highlighted how a dynamic learning experience, supported by live data analytics, teamwork and responsive content delivery support long-term engagement and learning. Adaptive learning interfaces are not static but are responsive to the needs of the learner, both to motivate and challenge learners, encourage social participation, mental development and deep learning. Through this, students engage more meaningfully with course material while their emotional needs are supported to fill the gap left in regular classrooms. Learning is student-focused therefore, tailored to their needs to foster an environment of innovation and collaboration. Engagement and motivation is therefore fostered, promoting the education of the students (Contrino et al., 2024).

Active engagement is also fostered by the adaptability of AI systems. When students continuously engage with the AI systems, the AI collects data on their performance, learning development and level of understanding of content to ensure they achieve an optimum rate of learning. This has been shown to not only promote academic success but also encourage participation, keeping a balance between the ease and difficulty of exercises *(Khosravi, Sadiq & Gasevic, 2020)*. This enables them to reach a state of 'flow', between appropriate competence and difficulty that promotes perseverance and participation *(Cziskzentmihalyi, 1990)*.

Instantaneous feedback mechanisms also support classroom engagement. When learners are able to get timely feedback on their mistakes, have their questions addressed and errors detected quickly, a continuous learning loop is created *(*Holmes et al., 2019*)*. This enables better mastery of concepts and supports autonomy and independence. Examples such as *ALEKS* and *MATHia* by *Carnegie Learning* provide continuous feedback to students. In addition to being adaptive to the student in terms of level of comprehension, providing appropriate level of difficulty of content to support learning, they provide better learning outcomes and support motivation *(Roll & Winne, 2015)*.

Group projects, which are important in teaching critical thinking and problem-solving, can also be supported by AI. This is not only by providing simulations to demonstrate processes within learning, but from the point of team formation where students with complementary skills and goals are matched to promote the best outcome *(*Chen et al., 2020*)*. Since remote learning is prevalent, Augmented Reality (AR) and Virtual Reality (VR) can support team projects in even these contexts, supporting project demonstrations through simulations *(*Lee & Martin, 2023*)*. These enable effective teambuilding and teamwork and promote participation and comprehension. An active mind support learning, since mastery is emphasized. It also promotes self-awareness, whereby the students is not a passive participant in their education but plays an active role, knows their strengths and weaknesses. AI supports this through tracking progress through visual dashboards, enabling students to think critically about their work. *Ifenthaler & Yau 2020* highlight that AI use can improve this self- awareness by facilitating independence and reflection, which signal engagement. This cultivates personal investment in the learning process and outcome, fostering intrinsic motivation in the process.

Affective AI systems also support learning by enabling detection of changing mental states. This includes frustration, boredom or confidence, which can be identified through keyboard patterns and facial expression and level of interaction, prompting the AI to provide emotional support (D'Mello & Graesser, 2015). The learning experience therefore becomes more empathic to promote emotional connection and motivation for students.

Safeguards are however necessary to prevent overreliance on AI tools, which can have detrimental effects. Partnership between human and AI in the process should therefore be fostered, since the human connection cannot be replaced (Holmes et al., 2021). Human facilitators can therefore foster problem solving, emotional development and student guidance.

To close, AI has potential to promote learning through fostering collaboration. It creates a dynamic learning environment where students are able to have complementary group dynamics towards a shared goal, with their individual learning needs met and cultivation of self-reliance in their educational trajectory. With ethical oversight and proper human collaboration, it can produce sustained benefits for the education of learners.

4. AI-DRIVEN SUPPORT AND MENTORSHIP

4.1 Data-Based Inventions

Students often experience challenges in learning, leading to dips in their performance and when detected by the institutions, interventions may be too late to make meaningful impact. AI however enables these challenges to be identified early enough that interventions can be engaged to change the learning trajectory. Through AI, predictive analytics can be used to catch bad performance early and intervene (Siemens & Baker, 2012). However, according to studies analytics without human mentorship are inadequate in improving student retention (Ferguson, 2012). Data analytics must be paired with guidance systems in order to enable the best solutions.

This is through predictive analysis, where students behaviour is monitored including attendance and participation, test performance and assignment performance, to detect indicators of a dip in performance before they are compounded. Poor performance, for example can be detected early by identifying downwards trends in engagement. For example, a 30% dip in engagement with a digital learning system over three weeks can be a signal for disengagement or non-comprehension of material. The student can then be engaged for mentorship, tailored remedial classes and appropriate quizzes to address gaps in learning. Chen & Lopez (2023) highlight a marked improvement in student retention and graduation rates in institutions that have engaged AI-driven data analytics. This shows the effectiveness of using AI in predictive analytics to promote engagement for students, not only for performance but for improving the educational trajectory of students. Applying analytics to promote learning, further supports student motivation, individualized support and equitable learning. To improve learning outcomes for students, data-backed inventions such as predictive analytics is essential. Vast datasets can be analyzed by AI within a short period and trends in performance, participation and student behaviour identified which would have otherwise have been an impossible or uphill task. They support preventive measures that can be instituted before the problems compound to create irreversible academic performance *(*Chen & Lopez, 2023*)*.

Since most educational institutions rely on digital systems to keep record of student data, these can be processed using AI processing to identify trends in student behaviour. These datasets include class attendance, assignment submission and academic performance as well as interaction with learning management systems (LMS). These can be analyzed to detect warning signs of disengagement and poor performance trends *(*Ifenthaler & Yau, 2020*)*. The institution can therefore provide appropriate responses to these trends, such as adaptive course modules, customized training and counselling to encourage improvement and retention *(Zawacki-Richter* et al., 2019).

The predictive capacity of AI's data analytics enables visualization of performance trends, which can be used by faculty and students in order to identify trends in learning. This enables these trends to be interpreted and analyzed accordingly, where learning gaps are identified and new solutions are thought up. This enables students to take an active role in their learning path, making informed data-backed choices in order to improve performance, promoting a sense of personal investment in their education since they become self-aware of their tendencies *(Khosravi et al., 2022)*. Assessments of performance therefore transform from static and periodic to continuous to promote the best outcomes.

Natural Language Processing is further able to analyze qualitative data from coursework, essay work and assignment inputs to examine the state of students' motivation, fulfilment and emotional support to better understand student behaviour *(*Holmes et al., 2021*)*. This has predictive value in enabling an all-rounded understanding of both academic trends and behaviour, as has been applied by the University of Arizona through its 'Smart Learning Analytics System', which has promoted a better understanding of risk factors for students and enabled proactive responses by faculty which has benefitted students by improving rates of retention and graduation rates.

Data-backed AI tools are also useful in promoting inclusivity in education, since they can be analysed to identify disparities along different demographics. Disaggregated datasets can therefore, be analysed to understand how certain obstacles affect people from certain groups, such as students from marginalized backgrounds or disabled students. The institution can therefore take a proactive approach to remedy these inequalities to prevent them from compounding and promote fairness (The Impact of AI on Inclusivity in Higher Education, 2025).

Sustainable and effective AI use in data analytics must however be backed by strong ethical oversight, which include data protection, preventing misuse and eliminating bias. As pointed out by Holmes et al., (2022), openness on implementation methods is central to build trust in the system, together with applying explainable AI (XAI).

AI inventions demonstrate important capabilities that have a revolutionary potential in education, as explained above. They are important in providing useful data that supports better results, timely interventions and reduce systemic inequality. This supports motivation by promoting active involvement in the education of students.

4.2 Improving Self-esteem and Reducing Anxiety

AI tools can offer support to promote self-confidence. This must however be done ethically, avoiding labelling systems that may stigmatize students (Selwyn, 2019). This is also dependent on the leadership strategy, promoting ethical labelling methods that build confidence.

Constructive feedback is important in promoting the confidence of the student. When guidance is paired with judgement, students are discouraged from seeking support from educators and even peers, which promotes feelings of isolation among students. AI assistants and virtual tutors provide this by giving objective feedback to students to support their learning journey. Students are able to continuously learn by making mistakes without being chastised or judged. This enables them to learn better and at the same time build confidence in themselves.

With individualized learning, learners have control over the pace of their learning. They study on their own and are able to address their mistakes privately so that they are proficient when they go back to the classroom. They are not a disturbance to the teachers by repeatedly seeking answers to the same questions or being stuck on a topic. They therefore build confidence in the classroom.

As reports have demonstrated, students who engage AI to assist their learning journey are more confident and suffer less anxiety (Mohamed et al., 2024). They control their own process and therefore have agency in their results. With agency over their work, they become more motivated and fulfilled.

AI-assisted learning is therefore able to build an all-rounded student. It supports both their educational journey and their mental strength so that they can face challenges with confidence. By building resilience when faced with difficulty, students develop skills that are applicable in other areas as well. They become curios and are able to take on challenges with confidence.

Intelligent Tutoring Systems, virtual tutors, adaptive learning tools all have the advantage of being responsive to the student's needs. Performance trends, rate of interaction and affective analysis of the students enable timely responses towards learning challenges that present themselves in the course of learning (Holmes et al., 2021). By providing continuous constructive feedback with no judgement, the students gain confidence in their studies since they are free to practice and make mistakes *(Zawacki-Richter et al., 2019).* Duolingo and Coursera for example utilize continuous reinforcement with appropriate level difficulty to promote mastery over the Course content and continuos improvement (Luckin et al., 2016).

With AI assistants, there is no expected judgement when students make mistakes since they provide objective feedback that is focused on teaching the student instead of having expectations of them *(Lee et al., 2022).* The student's self-esteem is built up, and they are able to enjoy the learning experience and can therefore ask questions freely, enabling them to become more competent in the process (Bandura, 1997).

Affective AI is able to detect stress and offer suggestions such as suggesting breaks and encouragement by using natural language processing and affective computing. Sentiment analysis is used by tools such as *Replika* and *Woebot* to provide emotional support for students, motivational prompts and emotional regulation (Inkster et al., 2018). This provides emotional support for struggling students not able to speak up.

AI assistance also teaches self-reliance and self-awareness, enabling them to learn how best they study to get the best results (Chen et al., 2020). Through tracking their progress with performance analytics and visual dashboards, their perceived competence is improved, which promotes self-confidence. They are therefore able to be proactive in their learning process, promoting feelings of autonomy and self-reliance that are pertinent in building intrinsic motivation (Xie et al., 2019).

Ethical integration and design of AI assistants is however key in maintaining inclusive learning. AI systems in schools should therefore be monitored in order to prevent bias in algorithmic data. Teachers can play this role in the classroom. This supports partnership between the AI and human educators. Students also learn how to identify bias with this guidance and develop critical thinking in the process. Responsible implementation of AI supports better outcomes for the students and avoids unnecessary harm that may come from misuse. AI presents opportunities to build a holistic learning experience that supports motivation in the student. This enables students to have better results and also have more confidence by achieving their goals.

5. ETHICAL CONSIDERATIONS AND CHALLENGES

With the potential for improvement that AI systems provide, there are also ethical concerns to consider in order to prevent unnecessary harm. This is important to prevent data misuse and unfairness in the education system.

5.1 Data Protection

Data management must adhere to principles of transparency and privacy to foster responsible implementation. AI is able to provide predictive analytics and adapt to the student since it processes large amounts of data. This data is of a variety of categories, in order to effectively respond to the student. Its misuse is therefore a major concern to both students and the institutions since it can open up avenues for exploitation. This defeats the purpose of promoting the learning experience if the data becomes threatening for the student.

Data protection has been identified as the biggest obstacle towards its integration, with responsible data governance through consent-based data collection, strict encryption and compliance with legal requirements highlighted as crucial in preventing misuse (OECD,2024).

This is governed by the General Data Protection Regulation (GDPR), but institutions must also show commitment in following these guidelines by instituting clear policies on data management. In addition to fostering trust with users, it is also imperative in protecting them from harm.

5.2 Algorithmic Bias and Fairness

Auditing AI system routinely and promoting inclusivity must be followed in AI integration by leadership (Williamson & Eynon, 2020). This prevents bias which may be inherent in analytical data from exacerbating inequality.

Data analytics of AI draw from historical data to learn. Existing biases in datasets may therefore be transferred to learning insights, fostering prejudice through bias learning materials and disadvantaging various social, cultural and gender groups. This may result in discrimination and unfairness within content suggestions, learning opportunity recommendation and grading.

AI trained on datasets for students from one racial group may for instance fail to take into account the context and needs of other racial groups, resulting in indirect discrimination. This perpetuates unfairness and exacerbates disparities of marginalized groups. Therefore, deliberate attempts have to be made to eliminate data by integrating inclusivity into datasets, conduct regular oversight and have ethical AI policies which incorporate accountability, transparency and non-discrimination.

5.3 Loss of Human Connection and Emotional Development

Student-teacher relationships must be maintained and not replaced by AI. This is important for motivation as it cultivates belonging and relatedness, which are key to motivation (Deci & Ryan, 2000). Increased dependence on AI systems reduces the need for human connection, which is central is fulfilling emotional needs and fostering emotional development of the student. AI mimicking of human emotion may foster connection but is not a substitute for human interactions. Overreliance may produce the isolating effects resulting from emotionally detached learning environments that affective AI systems seek to solve, defeating the purpose of emotional development as highlighted in OECD,2021. Balance is therefore recommended between interface with AI systems and human interaction to promote creativity, empathy and ethical understanding.

5.4 Digital Divide and Accessibility

The rates of economic and technological development vary across economic lines. This produces inequality in access to AI technology, the sophistication of AI systems and their sustainability within school environments. Educational leaders must entrench accessibility to AI-enhanced educational opportunities for learners from varied geographical and socio-economic backgrounds (Selwyn, 2019). This means that some students may benefit from AI assistance while others lag behind, unable to access its benefits, which prevents democratization of education.

Investment is therefore required in order to facilitate equitable access to AI technology by providing resources for infrastructure, training and equitable policies. Through this, challenges of AI access can be addressed to promote the best learning outcomes for students.

5.5 Accountability and Ethical Transparency

To foster effective AI integration, transparency of AI decision-making is key. There should be openness in the decision-making process where policy-makers gives reasons for their decisions. Students whose data is being affected are also owed transparency and accountability so that they can use AI systems without fear. Transparency and accountability must be entrenched in learning systems when implementing AI learning to foster confidence. Oversight committees should be instituted in order to provide this accountability, founded on open communication. AI systems should be audited continuously to eliminate risks of misuse and ensure the institutional policies are being followed. This enables students to build trust in the AI systems and therefore benefit from it.

CONCLUSION

From the preceding sections, it is clear that AI alone cannot deliver on the maximum goals for learning to promote motivation and retention for students. The decisions by leaders and the systems they implement are key in determining whether the resulting learning processes are sustainable. Leaders must align AI systems with teaching practices and the psychological needs of students to ensure that proficiency, human connection and autonomy are maintained, promoting intrinsic motivation (Deci & Ryan, 2000). Without effective leadership, inaccessibility, surveillance and a lack of motivation may be reinforced (Selwyn, 2019; Williamson & Eynon, 2020).

Considerations for Education Leaders

Perspective must be changed in implementation of AI, where it is not just a technical update to systems but a deliberate and responsible ethical endeavor. Institutional leaders must:

- *Define motivational goals* and then choose AI functions and systems that conform to them
- *Structure integration as a systemic change and* provide support to educators through upskilling and teamwork
- *Establish oversight systems* that are transparent, equitable and accountable
- *Build capacity in staff* to understand AI feedback and translate in line with motivational goals
- *Implement continuous audits* to ensure student needs, wellness and accessibility are being met as well as performance results

Through these strategies, human-centered learning is maintained with AI offering support rather than a replacement (Luckin et al., 2016; Holmes et al., 2019).

Policy and System Leadership Considerations

For motivation to be supported with AI-driven learning, policy-makers must implement:

- Clear management guidelines on responsible algorithmic management and data governance
- Funding resources to develop professional upskilling and infrastructure
- Practices maintaining ethics in AI procurement and conducting audits
- Information sharing across institutions to learn and maintain best practices

This holistic approach with leadership ensures that education can benefit from AI tools equitably to avoid worsening inequality (Selwyn, 2019).

REFERENCES

Aline Smadi, O.. (2025). Leveraging artificial intelligence for personalized learning pathways in higher education: A scoping review on digital transformation. *Informatics (MDPI)*, *16*(9), 819. DOI: 10.3390/info16090819

Ames, A. (2021). Adaptive e-learning environment based on learning styles and its impact on student engagement. *International Journal of Educational Technology in Higher Education*, *18*(1), 53. DOI: 10.1186/s41239-021-00289-4

Baker, T., & Smith, L. (2019). Educ-AI-tion rebooted? Exploring the future of artificial intelligence in schools and colleges. Nesta. https://www.nesta.org.uk/report/education-rebooted/

Bandura, A. (1997). *Self-efficacy: The exercise of control*. W. H. Freeman.

Bayly-Castaneda, K., Ramírez-Montoya, M.-S., & Morita-Alexander, A. (2024). Crafting personalized learning paths with AI for lifelong learning: A systematic literature review. *Frontiers in Education*, *9*, 1424386. Advance online publication. DOI: 10.3389/feduc.2024.1424386

Chen, L., Chen, P., & Lin, Z. (2020). Artificial intelligence in education: A review. *IEEE Access : Practical Innovations, Open Solutions*, *8*, 75264–75278. DOI: 10.1109/ACCESS.2020.2988510

Chen, R., & Lopez, M. (2023). Predictive analytics and student retention: Leveraging AI for academic success. *Journal of Educational Data Science*, *12*(2), 45–61.

Chen, X., Xie, H., & Hwang, G. J. (2020). A multi-perspective study on AI in education: Self-regulated learning and emotional engagement. *Computers & Education*, *157*, 103978. DOI: 10.1016/j.compedu.2020.103978

Chiu, T. K. F., Moorhouse, B. L., Chai, C. S., & Ismailov, M. (2023). Teacher support and student motivation to learn with artificial intelligence (AI)-based chatbot. *Interactive Learning Environments*. Advance online publication. DOI: 10.1080/10494820.2023.2172044

Contrino, M. F., Reyes-Millán, M., Vázquez-Villegas, P., & Membrillo-Hernández, J. (2024). Using an adaptive learning tool to improve student performance and satisfaction in online and face-to-face education for a more personalized approach. *Smart Learning Environments*, *11*(1), 6. Advance online publication. DOI: 10.1186/s40561-024-00292-y

D'Mello, S. K., Dieterle, E., & Duckworth, A. L. (2017). Advanced, analytic, automated (AAA) measurement of engagement during learning. *Educational Psychologist, 52*(2), 104–123. DOI: 10.1080/00461520.2017.1281747 PMID: 29038607

. D'Mello, S. K., & Graesser, A. C. (2015). Feeling, thinking, and computing with affect aware learning technologies.

Deci, E. L., & Ryan, R. M. (2000). The "what" and "why" of goal pursuits: Human needs and the self-determination of behavior. *Psychological Inquiry, 11*(4), 227–268. DOI: 10.1207/S15327965PLI1104_01

. Decisive. (2023). Integration of artificial intelligence performance prediction and learning analytics to improve student learning in online engineering course. International Journal of Educational Technology in Higher Education, 20(1),

DreamBox Learning. (n.d.). Continuous assessment and adaptivity in DreamBox Math. DreamBox Learning Help Center. https://dreamboxlearning.zendesk.com/hc/en-us/articles/27281596241043-DreamBox-Math-Continuous-Assessment-Adaptivity

Du Plooy, E., & van der Merwe, A. (2024). Personalized adaptive learning in higher education: A scoping review of key characteristics and impact on academic performance and engagement. *Education and Information Technologies*. Advance online publication. DOI: 10.1186/s PMID: 39524879

Ferguson, R. (2012). Learning Analytics: Drivers, Developments and Challenges. *International Journal of Technology Enhanced Learning*, *4*(5/6), 304–317. DOI: 10.1504/IJTEL.2012.051816

Gómez Martínez, R., Medrano García, M. L., & Aznar Sánchez, T. (2023). Motivation and personalization of teaching with machine learning. *Journal of Management and Business Education*, *26*(2), 1–18. DOI: 10.35564/jmbe.2023.0017

Hart, C. (2012). Factors associated with student persistence in an online program of study: A review of the literature. *Journal of Interactive Online Learning*, *11*(1), 19–42.

Holen, A., & Sortland, A. (2022). The Teamwork Indicator (TWI): A feedback inventory for students in active group learning and team projects. *European Journal of Engineering Education*, *47*(2), 230–244. Advance online publication. DOI: 10.1080/03043797.2021.1985435

Holmes, W., Bialik, M., & Fadel, C. (2019). *Artificial intelligence in education: Promises and implications for teaching and learning*. Center for Curriculum Redesign.

Holmes, W., Bialik, M., & Fadel, C. (2021). *Artificial intelligence in education: Promises and implications for teaching and learning*. Center for Curriculum Redesign.

Holmes, W., Luckin, R., & Griffiths, M. (2021). Responsible AI in education: Challenges and opportunities. *Computers and Education: Artificial Intelligence, 2*, 100018. DOI: 10.1016/j.caeai.2021.100018

Holmes, W., Porayska-Pomsta, K., Holstein, K., & Koedinger, K. (2022). Ethics of AI in education: Towards a community-wide framework. *International Journal of Artificial Intelligence in Education, 32*(3), 504–526. DOI: 10.1007/s40593-021-00239-1

Ifenthaler, D., & Yau, J. Y.-K. (2020). Utilising learning analytics to support study success in higher education: A systematic review. *Educational Technology Research and Development, 68*(4), 1961–1990. DOI: 10.1007/s11423-020-09788-z

Inkster, B., Sarda, S., & Subramanian, V. (2018). An empathy-driven, conversational artificial intelligence agent (WYSA) for digital mental well-being: Real-world data evaluation mixed-methods study. *JMIR mHealth and uHealth, 6*(11), e12106. DOI: 10.2196/12106 PMID: 30470676

Khosravi, H., Sadiq, S. W., & Gašević, D. (2020). Development and adoption of an adaptive learning system: Reflections and lessons learned. In *Proceedings of the 51st ACM Technical Symposium on Computer Science Education (SIGCSE '20)* (pp. 58–64). ACM. https://doi.org/DOI: 10.1145/3328778.3366900

Kuh, G. D. (2009). What student affairs professionals need to know about student engagement. *Journal of College Student Development, 50*(6), 683–706. DOI: 10.1353/csd.0.0099

Labadze, L., Grigolia, M., & Machaidze, L. (2023). Role of AI chatbots in education: Systematic literature review. *International Journal of Educational Technology in Higher Education, 20*(1), 56. Advance online publication. DOI: 10.1186/s41239-023-00426-1

Lee, J., & Martin, L. (2023). Artificial intelligence and immersive learning: The role of AI in enhancing student engagement through VR and AR. *Education and Information Technologies, 28*(4), 4873–4891. DOI: 10.1007/s10639-022-11249-4

Li, K., & Liu, J. (2020). A review on personalized learning technology based on artificial intelligence. *Symmetry, 12*(10), 1713. DOI: 10.3390/sym12101713

Luckin, R. (2018). *Machine learning and human intelligence: The future of education for the 21st century*. UCL Institute of Education Press.

Luckin, R., Holmes, W., Griffiths, M., & Forcier, L. B. (2016). *Intelligence unleashed: An argument for AI in education*. Pearson Education.

Mageira, K., Pittou, D., Papasalouros, A., Kotis, K., Zangogianni, P., & Daradoumis, A. (2022). Educational AI chatbots for content and language integrated learning. *Applied Sciences (Basel, Switzerland), 12*(7), 3239. Advance online publication. DOI: 10.3390/app12073239

Mohamed, A. M., Shaaban, T. S., Bakry, S. H., Guillén-Gámez, F. D., & Strzelecki, A. (2024). Empowering the Faculty of Education students: Applying AI's potential for motivating and enhancing learning. *Innovative Higher Education, 50*(2), 587–609. DOI: 10.1007/s10755-024-09747-z

Mousavinasab, E., Zarifsanaiey, N., Niakan Kalhori, S. R., Rakhshan, M., Keikha, L., & Saeedi, M. G. (2021). Intelligent tutoring systems: A systematic review of characteristics, applications, and evaluation methods. *Interactive Learning Environments, 29*(1), 142–163. DOI: 10.1080/10494820.2018.1558257

Nosenko, Yu. (2020). Knewton analytical review as a platform for personalization of learning content. [ITE]. *Journal of Information Technology Education*, (44), 65–76. DOI: 10.14308/ite000727

Organisation for Economic Co-operation and Development. (2024). AI, data governance & privacy: Synergies and areas of international co-operation (OECD Artificial Intelligence Papers). OECD Publishing. https://www.oecd.org/going-digital/ai/data-governance-privacy.htm

Selwyn, N. (2019). *Should robots replace teachers? AI and the future of education*. Polity Press.

Siemens, G., & Baker, R. S. D. (2012) Learning Analytics and Educational Data Mining: Towards Communication and Collaboration. *Proceedings of the 2nd International Conference on Learning Analytics and Knowledge*, Vancouver, 29 April-2 May 2012, 252-254. DOI: 10.1145/2330601.2330661

Siemens, G., & Long, P. (2011). Penetrating the fog: Analytics in learning and education. *EDUCAUSE Review, 46*(5), 30–40.

The Impact of AI on Inclusivity in Higher Education: A Rapid Review. (2025*Education Sciences15*91255https://doi.org/DOI: 10.3390/educsci15091255

Tinto, V. (2017). Reflections on student persistence. *Student Success, 8*(2), 1–8. DOI: 10.5204/ssj.v8i2.376

U.S. Department of Education, Office of Educational Technology. (2023). Artificial intelligence and the future of teaching and learning: Insights and recommendations. U.S. Department of Education. https://tech.ed.gov/ai/

Wei, X., Wang, L., Lee, L.-K., & Liu, R. (2025). The effects of generative AI on collaborative problem-solving and team creativity performance in digital story creation. *International Journal of Educational Technology in Higher Education*, *22*(1), 23. Advance online publication. DOI: 10.1186/s41239-025-00526-0

Williamson, B., & Eynon, R. (2020). Historical Threads, Missing Links, and Future Directions in AI in Education. *Learning, Media and Technology*, *45*(3), 223–235. DOI: 10.1080/17439884.2020.1798995

Xie, H., Chu, H.-C., Hwang, G.-J., & Wang, C.-C. (2019). Trends and development in technology-enhanced adaptive/personalized learning: A systematic review of journal publications from 2007 to 2017. *Computers & Education*, *140*, 103599. Advance online publication. DOI: 10.1016/j.compedu.2019.103599

Chapter 16
Rethinking Leadership in the Age of AI:
Strategic Approaches Toward Equity and Inclusion in the Classrooms

Hima Parameswaran
http://orcid.org/0000-0003-4816-5755
College of Business, City University, Ajman, UAE

ABSTRACT

Education is one of the many facets of our society that is changing, and the integration of artificial intelligence (AI) in education is having a profound impact. Adaptive leadership is crucial to the teaching and learning process in this context, as it influences student well-being, enthusiasm, and academic achievement. Consequently, there are several advantages to incorporating AI into emotional assessment in educational environments that could revolutionize understanding and approaches to students' socioemotional growth. Nevertheless, a comprehensive framework that organizes the subject's potential, challenges, and developments remains lacking. Students in the twenty-first century need more than standard academic instruction to succeed. They must be skilled in problem-solving, cooperation, communication, and social-emotional learning (SEL). Students with SEL and traditional skills will be better prepared to thrive in the rapidly changing digital economy. For thirty years, academics have been studying emotional intelligence (EI). The real-world setting in which emotional intelligence is produced and employed has, surprisingly, received little attention, even though there has been significant discussion about how to quantify it and about the validity of its assessment. More precisely, there is a substantial void in understanding the emergence and influence of digital interactions on emotional

DOI: 10.4018/979-8-3373-4908-4.ch016

intelligence. In this background, analyzing the literature from a broader perspective is imperative to enhance emotional intelligence in technology-rich classrooms. This comprehensive literature review examines the application of artificial intelligence (AI) to emotion assessment in educational settings. Additionally, it offers a comprehensive overview of the field, highlighting advancements, challenges, and opportunities in AI-powered emotional assessment in academic settings. By leveraging machine learning algorithms and natural language processing, AI systems can analyze human emotions across multiple modalities, including facial expressions, speech patterns, and text. This information can provide personalized feedback on emotional regulation, social interaction skills, and self-awareness. This study also examines the leadership styles that foster the use of Emotional Intelligence (EI) in classrooms. Hence, it guides teachers in developing strategies for transformational leadership within a digital learning context, addressing the challenges and ethical considerations associated with leveraging technology to cultivate emotional intelligence (EI) in the 21st-century classroom.

AN INTRODUCTION TO EDUCATIONAL LEADERSHIP

Educational leadership and practices serve as a transformative framework that integrates ethics, values, and scientific methods to enhance school systems and discipline. According to Mallillin (2020), this role involves employing targeted processes and techniques to go beyond traditional management, emphasizing behavioral traits that foster high-quality education. This leadership is inherently collaborative rather than individual; Mallillin and Mallillin (2019) emphasize that school leaders work together as active participants within the discipline to build a culture of care and trust. Additionally, this approach distributes leadership responsibilities among teachers, who act as mentors to peers and resources for students, thereby shaping behavioral norms and the overall school climate (Mallillin et al., 2021; Mallillin & Laurel, 2022). By aligning leadership strategies with the school's mission and vision, educational leaders can effectively address systemic challenges and prepare students to be future leaders (Harris & Jones, 2021; Nelson, 2022).

A snapshot of leadership and AI intervention in educational settings

The concept of leadership and its effectiveness within organizations remains uncertain, despite extensive research. Most studies focus on leadership traits, abilities, behaviors, power dynamics, and factors that influence organizational success. However, research on leadership effectiveness across different contexts remains limited, particularly in the current technology-driven era. Additionally, the role of education leadership has changed significantly with the rise of Artificial Intelligence (AI). Today, the education sector faces challenges related to student interactions with new technologies, including emotional intelligence, resource management, personalization, and accountability. Leadership now involves more than automation; it includes analyzing student performance data, employing predictive analytics, and addressing ethical considerations. Educational leaders should adopt diverse AI strategies to promote transparency, accountability, ethical standards, equity, diversity, and inclusion for all learners (Al-Ruheili & Al-Buraiki, 2025).

At the same time, technological literacy plays a pivotal role in advancing AI and generative AI (Gen AI) in academia. AI helps avoid monotony in a job and reduces mechanical, time-consuming tasks. However, this process necessitates empathy and fairness in all aspects. To clarify this point, the theory of job replacement emphasizes the importance of leadership in empathy and intuition as AI's role in academia progresses. As the fear of human replacement by AI persists, resistance to AI-driven technologies, such as ChatGPT, begins to interfere with more intricate aspects of academia. This understanding will enable academic leaders to navigate new curriculum mechanisms by strengthening their capabilities and creativity in student development. On the other hand, it enhances teachers' productivity by managing time and tasks effectively. Thus, a quality of work life can be maintained by alignment of interests. This enhances organizational effectiveness and business excellence.

In light of the background above, it is necessary to gain further insights into leadership traits across various situations and how they align with technological advancements in academia. Leadership roles among academics should be enhanced through new responsibilities and upskilling and reskilling, achieved by integrating technologies for change and risk management. Hence, this chapter highlights the leadership skills required in AI operations, their challenges, and monitoring and evaluation in academia.

Link between leadership and AI strategies

The literature suggests that AI can transform the scholastic environment by systematizing administrative processes, delivering instructions, enhancing personalized learning experiences, developing decision-making models, and advancing the core mission (Brusilovsky, 2024; Chen et al., 2020; Popenici & Kerr, 2017). Conversely, studies indicate that the application of AI in educational contexts is limited and lacks effective leadership (Sposato, 2024), particularly in understanding and implementing AI solutions within institutions (Nig et al., 2024). These aspects clarify the taxonomy of AI applications in educational leadership by providing a structured framework for understanding operational considerations and identifying potential areas for future development in classroom equity and inclusion. It was noted that the core concepts of AI's potential in higher education emphasize the balanced integration of technology into pedagogy. Later, these concepts were validated through empirical studies and theoretical developments (Popenici & Kerr, 2017). Moreover, a meta-synthetic review identified gaps in ethical frameworks and collective implementation strategies (Bond et al., 2024), underscoring the need for adaptive tools in educational processes (Zawacki-Richter et al., 2024). From an ethical perspective, governance has emerged as a critical area of focus. It not only underscores the importance of privacy, fairness, and transparency in AI development (Nguyen et al., 2022) but also highlights educational equity and the right to use, along with related challenges and opportunities (Xia et al., 2022). Another study highlighted the importance of effective leadership in developing a vision, managing expectations, and anticipating risks (Richardson et al., 2015). For instance, AI could automate 40 percent of administrative tasks in tracking student progress, in addition to taking attendance, generating reports with less time (Herold. 2019) managing library systems (Kuleto et al., 2021), adjusting content delivery and learning paths (Tang et al., 2020), including virtual teaching assistants for personalized interactions and feedback (Essel et al, 2022).

Application of educational leadership skills through AI

Ethical leadership involves fairness, honesty, altruism, and trustworthiness. However, leadership theories are not neutral; they involve morality, values, choice, and influence (Heifetz, 1994). In education, ethical leadership means maintaining integrity, promoting fair and inclusive curricula, and supporting acceptance, accessibility, and assessment reform (Mag et al., 2017). The UN (2017) stresses respecting diverse morals, norms, and practices—religious and non-religious—to foster inclusive, high-quality education, eliminating discrimination based on race, color, religion, and disability to support social inclusion. Strategies should improve understanding in large classes, provide resources for STEM (Wang, 2020), address biases, and remove barriers via intercultural dialogue (Dreamson, 2021). Academic leaders can promote diversity by using technology to enhance equity, creating authentic learning environments with real-world contexts, complex problems, resources, and assessments, which boost creativity, interaction, ownership, and multidisciplinary integration.

On the other hand, AI cannot fully replace human cognition because only humans possess emotional intelligence. AI algorithms deliver directions to students in a processed manner that may, unconsciously, lead to the loss of the nuanced approach that only human educators can offer. Inclusive education is more than a one-size-fits-all approach, as students come from diverse cultural, socioeconomic, and family backgrounds and exhibit varying emotional and social development, learning behaviors, skills, styles, and paces (Wang, 2020).

Developing a comprehensive Leadership–AI–EI–Equity framework requires moving beyond purely theoretical explanations toward a dynamic, adaptable system that prioritizes human judgment and ethical oversight to advance institutional progress. Recent research from 2024 to 2026 describes this as a "Systems Approach," where AI functions as the analytical core for extracting insights from data, while Emotional Intelligence (EI) manages the complex human elements of digital change. This approach ensures leaders act as empathetic mediators, helping to address employee concerns and foster psychological safety (Digital Promise, 2024; Okokoyo et al., 2025). Today, adaptive leadership is characterized by managerial agility and the integration of machine intelligence with "human-in-the-loop" decision-making, thereby preventing the reinforcement of systemic biases through predictive analytics (ResearchGate, 2025; UNESCO, 2026). Effective governance must shift from passive advice to active, real-time engagement.

Identifying the taxonomy for AI interventions

Today, rapid technological progress is transforming industries, making them reliant on these innovations for their survival. In a society driven by data and technology, maintaining the human touch is essential. While emotions are a vital part of daily life, people differ greatly in their ability to understand, process, regulate, and apply them constructively (Mayer et al., 2002). Emotional intelligence (EI) captures these differences, with strong evidence showing it enhances social-emotional traits like leadership and resilience, benefiting various areas of life (Grewal & Salovey, 2006). This highlights the importance of EI. Across sectors, EI is key to leadership, work design, job performance, and organizational success. It helps us understand what motivates others and how to collaborate effectively. Although intellectual and technical skills are critical, the role of EI in AI remains underexplored, despite its importance in understanding interpersonal dynamics and fostering well-being. AI has both strengths and weaknesses in developing EI in students. EI has been widely discussed for over two decades (Mathews, Roberts, and Zeidner, 2002). The unexpected digital shift in teaching caused by the global pandemic has created challenges for educators in addressing students' psychological needs. Online education now dominates pedagogical and technological discussions (Dhawan, 2020). Therefore, this section explores the background of EI, its importance in digital education, and strategies to develop both technical and emotional skills among educators, ultimately supporting student success.

McCarthy's 1955 conference, which explored the simulation of human intelligence through computational techniques, popularized the term "artificial intelligence" despite Turing's (1937; 1950) prior discussions on intelligent machines. Moreover, AI streamlines admissions processes, enhances accessibility through automated captioning, and enables AI-based plagiarism-detection systems (Kashishi & Hack, 2023).

The 2020 pandemic increased emphasis on online learning with a more homogeneous approach, aiming to tailor instruction to group needs through skill-based, learning-style, and pacing groupings. Learners with similar skills, preferences, or progress rates are grouped for focused practice and instruction, leveraging LMS tools, adaptive platforms, and data analytics, despite challenges such as preparation time, social isolation, discrimination, and heightened digital expectations. Today, AI enhances higher education through assessment, predictive modeling, chatbots, adaptive tutoring, and learning analytics, as noted by Crompton and Burke (2023).

HOW EMOTIONAL INTELLIGENCE AMONG LEADERS CONTRIBUTES TO LEARNING

The term "Emotional Intelligence" was first coined by psychologists Salovey and Mayer (1990). It emphasizes a person's ability to perceive, process, and manage emotional information accurately and effectively when dealing with oneself and others, as shown in Figure 1. This basic understanding fosters resilience in times of adversity, enabling individuals to make informed decisions rather than react impulsively. EI is not a fixed trait but a dynamic skill that can be cultivated and refined through situations. Maintaining composure and navigating challenging situations with poise requires effective self-management. In reality, EI encompasses a broader sense of social awareness, including empathy. This bridges the gap between misunderstandings and unfair or unethical communication by recognizing diverse perspectives. This entails creating an inclusive environment where individuals feel valued and respected. Moreover, EI improves social skills through conflict resolution, effective communication, network building, and collaboration (Chugh & Matchaba, 2024). Bar-On (1997) suggested that individuals with higher emotional intelligence tend to perform better in life than those with lower emotional intelligence; it has been shown to play a significant role in academic success, mental and physical health, and professional achievement.

Figure 1. The model of Emotional intelligence by Mayer and Salovey. 1997.

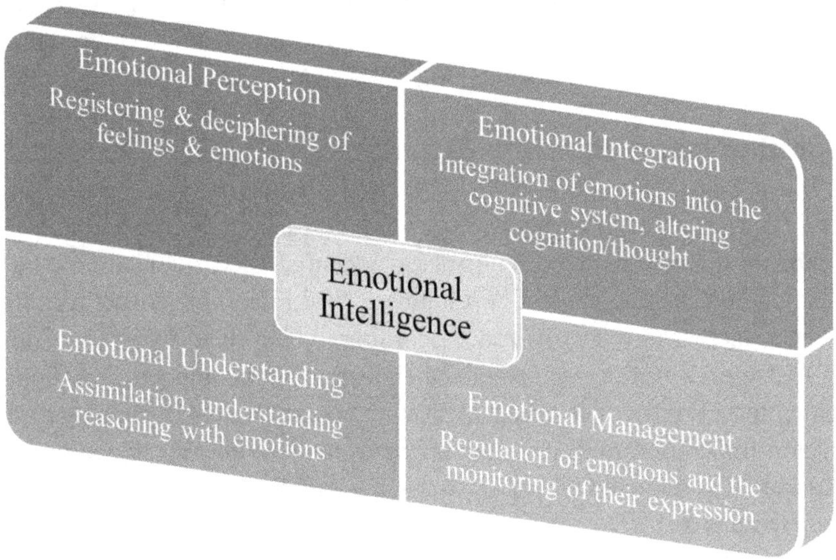

How can educational leaders create value through emotional intelligence?

Emotional intelligence confers substantial benefits, affecting both personal and professional success. It is a fundamental skill in many careers, enhancing communication, building stronger relationships, and supporting academic and professional achievement. EI underpins mutual respect, trust, and healthy relationships, while also fostering a sense of belonging and collective responsibility in society (Okolie, 2024). Additionally, it is closely linked to mental and physical health. Among teenagers, emotional intelligence is defined as the ability to use emotions effectively and adaptively (Sekhri, 2017). Research indicates a connection between EI and academic success (Fallahzadeh, 2011). Sanchez-Ruiz and colleagues (2013) found that emotional intelligence better predicts university students' academic performance than personality traits or cognitive skills. The study found that students' self-emotion appraisal was positively correlated with their academic results.

A study by Fasso and Knight (2018) found that identifying and managing emotions can positively affect online learning outcomes. It is essential to have positive emotions, such as attentiveness, keenness, and engagement, in the online learning environment, which leads to improved academic performance and better knowledge retention. Additionally, students could enhance their cognitive skills, participation, and motivation, thereby achieving greater academic success. On the other hand, a lack of concentration, enthusiasm, and frustration, as well as anxiety, hinders the achievement of desired outcomes. The latter can lead to reduced information processing and comprehension (Clarke, 2010; Wu & Yu, 2022).

Integrating leadership with EI and AI

Today's learning environments, which are increasingly integrating technology, recognize the importance of direct instructor-student contact in facilitating knowledge acquisition and shaping student development. The importance of EI for effective learning is increasingly recognized. According to Cleveland-Innes and Campbell (2012), EI refers to how individuals and their learning community express emotions, which, in turn, affects their engagement with course content, technology, and the instructor. In addition to Mayer and Salovey's model, other models of emotional intelligence (EI) include Goleman's, Bar-On's, and Wooff's. The concepts related to these models are;

a. Self-awareness defines the individual's internal state and resources. preferences, etc., with three competencies: emotional awareness, accurate self-assessment, and self-confidence;
b. Self-management refers to the ability to regulate one's behaviors, thoughts, and emotions effectively with competencies; emotional self-control, transparency, adaptability, achievement, initiative, and optimism;
c. Social awareness means the understanding of group dynamics and how individuals interact within social structures, with three competencies: empathy, organizational awareness, and service orientation, and
d. Relationship management refers to the set of skills and techniques used to communicate, collaborate, and build rapport with others effectively, with competencies such as change agent, conflict management, influence, inspirational leadership, teamwork, and collaboration (Wolff, 2005).

According to Bar-on, the other five elements are self-perception, emotional self-awareness, self-expression, interpersonal skills, decision-making skills, and stress management, which relate to the above EI competencies. An individual's emotional response to their learning environment and peers is seen as a key factor in learning (Flood, 2003). Researchers propose a relationship between emotionally designed e-platforms and enhanced student learning and satisfaction (Berenson et al., 2016). Furthermore, students with high emotional intelligence (EI) are typically more motivated and focused on achievement than those with low EI (Kumar et al., 2016).

The social constructivist approach proposes that knowledge is formed via social dialogue and cultural tools such as written and digital resources. Critics contend that these theories might neglect individual skills and the nuanced, sometimes ambiguous social signals encountered online (Bandura, 1977). Self-efficacy—the belief in one's capacity to learn—enhances motivation, participation, and self-regulation (Schunk & Pajares, 2009). Bandura (1977) characterized learning as a social cognitive process that takes place through observation or guidance. In online environments, strong self-efficacy and active engagement assist learners in managing their education through setting goals, tracking progress, receiving feedback, and comparing themselves with peers.

A practical approach to integrating leadership with AI, EI, and equity is for leaders to prioritize equity in classrooms through AI by placing robust ethical safeguards and stakeholder perspectives at the forefront of every decision. They safeguard student privacy by limiting the use of data and by clearly communicating AI practices to families. They assess potential biases by analyzing AI-generated insights with a diverse staff and by evaluating outcomes across different student groups (Smith, & Doe, 2025). They uphold accountability by ensuring that humans retain control over final decisions and by establishing straightforward avenues for students and parents to voice concerns. In everyday practice, this involves organizing conversations with parents before implementing new AI technologies, encouraging students to evaluate the systems and provide their input, and conducting frequent assessments to confirm that AI is benefiting all students equitably. By taking these specific steps, leaders foster trust and guarantee that AI enhances inclusion rather than detracting from it. By embedding these ethical mandates into quality assurance frameworks and prioritizing digital equity, institutional leaders can transition from mere experimentation to a sustainable, inclusive ecosystem that treats AI literacy as a foundational competency for the entire school community (AACSB, 2026; Athena Solutions, 2025).

AI AND ONLINE LEARNING

While distance learning has longstanding origins, the 2020 pandemic accelerated its adoption, making online education a standard in higher education. Even before the health crisis, academic leaders acknowledged its importance, with more than two-thirds having included it in their long-term plans by 2013. The pandemic caused a significant surge in online learning, with the percentage of undergraduates taking online classes more than doubling from 2019 to 2020, and nearly half of all college students enrolling in fully online degree programs. Online engagement among college students has steadily grown—from roughly 20% in 2007 to nearly 33% in 2012—and by 2021, more than 60% of undergraduates had taken at least one online course. Additionally, enrollment in full-time online degree programs exceeded 25% of all students in 2021. See the figures from Allen (2024) for detailed data. Research by Stolba et al. (2024) also explores this area, using the TIER Environmental Determinants and Emotional Response Framework, which expands on the Fully Online Learning Community (FOLC) model designed to foster cooperative learning and community in online settings (vanOostveen et al., 2016a). The growth of online enrollment in higher education is illustrated in Figure 2.

Figure 2. The growth of online enrollment in higher education from 2007 -2021.

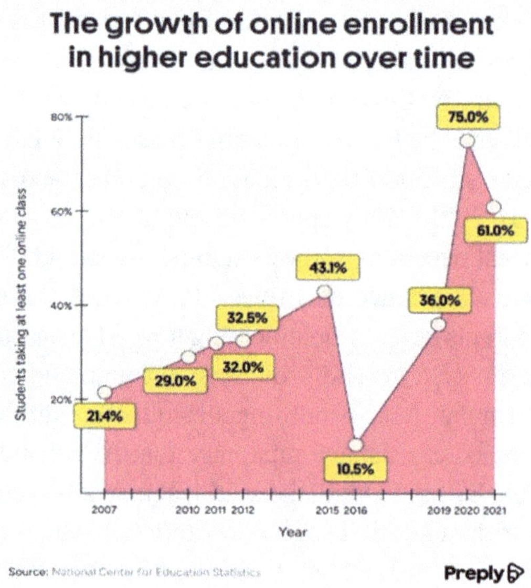

Source: https://preply.com/en/blog/online-learning-statistics/

The scenario depicts a school leader responding thoughtfully when an AI system mislabels a student as "at risk." Rather than acting on the alert alone, the leader gathers context from teachers, speaks directly with the student, and learns that the issue stems from a recent move and temporary loss of internet access—details the AI could not capture. The leader then adjusts the support plan to address the real barrier and shares the missing data with the AI team to improve the system. This response demonstrates ethical judgment, empathy, data literacy, and accountability, showing how emotionally intelligent leadership ensures that AI is used to promote equity and avoid mislabeling or harming students. This approach models the emerging competencies required for ethical and inclusive AI leadership:

- *Ethical judgment*, by questioning the validity and fairness of AI outputs
- *Empathy*, by centering the student's voice and circumstances
- *Data literacy*, by understanding the limitations of algorithmic predictions
- *Accountability*, by ensuring human oversight remains central to decision-making.

Ethical And Strategic Leadership In Online Learning

Online learning encompasses blended, hybrid, and fully online modes (Saichale, 2020; van Oostveen et al., 2016a). The Fully Online Learning Community (FOLC) emphasizes social constructivism, fostering collaborative knowledge creation and deeper understanding through cognitive presence. Social presence via videoconferencing enhances communication and peer connection. Using the FOLC model promotes active engagement with video, blogging, and dialogue, thereby reducing barriers to online interaction (McKeithan et al., 2021; Molinillo et al., 2018).

Grounded in the circumplex model of affect (Russel, 1980), emotional states are viewed as external expressions of internal psychological states influenced by pleasantness and activation (Barrett & Russell, 2015). Yagci and vanOostveen (2021) highlight that individual differences significantly impact emotional expression and interpretation. Cleveland-Innes and Campbell (2012) note that recognizing the link between emotions, engagement, and motivation is crucial for online learning communities, which depend on individuals forming connections and sharing vulnerabilities (van Oostveen et al., 2018). Online communities use synchronous and asynchronous tools within shared digital environments that leverage social and semantic web tools. While text and emoticons provide some emotional cues, audio-video communication captures facial expressions and body language effectively. Facial expressions are key to understanding human communication and relate to EI. Social actions improve emotions and serve as relationship-building tools. Positive emotions, like happiness and joy, enhance bonding (Meneghel et al., 2016). Negative emotions can reveal conflicts, aiding relationship development (Graham et al., 2008). Emotional support chatbots or virtual coaches offer guidance on relaxation, mindfulness, and emotional regulation (Zheng et al., 2023), helping students manage stress, build resilience, and control reactive behaviors.

The following scenario provides a nexus between leadership, equity, EI, and AI use:

Institutional Context: The Metropolitan University of Business (MUB)

1. The Strategic Dilemma

In early 2025, MUB faced a retention crisis. Data showed that first-generation and international students were 25% more likely to drop out than other students. At the same time, university leaders, including the Provost, rolled out an AI-based "Early Warning System" (EWS) to identify students at risk of failing. Unfortunately, the EWS mistakenly labeled students from lower-income backgrounds as "high-risk" based only on their past data. This created a "digital stigma" that deterred faculty from providing additional support to these students.

2. The Leadership Interpretation: Beyond Binary Logic

Applying a High-EI Leadership lens, the Provost interpreted this not as a technological failure but as an Equity crisis.

- *The Insight*: The AI was missing "Contextual Intelligence." It could identify the outcome (low grades) but failed to grasp the reasons behind it—such as financial stress, cultural displacement, or "imposter syndrome.'
- *The Decision*: Rather than turning off the AI, the Provost decided to "Humanize the Algorithm" by incorporating Emotional Intelligence into the technological process.

3. Navigating the AI–EI–Equity Landscape: Strategic Actions

Action A: Re-Coding for Equity (The "Weighted Resilience" Metric) The leadership collaborated with data scientists to adjust the AI's configuration. They shifted the focus from "Historical Deficits" (past grades) to "Indicators of Resilience." The AI was retrained to identify students balancing full-time work and studies, tagging them for "Potential Excellence Support" rather than "High-Risk Monitoring."

- *Goal:* To shift the narrative from deficit-based to asset-based equity.

Action B: The EI-Enabled Advising Protocol. The Provost required that AI "flags" remain inaccessible to faculty unless they complete mandatory EI and Empathy training. Advisors were instructed to use AI data as a tool to initiate conversations, not to draw conclusions.

- *Execution:* When the AI flagged a student, the advisor's role was to engage in "proactive outreach" by actively listening and offering emotional support, making sure the student felt "seen" by the institution instead of merely being "tracked" by a machine.

Action C: Ethical Governance (The Student AI-Ethics Board). To promote transparency within the institution, the Provost established a board comprising students, ethicists, and community leaders to conduct quarterly audits of the AI's decisions.

- *Goal:* To move ethics from a peripheral compliance task to a central pillar of institutional governance.

4. Critical Analysis: Outcomes and Leadership Reflections

By the 2026 academic cycle, MUB reported the following results:

- Retention Equilibrium: The 25% gap in retention for first-generation students was reduced to within 3% of the general student body.
- Faculty transformation revealed through surveys that educators felt more "connected" to students. The AI handled the "sorting" process, enabling humans to focus on "supporting".
- Economic Impact: The university experienced a 12% rise in external funding from industry partners, drawn to MUT's "Ethically-Certified" graduate talent.

Leadership Consideration

The MUB case demonstrates that educational leadership in the AI era is a *triadic performance*.

1. AI provided the scale, identifying thousands of students in real-time.
2. EI outlined the Method: it specified how the institution engaged with students—treating them with dignity rather than just as data points.
3. Equity served the Purpose by ensuring that technological power was used to create a level playing field, rather than exacerbating advantages for the privileged.

ADVANCEMENTS IN ONLINE LEARNING

E-learning is continually reshaping the educational landscape for learners across all demographic groups. Experiencing a remarkable surge since 2000, this lucrative industry continues to demonstrate momentum. Algorithms designed to detect emotions can analyze facial expressions, vocal intonation, and physiological responses (Middya, Nag, & Roy, 2022), providing individuals with insights into their emotional states. Through ongoing analysis and feedback, students can enhance their ability to identify and articulate their feelings, a critical component of emotional intelligence.

Although it is now a significant alternative to conventional education, online learning initially emerged from universities seeking to expand their reach. Its development began in 1982 with the establishment of computer-aided learning centers. It progressed through the introduction of the first online program in 1994, followed by the expansion of virtual course offerings by the late 1990s. The early 2000s saw the rise of open-access educational resources, such as MIT's OpenCourseWare, and the emergence of Massive Open Online Courses (MOOCs) in 2007, resulting in substantial growth in online course enrollment by 2009. In subsequent years, free online courses from prestigious institutions such as Stanford proliferated, and major online learning platforms, including Udacity and edX, were established. The accessibility of online education continued to grow, with nearly all U.S. public colleges offering online classes by 2014. The sector's growth accelerated dramatically in 2020, driven by the pandemic and increasing global skills gaps, which led to a surge in MOOC enrollments and the rise of online learning platforms. By 2024, platforms such as Udemy reported significant growth in skills-based learning, reflecting the industry's continued adaptation to evolving educational needs (Dean, 2024). It is also important to recognize that the FOLC model, grounded in constructivist theory, emphasizes social and cognitive presence and introduces collaborative learning in a digital setting to reduce transactional distance (Moore, 1993) and cultivate trust for effective communication (van Oostveen et al., 2016b). Additionally, AI supports emotional self-management by providing coping strategies (Ahmed et al., 2021). The following diagram presents McKinsey's findings on the dimensions that shape the online learning experiences of higher education students. (Figure 3).

Figure 3. Felipe Child, Marcus Frank, Jonathan Law, and Jimmy Sarakatsannis

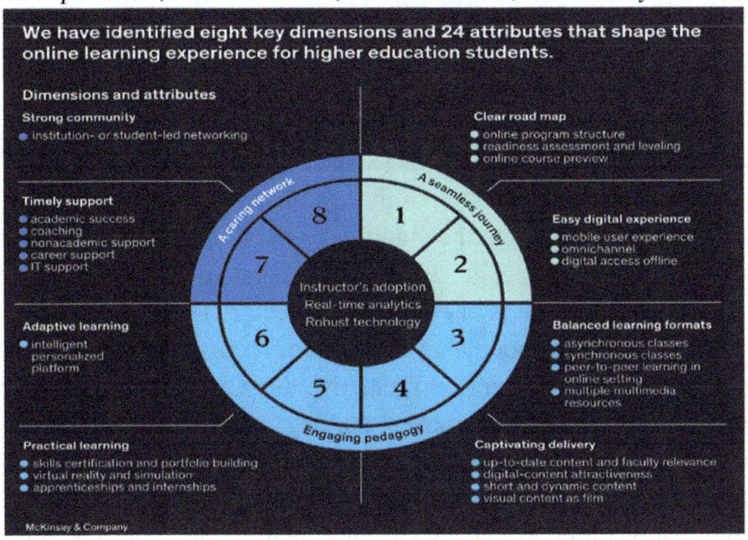

https://www.mckinsey.com/industries/public-sector/our-insights/what-do-higher-education-students-want-from-online-learning

The use of AI-driven simulations and role-playing exercises can foster the growth of empathy and social skills. Schutte and Stilinović (2017) have shown the efficacy of virtual reality in developing empathy. In the future, students may interact with AI-generated personas in situations that require them to interpret and respond to varied emotional signals and social interactions. This form of immersive learning provides a safe and controlled environment for students to hone their skills in empathy, attentive listening, and conflict resolution. AI can drive student motivation by dynamically adjusting educational content based on their emotional states and learning preferences. Through personalized learning platforms, task difficulty, relevant illustrations, and real-time support can be adapted, thereby enhancing student engagement and supporting the development of their emotional intelligence (Farrokhnia et al., 2023).

LEADERSHIP - ETHICAL GOVERNANCE AND AI INTERVENTIONS

Literature from various studies highlights the domains that encompass the full spectrum of AI applications in educational leadership, which confirms a significant nexus between ethical governance, strategic planning, and operational management (Sposato, 2024; Brusilovsky, 2024), and these domains can be utilized to emerging technologies and applications (Mao et al., 2024). The established taxonomy classifies the AI applications in educational leadership in areas such as ethical AI leadership and governance, governance and compliance, decision-making and policy formulation, organizational leadership and strategic planning, administrative efficiency, teaching practices, student support services, personalized learning, and diversity, equity, and inclusion (DEI) initiatives (Sposato, 2025). The next part provides a worm 's-eye view of the application of these domains.

The first domain highlights the significance of bias-detection algorithms and privacy safeguards (Nguyen et al., 2022). The second domain underscores the role of rules and regulations, and their effective enforcement in educational institutions through natural language processing and pattern recognition (Kaur et al., 2022). The subsequent domain centers on predictive analytics tools to analyze student outcomes and institutional performance, guiding policy adjustments and fostering an equitable education system (Wang, 2021). These AI strategies support strategic planning by assessing the achievement of goals for maintaining educational quality through optimal resource use. They can link internal and external factors in risk management and policymaking (Chiu et al., 2023). Modern scheduling systems help reduce administrative burdens for educators (Kuleto et al., 2021). Moreover, advanced pedagogical techniques using machine learning can identify learning gaps and improve classroom engagement through actionable feedback (Chiu et al., 2022). Student mental and cognitive abilities can also be supported by refined design recognition algorithms that analyze career paths, personalized activities, and extracurricular activities, thereby providing tailored recommendations. AI tools assist in creating personalized learning environments by analyzing patterns in student performance, thereby enhancing engagement and outcomes (Tang et al., 2020). Finally, these AI tools help address educational disparities across different groups (Xia et al., 2022).

EMPIRICAL EVIDENCE FOR THE APPLIED MODEL

Recent studies from 2024 to 2026 show that the practical use of the AI–EI–Equity framework is moving toward "Human-in-the-Loop" (HITL) models and ongoing algorithmic audits. For example, leadership in institutions is shifting from traditional oversight to a facilitator role, where administrators, such as those in the University of California System (2025), use AI as a pre-screener for admissions to identify non-traditional student strengths and apply emotional intelligence in making final decisions (Polat et al., 2025). In terms of equity, organizations like the New South Wales Department of Education (2025) employ predictive analytics to locate "staffing deserts," enabling proactive teacher placements to meet inclusive education goals in underserved communities (UNESCO, 2026). Additionally, ethical governance is being implemented through "Traceability Protocols" and "Algorithmic Red-Teaming," exemplified by the Singapore Ministry of Education (2026), which guarantees transparent, explainable AI-supported grading that is regularly checked for racial or socio-economic bias (Hummel, 2025; Digital Promise, 2024). This evolution ensures that technological progress acts as a tool for social justice, rather than a hidden system that deepens systemic inequalities (Okokoyo et al., 2025).

CONTRIBUTIONS TO AI INTERVENTIONS IN EDUCATIONAL SETTINGS: A COMPARATIVE APPROACH

To harness AI's full potential, policymakers play a crucial role in fostering equity and overcoming infrastructural challenges. The link between AI and educational inequality can be both beneficial and problematic. Without relevant algorithms, unbiased data, proper training datasets, and consideration of socioeconomic factors, AI's ability to promote equitable learning is limited. Regarding integrity, AI-driven plagiarism detectors support ethical standards; however, issues such as improper data collection, misleading content, and biased assessment methods require strict policies from governments, universities, and scholars. Additionally, project management tools and predictive analytics can monitor progress and identify risks, helping projects stay on track with minimal disruptions and improving student outcomes, including employability. The effectiveness of these measures depends on the availability of fair training data; otherwise, disparities in resource allocation may arise. Therefore, ethical issues concerning student welfare, equality, and data security are paramount. The educational sector must balance technological progress with strong ethical governance to uphold principles of equity.

A comparative analysis of AI education policies in the U.S., China, and Nigeria shows that in the U.S., AI strategies have improved access but also led to algorithmic biases that deepen economic and racial inequalities. In Nigeria, AI-supported Universal Basic Education (UBE) efforts have boosted school enrollment but have faced challenges with quality and funding (Sule, 2024). China prioritized student tracking and local intervention strategies over equity considerations (Zhang, 2024). Similarly, Australia's AI policies lean toward neoliberal economic goals, thereby limiting broader economic perspectives. Canada's market-driven AI approaches aim to enhance efficiency through democratic participation and equity, yet social justice and inclusion remain difficult to achieve (Lee & Johnstone, 2019). Regarding gender equity, AI fosters creativity and educational opportunities for girls but lacks long-term plans for sustainable development (Jones, 2011).

Umoke et al. (2025) conducted a study on AI-driven educational policy design, introducing an AI-Equity nexus model that emphasizes key AI concepts in education. These include machine learning, predictive analytics, Generative AI, and data-driven policy decisions. The model can analyze AI governance, policy implementation, ethical considerations, resource allocation, personalized and inclusive learning, impact assessments, and future outlooks.

PRACTICAL AND THEORETICAL IMPLICATIONS OF EDUCATIONAL LEADERSHIP IN EI, EQUITY, AND AI

An educational leadership model integrating AI, EI, and equity variables provides a transformative framework that bridges the gap between technical efficiency and human-centric values. Theoretically, it facilitates a shift toward *Adaptive-Hybrid Theory*, allowing researchers to explore how artificial intelligence's predictive power can be ethically balanced by emotional intelligence to mitigate "automation bias" (Okokoyo et al., 2025).

In practice, the model functions as a strategic toolkit for academics to optimize institutional decision-making. While AI streamlines administrative complexity and identifies points of student struggle, the EI and equity components ensure that resource allocation remains empathetic and adheres to inclusive education mandates. This multidisciplinary approach moves beyond descriptive policy, mandating actionable strategies like "Traceability Protocols" and live bias audits to ensure that technological advancements actively dismantle, rather than reinforce, systemic inequalities (Hummel, 2025).

AI-driven educational policymaking leverages complex datasets—including student performance, teacher evaluations, and demographic data—to generate actionable insights that traditional analytical methods often miss. By identifying learning gaps, predicting graduation trends, and optimizing equitable teacher placement in under-resourced communities, AI enables a shift toward more proactive, evidence-based resource planning and inclusive policy design. However, integrating these tools also poses significant ethical and practical hurdles, including algorithmic bias, sensitive data privacy concerns, and the potential for unpredictable outcomes. To navigate these challenges effectively, institutions must invest in robust technological infrastructure and comprehensive stakeholder training, ensuring that AI serves as a collaborative, transparent aid to human decision-making rather than a replacement for it.

SUMMARY

This chapter highlights the transformative power of AI-driven initiatives in promoting governance, resource optimization, and personalized learning, as well as leadership skills, from both objective and subjective perspectives. Various AI technologies, including predictive analytics, data analytics for decision-making, adaptive learning systems, and stakeholder engagement tools, can be integrated into educational strategies to maintain equity and inclusivity. Furthermore, in higher education settings, chatbots, intelligent tutoring systems, and adaptive learning platforms are being used to enhance student engagement and participation, yielding positive outcomes and long-term impact. Undoubtedly, these are promising elements for advancing educational policy and equity; however, obstacles such as algorithmic bias, insufficient training, inadequate infrastructure, and limited transparency and accountability must be addressed more effectively.

REFERENCES

AACSB. (2026). *A framework for artificial intelligence in business education: Exemplars and critical themes for successful integration.* AACSB Thought Leadership. https://www.aacsb.edu/insights/reports/2026/a-framework-for-artificial-intelligence-in-business-education

Ahmed, A., Ali, N., Aziz, S., Abd-Alrazaq, A. A., Hassan, A., Khalifa, M., Elhusein, B., Ahmed, M., Ahmed, M. A. S., & Househ, M. (2021). A review of mobile chatbot apps for anxiety and depression and their self-care features. *Computer Methods and Programs in Biomedicine Update, 1*, 100012. DOI: 10.1016/j.cmpbup.2021.100012

Al- Ruheili, H & Al-Buraiki (2025). *Optimizing Research Techniques and Learning Strategies with Digital Technologies.* IGI Global. DOI: DOI: 10.4018/979-8-3693-7863-2.ch009

Athena Infonomics. (2025). *Equitable AI in education: AI ethics guide for decision-makers.* Athena Infonomics Resources. https://www.athenainfonomics.com/resources/equitable-ai-in-education-ai-ethics-guide

Bandura, A. (1977). Self-efficacy: Toward a unifying theory of behavioral change. *Psychological Review, 84*(2), 191–215. DOI: 10.1037/0033-295X.84.2.191

Barrett, L. F., & Russell, J. A. (2015). An introduction to psychological construction. In Barrett, L. F., & Russell, J. A. (Eds.), *The psychological construction of emotion* (pp. 1–17). Guilford Press.

Berenson, R., Boyles, G., & Weaver, A. (2016). Age and gender differences in emotional intelligence in adults: A cross-sectional study. Emotional Intelligence as a Predictor for Success in Online Learning. https://www.irrodl.org/index.php/irrodl/article/viewArticle/385/1036

Bond, M., Khosravi, H., De Laat, M., Bergdahi, N., Negrea, V., Oxley, E., Pham, P., Chong, S. W., & Siemens, G. (2024). A meta-systematic review of artificial intelligence in higher education: A call for increased ethics, collaboration, and rigour. *International Journal of Educational Technology in Higher Education, 21*(1), 4. DOI: 10.1186/s41239-023-00436-z

Brusilovsky, P. (2024). AI in education, learner control, and human–AI collaboration. *International Journal of Artificial Intelligence in Education, 34*(1), 122–135. DOI: 10.1007/s40593-023-00356-z

Chen, L., Chen, P., & Lin, Z. (2020). Artificial Intelligence in Education [Review]. *IEEE Axess, 8*, 75764–75278.

Chugh, R., & Matchaba, P. (2024). *Adaptive Leadership in the Digital Age: Balancing AI and Human Empathy.* In *Cases on Leadership and Executive Coaching in the Era of AI* (pp. 45–67). IGI Global. DOI: 10.4018/979-8-3693-0240-8.ch003

Clarke, N. (2010). Emotional intelligence and learning in teams. *Journal of Workplace Learning, 22*(3), 125–145. DOI: 10.1108/13665621011028594

Cleveland-Innes, M., & Campbell, P. (2012). Emotional presence, learning, and the online learning environment. *International Review of Research in Open and Distance Learning, 13*(4), 269–292. DOI: 10.19173/irrodl.v13i4.1234

Crompton, H., & Burke, D. (2023). Artificial intelligence in higher education: The state of the field. *International Journal of Educational Technology in Higher Education, 20*(1), 22. DOI: 10.1186/s41239-023-00392-8

Digital Promise. (2024). *Educational leadership in the age of AI: A framework for powerful learning.* Digital Promise AI Portfolio. https://digitalpromise.org/initiative/artificial-intelligence-in-education/our-ai-portfolio/

Dreamson, N. (2021). *Cultural Diversity Pedagogy and Meta-Case Design: A New Approach to Diversity in Education.* Routledge. DOI: 10.4324/9781003096313

Essel, H. B., Vlachopoulos, D., Tachie-Menson, A., Johnson, E. E., & Baah, P. K. (2022). The impact of a virtual teaching assistant (chatbot) on students' learning in Ghanaian higher education. *International Journal of Educational Technology in Higher Education, 19*(1), 1–19. DOI: 10.1186/s41239-022-00362-6

Fallahzadeh, H. (2011). The relationship between emotional intelligence and academic achievement in medical science students in Iran. *Procedia: Social and Behavioral Sciences, 30*, 1461–1466. DOI: 10.1016/j.sbspro.2011.10.283

Farrokhnia, M., Banihashem, S. K., Noroozi, O., & Wals, A. (2023). A SWOT analysis of ChatGPT: Implications for educational practice and research. *Innovations in Education and Teaching International,* •••, 1–15.

Fasso, W., & Knight, B. A. (2018). Affect in Online Learning Outcomes, Emotions, and Affective States in Management Association (Ed). Innovative Applications of Online Pedagogy and Course Design. 131–151. DOI: 10.4018/978-1-525-5466-0ch007

Flood, J. (2003). Successful online learning: The five P's. Training Journal, 30–32.

Grewal, D. D., & Salovey, P. (2006). In Csikszentmihalyi, M., & Csikszentmihalyi, I. S. (Eds.), *"Benefits of emotional intelligence" in A life worth living: contributions to positive psychology* (pp. 104–119). Oxford University Press.

Harris, A., & Jones, M. (2021). Educational leadership: Knowledge, development, and challenges. *Journal of Educational Administration*, •••, 41–51.

Herold, B. (2019). Forty percent of elementary school teachers' work could be automated by 2030. McKinsey Global Institute predicts—education Week. https://edweek.org/education/forty-percent-of-elementary-scjool-teachers-work-could-be automated-by-2030-mckinsey-global-institute-predicts/2019/6

Hummel, S. (2025). Ethical and responsible AI in education: Situated ethics for democratic learning. *Education Sciences*, *15*(12), 1594. DOI: 10.3390/educsci15121594

Hummel, S. (2025). Ethical and responsible AI in education: Situated ethics for democratic learning. *Education Sciences*, *15*(12), 1594. DOI: 10.3390/educsci15121594

Jones, S. (2011). Girls' secondary education in Uganda: Assessing policy within the women's empowerment framework. *Gender and Education*, *23*(4), 385–413. DOI: 10.1080/09540253.2010.499854

Kashishi, N., & Hack, S. (2023). Emotional Intelligence in the Digital Age: Harnessing AI for students' inner development. *Journal of Perspectives in Applied Academic Practice*, *11*(3). Advance online publication. DOI: 10.56433/jpaap.v11i3.579

Kuleto, V., Ilic, M., Dumangiu, M., Rankovic, M., Martins, O. M., Paun, D., & Mihoreanu, L. (2021). Exploring opportunities and challenges of artificial intelligence and machine learning in higher education institutions. *Sustainability (Basel)*, *13*(18), 10424. DOI: 10.3390/su131810424

Kumar, J., Muniandy, B., Wan Yahaya, W., & Cowan, B. (2016). Emotional Design in Multimedia Learning: The Relationship between Emotional Intelligence and Learner Satisfaction, Conference paper, https://www.researchgate.net/publication/302574982

Mag, A. G., Sinfield, S., & Burns, T. (2017). The benefits of inclusive education: New challenges for university teachers. *MATEC Web of Conferences*, *121*, 12011. Advance online publication. DOI: 10.1051/matecconf/201712112011

Mallillin, L. L. (2020). Educational fields, processes, tools, and techniques in leadership. *IJMRA*, 1–11.

Mallillin, L. L.. (2021). *Teachers as educational leaders and resource providers*. IJMRA.

Mallillin, L. L., & Laurel, R. D. (2022). *Educational leadership transformation and quality systems*. IJMRA.

Mallillin, L. L., & Mallillin, J. B. (2019). *Transition behavior and traits of individual school leaders*. IJMRA.

Mao, J., Chen, B., & Liu, J. C. (2024). Generative artificial intelligence in education and its implications for assessment. *TechTrends*, *68*(1), 58–66. DOI: 10.1007/s11528-023-00911-4

Mayer, J. D., Salovey, P., & Caruso, D. R. (2002). *Mayer-Salovey-Caruso Emotional Intelligence Test (MCEIT) User's Manual*. MHS.

McCarthy, J., Minsky, M. L., Rochester, N., & Shannon, C. E. (1955). A proposal for the Dartmouth summer research project on artificial intelligence. Available at http://www-formal.stanford.edu/jmc/history/dartmouth/dartmouth.html

McKeithan, G. K., Rivera, M. O., Mann, L. E., & Mann, L. B. (2021). Strategies to promote meaningful student engagement in online settings. *Journal of Education and Training Studies*, *9*(4), 1. https://redfame.com/journal/index.php/jets/article/view/5135/5402. DOI: 10.11114/jets.v9i4.5135

Middya, A. I., Nag, B., & Roy, S. (2022). Deep learning based multimodal emotion recognition using model-level fusion of audio–visual modalities. *Knowledge-Based Systems*, *244*, 10858. DOI: 10.1016/j.knosys.2022.108580

Molinillo, S., Aguilar-Illescas, R., Anaya-Sánchez, R., & Vallespín-Arán, M. (2018). Exploring the impacts of interactions, social presence, and emotional engagement on active collaborative learning in a social web-based environment. *Computers & Education*, *123*, 41–52. DOI: 10.1016/j.compedu.2018.04.012

Moore, M. G. (1993). The theory of transactional distance. In Moore, M. G. (Ed.), *Handbook of distance education* (3rd ed., pp. 66–85). Routledge.

Nelson, S. (2022). The practice lens and values in educational leadership. *IJMRA*, 197–210.

Nguyen, A., Ngo, H. N., Hong, Y., Dang, B., & Nguyen, B. P. T. (2022). Ethical principles for artificial intelligence in education. *Education and Information Technologies*, *28*(4), 1–21.

Nig, D. T. K., Su, J., Leung, J. K. L., & Chu, S. K. W. (2024). Artificial Intelligence (AI) literacy education in secondary schools: A review. *Interactive Learning Environments*, *32*(10), 6204–6224. DOI: 10.1080/10494820.2023.2255228

Okokoyo, I. E.. (2025). Adaptive-Hybrid Theory: Navigating the transition from traditional to AI-integrated educational leadership. *Global Journal of Educational Leadership*, *9*(2), 45–68.

Okolie, U. C. (2024). The Role of Emotional Intelligence in Mitigating Algorithmic Bias: A Leadership Perspective. In *Artificial Intelligence for Social Justice and Sustainable Development* (pp. 156–178). IGI Global., DOI: 10.4018/979-8-3693-2015-0.ch008

Polat, M., Karataş, İ. H., & Varol, N. (2025). Ethical artificial intelligence (AI) in educational leadership: Literature review and bibliometric analysis. *Leadership and Policy in Schools*, *24*(1), 46–76. DOI: 10.1080/15700763.2024.2412204

Popenici, S. A. D., & Kerr, S. (2017). Exploring the impact of artificial intelligence on teaching and learning in higher education. *Research and Practice in Technology Enhanced Learning*, *12*(1), 22. DOI: 10.1186/s41039-017-0062-8

Richardson, J. W., McLeod, S., & Suers, N. (2015). Technology leadership is just good leadership: Dispositions of tech-savvy superintendents. AASA Journal of Scholarship & Practice, 12(1), 11–30. https://www.learntechlib.org/p/159574/

Salovey, P., & Mayer, J. D. (1990). Emotional Intelligence. *Imagination, Cognition and Personality*, *9*(3), 185–211. DOI: 10.2190/DUGG-P24E-52WK-6CDG

Sanchez-Ruiz, M. J., Mavroveli, S., & Poullis, J. (2013). Trait emotional intelligence and its links to university performance: An examination. *Personality and Individual Differences*, *54*(5), 658–662. DOI: 10.1016/j.paid.2012.11.013

Schunk, D. H., & Pajares, F. (2009). Self-efficacy theory. In Wentzel, K. R., & Wigfield, A. (Eds.), *Handbook of motivation at School*. Routledge.

Schutte, N. S., & Stilinović, E. J. (2017). Facilitating empathy through virtual reality. *Motivation and Emotion*, *41*(6), 708–712. DOI: 10.1007/s11031-017-9641-7

Sekhri, P., Sandhu, M., & Sachdev, V. (2017). Emerging Understanding of Emotional Intelligence of Teenagers. *International Journal of Clinical Pediatric Dentistry*, *10*(3), 289–292. DOI: 10.5005/jp-journals-10005-1452

Singapore Ministry of Education. (2026). *Traceability protocols in automated assessment: Standards for transparency and feedback*. MOE Singapore AI Literacy Initiative.

Smith, J. A., & Doe, R. (2025). *Decision-Making in the AI Era: Integrating Equity-Centered Leadership with Data Analytics*. In *Innovative Leadership and Policy for 21st Century Schools* (pp. 202–225). IGI Global.

Sposato, M. (2024). Leadership training and development in the age of artificial intelligence. *Development and Learning in Organizations*, *38*(4), 4–7. DOI: 10.1108/DLO-12-2023-0256

Sposato, M. (2025). Artificial intelligence in educational leadership: a comprehensive taxonomy and future directions. All Works. 7270. https://zuscholars.zu.ac.ae/works/7270

Stolba, A., Hope, A., Branch, J., Manoj, P., Trinier, J., Behboudi, A., vanOostveen, R., & Childs, E. (2024). Beyond content delivery: Harnessing emotional intelligence for community building in fully online digital spaces. *International Journal of Educational Technology in Higher Education*, *21*(1), 48. DOI: 10.1186/s41239-024-00481-2

Sule, J. O. (2024). Accessing the impact of policy reforms on the rights to education: A comparative study of emerging and developed economies (Nigeria and the U.S.). GSC Advanced Research and Reviews. 21(01). 056-064. https://doi/org/DOI: 10.30574/gscarr.2024.21.1.0359

Tang, Y., Liang, J., Hare, R., & Wang, F. Y. (2020). A personalized learning system for parallel intelligent education. *IEEE Transactions on Computational Social Systems*, *7*(2), 352–361. DOI: 10.1109/TCSS.2020.2965198

Turing, A. M. (1937). On computable numbers, with an application to the Entscheidungsproblem. *Proceedings of the London Mathematical Society*, *2*(1), 230–26. DOI: 10.1112/plms/s2-42.1.230

Turing, A. M. (1950). Computing machinery and intelligence. *Mind*, *59*, 443–460.

UNESCO. (2026). *Guidance for generative AI in education and research* (Updated ed.). UNESCO Digital Library. https://www.unesco.org/en/articles/guidance-generative-ai-education-and-research

United Nations. (2017). Toolkit on disability for Africa. Inclusive Education. Available at:https://www.un.org/esa/socdev/documents/disability/Toolkit/Inclusive-Education.pd

University of California System. (2025). *The co-pilot leadership initiative: AI-human collaboration in higher education admissions*. UC Office of the President (UCOP). *Research Reports (Montgomery).*

vanOostveen, R., DiGiuseppe, M., Barber, W., Blayone, T., & Childs, E. (2016a). New conceptions for digital technology sandboxes: Developing a Fully Online Learning Communities (FOLC) model. In *Proceedings of EdMedia: World Conference on Educational Media and Technology* 2016 (pp. 672–680). Association for the Advancement of Computing in Education (AACE), June 29, 2016, Vancouver, B.C. Retrieved from https://www.learntechlib.org/primary/p/173015/

Wang, P. (2020). On defining artificial intelligence. *Journal of Artificial General Intelligence, 11*(2), 73–86.

Wolff, S. (2005). *Emotional Competence Inventory: Technical manual.* The Hay Group.

Wu, R., & Yu, Z. (2022). Exploiting the effects of achievement emotions on online learning outcomes. A systematic review. *Frontiers in Psychology, 13*, 977931. Advance online publication. DOI: 10.3389/fpsyg.2022.977931

Xia, Q., Chiu, T. K., Zhou, X., Chai, C. S., & Cheng, M. (2022). Systematic literature review on opportunities, challenges, and future research recommendations of artificial intelligence in education. Computers and Education. *Artificial Intelligence, 4*, 10018.

Yagci, U., & vanOostveen, R. (2021). Developing coding structures for becoming effect-savvy in the fully Online Community Model. *Journal of Educational Informatics*, 2(1), 3–23. DOI: 10.51357/jei.v2i1.105

Zawacki-Richter, O., Bai, J. Y., Lee, K., Sagter van Tryon, P. J., & Prinsioo, P. (2024). New advances in artificial intelligence applications in higher education? *International Journal of Educational Technology in Higher Education*, 2(1), 32. DOI: 10.1186/s41239-024-00464-3

Zhang, H. (2024). *Equity Issues in Chinese Higher Education Policy: A Case Study of the Enrolment Expansion Policy* (1st ed.). Routledge., DOI: 10.4324/9781003328889

Zheng, Z., Liao, L., Deng, Y., & Nie, L. (2023). Building Emotional Support Chatbots in the Era of LLMs. /arXiv.2308.11584DOI: 10.48550

Chapter 17
The Perceptions of Students With Learning Difficulties Towards Developing Science Learning in Private Schools in Dubai

Muna AlSadoon
http://orcid.org/0009-0008-4722-5748
Zayed University, UAE

Sufian Forawi
British University in Dubai, UAE

ABSTRACT

This study aims to investigate students with learning difficulties (LD) 's perceptions of science learning in private schools in Dubai. Specifically, it examines critical factors such as intrinsic motivation, self-efficacy, and self-determination, which are crucial for understanding how these students engage with and develop an interest in science education. To achieve this, a quantitative research approach was employed using a structured questionnaire tailored for students with LD. The questionnaire was distributed online to ensure a broad, accessible reach, resulting in data collected from 110 students with learning difficulties. The findings show that students with LD generally have positive attitudes toward science learning. They exhibit a genuine interest and enthusiasm for developing their knowledge and skills in science. The

DOI: 10.4018/979-8-3373-4908-4.ch017

study emphasizes the importance of fostering these psychological factors and calls for collaboration among educational stakeholders to create an inclusive environment that supports all students' learning needs.

INTRODUCTION

The national agenda and the UAE Vision have set targets for the UAE to rank among the top 20 highest-achieving countries in PISA and the top 15 in TIMSS. (The Ministry of Education 2019). This improvement, beginning with Abu Dhabi and then Dubai and the Northern Emirates, has been dedicated to combining creativity and innovative thinking into school syllabuses. Also, government agencies have organized various activities to advance this agenda over the past 10 years. (Gulf News, 2018)

On the other hand, the Ministry of Education in the UAE has launched a distinguished program that aims to provide an exclusive educational system for talented Emirati students in cycles 2 and 3, including students from fifth to twelfth grade, in cooperation with the American College Board. (The Ministry of Education 2019). This vision can be achieved in a total learning opportunity involving access to scientific knowledge and actual discovery (Spooner et al., 2011).

Purpose of the Study

Research shows that students' interest in science learning declines gradually as they move from elementary to high school.(Yager & Bonnstetter, 1984; Osborne et al., 2003; van Griethuijsen et al., 2015). Supporters of students with LD (Learning Difficulties) have highlighted the value of science experiences for this group. (Osborne et al., 2003; Abell & Lederman, 2023), McGinnis (2003) stated that this experience was a moral consideration for this group of students when he/she was evaluated through a Scio- A scientific lens. Further, it will feed their wellness by allowing them to learn (Kwon, 2012). Additionally, students with LD need access to an extended core curriculum that supports them in contributing to hands-on science activities with their partners while making science learning approachable and meaningful for all learners, which remains a priority in the educational system. (Council, 1996). Also, AAAS (1993)Suggests that all students should have essential knowledge and skills to be scientifically well-educated citizens.

Science learning is an essential target for all students, including students with LD, since science is a typical subject that responds to students' curiosity and allows them to discover the surrounding world that fills them with new thoughts and ideas

(Mittal, 2013). Additionally, there is significant concern about the effects of science education in schools. Science influences many daily decisions.

STEM education relies on problem-solving skills related to real-life experiences that the students will face in their work experience later in life (Chen, 2013) . And students with LD who have problems developing these skills (Street et al., 2012). Furthermore, understanding the science syllabus enhances students' comprehension of the world's functions.(Mastropieri et al., 2006). The importance of this study lies in the extent to which students with LD are ready to engage in science learning.

Research Questions

This research study aims to investigate students with LD's perceptions of science learning in Dubai private schools, focusing on intrinsic motivation, self-efficacy, and self-determination. The quantitative research question has been addressed:

> What are students with LD's perceptions regarding developing science learning in middle schools in Dubai?

LITERATURE REVIEW

Theoretical Framework

This research study is underpinned by Social Cognitive Theory (SCT), as Bandura (1994) identified two basic concepts: efficacy expectations, which refer to a person's belief in their ability to perform the critical behaviors required to achieve a desired outcome (Chan & Lam, 2010). The second one is the result expectations: the belief that actions or behaviors will be effectively shown in these required results. (Palmer, 2006). (Bandura, 1994, 1997, 2012) suggests that a recognized sense of self-efficacy is built on and tied to four bases of information: indirect experience, verbal influence, psychological and emotional states, and mastery experiences. Of the four sources, Bandura (1997, 2008) argues that mastery experiences dominate the development of self-efficacy because they provide concrete indicators of personal competencies. These principles are part of this research when students with LD have self-efficacy and beliefs in their abilities to develop science learning. Social Cognitive Theory (SCT) provides the primary theoretical framework for this study, pointing out self-efficacy and the mutual interaction among personal, behavioral, and environmental components in learning (Bandura,1997). Its relevance is further strengthened when considered alongside Self-Determination Theory (SDT), which clarifies how intrinsic motivation and self-determination are supported by independence, ability, and relatedness (Deci & Ryan, 1985; Ryan & Deci, 2000). For students with LD, self-efficacy mirrors observed competence, autonomy supports self-regulated engagement in science learning, and relatedness reinforces motivation through supportive instructional relationships (Bureau et al., 2022). Together, SCT and SDT offer a coherent framework for understanding how motivation, self-efficacy, and self-determination interact to shape students' perceptions and engagement in science learning within inclusive educational environments (Ryan & Deci, 2000)

Context of the study

This research study aims to investigate students with LD's perceptions of science learning in Dubai private schools, focusing on intrinsic motivation, self-efficacy, and self-determination. The quantitative research question has been addressed:

> What are students with LD's perceptions regarding developing science learning in middle schools in Dubai?

Even though science has received much attention as one of the core subjects in policies and instructional activities, students with LD still perform lower than their non-disabled peers. (Taylor et al., 2010). In the UAE, inclusive education has become a strategic priority, particularly in private schools that implement international curricula such as the British, American, and IB curricula, as reflected in theDubai Inclusive Education Policy Framework, (2017). While national policies emphasize inclusion and equity, recent research highlights ongoing challenges in meeting the needs of students with LD in science classrooms, including limited differentiation, high curricular demands, and inconsistent access to specialized support services. These contextual factors underscore the importance of examining students' perceptions of science learning in Dubai's private school environment, where instructional expectations and support structures may vary significantly across schools.

Review of Literature

The organization, identification, and interpretation of sensory information to represent and understand the environment are characterized as perceptions (Schacter et al., 2011), cited in (Murtaza, 2018). Despite teachers' efforts to engage students, science and technology studies are unpopular (Osborne et al., 2003b; Birzina & Cedere, 2017). On the other hand, students can oversee and directly participate in their learning through inquiry- and project-based science, thereby fostering motivation and self-efficacy, especially for those who struggle academically (Malings, 2020).

Motivation, Self-Efficacy, and Self-Determination in Science Learning

Research grounded in SCT emphasizes that motivation, self-efficacy, and self-determination are correlated constructs rather than isolated learner characteristics (Bandura, 1989; Zimmerman, 2000). Motivation influences students' willingness to engage in science tasks, while self-efficacy determines the effort and persistence students put in when encountering academic challenges (Bandura, 1997). Self-determination further supports students' ability to regulate their learning, set goals, and seek assistance when needed (Ryan & Deci, 2000). For students with LD, these elements are particularly critical, as repeated academic challenges can negatively affect confidence and engagement if appropriate support is not provided(Zeng et al., 2018) .

Recent post-2020 studies in science education reinforce that students who experience supportive instructional environments—characterized by active learning, scaffolded instruction, and autonomy-supportive teaching—demonstrate higher levels of motivation and self-efficacy, leading to improved self-determination and academic engagement (Basileo et al., 2024; Reeve & Cheon, 2021). These findings suggest the need to examine science learning not only through performance outcomes but also through students' perceptions and psychological readiness to learn (Chiu, 2024; Joy et al., 2025).

Areepattamannil (2010) Focuses On how motivation, self-beliefs, and instructional techniques affect adolescent science achievement. A total of 13,985 fifteen-year-old adolescents from 431 schools across Canada participated in the survey. In science, the students' self-beliefs were assessed using self-efficacy and self-concept. Students' self-efficacy refers to their confidence in performing science-related tasks, whereas self-concept refers to their opinions of their capability to learn science. When students are allowed to develop their knowledge of the topic, they feel more at ease and secure in their abilities.

Self-determination is another factor that affects students' learning in science; it is a crucial notion that refers to an individual's ability to make decisions and manage their own lives. This skill is crucial to one's psychological health and well-being. People who have self-determination believe they have control over their choices and lives. It also affects motivation: people are more driven to act if they believe their actions will impact the outcome. (Cherry, 2023).

AI-Supported Tools in Science Education for Students with Learning Difficulties

Recent advancements in artificial intelligence (AI) have introduced new possibilities for supporting inclusive science education, particularly for students with LD. AI-supported tools such as adaptive learning platforms, intelligent tutoring systems, and data-driven feedback mechanisms enable personalized instruction tailored to students' learning pace, strengths, and challenges. In science education, these tools can support conceptual understanding through simulations, multimodal representations, and guided inquiry activities (Amouri et al., 2025; Kubsch et al., 2025a; Liu, 2023; Yılmaz & Yılmaz, 2024). From an SCT perspective, AI-supported learning environments can positively influence students' self-efficacy by providing immediate feedback and mastery-oriented learning experiences. These tools may also enhance motivation and self-determination by enabling students to take greater control over their learning processes. However, the effectiveness of AI in supporting students with LD depends on thoughtful implementation, teacher readiness, and alignment with inclusive pedagogical goals (Alsadoon & Forawi, 2024; Amouri et al., 2025; Cardona et al., 2023; Xia et al., 2022; Yılmaz & Yılmaz, 2024).

Educational Leadership and Challenges in Adopting AI for Inclusive Education

Educational leadership plays a critical role in the successful integration of AI technologies in inclusive science education. School leaders are responsible for launching a shared vision, confirming ethical and equitable use of AI tools, and supporting teachers through professional development. In diverse educational contexts, such as Dubai's private school sector, leaders face challenges related to resource allocation, teacher preparedness, data privacy, and resistance to technological change. Without strong leadership support, the potential of AI to enhance motivation, self-efficacy, and self-determination among students with learning difficulties may remain underutilized (Cardona et al., 2023; Kim, 2026; Kim & Wargo, 2025; Sposato, 2025; UNESCO, 2026).

Conceptual Framework of the Study

Guided by Social Cognitive Theory as the primary framework and informed by key principles of Self-Determination Theory, this study proposes a conceptual framework in which students' intrinsic motivation, self-efficacy, and self-determination function as interrelated personal factors that influence science learning. These factors interact reciprocally with environmental influences, including instructional practices, AI-supported learning tools, and educational leadership support, to shape students' perceptions, engagement, and readiness to develop science learning, particularly for students with LD in inclusive school settings.

Figure 1. Conceptual framework of the study

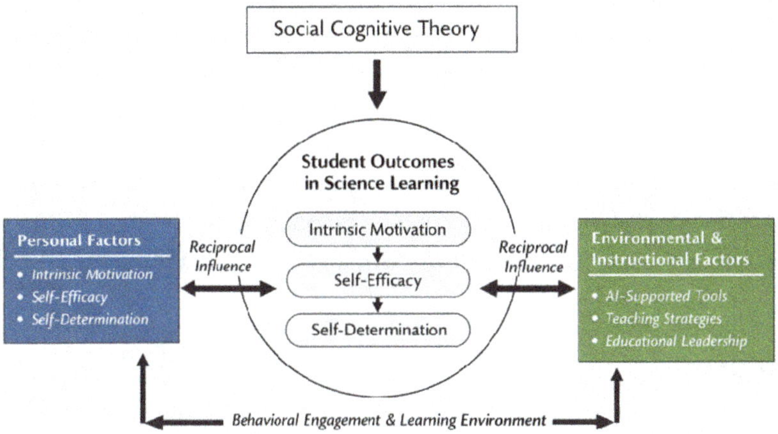

** This figure is generated by AI tools (OpenAI., 2024).*

METHODOLOGY

Study Design

This study employed a quantitative descriptive design to examine students with LD's perceptions of science learning.

Participants

The study took place in different private schools in Dubai that follow British, American, and IB curricula, since they are the most taught systems in the UAE, as international schools, according to the UAE curricula guides (Westley, 2022).The target population in this study is students with LD who are identified in school documents as having different learning difficulties in private schools in Dubai (middle stage, 6-8 grades). The sample in this research study is "convenience sampling," including 110 students with LD, and it reflects the accessible and willing participants who agreed to take part in this investigation. (Johnson et al., 2014).

Instrumentation

The students 'questionnaire used in this research study is a modified version of that used by Chumbley et al. (2015). Initially created by (Glynn et al., 2011), including 16 Items, it was distributed across three clusters to measure students with LD's intrinsic motivation, self-efficacy, and self-determination in learning science. The researcher revised the two versions and produced a version that measures the variables of this study. Further, the final version has been revised by experts in the education field and piloted with 26 students. The researcher did different descriptive analyses to answer the research question. A Likert scale format was utilized in the 16-item survey of students with LD to measure participants' levels of agreement or disagreement with various statements. Respondents were asked to choose from the following options: Strongly Agree (SA), Agree (A), Neutral, Disagree (D), and Strongly Disagree (SD).

Procedure

Data Collection

Ethical approval for this study was obtained from the British University in Dubai, since it is part of a PhD research study submitted to that university. Approval to conduct the research was also granted by the research and the grant office of the British University in Dubai. Participants were approached through their science or support teachers to help them complete the questionnaire, and these teachers were informed about the study's purpose, scope, and requirements.

Data Analysis

The first part of the data analysis includes calculating Cronbach's Alpha for the piloting sample (26 students) to examine the reliability of the instrument and the result, as shown in Table 1 below:

Table 1. Reliability Statistics of each Cluster of Students with LD Questionnaire

Cluster	Cronbach Alpha	Cronbach's Alpha Based on Standardized Items	N of Items
B: Intrinsic Motivation	.911	.912	5
C: Self-Efficacy	.872	.874	6
D: Self-Determination	.892	.893	5

The second part of the data analysis includes quantitative data were entered into SPSS (version 23) for analysis. Data cleaning was performed to identify and correct any missing or inconsistent responses. Descriptive statistics (mean, standard deviation, frequency, percentage) were calculated to summarize participant characteristics and key variables.

RESULTS

This section includes the reliability test of the students with the LD questionnaire (Table. 2) and descriptive data analysis.

The students with LD questionnaires are divided into three clusters: Intrinsic Motivation towards science learning, students' self-efficacy, and the students' self-determination. The analysis of the collected results and the distribution of students' response percentages are represented in Table 2. The highest frequency of responses was 'agree to totally agree' (56.1%), while the frequencies of disagreement and 'did not decide' (neutral) were close to each other (22.17% and 21.17%).

Additionally, item #15 showed the highest percentage of agreement at 74.54%. On the other hand, item #16 (47.27%) shows a high level of disagreement, indicating that students with LD need help with science.

Table 2. The Frequencies and Percentages of Students with LD Responses

Students with LD Questionnaire	Disagree		Neutral		Agree	
	#	%	#	%	#	%
1. Learning science is interesting and fun	25	22.72	18	16.36	67	60.91
2. I enjoy learning science because it teaches me new information	15	13.63	24	21.81	72	65.45
3. Learning science gives meaning to my life and the world around me	22	20	15	13.63	73	66.36
4. I am curious about discoveries in science Learning; I enjoy doing experiments and projects	21	19.09	15	13.63	74	67.27
5. Learning science is very meaningful. It gives me information and skills to help myself and others	22	20	14	12.72	74	67.27
6. I believe I can earn high grades in science.	21	19.09	34	30.90	55	50
7. I am sure I can understand science concepts easily.	36	32.72	20	18.18	54	49.09
8. I can discover new things.	25	22.72	37	33.63	48	43.63
9. I am confident that I can ask a question, form a hypothesis, predict, and test my prediction.	21	19.09	40	36.36	49	44.54
10. I believe I can master science knowledge and skills.	19	17.27	29	26.36	62	56.36
11. I am confident that I will do well on science tests	38	34.54	35	31.81	37	33.63
12. I always complete science assignments	21	19.09	26	23.63	63	57.27

continued on following page

Table 2. Continued

Students with LD Questionnaire	Disagree		Neutral		Agree	
	#	%	#	%	#	%
13. I always submit my science project on time	23	20.90	19	17.27	68	61.81
14. I study well for science tests.	17	15.45	24	21.81	69	62.72
15. I prepare well for my science experiment.	12	10.90	16	14.54	82	74.54
16. I ask for help to understand difficult ideas	52	47.27	17	15.45	41	37.27
Total of Each Frequency	390	22.17	383	21.17	988	56.1
Total of all Frequencies	1761					

Further descriptive analysis was performed using the students with LDs questionnaire to gain more details from the data. This analysis includes calculating the mean and standard deviation of each item's score in each cluster. In Cluster B, in general, all the mean scores are close to each other (between 3.66 and 3.87), with a range of standard deviation between 1.27 and 1.36; furthermore, the highest mean score is shown in item # 2 (M = 3.87, SD = 1.27), and the lowest mean score is shown in item # 1 (M = 3.66, SD = 1.363) as shown in the table below:

Table 3. The Descriptive Analysis of Cluster B that is related to the Intrinsic Motivation of Students with LD to Develop Science Learning

Cluster B: Intrinsic Motivation	N	Mean	Std. Deviation
1. Learning science is interesting and fun	110	3.66	1.36
2. I enjoy learning science because it teaches me new information	110	3.87	1.27
3. Learning science gives meaning to my life and the world around me	110	3.70	1.35
4. I am curious about discoveries in science Learning; I enjoy doing experiments and projects	110	3.80	1.34
5. Learning science is very meaningful. It gives me information and skills to help myself and others	110	3.82	1.34

The results of cluster C, which is related to the student's self-efficacy in developing science learning, show the same indicators as the previous cluster, with mean scores ranging from 3.29 to 3.85 and standard deviations ranging from 1.065 to 1.12. The highest mean score appears in item # 8 (M = 3.85, SD = 1.102), and the lowest score appears in item # 9 (M = 3.29, SD = 1.199). This result confirms that students with LD can earn high grades in science, understand science concepts, and follow up on scientific procedures (Table 4).

Table 4. The Descriptive Analysis of Cluster C is related to the Self-Efficacy of Students with LD in developing Science Learning

Cluster C: Self-Efficacy	Mean	Std. Deviation
6. I believe I can earn high grades in science.	3.45	1.194
7. I am sure I can understand science concepts easily.	3.36	1.254
8. I can discover new things.	3.85	1.102
9. I am confident that I can ask a question, form a hypothesis, predict, and test my prediction.	3.29	1.199
10. I believe I can master science knowledge and skills.	3.37	1.065

Furthermore, in Cluster D, which examines the self-determination of students with LD, the results are like the previous clusters (B and C), close to each other with slight differences in mean scores (between 3.62 and 4.14) and standard deviation (between 1.06 and 1.40). However, item #16 has the highest value (M = 4.14, SD = 1.14) across all clusters, indicating that this group of students requires extensive assistance with science (Table 4).

Table 5. The Descriptive Analysis of Cluster D is related to the Self-Determination of Students with LD to develop Science Learning

Cluster D: Self-Determination	Mean	Std. Deviation
11. I am confident that I will do well on science tests	3.63	1.057
12. I always complete science assignments	3.65	1.404
13. I always submit my science project on time	3.62	1.334
14. I study well for science tests.	3.71	1.280
15. I prepare well for my science experiment.	3.78	1.222
16. I ask for help to understand difficult ideas	4.14	1.137

DISCUSSION

Answering the research question is related to the students with LD's perceptions towards developing science learning. Beyond individual learner characteristics, this study's findings reflect broader trends and challenges in inclusive science education that are increasingly relevant to current educational systems. The moderate levels of motivation, self-efficacy, and self-determination reported by students with learning difficulties highlight the need for instructional environments that extend beyond traditional teaching approaches. Current trends in science education emphasize the integration of technology-enhanced and AI-supported learning tools to personalize instruction, scaffold complex scientific concepts, and provide timely feedback—factors that align closely with SCT's emphasis on mastery experiences and environmental supports (Bandura, 1997, 2008 (Amouri et al., 2025; Cardona et al., 2023; Xia et al., 2022; Yılmaz & Yılmaz, 2024). However, the effective implementation of such innovations requires strong educational leadership, teacher preparedness, and inclusive school policies (Amouri et al., 2025). Without systemic support, the potential of emerging technologies to enhance motivation and self-efficacy among students with learning difficulties may remain underutilized. This underscores the importance of aligning classroom practices, technological innovation, and leadership strategies to address persistent barriers in inclusive science education (Francesc et al., 2019; Kubsch et al., 2025b; Varsik & Vosberg, 2024).

There were no significant differences in the students' responses, as indicated by the general mean score, suggesting that these students have positive perceptions of developing science learning. However, the data from this study show moderate intrinsic motivation towards science learning, with 61-68% of students with LD agreeing with the items in cluster B (intrinsic motivation) of the questionnaire. Moderate motivation can be attributed to many reasons, such as the fact that science is an essential topic for students with LD to master (Mastropieri et al., 2006), and that science as a subject comprises challenging and unusual vocabulary and hard-to-understand scientific texts (Therrien et al., 2011). Also, science learning relies on lecturing and utilizing a textbook (Brigham et al., 2011), besides the perspective teachers have about students 'background (Mason & Hedin, 2011) that one (Mason & Hedin, 2011). Other hindrances that LD students face include limited focus during science classes, weaknesses in mathematical skills, and misbehavior in class (Taylor et al., 2010). All these issues reflect students with LD who are struggling and disinterested in meeting expectations in science classes. Furthermore, students' intellectual interest substantially affects their learning performance and their desire to participate in shaping their future. It is well-defined by their learning enthusiasm (what motivates learners to learn) and teaching/learning practice (how they learn). It shows a particular interaction between the growing personality and some life-space content (Aikenhead, 2005).

Some items show differences, such as Item #2, describing how students with LD enjoy learning science because it introduces new information. This lack of interest in science could be related to many factors, including the science teacher, the resources used, the type of activities, and the settings in the science class (Todd, 2020; Toli & Kallery, 2021).

The second cluster of the questionnaire concerns students' self-efficacy in developing science learning. The results show that 48.8% of students agreed with the items in this cluster that indicate low self-efficacy. Researchers hypothesize that a lack of science self-efficacy is a primary cause of this lack of interest (Lamb et al., 2014; Ballen et al., 2017; Blotnicky et al., 2018). A climate of discovery can be fostered by observations and queries, which are essential for scientific learning (Worth, 2010). The primary role of the science teacher is to enrich this motivation if they have the positive perceptions to do that (Mulholland & Wallace, 1996; Harlen, 1997; Harlen & Holroyd, 1997; van Aalderen-Smeets et al., 2012; Ualesi & Ward, 2018). Moreover, item # 10, which relates to the student's belief in his or her ability to master scientific knowledge and skills, has the highest percentage of agreement (56,36%) concerning the connection between mastering scientific knowledge and skills and the classroom environment, as Maranan (2017) mentioned in his/her thesis. Also, Stone (2014) claims that scientific skills can be improved when students receive clear instructions and guidance.

Science should be taught through hands-on activities (learning by doing) that include each learner directly, particularly those with LD (Malings, 2020). According to research, permitting students to "act like scientists" allows them to gain a greater understanding and become more involved in their science classes (McGrath & Hughes, 2018). Students can directly contribute to their learning through inquiry and project-based science learning (PBL). This offers motivation and self-efficacy, particularly for those who excel academically. Both of these instructional methods have helped teachers deliver more purposeful and engaging lessons while boosting academic performance. These interactive, content-rich lessons and activities provide students with fascinating and enjoyable learning opportunities. All learners can succeed to their fullest potential in the classroom and feel confident in their strengths, especially those with LD (Akınoğlu & Tandoğan, 2007; Merritt et al., 2017; Malings, 2020)

Additionally, numerous studies have shown that when the PBL strategy is used, students adopt a positive attitude, provide positive feedback on their collaborative efforts, and have a positive learning experience. Furthermore, it has been found that students with LD prefer PBL over the traditional approach and that using the former enhances their motivation and academic success(Baş & Beyhan, 2010; Filippatou & Kaldi, 2010; Kaldi et al., 2011).

Juan et al. (2018) also examined the connection between South African ninth-grade science achievement and self-efficacy. The survey found that students can develop self-efficacy and complete challenging tasks when appropriately directed and motivated. Additionally, Oje et al. (2021) found that students who participated in hands-on classroom learning may have higher motivation levels, independent of their academic level. Therefore, the teacher's strategies, the surrounding learning environment, the variability of resources, and the students themselves are factors that enrich or impair self-efficacy. This means that other factors play an essential role, as do the science teacher's perceptions of an inclusive setting, which Stinken-Rösner et al. (2020) summarize as "Acknowledging diversity, recognizing barriers, and enabling participation." This cannot be done by science teachers alone, since the goal of including this group of students in the mainstream setting requires providing an environment in schools, classes, programs, and activities where all students, including those with LD and those without, can participate and learn together(Dev & Kumar, 2014; Kalonde, 2019). Further, McKenzie (2016) claimed in her thesis that teachers and administrators lack teamwork and collaboration in creating a welcoming environment for students with LD.

The item with a low percentage of agreement (43.63%) is item #8, which states that science enables them to discover new things, and item # 9 (44.54%), which describes these students' ability to follow scientific procedures. This reflects their low self-efficacy in science. Item # 9 also contains the highest percentage of students who could not determine a response, one way or another (36%). In contrast to the researchers' assertion that student self-efficacy is a powerful predictor of academic performance and motivation, this demonstrates the students' lack of confidence in participating in science classes and following scientific methodologies. (Pintrich & De Groot, 1990; Graham & Weiner, 1996; Jackson, 2002; Pajares, 2003; Lane et al., 2004; Liu et al., 2006)

Cluster D of the questionnaire for students with LD involves self-determination. The results reveal that a low-to-moderate number of students with LD (37–63%) and an overall percentage (%) agreed with the items in this cluster (54.5). This percentage can be increased if schools and science teachers teach self-determination skills to students with or at risk for learning difficulties (LDs), who are more likely to fail in school (Didion et al., 2021).

While the findings of this study highlight learner-level challenges such as moderate motivation, variable self-efficacy, and reliance on external support, these issues should be understood within the context of broader trends in inclusive science education. Current educational developments emphasize the need for instructional innovation, technology-enhanced learning environments, and systemic support structures to address persistent barriers faced by students with LD. In particular, the increasing use of AI-supported and adaptive learning tools offers opportunities to personalize science instruction, strengthen mastery experiences, and promote greater learner autonomy—factors closely aligned with SCT. However, the successful translation of these trends into practice depends on school leadership, teacher preparedness, and institutional commitment to inclusion. Without coordinated leadership and professional development, learner-centered challenges are likely to persist despite advances in instructional technology.

Students can build self-determination skills in reading and beyond by emphasizing the core parts of these skills in elementary schools. Self-determination abilities evolve throughout time (Didion et al., 2021). Moreover, suppose students with LD develop self-determination skills, such as decision-making, problem-solving, goal setting and achievement, planning, self-management, self-advocacy, self-awareness, and self-knowledge. In that case, they will be better equipped to make prudent decisions and choices (Burke et al., 2020).

Further, item #4, which is linked to the students' thorough preparation for science experiments, shows strong agreement (75%). This indicates that this group of students engages in hands-on activities, which concurs with other studies that show PBL helps students with learning difficulties have more confidence when doing science (Gordon et al., 2001; Dunlap, 2005; Brown et al., 2013;).

According to research, being highly self-motivated can contribute to success in many different domains, including education (Cherry, 2021). Research demonstrates a significant relationship between reading achievement and self-directed learning for students with or at risk of disabilities (Didion et al., 2021).

Disability research has emphasized self-determination as an essential dimension because it affects the quality of life and the attainment of desired educational and adulthood-related goals. It is essential to foster self-determination through targeted strategies by providing opportunities for individuals to use the abilities they have developed. Offering these opportunities in various situations could be particularly important as a catalyst for the growth of self-determination (Vicente et al., 2020).

Further, some people use their abilities to motivate themselves, direct their behavior, and shape their attitudes. Because of this, self-efficacy belief is crucial for the self-regulation of motivation (Bandura, 1983). People are less willing to persevere through challenges when they believe they will not get the desired outcome. Self-efficacy is the cornerstone of motivation and success (Pajares, 2003). Some experts say self-efficacy predicts students' success (Schunk, 1989; Pajares, 1996; Long et al., 2007; Coutinho & Neuman, 2008).

The elements of this research study that cover the students' perceptions (intrinsic motivation, self-efficacy, and self-determination) can be pinned under the theoretical framework of SCT, as An & Meaney (2015) concluded. When inclusion practices in general education classes were studied, in a similar vein to this study, they established a link between the teacher's knowledge of the student's difficulties (teacher's behavior) and the motivation of these students to learn (personal elements), with these students' needs and learning objectives (environment). Additionally, the inability of these students to participate in class activities on an equal footing with their peers due to physical and social barriers can lower their motivation, self-efficacy, and self-determination. As a result, these students have an equal opportunity with their peers(Tugli et al., 2014). Students should be allowed to investigate, explore, and think like scientists(Gomez-Arizaga et al., 2016)The primary goal for students is to ask scientific questions, observe phenomena, collect evidence, and share this data with their classmates and teachers. This will help the students take ownership of their learning and become responsible (Council, 2000).

CONCLUSION

In conclusion, this chapter's primary strength lies in its learner-centered and empirically grounded examination of intrinsic motivation, self-efficacy, and self-determination in science learning among students with learning difficulties. The use of quantitative data and a clear theoretical foundation grounded in SCT enhances the rigor, coherence, and credibility of the findings, while the UAE-based context contributes valuable perspectives from an underrepresented educational setting. These strengths provide a solid platform for extending the chapter's analytical scope by more explicitly linking learner perceptions to instructional practices, emerging AI-supported learning tools, and educational leadership. Leveraging the existing theoretical and empirical foundation in this way would allow the chapter to address broader systemic and future-oriented dimensions of inclusive science education without detracting from its core focus.

Learning to adapt and change to succeed requires that students be proactive, and consistent success can boost self-efficacy. Teachers who provide their students with the chance to learn and do well are more likely to increase their students' self-efficacy for a future of a similar nature(Zimmerman & Dibenedetto, 2008).

The analysis of the data collected reveals that students with LD generally have positive attitudes toward science learning. They exhibit a genuine interest and enthusiasm for developing their knowledge in science, which is closely linked to their intrinsic motivation, a strong sense of self-efficacy, and self-determination. These findings highlight the importance of nurturing these psychological factors to enhance students' educational experiences with learning difficulties. Moreover, the study underscores the critical role of collaboration among educational stakeholders—teachers, parents, administrators, and policymakers—in fostering an inclusive and supportive learning environment. By working together, these stakeholders can implement strategies and interventions that improve students with LD's science learning outcomes and ensure they are actively and meaningfully involved in the learning process. This collaborative effort is essential for promoting a more inclusive educational framework that meets the diverse needs of all students.

Although this chapter emphasizes learner perceptions, these experiences are shaped by broader instructional and institutional contexts. Educational leadership plays a critical role in creating inclusive science learning environments by shaping decisions on curriculum design, teacher professional development, and access to supportive technologies. Without systemic and leadership support, efforts to enhance motivation and self-efficacy among students with LD may be limited in their long-term impact.

LIMITATIONS

This study took place during the COVID-19 lockdown, which extended the data collection process and limited access to participating schools. In addition, not all schools were permitted to participate due to institutional restrictions. The study relied on self-reported questionnaire data, which may be subject to response bias. Furthermore, the cross-sectional design and the focus on selected private schools in Dubai may limit the generalizability of the findings and prevent conclusions about temporal changes. Finally, the absence of qualitative data and the limited examination of instructional and leadership factors may have constrained a deeper understanding of the broader educational context influencing students' perceptions.

RECOMMENDATIONS

Based on the findings, it is recommended that educational leaders and policymakers strengthen inclusive science instruction through differentiated and scaffolded teaching approaches, invest strategically in AI-supported and adaptive learning tools, and prioritize professional development that supports teachers in addressing students' motivational and self-efficacy needs. Leadership support is essential to ensure that inclusive policies, instructional innovation, and technology adoption are coherently implemented across schools. Future research should build on this study by employing longitudinal and mixed-methods designs, examining instructional and leadership variables more directly, and evaluating the impact of AI-supported learning tools on students with learning difficulties' science learning outcomes across diverse educational contexts.

REFERENCES

AAAS. (1993). *Benchmarks for Science Literacy | American Association for the Advancement of Science (AAAS).* AMERICAN ASSOCIATION FOR THE ADVANCEMENT OF SCIENCE. https://www.aaas.org/resources/benchmarks-science-literacy

Abell, S. K., & Lederman, N. G. (2023). Handbook of Research on Science Education. *Handbook of Research on Science Education*, 1–1330. DOI: 10.4324/9780203824696

Aikenhead, G. S. (2005). RESEARCH INTO STS SCIENCE EDUCATION. *Educación Química, 16, 384-397, 16*, 384–397. chrome-extension://efaidnbmnnnibpcajpcglclefindmkaj/https://education.usask.ca/documents/profiles/aikenhead/research_sts_ed.pdf

Akınoğlu, O., & Tandoğan, R. Ö. (2007). The Effects of Problem-Based Active Learning in Science Education on Students' Academic Achievement, Attitude and Concept Learning. *Eurasia Journal of Mathematics, 3*(1), 71–81. chrome-extension://efaidnbmnnnibpcajpcglclefindmkaj/https://www.ejmste.com/download/the-effects-of-problem-basedactive-learning-in-scienceeducation-on-students-academicachievement-4048.pdf

Alsadoon, M., & Forawi, S. (2024). The Perceptions of Science Teachers in Improving and Developing Science Learning of Students with Learning Difficulties in the Middle Stage of Private Schools in Dubai. *Lecture Notes in Civil Engineering, 473 LNCE*, 149–161. DOI: 10.1007/978-3-031-56121-4_15

Amouri, H., Haroud, S., Ouchaouka, L., & Saqri, N. (2025). Acceptability of artificial intelligence in inclusive education: A TAM2-based study among preservice teachers. *Frontiers in Artificial Intelligence*, *8*, 1616327. DOI: 10.3389/frai.2025.1616327 PMID: 40918585

An, J., & Meaney, K. S. (2015). Inclusion Practices in Elementary Physical Education: A Social-cognitive Perspective. *International Journal of Disability Development and Education*, *62*(2), 143–157. DOI: 10.1080/1034912X.2014.998176

Areepattamannil, S. (2010). Parenting Practices, Parenting Style, and Children's School Achievement. *Psychological Studies*, *55*(4), 283–289. DOI: 10.1007/s12646-010-0043-0

Ballen, C. J., Wieman, C., Salehi, S., Searle, J. B., & Zamudio, K. R. (2017). Enhancing diversity in undergraduate science: Self-efficacy drives performance gains with active learning. *CBE Life Sciences Education*, *16*(4), ar56. Advance online publication. DOI: 10.1187/cbe.16-12-0344 PMID: 29054921

Bandura, A. (1983). Self-efficacy determinants of anticipated fears and calamities. *Journal of Personality and Social Psychology*, *45*(2), 464–469. DOI: 10.1037/0022-3514.45.2.464

Bandura, A. (1989). Social cognitive theory. In Vasta, R. (Ed.), *Annals of Child Development. Six Theories of Child Development* (Vol. 6, pp. 1–60). JAI Press.

Bandura, A. (1994). *Encyclopedia of mental health* (Vol. 4). Academic Press., http://www.des.emory.edu/mfp/BanEncy.html

Bandura, A. (1997). *Self-Efficacy: The Exercise of Control*. W.H. Freeman and Company.

Bandura, A. (1997). *Self-Efficacy_The Exercise of Control*. Freeman, W.H and Company. chrome-extension://efaidnbmnnnibpcajpcglclefindmkaj/https://edisciplinas.usp.br/pluginfile.php/7953477/mod_resource/content/1/Self-Efficacy_%20The%20Exercise%20of%20Control.pdf

Bandura, A. (2008). Toward an Agentic Theory of the Self. In Marsh, H. W., Craven, R. G., & McInerey, D. M. (Eds.), *Self-Processes, Learning, and Enabling Human Potential* (pp. 15–49). Information Age Publishing. DOI: 10.1108/978-1-60752-618-620251005

Bandura, A. (2012). On the functional properties of perceived self-efficacy revisited. *Journal of Management*, *38*(1), 9–44. DOI: 10.1177/0149206311410606

Baş, G., & Beyhan, Ö. (2010). Effects of multiple intelligences supported project-based learning on students' achievement levels and attitudes towards English lesson. *International Electronic Journal of Elementary Education, 2*(3), 365–386. chrome-extension://efaidnbmnnnibpcajpcglclefindmkaj/https://citeseerx.ist.psu.edu/document?repid=rep1&type=pdf&doi=ad064255d03c28cf158a80e58d852d8810108beb

Basileo, L. D., Otto, B., Lyons, M., Vannini, N., & Toth, M. D. (2024). The role of self-efficacy, motivation, and perceived support of students' basic psychological needs in academic achievement. *Frontiers in Education*, *9*, 1385442. Advance online publication. DOI: 10.3389/feduc.2024.1385442

Birzina, R., & Cedere, D. (2017). *The First Year Students' Perceptions of Higher Studies: a Case of University of Latvia* (pp. 40–50 B. (REEP).: Latvia University of Agriculture., Ed.; pp. 12–13). Jelgava. chrome-extension://efaidnbmnnnibpca-jpcglclefindmkaj/https://llufb.llu.lv/conference/REEP/2017/Latvia-Univ-Agricult-REEP-2017_proceedings-40-49.pdf

Blotnicky, K. A., Franz-Odendaal, T., French, F., & Joy, P. (2018). A study of the correlation between STEM career knowledge, mathematics self-efficacy, career interests, and career activities on the likelihood of pursuing a STEM career among middle school students. *International Journal of STEM Education*, *5*(1), 1–15. DOI: 10.1186/s40594-018-0118-3 PMID: 30631712

Brigham, F. J., Scruggs, T. E., & Mastropieri, M. A. (2011). Science Education and Students with Learning Disabilities. *Learning Disabilities Research & Practice*, *26*(4), 223–232. DOI: 10.1111/j.1540-5826.2011.00343.x

Brown, S. W., Lawless, K. A., & Boyer, M. A. (2013). Promoting Positive Academic Dispositions Using a Web-based PBL Environment: The GlobalEd 2 Project. *The Interdisciplinary Journal of Problem-Based Learning*, *7*(1). Advance online publication. DOI: 10.7771/1541-5015.1389

Burke, K., Raley, S. K., Shogren, K. A., Hagiwara, M., Mumbardó-Adam, C., Uyanik, H., & Behrens, S. (2020). A Meta-Analysis of Interventions to Promote Self-Determination for Students With Disabilities. Remedial and Special Education. *Vol. 41((3)), Pp. 176-188., 41*(3), 176–188.

Cardona, M. A., Rodríguez, R. J., & Ishmael, K. (2023). *Artificial Intelligence and the Future of Teaching and Learning Insights and Recommendations Artificial Intelligence and the Future of Teaching and Learning*. https://tech.ed.gov

Chan, J. C. Y., & Lam, S. (2010). Effects of different evaluative feedback on students' self-efficacy in learning. *Instructional Science*, *38*(1), 37–58. DOI: 10.1007/s11251-008-9077-2

Chen, X. (2013). *STEM Attrition: College Students' Paths into and out of STEM Fields. Statistical Analysis Report. NCES 2014-001*. National Center for Education Statistics.

Cherry, K. (2021, April 24). *Self-Determination Theory and Motivation.* Verywelll Mind. https://academicintegrity.org/resources/blog/98-2022/april-2022/365-self-determination-theory-and-academic-integrity#:~:text=According%20to%20self-%2Ddetermination%20theory,relatedness%20(Cherry%2C%202021)

Cherry, K. (2023, February 27). *Self Efficacy and Why Believing in Yourself Matters.* Verywell Mind. https://www.verywellmind.com/what-is-self-efficacy-2795954

Chiu, T. K. F. (2024). Using self-determination theory (SDT) to explain student STEM interest and identity development. *Instructional Science*, *52*(1), 89–107. DOI: 10.1007/s11251-023-09642-8

Chumbley, S. B., Haynes, J. C., & Stofer, K. A. (2015). A Measure of Students' Motivation to Learn Science through Agricultural STEM Emphasis. *Journal of Agricultural Education*, *56*(4), 107–122. DOI: 10.5032/jae.2015.04107

Council, N. R. (1996). *National Science Education Standards*. DOI: 10.17226/4962

Council, N. R. (2000). *Inquiry and the National Science Education Standards: A Guide for Teaching and Learning*. Inquiry and the National Science Education Standards., DOI: 10.17226/9596

Coutinho, S. A., & Neuman, G. (2008). A model of metacognition, achievement goal orientation, learning style and self-efficacy. *Learning Environments Research*, *11*(2), 131–151. DOI: 10.1007/s10984-008-9042-7

Deci, E. L., & Ryan, R. M. (1985). Education. In *Intrinsic Motivation and Self-Determination in Human Behavior Perspectives in Social Psychology* (Education). Springer, Boston, MA. DOI: 10.1007/978-1-4899-2271-7_9

Dev, S.., & Kumar, J. (2014). *(PDF) Teacher's perception towards the integration of students with Learning Disabilities into a regular classroom environment*. ResearchGate. https://www.researchgate.net/publication/287853414_Teacher's_perception_towards_the_integration_of_students_with_Learning_Disabilities_into_a_regular_classroom_environment

Didion, L., Toste, J. R., Benz, S. A., & Shogren, K. A. (2021). How Are Self-Determination Components Taught to Improve Reading Outcomes for Elementary Students With or At Risk for Learning Disabilities? *Learning Disability Quarterly*, *44*(4), 288–303. DOI: 10.1177/0731948721989328

Dubai Inclusive Education Policy Framework. (2017). *DUBAI INCLUSIVE ED UCATION POLICY FRAMEWORK*. https://share.google/xVs31k2Cs47vgvAKU

Dunlap, J. C. (2005). Problem-based learning and self-efficacy: How a capstone course prepares students for a profession. *Educational Technology Research and Development*, *53*(1), 65–83. DOI: 10.1007/BF02504858

Filippatou, D., & Kaldi, S. (2010). The effectiveness of project-based learning on pupils with learning difficulties regarding academic performance, group work and motivation The Effectiveness of Project-Based Learning on Pupils with Mild Learning Difficulties: A Preliminary Study. *Article in International Journal of Special Education*, 308–316. https://www.researchgate.net/publication/288070427_The_effectiveness_of_project-based_learning_on_pupils_with_learning_difficultics_regarding_academic_performance_group_work_and_motivation

Francesc, P. Subosa, M., Axel, R., & Paula, V. (2019). *Challenges and Opportunities for Sustainable Development Education Sector United Nations Educational, Scientific and Cultural Organization*. https://en.unesco.org/themes/education-policy-

Gomez-Arizaga, M. P., Kadir Bahar, A., June Maker, C., Zimmerman, R., & Pease, R. (2016). How does science learning occur in the classroom? Students' perceptions of science instruction during the implementation of the REAPS model. *Eurasia Journal of Mathematics, Science and Technology Education*, *12*(3), 431–455.

Gordon, P. R., Rogers, A. M., Comfort, M., Gavula, N., & McGee, B. P. (2001). A Taste of Problem-based Learning Increases Achievement of Urban Minority Middle-School Students. *Educational Horizons*, *79*(4), 171–175.

Graham, S., & Weiner, B. (1996). *Theories and principles of motivation*. Handbook of educational psychology. https://www.researchgate.net/publication/233896258

Gulf News. (2018). Mohammad Bin Rashid launches National Advanced Science Agenda 2031. *Gulf News*, 10.

Harlen, W. (1997). Primary teachers' understanding in science and its impact in the classroom. *Research in Science Education*, *27*(3), 323–337. DOI: 10.1007/BF02461757

Harlen, W., & Holroyd, C. (1997). Primary teachers' understanding of concepts of science: Impact on confidence and teaching. *International Journal of Science Education*, *19*(1), 93–105. DOI: 10.1080/0950069970190107

Jackson, J. W. (2002). Enhancing self-efficacy and learning performance. *Journal of Experimental Education*, *70*(3), 243–255. DOI: 10.1080/00220970209599508

Johnson, R. B., & Christensen, L. B. (2024). *Educational research: Quantitative, qualitative, and mixed approaches*. Sage publications.

Joy, A., Hartstone-Rose, A., Knox, J., Mathews, C. J., Cerda-Smith, J., & Mulvey, K. L. (2025). STEM ability perceptions, basic needs satisfaction, and intrinsic motivation in adolescents: The role of inclusive perceptions in self-determination. *PLoS ONE, 20*(3 March). DOI: 10.1371/journal.pone.0318266

Juan, A., Hannan, S., & Namome, C. (2018). I believe I can do science: Self-efficacy and science achievement of Grade 9 students in South Africa. *South African Journal of Science*, *114*(7–8). Advance online publication. DOI: 10.17159/sajs.2018/20170269

Kaldi, S., Filippatou, D., & Govaris, C. (2011). Project-based learning in primary schools: Effects on pupils' learning and attitudes. *Education*, *39*(1), 35–47.

Kalonde, G. (2019). *Inclusive Education in Science Education: Are Science Teachers Using Inclusive Technologies in Science Classrooms? Chapter 13* (pp. 261–273). DOI: 10.4018/978-1-5225-9438-3.ch013

Kim, J. (2026). School leaders and AI-driven education: a comparative study of readiness, perceptions and implementation strategies. *Artificial Intelligence in Education*, 1–17. DOI: 10.1108/AIIE-03-2025-0048

Kim, J., & Wargo, E. (2025). Empowering educational leaders for AI integration in rural STEM education: Challenges and strategies. *Frontiers in Education*, *10*, 1567698. Advance online publication. DOI: 10.3389/feduc.2025.1567698

Kubsch, M., Kastaun, M., Wulff, P., Graulich, N., Ariely, M., Bergmann-Gering, A., Gombert, S., Gregorcic, B., Härtig, H., Heuckmann, B., Horbach, A., Krist, C., Kortemeyer, G., Münch, B., Pazicni, S., Rosenberg, J. M., Schanze, S., Sbeglia, G., Skogvoll, V., . . . Zhai, X. (2025a). *Report on the Scoping Workshop on AI in Science Education Research 2025*. https://arxiv.org/pdf/2511.14318v2

Kubsch, M., Kastaun, M., Wulff, P., Graulich, N., Ariely, M., Bergmann-Gering, A., Gombert, S., Gregorcic, B., Härtig, H., Heuckmann, B., Horbach, A., Krist, C., Kortemeyer, G., Münch, B., Pazicni, S., Rosenberg, J. M., Schanze, S., Sbeglia, G., Skogvoll, V., & Zhai, X. (2025b). *Report on the Scoping Workshop on AI in Science Education Research 2025*. https://arxiv.org/abs/2511.14318

Kwon, H. J. (2012). The analysis of perception and the actual condition, needs of students with disabilities and related persons in general middle school. *Journal of Special Education: Theory and Practice*, *13*(4), 471–506.

Lamb, R. L., Vallett, D., & Annetta, L. (2014). Development of a short-form measure of science and technology self-efficacy using rasch analysis. *Journal of Science Education and Technology*, *23*(5), 641–657. DOI: 10.1007/s10956-014-9491-y

Lane, J., Lane, A. M., & Kyprianou, A. (2004). Self-efficacy, self-esteem and their impact on academic performance. *Social Behavior and Personality*, *32*(3), 247–256. DOI: 10.2224/sbp.2004.32.3.247

LIU. M., Hsieh, P., & Cho, Y. (2006). Middle School Students' Self-Efficacy, Attitudes, and Achievement in a Computer-Enhanced Problem-Based Learning Environment | Request PDF. *Journal of Interactive Learning Research*, *17*(3), 225–242. https://www.researchgate.net/publication/255645343_Middle_School_Students'_Self-Efficacy_Attitudes_and_Achievement_in_a_Computer-Enhanced_Problem-Based_Learning_Environment

Liu, R. (2023). *The Transformative Potential of Generative Artificial Intelligence (GAI) in STEM Learning, Equality, and Inclusion: A Student-Centered Mixed Methods Study – Institute for Diversity Science – UW–Madison*. Https://Ids.Wisc.Edu/Research/2023-Seed-Grant-Program/the-Transformative-Potential-of-Generative-Artificial-Intelligence-Gai-in-Stem-Learning-Equality-and-Inclusion-a-Student-Centered-Mixed-Methods-Study/. https://ids.wisc.edu/research/2023-seed-grant-program/the-transformative-potential-of-generative-artificial-intelligence-gai-in-stem-learning-equality-and-inclusion-a-student-centered-mixed-methods-study/

Long, J. F., Monoi, S., Harper, B., Knoblauch, D., & Murphy, P. K. (2007). Academic motivation and achievement among urban adolescents. *Urban Education, 42*(3), 196–222. DOI: 10.1177/0042085907300447

Malings, L. (2020). *How Inquiry-Based Instruction and Engineering-Based Activities Impact Science Abilities and Attitudes Toward Science Among Students with Learning Disabilities* [ProQuest Dissertations and Theses.]. Hofstra University.

Maranan, V. M. (2017). *Basic process skills and attitude toward science: inputs to an enhanced students' cognitive performance* [Unpublished Thesis, Laguna State Polytechnic University,]. https://www.sciepub.com/reference/324549

Mason, L. H., & Hedin, L. R. (2011). Reading Science Text: Challenges for Students with Learning Disabilities and Considerations for Teachers. *Learning Disabilities Research & Practice, 26*(4), 214–222. DOI: 10.1111/j.1540-5826.2011.00342.x

Mastropieri, M. A., Scruggs, T. E., Norland, J., S., B., McDuffie, K., & T., & Ornquist, E. H. (2006). Differentiated curriculum enhancement in inclusive middle school science: Effects on classroom and high stakes tests. *Journal of Special Education, 40,*(3), 130–137.

McGinnis, J. R. (2003). The Morality of Inclusive Verses Exclusive Settings. *The Role of Moral Reasoning on Socioscientific Issues and Discourse in Science Education*, 195–216. DOI: 10.1007/1-4020-4996-X_11

McGrath, A. L., & Hughes, M. T. (2018). Students With Learning Disabilities in Inquiry-Based Science Classrooms: A Cross-Case Analysis. *Learning Disability Quarterly, 41*(3), 131–143. DOI: 10.1177/0731948717736007

Mckenzie, R. (2016). Perceptions of Inclusion Factors by General Education Teachers and Administrators [Doctor of Education (Ed.D.), Walden University]. In *Walden Dissertations and Doctoral Studies*. https://scholarworks.waldenu.edu/dissertations/1908

Merritt, J., Lee, M. Y., Rillero, P., & Kinach, B. M. (2017). Problem-Based Learning in K–8 Mathematics and Science Education: A Literature Review. *The Interdisciplinary Journal of Problem-Based Learning, 11*(2), 3. DOI: 10.7771/1541-5015.1674

Mittal, R. (2013). Knowledge Builder"-The National Journal. *National Journal, 1*(1), 1–5. http://weschool.rtmonline.in

Mulholland, J., & Wallace, J. (1996). Breaking the cycle: Preparing elementary teachers to teach science. *Journal of Elementary Science Education, 8*(1), 17–38. DOI: 10.1007/BF03173739

Murtaza, N. (2018). *Perceptions of Students with Learning Disabilities Learning Science: A Narrative Study*. DOI: 10.20381/RUOR-22080

Oje, O. Adesope, Olusola., & Oje, A. Victor. (2021, July 26). Work in Progress: The Effects of Hands-on Learning on STEM Students' Motivation and Self-efficacy: A Meta-Analysis Work in Progress: The Effects of Hands-on Learning on STEM Students Motivation and Self-Efficacy: A Meta-Analysis. *American Society for Engineering Education Conference (Virtual, 07/19/2021 - 07/26/2021)*, Art. 34613. https://rex.libraries.wsu.edu/esploro/outputs/conferenceProceeding/Work-In-Progress-The-Effects-of-Hands-on-Learning/99900602846101842

Open, A. I. (2024). *ChatGPT (GPT-4) [Large language model]*. https://chat.openai.com/

Osborne, J., Simon, S., & Collins, S. (2003a). Attitudes towards science: A review of the literature and its implications. *International Journal of Science Education, 25*(9), 1049–1079. DOI: 10.1080/0950069032000032199

Osborne, J., Simon, S., & Collins, S. (2003b). Attitudes towards science: A review of the literature and its implications. *International Journal of Science Education, 25*(9), 1049–1079. DOI: 10.1080/0950069032000032199

Pajares, F. (1996). Self-Efficacy Beliefs in Academic Settings. https://Dx.Doi.Org/10.3102/00346543066004543, *66*(4), 543–578. DOI: 10.3102/00346543066004543

Pajares, F. (2003). SELF-EFFICACY BELIEFS, MOTIVATION, AND ACHIEVEMENT IN WRITING: A REVIEW OF THE LITERATURE. *Reading & Writing Quarterly, 19*(2), 139–158. DOI: 10.1080/10573560308222

Palmer, D. (2006). Durability of changes in self-efficacy of preservice primary teachers. *International Journal of Science Education, 28*(6), 655–671. DOI: 10.1080/09500690500404599

Pintrich, P. R., & De Groot, E. V. (1990). Motivational and Self-Regulated Learning Components of Classroom Academic Performance. *Journal of Educational Psychology, 82*(1), 33–40. chrome-extension://efaidnbmnnnibpcajpcglclefindmkaj/https://rhartshorne.com/fall-2012/eme6507-rh/cdisturco/eme6507-eportfolio/documents/pintrich%20and%20degroodt%201990.pdf

Reeve, J., & Cheon, S. H. (2021). Autonomy-supportive teaching: Its malleability, benefits, and potential to improve educational practice. *Educational Psychologist, 56*(1), 54–77. DOI: 10.1080/00461520.2020.1862657

Ryan, R. M., & Deci, E. L. (2000). Self-Determination Theory and the Facilitation of Intrinsic Motivation, Social Development, and Well-Being Self-Determination Theory. *The American Psychologist, 55*(1), 68–78. DOI: 10.1037/0003-066X.55.1.68 PMID: 11392867

Schunk, D. H. S. (1989). Self-efficacy and achievement behaviors.[]. *Educational Psychology Review, 1*(3), 173–208. http://www.springerlink.com. DOI: 10.1007/BF01320134

Spooner, F., Knight, V. F., Browder, D. M., Jimenez, B., & DiBiase, W. (2011). Evaluating evidence-based practice in teaching science content to students with severe developmental disabilities. *Research and Practice for Persons with Severe Disabilities : the Journal of TASH, 36*(1-2), 62–75. DOI: 10.2511/rpsd.36.1-2.62

Sposato, M. (2025). Artificial intelligence in educational leadership: A comprehensive taxonomy and future directions. *International Journal of Educational Technology in Higher Education, 22*(1), 1–8. DOI: 10.1186/s41239-025-00517-1

Stinken-Rösner, L., Rott, L., Hundertmark, S., Baumann, T., Menthe, J., Hoffmann, T., ... & Abels, S. (2020). Thinking inclusive science education from two perspectives: Inclusive pedagogy and science education. RISTAL. Research in Subject-matter Teaching and Learning, 3(1).

Stone, E. M. (2014). Guiding students to develop an understanding of scientific inquiry: A science skills approach to instruction and assessment. *CBE Life Sciences Education, 13*(1), 90–101. DOI: 10.1187/cbe-12-11-0198 PMID: 24591508

Street, C., Koff, R., Fields, H., Kuehne, L., Handlin, L., Getty, M., & Parker, D. (2012). Expanding Access to STEM for At-Risk Learners: A New Application of Universal Design for Instruction. *Journal of Postsecondary Education and Disability*.

Taylor, J., Therrien, W. J., Kaldenberg, E. R., Watt, S. J., Chanlen, N., & Hand, B. (2010a). Using An Inquiry-based Teaching Approach to Improve Science Outcomes for Students with Disabilities: Smapshot and Longitudinal Data. *Journal of Science Education for Students with Disabilities*, *15*(1), 27–39. DOI: 10.14448/jsesd.04.0003

Taylor, J., Therrien, W. J., Kaldenberg, E. R., Watt, S. J., Chanlen, N., & Hand, B. (2010b). Using An Inquiry-based Teaching Approach to Improve Science Outcomes for Students with Disabilities: Smapshot and Longitudinal Data. *Journal of Science Education for Students with Disabilities*, *15*(1), 27–39. DOI: 10.14448/jsesd.04.0003

The Ministry of Education. (2019). *Ministry of Education Strategic plan 2017-2021*. Online. https://www.moe.gov.ae/En/AboutTheMinistry/Pages/MinistryStrategy.aspx

Therrien, W. J., Hughes, C., & Hand, B. (2011). Introduction to Special Issue on Science Education and Students with Learning Disabilities. *Learning Disabilities Research & Practice*, *26*(4), 186–187. DOI: 10.1111/j.1540-5826.2011.00339.x

Todd, B. C. (2020). *Factors Influencing Student Interest in Science at School* [Master of Arts Degree In Education.]. California State University.

Toli, G., & Kallery, M. (2021). Enhancing student interest to promote learning in science: The case of the concept of energy. *Education Sciences*, *11*(5), 1–15. DOI: 10.3390/educsci11050220

Tugli, A. K., Klu, E. K., & Morwe, K. (2014). Critical Elements of the Social Model of Disability: Implications for Students with Disabilities in a South African Institution of Higher Education. *Journal of Social Sciences*, *39*(3), 331–336. DOI: 10.1080/09718923.2014.11893295

Ualesi, Y., & Ward, G. (2018). Teachers' attitudes toward teaching science in a New Zealand intermediate school. *The Australian Journal of Teacher Education*, *43*(6), 35–49. DOI: 10.14221/ajte.2018v43n6.3

UNESCO. (2026, January). *AI and the future of education. Disruptions, dilemmas and directions*. Https://Www.Unesco.Org/En/Articles/Ai-and-Future-Education-Disruptions-Dilemmas-and-Directions. https://www.unesco.org/en/articles/ai-and-future-education-disruptions-dilemmas-and-directions

van Aalderen-Smeets, S. I., Walma van der Molen, J. H., & Asma, L. J. F. (2012). Primary teachers' attitudes toward science: A new theoretical framework. *Science Education*, *96*(1), 158–182. DOI: 10.1002/sce.20467 van Griethuijsen, R. A. L. F., van Eijck, M. W., Haste, H., den Brok, P. J., Skinner, N. C., Mansour, N., Gencer, A. S., & BouJaoude, S. (2015). Global patterns in students' views of science and interest in science. *Research in Science Education, 45*(4), 581–603. DOI: 10.1007/s11165-014-9438-6

Varsik, S., & Vosberg, L. (2024). The potential impact of Artificial Intelligence on equity and inclusion in education. *OECD Artificial Intelligence Papers, OECD Artificial Intelligence Papers, 23*. DOI: 10.1787/dee339a8-en

Vicente, E., Mumbardó-Adam, C., Guillén, V. M., Coma-Roselló, T., Bravo-álvarez, M. Á., & Sánchez, S. (2020). Self-determination in people with intellectual disability: The mediating role of opportunities. *International Journal of Environmental Research and Public Health, 17*(17), 1–15. DOI: 10.3390/ijerph17176201 PMID: 32859080

Westley, D. (2022, November 24). *Which Curriculum is Dubai's Most Popular?* Which School Advisor. https://whichschooladvisor.com/uae/school-news/which-curriculum-is-dubais-most-popular

Worth, K. (2010, February 27). *Science in Early Childhood Classrooms: Content and Process*. Center for Science Education Education Development Center, Inc. https://ecrp.illinois.edu/beyond/seed/worth.html

Xia, Q., Chiu, T. K. F., Lee, M., Sanusi, I. T., Dai, Y., & Chai, C. S. (2022). A self-determination theory (SDT) design approach for inclusive and diverse artificial intelligence (AI) education. *Computers & Education, 189*, 104582. DOI: 10.1016/j.compedu.2022.104582

Yager, R. E., & Bonnstetter, R. J. (1984). Student Perceptions of Science Teachers, Classes, and Course Content. *School Science and Mathematics, 84*(5), 406–414. DOI: 10.1111/j.1949-8594.1984.tb09568.x

Yılmaz, Ö., & Yılmaz, Ö. (2024). Personalised learning and artificial intelligence in science education: Current state and future perspectives. *Educational Technology Quarterly, 2024*(3), 255–274. DOI: 10.55056/etq.744

Zeng, W., Ju, S., & Hord, C. (2018). A Literature Review of Academic Interventions for College Students With Learning Disabilities. *Learning Disability Quarterly, 41*(3), 159–169. DOI: 10.1177/0731948718760999

Zimmerman, B. J. (2000). Self-Efficacy: An Essential Motive to Learn. *Contemporary Educational Psychology, 25*(1), 82–91. DOI: 10.1006/ceps.1999.1016 PMID: 10620383

Zimmerman, B. J., & Dibenedetto, M. K. (2008). Mastery learning and assessment: Implications for students and teachers in an era of high-stakes testing. *Psychology in the Schools*, *45*(3), 206–216. DOI: 10.1002/pits.20291

Chapter 18
Faculty Perspectives on the Rollout of a New Arabic Language Program in UAE Higher Education and Its Implications for Leadership

Rehab AlKilani
http://orcid.org/0000-0002-8004-6476
Zayed University, UAE

Laila Mohebi
http://orcid.org/0000-0003-2640-4532
Zayed University, UAE

ABSTRACT

This study investigates faculty perceptions of the rollout of a newly mandated Arabic language program at a federal university in United Arab Emirates. Introduced in response to national concerns about declining Arabic proficiency, the reform required rapid curriculum redesign to serve both native and non-native learners. Guided by a qualitative constructivist–interpretivist approach, semi-structured interviews were conducted with seven instructors involved in delivery. Thematic analysis explored curriculum coherence, student engagement, and institutional supports shaping implementation. While faculty endorsed the national vision underpinning the reform, they reported gaps between learning outcomes, pedagogy, and assessment that constrained impact. Participants called for clearer guidance, better alignment

DOI: 10.4018/979-8-3373-4908-4.ch018

mechanisms, and sustained consultation. The findings highlight the central role of academic leadership in mediating policy into practice and emphasize the need for participatory governance in large-scale language reform.

INTRODUCTION

For centuries, Arabic has been far more than a tool for daily conversation; it is the beating heart of Islamic civilization (Ridwan, 2023). It serves as a vast, living library of the Muslim intellectual journey, weaving together how people think, how they pray, and how they understand their place in history (Abourehab & Azaz, 2023). In this sense, the language acts as a sacred vessel, carrying not just words but a collective identity and a shared spiritual heritage.

Yet, in the contemporary era, the pursuit of Arabic learning is marked by growing tensions. In an increasingly globalized world where English is widely positioned as the primary 'language of progress,' Arabic education is experiencing a subtle but profound crisis of relevance (Muhammad Zahid et al., 2025). In the United Arab Emirates, the expanding dominance of Western languages within higher education extends beyond curricular change; it risks creating a generational distance from the epistemological and cultural knowledge systems embedded in Arabic. This shift raises critical concerns about the preservation of linguistic heritage and the continuity of identity in rapidly modernizing societies (Thomure, 2019).

This challenge can be perceived worldwide, but it is especially *significant* for heritage learners and educators in the Gulf. In Western universities, even though political and strategic interest in the region remains resilient, fewer students are choosing to study Arabic (Khairanis et al., 2025). Meanwhile, educators must *address* the needs of students who are navigating complex linguistic and religious identities in an increasingly globalized setting. For these students and the faculty who lead them, learning Arabic is not merely an instrumental task; it is an act of reclaiming a sacred history. *In this context*, this study explores the direct perspectives of faculty members in the UAE, arguing that the success of new Arabic programs depends on a critical reassessment of how we sustain Islamic knowledge and identity in the modern world.

Many research studies have confirmed that literacy plays a vital role in improving language skills, including in Arabic language learning. Well-designed Arabic literacy programs allow students to better understand linguistic structures, expand their vocabulary, and improve their reading and writing abilities (Hijriyah et al., 2024). *Besides* literacy, learning motivation is extensively recognized as a crucial internal factor *influencing* students' academic success (Yundayani & Alghadari, 2025). The present study examines university faculty perspectives to inform the development of a new Arabic language program aimed at expanding learning opportunities for both native and non-native students. By foregrounding faculty insights, the study seeks to understand how Arabic can be positioned not only as a language of instruction but also as a vital carrier of cultural knowledge, identity, and heritage. These perspectives are intended to guide program design in ways that respond to contemporary educational needs while preserving the cultural richness embedded in the Arabic language.

LITERATURE REVIEW

In today's increasingly unified educational environment, teaching Arabic can serve as a meaningful pedagogical avenue for promoting cross-cultural understanding and strengthening students' global competencies (Wang et al., 2025). As educational institutions around the world seek to nurture intercultural literacy and bilingual awareness, Arabic language education offers substantial, yet often underutilized, opportunities to expand students' perspectives and challenge long-standing stereotypes about the Arab world (Rehman et al., 2025). With its profound linguistic roots, historical richness, and cultural complexity, *the* Arabic language provides valuable *insights* into Arab identity, philosophical traditions, and broader civilizational narratives that are frequently lacking from mainstream curricula in many non-Arab contexts.

Theoretical framework of the study

This study is grounded *in* the theory of "Curriculum Implementation Theory," which highlights the gap that often exists between *the* intended curriculum (policy and program design) and *the* enacted curriculum (classroom practice) (Fullan, 2007). This framework is highly pertinent to the present study, as faculty participants recognized misalignment between learning outcomes, classroom activities, and assessment mechanisms in the new Arabic language program. By *applying* this framework, the study examines how institutional support, pedagogical resources, and assessment structures influence faculty engagement with the new curriculum. It also *focuses on* the challenges that instructors encounter while executing top-down educational reforms, mainly in contexts shaped by national language policy mandates, such as those in the UAE.

Challenges to Learn Arabic Language Program

Previous studies reported that students learning Arabic encountered many challenges. These challenges can be divided into linguistic and non-linguistic difficulties (Norlaila, et al., 2025). Linguistic difficulties comprise the complexity of Arabic grammar, varied vocabulary, differences between Arabic and students' first language, and problems with reading and writing Arabic script. Non-linguistic challenges *include* limited learning resources, lack of study time, low motivation, weak support from the learning environment, issues related to teaching quality, and inadequate facilities and infrastructure. These challenges were identified among students at Sanggar Bimbingan Permai in Penang, Malaysia (Setianingsih & Robbani (2024). Likewise, in another study. Fatimah (2024) *assessed* the strategies used by students in the Arabic Language Education (PBA) program to master Arabic vocabulary. The study found that students from general school backgrounds used diverse learning strategies such as memory strategies *and* cognitive strategies to overcome their learning difficulties. Iqbal (2016) found that students' educational backgrounds *play* an important role in the difficulties they experience when learning Arabic as compared to those who had *an* earlier background *in the* Arabic language. Moreover, recent studies conducted by Pratama et al. (2022) and Setianingsih and Robbani (2024) generally defined the linguistic and non-linguistic difficulties faced by students learning Arabic. While these studies provide valuable insights into the nature of the learning difficulties, *they* do not provide practical solutions to improve learning outcomes.

Based on the earlier research studies, there is a clear research gap, some described students' difficulties or learning strategies, but few consider the role of students' educational backgrounds while also proposing concrete solutions. Thus, this study aims to address this gap by examining university faculty *perceptions regarding the introduction* of a new Arabic language course program in the universities of *the* UAE.

Context of the Study

New Arabic Language Program

In the United Arab Emirates, increasing concern has emerged regarding the declining proficiency of many young Emiratis in speaking and writing Arabic, a challenge largely linked to their schooling in private institutions where Arabic language instruction is often limited (Norlaila, et al., 2025). Although Arabic is a compulsory subject at the university level, many students enter higher education without an adequate linguistic foundation. Private schools in the UAE predominantly cater to expatriate communities and are generally oriented toward teaching Arabic as a second or foreign language, which may not sufficiently support the linguistic needs of Emirati students. Recognizing this issue, the UAE Ministry of Education has approved mandatory guidelines for the teaching of Arabic language, Islamic Studies, and Social Studies at the kindergarten level across all private schools, effective from the 2025/2026 academic year. This initiative aims to strengthen national identity from an early age, foster pride in the Arabic language, and enhance students' reading, writing, and communicative skills, thereby supporting their academic development and future participation in social and professional life within the UAE.

These national efforts align closely with the Arabic Language Charter introduced in 2012, which serves as a comprehensive framework guiding policies and legislation for the long-term preservation and modernization of Arabic in the UAE. The Charter outlines 13 key principles, beginning with the designation of Arabic as the official language of the state and the language of all official communication, laws, and government services (Thomure, 2019). It further encourages private schools and language centers to provide Arabic instruction for non-native learners, expanding access to the language beyond native-speaking communities (Emirates News, 2012). At the higher education level, the Charter assigns universities and research institutions a critical role in enriching Arabic through the development of new terminology, academic research in Arabic language education, and the translation of international literary and scientific works into Arabic. Within this policy context, the present study explores university faculty perceptions of a newly designed Arabic language program intended for both native and non-native students, with the aim of enhancing Arabic proficiency as a vital tool for communication, cultural continuity, and professional engagement in a globalized UAE.

Research Questions

1. How do university instructors perceive the design, coherence, and academic suitability of the new Arabic language curriculum?
2. How has the implementation of the new Arabic curriculum influenced students' engagement, motivation, and linguistic development from instructors' perspectives?
3. What challenges, supports, and institutional factors have shaped the implementation of the new Arabic language curriculum, and how can alignment with national language strategies be strengthened?

Research Method

This study adopted a qualitative research design (Lim, 2025) to explore university faculty perceptions of a newly introduced Arabic language program at a public university in Abu Dhabi, United Arab Emirates. A qualitative approach was suitable as it allows for an in-depth understanding of teachers' lived experiences and perspectives, which are influenced by sociocultural, institutional, and linguistic factors that cannot be fully captured through quantitative methods (Achruh & Sukirman, 2024). The study examined faculty views on curriculum coherence and academic suitability, the program's impact on students' engagement, motivation, and linguistic development, and the institutional and pedagogical factors affecting its implementation. Data were collected through in-depth, semi-structured interviews with faculty members across different disciplines and academic levels (Lim, 2025), enabling the collection of rich, descriptive insights. This research was grounded in the interpretivist paradigm (Alharahsheh & Pius, 2020), which emphasizes subjective meaning and contextual understanding in knowledge construction (Aguzzoli et al., 2024). Within this framework, teachers are viewed as active agents whose perspectives are essential for understanding the realities of Arabic language education in higher education.

Ethical approval was obtained in accordance with the relevant university protocols prior to data collection. Participants were then recruited and interviewed following institutional ethical guidelines. All participants received information sheets explaining the study's purpose, procedures, potential risks, and their rights. Informed consent was obtained, and confidentiality and anonymity were assured using pseudonyms and the removal of identifying details. Participants were informed of their right to withdraw at any time without penalty. All data were stored securely in password-protected files and accessed only by the researchers and authorized academic advisors. The interviews were conducted online via Zoom or Google Meet, depending on participants' availability and location. Each interview lasted between 45 and 60 minutes and was audio-recorded with participants' informed consent to ensure accurate transcription and analysis.

Sample

Table 1. Demographic Background of the Participants

University Respondents	Gender		Age group	Academic Degree	Academic Experience	Academic Rank
	Male	Female				
1	Male	------	45-54	PhD	≥10 years	Associate Professor
2	---- ---	Female	45-54	PhD	≤6 years	Assistant Professor
3	Male	-------	45-54	PhD	≥10 years	Associate Professor
4	Male	-------	45-54	PhD	≥10 years	Associate Professor
5	---- ---	Female	35-44	PhD	≥10 years	Assistant Professor
6	Male	-------	45-54	PhD	≥10 years	Lecturer
7	---- ---	Female	35-44	PhD	≥10 years	Lecturer

Participants were selected through purposive sampling to recruit individuals with direct experience of the phenomenon under study. To ensure a range of perspectives, participants were drawn from the department of Social Sciences and eligibility criteria required a minimum of five years of Arabic teaching experience and involvement in curriculum implementation or instructional design. In total, seven participants were interviewed, with data collection continuing until data saturation was achieved. This sample size aligns with qualitative research principles, which prioritize depth and contextual understanding over generalizability (Braun & Clarke, 2025).

Data analysis

Data analysis was conducted using thematic analysis, following Braun and Clarke's (2025) six-phase approach. This process involved familiarization with the data through repeated reading of transcripts, generating initial codes, and organizing these codes into broader themes. The themes were then reviewed, refined, and defined before being synthesized into a coherent narrative addressing the research questions and theoretical framework. To ensure trustworthiness, strategies outlined by Lincoln and Guba (1985) were applied. Credibility was enhanced through member checking and peer debriefing with academic colleagues was used to reduce researcher bias and enhance analytical rigor. Through the thematic analysis ten themes were extracted from the data. These are presented below in the findings section.

FINDINGS

Theme 1: Questioning Innovation and the Perceived Lack of Academic Depth

The main theme emerging from the respondents' responses was uncertainty toward the Arabic curriculum's claimed for innovation, with respective faculty both male and female questioned whether the new Arabic course design represents meaningful pedagogical advancement? Though some experimental elements such as image analysis and reading aloud were acknowledged that were embedded in the curriculum, these elements were frequently considered as experimental and inconsistently applied, rather than being analytically effective. A middle-aged male faculty member with more than ten years' teaching Arabic language experience narrated his experience by saying this:

'The most innovative aspects include incorporating experimental elements into the content, such as image analysis, the inclusion of theatrical elements, and reading aloud. However, innovation doesn't necessarily mean effectiveness or goodness; it's subject to experimentation' (Male-Associate Professor).

It reflects that faculty did not find innovation in the new Arabic course to focus on the Emirates traditional culture, customs and cultural values, however they believed that this course was designed to the foreign students so they can develop their interest in the Arabic language. Another male respondent described his views regarding this course:

If we're talking about innovative aspects, I don't find anything truly innovative. The word 'innovative' implies a kind of renewal or a distinctive feature, and that noticeable distinction is missing (Male-Lecturer).

However, female respondents, in particular, expressed strong criticism, arguing that the curriculum appears innovative in form but regresses in practice, even resembling pre-secondary instruction. A female faculty with having 6 years of teaching Arabic language said:

'Honestly, I don't see any creativity in this new program. When we start teaching it, the curriculum is poor and takes students back to pre-secondary levels' (Female-Assistant Professor)

Female respondents' main concern was the absence of a dedicated Arabic textbook, which places a substantial burden on instructors to independently source teaching materials. As a result, innovation in the course relied largely on individual effort rather than being embedded within the curriculum design. Contrary to female respondents, male respondents echoed this concern by emphasizing that true innovation requires clear differentiation and renewal, not simply flexibility. Some considered the openness of the curriculum as a double-edged sword: while it allows instructors to "think outside the box," it concurrently creates pressure due to the lack of planned guidance. In general, innovation was often perceived as superficial especially for native Arabic-speaking university students, some respondents recommended that this approach might be more suitable for non-native learners than for Emirati or Arab students.

Innovation as Alignment with Students' Needs, Practical Language, and Skills-Based Learning

Several respondents emphasized that effective curriculum design must begin with identifying the target audience, intended level, and institutional context. Innovation, from this perspective, lies in tailoring content to students who primarily study in English and require functional Arabic applicable to real-life contexts, such as media and professional communication, rather than heavy classical or poetic language. One senior male faculty explained his thoughts:

'Curriculum design isn't a one-size-fits-all approach. The most crucial thing is identifying the target group—the students (Male-Associate Professor).

Respondents' apprehensions primarily concerned the alignment of the Arabic curriculum with societal needs, considering the same another senior male faculty reflected:

'It should always be close to people's everyday lives—the language of media and news—away from classical Arabic' (Male- Associate Professor).

Besides, male respondents' perspective, female respondents were more likely to highlighted project-based learning and skills-focused instruction particularly in speaking and writing as genuinely innovative and effective. A young female respondent teaching Arabic course explained:

'The emphasis on projects, presentations, and speaking was excellent. Students are eager to move away from exams and showcase their actual talent' (Female-Lecturer).

These elements were seen to enhance student engagement, motivation, and confidence, especially in an era shaped by artificial intelligence where traditional exams are increasingly limited. The integration of projects, presentations, and performance-based assessment was viewed as a meaningful shift that allows students to demonstrate authentic linguistic competence. This analysis suggests that where innovation was positively perceived, it was closely tied to applied Arabic, long-term learning outcomes, and active learning strategies, rather than content novelty alone. Aligned with this scenario, a young female faculty revealed her views as:

'What matters to me in a curriculum is that it covers long-term objectives, not just grades. The student should gain confidence and be able to apply what they learned in real life' (Female- Assistant professor).

Theme 2: Dependence on Institutional Curriculum and Textbooks

Respective respondents emphasized the significance of organized course materials and institutional procedures as the backbone of their teaching Arabic course. The course syllabus, departmental texts, and official textbooks were frequently cited as primary references. One senior male respondent described:

'The primary sources are, first and foremost, the course textbook... We adhere to basic guidelines set according to the day and date. This is considered a primary reference' (Male-Associate Professor).

Another senior male faculty emphasized the collaborative work involved in the curriculum development:

'We formed several committees that developed the course content to assist the instructors in teaching this course. Otherwise, there is no single textbook that can encompass all the course content. Other resources include audio recordings, YouTube videos, and similar materials' (Male-Associate Professor).

These responses specify a reliance on structured, committee-developed materials, especially in the institutions handling large student cohorts, ensuring uniformity in learning outcomes across educational programs. Another male perspective added and explained that some institutions, like XYZ University, designed their own curriculum, integrated multiple text types and practical applications for teaching Arabic course.

Limitations, Variability, and Instructor-Led Resource Selection

Female respondents stressed the limitations in the accessibility of standardized materials and consistency with learning outcomes. One female faculty with less than six years' teaching of Arabic experience explained:

'I mean, not entirely, because the learning outcomes are one thing, and what we actually teach is another... an hour and a half isn't enough for us to cover all of that, reading and writing... There's a lot of randomness in the approach' (Female-Associate Professor).

Another female pointed out that resources often depend on individual instructors rather than a fixed curriculum. Many of us do not follow the standardized curriculum, like a textbook as a reference book to the students. We share different sources of information related to the course with the students extracted from the media, books, stories etc. The major concern of the female faculty was the evolving nature of course resources and the need for continuous updates to match contemporary developments in the domain of Arabic language. A relatively less -experienced female faculty explained her perspective by saying:

'In some of the courses we study, the sources and references are constantly changing... We must add videos and sources that we used previously; new, very different, and useful ones will emerge that keep pace with modern developments (Female-Lecturer).

This highlights the challenges in the alignment with intended learning outcomes of Arabic course, exhibiting a tension between institutional guidelines and practical classroom realities.

Theme 3: Lack of Alignment Between Curriculum Depth and University Assessment Practices

Respondents' responses revealed a mutual concern among both male and female faculty members that the existing Arabic curriculum content only partially meets university-level expectations, particularly in terms of depth, coherence, and alignment between lessons, activities, and assessments. Almost all male described the curriculum as:

'Only average in its alignment with university students," noting that while some ideas are "somewhat bold," they require "testing and re-evaluation'.

This perceives a lack of harmony in the curriculum that was also echoed by a middle-aged female respondent who strongly argued that the curriculum is

'Suitable even for middle school or high school students' (Female- Assistant Professor).

It stresses that many components such as oral reading, basic grammar rules like *"kana and its sisters,"* and punctuation are repetitions of prior schooling rather than academically challenging university content. She further disapproved the discrepancy between teaching and assessment, perceiving that

'We study theater and poetry, but there was no exam on either,'

At the same time, some male respondents contextualized these deficiencies by directing to students' weak entry-level proficiency, describing this situation as:

'Huge paradox between what should be happening at university and what I see,'

This directs instructors to adhere to *the bare minimum requirements for student development* rather than offering depth-oriented, critical, and literary-focused instruction. From this viewpoint, the curriculum is considered as being in a phase of *re-establishment,* constrained by students inflated prior grades and low real ability. Both male and female respondents took a more composed view, explaining that although the curriculum meets essential requirements, its effectiveness depends on students' ability levels. One female respondent pronounced this by saying it is like

'Trying to pour a one-liter bottle into a 150 ml cup'.

However, there was an agreement that improvement is necessary in the curriculum, particularly in diversifying activities and aligning assessments with intended skills. One senior male respondent emphasized that the curriculum:

'shouldn't revolve solely around reading and analysis' (Male- Senior Lecturer).

It calls for precise assessment of speaking and writing skills, while an experienced female faculty emphasized the need to move away from traditional exams toward projects that develop

'Practical writing, speaking, presentation, persuasion, and argumentation' (Female-Lecturer).

These perspectives propose that the curriculum's appropriateness is constrained not only by design issues and discrepancies but also by contextual realities of student readiness, resulting in a curriculum that struggles to balance university-level precision with foundational remediation.

Theme 4: Fragmented Alignment and the Need for Contextually Grounded Curriculum Coherence

The analysis of responses signifies a main perception among both male and female respondents that the curriculum elements 'objectives', 'content', 'activities', and 'assessment 'are only moderately integrated, with rationality often challenged by disintegrated implementation, weak content structure, and contextual limitations associated with student preparedness. Some male respondents recognized that the curriculum *'appears to follow a single path'* yet emphasized that *'the content needs a complete overhaul',* arguing that while alignment may exist at a practical level, the functional academic depth entails serious review by subject experts. In contrast, a female respondent proposed a sharply critical perspective, labelling the curriculum as *"inconsistent and disproportionate,"* where *"every week we study something different, like a* stemming in a lack of continuity, absence of a core textbook, and no cumulative learning. She emphasized that *"there's no integration... no lesson that can be taught today and then, after a month, we can observe how the student develops* (female- Assistant Professor)

It highlights a disconnection between what is taught and what can be meaningfully assessed.

Hence, male respondents enclosed the issue more carefully, recommending that coherence must be evaluated in relation to the course's foundational nature, observing that the curriculum is *"open to development"* and still in a *"pilot phase,"* formed by time pressures and evolving pedagogical approaches.

One senior male participant defended the principle of integration, stating that:

Every test we conduct, and every activity we undertake, must align with one of the course objectives (Male- Associate Professor).

Female respondents explained that even if the curriculum is designed to match university goals, it does not work well in practice because many students do not have fundamental language skills. Respondents felt that to make the curriculum more linked and effective, it should be designed based on real classroom situations rather than ideal or theoretical ideas. Some respondents, especially male participants, suggested practical ways to improve it, such as organizing the curriculum into clear sections like short stories, poetry, and functional writing, adding useful skills like email writing and public speaking, and arranging content in a gradual, step-by-step way. They also believed that this approach would work better than using many short and incoherent texts. Overall, these interpretations show that although curriculum coherence is an official goal, it is not fully achieved yet because of issues with content design, students' skill levels, and the need for a more planned, practical, and context-based curriculum.

Theme 5: Student Engagement and Motivation in the New Curriculum

The responses indicate that student interest in the new Arabic curriculum is uneven but generally positive, with engagement largely influenced by assessment relevance, instructor delivery, and differentiated student levels. Respective respondents noted that students tend to prioritize course components linked directly to tests or exams, A male faculty mentioned in his views:

'Any part of the course that doesn't constitute a test in the assessments is superfluous'. (Male- Associate Professor).

Motivation also appears to correlate with the personal engagement of the instructor, as one participant observed, the same respondent said further:

'Sometimes the instructor's performance and explanations compensate for the course's shortcomings and gaps.

It reflects from male responses that students' initial interest is often strengthened by preconceptions of Arabic as a challenging language, especially regarding grammar and syntax, which they approach with uneasiness. However, with tailored interventions, such as reading aloud tests, projects on influential Arab figures, and individualized presentations, students demonstrated meaningful improvement in both confidence and Arabic proficiency. For example, one female respondent emphasized:

'Some students even reached the point of standing before the class and delivering impromptu speeches spontaneously, without prior preparation' (Female, Lecturer).

Respondents also repeated these observations, observing that student motivation can vary extensively depending on the academic preparedness and preliminary skill level, and that engaging activities such as practical projects and varied exercises are fundamental for enhancing both interest and learning outcomes. One male faculty reported:

'Students should deliver speeches, write emails, participate in dialogues or debates, and undertake projects... shifting the subject from a mere university requirement to a dynamic course' (Male- Lecturer).

This analysis proposes that while some students show high commitment and improvement, others remain uncertain due to foundational weaknesses or low academic motivation. Strategic curriculum design, active instructor contribution, and skill-based projects appear key to sustaining motivation and refining perception of the Arabic language.

Theme 6: Student-Centered, Active Learning Strategies for Arabic linguistic Skills

The respondents emphasized student-centered, active learning strategies as the most effective for developing linguistic and intellectual skills. Traditional oral reading is seen as inadequate for promoting speaking fluency, so methods such as oral presentations, debates, podcasts, and flipped classroom activities are emphasized. A recurring theme is student involvement in the assessment process, which encourages responsibility and reflection, A female respondent expressed her feelings by saying:

'I always let them evaluate their classmates or themselves...which makes them feel that we have a responsibility in the classroom' (Female-Assistant Professor).

It shows that Interactive and collaborative activities are emphasized as crucial, A senior male faculty reported as:

'The student doesn't just receive information; they experiment. They experiment with speaking; they experiment with application' (Male-Associate Professor).

Discussion and engagement are central for keeping students motivated and focused. A senior female revealed his experiences by saying:

'Any activity that gets the student involved in the learning process makes them feel present...they respond well and don't get distracted' (Female-Associate Professor).

The faculty also stressed on the relevance and variety associated with adapting materials to students' interests through podcasts or thematic weekly focuses and incorporating field trips or guest speakers. Gamification and small rewards are used to maintain motivation and a playful spirit:

'Everyone...will always have a childlike side, we love motivation, we love challenges' (Female- Lecturer).

Overall, the analysis highlights that a combination of interactive, collaborative, reflective, and relevant activities advances both linguistic competence and intellectual growth while promoting student independence.

Theme 7: Project-Based Assessment for Cognitive and Skill Development

The respondents reflected unfavorably on the current exam and assessment system, perceiving those traditional exams, while prevailing, often fail to capture students' accurate understanding and skill development. While multiple-choice tests are commonly used to measure understanding, the female faculty expressed reservations for instance:

'I would replace these tests with short-answer formats...continuous multiple-choice questions sometimes lead them to finish quickly' (Female -Assistant Professor).

She emphasized the need for assessments that genuinely reflect cognitive understanding. Reading tests are better to assess students' reading skills. However, a main concern is the disproportion between knowledge-based and skill-based assessment, with grammar comprising only a quarter of the grade while three-quarters are based on broader comprehension and external knowledge said by senior male faculty

'Three-quarters of the mark is based on external knowledge...the only studied and tested part is grammar, just a quarter of the mark' (Male- Associate Professor).

To address this disproportion, the faculty member strongly advocates for project-based and applied assessments, emphasizing that such methods uncover not only understanding but also presentation, communication, and analytical skills said by female respondent.

'The academic project is excellent; it reveals the student's presentation skills, their posture, eye contact, and communication abilities (Female-Assistant Professor).

However, state-of-the-art approaches like video presentations, debates, and applied tasks are suggested as alternatives to traditional exams, said by male lecturer:

'We could reduce the number of exams and replace them with direct application...a student could prepare a video on a specific topic...or present a debate' (Male- Lecturer).

Another male faculty reported that:

'The assessments are too numerous compared to the weeks...I suggested removing the second activity related to the content because it's redundant' (Male-Lecturer).

He further explained that:

'The more we try to regulate exams...the more we unfortunately find new ways to use chatbots for cheating' (Male- Lecturer).

It reflects that assessment should be aligned with the curriculum, balance cognitive knowledge with skill-based performance and student-centered tasks. By reducing reliance on traditional exams and increasing project-oriented evaluations, students are more likely to develop both intellectual abilities and practical competencies, leading to more meaningful and authentic learning outcomes.

Theme 8: Curriculum Overload and Implementation Challenges in a Transitional Learning Context

The analysis of the responses unveiled that the most substantial challenges in instigating the new curriculum derived from curriculum overload, constant changes, limited resources, and wide variations in student proficiency levels, all of which place considerable pressure on both teachers and students. Though the curriculum appears simple on the surface, it is labelled as 'quite dense', covering many large topics within a limited time, which forces instructors to rush through content and negotiates depth of learning. Numerous revisions to course plans and assessment structures further confuse implementation, as instructors struggle to prepare effectively amid ongoing experimentation. The absence of a clear textbook and the dependance on weak or non-academic materials add to the struggle, pushing teachers to pursue external resources to maintain instructional quality. Another main challenge is the substantial discrepancy in students' Arabic language abilities due to the removal of placement tests, stemming in classrooms that comprise both highly proficient and extremely weak learners. This situation makes it challenging to achieve learning outcomes fairly and diminishes the effectiveness of instruction. Moreover, unnecessary assessments and exam pressure undesirably affect motivation and focus, reducing enjoyment in the learning process for both teachers and students. As one male participant noticed:

'There are far too many topics…and there isn't enough time to cover them all," while another emphasized the instability of implementation, stating (Male- Associate Professor).

And senior female participant said:

'Pressure takes away the enjoyment from the teaching and learning process' (Female -Associate Professor).

In general, the responses highlight the urgent need for a more coherent, focused curriculum supported by appropriate resources, balanced assessment, and strategies that account for learner diversity.

Theme 9: Reliance on Collegial Support amid Limited Institutional Guidance

The responses suggested that support during Arabic curriculum implementation was largely informal, unreliable, and deeply dependent on individual or collegial effort rather than structured institutional planning. While some participants recognized the availability of general university training and technical assistance, these were labeled as optional and not precisely tailored to the needs of curriculum implementation. The most significant support came from colleagues within the department through collaboration, material sharing, and unceasing guidance for teaching Arabic course, which assisted compensate for the absence of administrative training, feedback, and resources. Respective respondents expressed frustration over the lack of formal follow-up, especially during curriculum development, mentioning that significant academic work was submitted without receiving any feedback. Others highlighted unmet needs such as specialized facilities, platforms for Arabic language learning, and skill-based training. As one participant stated:

'There was, no resources, no assistance from any quarter—just our own efforts as a team' (Male-Associate Professor).

Although another emphasized the value of peer collaboration by saying,

'We received real support from our colleagues in the department, not from the administration' (Female- Associate Professor).

The need for targeted skill-based support is captured in the remark said by one participant:

'The simplest support I need is feedback' (Male- Associate Professor).

Generally, it shows that although informal and technical support occurs, the absence of structured, curriculum-specific institutional support considerably affects effective execution.

Theme 10: Partial Alignment with State Vision amid Calls for Deeper Linguistic and Cultural Integration

The participants' responses signify that the new curriculum is generally perceived as supporting with the state's strategy of promoting the Arabic language, but this alignment is often observed as partial and in need of deeper development. Respective participants recognized that the curriculum carries positive intentions yet questioned its effectiveness in achieving long-term linguistic outcomes. One male participant described this balanced view by stating that

'there's no doubt that this course aims for that, but does it fully achieve that goal? ... I'd put it at an intermediate level' (Male- Associate Professor).

He suggested that the curriculum aligns theoretically but lacks depth. Similarly, a female participant emphasized that the issue lies not in policy but in structural continuity, arguing that

'Three credit hours aren't enough for a student to graduate with a strong level of Arabic... each course should build upon the previous ones (Female- Assistant Professor).

It reflects the need for a coherent sequence of Arabic courses rather than a single isolated offering.

However, in contrast, another male participant expressed strong confidence in the curriculum's alignment, noting that

'This learning is project-based, based on valuing the Arabic language... and directly aligned with the state's interests' (Male-Assistant Professor).

Across responses, there was also a strong call especially from female participants to move beyond technical language skills toward promoting cultural belonging, social awareness, and identity preservation, reinforcing the idea that meaningful language promotion must integrate content, culture, and continuity rather than remain limited to surface-level activities.

DISCUSSION

The findings of this qualitative study reveal a nuanced and multifaceted picture of the implementation of the new Arabic language curriculum, emphasizing both its alignment with state policies and leadership priorities and the significant challenges that limit its efficiency in practice. While participants usually recognized that the curriculum reflects national goals associated with promoting the Arabic language, cultural identity, and citizenship, this alignment was often described as partial rather than fully realized (Kamal, 2025). Participants frequently referred to the importance of clearer academic leadership in translating policy ambition into classroom practice.

A main theme emerging from this data is the stress between curriculum breadth and instructional depth. Participants consistently reported that the curriculum is dense, overloaded with content, and constrained by time, which forces instructors to prioritize coverage over mastery (Khairanis et al., 2025). This stress undermines both teaching quality and student engagement, resonating with previous research that warns against overambitious curriculum design in language education (Norlaila et al., 2025). The emphasis on multiple assessments, activities, and projects within a short timeframe was perceived as particularly detrimental, as it created stress for both students and teachers and reduced the enjoyment of the learning process, an element widely recognized as essential for effective language acquisition. Several instructors connected these pressures to top-down leadership decisions regarding pacing and performance expectations.

Respondents' perspectives also indicate a critical gap between innovative pedagogical approaches and linguistic relevance (Ilmiani, 2022). Though project-based learning and practice-based activities were acknowledged as valuable in principle, several participants questioned their effectiveness when projects were not directly connected to Arabic language skills. Assignments focusing on presentations about historical figures or non-linguistic content were seen as superficial, especially when students relied on ready-made materials without meaningful language practice. This finding aligns with literature suggesting that applied learning in language education must be carefully scaffolded to ensure that communicative competence, vocabulary development, and structural accuracy remain central (Hossain, 2024). Faculty members emphasized that stronger pedagogical leadership and guidance could better align innovation with language mastery.

Another important finding is associated with learners' diverse backgrounds and the lack of placement mechanisms. The removal of placement testing has led to classes with wide proficiency differences, making it difficult to achieve reasonable learning outcomes. Participants identified this as a major barrier to curriculum effectiveness, as instructors are required to teach the same content to students with vastly diverse Arabic proficiency levels. This finding aligns with previous research emphasizing the importance of diagnostic assessment and differentiated instruction in language programs, particularly in higher education contexts (Alderson, 2005; Tomlinson, 2014). Participants suggested that leadership intervention in policy revision and resource allocation would be necessary to address this structural issue.

The findings emphasize instructors' roles as both curriculum implementers and informal curriculum developers. Although institutional support was perceived as partial, particularly regarding training and resources, strong collegial collaboration emerged as a key coping strategy. Faculty relied on peer support, shared materials, and collaborative problem-solving to address curriculum challenges. This aligns with prior research emphasizing the role of professional learning communities in supporting curriculum reform, particularly during stages of transition (DuFour, 2004; Hargreaves & O'Connor, 2018). In the absence of consistent formal direction, distributed forms of leadership among colleagues became essential.

CONCLUSION

This study concludes that although the new Arabic language curriculum aligns with state-level educational strategies at the level of the UAE vision, its effectiveness is restricted by structural, pedagogical, and institutional limitations. *A central issue concerns the translation of policy leadership into sustained instructional leadership.* To enhance its influence, there is a need for a more comprehensive program design with stronger institutional support, effective feedback mechanisms, and greater emphasis on linguistic depth and cultural significance. *Strengthening coordination between decision makers, program leaders, and classroom instructors appears critical.* Addressing these areas is indispensable for ensuring that Arabic language programs in higher education move beyond symbolic alignment and achieve sustainable and transformative learning outcomes.

This study presents implications for future research based on these insights. Conducting comparative studies with other higher education institutions in the UAE or across the Gulf region could clarify contextual similarities and differences in faculty experiences and curriculum implementation. Moreover, longitudinal research following faculty development and student outcomes over time would help evaluate the sustainability and effectiveness of the curriculum reforms while supporting ongoing improvements in Arabic language instruction and faculty professional development, particularly in relation to evolving leadership models.

REFERENCES

Abourehab, Y., & Azaz, M. (2023). Pedagogical translanguaging in community/heritage Arabic language learning. *Journal of Multilingual and Multicultural Development*, *44*(5), 398–411. DOI: 10.1080/01434632.2020.1826496

Achruh, A., & Sukirman, S. (2024). An analysis of Indonesian Islamic higher education institutions in the era of globalization. *International Journal of Learning. Teaching and Educational Research*, *23*(9), 78–102.

Aguzzoli, R., Lengler, J., Miller, S. R., & Chidlow, A. (2024). Paradigms in qualitative IB research: Trends, analysis, and recommendations. *MIR. Management International Review*, *64*(2), 165–198. DOI: 10.1007/s11575-024-00529-5

Alderson, J. C. (2005). *Diagnosing foreign language proficiency: The interface between learning and assessment*. Continuum.

Alharahsheh, H. H., & Pius, A. (2020). A review of key paradigms: Positivism vs. interpretivism. *Global Academic Journal of Humanities and Social Sciences, 2*(3), 39–43. https://gajrc.com/media/articles/GAJHSS_23_39-43_VMGJbOK.pdf

Braun, V., & Clarke, V. (2025). Reporting guidelines for qualitative research: A values-based approach. *Qualitative Research in Psychology*, *22*(2), 399–438. DOI: 10.1080/14780887.2024.2382244

DuFour, R. (2004). What is a professional learning community? *Educational Leadership*, *61*, 6–11.

Emirates News. (2012, April 23). Mohamed unveils the Arabic language charter._https://www.emirates247.com/news/government/mohammed-unveils-arabic-language-charter-2012-04-23-1.455274

Fatimah. (2024). *Istratijiyah al-Thalabah 'ala Ta'allum Itqan al-Mufradat fi Qism Ta'lim al-Lugah al-Arabiyyah bi Jamiah Antasari al-Islamiyah al-Hukumiyah.* Pendidikan Bahasa Arab: UIN Antasari Banjarmasin.

Fullan, M. (2007). *The new meaning of educational change* (4th ed.). Teachers College Press.

Hargreaves, A., & O'Connor, M. T. (2018). *Collaborative professionalism: When teaching together means learning for all*. Corwin. DOI: 10.4135/9781506328133

Hijriyah, U., Edi, R. N., Erlina, E., Kesuma, G. C., & Saâ, T. (2024). Innovative approaches to Arabic vocabulary learning for Islamic senior high school students with Lectora Inspire. *Journal Pendidikan Islam, 10*(2), 218–233. DOI: 10.15575/jpi.v10i2.28754

Hossain, I. K. (2024). Literature-based language learning: Challenges and opportunities for English learners. *Ampersand (Oxford, UK), 13*, 100201. DOI: 10.1016/j.amper.2024.100201

Ilmiani, A. M., Miolo, M. I., Hunainah, H., & Maghfurin, A. (2022). Building literacy in reading foreign language books for Arabic education students. *Arabiyat: Jurnal Pendidikan Bahasa Arab dan Kebahasaaraban, 9*(1), 44–55. https://doi.org/DOI: 10.15408/a.v9i1.20312

Iqbal, M. (2016). Studi komparasi prestasi belajar mata kuliah bahasa Arab antara mahasiswa lulusan pondok pesantren dengan mahasiswa non-pondok pesantren di Jurusan Pendidikan Bahasa Arab Fakultas Ilmu Tarbiyah dan Keguruan UIN Sunan Kalijaga Yogyakarta. *Pendidikan Bahasa Arab: UIN Sunan Kalijaga Yogyakarta.*

Khairanis, R., & Aldi, M., Aziz, A. S. (2025). The role of Arabic in strengthening cultural identity in the digital age. *CARONG: Jurnal Pendidikan, Sosial dan Humaniora, 1*(3), 119–130. https://doi.org/DOI: 10.62710/annx2098

Lim, W. M. (2025). What is qualitative research? An overview and guidelines. *Australasian Marketing Journal, 33*(2), 199–229. DOI: 10.1177/14413582241264619

Lincoln, Y., & Guba, E. (1985). Naturalistic inquiry. *Sage (Atlanta, Ga.).*

Norlaila, N., Muradi, A., Oensyar, M. K., & Arifin, A. (2025). *Students' difficulties in Arabic: A study of the background of student's Arabic language education*. Ijaz Arabi Journal of Arabic Learning.

Rehman, I. U., Malik, U., Khan, A. A., & Hayat, A. (2025). Reinventing stereotypes: An exploration of digital orientalism in Western media representation of the Middle East. *The Journal of Research Review, 2*(1), 36–43. https://thejrr.com/index.php/39/article/view/80

Ridwan, M. (2023). Membuka wawasan keislaman: Kebermaknaan bahasa Arab dalam pemahaman Islam. *Jazirah: Jurnal Peradaban dan Kebudayaan, 4*(2), 102–115. https://doi.org/DOI: 10.51190/jazirah.v4i2.100

Setianingsih, R., & Robbani, A. S. (2024). Problematika pembelajaran bahasa Arab: Studi kasus pada siswa Sanggar Bimbingan Permai Penang Malaysia. *Diglosia: Jurnal Kajian Bahasa, Sastra, dan Pengajarannya, 7*(4), 655–664. https://doi.org/DOI: 10.30872/diglosia.v7i4.1065

Taha-Thomure, H. (2019). Arabic language education in the UAE. In Gallagher, K. (Ed.), *Education in the UAE: Innovation and transformation* (pp. 87–104). Springer., DOI: 10.1007/978-981-13-7736-5_5

Tomlinson, C. A. (2014). *The differentiated classroom: Responding to the needs of all learners* (2nd ed.). ASCD.

Wang, J. Q., Liu, G., & Lei, Y. (2025). Reaffirming the importance of traditional humanities in the era of AI-enhanced translation and transcultural communication. *International Communication of Chinese Culture, 12*(2), 277–311. DOI: 10.1007/s40636-025-00334-1

Yundayani, A., & Alghadari, F. (2025). The reflective factors of students' determination for effective learning in higher education. *Eureka: Journal of Educational Research, 3*(2), 115–127. DOI: 10.56773/ejer.v3i2.40

Zahid, M., & Rahimadinullah, A., & Kholisin. (2025). Arabic language education in Islamic higher education. *Journal of Arabic Language. Literature and Education, 6*(2), 535–550.

Chapter 19

Sustainable AI Literacy in Higher Education Through Awareness, Ethics, and Curriculum Design

Nadine Jaafarawi
http://orcid.org/0000-0002-6855-1461
Zayed University, UAE

Rima Al Chaar
http://orcid.org/0000-0002-1810-9827
Zayed University, UAE

ABSTRACT

Artificial intelligence (AI) continues to reshape higher education, influencing how students learn and how educators design and deliver instruction. While its pedagogical and operational effects have been widely discussed, much less attention has been given to its environmental footprint. This chapter presents AWARE-AI (Assessing Awareness and Attitudes toward Responsible Environmental Use of AI), a study exploring how undergraduate students understand the ecological costs of AI technologies and how these insights can inform more sustainable curriculum design. The project brings together perspectives from technology, sustainability, and education, targeting foundational courses at a federal university in the United Arab Emirates. Through linking AI literacy with environmental responsibility, the

DOI: 10.4018/979-8-3373-4908-4.ch019

study introduces the concept of Sustainable AI Literacy (SAIL) and highlights ways in which higher education can integrate sustainability principles into teaching, learning, and policy in an ethically grounded and interdisciplinary manner.

INTRODUCTION

Artificial Intelligence (AI) is now deeply connected with the way higher education systems operate. Over the past two decades, universities have seen the fast growth of AI applications in teaching, learning, and administration. At first, AI was mainly linked to small experiments such as intelligent tutoring systems or adaptive platforms that tried to guide students through step-by-step practice. These early systems were useful but limited. They did not transform the structure of higher education, but they gave a signal that machines could support teachers in providing feedback and in adapting learning to student needs (Alzahrani, 2023).

Later, as universities adopted large digital platforms, AI became part of the infrastructure. It was embedded in plagiarism detection, learning analytics, automatic grading, and even student advising services. This changed the role of AI from being an "extra tool" into something that is part of the daily life of universities. Today, with the rise of generative AI (GenAI), this role has expanded again. Students now use several tools for writing support, translation, brainstorming, or quick information access (Xiao et al., 2025). In this chapter, the term AI refers mainly to generative and language-based systems such as ChatGPT, Google Bard, and Microsoft Copilot, along with AI-supported applications like Grammarly, Canva, and Turnitin Draft Coach that are commonly used in higher education. This definition reflects the tools that students in the study reported using most frequently for academic and creative work. Evidence shows that more than 70% of students in China already use GenAI, but many still say their skills are not fully developed, which means adoption is high but real literacy is not (Xiao et al., 2025). Similar studies in other regions confirm that students see AI as useful but at the same time raise concerns about plagiarism, misinformation, and too much dependence on automated systems (Gherhe & Obrad, 2018).

This growing use of AI in universities has generated a lot of research. Most studies focus on pedagogy, personalization, ethics, or academic integrity. However, there is a missing link in these discussions: the environmental implications of AI. Training and running large AI models require a massive amount of energy and resources. For example, a recent analysis of 79 AI systems released between 2020 and 2024 estimated that their combined carbon emissions could reach over 100 million tons of CO_2 equivalent per year, a number that is close to the yearly emissions of some small countries (Yu et al., 2024). Other reports confirm that AI is extremely compute and hardware-intensive, depending on specialized chips, large data centers, and vast water supplies for cooling (Delort et al., 2023; Simpson, 2025). As much as energy and emissions are responsible for a big part of this footprint, yet hidden costs such as rare mineral extraction, electronic waste, and water depletion from cloud-scale data centers should not be excluded (Delort et al., 2023; Simpson, 2025). While such global statistics are alarming, little is known about how students in rapidly digitalizing regions, such as the United Arab Emirates (UAE), perceive these environmental consequences.

As AI is currently presented as a solution to climate change and sustainability challenges, its own costs are rarely discussed in higher education contexts. Universities around the world are setting strong sustainability goals, but most of the digital tools they use, including AI, are not assessed for their environmental footprint. Recent studies warn that even when AI is applied for positive purposes, like improving public health, its long-term environmental costs can create new inequalities and undermine future health justice (Moyano-Fernández et al., 2024). This riddle is important for education because it shows that students need to be thoughtful about the broader ecological implications of AI and not merely learning how to use AI effectively. This concern holds particular relevance in the UAE, where sustainability has become a national priority under the UAE Green Agenda 2030 and the National Climate Change Plan. Higher education institutions, including federal Universities, have aligned their strategies with the Ministry of Education (MoE) and Abu Dhabi Department of Education and Knowledge (ADEK) initiatives promoting environmental responsibility, digital transformation, and innovation-driven sustainability. Yet, despite these strong policy frameworks, limited research has explored how students themselves understand the environmental dimension of AI use within these green higher education agendas.

At the same time, emerging research suggests that student awareness alone is not sufficient to address the environmental and ethical implications of AI use in higher education. Strategic leadership and institutional governance play a critical role in shaping how AI is adopted, regulated, and embedded within teaching and learning practices. Without clear leadership direction, sustainability commitments risk remaining symbolic rather than operational, particularly when AI technologies are introduced at scale across academic and administrative systems (Tarisayi, 2024; Arar et al., 2025).

Furthermore, the recent UAE AI Policy for Education, which mandates the gradual incorporation of AI studies and tools across K-12 curricula, is expected to expand AI usage among future university cohorts. This policy momentum makes it essential to begin introducing sustainable AI awareness now, before this next generation of learners enters higher education already immersed in AI technologies. The authors view this chapter as a timely response to this national shift, which is an attempt to ensure that the country's ambitious AI integration is accompanied by equal attention to environmental and ethical responsibility.

The purpose of this chapter is to introduce AWARE-AI (Assessing Awareness and Attitudes toward Responsible Environmental Use of AI), as a conceptual and pedagogical framework that links AI literacy with sustainability thinking in higher education. Developed in the context of a federal university in the UAE, AWARE-AI is intended as a guiding lens for curriculum design and reflection, rather than as a validated measurement or evaluation model. It emphasizes that responsible AI literacy should extend beyond technical and ethical competence to include awareness of environmental responsibility (Bolte et al., 2022; Sætra, 2021).

The significance of this approach is threefold. First, it addresses a gap in research. Current studies on AI in higher education pay attention to student attitudes and adoption (Alzahrani, 2023; Xiao et al., 2025), but very few examine how students connect AI with sustainability or climate change. Second, it offers a pathway to embed ecological awareness into digital literacy courses, which are often part of general education requirements. If students learn to see the environmental price tag that comes with AI productivity, they can develop more responsible behaviors. Third, it connects higher education to global goals. By aligning AI literacy with Sustainable Development Goal (SDG) 4: Quality Education and SDG 13: Climate Action, universities can play a stronger role in addressing both educational and environmental challenges together (Kumar, 2024; Sætra, 2021). Accordingly, the research questions focus on students' awareness and attitudes, rather than on testing or validating the framework itself.

This study is guided by three research questions:

1. How do students from different academic backgrounds understand the environmental impact of AI?
2. What attitudes do they show toward sustainable digital behaviors?
3. How can curriculum design integrate sustainability and AI ethics into general education?

These questions are designed to assess both students' awareness (what students know) and attitudes (how they feel and act). Together, they support the goal of linking AI literacy with environmental responsibility and guide the review of existing studies on sustainable AI education presented in the next section.

LITERATURE REVIEW

The Evolution of AI in Higher Education

The use of intelligence in education has been a gradual process, evolving from a small-scale experiment to a widespread presence in universities. Initially, AI tools were sparingly used, such as in tutoring systems or programs that provided students with automated feedback. Researchers like Alzahrani (2023) have noted that these early systems demonstrated the potential for technology to assist teachers by streamlining their workload and supporting students. Although these initial systems were relatively simple, they paved the way for the integration of AI in educational settings, laying the groundwork for further innovation.

In the early 2000s, AI became a staple in learning management systems. This marked a change as AI was no longer a supplementary tool but an integral part of daily university life. Chatbots also emerged, addressing student queries and providing support, which quickly made them a familiar fixture in the student experience.

When it comes to students' attitudes towards AI, some are excited about the possibilities, while others are anxious about what it might mean for them. A study of students in Romania done by Gherhe & Obrad (2018) found some differences in how they view AI. Students in fields like engineering or computer science tend to feel more informed and positive about AI compared to their peers in the humanities. There is also a gender gap, with male students feeling more confident about AI than female students, as research by Gherhe and Obrad back in 2018 highlighted. What is clear from all this is that just having access to AI is not enough; how students think and feel about it plays a role in how they use it. Research has also shown that many students express concerns about plagiarism, misinformation, and an overreliance on intelligence. If not properly managed, this could hinder creativity and reduce critical thinking skills, which highlights the need for explicit guidelines on responsible AI use, as noted by Xio et al. (2025).

In parallel, AI is also being connected to sustainability efforts in education. A trend that has been noted by Al-Zahrani (2024) is that universities are experimenting with AI to cut down on energy consumption, manage waste effectively, and develop eco-friendly transportation systems. This shows that AI is no longer just a learning tool; it's actually becoming an integral part of how universities run on a day-to-day basis. However, it became noticeable that AI itself has a footprint, starting from the amount of electricity it uses and not ending by the electronic waste it generates. As a result, as time passes, it shows that AI can be considered as a mixed blessing or two-edged blade. On the one hand, it can help universities become greener and achieve their sustainability goals. On the other hand, bringing in AI also means becoming a contributor to new environmental challenges. This dual role of AI represents the latest stage in its evolutionary journey, preparing the ground for discussions in upcoming sections of this chapter.

Environmental Dimensions of Artificial Intelligence

The environmental dimension of AI is becoming increasingly important as generative models increase in size, reliance, and adoption. While universities often mark AI as a digital innovation, the ecological cost of building and running these systems is significant. These impacts can be grouped into energy use, water consumption, emissions, e-waste, and resource extraction.

Energy-Intensive Computing

Training and using large language models (LLMs) require extreme amounts of electricity. Training GPT-3 consumed 1,287 MWh and released about 552 tons of CO_2, while GPT-4 consumed around 7,200 MWh, almost six times more (Håkans, 2025). According to new studies, training state-of-the-art models can generate emissions comparable to multiple transatlantic flights (Chowdhury et al., 2025). The costs do not stop after training, an inference which is the everyday use of AI systems, requires continuous high-performance computing. A ChatGPT query consumes almost ten times more energy than a Google search (Håkans, 2025). With millions of users worldwide, the cumulative energy demand is projected to reach over 100 terawatt hours (TWh) annually by 2027, which is equivalent to the electricity consumption of medium-sized countries (Li et al., 2025). This trend is also reflected in sustainability dashboards such as Power BI reports, which show steep annual growth in AI-related electricity demand (Jegham et al., 2025, preprint). (Note: Some of the data cited in this section are drawn from preprint sources that have not yet undergone peer review. Given the rapid pace of AI research, many studies are first shared in preprint form to ensure timely dissemination before formal publication.)

Water Consumption and Hidden Footprints

Alongside energy, water is another critical resource for AI. Data centers depend on large volumes of freshwater to cool servers. Training GPT-3 alone evaporated 700,000 liters of clean water, an amount equivalent to the annual use of several households (Li et al., 2025). By 2027, global AI could withdraw between 4.2 and 6.6 billion cubic meters of water, more than the annual water use of Denmark or half of the United Kingdom (Li et al., 2025). Studies gauging users' environmental awareness of AI usage, more specifically ChatGPT, show that this impact is largely unnoticed. In one survey, 80% of ChatGPT users said they never thought about environmental costs while using the tool, and only 25% said they would change their habits if informed (Håkans, 2025; Graves et al., 2025).

E-Waste, Emissions, and Rare Earth Metals

AI requires specialized chips and servers made from rare materials such as cobalt, lithium, and tantalum. Extracting these minerals is linked to water pollution, deforestation, and human rights issues (Hosseini et al., 2025). Frequent hardware upgrades in data centers generate large amounts of e-waste, much of which is not recycled. Data centers themselves emit carbon dioxide and, according to projections, could consume 8% of U.S. electricity and 5% of Europe's by 2030 if growth continues unchecked (Senyapar & Bayindir, 2025). These numbers show that AI's environmental burden extends beyond software into the global supply chain.

Carbon Literacy and Digital Sustainability in Education

Despite these impacts, there are few examples of carbon or water literacy being included in higher education. Universities teach digital literacy and, more recently, AI ethics, but they rarely connect AI use with ecological responsibility. Scholars argue that raising awareness through transparent reporting, dashboards, and classroom activities can help students see the hidden costs of their online actions (Lo, 2024; Graves et al., 2025). Such approaches can build the idea of "digital sustainability," where technical skills are accompanied with an understanding of environmental footprints.

Dual Lens: AI for Sustainability vs. Sustainability of AI

AI is often promoted as a tool for sustainability. For example, in energy optimization, precision agriculture, or climate modelling (Chaudhary, 2023). At the same time, the "sustainability of AI" emphasizes reducing its own environmental burden. Researchers argue that both views must be considered together. If not, AI could create a paradox where it helps reduce emissions in one sector while increasing them in another (van Wynsberghe, 2021).

Scarcity of Student-Centered Research

A striking gap in the literature is the absence of student voices. Most environmental studies of AI come from engineering or policy fields, but we know little about how students perceive these issues. Early surveys show limited awareness, with many students associating AI only with academic benefits and not with environmental costs (Håkans, 2025). Since students are the main users of generative AI in universities, closing this gap is critical by including them in sustainability discussions, which will help eventually align higher education with SDG 4 (Quality Education) and SDG 13 (Climate Action).

In summary, AI's environmental dimensions present a double challenge: it is both an enabler of sustainability and a source of new ecological pressures. As energy use, water scarcity, emissions, and e-waste rise while user awareness remains limited, higher education requires a conceptual lens through which AI literacy extends beyond technical and ethical concerns to include ecological responsibility.

Leadership, Governance, and Institutional Responsibility for AI Adoption

Beyond governance structures, leadership scholarship in higher education emphasizes the role of institutional leaders in shaping strategic direction, institutional culture, and the responsible integration of emerging technologies. Research on AI leadership and sustainability highlights that effective implementation depends on coordinated leadership, faculty capacity-building, and alignment between institutional policy and educational practice rather than isolated or ad hoc initiatives (Tarisayi, 2024; Arar et al., 2025; Leal Filho et al., 2023).

While much of the literature on AI in higher education focuses on pedagogy, student behavior, and ethical awareness, a growing body of research emphasizes that the adoption of AI is ultimately shaped by institutional leadership and governance structures. Strategic leadership determines not only which AI tools are adopted, but also how they are regulated, supported, and aligned with institutional values. Studies on responsible AI adoption in higher education highlight that without clear governance frameworks, universities risk fragmented practices, inconsistent ethical standards, and sustainability commitments that remain aspirational rather than operational (Tarisayi, 2024; Arar et al., 2025).

Leadership scholarship further suggests that AI integration requires coordinated decision-making across academic, administrative, and technological domains. This includes the development of institutional policies, faculty capacity-building initiatives, and accountability mechanisms that guide ethical and sustainable AI use at scale (Hojeij, 2025; Khairullah et al., 2025). In this sense, AI literacy and sustainability cannot be addressed solely at the level of individual courses or student awareness. Instead, they depend on institutional leadership that frames AI as a socio-technical system requiring governance, ethical oversight, and long-term sustainability planning.

AI Literacy and Responsible Digital Engagement

Higher education institutions have established AI literacy as a core educational goal because students, along with faculty members, must understand both the technical aspects and ethical and civic responsibilities of working with intelligent systems. Research indicates literacy extends beyond operational abilities because it incorporates both critical thinking and reflective practices along with sustainable methods.

Frameworks for AI Literacy

Three essential components that form the foundation of AI literacy, according to Ma and Chen (2024), include technical competence, ethical awareness, and civic responsibility. According to UNESCO, AI literacy requires students to develop competencies that teach them both AI usage and evaluation of equity effects alongside privacy protection and sustainability management. The ChatGPT literacy model developed by Ma et al. (2024) introduces six essential competencies to understand benefits, limitations, prompt crafting, output evaluation, relevance assessment, and ethical considerations. These frameworks demonstrate that literacy requires technical expertise alongside thoughtful decision-making abilities.

Technical vs. Ethical and Civic Literacy

The early definitions of AI literacy emphasized computational capabilities and system access, but current research indicates that technical knowledge by itself is insufficient without ethical and civic perspectives (Long & Magerko, 2020). Research by Zhang et al. (2025) demonstrates that teaching students to detect plagiarism through AI tools enables them to view academic integrity as both ethical conduct and non-punishable behavior. Research on pre-service teacher education reveals that future educators possess skills to operate AI tools, yet they receive inadequate training regarding ethical and pedagogical aspects (Guan & Zhang, 2025). The existing gap demonstrates how people understand AI usage methods but remain uncertain about proper times and reasons for implementing such systems.

Awareness and Digital Behavior

User conduct depends heavily on their understanding of AI-related effects. According to Foroughi et al. (2025) students who use generative AI for sustainability information tend to convert their awareness into green purchasing habits. The relationship between literacy and sustainability or ethics teaching demonstrates its power to expand academic learning into real-life decision-making. Students' adoption behavior depends on their expectations, along with peer influence, but awareness acts as a moderating factor that determines responsible versus careless adoption behavior according to Milicevic et al. (2024).

Student Perceptions Across Contexts

Different cultural groups and academic fields demonstrate unique perspectives on artificial intelligence. Romanian students showed positive attitudes toward using AI in academics, yet they had doubts regarding its moral implications (Gherhe & Obrad, 2018). Research indicates that more than 70% of Chinese students use GenAI, yet their literacy skills vary widely, while their ability to think ethically about AI remains narrow (Xiao et al., 2025). The UAE shows evidence of extensive and regular usage of AI tools throughout its population. A survey of 822 students from seven universities revealed that 80 percent of students use AI tools while more than two-thirds of them use them daily or weekly (Swidan et al., 2025). Students utilized AI tools for efficiency and writing assistance and creative work, yet expressed deep concerns about plagiarism issues, data privacy risks, and unclear institutional guidelines. The students remained uncertain about university policies, which generated ethical challenges along with different operational practices. A study involving 225 UAE higher education educators and leaders showed that public universities adopted AI tools at a higher rate (58%) than private institutions (33%) but formal AI training programs sometimes decreased adoption through increased AI skepticism among educators (Al-Jenaibi, 2024). The research demonstrates an interesting situation because UAE students and educators experience high AI exposure, yet insufficient guidance and training, and unclear policies restrict their responsible usage.

Toward Responsible Digital Engagement

The research demonstrates the requirement for AI literacy which must include ethical reasoning abilities together with clear policies and sustainability awareness. The AI competency guidelines of UNESCO and tools such as GPTFootprint support responsible digital practices by translating ethical and sustainability principles into actionable guidance (Graves et al., 2025). According to Tan and Tang (2025), literacy development needs to progress through stages from knowledge to application and evaluation, and finally to ethics. Universities must establish programs that help students and educators develop the ability to use AI tools effectively and to consider their broader effects on academic ethics, environmental sustainability, and social structures.

The process of AI literacy extends beyond the basic instruction of technical competencies. Students, along with educators, need training to use AI tools responsibly, balancing operational efficiency with ethical practices while pursuing innovation and sustainability. The UAE situation displays how students and teachers use AI tools daily at school, yet require organized literacy education that combines access to education with responsible AI use training.

Curriculum, Ethics, and the Role of General Education

Higher education institutions utilize AI for educational purposes, which now includes value-based learning and global citizenship development. The educational curriculum provides essential learning spaces for students to acquire technical skills while building their moral understanding of new technologies. Universities now teach AI through ethical and social frameworks that incorporate environmental sustainability.

Through their educational curriculum, institutions teach essential values to their students. Research demonstrates that when sustainability education is integrated into curricula, students establish connections between their digital actions and environmental issues that need addressing. According to Nordgren (2023), AI operates as two opposing agents that both produce environmental harm by emitting pollutants and develop solutions to combat climate change, so students must understand these opposing effects. Similarly, UNESCO's AI in Education guidelines encourage educational institutions to teach students about AI ethics along with societal impacts, climate responsibility, and sustainability (UNESCO, 2023).

Traditionally, general education programs have always aimed to teach civic values and interdisciplinary awareness. The integration of AI and sustainability education through general education programs supports institutional missions by teaching digital competence from planetary perspectives. The proposal of Raper et al. (2022) shows that "sustainability budgets" operate as a governance system for AI through their educational planning, which enables non-experts to understand technical concepts. Similarly, Allam et al. (2025) introduced the concept of "living intelligence", a concept that perceives AI as a system that co-evolves with humans, not replaces them, and has a shared responsibility with humans to support sustainable education.

Building on how awareness shapes individual behavior, it is also important to examine how broader perceptions and institutional policies influence responsible engagement with AI. Research suggests that the absence of clear institutional guidelines undermines responsible engagement. In the UAE, for example, Swidan et al. (2025) report that students who use AI tools without ethical awareness have done so because their educational institutions fail to provide specific guidelines. As mentioned above, Al-Jenaibi (2024) showed that public universities and private universities have different AI adoption rates, with public universities showing a higher percentage of AI usage among educators in comparison to the private sector. This discrepancy could be explained by the fact that formal training programs sometimes caused instructors to use AI less frequently due to increased caution about AI's risks. These findings highlight how institutional culture and policies influence educators' engagement with AI. In response, universities use the curriculum to articulate and embed institutional values, such as ethics and sustainability, into learning outcomes that students can clearly understand and meaningfully apply.

While students and educators call for clearer policies in their own institutions, these concerns also echo at the global level, where AI ethics and sustainability are increasingly tied to the UN SDGs, according to expanding research findings. The United Nations Sustainable Development Goal 4 establishes quality education standards that teach sustainable development principles to learners, and Goal 13 sets immediate requirements for global warming climate action. Consequently, academic programs gain specific targets when they implement AI ethics and sustainability education. Building on the perspectives of Dhiman et al. (2024) and van Wynsberghe (2021), two complementary aims emerge within AI ethics education: to employ AI for environmental benefit and to mitigate the ecological harm generated by AI technologies. This dual focus supports the current necessity for an "ethics of carefulness" which combines justice with transparent and ecologically protective principles.

The main challenge arises from incorporating sustainability principles into AI course development instead of merely incorporating sustainability content. According to Chan and Hu (2023) student attitudes toward generative AI determine their willingness to practice responsible AI use through hands-on ethical education in learning environments. The research by Herawati et al. (2024) indicates that Indonesian students endorse AI in education, yet express concerns about its effects on employment and data privacy, thus necessitating educational methods that respect cultural traditions. Universities can achieve student understanding of AI as a societal and environmental practice by integrating sustainability and ethics into their core educational programs. This approach can support students in engaging with digital transformation and climate change issues through AI education, while fostering responsible decision-making and sound judgment.

Undoubtedly, the structure of educational curricula shapes how graduates of the future will understand and manage AI-related difficulties. Higher education institutions can implement AI literacy by integrating sustainability and ethics and global citizenship into general education programs which follow international policy guidelines and address student needs in their local context. This educational approach teaches students to manage digital transformation challenges and climate change impacts through AI instruction, while building their capability for ethical decision-making.

At the national level, the UAE educational system requires these specific learning objectives to be implemented. ADEK and the UAE National Agenda for Sustainable Development support the digital transformation of higher education in the nation. Federal universities have the opportunity to drive this change through AI literacy programs that teach sustainability and ethics while following global standards and local needs. The implementation of these values in general education serves both educational and cultural purposes because it trains students to understand technology through sustainable practices and social accountability.

METHODOLOGY

Research Design

The study used a convergent parallel mixed-methods design to examine undergraduate students' understanding and awareness of AI's environmental implications, alongside their related attitudes, using both quantitative and qualitative approaches.

Participants

The research included 180 students who studied basic general education subjects at a UAE federal university. Of these, 177 students consented to participate and successfully completed the survey, yielding a response rate of 98%. Participants represented a range of academic disciplines, including business, media and communication, psychology, information technology, natural sciences, art, and international studies, providing an interdisciplinary perspective on the topic. The majority were in their first or second year of study, who had similar digital learning experiences with basic education about AI.

The sample included 89 females (50.3%) and 88 males (49.7%) participants, indicating a nearly balanced gender distribution. They were aged between 18 and 22 years, and all were UAE nationals who provided insights based on the UAE higher education system and cultural background. This balanced and interdisciplinary sample provided a robust foundation for examining student attitudes, awareness, and ethical orientations toward the environmental implications of AI in higher education.

Research Instruments

The research tool used the AI literacy framework developed by Wang et al. (2023), which conceptualizes AI literacy through four interconnected elements: awareness, usage, evaluation, and ethics. Based on this model, the student questionnaire followed the original structure and conceptual domains. However, the instrument was intentionally adapted for this study in two key ways.

First, the researchers extended the framework to incorporate environmental sustainability dimensions, which received limited attention in the original framework. Specifically, new awareness items were developed to explore students' understanding of AI's environmental implications, including data center energy consumption and electronic waste production. Second, the instrument was linguistically and cognitively adapted to suit UAE higher education students, ensuring accessibility for first-year and second-year undergraduates.

For this study, AI was defined as digital tools that use machine learning or language models to generate, assist, or evaluate academic content. Examples shared with participants included ChatGPT, Google Bard, Microsoft Copilot, Grammarly, Canva, and Turnitin Draft Coach to ensure a shared understanding of the term.

The AWARE-AI Student Questionnaire was developed as a study-specific instrument. The final questionnaire consisted of six sections:

- Section A gathered demographic data, including field of study, semester, age, and gender.
- Section B addressed AI awareness, particularly environmental implications. This section incorporated Likert-scale statements, yes/no items, open-ended responses, and true/false knowledge checks.
- Section C examined the frequency and nature of AI tool usage.
- Section D evaluated students' interpretations of AI's environmental effects.
- Section E assessed ethical attitudes and responsible digital behaviors.
- Section F collected curriculum-related preferences and suggestions.

Section B underwent the most substantial modification to accommodate varying levels of digital and scientific literacy among participants. To ensure content validity, an expert in natural sciences and sustainability reviewed the newly developed items. The questionnaire was also piloted prior to distribution to confirm clarity, accessibility, and the absence of leading questions.

Procedure

Data Collection

Ethical approval for the study was granted by the university's institutional research ethics review board. At the start of the questionnaire, participants provided informed consent and were reminded that they could withdraw at any time without consequence. Survey data were collected through an online questionnaire distributed across the 8 classes.

Data Analysis

Quantitative analyses were used to identify broad patterns, group differences, and relationships among students' AI awareness, use, and ethical orientation. Qualitative analysis focused on recurring themes in students' open-ended reflections to provide contextual depth and support interpretation of the quantitative trends.

For the qualitative strand, the researchers conducted inductive thematic analysis of open-ended survey responses to identify recurring patterns related to AI environmental awareness. Manual coding was used to preserve contextual meaning and support a nuanced interpretation of students' reflections.

RESULTS

The findings of the AWARE-AI study present an integrated overview of students' levels of awareness, behavioral patterns, and ethical orientations toward the environmental implications of AI. Quantitative results from the student questionnaire are first summarized to illustrate broad trends in AI familiarity, use, and sustainability attitudes across the sample. These are followed by inferential analyses examining potential differences among academic disciplines, and qualitative insights derived from open-ended responses. Together, these findings illustrate how undergraduate students in a UAE federal university perceive the ecological impact of AI technologies and how such perceptions can inform sustainable curriculum design. For institutional leaders, these findings underscore the need to support structures that translate awareness into sustained, responsible AI practices.

Quantitative Findings

The research results showed that students at the undergraduate level showed relatively high levels of engagement and awareness regarding AI. The mean values for the main constructs, as shown in Table 1, ranged from moderate to high. Students reported relatively strong awareness of AI basics through their second-highest mean score of 3.53 (SD = 0.70), which indicates their growing understanding of AI environmental effects, including energy usage, water consumption, and electronic waste generation. The results show students understand the value of responsible AI usage, but they need more development in their understanding of sustainability aspects.

Table 1. Means and Standard Deviations for Awareness, Behavioral, and Ethical Constructs (N = 177)

Construct	N	M	SD
AI Awareness	177	3.53	0.70
AI Use & Behavior	177	3.62	0.80
Ethical & Sustainability Orientation	177	3.20	0.76

Group Differences in AI Awareness (ANOVA t-tests)

The research team performed multiple inferential tests to establish if student backgrounds affected their knowledge about AI environmental effects and their related opinions. The study used one-way analysis of variance (ANOVA) to determine if academic background influenced students' comprehension of AI environmental implications (Table 2). The test compared mean awareness scores across six academic groups, which included business, media and communication, psychology, information technology, natural sciences, and international studies. This analysis aimed to identify potential patterns of disciplinary variation in students' environmental AI literacy, reflecting how exposure to technology-oriented or socially oriented curricula may shape their awareness levels.

Table 2. One-Way ANOVA Results Comparing AI Environmental Awareness Across Academic Disciplines (N = 173)

Discipline	N	M	SD
Art	2	4.20	0.00
Business	56	3.54	0.69
Information Technology	58	3.55	0.71
International Studies	26	3.33	0.70
Media and Communication	11	3.71	0.71

continued on following page

Table 2. Continued

Discipline	N	M	SD
Natural Sciences	11	3.02	0.74
Psychology	9	3.98	0.43
Total / F(6,166)	173	3.52	0.71

Note. The ANOVA included 173 participants with complete data for discipline and awareness; four cases with missing values were excluded listwise. F(6, 166) = 2.44, p = .027. All items were rated or converted to a 5-point scale (1 = Strongly Disagree/No, 5 = Strongly Agree/Yes).

The inferential analyses revealed meaningful differences by discipline but not by gender or academic level. The ANOVA results in Table 2 indicated a statistically significant effect of discipline on AI environmental awareness, $F(6, 166) = 2.44$, $p = .027$. Psychology (M = 3.98) and Art (M = 4.20) students reported the highest awareness, whereas Natural Sciences (M = 3.02) and International Studies (M = 3.33) reported comparatively lower scores.

In contrast, *t*-tests (Table 3) showed no significant gender-based variation in awareness, behavior, or ethical orientation, indicating similar patterns across male and female respondents.

Table 3. Independent-Samples t-Tests Comparing AI Awareness, Behavior, and Ethics by Gender (N = 177)

Construct	Male M	Female M	*t*(175)	*p*
AI Awareness	3.51	3.55	0.41	.682
AI Use & Behavior	3.60	3.64	0.28	.780
Ethical & Sustainability Orientation	3.18	3.21	0.17	.863

Note. No significant gender differences emerged across constructs; means are based on 5-point composite scores.

Additional analyses indicated that greater environmental awareness was associated with stronger ethical and sustainability orientation, but did not significantly reduce AI usage frequency, highlighting a gap between knowledge and behavioral change.

Qualitative Findings

To complement the quantitative strand, open-ended questions in the AWARE-AI student questionnaire invited participants to describe, in their own words, the environmental effects of AI and how universities could raise awareness about them. These written reflections were analysed using inductive thematic analysis. Five interrelated themes emerged, capturing both students' conceptual understanding of AI's ecological footprint and their suggestions for educational action, as seen in Table 4 below.

Table 4. Summary of Emergent Themes from Students' Open-Ended Responses

Theme	Core Idea	Representative Quotations (anonymized)
1. Environmental costs of AI	Students identified high energy use, carbon emissions, and water consumption as the main environmental burdens of AI operations and data centers.	*"AI needs a lot of power, and this increases pollution." / "Big AI systems use too much water and electricity for cooling."*
2. Hardware waste and resource extraction	Frequent upgrades and hardware dependence were linked to e-waste and mining of rare minerals.	*"Old devices become waste because of new AI updates." / "Making chips and machines uses materials that harm the environment."*
3. Limited literacy and uncertainty	Several participants expressed confusion or limited knowledge about AI's environmental effects.	*"I'm not sure how AI affects the environment." / "Maybe it uses too much electricity or costs a lot to run."*
4. Integrating sustainability into learning	Students suggested embedding AI-and-environment topics into university curricula through courses, workshops, and guest talks.	*"We can add short lessons about AI and the environment in our classes." / "The university can make workshops to teach about this topic."*
5. Campus awareness and action	Respondents recommended awareness campaigns, competitions, and transparent communication of the university's digital footprint.	*"Put posters or videos around the campus to show how AI affects nature." / "Show how much energy the university uses from AI tools."*

Note. Themes were derived from inductive coding of 177 students' open-ended survey responses; quotations are paraphrased for clarity and anonymity.

Students' qualitative reflections revealed a developing yet genuine awareness of how AI affects the environment. Many students acknowledged that AI technologies require substantial energy to operate, linking this to pollution and resource use. Comments such as *"AI needs a lot of power, and this increases pollution"* and *"Big AI systems use too much water and electricity for cooling"* illustrate that students are beginning to connect digital consumption with real environmental costs. Others drew attention to hardware dependency, noting that frequent upgrades and the production of new devices contribute to electronic waste and the depletion of natural materials, as one student put it, "*Old devices become waste because of new AI updates.*"

At the same time, several students expressed their uncertainty or limited understanding of these matters. Statements like *"I'm not sure how AI affects the environment"* suggest that while awareness exists, it remains uneven, reflecting the moderate levels of ethical and sustainability orientation found in the quantitative results.

When invited to propose actions, students offered practical and contextually grounded ideas. They recommended integrating AI and environment topics into regular coursework, guest lectures, and workshops: *"We can add short lessons about AI and the environment in our classes"*, showing a desire for more structured learning. Others envisioned collective campus initiatives such as poster campaigns or visual displays of energy use to make sustainability efforts visible: *"Show how much energy the university uses from AI tools."*

These reflections indicate that students view responsibility for AI's environmental impact as shared between individuals and institutions. They also point to the need for curriculum-level sustainability discussions and hands-on experiences to translate awareness into informed, responsible practice.

DISCUSSION

Integrating Student Awareness With Global AI Literacy Trends

The findings of this study indicate that while students in the UAE exhibit strong engagement with AI tools, their awareness of the environmental implications of AI use remains limited and uneven across disciplines. Quantitative results showed that students from psychology and art disciplines reported higher environmental awareness results than students from other academic fields, possibly because their majors focus on ethical reflection, sustainability, and human impact. Qualitative data reinforced this trend, showing that even if students could identify electricity consumption, e-waste, and carbon emissions as major problems, their answers displayed uncertainty or limited understanding of the deeper ecological processes involved.

These patterns align with international studies emphasizing that AI literacy extends beyond operational competence. As noted by Ma and Chen (2024) and UNESCO (2023), literacy in AI education requires students to develop ethical reasoning, sustainability awareness, and civic responsibility. While most students are proficient in using tools such as ChatGPT, they often overlook the environmental cost of their digital behavior, which is a tendency also reported globally by Håkans (2025) and Li et al. (2025), who found that over 80% of users had never considered AI's ecological footprint.

For institutional leaders and academic governance bodies in the UAE, these findings point to a leadership and policy challenge: repositioning AI literacy as institutionally coordinated ethical and environmental education, rather than relying solely on individual courses to foster responsible digital conduct.

Understanding the Environmental Paradox of AI in Higher Education

The results also highlight a tension that van Wynsberghe (2021) describes above as the "AI sustainability paradox." Students viewed AI as both a solution and a source of environmental harm, reflecting the dual role discussed in the literature, which is AI for sustainability versus the sustainability of AI. This paradox emerged strongly in student narratives, which recognized AI's potential for optimizing learning and energy efficiency while simultaneously consuming vast resources in data centers. Such ambivalence illustrates how young adults are beginning to internalize AI's two-edged nature: a driver of innovation and a consumer of planetary resources.

At the institutional level, this duality positions AI as a governance issue rather than a purely technical one, requiring leadership oversight within sustainability and digital transformation frameworks. Al-Zahrani (2024) demonstrated how universities worldwide now use AI to support campus sustainability through smart energy systems and waste reduction initiatives, yet those same technologies contribute to new emissions and electronic waste. These tensions require transparent leadership-led discussions and policy alignment within UAE higher education systems, particularly as AI integration is guided by the UAE National Strategy for Artificial Intelligence (2031) and ADEK's digital transformation agenda.

In this context, environmental literacy related to AI should become a strategic priority within the UAE's higher education transformation. Students' awareness of AI's ecological costs represents a critical step toward cultivating what Graves et al. (2025) term "digital sustainability", which is the capacity to understand, critically evaluate, and mitigate the environmental consequences of digital technologies through institutionally supported practices rather than individual awareness alone.

From Awareness to Action: Embedding Sustainability in UAE Curricula

A key implication of this study is the need to translate student awareness into institutionally supported educational action. The open-ended responses revealed strong demand for workshops, lectures, and curricular activities that connect AI use to sustainability practices. Students' suggestions, ranging from awareness campaigns to integrating "Green AI" topics into general education courses, mirror global trends highlighted by Nordgren (2023) and UNESCO (2023), who emphasize that climate literacy should be linked with AI ethics to produce responsible digital citizens.

The UAE context provides a policy-aligned foundation for implementing such initiatives. Federal universities operate under policy frameworks that already prioritize sustainability and innovation. The UAE National Agenda for Sustainable

Development, together with ADEK, explicitly supports the digital transformation of higher education to meet *SDG 4 (Quality Education)* and *SDG 13 (Climate Action)*. Leadership alignment of AI literacy initiatives with these national priorities is therefore critical to ensuring that sustainability considerations extend beyond technical competence to include AI's planetary consequences.

Furthermore, the institutional disparity identified by Al-Jenaibi (2024), whereby public universities adopt AI tools more readily than private institutions, suggests that leadership-led coordination is required to ensure system-wide and equitable AI literacy implementation. In response, embedding sustainability through interdisciplinary modules can reduce fragmentation across institutions. As Raper et al. (2022) and Allam et al. (2025) propose, "living intelligence" curricula, where AI is seen as co-evolving with human responsibility, provide a model through which institutional leadership can reframe environmental and digital accountability as shared educational commitments rather than isolated instructional efforts.

Toward a Conceptual Model of Sustainable AI Literacy

Drawing on these findings, this study proposes a conceptual *Sustainable AI Literacy (SAIL)* model, as shown in figure 1, that brings together awareness, ethics, and ecological responsibility. Such a model builds upon existing frameworks by Ma and Chen (2024) and Tan and Tang (2025), which describe AI literacy as a continuum from knowledge to evaluation and ethical application. The present study extends this continuum by embedding sustainability as an explicit learning outcome, positioning environmental responsibility as a core dimension of AI literacy rather than a peripheral concern.

Figure 1. The Sustainable AI Literacy (SAIL) Framework: Illustrating the Intersection of AI Literacy, Ethical Responsibility, and Environmental Sustainability

SAIL is informed by the AWARE-AI framework and the study's findings, and is presented as a pedagogical synthesis rather than a validated, predictive, or evaluative model. Its realization depends on institutional leadership and governance structures that enable curriculum integration, resourcing, and ethical alignment at scale. In the UAE context, this model could be operationalized through three leadership-enabled pedagogical pillars:

1. Curricular Integration: Embedding AI and environmental sustainability modules within general education and disciplinary courses.
2. Experiential Learning: Engaging students in sustainability-focused projects, hackathons, and campus initiatives addressing AI's energy and resource use.
3. Ethical Reflection and Policy Alignment: Encouraging students to connect institutional AI policies with personal responsibility through case-based learning and cross-disciplinary discussions.

The model follows UNESCO AI in Education guidelines and the UAE AI Strategy 2031 to fulfill both national and international requirements. It conceptually reflects what Dhiman et al. (2024) describe as the "ethics of carefulness," encouraging universities to adopt transparent, justice-oriented, and ecologically aware pedagogies.

Taken together, the study's findings identify the UAE as a promising context for advancing sustainable AI literacy in higher education. Students' partial awareness, along with their enthusiasm for learning, reflects both the challenges and opportunities of embedding sustainability in digital education. Institutional leaders and academic governance bodies are therefore positioned to recognize AI not only as a pedagogical resource but also as an environmental actor, requiring strategic oversight to cultivate graduates who understand responsible innovation and environmental stewardship as inseparable.

Leadership Enablers for Implementing the *SAIL* Framework

While the *SAIL* framework outlines pedagogical pathways for embedding sustainability within AI literacy, its successful implementation depends on institutional leadership and governance. From a leadership perspective, sustainable AI literacy requires coordinated action across vision-setting, policy development, faculty capacity-building, and resource allocation. Educational leaders play a central role in translating sustainability goals into operational practice by setting strategic priorities, allocating resources, and establishing clear institutional policies around AI use. Without such coordination, sustainability-oriented AI initiatives risk remaining isolated at the course level rather than becoming embedded across programs and faculties. This positions educational leaders as key agents in aligning AI innovation with institutional sustainability commitments.

At the senior leadership level, deans and provosts are positioned to support *SAIL* through curriculum oversight, faculty development initiatives, and cross-unit collaboration that aligns teaching, technology, and sustainability agendas. This includes investing in professional development that equips educators to integrate environmental considerations into AI-related teaching and providing institutional guidance that clarifies ethical and sustainable expectations for AI use. At the administrative level, governance structures are needed to ensure transparency, accountability, and consistency in how AI tools are adopted and evaluated across the university.

Implementing *SAIL* also presents practical challenges for leadership, including infrastructure demands, competing institutional priorities, and equity considerations related to access and digital resource use. Addressing these challenges requires strategic decision-making that balances innovation with responsibility, ensuring that environmental awareness is sustained rather than symbolic. In this sense, *SAIL* should be understood not only as a curriculum framework, but as a leadership-enabled model that depends on institutional commitment, capacity-building, and long-term planning.

CONCLUSION

This chapter investigated UAE students' awareness of the environmental implications of AI within the context of higher education. The study found that while students display high levels of AI adoption for learning and productivity, their understanding of AI's ecological footprint remains limited. The research data showed variations across disciplines, with psychology and art students reporting higher levels of awareness of sustainability issues, whereas qualitative responses reflected general uncertainty about how AI systems impact the environment.

The UAE, through its National AI Strategy 2031 and Sustainable Development Goals (SDGs 4 and 13), provides a strong policy foundation for such integration. Hence, institutional leaders and academic governance bodies can transform awareness into responsible digital engagement through sustainability-focused AI curricula that link classroom education to the UAE's broader sustainability agenda.

Equally important, the findings suggest that sustainable AI literacy extends beyond student knowledge and depends on how AI education is framed, delivered, and modeled through institutional leadership and faculty practice.

Limitations

This study relied on self-reported data gathered through a single questionnaire, which naturally reflects students' perceptions more than their actual classroom practices. While the responses offered useful indications of how undergraduates view AI and sustainability, future research could draw from a wider range of courses and student levels. Gathering data from advanced or discipline-specific classes, or conducting comparative studies across cohorts, could reveal how awareness deepens with experience. Follow-up interviews and more extended engagement with participants would also help trace how students' views evolve over time.

A second limitation concerns the scope of participation. The sample represented one federal university, which provides a valuable but narrow snapshot of the UAE's higher education system. Including students from other institutions, particularly from private or specialized universities, would strengthen generalizability. The absence of faculty input is another constraint, as instructors' perspectives could shed light on institutional readiness and on how sustainable AI practices are modeled in teaching.

Finally, while this chapter raises the possibility that course-specific or fine-tuned AI tools may reduce energy demands compared to large, general-purpose models, this assumption was not empirically examined in the present study. Existing literature suggests potential efficiency gains, but systematic investigation in educational contexts remains limited. Future research could explore how AI design choices in curriculum settings relate to environmental efficiency.

Recommendations

From a leadership and governance perspective, the following recommendations outline actionable pathways for institutional decision-makers. They highlight the need to move environmental awareness beyond technical proficiency and embed it within everyday academic decision-making.

Institutional Policy and Collaboration

Institutional leaders and academic governance bodies should develop internal policies that assess the environmental impact of AI systems while collaborating with external partners, including ADEK, MoE, and sustainability organizations, to align with national initiatives such as the UAE National Strategy for Artificial Intelligence (2031) and Sustainable Development Goal 13. Joint frameworks for monitoring and reporting can strengthen ecological accountability across the education sector and ensure digital transformation supports climate action and responsible resource use. Such coordination requires senior academic leadership, including provosts and deans, to oversee governance structures, ensure resourcing, and align institutional AI practices with national sustainability priorities.

Faculty Professional Development

When institutional leaders support faculty professional development that integrates sustainability into pedagogical practice, educators can model and discuss sustainable AI practices with their students with confidence. These professional learning opportunities can introduce faculty to AI environmental impacts while helping them reflect on their teaching methods and design activities that limit unnecessary data use or computation. For these initiatives to be sustained, institutional leaders must formally recognize professional development in sustainable AI as part of faculty workload, evaluation, and teaching innovation strategies.

Sustainable AI Infrastructure

The energy load of academic computing can be reduced through the development of smaller, purpose-built AI systems for specific courses. Such systems may require fewer resources than large general models while still maintaining their ability to support learning goals effectively. The development of this technology requires institutional leaders and academic governance bodies to work together with software developers and policymakers. For that, empirical research is needed to determine how far course-specific AI designs can actually lower consumption, although the environmental and educational advantages make further investigation essential.

Curricular Integration and Student Engagement

Integrating sustainability into AI-related courses helps students connect technological innovation with environmental stewardship. Awareness campaigns, coding challenges, and "Green AI" competitions can transform theory into practice, promoting responsibility and creative thinking.

In parallel, the recent UAE AI Policy for Education, which mandates the introduction of AI learning components across K-12 curricula, reinforces the urgency of conceptual *SAIL* principles at earlier educational stages. The authors view this as an opportunity to align national reform with sustainability education to ensure that, as AI becomes integral to school learning, environmental responsibility grows alongside digital competence. Embedding *SAIL* principles into the national curriculum would create a continuous learning pathway from school to university, shaping a generation that understands both the power and the ecological cost of intelligent technologies.

These recommendations underscore that sustainability cannot be treated as separate from how AI is taught or used in higher education. When institutional leaders and academic governance bodies position AI as both an educational resource and a shared responsibility, students are more likely to develop informed awareness of the environmental consequences of their digital choices. Embedding these principles across teaching, research, and campus operations can cultivate graduates who are technologically capable while remaining critically aware of AI's ecological impact, capturing the core intent of sustainable AI literacy.

REFERENCES

Al-Jenaibi, B. (2024). Evaluating the influences on AI adoption in higher education in the UAE: Students' utilization of AI. *South Eastern European Journal of Public Health, 25*(S2), 1612–1624. https://www.seejph.com/index.php/seejph/article/view/2932/1967

Al-Zahrani, A. M. (2024). Harnessing AI for sustainable university practices: Toward a greener campus. *International Journal of Sustainability in Higher Education.* Advance online publication. DOI: 10.1108/IJSHE-08-2024-0566

Allam, H. M., Gyamfi, B., & AlOmar, B. (2025). Sustainable innovation: Harnessing AI and living intelligence to transform higher education. *Education Sciences, 15*(4), 398. DOI: 10.3390/educsci15040398

Alzahrani, L. (2023). Analyzing students' attitudes and behavior toward artificial intelligence technologies in higher education. *International Journal of Recent Technology and Engineering, 11*(6), 65–73. DOI: 10.35940/ijrte.F7475.0311623

Arar, K., Tlili, A., Schunka, L., Salha, S., & Saiti, A. (2025). Reimagining Educational Leadership and Management Through Artificial Intelligence: An Integrative Systematic Review. *Leadership and Policy in Schools, 24*(1), 4–26. DOI: 10.1080/15700763.2025.2451982

Bolte, L., Vandemeulebroucke, T., & van Wynsberghe, A. (2022). From an ethics of carefulness to an ethics of desirability: Going beyond current ethics approaches to sustainable AI. *Sustainability (Basel), 14*(8), 4472. DOI: 10.3390/su14084472

Chan, C. K. Y., & Hu, W. (2023). Students' voices on generative AI: Perceptions, benefits, and challenges in higher education. *International Journal of Educational Technology in Higher Education, 20*(43), 1–20. DOI: 10.1186/s41239-023-00411-8

Chowdhury, M. N. U. R., Haque, A., & Soliman, H. (2025). The hidden cost of AI: Unraveling the power-hungry nature of large language models. *Preprints.* https://doi.org/DOI: 10.20944/preprints202502.1676.v1

Delort, E., Riou, L., & Srivastava, A. (2023). Environmental impact of artificial intelligence. INRIA; CEA Leti. https://inria.hal.science/hal-04283245/document

Dhiman, R., Miteff, S., Wang, Y., Ma, S.-C., Amirikas, R., & Fabian, B. (2024). Artificial intelligence and sustainability-A review. *Analytics, 3*(1), 140–164. DOI: 10.3390/analytics3010008

Durmus Senyapar, H. N., & Bayindir, R. (2025). The energy hunger paradox of artificial intelligence: End of clean energy or magic wands for sustainability? *Sustainability (Basel), 17*(7), 2887. DOI: 10.3390/su17072887

Gherhe , V., & Obrad, C. (2018). Technical and humanities students' perspectives on the development and sustainability of artificial intelligence (AI). *Sustainability (Basel), 10*(9), 3066. DOI: 10.3390/su10093066

Graves, N., Larrieu, V., Zhang, Y. T., Peng, J., Rao, V. N., Liu, Y., & Monroy-Hernández, A. (2025). GPTFootprint: Increasing consumer awareness of the environmental impacts of LLMs. In *CHI EA '25: Extended Abstracts of the CHI Conference on Human Factors in Computing Systems* (Article 296, pp. 1-16). ACM. DOI: 10.1145/3706599.3719708

Håkans, O. (2025). The environmental impact of using artificial intelligence : Exploring the environmental impact of ChatGPT: A literature study and user perception analysis (Dissertation). https://urn.kb.se/resolve?urn=urn:nbn:se:kth:diva-361831

Herawati, A. A., Yusuf, S., Ilfiandra, I., Taufik, A., & Habibi, A. S. Y. (2024). Exploring the role of artificial intelligence in education: Students' preferences and perceptions. *Al-Ishlah: Jurnal Pendidikan, 16*(2), 1029–1040. DOI: 10.35445/alishlah.v16i2.4784

Hojeij, Z. (2025). Strategic Leadership for AI Integration in Higher Education. In ElSayary, A. (Ed.), *Prompt Engineering and Generative AI Applications for Teaching and Learning* (pp. 329–348). IGI Global Scientific Publishing. DOI: 10.4018/979-8-3693-7332-3.ch020

Hosseini, M., Gao, P., & Vivas-Valencia, C. (2025). A social-environmental impact perspective of generative artificial intelligence. *Environmental Science and Ecotechnology, 23*, 100520. Advance online publication. DOI: 10.1016/j.ese.2024.100520 PMID: 39811486

Jegham, N., Abdelatti, M., Elmoubarki, L., & Hendawi, A. (2025). How hungry is AI? Benchmarking energy, water, and carbon footprint of LLM inference. *arXiv preprint arXiv:2505.09598.* https://arxiv.org/abs/2505.09598

Khairullah, S. A., Harris, S., Hadi, H. J., Sandhu, R. A., Ahmad, N., & Alshara, M. A. (2025). Implementing artificial intelligence in academic and administrative processes through responsible strategic leadership in the higher education institutions. *Frontiers in Education, 10*, 1548104. DOI: 10.3389/feduc.2025.1548104

Kumar, M. (2024). AI for climate change: Predicting environmental impact and developing sustainable solutions. *ESP Journal of Engineering & Technology Advancements*, *4*(3), 127–133. DOI: 10.56472/25832646/JETA-V4I3P112

Leal Filho, W., Simaens, A., Paço, A., Hernandez-Diaz, P. M., Vasconcelos, C. R. P., Fritzen, B., & Mac-Lean, C. (2023). Integrating the Sustainable Development Goals into the strategy of higher education institutions. *International Journal of Sustainable Development and World Ecology*, *30*(5), 564–575. DOI: 10.1080/13504509.2023.2167884

Li, P., Yang, J., Islam, M. A., & Ren, S. (2025). Making AI less "thirsty": Uncovering and addressing the secret water footprint of AI models. *arXiv preprint arXiv:2304.03271*. https://arxiv.org/pdf/2304.03271

Lo, N. P.-K. (2024). The confluence of digital literacy and eco-consciousness: Harmonizing digital skills with sustainable practices in education. *Platforms*, *2*(1), 15–32. DOI: 10.3390/platforms2010002

Long, D., & Magerko, B. (2020, April). What is AI literacy? Competencies and design considerations. *Proceedings of the 2020 CHI conference on human factors in computing systems*, 1-16. DOI: 10.1145/3313831.3376727

Ma, Q., Crosthwaite, P., Sun, D., & Zou, D. (2024). Exploring ChatGPT literacy in language education: A global perspective and comprehensive approach. *Computers and Education: Artificial Intelligence*, *7*, 100278. Advance online publication. DOI: 10.1016/j.caeai.2024.100278

Ma, S., & Chen, Z. (2024). The development and validation of the artificial intelligence literacy scale for Chinese college students (AILS-CCS). *IEEE Access : Practical Innovations, Open Solutions*, *12*, 146419–146429. DOI: 10.1109/ACCESS.2024.3468378

Milicevic, N., Kalas, B., Djokic, N., Malcic, B., & Djokic, I. (2024). Students' intention toward artificial intelligence in the context of digital transformation. *Sustainability (Basel)*, *16*(9), 3554. DOI: 10.3390/su16093554

Moyano-Fernández, C., Rueda, J., Delgado, J., & Ausín, T. (2024). May artificial intelligence take health and sustainability on a honeymoon? Towards green technologies for multidimensional health and environmental justice. *Global Bioethics = Problemi di Bioetica*, *35*(1), 2322208. DOI: 10.1080/11287462.2024.2322208 PMID: 38476503

Nordgren, A. (2023). Artificial intelligence and climate change: Ethical issues. *Journal of Information. Communication and Ethics in Society*, *21*(1), 1–15. DOI: 10.1108/JICES-11-2021-0106

Raper, R., Boeddinghaus, J., Coeckelbergh, M., Gross, W., Campigotto, P., & Lincoln, C. N. (2022). Sustainability budgets: A practical management and governance method for achieving Goal 13 of the Sustainable Development Goals for AI development. *Sustainability (Basel)*, *14*(7), 4019. DOI: 10.3390/su14074019

Sætra, H. S. (2021). A framework for evaluating and disclosing the ESG related impacts of AI with the SDGs. *Sustainability (Basel)*, *13*(15), 8503. DOI: 10.3390/su13158503

Simpson, W. (2025). A need to regulate the environmental impacts of AI: Preserving clean water for humans, not robots. *Tulane Environmental Law Journal*, *38*(1), 133–147.

Swidan, A., Lee, S. Y., & Romdhane, S. B. (2025). College students' use and perceptions of AI tools in the UAE: Motivations, ethical concerns and institutional Guidelines. *Education Sciences*, *15*(4), 461. DOI: 10.3390/educsci15040461

Tan, Q., & Tang, X. (2025). Unveiling AI literacy in K-12 education: A systematic literature review of empirical research. *Interactive Learning Environments*, *33*(9), 1–17. DOI: 10.1080/10494820.2025.2482586

Tarisayi, K. S. (2024). Strategic leadership for responsible artificial intelligence adoption in higher education. *CTE Workshop Proceedings*, *11*, 4-14. DOI: 10.55056/cte.616

UNESCO. (2023). *AI and education: Guidance for policy-makers*. UNESCO Publishing. DOI: 10.54675/PCSP7350

van Wynsberghe, A. (2021). Sustainable AI: AI for sustainability and the sustainability of AI. *AI and Ethics*, *1*(3), 213–218. DOI: 10.1007/s43681-021-00043-6

Wang, B., Rau, P. L. P., & Yuan, T. (2023). Measuring user competence in using artificial intelligence: Validity and reliability of artificial intelligence literacy scale. *Behaviour & Information Technology*, *42*(9), 1324–1337. DOI: 10.1080/0144929X.2022.2072768

Xiao, L., Pyng, H. S., Ayub, A. F. M., Zhu, Z., Gao, J., & Qing, Z. (2025). University students' usage of generative artificial intelligence for sustainability: A cross-sectional survey from China. *Sustainability (Basel)*, *17*(8), 3541. DOI: 10.3390/su17083541

Yu, Y., Wang, J., Liu, Y., Yu, P., Wang, D., Zheng, P., & Zhang, M. (2024). Revisit the environmental impact of artificial intelligence: The overlooked carbon emission source? *Frontiers of Environmental Science & Engineering*, *18*(12), 158. DOI: 10.1007/s11783-024-1918-y

Zhang, Y., Liu, Y., & Wang, X. (2025). Enhancing anti-plagiarism literacy practices among undergraduates with AI. *Interactive Learning Environments*, 1–15. DOI: 10.1080/10494820.2025.2492783

About the Contributors

Areej ElSayary is an Associate Professor and Chair of the General Education department within the College of Interdisciplinary Studies. She previously served as the Graduate Program Coordinator within Zayed University's College of Education. She is a distinguished academic experienced in STE(A)M Education, curriculum design, teaching methodologies, assessment strategies, and school accreditation. Her knowledge and experience extend to her role as a certified associate of the Blackboard Academy, a recognized Fellow of the Higher Education Academy (FHEA), and a respected Editor and researcher. Dr. Areej has conducted numerous impactful teacher training programs across the United Arab Emirates, further elevating the region's education quality. Beyond academia, she is a Mental Health Ambassador at Zayed University, an ICF Coach Member, and a cyberpsychologist bringing her specialized expertise in positive psychology to promote holistic well-being. Her research interests encompass a wide spectrum, spanning cognitive development, cyberpsychology, human-computer interaction, entrepreneurship, innovation, design-thinking, interdisciplinary STE(A)M approaches, and advanced assessment methodologies.

Ghadah Al Murshidi is Associate Professor in Language and Literacy, Curriculum and Instruction, at the College of Education, and previously was in Applied Linguistics, UAE University. She taught some graduate and undergraduate courses such as Thesis: Seminar 1(Master degree course), Emirates studies, Professional ethics in Education, Children play, Student teaching in elementary School/English, Introduction to Language and Communication, Critical and Creative Thinking, Classroom Environment and Assessment in Elementary Education, Language Development and emergent Litcracy in Early Childhood, Capstone experience of teaching English language, Current trends and issues in teaching English language .Her recent interests are in Early childhood literacy, online learning, teachers' professional development. She has published extensively in the area of language and literacy. Dr Al Murshidi received award for her book "The Guide of Creativity and Innovation in the UAE", by His Highness Sheikh Hamad bin Mohammed Al Sharqi, the Ruler of the emirate Fujairah and a member of the Supreme Council in the UAE. She led a national, multidisciplinary research project "A Comparative Study of Emirati students' Academic Experiences atUAE University, Zayed University and Higher College of Technology" which was funded by United Arab Emirates University - National Research Foundation. She was the Emirati expert in international research project "A Comparative Study of global citizenship in Arabic Countries Education" which was funded by Regional Centre of Quality and Excellence in Education, KSA. She received the YoungEmirati Researcher Prize and the best Young researcher award. For her community service, she received Emirati women award. she received the best academic woman achiever award.

Karim Ragab is a UAE-based school leader and STEM educator with 22 years' experience spanning teaching, curriculum development, and K–12 leadership. He is Vice Principal at Ittihad Private School–Mamzar, where he has led literacy/numeracy initiatives, strengthened instructional quality, and driven measurable gains. Previously, Karim served as Principal for the Applied Technology High Schools (Dubai and Umm Al Quwain). An active IEEE member, he previously developed national Applied Technology curricula and mentored students for Emirates/WorldSkills competitions. He represented the UAE as the CNC turning expert in the WorldSkills competitions (Leipzig 2013 and São Paulo 2015). Karim holds an MSc in Mechanical Engineering (American University of Sharjah) and a BSc from Alexandria University, and he is completing a PhD in Educational Technology (Universidad de Córdoba, expected June 2026). His recent publications focus on interactive technology in STEM education and energy efficiency in schools.

* * *

Abdulai Abukari is currently Professor, Education Management, Leadership and Policy, a Visiting Fellow at the University of Glasgow and Coordinator of a number of modules in the Faculty of Education at the British University in Dubai (BUiD). Prof. Abdulai Abukari completed his PhD in Comparative and International Education at Middlesex University and Master of Philosophy at the University of Oslo in the same discipline. He specialises in Comparative and International Education (Policy, Leadership and Management); Quality Assurance in education particularly higher education; Workplace Learning and Teacher Education. Before joining BUiD, he worked for Middlesex University in different capacities for over ten years with at least the last five years as a senior lecturer and a programme leader for undergraduate and postgraduate professional development programmes at the Institute for Work Based Learning (IWBL). He also taught at different levels of educational systems including Key stage 2 (UK), Teacher training college and Senior high school (Ghana).

Noor Aisha is a decennary experienced professional, serving in Basic Education Department, Governmentof Uttar Pradesh, India. She has completed her doctorate in Educational Technology and Instructional Design from Indira Gandhi National Open University, New Delhi, (India). Her teaching philosophy is to impart education while fulfilling the student's specific learning needs and realizing teachers' crucial role in a technology enabled learning environment. Her sincere efforts have always been in the direction to harmonize theory and practice in the process of teaching and learning.

Ahmed Al Zaabi is an Emirati academic who holds a PhD in Business Management and Strategic Leadership from Universiti Utara Malaysia. He also holds a Master's in Strategic Management from Dubai Men's College, Higher Colleges of Technology, UAE, and a Master's in International Business Administration from the University of Wollongong in Dubai, enhancing his expertise in global business strategies. As a researcher, Dr. Al Zaabi has published influential papers such as "The Effect of E-Learning Training Program on Organizational Performance Through Underlying Mechanisms of Capacity Building of Dubai Police Force," "Do Job Performance Mediates between E-Learning Training Program and Organizational Performance: A Case of Dubai Police Force," among others. He has completed numerous specialized courses across various fields, particularly in administrative and security-related disciplines. His blend of advanced academic qualifications and practical experience positions him as a knowledgeable and skilled professional in strategic management, business administration, and organizational performance, making impactful contributions to the field.

Maram Alaqra has over 17 years' experience in education, working across higher education and K-12 settings. Dr. Alaqra has taught graduate and undergraduate courses at Texas A&M University, which included over eight years of research experience on STEM education. Having spoken widely on STEM education internationally and throughout the US, Dr. Alaqra has also been part of large-scale STEM education research projects funded by the National Science Foundation, National Institute of Health, and Department of Education. Dr. Alaqra's research agenda has emphasized culturally relevant teaching and learning through designing culturally sensitive learning environments for students to improve STEM self-efficacies and interests. Research interests include: STEM education, culturally relevant instruction, STEM self-efficacy, community-based learning, and 21st Century skills.

Rima Al Chaar is a Senior Instructor and Fellow of the Higher Education Academy (FHEA) at Zayed University's College of Natural and Health Sciences in the United Arab Emirates. She teaches undergraduate courses in environmental sustainability, health, and data reasoning, and is actively involved in curriculum development, quality assurance, and student-centered learning. Her research focuses on ethical artificial intelligence integration in higher education, sustainability literacy, and experiential learning frameworks. With academic training in Chemistry and Microbiology of Water, she contributes to institutional sustainability initiatives and interdisciplinary collaboration, while continually advancing professional practice aligned with evidence-based teaching and assessment.

Hend Al Mazmi is currently a doctoral candidate at the British University in Dubai, pursuing a PhD in Education.

Rehab AlKilani is an Assistant Professor of Arabic Language and Literature at Zayed University, UAE. She holds a PhD in Literature and Criticism and specializes in literary studies, identity and cultural analysis, and contemporary Arabic literature. Her research and creative interests include narrative studies, screenwriting, television writing, and script development, alongside semiotics and language pedagogy.

Badria Almurshidi is a Clinical Scientist and assistant professor, Field of expertise Nanotechnology in medicine and Environmental Health and Toxicology. One of the outstanding researchers in University of South Carolina 2019 in the field of Nanomedicine and winner of the first research prize in the Rare genetic diseases conference in 2024. Worked as specialist in forensic medicine at branch of Paternity and disaster victim identification for 2 years.

Muna AlSadoon is a PhD holder in Science Education and Learning Difficulties from The British University in Dubai/United Arab Emirates, an adjunct faculty member at Zayed University, an active member in quality matters as an online course evaluator, and a Certified Associate in Digital Teaching and Learning, Blackboard Academy. Muna AlSadoon is an educator who has more than 25 years of experience as a science and biology teacher, Science HoD, and Academic Advisor in different private schools and education centers in Dubai. Her journey in the education field includes teaching in American curriculum schools and training science teachers. Research Interests: Education, Science Education, Learning Difficulties.

Khushboo Bhatt is an Assistant Professor in Management with a doctoral degree in Management Psychology, specializing in Organizational Behaviour and Spiritual Psychology. Her academic and research interests include emotional intelligence, leadership, workplace well-being, career management, and the integration of indigenous knowledge systems with contemporary management theories. She has published research articles and book chapters in peer-reviewed and Scopus-indexed outlets, presented her work at national and international conferences, and received best paper awards. Dr. Bhatt actively engages in interdisciplinary research and mentoring, with a strong focus on applying psychological and ethical perspectives to management education and practice.

Tendai Charles is an Assistant Professor of Education at the British University in Dubai. He holds an MSc in Data Analytics & Social Statistics from the University of Manchester and a PhD in Education from the University of York. He is an accredited researcher with the Office for National Statistics and is a Fellow of the Royal Statistical Society. He is a post-positivist researcher who specialises in evidence-based education and uses computational statistics for secondary data analyses.

Mona El Samaty is an Assistant Professor at Sharjah Education Academy in the United Arab Emirates. Her research focuses on teacher education, and sociolinguistics, with particular attention to equity, multilingualism, and critical pedagogy. She has presented her work at over 30 international conferences and published across peer-reviewed venues. Dr. El Samaty has extensive teaching and supervisory experience, having served in higher education institutions in Egypt, the UAE, and Canada, and is the recipient of multiple academic awards, including recognition for her doctoral research at the University of Toronto.

Rolla Elsaiary is an educational leader and scholar specializing in culturally responsive leadership, multilingual education, and ethical AI integration in schools. She serves as an Assistant Principal at an Arabic immersion magnet school in Texas, where she leads instructional innovation and equity-centered initiatives. Dr. Elsaiary holds a Doctor of Education from the University of South Carolina, a Master's degree in Educational Leadership, and a Master's in Curriculum and Instruction. She is currently pursuing an MBA in Artificial Intelligence. Her research examines how school leaders can responsibly integrate AI while preserving teacher agency, student voice, and linguistic identity.

Nadine Jaafarawi is an Associate Professor of Applied Linguistics at Zayed University in Abu Dhabi, United Arab Emirates. With over 25 years of teaching experience, she has contributed to national and international initiatives, including the

EmSAT National Committee for Grade 1 Baseline Assessment at the UAE Ministry of Education. A Fellow of the Higher Education Academy (Advance HE), she previously served as a trainer in the Child Protection Training Certification Program with Georgetown University and the Abu Dhabi Early Childhood Authority. Her research focuses on bilingual language acquisition, sociolinguistic discourse, and innovative language pedagogy in the Arabian Peninsula.

Aileen Wanli Lam is a Senior Lecturer from the National University of Singapore. She teaches business communications, critical thinking and academic writing, and is fascinated with educational technology which has led to the development of blended and online courses. She continues to keep up with developments in Generative AI and its impact on industries and education. Aileen's research interests lie in educational technology, leadership, pedagogy and student life.

Daron Benjamin Loo received his PhD in applied linguistics from King Mongkut's University of Technology Thonburi. He is currently senior lecturer at Universiti Malaysia Sabah, where he teaches English for academic and specific purposes at the undergraduate level. He supervises research on the intersection between language and society at the postgraduate level. Daron has published in indexed journal on topics ranging from language teaching practice to language and identity in public discourse.

Enrico Moch holds a doctorate in economics. He works as a lecturer at various universities in Germany, including the DHBW Ravensburg. He is Academic Director of the GrandEdu Research School based in Herford. His research focuses on AI governance, technical data protection and the institutional governance of digital platforms. Mr. Moch regularly publishes specialist articles, is involved in interdisciplinary book projects and runs the podcast "GrandEdu Research School - Der Wirtschaft auf der Spur!". He is also involved in academic peer review and knowledge transfer between research and practice.

Laila Mohebi stands out in the education sector, particularly in early childhood education and the role of technology in teaching. Holding a PhD from the British University in Dubai, her focus is on leadership and educational policy. As an associate professor at Zayed University, Dr. Mohebi is deeply involved in both teaching and research. Her scholarly contributions, highlighted by numerous publications in prestigious journals, center on utilizing technology in education, enhancing teacher training, and developing cutting-edge educational methods. Dr. Mohebi is dedicated to educational advancement, evidenced by her active participation in major projects and mentorship in teacher training initiatives. Her efforts are not just academic; they significantly influence future educational strategies and practices.

Tobias Oberdieck is Managing Director of GrandEdu GmbH, a leading further education institution that specialises in preparing professionals for degrees such as the Bachelor Professional, Master Professional and Master of Business Administration (MBA). In his role at GrandEdu, he drives innovative educational strategies to actively support the recruitment of skilled labour in Germany. During his doctorate, Dr. Oberdieck worked as a research assistant at the Department of Business Administration and Economics at the Niederrhein University of Applied Sciences in Germany. During this time, he deepened his expertise in the areas of education management, labour market research and economic education models, which he now brings to his work at GrandEdu. His research focuses on the interface between continuing vocational training, academic education and the challenges of the modern labour market.

Maxwell Peprah Opoku is currently an Associate Professor in Special Education at the United Arab Emirates University. He holds a PhD in Education from University of Tasmania, Australia. Before Joining UAEU, he worked as casual academic, teaching undergraduate and graduate courses at Faculty of Education, University of Tasmania, Australia. Maxwell has passion for research and his research interests includes: gifted education, disability research, special education, cerebral palsy, autism, Down Syndrome, intellectual disability, mental health, Deaf research, visual impairment, professional development, inclusive leadership, rural education, teacher education, parenting, human development, gender and inclusive research, community-based rehabilitation, education and social justice, inclusive education, disability and behavior management, trauma-informed practice, classroom management, health research, human rights, social policies and public policy.

Hima Parameswaran is an Associate Professor of Human Resource Management at the College of Business, City University Ajman, United Arab Emirates. She holds a Ph.D. in Public Administration and an Associate CIPD (Level 7) from the Chartered Institute of Personnel Development, UK. Her academic expertise encompasses strategic HRM, leadership, organizational development, performance management, and quality work-life, complemented by her research on talent management, transformational leadership, flexible workforces, and employee value propositions. A prolific scholar, she has published extensively in reputed international journals, reviewed for several scholarly publications, and presented at more than thirty national and international conferences, often serving as keynote speaker, session chair, and organizing committee member. Her intellectual pursuits extend into collaborative research with international universities, reflecting her global academic engagement. She actively contributes to community development through workshops and training programs for schools and industries across the UAE, nurturing administrative capability and psychological well-being. Beyond academia, her diverse professional journey spans the healthcare sector and television media, enriching her perspective with multidimensional experience. With over sixteen years of excellence in teaching, research, and service, Dr. Parameswaran exemplifies a rare synthesis of scholarship, leadership, and societal contribution.

Dhartiben Patel is working with Indukaka Ipcowala Institute of Management, Faculty of Management Studies, as an Assistant Professor. She carries 1 year of experience in banking field, 4 years of experience in corporate field and 4 years of experience in education field. Her teaching interest lie in the areas of Finance, Accounts and Logical Thinking. Her educational background includes Pursuing Doctorate in Management (PhD), Masters in Business Administration (MBA-FINANCE), Bachelors in Commerce (B. Com). She is dedicated to advancing knowledge in the field through both teaching and research.

Foram Pathak is an educator and researcher in Organisational Behaviour, Human Resource, Neuroscience and Positive Psychology. Her work explores Happiness, Success, Lifestyle, Ancient teachings, Neuroplasticity, mentoring, coaching, counselling, emotional intelligence, mindsets, and well-being through a blend of behavioural science, value education, Training and Development and Indian Knowledge Systems. She is committed to nurturing reflective, value-driven learners and leaders.

Subhashree S. is a dedicated academic and researcher currently pursuing a Ph.D. in Commerce at Sardar Patel University, VV Nagar, Gujarat. With over a decade of experience in commerce education, she has served as a faculty member at esteemed institutions including Sri G.V.G. Visalakshi College for Women (2014–2019), Parul Institute of Commerce (2021–2024), and currently at Indukaka Ipcowala Institute of Management, Charotar University of Science and Technology, Changa. Her research interests encompass consumer behavior in online shopping—particularly personal care products among millennials—AI applications in marketing and education, forensic accounting, and technology adoption models. She holds an M.Com (80.17%, First Class) and M.Phil, along with qualifications like TNSET and diplomas in child care management and business skills. Subhashree has authored/co-authored 20+ Scopus/UGC-indexed journal articles, 7 book chapters, and a research book on online shopping preferences. Notable publications include works on AR/VR in cosmetics purchases (2026, International Journal of Accounting and Economic

Studies) and e-WOM's impact on consumer intentions (2025 book chapter). She has presented at 15+ national/international conferences, securing multiple Best Paper Awards, such as at CHARUSAT (2025, 2024) and GLS University (2025). Additionally, she has contributed as a reviewer/editor for journals like Computers in Human Behavior (Elsevier) and delivered expert lectures on AI in business and NEP 2020. Her academic contributions are recognized with awards like Parul University's Academic Excellence (2023–2024) and I2OR National Eminent Academic Leader (2021). Proficient in Power BI, SPSS, and R, she coordinates IQAC, innovation clubs, and mentorship programs, fostering outcome-based education.

Reshma G. Sable is the Professor of Management at Charotar University of Science and Technology, with over 17 years of experience in the field of education. Her academic interests include Organizational Behaviour, Human Resource Management, General Management, Critical Thinking and Logic, and Emotional Intelligence. She holds a Doctorate in Management (PhD – Learning Organization), along with an MBA (Human Resource Management), MEd, MSc (Inorganic Chemistry), BEd, and BSc. She has also qualified NET in Human Resource Management and Education, SET in Education, and is an Accredited Management Teacher (AMT) certified by the All India Management Association, New Delhi. Dr. Sable has published several research papers in reputed journals and has chaired sessions at national and international conferences. Her strengths include critical thinking, interpersonal communication, and analytical skills, and she is proficient in English, Hindi, and Marathi. Beyond academia, Dr. Sable leads impactful community initiatives focusing on surveys and awareness programs on superstitions and traditional beliefs in villages across Gujarat, helping communities understand the science behind these practices. She is also actively engaged in developing emotional intelligence and personality development among adolescents, particularly girls in rural areas, through interactive workshops and training sessions. Additionally, she conducts corporate training programmes on enhancing emotional intelligence, employee motivation, workplace morale, and offers consultancy in areas such as 5S implementation, defining KPAs and KPIs, and designing performance appraisal and compensation systems.

Nada Sarkis is an Associate Professor of Marketing at the USEK Business School. Over the course of her academic career, she has played a pivotal part in program development, & curriculum design. Her research expertise lies at the intersection of digital marketing, consumer behavior, sustainability, and business analytics, with a strong focus on how organizations & consumers adapt to technological disruption. Her research output includes peer-reviewed journal articles, international conference contributions, book chapters, & teaching cases, notably featured in Essentials of Modern Marketing (Kotler & Partners). She is also actively involved in international research collaborations & development projects that bridge academia and industry. These include consultancy and training programs in Lebanon & across the region, focusing on entrepreneurship, digital transformation, and resilience-building among SMEs & business communities. Her academic achievements are complemented by a series of prestigious scholarships & fellowships, including the Fulbright Junior Faculty Development Program at the University of Illinois Urbana-Champaign. She holds a PhD from Paul Cezanne University, France.

Satya Subrahmanyam is a distinguished academic leader, researcher, and institutional strategist with over 27 years of experience in higher education, leadership, and research management. He holds two PhDs and a Postdoctoral qualification from the Polytechnic Institute of Leiria, Portugal. Currently serving as Professor and Dean (Research) at Holy Spirit University of Kaslik (USEK), Lebanon, he spearheads research initiatives that enhance academic excellence and institutional reputation. He played a pivotal role in the development of the Catholic University in Erbil, Kurdistan, where he established new departments, led research programs, and collaborated on international educational projects. As a founding member and Managing Partner of Vignan Institute of Technology and Management, India, he contributed to its transformation into a premier institution. With expertise in AI-driven business strategies, HR analytics, and leadership in technology adoption, he has published extensively, guided PhD research, and led training programs in corporate and academic settings.

Index

A

C

D

E

F

G

H

L

P

S

T

U

www.ingramcontent.com/pod-product-compliance
Lightning Source LLC
LaVergne TN
LVHW061531290926
849162LV00004B/749